MICHIGAN COURT RULES
2015 Edition

Updated through January 1, 2015

Michigan Legal Publishing Ltd.

Academic and bulk discounts available at
www.michlp.com

WE WELCOME YOUR FEEDBACK: info@michlp.com

ISBN-13: 978-1-942842-00-2
ISBN-10: 1942842007

Table of Contents

Table of Contents

CHAPTER 1. GENERAL PROVISIONS

Subchapter 1.100 Applicability; Construction

Rule 1.101 Title; Citation

These rules are the "Michigan Court Rules of 1985." An individual rule may be referred to as "Michigan Court Rule __________," and cited by the symbol "MCR __________." For example, this rule may be cited as MCR 1.101.

Rule 1.102 Effective Date

These rules take effect on March 1, 1985. They govern all proceedings in actions brought on or after that date, and all further proceedings in actions then pending. A court may permit a pending action to proceed under the former rules if it finds that the application of these rules to that action would not be feasible or would work injustice.

Rule 1.103 Applicability

The Michigan Court Rules govern practice and procedure in all courts established by the constitution and laws of the State of Michigan. Rules stated to be applicable only in a specific court or only to a specific type of proceeding apply only to that court or to that type of proceeding and control over general rules.

Rule 1.104 Statutory Practice Provisions

Rules of practice set forth in any statute, if not in conflict with any of these rules, are effective until superseded by rules adopted by the Supreme Court.

Rule 1.105 Construction

These rules are to be construed to secure the just, speedy, and economical determination of every action and to avoid the consequences of error that does not affect the substantial rights of the parties.

Rule 1.106 Catch Lines

The catch lines of a rule are not part of the rule and may not be used to construe the rule more broadly or more narrowly than the text indicates.

Rule 1.107 Number

Words used in the singular also apply to the plural, where appropriate.

Rule 1.108 Computation of Time

In computing a period of time prescribed or allowed by these rules, by court order, or by statute, the following rules apply:

(1) The day of the act, event, or default after which the designated period of time begins to run is not included. The last day of the period is included, unless it is a Saturday, Sunday, legal holiday, or day on which the court is closed pursuant to court order; in that event the period runs until the end of the next day that is not a Saturday, Sunday, legal holiday, or day on which the court is closed pursuant to court order.

(2) If a period is measured by a number of weeks, the last day of the period is the same day of the week as the day on which the period began.

(3) If a period is measured by months or years, the last day of the period is the same day of the month as the day on which the period began. If what would otherwise be the final month does not include that day, the last day of the period is the last day of that month. For example, "2 months" after January 31 is March 31, and "3 months" after January 31 is April 30.

Rule 1.109 Court Records Defined; Document Defined; Filing Standards; Signatures; and Access

(A) **Court Records Defined.**

(1) Court records are defined by MCR 8.119 and this subrule. Court records are recorded information of any kind that has been created by the court or filed with the court in accordance with Michigan Court Rules. Court records may be created using any means and may be maintained in any medium authorized by these court rules provided those records comply with other provisions of law and these court rules.

(a) Court records include, but are not limited to:

(i) documents, attachments to documents, discovery materials, and other materials filed with the clerk of the court,

(ii) documents, recordings, data, and other recorded information created or handled by the court, including all data produced in conjunction with the use of any system for the purpose of transmitting, accessing, reproducing, or maintaining court records.

(b) For purposes of this subrule:

(i) Documents include, but are not limited to, pleadings, orders, and judgments.

(ii) Recordings refer to audio and video recordings (whether analog or digital), stenotapes, log notes, and other related records.

(iii) Data refers to any information entered in the case management system that is not ordinarily reduced to a document, but that is still recorded information.

(iv) Other recorded information includes, but is not limited to, notices, bench warrants, arrest warrants, and other process issued by the court that do not have to be maintained on paper or digital image.

(2) Discovery materials that are not filed with the clerk of the court are not court records. Exhibits that are maintained by the court reporter or other authorized staff pursuant to MCR 2.518 or MCR 3.930 during the pendency of a proceeding are not court records.

(B) **Document Defined**. A document means a record produced on paper or a digital image of a record originally produced on paper or originally created by an approved electronic means, the output of which is readable by sight and can be printed to paper.

(C) **Filing Standards**.

(1) All pleadings and other documents prepared for filing in the courts of this state must comply with MCR 8.119(C) and be filed on good quality 8½ by 11 inch paper or transmitted through an approved electronic means or created electronically by the court and maintained in a digital image. The print must be no smaller than 10 characters per inch (nonproportional) or 12-point (proportional), except with regard to forms approved by the State Court Administrative Office.

(2) All other materials submitted for filing shall be prepared in accordance with this subrule and standards established by the state court administrative office. An attachment or discovery material that is submitted for filing shall be made part of the public case file unless otherwise confidential.

(3) All original documents filed on paper may be reproduced and maintained by the court as a digital image in place of the paper original in accordance with standards and guidelines established by the state court administrative office.

(4) A clerk of the court may reject nonconforming documents as prescribed by MCR 8.119.

(D) **Signatures**.

(1) A signature, as required by these court rules and law, means a written signature as defined by MCL 8.3q or an electronic signature as defined by this subrule.

(2) An electronic signature means an electronic sound, symbol, or process, attached to or logically associated with a record and executed or adopted by a person with the intent to sign the record.

(3) If a law or court rule requires a signature to be notarized or made under oath, the requirement is satisfied if the electronic signature of the person authorized to perform those acts, together with all other information required to be included by other applicable law or court rule, is attached to or logically associated with the signature.

(4) Retention of a signature electronically affixed to a document that will be retained by the court in electronic format must not be dependent upon the mechanism that was used to affix that signature.

(E) Requests for access to public court records shall be granted in accordance with MCR 8.119(H).

Rule 1.110 Collection of Fines and Costs

Fines, costs, and other financial obligations imposed by the court must be paid at the time of assessment, except when the court allows otherwise, for good cause shown.

Rule 1.111 Foreign Language Interpreters

(A) **Definitions**. When used in this rule, the following words and phrases have the following definitions:

(1) "Case or Court Proceeding" means any hearing, trial, or other appearance before any court in this state in an action, appeal, or other proceeding, including any matter conducted by a judge, magistrate, referee, or other hearing officer.

(2) "Party" means a person named as a party or a person with legal decision-making authority in the case or court proceeding.

(3) A person is "financially able to pay for interpretation costs" if the court determines that requiring reimbursement of interpretation costs will not pose an unreasonable burden on the person's ability to have meaningful access to the court. For purposes of this rule, a person is financially able to pay for interpretation costs when:

(a) The person's family or household income is greater than 125% of the federal poverty level; and

(b) An assessment of interpretation costs at the conclusion of the litigation would not unreasonably impede the person's ability to defend or pursue the claims involved in the matter.

(4) "Certified foreign language interpreter" means a person who has:

(a) passed a foreign language interpreter test administered by the State Court Administrative Office or a similar state or federal test approved by the state court administrator,

(b) met all the requirements established by the state court administrator for this interpreter classification, and

(c) registered with the State Court Administrative Office.

(5) "Interpret" and "interpretation" mean the oral rendering of spoken communication from one language to another without change in meaning.

(6) "Qualified foreign language interpreter" means:

(a) A person who provides interpretation services, provided that the person has:

(i) registered with the State Court Administrative Office; and

(ii) met the requirements established by the state court administrator for this interpreter classification; and

(iii) been determined by the court after voir dire to be competent to provide interpretation services for the proceeding in which the interpreter is providing services, or

(b) A person who works for an entity that provides in-person interpretation services provided that:

(i) both the entity and the person have registered with the State Court Administrative Office; and

(ii) the person has met the requirements established by the state court administrator for this interpreter classification; and

(iii) the person has been determined by the court after voir dire to be competent to provide interpretation services for the proceeding in which the interpreter is providing services, or

(c) A person who works for an entity that provides interpretation services by telecommunication equipment, provided that:

(i) the entity has registered with the State Court Administrative Office; and

(ii) the entity has met the requirements established by the state court administrator for this interpreter classification; and

(iii) the person has been determined by the court after voir dire to be competent to provide interpretation services for the proceeding in which the interpreter is providing services

(B) **Appointment of a Foreign Language Interpreter**.

(1) If a person requests a foreign language interpreter and the court determines such services are necessary for the person to meaningfully participate in the case or court proceeding, or on the court's own determination that foreign language interpreter services are necessary for a person to meaningfully participate in the case or court proceeding, the court shall appoint a foreign language interpreter for that person if the person is a witness testifying in a civil or criminal case or court proceeding or is a party.

(2) The court may appoint a foreign language interpreter for a person other than a party or witness who has a substantial interest in the case or court proceeding.

(3) In order to determine whether the services of a foreign language interpreter are necessary for a person to meaningfully participate under subrule (B)(1), the court shall rely upon a request by an LEP individual (or a request made on behalf of an LEP individual) or prior notice in the record. If no such requests have been made, the court may conduct an examination of the person on the record to determine whether such services are necessary. During the examination, the court may use a foreign language interpreter. For purposes of this examination, the court is not required to comply with the requirements of subrule (F) and the foreign language interpreter may participate remotely.

(C) **Waiver of Appointment of Foreign Language Interpreter**. A person may waive the right to a foreign language interpreter established under subrule (B)(1) unless the court determines that the interpreter is required for the protection of the person's rights and the integrity of the case or court proceeding. The court must find on the record that a person's waiver of an interpreter is knowing and voluntary. When accepting the person's waiver, the court may use a foreign language interpreter. For purposes of this waiver, the court is not required to comply with the requirements of subrule (F) and the foreign language interpreter may participate remotely.

(D) **Recordings**. The court may make a recording of anything said by a foreign language interpreter or a limited English proficient person while testifying or responding to a colloquy during those portions of the proceedings.

(E) **Avoidance of Potential Conflicts of Interest**.

(1) The court should use all reasonable efforts to avoid potential conflicts of interest when appointing a person as a foreign language interpreter and shall state its reasons on the record for appointing the person if any of the following applies:

(a) The interpreter is compensated by a business owned or controlled by a party or a witness;

(b) The interpreter is a friend, a family member, or a household member of a party or witness;

(c) The interpreter is a potential witness;

(d) The interpreter is a law enforcement officer;

(e) The interpreter has a pecuniary or other interest in the outcome of the case;

(f) The appointment of the interpreter would not serve to protect a party's rights or ensure the integrity of the proceedings;

(g) The interpreter does have, or may have, a perceived conflict of interest;

(h) The appointment of the interpreter creates an appearance of impropriety.

(2) A court employee may interpret legal proceedings as follows:

(a) The court may employ a person as an interpreter. The employee must meet the minimum requirements for interpreters established by subrule (A)(4). The state court administrator may authorize the court to hire a person who does not meet the minimum requirements established by subrule (A)(4) for good cause including the unavailability of a certification test for the foreign language and the absence of certified interpreters for the foreign language in the geographic area in which the court sits. The court seeking authorization from the state court administrator shall provide proof of the employee's competency to act as an interpreter and shall submit a plan for the employee to meet the minimum requirements established by subrule (A)(4) within a reasonable time.

(b) The court may use an employee as an interpreter if the employee meets the minimum requirements for interpreters established by this rule and is not otherwise disqualified.

(F) **Appointment of Foreign Language Interpreters**.

(1) When the court appoints a foreign language interpreter under subrule (B)(1), the court shall appoint a certified foreign language interpreter whenever practicable. If a certified foreign language interpreter is not reasonably available, and after considering the gravity of the proceedings and whether the matter should be rescheduled, the court may appoint a qualified foreign language interpreter who meets the qualifications in (A)(6). The court shall make a record of its reasons for using a qualified foreign language interpreter.

(2) If neither a certified foreign language interpreter nor a qualified foreign language interpreter is reasonably available, and after considering the gravity of the proceeding and whether the matter should be rescheduled, the court may appoint a person whom the court determines through voir dire to be capable of conveying the intent and content of the speaker's words sufficiently to allow the court to conduct the proceeding without prejudice to the limited English proficient person.

(3) The court shall appoint a single interpreter for a case or court proceeding. The court may appoint more than one interpreter after consideration of the nature and duration of the proceeding; the number of parties in interest and witnesses requiring an interpreter; the primary languages of those persons; and the quality of the remote technology that may be utilized when deemed necessary by the court to ensure effective communication in any case or court proceeding.

(4) The court may set reasonable compensation for interpreters who are appointed by the court. Court-appointed interpreter costs are to be paid out of funds provided by law or by the court.

(5) If a party is financially able to pay for interpretation costs, the court may order the party to reimburse the court for all or a portion of interpretation costs.

(6) Any doubts as to eligibility for interpreter services should be resolved in favor of appointment of an interpreter.

(7) At the time of determining eligibility, the court shall inform the party or witness of the penalties for making a false statement. The party has the continuing obligation to inform the court of any change in financial status and, upon request of the court, the party must submit financial information.

(G) **Administration of Oath or Affirmation to Interpreters**. The court shall administer an oath or affirmation to a foreign language interpreter substantially conforming to the following: "Do you solemnly swear or affirm that you will truly, accurately, and impartially interpret in the matter now before the court and not divulge confidential communications, so help you God?"

(H) **Request for Review**.

(1) Any time a court denies a request for the appointment of a foreign language interpreter or orders reimbursement of interpretation costs, it shall do so by written order.

(2) An LEP individual may immediately request review of the denial of appointment of a foreign language interpreter or an assessment for the reimbursement of interpretation costs. A request for review must be submitted to the court within 56 days after entry of the order.

(a) In a court having two or more judges, the chief judge shall decide the request for review de novo.

(b) In a single-judge court, or if the denial was issued by a chief judge, the judge shall refer the request for review to the state court administrator for assignment to another judge, who shall decide the request de novo.

(c) A pending request for review under this subrule stays the underlying litigation.

(d) A pending request for review under this subrule must be decided on an expedited basis.

(e) No motion fee is required for a request for review made under this subrule.

Subchapter 1.200 Amendment of Michigan Court Rules

Rule 1.201 Amendment Procedure

(A) **Notice of Proposed Amendment**. Before amending the Michigan Court Rules or other sets of rules within its jurisdiction, the Supreme Court will notify the secretary of the State Bar of Michigan and the state court administrator of the proposed amendment, and the manner and date for submitting comments. The notice also will be posted on the Court's website, http://courts.mi.gov/courts/michigansupremecourt/rules/court-rules-admin-matters/pages/default.aspx.

(B) **Notice to Bar**. The state bar secretary shall notify the appropriate state bar committees or sections of the proposed amendment, and the manner and date for submitting comments. Unless otherwise directed by the Court, the proposed amendment shall be published in the Michigan Bar Journal.

(C) **Notice to Judges**. The state court administrator shall notify the presidents of the Michigan Judges Association, the Michigan District Judges Association, and the Michigan Probate and Juvenile Court Judges Association of the proposed amendment, and the manner and date for submitting comments.

(D) **Exceptions**. The Court may modify or dispense with the notice requirements of this rule if it determines that there is a need for immediate action or if the proposed amendment would not significantly affect the delivery of justice.

(E) **Administrative Public Hearings**. The Court will conduct a public hearing pursuant to Supreme Court Administrative Order 1997-11 before acting on a proposed amendment that requires notice, unless there is a need for immediate action, in which event the amendment will be considered at a public hearing following adoption. Public hearing agendas will be posted on the Court's website.

CHAPTER 2 CIVIL PROCEDURE

Subchapter 2.000 General Provisions

Rule 2.001 Applicability

The rules in this chapter govern procedure in all civil proceedings in all courts established by the constitution and laws of the State of Michigan, except where the limited jurisdiction of a court makes a rule inherently inapplicable or where a rule applicable to a specific court or a specific type of proceeding provides a different procedure.

Rule 2.002 Waiver or Suspension of Fees and Costs for Indigent Persons

(A) **Applicability**.

(1) Only a natural person is eligible for the waiver or suspension of fees and costs under this rule.

(2) Except as provided in subrule (F), for the purpose of this rule "fees and costs" applies only to filing fees required by law.

(B) **Execution of Affidavits**. An affidavit required by this rule may be signed either

(1) by the party in whose behalf the affidavit is made; or

(2) by a person having personal knowledge of the facts required to be shown, if the person in whose behalf the affidavit is made is unable to sign it because of minority or other disability. The affidavit must recite the minority or other disability.

(C) **Persons Receiving Public Assistance**. If a party shows by ex parte affidavit or otherwise that he or she is receiving any form of public assistance, the payment of fees and costs as to that party shall be suspended.

(D) **Other Indigent Persons**. If a party shows by ex parte affidavit or otherwise that he or she is unable because of indigency to pay fees and costs, the court shall order those fees and costs either waived or suspended until the conclusion of the litigation.

(E) **Domestic Relations Cases; Payment of Fees and Costs by Spouse**.

(1) In an action for divorce, separate maintenance, or annulment or affirmation of marriage, the court shall order suspension of payment of fees and costs required to be paid by a party and order that they be paid by the spouse, if that party

(a) is qualified for a waiver or suspension of fees and costs under subrule (C) or (D), and

(b) is entitled to an order requiring the spouse to pay attorney fees.

(2) If the spouse is entitled to have the fees and costs waived or suspended under subrule (C) or (D), the fees and costs are waived or suspended for the spouse.

(F) **Payment of Service Fees and Costs of Publication for Indigent Persons**. If payment of fees and costs has been waived or suspended for a party and service of process must be made by an official process server or by publication, the court shall order the service fees or costs of publication paid by the county or funding unit in which the action is pending, if the party submits an ex parte affidavit stating facts showing the necessity for that type of service of process.

(G) **Reinstatement of Requirement for Payment of Fees and Costs**. If the payment of fees or costs has been waived or suspended under this rule, the court may on its own initiative order the person for whom the fees or costs were waived or suspended to pay those fees or costs when the reason for the waiver or suspension no longer exists.

Rule 2.003 Disqualification of Judge

(A) **Applicability**. This rule applies to all judges, including justices of the Michigan Supreme Court, unless a specific provision is stated to apply only to judges of a certain court. The word "judge" includes a justice of the Michigan Supreme Court.

(B) **Who May Raise**. A party may raise the issue of a judge's disqualification by motion or the judge may raise it.

(C) **Grounds**.

(1) Disqualification of a judge is warranted for reasons that include, but are not limited to, the following:

(a) The judge is biased or prejudiced for or against a party or attorney.

(b) The judge, based on objective and reasonable perceptions, has either (i) a serious risk of actual bias impacting the due process rights of a party as enunciated in Caperton v Massey, ____US____; 129 S Ct 2252; 173 L Ed 2d 1208 (2009), or (ii) has failed to adhere to the appearance of impropriety standard set forth in Canon 2 of the Michigan Code of Judicial Conduct.

(c) The judge has personal knowledge of disputed evidentiary facts concerning the proceeding.

(d) The judge has been consulted or employed as an attorney in the matter in controversy.

(e) The judge was a partner of a party, attorney for a party, or a member of a law firm representing a party within the preceding two years.

(f) The judge knows that he or she, individually or as a fiduciary, or the judge's spouse, parent or child wherever residing, or any other member of the judge's family residing in the judge's household, has more than a de minimis economic interest in the subject matter in controversy that could be substantially impacted by the proceeding.

(g) The judge or the judge's spouse, or a person within the third degree of relationship to either of them, or the spouse of such a person:
 (i) is a party to the proceeding, or an officer, director, or trustee of a party;
 (ii) is acting as a lawyer in the proceeding;
 (iii) is known by the judge to have a more than de minimis interest that could be substantially affected by the proceeding;
 (iv) is to the judge's knowledge likely to be a material witness in the proceeding.

(2) *Disqualification not warranted.*
 (a) A judge is not disqualified merely because the judge's former law clerk is an attorney of record for a party in an action that is before the judge or is associated with a law firm representing a party in an action that is before the judge.
 (b) A judge is not disqualified based solely upon campaign speech protected by Republican Party of Minn v White, 536 US 765 (2002), so long as such speech does not demonstrate bias or prejudice or an appearance of bias or prejudice for or against a party or an attorney involved in the action.

(D) **Procedure**.
(1)
 (a) Time for Filing in the Trial Courts. To avoid delaying trial and inconveniencing the witnesses, all motions for disqualification must be filed within 14 days of the discovery of the grounds for disqualification. If the discovery is made within 14 days of the trial date, the motion must be made forthwith.
 (b) Time for Filing in the Court of Appeals. All motions for disqualification must be filed within 14 days of disclosure of the judges' assignment to the case or within 14 days of the discovery of the grounds for disqualification. If a party discovers the grounds for disqualification within 14 days of a scheduled oral argument or argument on the application for leave to appeal, the motion must be made forthwith.
 (c) Time for Filing in the Supreme Court. If an appellant is aware of grounds for disqualification of a justice, the appellant must file a motion to disqualify with the application for leave to appeal. All other motions must be filed within 28 days after the filing of the application for leave to appeal or within 28 days of the discovery of the grounds for disqualification. If a party discovers the grounds for disqualification within 28 days of a scheduled oral argument or argument on the application for leave to appeal, the motion must be made forthwith.
 All requests for review by the entire Court pursuant to subsection (3)(b) must be made within 14 days of the entry of the decision by the individual justice.
 (d) Untimely Motions. Untimely motions in the trial court, the Court of Appeals, and the Supreme Court may be granted for good cause shown. If a motion is not timely filed in the trial court, the Court of Appeals, or the Supreme Court, untimeliness is a factor in deciding whether the motion should be granted.

(2) *All Grounds to be Included; Affidavit.* In any motion under this rule, the moving party must include all grounds for disqualification that are known at the time the motion is filed. An affidavit must accompany the motion.

(3) *Ruling.*
 (a) For courts other than the Supreme Court, the challenged judge shall decide the motion. If the challenged judge denies the motion,
 (i) in a court having two or more judges, on the request of a party, the challenged judge shall refer the motion to the chief judge, who shall decide the motion de novo;
 (ii) in a single-judge court, or if the challenged judge is the chief judge, on the request of a party, the challenged judge shall refer the motion to the state court administrator for assignment to another judge, who shall decide the motion de novo.
 (b) In the Supreme Court, if a justice's participation in a case is challenged by a written motion or if the issue of participation is raised by the justice himself or herself, the challenged justice shall decide the issue and publish his or her reasons about whether to participate.

If the challenged justice denies the motion for disqualification, a party may move for the motion to be decided by the entire Court. The entire Court shall then decide the motion for disqualification de novo. The Court's decision shall include the reasons for its grant or denial of the motion for disqualification. The Court shall issue a written order containing a statement of reasons for its grant or denial of the motion for disqualification. Any concurring or dissenting statements shall be in writing.

(4) *If Disqualification Motion is Granted.*
 (a) For courts other than the Supreme Court, when a judge is disqualified, the action must be assigned to another judge of the same court, or, if one is not available, the state court administrator shall assign another judge.

(b) In the Supreme Court, when a justice is disqualified, the underlying action will be decided by the remaining justices of the Court.

(E) **Waiver of Disqualification**. Parties to the proceeding may waive disqualification even where it appears that there may be grounds for disqualification of the judge. Such waiver may occur whether the grounds for disqualification were raised by a party or by the judge, so long as the judge is willing to participate. Any agreement to waive the disqualification must be made by all parties to the litigation and shall be in writing or placed on the record.

Rule 2.004 Incarcerated Parties

(A) This subrule applies to

(1) domestic relations actions involving minor children, and

(2) other actions involving the custody, guardianship, neglect, or foster-care placement of minor children, or the termination of parental rights,

in which a party is incarcerated under the jurisdiction of the Department of Corrections.

(B) The party seeking an order regarding a minor child shall

(1) contact the department to confirm the incarceration and the incarcerated party's prison number and location;

(2) serve the incarcerated person with the petition or motion seeking an order regarding the minor child, and file proof with the court that the papers were served; and

(3) file with the court the petition or motion seeking an order regarding the minor child, stating that a party is incarcerated and providing the party's prison number and location; the caption of the petition or motion shall state that a telephonic or video hearing is required by this rule.

(C) When all the requirements of subrule (B) have been accomplished to the court's satisfaction, the court shall issue an order requesting the department, or the facility where the party is located if it is not a department facility, to allow that party to participate with the court or its designee by way of a noncollect and unmonitored telephone call or by video conference in a hearing or conference, including a friend of the court adjudicative hearing or meeting. The order shall include the date and time for the hearing, and the prisoner's name and prison identification number, and shall be served by the court upon the parties and the warden or supervisor of the facility where the incarcerated party resides.

(D) All court documents or correspondence mailed to the incarcerated party concerning any matter covered by this rule shall include the name and the prison number of the incarcerated party on the envelope.

(E) The purpose of the telephone call or video conference described in this subrule is to determine

(1) whether the incarcerated party has received adequate notice of the proceedings and has had an opportunity to respond and to participate,

(2) whether counsel is necessary in matters allowing for the appointment of counsel to assure that the incarcerated party's access to the court is protected,

(3) whether the incarcerated party is capable of self-representation, if that is the party's choice,

(4) how the incarcerated party can communicate with the court or the friend of the court during the pendency of the action, and whether the party needs special assistance for such communication, including participation in additional telephone calls or video conferences, and

(5) the scheduling and nature of future proceedings, to the extent practicable, and the manner in which the incarcerated party may participate.

(F) A court may not grant the relief requested by the moving party concerning the minor child if the incarcerated party has not been offered the opportunity to participate in the proceedings, as described in this rule. This provision shall not apply if the incarcerated party actually does participate in a telephone call or video conference, or if the court determines that immediate action is necessary on a temporary basis to protect the minor child.

(G) The court may impose sanctions if it finds that an attempt was made to keep information about the case from an incarcerated party in order to deny that party access to the courts.

Subchapter 2.100 Commencement of Action; Service of Process; Pleadings; Motions

Rule 2.101 Form and Commencement of Action

(A) **Form of Action**. There is one form of action known as a "civil action."

(B) **Commencement of Action**. A civil action is commenced by filing a complaint with a court.

Rule 2.102 Summons; Expiration of Summons; Dismissal of Action for Failure to Serve

(A) **Issuance**. On the filing of a complaint, the court clerk shall issue a summons to be served as provided in MCR 2.103 and 2.105. A separate summons may issue against a particular defendant or group of defendants. A duplicate summons may be issued from time to time and is as valid as the original summons.

(B) **Form**. A summons must be issued "In the name of the people of the State of Michigan," under the seal of the court that issued it. It must be directed to the defendant, and include

(1) the name and address of the court,

(2) the names of the parties,

(3) the file number,

(4) the name and address of the plaintiff's attorney or the address of a plaintiff appearing without an attorney,
(5) the defendant's address, if known,
(6) the name of the court clerk,
(7) the date on which the summons was issued,
(8) the last date on which the summons is valid,
(9) a statement that the summons is invalid unless served on or before the last date on which it is valid,
(10) the time within which the defendant is required to answer or take other action, and
(11) a notice that if the defendant fails to answer or take other action within the time allowed, judgment may be entered against the defendant for the relief demanded in the complaint.

(C) **Amendment**. At any time on terms that are just, a court may allow process or proof of service of process to be amended, unless it clearly appears that to do so would materially prejudice the substantive rights of the party against whom the process issued. An amendment relates back to the date of the original issuance or service of process unless the court determines that relation back would unfairly prejudice the party against whom the process issued.

(D) **Expiration**. A summons expires 91 days after the date the complaint is filed. However, within those 91 days, on a showing of due diligence by the plaintiff in attempting to serve the original summons, the judge to whom the action is assigned may order a second summons to issue for a definite period not exceeding 1 year from the date the complaint is filed. If such an extension is granted, the new summons expires at the end of the extended period. The judge may impose just conditions on the issuance of the second summons. Duplicate summonses issued under subrule (A) do not extend the life of the original summons. The running of the 91-day period is tolled while a motion challenging the sufficiency of the summons or of the service of the summons is pending.

(E) **Dismissal as to Defendant Not Served**.
(1) On the expiration of the summons as provided in subrule (D), the action is deemed dismissed without prejudice as to a defendant who has not been served with process as provided in these rules, unless the defendant has submitted to the court's jurisdiction. As to a defendant added as a party after the filing of the first complaint in the action, the time provided in this rule runs from the filing of the first pleading that names that defendant as a party.
(2) After the time stated in subrule (E)(1), the clerk shall examine the court records and enter an order dismissing the action as to a defendant who has not been served with process or submitted to the court's jurisdiction. The clerk's failure to enter a dismissal order does not continue an action deemed dismissed.
(3) The clerk shall give notice of the entry of a dismissal order under MCR 2.107 and record the date of the notice in the case file. The failure to give notice does not affect the dismissal.

(F) **Setting Aside Dismissal**. A court may set aside the dismissal of the action as to a defendant under subrule (E) only on stipulation of the parties or when all of the following conditions are met:
(1) within the time provided in subrule (D), service of process was in fact made on the dismissed defendant, or the defendant submitted to the court's jurisdiction;
(2) proof of service of process was filed or the failure to file is excused for good cause shown;
(3) the motion to set aside the dismissal was filed within 28 days after notice of the order of dismissal was given, or, if notice of dismissal was not given, the motion was promptly filed after the plaintiff learned of the dismissal.

(G) **Exception; Summary Proceedings to Recover Possession of Realty**. Subrules (D), (E), and (F) do not apply to summary proceedings governed by MCL 600.5701-600.5759 and by subchapter 4.200 of these rules.

Rule 2.103 Process; Who May Serve

(A) **Service Generally**. Process in civil actions may be served by any legally competent adult who is not a party or an officer of a corporate party.

(B) **Service Requiring Seizure of Property**. A writ of restitution or process requiring the seizure or attachment of property may only be served by
(1) a sheriff or deputy sheriff, or a bailiff or court officer appointed by the court for that purpose,
(2) an officer of the Department of State Police in an action in which the state is a party, or
(3) a police officer of an incorporated city or village in an action in which the city or village is a party.
A writ of garnishment may be served by any person authorized by subrule (A).

(C) **Service in a Governmental Institution**. If personal service of process is to be made on a person in a governmental institution, hospital, or home, service must be made by the person in charge of the institution or by someone designated by that person.

(D) **Process Requiring Arrest**. Process in civil proceedings requiring the arrest of a person may be served only by a sheriff, deputy sheriff, or police officer, or by a court officer appointed by the court for that purpose.

Rule 2.104 Process; Proof of Service

(A) **Requirements**. Proof of service may be made by

(1) written acknowledgment of the receipt of a summons and a copy of the complaint, dated and signed by the person to whom the service is directed or by a person authorized under these rules to receive the service of process;

(2) a certificate stating the facts of service, including the manner, time, date, and place of service, if service is made within the State of Michigan by

(a) a sheriff,

(b) a deputy sheriff or bailiff, if that officer holds office in the county in which the court issuing the process is held,

(c) an appointed court officer,

(d) an attorney for a party; or

(3) an affidavit stating the facts of service, including the manner, time, date, and place of service, and indicating the process server's official capacity, if any.

The place of service must be described by giving the address where the service was made or, if the service was not made at a particular address, by another description of the location.

(B) **Failure to File**. Failure to file proof of service does not affect the validity of the service.

(C) **Publication, Posting, and Mailing**. If the manner of service used requires sending a copy of the summons and complaint by mail, the party requesting issuance of the summons is responsible for arranging the mailing and filing proof of service. Proof of publication, posting, and mailing under MCR 2.106 is governed by MCR 2.106(G).

Rule 2.105 Process; Manner of Service

(A) **Individuals**. Process may be served on a resident or nonresident individual by

(1) delivering a summons and a copy of the complaint to the defendant personally; or

(2) sending a summons and a copy of the complaint by registered or certified mail, return receipt requested, and delivery restricted to the addressee. Service is made when the defendant acknowledges receipt of the mail. A copy of the return receipt signed by the defendant must be attached to proof showing service under subrule (A)(2).

(B) **Individuals; Substituted Service.** Service of process may be made

(1) on a nonresident individual, by

(a) serving a summons and a copy of the complaint in Michigan on an agent, employee, representative, sales representative, or servant of the defendant, and

(b) sending a summons and a copy of the complaint by registered mail addressed to the defendant at his or her last known address;

(2) on a minor, by serving a summons and a copy of the complaint on a person having care and control of the minor and with whom he or she resides;

(3) on a defendant for whom a guardian or conservator has been appointed and is acting, by serving a summons and a copy of the complaint on the guardian or conservator;

(4) on an individual doing business under an assumed name, by

(a) serving a summons and copy of the complaint on the person in charge of an office or business establishment of the individual, and

(b) sending a summons and a copy of the complaint by registered mail addressed to the individual at his or her usual residence or last known address.

(C) **Partnerships; Limited Partnerships**. Service of process on a partnership or limited partnership may be made by

(1) serving a summons and a copy of the complaint on any general partner; or

(2) serving a summons and a copy of the complaint on the person in charge of a partnership office or business establishment and sending a summons and a copy of the complaint by registered mail, addressed to a general partner at his or her usual residence or last known address.

(D) **Private Corporations, Domestic and Foreign**. Service of process on a domestic or foreign corporation may be made by

(1) serving a summons and a copy of the complaint on an officer or the resident agent;

(2) serving a summons and a copy of the complaint on a director, trustee, or person in charge of an office or business establishment of the corporation and sending a summons and a copy of the complaint by registered mail, addressed to the principal office of the corporation;

(3) serving a summons and a copy of the complaint on the last presiding officer, president, cashier, secretary, or treasurer of a corporation that has ceased to do business by failing to keep up its organization by the appointment of officers or otherwise, or whose term of existence has expired;

(4) sending a summons and a copy of the complaint by registered mail to the corporation or an appropriate corporation officer and to the Michigan Bureau of Commercial Services, Corporation Division if

(a) the corporation has failed to appoint and maintain a resident agent or to file a certificate of that appointment as required by law;

(b) the corporation has failed to keep up its organization by the appointment of officers or otherwise; or

(c) the corporation's term of existence has expired.

(E) **Partnership Associations; Unincorporated Voluntary Associations**. Service of process on a partnership association or an unincorporated voluntary association may be made by
(1) serving a summons and a copy of the complaint on an officer, director, trustee, agent, or person in charge of an office or business establishment of the association, and
(2) sending a summons and a copy of the complaint by registered mail, addressed to an office of the association. If an office cannot be located, a summons and a copy of the complaint may be sent by registered mail to a member of the association other than the person on whom the summons and complaint was served.

(F) **Service on Insurer**. To the extent that it is permitted by statute, service on an insurer may be satisfied by providing two summonses and a copy of the complaint to the Commissioner of the Office of Financial and Insurance Regulation via delivery or registered mail.

(G) **Public Corporations**. Service of process on a public, municipal, quasi-municipal, or governmental corporation, unincorporated board, or public body may be made by serving a summons and a copy of the complaint on:
(1) the chairperson of the board of commissioners or the county clerk of a county;
(2) the mayor, the city clerk, or the city attorney of a city;
(3) the president, the clerk, or a trustee of a village;
(4) the supervisor or the township clerk of a township;
(5) the president, the secretary, or the treasurer of a school district;
(6) the president or the secretary of the Michigan State Board of Education;
(7) the president, the secretary, or other member of the governing body of a corporate body or an unincorporated board having control of a state institution;
(8) the president, the chairperson, the secretary, the manager, or the clerk of any other public body organized or existing under the constitution or laws of Michigan, when no other method of service is specially provided by statute.
The service of process may be made on an officer having substantially the same duties as those named or described above, irrespective of title. In any case, service may be made by serving a summons and a copy of the complaint on a person in charge of the office of an officer on whom service may be made and sending a summons and a copy of the complaint by registered mail addressed to the officer at his or her office.

(H) **Agent Authorized by Appointment or by Law**.
(1) Service of process on a defendant may be made by serving a summons and a copy of the complaint on an agent authorized by written appointment or by law to receive service of process.
(2) Whenever, pursuant to statute or court rule, service of process is to be made on a nongovernmental defendant by service on a public officer, service on the public officer may be made by registered mail addressed to his or her office.

(I) **Discretion of the Court**.
(1) On a showing that service of process cannot reasonably be made as provided by this rule, the court may by order permit service of process to be made in any other manner reasonably calculated to give the defendant actual notice of the proceedings and an opportunity to be heard.
(2) A request for an order under the rule must be made in a verified motion dated not more than 14 days before it is filed. The motion must set forth sufficient facts to show that process cannot be served under this rule and must state the defendant's address or last known address, or that no address of the defendant is known. If the name or present address of the defendant is unknown, the moving party must set forth facts showing diligent inquiry to ascertain it. A hearing on the motion is not required unless the court so directs.
(3) Service of process may not be made under this subrule before entry of the court's order permitting it.

(J) **Jurisdiction; Range of Service; Effect of Improper Service**.
(1) Provisions for service of process contained in these rules are intended to satisfy the due process requirement that a defendant be informed of an action by the best means available under the circumstances. These rules are not intended to limit or expand the jurisdiction given the Michigan courts over a defendant. The jurisdiction of a court over a defendant is governed by the United States Constitution and the constitution and laws of the State of Michigan. See MCL 600.701 et seq.
(2) There is no territorial limitation on the range of process issued by a Michigan court.
(3) An action shall not be dismissed for improper service of process unless the service failed to inform the defendant of the action within the time provided in these rules for service.

(K) **Registered and Certified Mail**.
(1) If a rule uses the term "registered mail," that term includes the term "certified mail," and the term "registered mail, return receipt requested" includes the term "certified mail, return receipt requested." However, if certified mail is used, the receipt of mailing must be postmarked by the post office.
(2) If a rule uses the term "certified mail," a postmarked receipt of mailing is not required.

Registered mail may be used when a rule requires certified mail.

Rule 2.106 Notice by Posting or Publication

(A) **Availability**. This rule governs service of process by publication or posting pursuant to an order under MCR 2.105(I).

(B) **Procedure**. A request for an order permitting service under this rule shall be made by motion in the manner provided in MCR 2.105(I). In ruling on the motion, the court shall determine whether mailing is required under subrules (D)(2) or (E)(2).

(C) **Notice of Action; Contents**.

(1) The order directing that notice be given to a defendant under this rule must include

(a) the name of the court,

(b) the names of the parties,

(c) a statement describing the nature of the proceedings,

(d) directions as to where and when to answer or take other action permitted by law or court rule, and

(e) a statement as to the effect of failure to answer or take other action.

(2) If the names of some or all defendants are unknown, the order must describe the relationship of the unknown defendants to the matter to be litigated in the best way possible, as, for example, unknown claimants, unknown owners, or unknown heirs, devisees, or assignees of a named person.

(D) **Publication of Order; Mailing**. If the court orders notice by publication, the defendant shall be notified of the action by

(1) publishing a copy of the order once each week for 3 consecutive weeks, or for such further time as the court may require, in a newspaper in the county where the defendant resides, if known, and if not, in the county where the action is pending; and

(2) sending a copy of the order to the defendant at his or her last known address by registered mail, return receipt requested, before the date of the last publication. If the plaintiff does not know the present or last known address of the defendant, and cannot ascertain it after diligent inquiry, mailing a copy of the order is not required. The moving party is responsible for arranging for the mailing and proof of mailing.

(E) **Posting; Mailing**. If the court orders notice by posting, the defendant shall be notified of the action by

(1) posting a copy of the order in the courthouse and 2 or more other public places as the court may direct for 3 continuous weeks or for such further time as the court may require; and

(2) sending a copy of the order to the defendant at his or her last known address by registered mail, return receipt requested, before the last week of posting. If the plaintiff does not know the present or last known address of the defendant, and cannot ascertain it after diligent inquiry, mailing a copy of the order is not required. The moving party is responsible for arranging for the mailing and proof of mailing.

The order must designate who is to post the notice and file proof of posting. Only a person listed in MCR 2.103(B)(1), (2), or (3) may be designated.

(F) **Newspaper Defined**.

(1) The term "newspaper" as used in this rule is limited to a newspaper published in the English language for the dissemination of general news and information or for the dissemination of legal news. The newspaper must have a bona fide list of paying subscribers or have been published at least once a week in the same community without interruption for at least 2 years, and have been established, published, and circulated at least once a week without interruption for at least 1 year in the county where publication is to occur.

(2) If no newspaper qualifies in the county where publication is to be made under subrule (D)(1) the term "newspaper" includes a newspaper that by this rule is qualified to publish notice of actions commenced in an adjoining county.

(G) **Proof of Service**. Service of process made pursuant to this rule may be proven as follows:

(1) Publication must be proven by an affidavit of the publisher or the publisher's agent

(a) stating facts establishing the qualification of the newspaper in which the order was published,

(b) setting out a copy of the published order, and

(c) stating the dates on which it was published.

(2) Posting must be proven by an affidavit of the person designated in the order under subrule (E) attesting that a copy of the order was posted for the required time in the courthouse in a conspicuous place open to the public and in the other places as ordered by the court.

(3) Mailing must be proven by affidavit. The affiant must attach a copy of the order as mailed, and a return receipt.

Rule 2.107 Service and Filing of Pleadings and Other Papers

(A) **Service; When Required**.

(1) Unless otherwise stated in this rule, every party who has filed a pleading, an appearance, or a motion must be served with a copy of every paper later filed in the action. A nonparty who has filed a motion or appeared in response to a motion need

only be served with papers that relate to that motion.

(2) Except as provided in MCR 2.603, after a default is entered against a party, further service of papers need not be made on that party unless he or she has filed an appearance or a written demand for service of papers. However, a pleading that states a new claim for relief against a party in default must be served in the manner provided by MCR 2.105.

(3) If an attorney appears on behalf of a person who has not received a copy of the complaint, a copy of the complaint must be delivered to the attorney on request.

(4) All papers filed on behalf of a defendant must be served on all other defendants not in default.

(B) **Service on Attorney or Party**.

(1) Service required or permitted to be made on a party for whom an attorney has appeared in the action must be made on the attorney except as follows:

(a) The original service of the summons and complaint must be made on the party as provided by MCR 2.105;

(b) When a contempt proceeding for disobeying a court order is initiated, the notice or order must be personally delivered to the party, unless the court orders otherwise;

(c) After a final judgment or final order has been entered and the time for an appeal of right has passed, papers must be served on the party unless the rule governing the particular postjudgment procedure specifically allows service on the attorney;

(d) The court may order service on the party.

(2) If two or more attorneys represent the same party, service of papers on one of the attorneys is sufficient. An attorney who represents more than one party is entitled to service of only one copy of a paper.

(3) If a party prosecutes or defends the action on his or her own behalf, service of papers must be made on the party in the manner provided by subrule (C).

(C) **Manner of Service**. Service of a copy of a paper on an attorney must be made by delivery or by mailing to the attorney at his or her last known business address or, if the attorney does not have a business address, then to his or her last known residence address. Service on a party must be made by delivery or by mailing to the party at the address stated in the party's pleadings.

(1) *Delivery to Attorney*. Delivery of a copy to an attorney within this rule means

(a) handing it to the attorney personally, or, if agreed to by the parties, e-mailing it to the attorney as allowed under MCR 2.107(C)(4);

(b) leaving it at the attorney's office with the person in charge or, if no one is in charge or present, by leaving it in a conspicuous place; or

(c) if the office is closed or the attorney has no office, by leaving it at the attorney's usual residence with some person of suitable age and discretion residing there.

(2) *Delivery to Party*. Delivery of a copy to a party within this rule means

(a) handing it to the party personally, or, if agreed to by the parties, e-mailing it to the party as allowed under MCR 2.107(C)(4); or

(b) leaving it at the party's usual residence with some person of suitable age and discretion residing there.

(3) *Mailing*. Mailing a copy under this rule means enclosing it in a sealed envelope with first class postage fully prepaid, addressed to the person to be served, and depositing the envelope and its contents in the United States mail. Service by mail is complete at the time of mailing.

(4) *E-mail*. Some or all of the parties may agree to e-mail service among themselves by filing a stipulation in that case. Some or all of the parties may agree to e-mail service by a court by filing an agreement with the court to do so. E-mail service shall be subject to the following conditions:

(a) The stipulation or agreement for service by e-mail shall set forth the e-mail addresses of the parties or attorneys that agree to e-mail service, which shall include the same e-mail address currently on file with the State Bar of Michigan. If an attorney is not a member of the State Bar of Michigan, the e-mail address shall be the e-mail address currently on file with the appropriate registering agency in the state of the attorney's admission. Parties and attorneys who have stipulated or agreed to service by e-mail under this subsection shall immediately notify all other parties and the court if the party's or attorney's e-mail address changes.

(b) The parties shall set forth in the stipulation or agreement all limitations and conditions concerning e-mail service, including but not limited to:

(i) the maximum size of the document that may be attached to an e-mail;

(ii) designation of exhibits as separate documents;

(iii) the obligation (if any) to furnish paper copies of e-mailed documents; and

(iv) the names and e-mail addresses of other individuals in the office of an attorney of record designated to receive e-mail service on behalf of a party.

(c) Documents served by e-mail must be in PDF format or other format that prevents the alteration of the document contents.

(d) A paper served by e-mail that an attorney is required to sign may include the attorney's actual signature or a signature block with the name of the signatory accompanied by "s/" or "/s/." That designation shall constitute a signature for all purposes, including those contemplated by MCR 2.114(C) and (D).

(e) Each e-mail that transmits a document shall include a subject line that identifies the case by court, party name, case number, and the title or legal description of the document(s) being sent.

(f) An e-mail transmission sent after 4:30 p.m. Eastern Time shall be deemed to be served on the next day that is not a Saturday, Sunday, or legal holiday. Service by e-mail under this subrule is treated as service by delivery under MCR 2.107(C)(1).

(g) A party may withdraw from a stipulation or agreement for service by e-mail if that party notifies the other party or parties and the court in writing at least 28 days in advance of the withdrawal.

(h) Service by e-mail is complete upon transmission, unless the party making service learns that the attempted service did not reach the e-mail address of the intended recipient. If an e-mail is returned as undeliverable, the party, attorney, or court must serve the paper or other document by regular mail under MCR 2.107(C)(3), and include a copy of the return notice indicating that the e-mail was undeliverable. A party, attorney, or court must also retain a notice that the e-mail was undeliverable.

(i) The e-mail sender shall maintain an archived record of sent items that shall not be purged until the conclusion of the case, including the disposition of all appeals.

(D) **Proof of Service**. Except as otherwise provided by MCR 2.104, 2.105, or 2.106, proof of service of papers required or permitted to be served may be by written acknowledgment of service, affidavit of the person making the service, a statement regarding the service verified under MCR 2.114(B), or other proof satisfactory to the court. The proof of service may be included at the end of the paper as filed. Proof of service must be filed promptly and at least at or before a hearing to which the paper relates.

(E) **Service Prescribed by Court**. When service of papers after the original complaint cannot reasonably be made because there is no attorney of record, because the party cannot be found, or for any other reason, the court, for good cause on ex parte application, may direct in what manner and on whom service may be made.

(F) **Numerous Parties**. In an action in which there is an unusually large number of parties on the same side, the court on motion or on its own initiative may order that

(1) they need not serve their papers on each other;

(2) responses to their pleadings need only be served on the party to whose pleading the response is made;

(3) a cross-claim, counterclaim, or allegation in an answer demanding a reply is deemed denied by the parties not served; and

(4) the filing of a pleading and service on an adverse party constitutes notice of it to all parties.

A copy of the order must be served on all parties in the manner the court directs.

(G) **Filing With Court Defined**. Pleadings and other materials filed with the court as required by these rules must be filed with the clerk of the court in accordance with standards prescribed by MCR 1.109(C), except that the judge to whom the case is assigned may accept materials for filing when circumstances warrant. A judge who does so shall note the filing date on the materials and immediately transmit them to the clerk. It is the responsibility of the party who presented the materials to confirm that they have been filed with the clerk. If the clerk records the receipt of materials on a date other than the filing date, the clerk shall record the filing date on the register of actions.

Rule 2.108 Time

(A) **Time for Service and Filing of Pleadings**.

(1) A defendant must serve and file an answer or take other action permitted by law or these rules within 21 days after being served with the summons and a copy of the complaint in Michigan in the manner provided in MCR 2.105(A)(1).

(2) If service of the summons and a copy of the complaint is made outside Michigan, or if the manner of service used requires the summons and a copy of the complaint to be sent by registered mail addressed to the defendant, the defendant must serve and file an answer or take other action permitted by law or these rules within 28 days after service.

(3) When service is made in accordance with MCR 2.106, the court shall allow a reasonable time for the defendant to answer or take other action permitted by law or these rules, but may not prescribe a time less than 28 days after publication or posting is completed.

(4) A party served with a pleading stating a cross-claim or counterclaim against that party must serve and file an answer or take other action permitted by law or these rules within 21 days after service.

(5) A party served with a pleading to which a reply is required or permitted may serve and file a reply

within 21 days after service of the pleading to which it is directed.

(6) In an action alleging medical malpractice filed on or after October 1, 1986, unless the defendant has responded as provided in subrule (A)(1) or (2), the defendant must serve and file an answer within 21 days after being served with the notice of filing the security for costs or the affidavit in lieu of such security required by MCL 600.2912d.

(B) **Time for Filing Motion in Response to Pleading**. A motion raising a defense or an objection to a pleading must be served and filed within the time for filing the responsive pleading or, if no responsive pleading is required, within 21 days after service of the pleading to which the motion is directed.

(C) **Effect of Particular Motions and Amendments**. When a motion or an amended pleading is filed, the time for pleading set in subrule (A) is altered as follows, unless a different time is set by the court:

(1) If a motion under MCR 2.116 made before filing a responsive pleading is denied, the moving party must serve and file a responsive pleading within 21 days after notice of the denial. However, if the moving party, within 21 days, files an application for leave to appeal from the order, the time is extended until 21 days after the denial of the application unless the appellate court orders otherwise.

(2) An order granting a motion under MCR 2.116 must set the time for service and filing of the amended pleading, if one is allowed.

(3) The response to a supplemental pleading or to a pleading amended either as of right or by leave of court must be served and filed within the time remaining for response to the original pleading or within 21 days after service of the supplemental or amended pleading, whichever period is longer.

(4) If the court has granted a motion for more definite statement, the responsive pleading must be served and filed within 21 days after the more definite statement is served.

(D) **Time for Service of Order to Show Cause**. An order to show cause must set the time for service of the order and for the hearing, and may set the time for answer to the complaint or response to the motion on which the order is based.

(E) **Extension of Time**. A court may, with notice to the other parties who have appeared, extend the time for serving and filing a pleading or motion or the doing of another act, if the request is made before the expiration of the period originally prescribed. After the expiration of the original period, the court may, on motion, permit a party to act if the failure to act was the result of excusable neglect. However, if a rule governing a particular act limits the authority to extend the time, those limitations must be observed. MCR 2.603(D) applies if a default has been entered.

(F) **Unaffected by Expiration of Term**. The time provided for the doing of an act or the holding of a proceeding is not affected or limited by the continuation or expiration of a term of court. The continuation or expiration of a term of court does not affect the power of a court to do an act or conduct a proceeding in a civil action pending before it.

Rule 2.109 Security for Costs

(A) **Motion**. On motion of a party against whom a claim has been asserted in a civil action, if it appears reasonable and proper, the court may order the opposing party to file with the court clerk a bond with surety as required by the court in an amount sufficient to cover all costs and other recoverable expenses that may be awarded by the trial court, or, if the claiming party appeals, by the trial and appellate courts. The court shall determine the amount in its discretion. MCR 3.604(E) and (F) govern objections to the surety.

(B) **Exceptions**. Subrule (A) does not apply in the following circumstances:

(1) The court may allow a party to proceed without furnishing security for costs if the party's pleading states a legitimate claim and the party shows by affidavit that he or she is financially unable to furnish a security bond.

(2) Security shall not be required of

(a) the United States or an agency or instrumentality of the United States;

(b) the State of Michigan or a governmental unit of the state, including but not limited to a public, municipal, quasi-municipal or governmental corporation, unincorporated board, public body, or political subdivision; or

(c) an officer of a governmental unit or agency exempt from security who brings an action in his or her official capacity.

(C) **Modification of Order**. The court may order new or additional security at any time on just terms,

(1) if the party or the surety moves out of Michigan, or

(2) if the original amount of the bond proves insufficient.

A person who becomes a new or additional surety is liable for all costs from the commencement of the action, as if he or she had been the original surety.

Rule 2.110 Pleadings

(A) **Definition of "Pleading."** The term "pleading" includes only:

(1) a complaint,

(2) a cross-claim,

(3) a counterclaim,

(4) a third-party complaint,

(5) an answer to a complaint, cross-claim, counterclaim, or third-party complaint, and
(6) a reply to an answer.
No other form of pleading is allowed.

(B) **When Responsive Pleading Required**. A party must file and serve a responsive pleading to
(1) a complaint,
(2) a counterclaim,
(3) a cross-claim,
(4) a third-party complaint, or
(5) an answer demanding a reply.

(C) **Designation of Cross-Claim or Counterclaim**. A cross-claim or a counterclaim may be combined with an answer. The counterclaim or cross-claim must be clearly designated as such.
(1) A responsive pleading is not required to a cross-claim or counterclaim that is not clearly designated as such in the answer.
(2) If a party has raised a cross-claim or counterclaim in the answer, but has not designated it as such, the court may treat the pleading as if it had been properly designated and require the party to amend the pleading, direct the opposing party to file a responsive pleading, or enter another appropriate order.
(3) The court may treat a cross-claim or counterclaim designated as a defense, or a defense designated as a cross-claim or counterclaim, as if the designation had been proper and issue an appropriate order.

Rule 2.111 General Rules of Pleading

(A) **Pleading to be Concise and Direct; Inconsistent Claims.**
(1) Each allegation of a pleading must be clear, concise, and direct.
(2) Inconsistent claims or defenses are not objectionable. A party may
(a) allege two or more statements of fact in the alternative when in doubt about which of the statements is true;
(b) state as many separate claims or defenses as the party has, regardless of consistency and whether they are based on legal or equitable grounds or on both.
All statements made in a pleading are subject to the requirements of MCR 2.114.

(B) **Statement of Claim**. A complaint, counterclaim, cross-claim, or third-party complaint must contain the following:
(1) A statement of the facts, without repetition, on which the pleader relies in stating the cause of action, with the specific allegations necessary reasonably to inform the adverse party of the nature of the claims the adverse party is called on to defend; and
(2) A demand for judgment for the relief that the pleader seeks. If the pleader seeks an award of money, a specific amount must be stated if the claim is for a sum certain or a sum that can by computation be made certain, or if the amount sought is $25,000 or less. Otherwise, a specific amount may not be stated, and the pleading must include allegations that show that the claim is within the jurisdiction of the court. Declaratory relief may be claimed in cases of actual controversy. See MCR 2.605. Relief in the alternative or relief of several different types may be demanded.

(C) **Form of Responsive Pleading**. As to each allegation on which the adverse party relies, a responsive pleading must
(1) state an explicit admission or denial;
(2) plead no contest; or
(3) state that the pleader lacks knowledge or information sufficient to form a belief as to the truth of an allegation, which has the effect of a denial.

(D) **Form of Denials**. Each denial must state the substance of the matters on which the pleader will rely to support the denial.

(E) **Effect of Failure to Deny**.
(1) Allegations in a pleading that requires a responsive pleading, other than allegations of the amount of damage or the nature of the relief demanded, are admitted if not denied in the responsive pleading.
(2) Allegations in a pleading that does not require a responsive pleading are taken as denied.
(3) A pleading of no contest, provided for in subrule (C)(2), permits the action to proceed without proof of the claim or part of the claim to which the pleading is directed. Pleading no contest has the effect of an admission only for purposes of the pending action.

(F) **Defenses; Requirement That Defense Be Pleaded**.
(1) *Pleading Multiple Defenses*. A pleader may assert as many defenses, legal or equitable or both, as the pleader has against an opposing party. A defense is not waived by being joined with other defenses.
(2) *Defenses Must Be Pleaded; Exceptions*. A party against whom a cause of action has been asserted by complaint, cross-claim, counterclaim, or third-party claim must assert in a responsive pleading the defenses the party has against the claim. A defense not asserted in the responsive pleading or by motion as provided by these rules is waived, except for the defenses of lack of jurisdiction over the subject matter of the action, and failure to state a claim on which relief can be granted. However,
(a) a party who has asserted a defense by motion filed pursuant to MCR 2.116 before filing a

responsive pleading need not again assert that defense in a responsive pleading later filed;

(b) if a pleading states a claim for relief to which a responsive pleading is not required, a defense to that claim may be asserted at the trial unless a pretrial conference summary pursuant to MCR 2.401(C) has limited the issues to be tried.

(3) *Affirmative Defenses*. Affirmative defenses must be stated in a party's responsive pleading, either as originally filed or as amended in accordance with MCR 2.118. Under a separate and distinct heading, a party must state the facts constituting

(a) an affirmative defense, such as contributory negligence; the existence of an agreement to arbitrate; assumption of risk; payment; release; satisfaction; discharge; license; fraud; duress; estoppel; statute of frauds; statute of limitations; immunity granted by law; want or failure of consideration; or that an instrument or transaction is void, voidable, or cannot be recovered on by reason of statute or nondelivery;

(b) a defense that by reason of other affirmative matter seeks to avoid the legal effect of or defeat the claim of the opposing party, in whole or in part;

(c) a ground of defense that, if not raised in the pleading, would be likely to take the adverse party by surprise.

Rule 2.112 Pleading Special Matters

(A) **Capacity; Legal Existence**.

(1) Except to the extent required to show jurisdiction of a court, it is not necessary to allege

(a) the capacity of a party to sue,

(b) the authority of a party to sue or be sued in a representative capacity, or

(c) the legal existence of an organized association of persons that is made a party.

(2) A party wishing to raise an issue about

(a) the legal existence of a party,

(b) the capacity of a party to sue or be sued, or

(c) the authority of a party to sue or be sued in a representative capacity,

must do so by specific allegation, including supporting facts peculiarly within the pleader's knowledge.

(B) **Fraud, Mistake, or Condition of Mind**.

(1) In allegations of fraud or mistake, the circumstances constituting fraud or mistake must be stated with particularity.

(2) Malice, intent, knowledge, and other conditions of mind may be alleged generally.

(C) **Conditions Precedent**.

(1) In pleading performance or occurrence of conditions precedent, it is sufficient to allege generally that all conditions precedent have been performed or have occurred.

(2) A denial of performance or occurrence must be made specifically and with particularity.

(D) **Action on Policy of Insurance**.

(1) In an action on a policy of insurance, it is sufficient to allege

(a) the execution, date, and amount of the policy,

(b) the premium paid or to be paid,

(c) the property or risk insured,

(d) the interest of the insured, and

(e) the loss.

(2) A defense of

(a) breach of condition, agreement, representation, or warranty of a policy of insurance or of an application for a policy; or

(b) failure to furnish proof of loss as required by the policy must be stated specifically and with particularity.

(E) **Action on Written Instrument**.

(1) In an action on a written instrument, the execution of the instrument and the handwriting of the defendant are admitted unless the defendant specifically denies the execution or the handwriting and supports the denial with an affidavit filed with the answer. The court may, for good cause, extend the time for filing the affidavits.

(2) This subrule also applies to an action against an indorser and to a party against whom a counterclaim or a cross-claim on a written instrument is filed.

(F) **Official Document or Act**. In pleading an official document or official act, it is sufficient to allege that the document was issued or the act done in compliance with law.

(G) **Judgment**. A judgment or decision of a domestic or foreign court, a tribal court of a federally recognized Indian tribe, a judicial or quasi-judicial tribunal, or a board or officer, must be alleged with sufficient particularity to identify it; it is not necessary to state facts showing jurisdiction to render it.

(H) **Statutes, Ordinances, or Charters**. In pleading a statute, ordinance, or municipal charter, it is sufficient to identify it, without stating its substance, except as provided in subrule (M).

(I) **Special Damages**. When items of special damage are claimed, they must be specifically stated.

(J) **Law of Other Jurisdictions; Notice in Pleadings**. A party who intends to rely on or raise an issue concerning the law of

(1) a state other than Michigan,

(2) a United States territory,

(3) a foreign nation or unit thereof, or

(4) a federally recognized Indian tribe

must give notice of that intention either in his or her pleadings or in a written notice served by the close of discovery.

(K) **Fault of Nonparties; Notice**.

(1) *Applicability*. This subrule applies to actions based on tort or another legal theory seeking damages for personal injury, property damage, or wrongful death to which MCL 600.2957 and MCL 600.6304, as amended by 1995 PA 249, apply.

(2) *Notice Requirement*. Notwithstanding MCL 600.6304, the trier of fact shall not assess the fault of a nonparty unless notice has been given as provided in this subrule.

(3) *Notice*.

(a) A party against whom a claim is asserted may give notice of a claim that a nonparty is wholly or partially at fault. A notice filed by one party identifying a particular nonparty serves as notice by all parties as to that nonparty.

(b) The notice shall designate the nonparty and set forth the nonparty's name and last known address, or the best identification of the nonparty that is possible, together with a brief statement of the basis for believing the nonparty is at fault.

(c) The notice must be filed within 91 days after the party files its first responsive pleading. On motion, the court shall allow a later filing of the notice on a showing that the facts on which the notice is based were not and could not with reasonable diligence have been known to the moving party earlier, provided that the late filing of the notice does not result in unfair prejudice to the opposing party.

(4) *Amendment Adding Party*. A party served with a notice under this subrule may file an amended pleading stating a claim or claims against the nonparty within 91 days of service of the first notice identifying that nonparty. The court may permit later amendment as provided in MCR 2.118.

(L) **Medical Malpractice Actions**.

(1) In an action alleging medical malpractice filed on or after October 1, 1993, each party must file an affidavit as provided in MCL 600.2912d and 600.2912e. Notice of filing the affidavit must be promptly served on the opposing party. If the opposing party has appeared in the action, the notice may be served in the manner provided by MCR 2.107. If the opposing party has not appeared, the notice must be served in the manner provided by MCR 2.105. Proof of service of the notice must be promptly filed with the court.

(2) In a medical malpractice action, unless the court allows a later challenge for good cause:

(a) all challenges to a notice of intent to sue must be made by motion, filed pursuant to MCR 2.119, at the time the defendant files its first response to the complaint, whether by answer or motion, and

(b) all challenges to an affidavit of merit or affidavit of meritorious defense, including challenges to the qualifications of the signer, must be made by motion, filed pursuant to MCR 2.119, within 63 days of service of the affidavit on the opposing party. An affidavit of merit or meritorious defense may be amended in accordance with the terms and conditions set forth in MCR 2.118 and MCL 600.2301.

(M) **Headlee Amendment Actions**. In an action brought pursuant to Const 1963, art 9, § 32, alleging a violation of Const 1963, art 9, §§ 25-34, the pleadings shall set forth with particularity the factual basis for the alleged violation or a defense and indicate whether there are any factual questions that are anticipated to require resolution by the court. In an action involving Const 1963, art 9, § 29, the plaintiff shall state with particularity the type and extent of the harm and whether there has been a violation of either the first or second sentence of that section. In an action involving the second sentence of Const 1963, art 9, §29, the plaintiff shall state with particularity the activity or service involved. The pleadings shall identify all statutes involved in the case, and the parties shall append to their pleadings copies of all ordinances and municipal charter provisions involved, and any available documentary evidence supportive of a claim or defense. The parties may supplement their pleadings with additional documentary evidence as it becomes available to them.

(N) A party whose cause of action is to collect a consumer debt as defined in the Michigan collection practices act (MCL 445.251[a] and [d]) must also include the following information in its complaint:

(1) the name of the creditor (as defined in MCL 445.251[e] and [f]), and

(2) the corresponding account number or identification number, or if none is available, information sufficient to identify the alleged debt, and

(3) the balance due to date.

(O) **Business and Commercial Disputes**.

(1) If a case involves a business or commercial dispute as defined in MCL 600.8031 and the court maintains a business court docket, a party shall verify on the face of the party's initial pleading that the case meets the statutory requirements to be assigned to the business court. If a cross-claim, counterclaim, third-party complaint, amendment, or any other modification of the action includes a business or commercial dispute, a party shall verify on the face of the party's pleading that the case meets the statutory requirements to be assigned to the business court.

(2) If a party files a pleading alleging a business or commercial dispute as defined in MCL 600.8031 but fails to verify that the case meets the statutory requirements to be assigned to the business court as required in subsection (1) of this subrule, any party to the action may thereafter file a motion for determination that the case is eligible for assignment to the business court.

(3) On the motion of a party or the court's own initiative, if the court determines that the action meets the statutory requirements of MCL 600.8031, the court shall assign the case to the business court.

(4) A party may file a motion requesting the chief judge review a decision made under subsection 3. The chief judge's ruling is not an order that may be appealed.

Rule 2.113 Form of Pleadings and Other Papers

(A) **Applicability**. The rules on the form, captioning, signing, and verifying of pleadings apply to all motions, affidavits, and other papers provided for by these rules. However, an affidavit must be verified by oath or affirmation.

(B) **Preparation**. Every pleading must be legibly printed in the English language and in compliance with MCR 1.109.

(C) **Captions**.

(1) The first part of every pleading must contain a caption stating

(a) the name of the court;

(b) the names of the parties or the title of the action, subject to subrule (D);

(c) the case number, including a prefix of the year filed and a two-letter suffix for the case-type code from a list provided by the State Court Administrator pursuant to MCR 8.117 according to the principal subject matter of the proceeding;

(d) the identification of the pleading (see MCR 2.110[A]);

(e) the name, business address, telephone number, and state bar number of the pleading attorney;

(f) the name, address, and telephone number of a pleading party appearing without an attorney; and

(g) the name and state bar number of each other attorney who has appeared in the action.

(2) The caption of a complaint must also contain either (a) or (b) as a statement of the attorney for the plaintiff, or of a plaintiff appearing without an attorney:

(a) There is no other pending or resolved civil action arising out of the transaction or occurrence alleged in the complaint.

(b) A civil action between these parties or other parties arising out of the transaction or occurrence alleged in the complaint has been previously filed in [this court]/[______ Court], where it was given docket number ______ and was assigned to Judge ______. The action [remains]/[is no longer] pending.

(3) If an action has been assigned to a particular judge in a multi-judge court, the name of that judge must be included in the caption of a pleading later filed with the court.

(D) **Names of Parties**.

(1) In a complaint, the title of the action must include the names of all the parties, with the plaintiff's name placed first.

(2) In other pleadings, it is sufficient to state the name of the first party on each side with an appropriate indication of other parties, such as "et al."

(E) **Paragraphs; Separate Statements**.

(1) All allegations must be made in numbered paragraphs, and the paragraphs of a responsive pleading must be numbered to correspond to the numbers of the paragraphs being answered.

(2) The content of each paragraph must be limited as far as practicable to a single set of circumstances.

(3) Each statement of a claim for relief founded on a single transaction or occurrence or on separate transactions or occurrences, and each defense other than a denial, must be stated in a separately numbered count or defense.

(F) **Exhibits; Written Instruments**.

(1) If a claim or defense is based on a written instrument, a copy of the instrument or its pertinent parts must be attached to the pleading as an exhibit unless the instrument is

(a) a matter of public record in the county in which the action is commenced and its location in the record is stated in the pleading;

(b) in the possession of the adverse party and the pleading so states;

(c) inaccessible to the pleader and the pleading so states, giving the reason; or

(d) of a nature that attaching the instrument would be unnecessary or impractical and the pleading so states, giving the reason.

(2) An exhibit attached or referred to under subrule (F)(1)(a) or (b) is a part of the pleading for all purposes.

(G) **Adoption by Reference**. Statements in a pleading may be adopted by reference only in another part of the same pleading.

Rule 2.114 Signatures of Attorneys and Parties; Verification; Effect; Sanctions

(A) **Applicability**. This rule applies to all pleadings, motions, affidavits, and other papers provided for by these rules. See MCR 2.113(A). In this rule, the term "document" refers to all such papers.

(B) **Verification.**

(1) Except when otherwise specifically provided by rule or statute, a document need not be verified or accompanied by an affidavit.

(2) If a document is required or permitted to be verified, it may be verified by

(a) oath or affirmation of the party or of someone having knowledge of the facts stated; or

(b) except as to an affidavit, including the following signed and dated declaration: "I declare that the statements above are true to the best of my information, knowledge, and belief."

In addition to the sanctions provided by subrule (E), a person who knowingly makes a false declaration under subrule (B)(2)(b) may be found in contempt of court.

(C) **Signature.**

(1) Requirement. Every document of a party represented by an attorney shall be signed by at least one attorney of record. A party who is not represented by an attorney must sign the document.

(2) Failure to Sign. If a document is not signed, it shall be stricken unless it is signed promptly after the omission is called to the attention of the party.

(3) An electronic signature is acceptable provided it complies with MCR 1.109(D).

(D) **Effect of Signature**. The signature of an attorney or party, whether or not the party is represented by an attorney, constitutes a certification by the signer that

(1) he or she has read the document;

(2) to the best of his or her knowledge, information, and belief formed after reasonable inquiry, the document is well grounded in fact and is warranted by existing law or a good-faith argument for the extension, modification, or reversal of existing law; and

(3) the document is not interposed for any improper purpose, such as to harass or to cause unnecessary delay or needless increase in the cost of litigation.

(E) **Sanctions for Violation**. If a document is signed in violation of this rule, the court, on the motion of a party or on its own initiative, shall impose upon the person who signed it, a represented party, or both, an appropriate sanction, which may include an order to pay to the other party or parties the amount of the reasonable expenses incurred because of the filing of the document, including reasonable attorney fees. The court may not assess punitive damages.

(F) **Sanctions for Frivolous Claims and Defenses**. In addition to sanctions under this rule, a party pleading a frivolous claim or defense is subject to costs as provided in MCR 2.625(A)(2). The court may not assess punitive damages.

Rule 2.115 Motion to Correct or to Strike Pleadings

(A) **Motion for More Definite Statement**. If a pleading is so vague or ambiguous that it fails to comply with the requirements of these rules, an opposing party may move for a more definite statement before filing a responsive pleading. The motion must point out the defects complained of and the details desired. If the motion is granted and is not obeyed within 14 days after notice of the order, or within such other time as the court may set, the court may strike the pleading to which the motion was directed or enter an order it deems just.

(B) **Motion to Strike**. On motion by a party or on the court's own initiative, the court may strike from a pleading redundant, immaterial, impertinent, scandalous, or indecent matter, or may strike all or part of a pleading not drawn in conformity with these rules.

Rule 2.116 Summary Disposition

(A) **Judgment on Stipulated Facts.**

(1) The parties to a civil action may submit an agreed-upon stipulation of facts to the court.

(2) If the parties have stipulated to facts sufficient to enable the court to render judgment in the action, the court shall do so.

(B) **Motion.**

(1) A party may move for dismissal of or judgment on all or part of a claim in accordance with this rule. A party against whom a defense is asserted may move under this rule for summary disposition of the defense. A request for dismissal without prejudice under MCL 600.2912c must be made by motion under MCR 2.116 and MCR 2.119.

(2) A motion under this rule may be filed at any time consistent with subrule (D) and subrule (G)(1), but the hearing on a motion brought by a party asserting a claim shall not take place until at least 28 days after the opposing party was served with the pleading stating the claim.

(C) **Grounds**. The motion may be based on one or more of these grounds, and must specify the grounds on which it is based:

(1) The court lacks jurisdiction over the person or property.

(2) The process issued in the action was insufficient.

(3) The service of process was insufficient.

(4) The court lacks jurisdiction of the subject matter.

(5) The party asserting the claim lacks the legal capacity to sue.

(6) Another action has been initiated between the same parties involving the same claim.
(7) Entry of judgment, dismissal of the action, or other relief is appropriate because of release, payment, prior judgment, immunity granted by law, statute of limitations, statute of frauds, an agreement to arbitrate or to litigate in a different forum, infancy or other disability of the moving party, or assignment or other disposition of the claim before commencement of the action.
(8) The opposing party has failed to state a claim on which relief can be granted.
(9) The opposing party has failed to state a valid defense to the claim asserted against him or her.
(10) Except as to the amount of damages, there is no genuine issue as to any material fact, and the moving party is entitled to judgment or partial judgment as a matter of law.

(D) **Time to Raise Defenses and Objections**. The grounds listed in subrule (C) must be raised as follows:
(1) The grounds listed in subrule (C)(1), (2), and (3) must be raised in a party's first motion under this rule or in the party's responsive pleading, whichever is filed first, or they are waived.
(2) The grounds listed in subrule (C)(5), (6), and (7) must be raised in a party's responsive pleading, unless the grounds are stated in a motion filed under this rule prior to the party's first responsive pleading. Amendment of a responsive pleading is governed by MCR 2.118.
(3) The grounds listed in subrule (C)(4) and the ground of governmental immunity may be raised at any time, regardless of whether the motion is filed after the expiration of the period in which to file dispositive motions under a scheduling order entered pursuant to MCR 2.401.
(4) The grounds listed in subrule (C)(8), (9), and (10) may be raised at any time, unless a period in which to file dispositive motions is established under a scheduling order entered pursuant to MCR 2.401. It is within the trial court's discretion to allow a motion filed under this subsection to be considered if the motion is filed after such period.

(E) **Consolidation; Successive Motions**.
(1) A party may combine in a single motion as many defenses or objections as the party has based on any of the grounds enumerated in this rule.
(2) No defense or objection is waived by being joined with one or more other defenses or objections.
(3) A party may file more than one motion under this rule, subject to the provisions of subrule (F).

(F) **Motion or Affidavit Filed in Bad Faith**. A party or an attorney found by the court to have filed a motion or an affidavit in violation of the provisions of MCR 2.114 may, in addition to the imposition of other penalties prescribed by that rule, be found guilty of contempt.

(G) **Affidavits; Hearing**.
(1) Except as otherwise provided in this subrule, MCR 2.119 applies to motions brought under this rule.
(a) Unless a different period is set by the court,
(i) a written motion under this rule with supporting brief and any affidavits must be filed and served at least 21 days before the time set for the hearing, and
(ii) any response to the motion (including brief and any affidavits) must be filed and served at least 7 days before the hearing.
(b) If the court sets a different time for filing and serving a motion or a response, its authorization must be endorsed in writing on the face of the notice of hearing or made by separate order.
(c) A copy of a motion or response (including brief and any affidavits) filed under this rule must be provided by counsel to the office of the judge hearing the motion. The judge's copy must be clearly marked JUDGE'S COPY on the cover sheet; that notation may be handwritten.
(2) Except as to a motion based on subrule (C)(8) or (9), affidavits, depositions, admissions, or other documentary evidence may be submitted by a party to support or oppose the grounds asserted in the motion.
(3) Affidavits, depositions, admissions, or other documentary evidence in support of the grounds asserted in the motion are required
(a) when the grounds asserted do not appear on the face of the pleadings, or
(b) when judgment is sought based on subrule (C)(10).
(4) A motion under subrule (C)(10) must specifically identify the issues as to which the moving party believes there is no genuine issue as to any material fact. When a motion under subrule (C)(10) is made and supported as provided in this rule, an adverse party may not rest upon the mere allegations or denials of his or her pleading, but must, by affidavits or as otherwise provided in this rule, set forth specific facts showing that there is a genuine issue for trial. If the adverse party does not so respond, judgment, if appropriate, shall be entered against him or her.
(5) The affidavits, together with the pleadings, depositions, admissions, and documentary evidence then filed in the action or submitted by the parties, must be considered by the court when the motion is based on subrule (C)(1)-(7) or (10). Only the pleadings may be considered when the motion is based on subrule (C)(8) or (9).
(6) Affidavits, depositions, admissions, and documentary evidence offered in support of or in

opposition to a motion based on subrule (C)(1)-(7) or (10) shall only be considered to the extent that the content or substance would be admissible as evidence to establish or deny the grounds stated in the motion.

(H) **Affidavits Unavailable**.

(1) A party may show by affidavit that the facts necessary to support the party's position cannot be presented because the facts are known only to persons whose affidavits the party cannot procure. The affidavit must

(a) name these persons and state why their testimony cannot be procured, and

(b) state the nature of the probable testimony of these persons and the reason for the party's belief that these persons would testify to those facts.

(2) When this kind of affidavit is filed, the court may enter an appropriate order, including an order

(a) denying the motion, or

(b) allowing additional time to permit the affidavit to be supported by further affidavits, or by depositions, answers to interrogatories, or other discovery.

(I) **Disposition by Court; Immediate Trial**.

(1) If the pleadings show that a party is entitled to judgment as a matter of law, or if the affidavits or other proofs show that there is no genuine issue of material fact, the court shall render judgment without delay.

(2) If it appears to the court that the opposing party, rather than the moving party, is entitled to judgment, the court may render judgment in favor of the opposing party.

(3) A court may, under proper circumstances, order immediate trial to resolve any disputed issue of fact, and judgment may be entered forthwith if the proofs show that a party is entitled to judgment on the facts as determined by the court. An immediate trial may be ordered if the grounds asserted are based on subrules (C)(1) through (C)(6), or if the motion is based on subrule (C)(7) and a jury trial as of right has not been demanded on or before the date set for hearing. If the motion is based on subrule (C)(7) and a jury trial has been demanded, the court may order immediate trial, but must afford the parties a jury trial as to issues raised by the motion as to which there is a right to trial by jury.

(4) The court may postpone until trial the hearing and decision on a matter involving disputed issues of fact brought before it under this rule.

(5) If the grounds asserted are based on subrule (C)(8), (9), or (10), the court shall give the parties an opportunity to amend their pleadings as provided by MCR 2.118, unless the evidence then before the court shows that amendment would not be justified.

(J) **Motion Denied; Case Not Fully Adjudicated on Motion**.

(1) If a motion under this rule is denied, or if the decision does not dispose of the entire action or grant all the relief demanded, the action must proceed to final judgment. The court may:

(a) set the time for further pleadings or amendments required;

(b) examine the evidence before it and, by questioning the attorneys, ascertain what material facts are without substantial controversy, including the extent to which damages are not disputed; and

(c) set the date on which all discovery must be completed.

(2) A party aggrieved by a decision of the court entered under this rule may:

(a) seek interlocutory leave to appeal as provided for by these rules;

(b) claim an immediate appeal as of right if the judgment entered by the court constitutes a final judgment under MCR 2.604(B); or

(c) proceed to final judgment and raise errors of the court committed under this rule in an appeal taken from final judgment.

Rule 2.117 Appearances

(A) **Appearance by Party**.

(1) A party may appear in an action by filing a notice to that effect or by physically appearing before the court for that purpose. In the latter event, the party must promptly file a written appearance and serve it on all persons entitled to service. The party's address and telephone number must be included in the appearance.

(2) Filing an appearance without taking any other action toward prosecution or defense of the action neither confers nor enlarges the jurisdiction of the court over the party. An appearance entitles a party to receive copies of all pleadings and papers as provided by MCR 2.107(A). In all other respects, the party is treated as if the appearance had not been filed.

(B) **Appearance by Attorney**.

(1) *In General*. An attorney may appear by an act indicating that the attorney represents a party in the action. An appearance by an attorney for a party is deemed an appearance by the party. Unless a particular rule indicates otherwise, any act required to be performed by a party may be performed by the attorney representing the party.

(2) *Notice of Appearance*.

(a) If an appearance is made in a manner not involving the filing of a paper with the court, the attorney must promptly file a written appearance and serve it on the parties entitled to service. The attorney's address and telephone number must be included in the appearance.

(b) If an attorney files an appearance, but takes no other action toward prosecution or defense of the action, the appearance entitles the attorney to service of pleadings and papers as provided by MCR 2.107(A).

(3) *Appearance by Law Firm.*

(a) A pleading, appearance, motion, or other paper filed by a law firm on behalf of a client is deemed the appearance of the individual attorney first filing a paper in the action. All notices required by these rules may be served on that individual. That attorney's appearance continues until an order of substitution or withdrawal is entered. This subrule is not intended to prohibit other attorneys in the law firm from appearing in the action on behalf of the party.

(b) The appearance of an attorney is deemed to be the appearance of every member of the law firm. Any attorney in the firm may be required by the court to conduct a court ordered conference or trial.

(C) **Duration of Appearance by Attorney**.

(1) Unless otherwise stated or ordered by the court, an attorney's appearance applies only in the court in which it is made, or to which the action is transferred, until a final judgment or final order is entered disposing of all claims by or against the party whom the attorney represents and the time for appeal of right has passed. The appearance applies in an appeal taken before entry of final judgment or final order by the trial court.

(2) An attorney who has entered an appearance may withdraw from the action or be substituted for only on order of the court.

Rule 2.118 Amended and Supplemental Pleadings

(A) **Amendments**.

(1) A party may amend a pleading once as a matter of course within 14 days after being served with a responsive pleading by an adverse party, or within 14 days after serving the pleading if it does not require a responsive pleading.

(2) Except as provided in subrule (A)(1), a party may amend a pleading only by leave of the court or by written consent of the adverse party. Leave shall be freely given when justice so requires.

(3) On a finding that inexcusable delay in requesting an amendment has caused or will cause the adverse party additional expense that would have been unnecessary had the request for amendment been filed earlier, the court may condition the order allowing amendment on the offending party's reimbursing the adverse party for the additional expense, including reasonable attorney fees.

(4) Amendments must be filed in writing, dated, and numbered consecutively, and must comply with MCR 2.113. Unless otherwise indicated, an amended pleading supersedes the former pleading.

(B) **Response to Amendments**. Within the time prescribed by MCR 2.108, a party served with an amendment to a pleading requiring a response under MCR 2.110(B) must

(1) serve and file a pleading in response to the amended pleading, or

(2) serve and file a notice that the party's pleading filed in response to the opposing party's earlier pleading will stand as the response to the amended pleading.

(C) **Amendments to Conform to the Evidence**.

(1) When issues not raised by the pleadings are tried by express or implied consent of the parties, they are treated as if they had been raised by the pleadings. In that case, amendment of the pleadings to conform to the evidence and to raise those issues may be made on motion of a party at any time, even after judgment.

(2) If evidence is objected to at trial on the ground that it is not within the issues raised by the pleadings, amendment to conform to that proof shall not be allowed unless the party seeking to amend satisfies the court that the amendment and the admission of the evidence would not prejudice the objecting party in maintaining his or her action or defense on the merits. The court may grant an adjournment to enable the objecting party to meet the evidence.

(D) **Relation Back of Amendments**. An amendment that adds a claim or a defense relates back to the date of the original pleading if the claim or defense asserted in the amended pleading arose out of the conduct, transaction, or occurrence set forth, or attempted to be set forth, in the original pleading. In a medical malpractice action, an amendment of an affidavit of merit or affidavit of meritorious defense relates back to the date of the original filing of the affidavit.

(E) **Supplemental Pleadings**. On motion of a party the court may, on reasonable notice and on just terms, permit the party to serve a supplemental pleading to state transactions or events that have happened since the date of the pleading sought to be supplemented, whether or not the original pleading is defective in its statement of a claim for relief or a defense. The court may order the adverse party to plead, specifying the time allowed for pleading.

Rule 2.119 Motion Practice

(A) **Form of Motions.**

(1) An application to the court for an order in a pending action must be by motion. Unless made during a hearing or trial, a motion must

(a) be in writing,

(b) state with particularity the grounds and authority on which it is based,

(c) state the relief or order sought, and

(d) be signed by the party or attorney as provided in MCR 2.114.

(2) A motion or response to a motion that presents an issue of law must be accompanied by a brief citing the authority on which it is based. Except as permitted by the court, the combined length of any motion and brief, or of a response and brief, may not exceed 20 pages double spaced, exclusive of attachments and exhibits. Quotations and footnotes may be single-spaced. At least one-inch margins must be used, and printing shall not be smaller than 12-point type. A copy of a motion or response (including brief) filed under this rule must be provided by counsel to the office of the judge hearing the motion. The judge's copy must be clearly marked judge's copy on the cover sheet; that notation may be handwritten.

(3) A motion and notice of the hearing on it may be combined in the same document.

(4) If a contested motion is filed after rejection of a proposed order under subrule (D), a copy of the rejected order and an affidavit establishing the rejection must be filed with the motion.

(B) **Form of Affidavits.**

(1) If an affidavit is filed in support of or in opposition to a motion, it must:

(a) be made on personal knowledge;

(b) state with particularity facts admissible as evidence establishing or denying the grounds stated in the motion; and

(c) show affirmatively that the affiant, if sworn as a witness, can testify competently to the facts stated in the affidavit.

(2) Sworn or certified copies of all papers or parts of papers referred to in an affidavit must be attached to the affidavit unless the papers or copies:

(a) have already been filed in the action;

(b) are matters of public record in the county in which the action is pending;

(c) are in the possession of the adverse party, and this fact is stated in the affidavit or the motion; or

(d) are of such nature that attaching them would be unreasonable or impracticable, and this fact and the reasons are stated in the affidavit or the motion.

(C) **Time for Service and Filing of Motions and Responses.**

(1) Unless a different period is set by these rules or by the court for good cause, a written motion (other than one that may be heard ex parte), notice of the hearing on the motion, and any supporting brief or affidavits must be served as follows:

(a) at least 9 days before the time set for the hearing, if served by mail, or

(b) at least 7 days before the time set for the hearing, if served by delivery under MCR 2.107(C)(1) or (2).

(2) Unless a different period is set by these rules or by the court for good cause, any response to a motion (including a brief or affidavits) required or permitted by these rules must be served as follows:

(a) at least 5 days before the hearing, if served by mail, or

(b) at least 3 days before the hearing, if served by delivery under MCR 2.107(C)(1) or (2).

(3) If the court sets a different time for serving a motion or response its authorization must be endorsed in writing on the face of the notice of hearing or made by separate order.

(4) Unless the court sets a different time, a motion must be filed at least 7 days before the hearing, and any response to a motion required or permitted by these rules must be filed at least 3 days before the hearing.

(D) **Uncontested Orders.**

(1) Before filing a motion, a party may serve on the opposite party a copy of a proposed order and a request to stipulate to the court's entry of the proposed order.

(2) On receipt of a request to stipulate, a party may

(a) stipulate to the entry of the order by signing the following statement at the end of the proposed order: “I stipulate to the entry of the above order”; or

(b) waive notice and hearing on the entry of an order by signing the following statement at the end of the proposed order: “Notice and hearing on entry of the above order is waived.”

A proposed order is deemed rejected unless it is stipulated to or notice and hearing are waived within 7 days after it is served.

(3) If the parties have stipulated to the entry of a proposed order or waived notice and hearing, the court may enter the order. If the court declines to enter the order, it shall notify the moving party that a hearing on the motion is required. The matter then proceeds as a contested motion under subrule (E).

(4) The moving party must serve a copy of an order entered by the court pursuant to subrule (D)(3) on the parties entitled to notice under MCR 2.107, or

notify them that the court requires the matter to be heard as a contested motion.

(5) Notwithstanding the provisions of subrule (D)(3), stipulations and orders for adjournment are governed by MCR 2.503.

(E) **Contested Motions**.

(1) Contested motions should be noticed for hearing at the time designated by the court for the hearing of motions. A motion will be heard on the day for which it is noticed, unless the court otherwise directs. If a motion cannot be heard on the day it is noticed, the court may schedule a new hearing date or the moving party may renotice the hearing.

(2) When a motion is based on facts not appearing of record, the court may hear the motion on affidavits presented by the parties, or may direct that the motion be heard wholly or partly on oral testimony or deposition.

(3) A court may, in its discretion, dispense with or limit oral arguments on motions, and may require the parties to file briefs in support of and in opposition to a motion.

(4) Appearance at the hearing is governed by the following:

(a) A party who, pursuant to subrule (D)(2), has previously rejected the proposed order before the court must either

(i) appear at the hearing held on the motion, or

(ii) before the hearing, file a response containing a concise statement of reasons in opposition to the motion and supporting authorities.

A party who fails to comply with this subrule is subject to assessment of costs under subrule (E)(4)(c).

(b) Unless excused by the court, the moving party must appear at a hearing on the motion. A moving party who fails to appear is subject to assessment of costs under subrule (E)(4)(c); in addition, the court may assess a penalty not to exceed $100, payable to the clerk of the court.

(c) If a party violates the provisions of subrule (E)(4)(a) or (b), the court shall assess costs against the offending party, that party's attorney, or both, equal to the expenses reasonably incurred by the opposing party in appearing at the hearing, including reasonable attorney fees, unless the circumstances make an award of expenses unjust.

(F) **Motions for Rehearing or Reconsideration**.

(1) Unless another rule provides a different procedure for reconsideration of a decision (see, e.g., MCR 2.604[A], 2.612), a motion for rehearing or reconsideration of the decision on a motion must be served and filed not later than 21 days after entry of an order deciding the motion.

(2) No response to the motion may be filed, and there is no oral argument, unless the court otherwise directs.

(3) Generally, and without restricting the discretion of the court, a motion for rehearing or reconsideration which merely presents the same issues ruled on by the court, either expressly or by reasonable implication, will not be granted. The moving party must demonstrate a palpable error by which the court and the parties have been misled and show that a different disposition of the motion must result from correction of the error.

(G) **Motion Fees**. The following provisions apply to actions in which a motion fee is required:

(1) A motion fee must be paid on the filing of any request for an order in a pending action, whether the request is entitled "motion," "petition," "application," or otherwise.

(2) The clerk shall charge a single motion fee for all motions filed at the same time in an action regardless of the number of separately captioned documents filed or the number of distinct or alternative requests for relief included in the motions.

(3) A motion fee may not be charged:

(a) in criminal cases;

(b) for a notice of settlement of a proposed judgment or order under MCR 2.602(B);

(c) for a request for an order waiving fees under MCR 2.002 or MCL 600.2529(4) or MCL 600.8371(6);

(d) if the motion is filed at the same time as another document in the same action as to which a fee is required; or

(e) for entry of an uncontested order under subrule (D).

Subchapter 2.200 Parties; Joinder of Claims and Parties; Venue; Transfer of Actions

Rule 2.201 Parties Plaintiff and Defendant; Capacity

(A) **Designation of Parties**. The party who commences a civil action is designated as plaintiff and the adverse party as defendant. In an appeal the relative position of the parties and their designations as plaintiff and defendant are the same, but they are also designated as appellant and appellee.

(B) **Real Party in Interest**. An action must be prosecuted in the name of the real party in interest, subject to the following provisions:

(1) A personal representative, guardian, conservator, trustee of an express trust, a party with whom or in

whose name a contract has been made for the benefit of another, or a person authorized by statute may sue in his or her own name without joining the party for whose benefit the action is brought.

(2) An action on the bond of a public officer required to give bond to the people of the state may be brought in the name of the person to whom the right on the bond accrues.

(3) An action on a bond, contract, or undertaking made with an officer of the state or of a governmental unit, including but not limited to a public, municipal, quasi-municipal, or governmental corporation, an unincorporated board, a public body, or a political subdivision, may be brought in the name of the state or the governmental unit for whose benefit the contract was made.

(4) An action to prevent illegal expenditure of state funds or to test the constitutionality of a statute relating to such an expenditure may be brought:

(a) in the name of a domestic nonprofit corporation organized for civic, protective, or improvement purposes; or

(b) in the names of at least 5 residents of Michigan who own property assessed for direct taxation by the county where they reside.

(C) **Capacity to Sue or be Sued.**

(1) A natural person may sue or be sued in his or her own name.

(2) A person conducting a business under a name subject to certification under the assumed name statute may be sued in that name in an action arising out of the conduct of that business.

(3) A partnership, partnership association, or unincorporated voluntary association having a distinguishing name may sue or be sued in its partnership or association name, in the names of any of its members designated as such, or both.

(4) A domestic or a foreign corporation may sue or be sued in its corporate name, unless a statute provides otherwise.

(5) Actions to which the state or a governmental unit (including but not limited to a public, municipal, quasi-municipal, or governmental corporation, an unincorporated board, a public body, or a political subdivision) is a party may be brought by or against the state or governmental unit in its own name, or in the name of an officer authorized to sue or be sued on its behalf. An officer of the state or governmental unit must be sued in the officer's official capacity to enforce the performance of an official duty. An officer who sues or is sued in his or her official capacity may be described as a party by official title and not by name, but the court may require the name to be added.

(D) **Unknown Parties; Procedure**.

(1) Persons who are or may be interested in the subject matter of an action, but whose names cannot be ascertained on diligent inquiry, may be made parties by being described as:

(a) unknown claimants;

(b) unknown owners; or

(c) unknown heirs, devisees, or assignees of a deceased person who may have been interested in the subject matter of the action.

If it cannot be ascertained on diligent inquiry whether a person who is or may be interested in the subject matter of the action is alive or dead, what disposition the person may have made of his or her interest, or where the person resides if alive, the person and everyone claiming under him or her may be made parties by naming the person and adding "or [his or her] unknown heirs, devisees, or assignees."

(2) The names and descriptions of the persons sought to be made parties, with a statement of the efforts made to identify and locate them, must be stated in the complaint and verified by oath or affirmation by the plaintiff or someone having knowledge of the facts in the plaintiff's behalf. The court may require a more specific description to be made by amendment.

(3) A publication giving notice to persons who cannot be personally served must include the description of unknown persons as set forth in the complaint or amended complaint.

(4) The publication and all later proceedings in the action are conducted as if the unknown parties were designated by their proper names. The judgment rendered determines the nature, validity, and extent of the rights of all parties.

(5) A person desiring to appear and show his or her interest in the subject matter of the action must proceed under MCR 2.209. Subject to that rule, the person may be made a party in his or her proper name.

(E) **Minors and Incompetent Persons**. This subrule does not apply to proceedings under chapter 5.

(1) *Representation.*

(a) If a minor or incompetent person has a conservator, actions may be brought and must be defended by the conservator on behalf of the minor or incompetent person.

(b) If a minor or incompetent person does not have a conservator to represent the person as plaintiff, the court shall appoint a competent and responsible person to appear as next friend on his or her behalf, and the next friend is responsible for the costs of the action.

(c) If the minor or incompetent person does not have a conservator to represent the person as defendant, the action may not proceed until the court appoints a guardian ad litem, who is not responsible for the costs of the action unless, by reason of personal misconduct, he or she is specifically charged costs by the court. It is unnecessary to appoint a representative for a minor accused of a civil infraction.

(2) *Appointment of Representative.*

(a) Appointment of a next friend or guardian ad litem shall be made by the court as follows:

(i) if the party is a minor 14 years of age or older, on the minor's nomination, accompanied by a written consent of the person to be appointed;

(ii) if the party is a minor under 14 years of age or an incompetent person, on the nomination of the party's next of kin or of another relative or friend the court deems suitable, accompanied by a written consent of the person to be appointed; or

(iii) if a nomination is not made or approved within 21 days after service of process, on motion of the court or of a party.

(b) The court may refuse to appoint a representative it deems unsuitable.

(c) The order appointing a person next friend or guardian ad litem must be promptly filed with the clerk of the court.

(3) *Security.*

(a) Except for costs and expenses awarded to the next friend or guardian ad litem or the represented party, a person appointed under this subrule may not receive money or property belonging to the minor or incompetent party or awarded to that party in the action, unless he or she gives security as the court directs.

(b) The court may require that the conservator representing a minor or incompetent party give security as the court directs before receiving the party's money or property.

(4) Incompetency While Action Pending. A party who becomes incompetent while an action is pending may be represented by his or her conservator, or the court may appoint a next friend or guardian ad litem as if the action had been commenced after the appointment.

Rule 2.202 Substitution of Parties

(A) **Death.**

(1) If a party dies and the claim is not thereby extinguished, the court may order substitution of the proper parties.

(a) A motion for substitution may be made by a party, or by the successor or representative of the deceased party.

(b) Unless a motion for substitution is made within 91 days after filing and service of a statement of the fact of the death, the action must be dismissed as to the deceased party, unless the party seeking substitution shows that there would be no prejudice to any other party from allowing later substitution.

(c) Service of the statement or motion must be made on the parties as provided in MCR 2.107, and on persons not parties as provided in MCR 2.105.

(2) If one or more of the plaintiffs or one or more of the defendants in an action dies, and the right sought to be enforced survives only to the surviving plaintiffs or only against the surviving defendants, the action does not abate. A party or attorney who learns that a party has died must promptly file a notice of the death.

(B) **Transfer or Change of Interest**. If there is a change or transfer of interest, the action may be continued by or against the original party in his or her original capacity, unless the court, on motion supported by affidavit, directs that the person to whom the interest is transferred be substituted for or joined with the original party, or directs that the original party be made a party in another capacity. Notice must be given as provided in subrule (A)(1)(c).

(C) **Public Officers; Death or Separation From Office**. When an officer of the class described in MCR 2.201(C)(5) is a party to an action and during its pendency dies, resigns, or otherwise ceases to hold office, the action may be continued and maintained by or against the officer's successor without a formal order of substitution.

(D) **Substitution at Any Stage**. Substitution of parties under this rule may be ordered by the court either before or after judgment or by the Court of Appeals or Supreme Court pending appeal. If substitution is ordered, the court may require additional security to be given.

Rule 2.203 Joinder of Claims, Counterclaims, and Cross-Claims

(A) **Compulsory Joinder**. In a pleading that states a claim against an opposing party, the pleader must join every claim that the pleader has against that opposing party at the time of serving the pleading, if it arises out of the transaction or occurrence that is the subject matter of the action and does not require for its adjudication the presence of third parties over whom the court cannot acquire jurisdiction.

(B) **Permissive Joinder**. A pleader may join as either independent or alternate claims as many claims, legal or equitable, as the pleader has against an opposing party. If a claim is one previously cognizable only after another claim has been prosecuted to a conclusion, the two claims may be joined in a single action; but the court may grant relief only in accordance with the substantive rights of the parties.

(C) **Counterclaim Exceeding Opposing Claim**. A counterclaim may, but need not, diminish or defeat the recovery sought by the opposing party. It may claim relief exceeding in amount or different in kind from that sought in the pleading of the opposing party.

(D) **Cross-Claim Against Co-Party**. A pleading may state as a cross-claim a claim by one party against a co-party arising out of the transaction or occurrence that is the subject matter of the original action or of a counterclaim, or that relates to property that is the subject matter of the original action. The cross-claim may include a claim that the party against whom it is asserted is or may be liable to the cross-claimant for all or part of a claim asserted in the action against the cross-claimant.

(E) **Time for Filing Counterclaim or Cross-Claim**. A counterclaim or cross-claim must be filed with the answer or filed as an amendment in the manner provided by MCR 2.118. If a motion to amend to state a counterclaim or cross-claim is denied, the litigation of that claim in another action is not precluded unless the court specifies otherwise.

(F) **Separate Trials; Separate Judgment**. If the court orders separate trials as provided in MCR 2.505(B), judgment on a claim, counterclaim, or cross-claim may be rendered in accordance with the terms of MCR 2.604 when the court has jurisdiction to do so. The judgment may be rendered even if the claims of the opposing party have been dismissed or otherwise disposed of.

(G) **Joining Additional Parties**.

(1) *Persons Who May be Joined*. Persons other than those made parties to the original action may be made parties to a counterclaim or cross-claim, subject to MCT 2.205 and 2.206.

(2) *Summons*. On the filing of a counterclaim or cross-claim adding new parties, the court clerk shall issue a summons for each new party in the same manner as on the filing of a complaint, as provided in MCR 2.102(A)-(C). Unless the court order otherwise, the summons is valid for 21 days after the court issues it.

Rule 2.204 Third-Party Practice

(A) **When Defendant May Bring in Third Party**.

(1) Subject to the provisions of MCL 500.3030, any time after commencement of an action, a defending party, as a third-party plaintiff, may serve a summons and complaint on a person not a party to the action who is or may be liable to the third-party plaintiff for all or part of the plaintiff's claim. The third-party plaintiff need not obtain leave to make the service if the third-party complaint is filed within 21 days after the third-party plaintiff's original answer was filed. Otherwise, leave on motion with notice to all parties is required. Unless the court orders otherwise, the summons issued on the filing of a third-party complaint is valid for 21 days after it is issued, and must include the expiration date. See MCR 2.102(B)(8).

(2) Within the time provided by MCR 2.108(A)(1)-(3), the person served with the summons and third-party complaint (the "third-party defendant") must respond to the third-party plaintiff's claim as provided in MCR 2.111, and may file counterclaims against the third-party plaintiff and cross-claims against other parties as provided in MCR 2.203. The third-party defendant may assert against the plaintiff any defenses which the third-party plaintiff has to the plaintiff's claim. The third-party defendant may also assert a claim against the plaintiff arising out of the transaction or occurrence that is the subject matter of the plaintiff's claim against the third-party plaintiff.

(3) The plaintiff may assert a claim against the third-party defendant arising out of the transaction or occurrence that is the subject matter of the plaintiff's claim against the third-party plaintiff, and the third-party defendant must respond as provided in MCR 2.111 and may file counterclaims and cross-claims as provided in MCR 2.203.

(4) A party may move for severance, separate trial, or dismissal of the third-party claim. The court may direct entry of a final judgment on either the original claim or the third-party claim, in accordance with MCR 2.604(B).

(5) A third-party defendant may proceed under this rule against a person not a party to the action who is or may be liable to the third-party defendant for all or part of a claim made in the action against the third-party defendant.

(B) **When Plaintiff May Bring in Third Party**. A plaintiff against whom a claim or counterclaim is asserted may bring in a third party under this rule to the same extent as a defendant.

(C) **Exception; Small Claims**. The provisions of this rule do not apply to actions in the small claims division of the district court.

Rule 2.205 Necessary Joinder of Parties

(A) **Necessary Joinder**. Subject to the provisions of subrule (B) and MCR 3.501, persons having such interests in the subject matter of an action that their presence in the action is essential to permit the court to render complete relief must be made parties and aligned as plaintiffs or defendants in accordance with their respective interests.

(B) **Effect of Failure to Join**. When persons described in subrule (A) have not been made parties and are subject to the jurisdiction of the court, the court shall order them summoned to appear in the action, and may prescribe the time and order of pleading. If jurisdiction over those persons can be acquired only by their consent or voluntary appearance, the court may proceed with the action and grant appropriate relief to persons who are parties to prevent a failure of justice. In determining whether to proceed, the court shall consider

(1) whether a valid judgment may be rendered in favor of the plaintiff in the absence of the person not joined;

(2) whether the plaintiff would have another effective remedy if the action is dismissed because of the nonjoinder;

(3) the prejudice to the defendant or to the person not joined that may result from the nonjoinder; and

(4) whether the prejudice, if any, may be avoided or lessened by a protective order or a provision included in the final judgment.

(C) Notwithstanding the failure to join a person who should have been joined, the court may render a judgment against the plaintiff whenever it is determined that the plaintiff is not entitled to relief as a matter of substantive law.

(D) **Names of Omitted Persons and Reasons for Nonjoinder to be Pleaded**. In a pleading in which relief is asked, the pleader must state the names, if known, of persons who are not joined, but who ought to be parties if complete relief is to be accorded to those already parties, and must state why they are not joined.

Rule 2.206 Permissive Joinder of Parties

(A) **Permissive Joinder**.

(1) All persons may join in one action as plaintiffs

(a) if they assert a right to relief jointly, severally, or in the alternative, in respect of or arising out of the same transaction, occurrence, or series of transactions or occurrences and if a question of law or fact common to all of the plaintiffs will arise in the action; or

(b) if their presence in the action will promote the convenient administration of justice.

(2) All persons may be joined in one action as defendants

(a) if there is asserted against them jointly, severally, or in the alternative, a right to relief in respect of or arising out of the same transaction, occurrence, or series of transactions or occurrences and if a question of law or fact common to all of the defendants will arise in the action; or

(b) if their presence in the action will promote the convenient administration of justice.

(3) A plaintiff or defendant need not be interested in obtaining or defending against all the relief demanded. Judgment may be rendered for one or more of the parties against one or more of the parties as the rights and liabilities of the parties are determined.

(B) **Separate Trials**. The court may enter orders to prevent a party from being embarrassed, delayed, or put to expense by the joinder of a person against whom the party asserts no claim and who asserts no claim against the party, and may order separate trials or enter other orders to prevent delay or prejudice.

Rule 2.207 Misjoinder and Nonjoinder of Parties

Misjoinder of parties is not a ground for dismissal of an action. Parties may be added or dropped by order of the court on motion of a party or on the court's own initiative at any stage of the action and on terms that are just. When the presence of persons other than the original parties to the action is required to grant complete relief in the determination of a counterclaim or cross-claim, the court shall order those persons to be brought in as defendants if jurisdiction over them can be obtained. A claim against a party may be severed and proceeded with separately.

Rule 2.209 Intervention

(A) **Intervention of Right**. On timely application a person has a right to intervene in an action:

(1) when a Michigan statute or court rule confers an unconditional right to intervene;

(2) by stipulation of all the parties; or

(3) when the applicant claims an interest relating to the property or transaction which is the subject of the action and is so situated that the disposition of the action may as a practical matter impair or impede the applicant's ability to protect that interest, unless the applicant's interest is adequately represented by existing parties.

(B) **Permissive Intervention**. On timely application a person may intervene in an action

(1) when a Michigan statute or court rule confers a conditional right to intervene; or

(2) when an applicant's claim or defense and the main action have a question of law or fact in common. In exercising its discretion, the court shall consider whether the intervention will unduly delay or prejudice the adjudication of the rights of the original parties.

(C) **Procedure**. A person seeking to intervene must apply to the court by motion and give notice in writing to all parties under MCR 2.107. The motion must

(1) state the grounds for intervention, and

(2) be accompanied by a pleading stating the claim or defense for which intervention is sought.

(D) **Notice to Attorney General**. When the validity of a Michigan statute or a rule or regulation included in the Michigan Administrative Code is in question in an action to which the state or an officer or agency of the state is not a party, the court may require that notice be given to the Attorney General, specifying the pertinent statute, rule, or regulation.

Rule 2.221 Motion for Change of Venue

(A) **Time to File**. A motion for change of venue must be filed before or at the time the defendant files an answer.
(B) **Late Motion**. Untimeliness is not a ground for denial of a motion filed after the answer if the court is satisfied that the facts on which the motion is based were not and could not with reasonable diligence have been known to the moving party more than 14 days before the motion was filed.
(C) **Waiver**. An objection to venue is waived if it is not raised within the time limits imposed by this rule.

Rule 2.222 Change of Venue; Venue Proper

(A) **Grounds**. The court may order a change of venue of a civil action, or of an appeal from an order or decision of a state board, commission, or agency authorized to promulgate rules or regulations, for the convenience of parties and witnesses or when an impartial trial cannot be had where the action is pending. In the case of appellate review of administrative proceedings, venue may also be changed for the convenience of the attorneys.
(B) **Motion Required**. If the venue of the action is proper, the court may not change the venue on its own initiative, but may do so only on motion of a party.
(C) **Multiple Claims**. If multiple claims are joined in an action, and the venue of one or more of them would have been improper if the claims had been brought in separate actions, the defendant may move to separate the claims and to transfer those as to which venue would have been improper. The court has discretion to
   (1) order the transfer of all claims,
   (2) order the separation and transfer moved for, or
   (3) retain the entire action for trial.
(D) **Filing and Jury Fees After Change of Venue**.
   (1) At or before the time the order changing venue is entered, the party that moved for change of venue shall tender a negotiable instrument in the amount of the applicable filing fee, payable to the court to which the case is to be transferred. The transferring court shall send the negotiable instrument with the case documents to the transferee court.
   (2) If the jury fee has been paid, the clerk of the transferring court shall forward it to the clerk of the court to which the action is transferred.
(E) In tort actions filed between October 1, 1986, and March 28, 1996, if venue is changed because of hardship or inconvenience, the action may be transferred only to the county in which the moving party resides.

Rule 2.223 Change of Venue; Venue Improper

(A) **Motion; Court's Own Initiative**. If the venue of a civil action is improper, the court
   (1) shall order a change of venue on timely motion of a defendant, or
   (2) may order a change of venue on its own initiative with notice to the parties and opportunity for them to be heard on the venue question.
   If venue is changed because the action was brought where venue was not proper, the action may be transferred only to a county in which venue would have been proper.
(B) **Costs; Fees**.
   (1) The court shall order the change at the plaintiff's cost, which shall include the statutory filing fee applicable to the court to which the action is transferred, and which may include reasonable compensation for the defendant's expense, including reasonable attorney fees, in attending in the wrong court.
   (2) After transfer, no further proceedings may be had in the action until the costs and expenses allowed under this rule have been paid. If they are not paid within 56 days from the date of the order changing venue, the action must be dismissed by the court to which it was transferred.
   (3) If the jury fee has been paid, the clerk of the transferring court shall forward it to the clerk of the court to which the action is transferred.
   (4) MCL 600.1653 applies to tort actions filed on or after October 1, 1986.

Rule 2.224 Change of Venue in Tort Actions (*repealed*)

Rule 2.225 Joinder of Party to Control Venue

(A) **Joinder Not in Good Faith**. On a defendant's motion, venue must be changed on a showing that the venue of the action is proper only because of the joinder of a codefendant who was not joined in good faith but only to control venue.
(B) **Transfer Costs**. A transfer under this rule must be made at the plaintiff's cost, which shall include the statutory filing fee applicable to the court to which the action is transferred, and which may include reasonable compensation for the defendant's expense, including reasonable attorney fees, necessary to accomplish the transfer.

(C) **Jury Fee**. If the jury fee has been paid, the clerk of the transferring court shall forward it to the clerk of the court to which the action is transferred.

Rule 2.226 Change of Venue; Orders

The court ordering a change of venue shall enter all necessary orders pertaining to the certification and transfer of the action to the court to which the action is transferred.

Rule 2.227 Transfer of Actions on Finding of Lack of Jurisdiction

(A) **Transfer to Court Which Has Jurisdiction**.

(1) When the court in which a civil action is pending determines that it lacks jurisdiction of the subject matter of the action, but that some other Michigan court would have jurisdiction of the action, the court may order the action transferred to the other court in a place where venue would be proper. If the question of jurisdiction is raised by the court on its own initiative, the action may not be transferred until the parties are given notice and an opportunity to be heard on the jurisdictional issue.

(2) As a condition of transfer, the court shall require the plaintiff to pay the statutory filing fee applicable to the court to which the action is to be transferred, and to pay reasonable compensation for the defendant's expense, including reasonable attorney fees, in attending in the wrong court.

(3) If the plaintiff does not pay the filing fee to the clerk of the court transferring the action and submit proof to the clerk of the payment of any other costs imposed within 28 days after entry of the order of transfer, the clerk shall notify the judge who entered the order, and the judge shall dismiss the action for lack of jurisdiction. The clerk shall notify the parties of the entry of the dismissal.

(4) After the plaintiff pays the fee and costs, the clerk of the court transferring the action shall promptly forward to the clerk of the court to which the action is transferred the original papers filed in the action and the filing fee and shall send written notice of this action to the parties. If part of the action remains pending in the transferring court, certified copies of the papers filed may be forwarded, with the cost to be paid by the plaintiff.

(B) **Procedure After Transfer**.

(1) The action proceeds in the court to which it is transferred as if it had been originally filed there. If further pleadings are required or allowed, the time for filing them runs from the date the clerk sends notice that the file has been forwarded under subrule (A)(4). The court to which the action is transferred may order the filing of new or amended pleadings.

(2) If a defendant had not been served with process at the time the action was transferred, the plaintiff must obtain the issuance of a new summons by the court to which the action is transferred.

(3) A waiver of jury trial in the court in which the action was originally filed is ineffective after transfer. A party who had waived trial by jury may demand a jury trial after transfer by filing a demand and paying the applicable jury fee within 28 days after the clerk sends the notice that the file has been forwarded under subrule (A)(4). A demand for a jury trial in the court in which the action was originally filed is preserved after transfer. If the jury fee had been paid, the clerk shall forward it with the file to the clerk of the court to which the action is transferred.

(C) **Relation to Other Transfer Provisions**. This rule does not affect transfers (pursuant to other rules or statutes) of actions over which the transferring court had jurisdiction.

Subchapter 2.300 Discovery

Rule 2.301 Completion of Discovery

(A) In circuit and probate court, the time for completion of discovery shall be set by an order entered under MCR 2.401(B)(2)(a).

(B) In an action in which discovery is available only on leave of the court or by stipulation, the order or stipulation shall set a time for completion of discovery. A time set by stipulation may not delay the scheduling of the action for trial.

(C) After the time for completion of discovery, a deposition of a witness taken solely for the purpose of preservation of testimony may be taken at any time before commencement of trial without leave of court.

Rule 2.302 General Rules Governing Discovery

(A) **Availability of Discovery**.

(1) After commencement of an action, parties may obtain discovery by any means provided in subchapter 2.300 of these rules.

(2) In actions in the district court, no discovery is permitted before entry of judgment except by leave of the court or on the stipulation of all parties. A motion for discovery may not be filed unless the discovery sought has previously been requested and refused.

(3) Notwithstanding the provisions of this or any other rule, discovery is not permitted in actions in the small claims division of the district court or in civil infraction actions.

(4) After a postjudgment is filed pursuant to a domestic relations action as defined by subchapter 3.200 of

these rules, parties may obtain discovery by any means provided in subchapter 2.300 of these rules.

(B) **Scope of Discovery**.

(1) *In General*. Parties may obtain discovery regarding any matter, not privileged, which is relevant to the subject matter involved in the pending action, whether it relates to the claim or defense of the party seeking discovery or to the claim or defense of another party, including the existence, description, nature, custody, condition, and location of books, documents, or other tangible things, or electronically stored information and the identity and location of persons having knowledge of a discoverable matter. It is not ground for objection that the information sought will be inadmissible at trial if the information sought appears reasonably calculated to lead to the discovery of admissible evidence.

(2) *Insurance Agreements*. A party may obtain discovery of the existence and contents of an insurance agreement under which a person carrying on an insurance business may be liable to satisfy part or all of a judgment which may be entered in the action or to indemnify or reimburse for payments made to satisfy the judgment. Information concerning the insurance agreement is not by reason of disclosure admissible at trial. For purposes of this subrule, an application for insurance is not part of an insurance agreement.

(3) *Trial Preparation; Materials*.

(a) Subject to the provisions of subrule (B)(4), a party may obtain discovery of documents and tangible things otherwise discoverable under subrule (B)(1) and prepared in anticipation of litigation or for trial by or for another party or another party's representative (including an attorney, consultant, surety, indemnitor, insurer, or agent) only on a showing that the party seeking discovery has substantial need of the materials in the preparation of the case and is unable without undue hardship to obtain the substantial equivalent of the materials by other means. In ordering discovery of such materials when the required showing has been made, the court shall protect against disclosure of the mental impressions, conclusions, opinions, or legal theories of an attorney or other representative of a party concerning the litigation.

(b) Without the showing required by subrule (B)(3)(a), a party or a nonparty may obtain a statement concerning the action or its subject matter previously made by the person making the request. A nonparty whose request is refused may move for a court order. The provisions of MCR 2.313(A)(5) apply to the award of expenses incurred in relation to the motion.

(c) For purposes of subrule (B)(3)(b), a statement previously made is

(i) a written statement signed or otherwise adopted or approved by the person making it; or

(ii) a stenographic, mechanical, electrical, or other recording, or a transcription of it, which is a substantially verbatim recital of an oral statement by the person making it and contemporaneously recorded.

(4) *Trial Preparation; Experts*. Discovery of facts known and opinions held by experts, otherwise discoverable under the provisions of subrule (B)(1) and acquired or developed in anticipation of litigation or for trial, may be obtained only as follows:

(a)

(i) A party may through interrogatories require another party to identify each person whom the other party expects to call as an expert witness at trial, to state the subject matter about which the expert is expected to testify, and to state the substance of the facts and opinions to which the expert is expected to testify and a summary of the grounds for each opinion.

(ii) A party may take the deposition of a person whom the other party expects to call as an expert witness at trial. The party taking the deposition may notice that the deposition is to be taken for the purpose of discovery only and that it shall not be admissible at trial except for the purpose of impeachment, without the necessity of obtaining a protective order as set forth in MCR 2.302(C)(7).

(iii) On motion, the court may order further discovery by other means, subject to such restrictions as to scope and such provisions (pursuant to subrule [B][4][C]) concerning fees and expenses as the court deems appropriate.

(b) A party may not discover the identity of and facts known or opinions held by an expert who has been retained or specially employed by another party in anticipation of litigation or preparation for trial and who is not expected to be called as a witness at trial, except

(i) as provided in MCR 2.311, or

(ii) where an order has been entered on a showing of exceptional circumstances under which it is impracticable for the party seeking discovery to obtain facts or opinions on the same subject by other means.

(c) Unless manifest injustice would result

(i) the court shall require that the party seeking discovery under subrules (B)(4)(a)(ii) or (iii) or (B)(4)(b) pay the expert a reasonable fee for time spent in a deposition, but not including preparation time; and

(ii) with respect to discovery obtained under subrule (B)(4)(a)(ii) or (iii), the court may require, and with respect to discovery obtained under subrule (B)(4)(b) the court shall require, the party seeking discovery to pay the other party a fair portion of the fees and expenses reasonably incurred by the latter party in obtaining facts and opinions from the expert.

(d) A party may depose a witness that he or she expects to call as an expert at trial. The deposition may be taken at any time before trial on reasonable notice to the opposite party, and may be offered as evidence at trial as provided in MCR 2.308(A). The court need not adjourn the trial because of the unavailability of expert witnesses or their depositions.

(5) *Electronically Stored Information.* A party has the same obligation to preserve electronically stored information as it does for all other types of information. Absent exceptional circumstances, a court may not impose sanctions under these rules on a party for failing to provide electronically stored information lost as a result of the routine, good-faith operation of an electronic information system.

(6) *Limitation of Discovery of Electronic Materials.* A party need not provide discovery of electronically stored information from sources that the party identifies as not reasonably accessible because of undue burden or cost. On motion to compel discovery or for a protective order, the party from whom discovery is sought must show that the information is not reasonably accessible because of undue burden or cost. If that showing is made, the court may nonetheless order discovery from such sources if the requesting party shows good cause, considering the limitations of MCR 2.302(C). The court may specify conditions for the discovery.

(7) *Information Inadvertently Produced.* If information that is subject to a claim of privilege or of protection as trial-preparation material is produced in discovery, the party making the claim may notify any party that received the information of the claim and the basis for it. After being notified, a party must promptly return, sequester, or destroy the specified information and any copies it has and may not use or disclose the information until the claim is resolved. A receiving party may promptly present the information to the court under seal for a determination of the claim. If the receiving party disclosed the information before being notified, it must take reasonable steps to retrieve it. The producing party must preserve the information until the claim is resolved.

(C) **Protective Orders.** On motion by a party or by the person from whom discovery is sought, and on reasonable notice and for good cause shown, the court in which the action is pending may issue any order that justice requires to protect a party or person from annoyance, embarrassment, oppression, or undue burden or expense, including one or more of the following orders:

(1) that the discovery not be had;

(2) that the discovery may be had only on specified terms and conditions, including a designation of the time or place;

(3) that the discovery may be had only by a method of discovery other than that selected by the party seeking discovery;

(4) that certain matters not be inquired into, or that the scope of the discovery be limited to certain matters;

(5) that discovery be conducted with no one present except persons designated by the court;

(6) that a deposition, after being sealed, be opened only by order of the court;

(7) that a deposition shall be taken only for the purpose of discovery and shall not be admissible in evidence except for the purpose of impeachment;

(8) that a trade secret or other confidential research, development, or commercial information not be disclosed or be disclosed only in a designated way;

(9) that the parties simultaneously file specified documents or information enclosed in sealed envelopes to be opened as directed by the court.

If the motion for a protective order is denied in whole or in part, the court may, on terms and conditions as are just, order that a party or person provide or permit discovery. The provisions of MCR 2.313(A)(5) apply to the award of expenses incurred in relation to the motion.

(D) **Sequence and Timing of Discovery**. Unless the court orders otherwise, on motion, for the convenience of parties and witnesses and in the interests of justice, methods of discovery may be used in any sequence, and the fact that a party is conducting discovery, whether by deposition or otherwise, does not operate to delay another party's discovery.

(E) **Supplementation of Responses**.

(1) *Duty to Supplement.* A party who has responded to a request for discovery with a response that was complete when made is under no duty to

supplement the response to include information acquired later, except as follows:

(a) A party is under a duty seasonably to supplement the response with respect to a question directly addressed to

(i) the identity and location of persons having knowledge of discoverable matters; and

(ii) the identity of each person expected to be called as an expert witness at trial, the subject matter on which the expert is expected to testify, and the substance of the expert's testimony.

(b) A party is under a duty seasonably to amend a prior response if the party obtains information on the basis of which the party knows that

(i) the response was incorrect when made; or

(ii) the response, though correct when made, is no longer true and the circumstances are such that a failure to amend the response is in substance a knowing concealment.

(c) A duty to supplement responses may be imposed by order of the court, agreement of the parties, or at any time before trial through new requests for supplementation of prior responses.

(2) *Failure to Supplement*. If the court finds, by way of motion or otherwise, that a party has not seasonably supplemented responses as required by this subrule the court may enter an order as is just, including an order providing the sanctions stated in MCR 2.313(B), and, in particular, MCR 2.313(B)(2)(b).

(F) **Stipulations Regarding Discovery Procedure**. Unless the court orders otherwise, the parties may by written stipulation:

(1) provide that depositions may be taken before any person, at any time or place, on any notice, and in any manner, and when so taken may be used like other depositions; and

(2) modify the procedures of these rules for other methods of discovery, except that stipulations extending the time within which discovery may be sought or for responses to discovery may be made only with the approval of the court.

(G) **Signing of Discovery Requests, Responses, and Objections; Sanctions**.

(1) In addition to any other signature required by these rules, every request for discovery and every response or objection to such a request made by a party represented by an attorney shall be signed by at least one attorney of record. A party who is not represented by an attorney must sign the request, response, or objection.

(2) If a request, response, or objection is not signed, it shall be stricken unless it is signed promptly after the omission is called to the attention of the party making the request, response, or objection, and another party need not take any action with respect to it until it is signed.

(3) The signature of the attorney or party constitutes a certification that he or she has read the request, response, or objection, and that to the best of the signer's knowledge, information, and belief formed after a reasonable inquiry it is:

(a) consistent with these rules and warranted by existing law or a good-faith argument for the extension, modification, or reversal of existing law;

(b) not interposed for any improper purpose, such as to harass or to cause unnecessary delay or needless increase in the cost of litigation; and

(c) not unreasonable or unduly burdensome or expensive, given the needs of the case, the discovery already had in the case, the amount in controversy, and the importance of the issues at stake in the litigation.

(4) If a certification is made in violation of this rule, the court, on the motion of a party or on its own initiative, shall impose upon the person who made the certification, the party on whose behalf the request, response, or objection is made, or both, an appropriate sanction, which may include an order to pay the amount of the reasonable expenses incurred because of the violation, including reasonable attorney fees.

(H) **Filing and Service of Discovery Materials**.

(1) Unless a particular rule requires filing of discovery materials, requests, responses, depositions, and other discovery materials may not be filed with the court except as follows:

(a) If discovery materials are to be used in connection with a motion, they must either be filed separately or be attached to the motion or an accompanying affidavit;

(b) If discovery materials are to be used at trial they must be made an exhibit pursuant to MCR 2.518 or MCR 3.930;

(c) The court may order discovery materials to be filed.

(2) Copies of discovery materials served under these rules must be served on all parties to the action, unless the court has entered an order under MCR 2.107(F).

(3) On appeal, only discovery materials that were filed or made exhibits are part of the record on appeal.

(4) Removal and destruction of discovery materials are governed by MCR 2.316.

Rule 2.303 Depositions Before Action or Pending Appeal

(A) **Before Action.**

(1) *Petition*. A person who desires to perpetuate his or her own testimony or that of another person, for use as evidence and not for the purpose of discovery, regarding a matter that may be cognizable in a Michigan court may file a verified petition in the circuit court of the county of the residence of an expected adverse party. The petition must be entitled in the name of the petitioner and must show:

(a) that the petitioner expects to be a party to an action cognizable in a Michigan court but is presently unable to bring it or cause it to be brought and the reasons why;

(b) the subject matter of the expected action and the petitioner's interest in it;

(c) the facts sought to be established by the proposed testimony and the reasons for desiring to perpetuate it;

(d) the names or a description of the persons that the petitioner expects will be adverse parties and their addresses so far as known; and

(e) the names and addresses of the persons to be examined and the substance of the testimony that the petitioner expects to elicit from each.

The petition must ask for an order authorizing the petitioner to take the depositions of the persons to be examined named in the petition for the purpose of perpetuating their testimony.

(2) *Notice and Service*. The petitioner shall serve a notice on each person named in the petition as an expected adverse party, together with a copy of the petition, stating that the petitioner will apply to the court, at a specified time and place, for the order described in the petition. At least 21 days before the date of hearing, the notice must be served in the manner provided in MCR 2.105 for service of summons. If service cannot be made on an expected adverse party with due diligence, the court may issue an order as is just for service by publication or otherwise, and shall appoint, for persons not served in the manner provided in MCR 2.105, an attorney to represent them, and to cross-examine the deponent. If an expected adverse party is a minor or an incompetent person, the law relating to minors and incompetents, including MCR 2.201(E), applies.

(3) *Order and Examination*. If the court is satisfied that the perpetuation of the testimony may prevent a failure or delay of justice, it shall issue an order designating or describing the persons whose depositions may be taken and specifying the subject matter of the examination and whether the depositions are to be taken on oral examination or written interrogatories. The depositions may then be taken in accordance with these rules. In addition the court may issue orders of the character provided for by MCR 2.310 and 2.311.

(4) *Use of Deposition*.

(a) If a deposition to perpetuate testimony is taken under these rules, it may be used in an action involving the same subject matter subsequently brought in a Michigan court, in accordance with MCR 2.308.

(b) If a deposition to perpetuate testimony has been taken under the Federal Rules of Civil Procedure, or the rules of another state, the court may, if it finds that the deposition was taken in substantial compliance with these rules, allow the deposition to be used as if it had been taken under these rules.

(B) **Pending Appeal**. If an appeal has been taken from a judgment of a trial court, or before the taking of an appeal if the time for appeal has not expired, the court in which the judgment was rendered may allow the taking of the depositions of witnesses to perpetuate their testimony for use if there are further proceedings in that court. The party who wishes to perpetuate the testimony may move for leave to take the depositions, with the same notice and service of the motion as if the action were then pending in the trial court. The motion must show

(1) the names and addresses of the persons to be examined and the substance of the testimony that the party expects to elicit from each; and

(2) the reasons for perpetuating their testimony.

If the court finds that the perpetuation of testimony is proper to avoid a failure or delay of justice, it may issue an order allowing the depositions to be taken and may issue orders of the character provided for by MCR 2.310 and 2.311. The depositions may then be taken and used in the same manner and under the same conditions prescribed in these rules for depositions taken in actions pending before the court.

Rule 2.304 Persons Before Whom Depositions May Be Taken

(A) **Within the United States**. Within the United States or within a territory or insular possession subject to the dominion of the United States, depositions may be taken

(1) before a person authorized to administer oaths by the laws of Michigan, the United States, or the place where the examination is held;

(2) before a person appointed by the court in which the action is pending; or

(3) before a person on whom the parties agree by stipulation under MCR 2.302(F)(1).

A person acting under subrule (A)(2) or (3) has the power to administer oaths, take testimony, and do all other acts necessary to take a deposition.

(B) **In Foreign Countries**. In a foreign country, depositions may be taken

(1) on notice before a person authorized to administer oaths in the place in which the examination is held, by either the law of that place or of the United States; or

(2) before a person commissioned by the court, and a person so commissioned has the power by virtue of the commission to administer a necessary oath and take testimony; or

(3) pursuant to a letter rogatory.

A commission or a letter rogatory may be issued on motion and notice and on terms that are just and appropriate. It is not requisite to the issuance of a commission or a letter rogatory that the taking of the deposition in another manner is impracticable or inconvenient; both a commission and a letter rogatory may be issued in a proper case. A notice or commission may designate the person before whom the deposition is to be taken either by name or descriptive title. A letter rogatory may be addressed "To the Appropriate Authority in [name of country]." Evidence obtained in response to a letter rogatory need not be excluded merely because it is not a verbatim transcript or the testimony was not taken under oath, or because of a similar departure from the requirements for depositions taken within the United States under these rules.

(C) **Disqualification for Interest**. Unless the parties agree otherwise by stipulation in writing or on the record, a deposition may not be taken before a person who is

(1) a relative or employee of or an attorney for a party,

(2) a relative or employee of an attorney for a party, or

(3) financially interested in the action.

Rule 2.305 Subpoena for Taking Deposition

(A) **General Provisions.**

(1) After serving the notice provided for in MCR 2.303(A)(2), 2.306(B), or 2.307(A)(2), a party may have a subpoena issued in the manner provided by MCR 2.506 for the person named or described in the notice. Service on a party or a party's attorney of notice of the taking of the deposition of a party, or of a director, trustee, officer, or employee of a corporate party, is sufficient to require the appearance of the deponent; a subpoena need not be issued.

(2) The subpoena may command the person to whom it is directed to produce and permit inspection and copying of designated documents or other tangible things relevant to the subject matter of the pending action and within the scope of discovery under MCR 2.302(B). The procedures in MCR 2.310 apply to a party deponent.

(3) A deposition notice and a subpoena under this rule may provide that the deposition is solely for producing documents or other tangible things for inspection and copying, and that the party does not intend to examine the deponent.

(4) A subpoena issued under this rule is subject to the provisions of MCR 2.302(C), and the court in which the action is pending, on timely motion made before the time specified in the subpoena for compliance, may

(a) quash or modify the subpoena if it is unreasonable or oppressive;

(b) enter an order permitted by MCR 2.302(C); or

(c) condition denial of the motion on prepayment by the person on whose behalf the subpoena is issued of the reasonable cost of producing books, papers, documents, or other tangible things.

(5) Service of a subpoena on the deponent must be made as provided in MCR 2.506. A copy of the subpoena must be served on all other parties in the same manner as the deposition notice.

(B) **Inspection and Copying of Documents**. A subpoena issued under subrule (A) may command production of documents or other tangible things, but the following rules apply:

(1) The subpoena must be served at least 14 days before the time for production. The subpoenaed person may, not later than the time specified in the subpoena for compliance, serve on the party serving the subpoena written objection to inspection or copying of some or all of the designated materials.

(2) If objection is made, the party serving the subpoena is not entitled to inspect and copy the materials without an order of the court in which the action is pending.

(3) The party serving the subpoena may, with notice to the deponent, move for an order compelling production of the designated materials. MCR 2.313(A)(5) applies to motions brought under this subrule.

(C) **Place of Examination.**

(1) A deponent may be required to attend an examination in the county where the deponent resides, is employed, or transacts business in person, or at another convenient place specified by order of the court.

(2) In an action pending in Michigan, the court may order a nonresident plaintiff or an officer or managing agent of the plaintiff to appear for a deposition at a designated place in Michigan or elsewhere on terms and conditions that are just, including payment by the defendant of the

reasonable expenses of travel, meals, and lodging incurred by the deponent in attending.

(3) If it is shown that the deposition of a nonresident defendant cannot be taken in the state where the defendant resides, the court may order the defendant or an officer or managing agent of the defendant to appear for a deposition at a designated place in Michigan or elsewhere on terms and conditions that are just, including payment by the plaintiff of the reasonable expenses of travel, meals, and lodging incurred by the deponent in attending.

(D) **Petition to Courts Outside Michigan to Compel Testimony**. When the place of examination is in another state, territory, or country, the party desiring to take the deposition may petition a court of that state, territory, or country for a subpoena or equivalent process to require the deponent to attend the examination.

(E) **Action Pending in Another Country**. An officer or a person authorized by the laws of another country to take a deposition in Michigan, with or without a commission, in an action pending in a court of that country may submit an application to a court of record in the county in which the deponent resides, is employed, transacts business in person, or is found, for a subpoena to compel the deponent to give testimony. The court may hear and act on the application with or without notice, as the court directs.

(F) **Action Pending in Another State or Territory**. A person may request issuance of a subpoena in this state for an action pending in another state or territory under the Uniform Interstate Depositions and Discovery Act, MCL 600.2201 et seq., to require a person to attend a deposition, to produce and permit inspection and copying of materials, or to permit inspection of premises under the control of the person.

Rule 2.306 Depositions on Oral Examination

(A) **When Depositions May Be Taken**.

(1) After commencement of the action, a party may take the testimony of a person, including a party, by deposition on oral examination. Leave of court, granted with or without notice, must be obtained only if the plaintiff seeks to take a deposition before the defendant has had a reasonable time to obtain an attorney. A reasonable time is deemed to have elapsed if:

(a) the defendant has filed an answer;

(b) the defendant's attorney has filed an appearance;

(c) the defendant has served notice of the taking of a deposition or has taken other action seeking discovery;

(d) the defendant has filed a motion under MCR 2.116; or

(e) 28 days have expired after service of the summons and complaint on a defendant or after service made under MCR 2.106.

(2) The deposition of a person confined in prison or of a patient in a state home, institution, or hospital for the mentally ill or mentally handicapped, or any other state hospital, home, or institution, may be taken only by leave of court on terms as the court provides.

(B) **Notice of Examination; Subpoena; Production of Documents and Things**.

(1) A party desiring to take the deposition of a person on oral examination must give reasonable notice in writing to every other party to the action. The notice must state

(a) the time and place for taking the deposition, and

(b) the name and address of each person to be examined, if known, or, if the name is not known, a general description sufficient to identify the person or the particular class or group to which the person belongs.

If the subpoena to be served directs the deponent to produce documents or other tangible things, the designation of the materials to be produced as set forth in the subpoena must be attached to or included in the notice.

(2) On motion for good cause, the court may extend or shorten the time for taking the deposition. The court may regulate the time and order of taking depositions to best serve the convenience of the parties and witnesses and the interests of justice.

(3) The attendance of witness may be compelled by subpoena as provided in MCR 2.305.

(4) The notice to a party deponent may be accompanied by a request for the production of documents and tangible things at the taking of the deposition. MCR 2.310 applies to the request.

(5) In a notice and subpoena, a party may name as the deponent a public or private corporation, partnership, association, or governmental agency and describe with reasonable particularity the matters on which examination is requested. The organization named must designate one or more officers, directors, or managing agents, or other persons, who consent to testify on its behalf, and may set forth, for each person designated, the matters on which the person will testify. A subpoena must advise a nonparty organization of its duty to make the designation. The persons designated shall testify to matters known or reasonably available to the organization. This subrule does not preclude taking a deposition by another procedure authorized in these rules.

(C) **Conduct of Deposition; Examination and Cross-Examination; Manner of Recording; Objections; Conferring with Deponent**.

(1) *Examination of Deponent*.

(a) The person before whom the deposition is to be taken must put the witness on oath.

(b) Examination and cross-examination of the witness shall proceed as permitted at a trial under the Michigan Rules of Evidence.

(c) In lieu of participating in the oral examination, a party may send written questions to the person conducting the examination, who shall propound them to the witness and record the witness's answers.

(2) *Recording of Deposition*. The person before whom the deposition is taken shall personally, or by someone acting under his or her direction and in his or her presence, record the testimony of the witness.

(a) The testimony must be taken stenographically or recorded by other means in accordance with this subrule. The testimony need not be transcribed unless requested by one of the parties.

(b) While the testimony is being taken, a party, as a matter of right, may also make a record of it by nonsecret mechanical or electronic means, except that video recording is governed by MCR 2.315. Any use of the recording in court is within the discretion of the court. A person making such a record must furnish a duplicate of the record to another party at the request and expensed of the other party.

(3) *Recording by Nonstenographic Means*. The court may order, or the parties may stipulate, that the testimony at a deposition be recorded by other than stenographic means.

(a) The order or stipulation must designate the manner of recording and preserving the deposition, and may include other provisions to assure that the recorded testimony will be accurate and trustworthy. A deposition in the form of a recording may be filed with the court as are other depositions.

(b) If a deposition is taken by other than stenographic means on order of the court, a party may nevertheless arrange to have a stenographic transcription made at that party's own expense.

(c) Before a deposition taken by other than stenographic means may be used in court it must be transcribed unless the court enters an order waiving transcription. The costs of transcription are borne by the parties as determined by the court.

(d) Subrule (C)(3) does not apply to video depositions, which are governed by MCR 2.315.

(4) *Objections During Deposition*.

(a) All objections made at the deposition, including objections to

(i) the qualifications of the person taking the deposition,

(ii) the manner of taking it,

(iii) the evidence presented, or

(iv) the conduct of a party,

must be noted on the record by the person before whom the deposition is taken.

Subject to limitation imposed by an order under MCR 2.302(C) or subrule (D) of this rule, evidence objected to on grounds other than privilege shall be taken subject to the objections.

(b) An objection during a deposition must be stated concisely in a civil and nonsuggestive manner.

(c) Objections are limited to

(i) objections that would be waived under MCR 2.308(C)(2) or (3), and

(ii) those necessary to preserve a privilege or other legal protection or to enforce a limitation ordered by the court.

(5) *Conferring with Deponent*.

(a) A person may instruct a deponent not to answer only when necessary to preserve a privilege or other legal protection, to enforce a limitation ordered by the court, or to present a motion under MCR 2.306(D)(1).

(b) A deponent may not confer with another person while a question is pending, except to decide whether to assert a privilege or other legal protection.

(D) **Motion to Terminate or Limit Examination; Sanctions; Asserting Privilege**.

(1) *Motion*. At any time during the taking of the deposition, on motion of a party or of the deponent and on a showing that the examination is being conducted in bad faith or in a manner unreasonably to annoy, embarrass, or oppress the deponent or party, or that the matter inquired about is privileged, a court in which the action is pending or the court in the county or district where the deposition is being taken may order the person conducting the examination to cease taking the deposition, or may limit the scope and manner of the taking of the deposition as provided in MCR 2.302(C). If the order entered terminates the examination, it may resume only on order of the court in which the action is pending.

(2) *Sanctions*. On motion, the court may impose an appropriate sanction- including the reasonable expenses and attorney fees incurred by any party-

on a person who impedes, delays, or frustrates the fair examination of the deponent or otherwise violates this rule.

(3) *Suspending Deposition*. On demand of the objecting party or deponent, the taking of the deposition must be suspended for the time necessary to move for an order. MCR 2.313(A)(5) applies to the award of expenses incurred in relation to the motion.

(4) *Raising Privilege before Deposition*. If a party knows before the time scheduled for the taking of a deposition that he or she will assert that the matter to be inquired about is privileged, the party must move to prevent the taking of the deposition before its occurrence or be subject to costs under subrule (G).

(5) *Failure to Assert Privilege*. A party who has a privilege regarding part or all of the testimony of a deponent must either assert the privilege at the deposition or lose the privilege as to that testimony for purposes of the action. A party who claims a privilege at a deposition may not at the trial offer the testimony of the deponent pertaining to the evidence objected to at the deposition. A party who asserts a privilege regarding medical information is subject to the provisions of MCR 2.314(B).

(E) **Exhibits**. Documents and things produced for inspection during the examination of the witness must, on the request of a party, be marked for identification and annexed to the deposition, if practicable, and may be inspected and copied by a party, except as follows:

(1) The person producing the materials may substitute copies to be marked for identification, if he or she affords to all parties fair opportunity to verify the copies by comparison with the originals.

(2) If the person producing the materials requests their return, the person conducting the examination or the stenographer must mark them, give each party an opportunity to inspect and copy them, and return them to the person producing them, and the materials may then be used in the same manner as if annexed to the deposition. A party may move for an order that the original be annexed to and filed with the deposition, pending final disposition of the action.

(F) **Certification and Transcription; Filing; Copies**.

(1) If transcription is requested by a party, the person conducting the examination or the stenographer must certify on the deposition that the witness was duly sworn and that the deposition is a true record of the testimony given by the witness. A deposition transcribed and certified in accordance with subrule (F) need not be submitted to the witness for examination and signature.

(2) On payment of reasonable charges, the person conducting the examination shall furnish a copy of the deposition to a party or to the deponent. Where transcription is requested by a party other than the party requesting the deposition, the court may order, or the parties may stipulate, that the expense of transcription or a portion of it be paid by the party making the request.

(3) Except as provided in subrule (C)(3) or in MCR 2.315(E), a deposition may not be filed with the court unless it has first been transcribed. If a party requests that the transcript be filed, the person conducting the examination or the stenographer shall, after transcription and certification:

(a) securely seal the transcript in an envelope endorsed with the title and file number of the action and marked "Deposition of [name of witness]," and promptly file it with the court in which the action is pending or send it by registered or certified mail to the clerk of that court for filing;

(b) give prompt notice of its filing to all other parties, unless the parties agree otherwise by stipulation in writing or on the record.

(G) **Failure to Attend or to Serve Subpoena; Expenses**.

(1) If the party giving the notice of the taking of a deposition fails to attend and proceed with the deposition and another party attends in person or by attorney pursuant to the notice, the court may order the party giving the notice to pay to the other party the reasonable expenses incurred in attending, including reasonable attorney fees.

(2) If the party giving the notice of the taking of a deposition of a witness fails to serve a subpoena on the witness, and the witness because of the failure does not attend, and if another party attends in person or by attorney because he or she expects the deposition of that witness to be taken, the court may order the party giving the notice to pay to the other party the reasonable expenses incurred in attending, including reasonable attorney fees.

Rule 2.307 Depositions on Written Questions

(A) **Serving Questions; Notice**.

(1) Under the same circumstances as set out in MCR 2.306(A), a party may take the testimony of a person, including a party, by deposition on written questions. The attendance of the witnesses may be compelled by the use of a subpoena as provided in MCR 2.305. A deposition on written questions may be taken of a public or private corporation or partnership or association or governmental agency in accordance with the provisions of MCR 2.306(B)(5).

(2) A party desiring to take a deposition on written questions shall serve them on every other party with a notice stating

(a) the name and address of the person who is to answer them, if known, and, if the name is not known, a general description sufficient to identify the person or the particular class or group to which the person belongs; and

(b) the name or descriptive title and address of the person before whom the deposition is to be taken.

(3) Within 14 days after the notice and written questions are served, a party may serve cross-questions on all other parties. Within 7 days after being served with cross-questions, a party may serve redirect questions on all other parties. Within 7 days after being served with redirect questions, a party may serve recross-questions on all other parties. The parties, by stipulation in writing, or the court, for cause shown, may extend or shorten the time requirements.

(B) **Taking of Responses and Preparation of Record.** A copy of the notice, any stipulation, and copies of all questions served must be delivered by the party who proposed the deposition to the person before whom the deposition will be taken as stated in the notice. The person before whom the deposition is to be taken must proceed promptly to take the testimony of the witness in response to the questions, and, if requested, to transcribe, certify, and file the deposition in the manner provided by MCR 2.306(C), (E), and (F), attaching the copy of the notice, the questions, and any stipulations of the parties.

Rule 2.308 Use of Depositions in Court Proceedings

(A) **In General.** Depositions or parts thereof shall be admissible at trial or on the hearing of a motion or in an interlocutory proceeding only as provided in the Michigan Rules of Evidence.

(B) **Objections to Admissibility.** Subject to the provisions of subrule (C) and MCR 2.306(C)(4), objection may be made at the trial or hearing to receiving in evidence a deposition or part of a deposition for any reason that would require the exclusion of the evidence.

(C) **Effect of Errors or Irregularities in Depositions.**

(1) *Notice.* Errors or irregularities in the notice for taking a deposition are waived unless written objection is promptly served on the party giving notice.

(2) *Disqualification of Person Before Whom Taken.* Objection to taking a deposition because of disqualification of the person before whom it is to be taken is waived unless made before the taking of the deposition begins or as soon thereafter as the disqualification becomes known or could be discovered with reasonable diligence.

(3) *Taking of Deposition.*

(a) Objections to the competency of a witness or to the competency, relevancy, or materiality of testimony are not waived by failure to make them before or during the taking of a deposition, unless the ground of the objection is one which might have been obviated or removed if presented at that time.

(b) Errors and irregularities occurring at the deposition in the manner of taking the deposition, in the form of the questions or answers, in the oath or affirmation, or in the conduct of parties and errors of any other kind which might be cured if promptly presented, are waived unless seasonable objection is made at the taking of the deposition.

(c) Objections to the form of written questions submitted under MCR 2.307 are waived unless served in writing on the party propounding them within the time allowed for serving the succeeding cross-questions or other questions and within 7 days after service of the last questions authorized.

(d) On motion and notice a party may request a ruling by the court on an objection in advance of the trial.

(4) *Certification, Transcription, and Filing of Deposition.* Errors and irregularities in the manner in which the testimony is transcribed or the deposition is prepared, signed, certified, sealed, endorsed, transmitted, filed, or otherwise dealt with by the person before whom it was taken are waived unless a motion objecting to the deposition is filed within a reasonable time.

(5) *Harmless Error.* None of the foregoing errors or irregularities, even when not waived, or any others, preclude or restrict the use of the deposition, except insofar as the court finds that the errors substantially destroy the value of the deposition as evidence or render its use unfair or prejudicial.

Rule 2.309 Interrogatories to Parties

(A) **Availability; Procedure for Service.** A party may serve on another party written interrogatories to be answered by the party served or, if the party served is a public or private corporation, partnership, association, or governmental agency, by an officer or agent. Interrogatories may, without leave of court, be served:

(1) on the plaintiff after commencement of the action;

(2) on a defendant with or after the service of the summons and complaint on that defendant.

(B) **Answers and Objections.**

(1) Each interrogatory must be answered separately and fully in writing under oath. The answers must include such information as is available to the party

served or that the party could obtain from his or her employees, agents, representatives, sureties, or indemnitors. If the answering party objects to an interrogatory, the reasons for the objection must be stated in lieu of an answer.

(2) The answering party shall repeat each interrogatory or subquestion immediately before the answer to it.

(3) The answers must be signed by the person making them and the objections signed by the attorney or an unrepresented party making them.

(4) The party on whom the interrogatories are served must serve the answers and objections, if any, on all other parties within 28 days after the interrogatories are served, except that a defendant may serve answers within 42 days after being served with the summons and complaint. The court may allow a longer or shorter time and, for good cause shown, may excuse service on parties other than the party who served the interrogatories.

(C) **Motion to Compel Answers**. The party submitting the interrogatories may move for an order under MCR 2.313(A) with respect to an objection to or other failure to answer an interrogatory. If the motion is based on the failure to serve answers, proof of service of the interrogatories must be filed with the motion. The motion must state that the movant has in good faith conferred or attempted to confer with the party not making the disclosure in an effort to secure the disclosure without court action.

(D) **Scope; Use at Trial**.

(1) An interrogatory may relate to matters that can be inquired into under MCR 2.302(B).

(2) An interrogatory otherwise proper is not necessarily objectionable merely because an answer to the interrogatory involves an opinion or contention that relates to fact or the application of law to fact, but the court may order that an interrogatory need not be answered until after designated discovery has been completed or until a pretrial conference or other later time.

(3) The answer to an interrogatory may be used to the extent permitted by the rules of evidence.

(E) **Option to Produce Business Records**. Where the answer to an interrogatory may be derived from

(1) the business records of the party on whom the interrogatory has been served,

(2) an examination, audit, or inspection of business records, or

(3) a compilation, abstract, or summary based on such records,

and the burden of deriving the answer is substantially the same for the party serving the interrogatory as for the party served, it is a sufficient answer to the interrogatory to specify the records from which the answer may be derived and to afford to the party serving the interrogatory reasonable opportunity to examine, audit, or inspect the records and to make copies, compilations, abstracts, or summaries. A specification shall be in sufficient detail to permit the interrogating party to identify, as readily as can the party served, the records from which the answer may be derived.

Rule 2.310 Requests for Production of Documents and Other Things; Entry on Land for Inspection and Other Purposes

(A) **Definitions**. For the purpose of this rule,

(1) "Documents" includes writings, drawings, graphs, charts, photographs, phono records, and other data compilations from which information can be obtained, translated, if necessary, by the respondent through detection devices into reasonably usable form.

(2) "Entry on land" means entry upon designated land or other property in the possession or control of the person on whom the request is served for the purpose of inspecting, measuring, surveying, photographing, testing, or sampling the property or a designated object or operation on the property, within the scope of MCR 2.302(B).

(B) **Scope**.

(1) A party may serve on another party a request

(a) to produce and permit the requesting party, or someone acting for that party,

(i) to inspect and copy designated documents or

(ii) to inspect and copy, test, or sample other tangible things

that constitute or contain matters within the scope of MCR 2.302(B) and that are in the possession, custody, or control of the party on whom the request is served; or

(b) to permit entry on land.

(2) A party may serve on a nonparty a request

(a) to produce and permit the requesting party or someone acting for that party to inspect and test or sample tangible things that constitute or contain matters within the scope of MCR 2.302(B) and that are in the possession, custody, or control of the person on whom the request is served; or

(b) to permit entry on land.

(C) **Request to Party**.

(1) The request may, without leave of court, be served on the plaintiff after commencement of the action and on the defendant with or after the service of the summons and complaint on that defendant. The request must list the items to be inspected, either by individual item or by category, and describe each item and category with reasonable particularity. The request must specify a reasonable time, place,

and manner of making the inspection and performing the related acts, as well as the form or forms in which electronically stored information is to be produced, subject to objection.

(2) The party on whom the request is served must serve a written response within 28 days after service of the request, except that a defendant may serve a response within 42 days after being served with the summons and complaint. The court may allow a longer or shorter time. With respect to each item or category, the response must state that inspection and related activities will be permitted as requested or that the request is objected to, in which event the reasons for objection must be stated. If objection is made to part of an item or category, the part must be specified. If the request does not specify the form or forms in which electronically stored information is to be produced, the party responding to the request must produce the information in a form or forms in which the party ordinarily maintains it, or in a form or forms that is or are reasonably usable. A party producing electronically stored information need only produce the same information in one form.

(3) The party submitting the request may move for an order under MCR 2.313(A) with respect to an objection to or a failure to respond to the request or a part of it, or failure to permit inspection as requested. If the motion is based on a failure to respond to a request, proof of service of the request must be filed with the motion. The motion must state that the movant has in good faith conferred or attempted to confer with the party not making the disclosure in an effort to secure the disclosure without court action.

(4) The party to whom the request is submitted may seek a protective order under MCR 2.302(C).

(5) A party who produces documents for inspection shall produce them as they are kept in the usual course of business or shall organize and label them to correspond with the categories in the request.

(6) Unless otherwise ordered by the court for good cause, the party producing items for inspection shall bear the cost of assembling them and the party requesting the items shall bear any copying costs.

(D) **Request to Nonparty**.

(1) A request to a nonparty may be served at any time, except that leave of the court is required if the plaintiff seeks to serve a request before the occurrence of one of the events stated in MCR 2.306(A)(1).

(2) The request must be served on the person to whom it is directed in the manner provided in MCR 2.105, and a copy must be served on the other parties.

(3) The request must

(a) list the items to be inspected and tested or sampled, either by individual item or by category, and describe each item and category with reasonable particularity,

(b) specify a reasonable time, place, and manner of making the inspection and performing the related acts, and

(c) inform the person to whom it is directed that unless he or she agrees to allow the inspection or entry at a reasonable time and on reasonable conditions, a motion may be filed seeking a court order to require the inspection or entry.

(4) If the person to whom the request is directed does not permit the inspection or entry within 14 days after service of the request (or a shorter time if the court directs), the party seeking the inspection or entry may file a motion to compel the inspection or entry under MCR 2.313(A). The motion must include a copy of the request and proof of service of the request. The movant must serve the motion on the person from whom discovery is sought as provided in MCR 2.105.

(5) The court may order the party seeking discovery to pay the reasonable expenses incurred in complying with the request by the person from whom discovery is sought.

(6) This rule does not preclude an independent action against a nonparty for production of documents and other things and permission to enter on land or a subpoena to a nonparty under MCR 2.305.

Rule 2.311 Physical and Mental Examination of Persons

(A) **Order for Examination**. When the mental or physical condition (including the blood group) of a party, or of a person in the custody or under the legal control of a party, is in controversy, the court in which the action is pending may order the party to submit to a physical or mental or blood examination by a physician (or other appropriate professional) or to produce for examination the person in the party's custody or legal control. The order may be entered only on motion for good cause with notice to the person to be examined and to all parties. The order must specify the time, place, manner, conditions, and scope of the examination and the person or persons by whom it is to be made, and may provide that the attorney for the person to be examined may be present at the examination.

(B) **Report of Examining Physician**.

(1) If requested by the party against whom an order is entered under subrule (A) or by the person examined, the party causing the examination to be made must deliver to the requesting person a copy of a detailed written report of the examining

physician setting out the findings, including results of all tests made, diagnosis, and conclusions, together with like reports on all earlier examinations of the same condition, and must make available for inspection and examination x-rays, cardiograms, and other diagnostic aids.

(2) After delivery of the report, the party causing the examination to be made is entitled on request to receive from the party against whom the order is made a similar report of any examination previously or thereafter made of the same condition, and to a similar inspection of all diagnostic aids unless, in the case of a report on the examination of a nonparty, the party shows that he or she is unable to obtain it.

(3) If either party or a person examined refuses to deliver a report, the court on motion and notice may enter an order requiring delivery on terms as are just, and if a physician refuses or fails to comply with this rule, the court may order the physician to appear for a discovery deposition.

(4) By requesting and obtaining a report on the examination ordered under this rule, or by taking the deposition of the examiner, the person examined waives any privilege he or she may have in that action, or another action involving the same controversy, regarding the testimony of every other person who has examined or may thereafter examine the person as to the same mental or physical condition.

(5) Subrule (B) applies to examinations made by agreement of the parties, unless the agreement expressly provides otherwise.

(6) Subrule (B) does not preclude discovery of a report of an examining physician or the taking of a deposition of the physician under any other rule.

Rule 2.312 Request for Admission

(A) **Availability; Scope**. Within the time for completion of discovery, a party may serve on another party a written request for the admission of the truth of a matter within the scope of MCR 2.302(B) stated in the request that relates to statements or opinions of fact or the application of law to fact, including the genuineness of documents described in the request. Copies of the documents must be served with the request unless they have been or are otherwise furnished or made available for inspection and copying. Each matter of which an admission is requested must be stated separately.

(B) **Answer; Objection**.

(1) Each matter as to which a request is made is deemed admitted unless, within 28 days after service of the request, or within a shorter or longer time as the court may allow, the party to whom the request is directed serves on the party requesting the admission a written answer or objection addressed to the matter. Unless the court orders a shorter time a defendant may serve an answer or objection within 42 days after being served with the summons and complaint.

(2) The answer must specifically deny the matter or state in detail the reasons why the answering party cannot truthfully admit or deny it. A denial must fairly meet the substance of the request, and when good faith requires that a party qualify an answer or deny only part of the matter of which an admission is requested, the party must specify the parts that are admitted and denied.

(3) An answering party may not give lack of information or knowledge as a reason for failure to admit or deny unless the party states that he or she has made reasonable inquiry and that the information known or readily obtainable is insufficient to enable the party to admit or deny.

(4) If an objection is made, the reasons must be stated. A party who considers that a matter of which an admission has been requested presents a genuine issue for trial may not, on that ground alone, object to the request. The party may, subject to the provisions of MCR 2.313(C), deny the matter or state reasons why he or she cannot admit or deny it.

(C) **Motion Regarding Answer or Objection**. The party who has requested the admission may move to determine the sufficiency of the answer or objection. The motion must state that the movant has in good faith conferred or attempted to confer with the party not making the disclosure in an effort to secure the disclosure without court action. Unless the court determines that an objection is justified, it shall order that an answer be served. If the court determines that an answer does not comply with the requirements of the rule, it may order either that the matter is admitted, or that an amended answer be served. The court may, in lieu of one of these orders, determine that final disposition of the request be made at a pretrial conference or at a designated time before trial. The provisions of MCR 2.313(A)(5) apply to the award of expenses incurred in relation to the motion.

(D) **Effect of Admission**.

(1) A matter admitted under this rule is conclusively established unless the court on motion permits withdrawal or amendment of an admission. For good cause the court may allow a party to amend or withdraw an admission. The court may condition amendment or withdrawal of the admission on terms that are just.

(2) An admission made by a party under this rule is for the purpose of the pending action only and is not an admission for another purpose, nor may it be used against the party in another proceeding.

(E) **Public Records.**
(1) A party intending to use as evidence
(a) a record that a public official is required by federal, state, or municipal authority to receive for filing or recording or is given custody of by law, or
(b) a memorial of a public official,
may prepare a copy, synopsis, or abstract of the record, insofar as it is to be used, and serve it on the adverse party sufficiently in advance of trial to allow the adverse party a reasonable opportunity to determine its accuracy.
(2) The copy, synopsis, or abstract is then admissible in evidence as admitted facts in the action, if otherwise admissible, except insofar as its inaccuracy is pointed out by the adverse party in an affidavit filed and served within a reasonable time before trial.
(F) **Filing With Court**. Requests and responses under this rule must be filed with the court either before service or within a reasonable time thereafter.

Rule 2.313 Failure to Provide or to Permit Discovery; Sanctions

(A) **Motion for Order Compelling Discovery**. A party, on reasonable notice to other parties and all persons affected, may apply for an order compelling discovery as follows:
(1) *Appropriate Court*. A motion for an order under this rule may be made to the court in which the action is pending, or, as to a matter relating to a deposition, to a court in the county or district where the deposition is being taken.
(2) *Motion*. If
(a) a deponent fails to answer a question propounded or submitted under MCR 2.306 or 2.307,
(b) a corporation or other entity fails to make a designation under MCR 2.306(B)(5) or 2.307(A)(1),
(c) a party fails to answer an interrogatory submitted under MCR 2.309, or
(d) in response to a request for inspection submitted under MCR 2.310, a person fails to respond that inspection will be permitted as requested, the party seeking discovery may move for an order compelling an answer, a designation, or inspection in accordance with the request. When taking a deposition on oral examination, the proponent of the question may complete or adjourn the examination before applying for an order.
(3) *Ruling; Protective Order*. If the court denies the motion in whole or in part, it may enter a protective order that it could have entered on motion made under MCR 2.302(C).
(4) *Evasive or Incomplete Answer*. For purposes of this subrule an evasive or incomplete answer is to be treated as a failure to answer.
(5) *Award of Expenses of Motion*.
(a) If the motion is granted, the court shall, after opportunity for hearing, require the party or deponent whose conduct necessitated the motion or the party or attorney advising such conduct, or both, to pay to the moving party the reasonable expenses incurred in obtaining the order, including attorney fees, unless the court finds that the opposition to the motion was substantially justified or that other circumstances make an award of expenses unjust.
(b) If the motion is denied, the court shall, after opportunity for hearing, require the moving party or the attorney advising the motion, or both, to pay to the person who opposed the motion the reasonable expenses incurred in opposing the motion, including attorney fees, unless the court finds that the making of the motion was substantially justified or that other circumstances make an award of expenses unjust.
(c) If the motion is granted in part and denied in part, the court may apportion the reasonable expenses incurred in relation to the motion among the parties and other persons in a just manner.

(B) **Failure to Comply With Order**.
(1) *Sanctions by Court Where Deposition Is Taken*. If a deponent fails to be sworn or to answer a question after being directed to do so by a court in the county or district in which the deposition is being taken, the failure may be considered a contempt of that court.
(2) *Sanctions by Court in Which Action Is Pending*. If a party or an officer, director, or managing agent of a party, or a person designated under MCR 2.306(B)(5) or 2.307(A)(1) to testify on behalf of a party, fails to obey an order to provide or permit discovery, including an order entered under subrule (A) of this rule or under MCR 2.311, the court in which the action is pending may order such sanctions as are just, including, but not limited to the following:
(a) an order that the matters regarding which the order was entered or other designated facts may be taken to be established for the purposes of the action in accordance with the claim of the party obtaining the order;
(b) an order refusing to allow the disobedient party to support or oppose designated claims or

defenses, or prohibiting the party from introducing designated matters into evidence;

(c) an order striking pleadings or parts of pleadings, staying further proceedings until the order is obeyed, dismissing the action or proceeding or a part of it, or rendering a judgment by default against the disobedient party;

(d) in lieu of or in addition to the foregoing orders, an order treating as a contempt of court the failure to obey an order, except an order to submit to a physical or mental examination;

(e) where a party has failed to comply with an order under MCR 2.311(A) requiring the party to produce another for examination, such orders as are listed in subrules (B)(2)(a), (b), and (c), unless the party failing to comply shows that he or she is unable to produce such person for examination.

In lieu of or in addition to the foregoing orders, the court shall require the party failing to obey the order or the attorney advising the party, or both, to pay the reasonable expenses, including attorney fees, caused by the failure, unless the court finds that the failure was substantially justified or that other circumstances make an award of expenses unjust.

(C) **Expenses on Failure to Admit**. If a party denies the genuineness of a document, or the truth of a matter as requested under MCR 2.312, and if the party requesting the admission later proves the genuineness of the document or the truth of the matter, the requesting party may move for an order requiring the other party to pay the expenses incurred in making that proof, including attorney fees. The court shall enter the order unless it finds that

(1) the request was held objectionable pursuant to MCR 2.312,

(2) the admission sought was of no substantial importance,

(3) the party failing to admit had reasonable ground to believe that he or she might prevail on the matter, or

(4) there was other good reason for the failure to admit.

(D) **Failure of Party to Attend at Own Deposition, to Serve Answers to Interrogatories, or to Respond to Request for Inspection**.

(1) If a party; an officer, director, or managing agent of a party; or a person designated under MCR 2.306(B)(5) or 2.307(A)(1) to testify on behalf of a party fails

(a) to appear before the person who is to take his or her deposition, after being served with a proper notice;

(b) to serve answers or objections to interrogatories submitted under MCR 2.309, after proper service of the interrogatories; or

(c) to serve a written response to a request for inspection submitted under MCR 2.310, after proper service of the request,

on motion, the court in which the action is pending may order such sanctions as are just. Among others, it may take an action authorized under subrule (B)(2)(a), (b), and (c).

(2) In lieu of or in addition to an order, the court shall require the party failing to act or the attorney advising the party, or both, to pay the reasonable expenses, including attorney fees, caused by the failure, unless the court finds that the failure was substantially justified or that other circumstances make an award of expenses unjust.

(3) A failure to act described in this subrule may not be excused on the ground that the discovery sought is objectionable unless the party failing to act has moved for a protective order as provided by MCR 2.302(C).

(E) Absent exceptional circumstances, a court may not impose sanctions under these rules on a party for failing to provide electronically stored information lost as a result of the routine, good-faith operation of an electronic information system.

Rule 2.314 Discovery of Medical Information Concerning Party

(A) **Scope of Rule**.

(1) When a mental or physical condition of a party is in controversy, medical information about the condition is subject to discovery under these rules to the extent that

(a) the information is otherwise discoverable under MCR 2.302(B), and

(b) the party does not assert that the information is subject to a valid privilege.

(2) Medical information subject to discovery includes, but is not limited to, medical records in the possession or control of a physician, hospital, or other custodian, and medical knowledge discoverable by deposition or interrogatories.

(3) For purposes of this rule, medical information about a mental or physical condition of a party is within the control of the party, even if the information is not in the party's immediate physical possession.

(B) **Privilege; Assertion; Waiver; Effects**.

(1) A party who has a valid privilege may assert the privilege and prevent discovery of medical information relating to his or her mental or physical condition. The privilege must be asserted in the party's written response to a request for production

of documents under MCR 2.310, in answers to interrogatories under MCR 2.309(B), before or during the taking of a deposition, or by moving for a protective order under MCR 2.302(C). A privilege not timely asserted is waived in that action, but is not waived for the purposes of any other action.

(2) Unless the court orders otherwise, if a party asserts that the medical information is subject to a privilege and the assertion has the effect of preventing discovery of medical information otherwise discoverable under MCR 2.302(B), the party may not thereafter present or introduce any physical, documentary, or testimonial evidence relating to the party's medical history or mental or physical condition.

(C) **Response by Party to Request for Medical Information.**

(1) A party who is served with a request for production of medical information under MCR 2.310 must either:

(a) make the information available for inspection and copying as requested;

(b) assert that the information is privileged;

(c) object to the request as permitted by MCR 2.310(C)(2); or

(d) furnish the requesting party with signed authorizations in the form approved by the state court administrator sufficient in number to enable the requesting party to obtain the information requested from persons, institutions, hospitals, and other custodians in actual possession of the information requested.

(2) A party responding to a request for medical information as permitted by subrule (C)(1)(d) must also inform the adverse party of the physical location of the information requested.

(D) **Release of Medical Information by Custodian.**

(1) A physician, hospital, or other custodian of medical information (referred to in this rule as the "custodian") shall comply with a properly authorized request for the medical information within 28 days after the receipt of the request, or, if at the time the request is made the patient is hospitalized for the mental or physical condition for which the medical information is sought, within 28 days after the patient's discharge or release. The court may extend or shorten these time limits for good cause.

(2) In responding to a request for medical information under this rule, the custodian will be deemed to have complied with the request if the custodian

(a) makes the information reasonably available for inspection and copying; or

(b) delivers to the requesting party the original information or a true and exact copy of the original information accompanied by a sworn certificate in the form approved by the state court administrator, signed by the custodian verifying that the copy is a true and complete reproduction of the original information.

(3) If it is essential that an original document be examined when the authenticity of the document, questions of interpretation of handwriting, or similar questions arise, the custodian must permit reasonable inspection of the original document by the requesting party and by experts retained to examine the information.

(4) If x-rays or other records incapable of reproduction are requested, the custodian may inform the requesting party that these records exist, but have not been delivered pursuant to subrule (D)(2). Delivery of the records may be conditioned on the requesting party or the party's agent signing a receipt that includes a promise that the records will be returned to the custodian after a reasonable time for inspection purposes has elapsed.

(5) In complying with subrule (D)(2), the custodian is entitled to receive reasonable reimbursement in advance for expenses of compliance.

(6) If a custodian does not respond within the time permitted by subrule (D)(1) to a party's authorized request for medical information, a subpoena may be issued under MCR 2.305(A)(2), directing that the custodian present the information for examination and copying at the time and place stated in the subpoena.

(E) **Persons Not Parties.** Medical information concerning persons not parties to the action is not discoverable under this rule.

Rule 2.315 Video Depositions

(A) **When Permitted.** Depositions authorized under MCR 2.303 and 2.306 may be taken by means of simultaneous audio and visual electronic recording without leave of the court or stipulation of the parties, provided the deposition is taken in accordance with this rule.

(B) **Rules Governing.** Except as provided in this rule, the taking of video depositions is governed by the rules governing the taking of other depositions unless the nature of the video deposition makes compliance impossible or unnecessary.

(C) **Procedure.**

(1) A notice of the taking of a video deposition and a subpoena for attendance at the deposition must state that the deposition is to be visually recorded.

(2) A video deposition must be timed by means of a digital clock or clocks capable of displaying the hours, minutes, and seconds. The clock or clocks

must be in the picture at all times during the taking of the deposition.

(3) A video deposition must begin with a statement on camera of the date, time, and place at which the recording is being made, the title of the action, and the identification of the attorneys.

(4) The person being deposed must be sworn as a witness on camera by an authorized person.

(5) More than one camera may be used, in sequence or simultaneously.

(6) The parties may make audio recordings while the video deposition is being taken.

(7) At the conclusion of the deposition a statement must be made on camera that the deposition is completed.

(D) **Custody of Tape and Copies**.

(1) The person making the video recording must retain possession of it. The video recording must be securely sealed and marked for identification purposes.

(2) The parties may purchase audio or audio-visual copies of the recording from the operator.

(E) **Filing; Notice of Filing**. If a party requests that the deposition be filed, the person who made the recording shall

(1) file the recording with the court under MCR 2.306(F)(3), together with an affidavit identifying the recording, stating the total elapsed time, and attesting that no alterations, additions, or deletions other than those ordered by the court have been made;

(2) give the notice required by MCR 2.306(F)(3), and

(3) serve copies of the recording on all parties who have requested them under MCR 2.315(D)(2).

(F) **Use as Evidence; Objections**.

(1) A video deposition may not be used in a court proceeding unless it has been filed with the court.

(2) Except as modified by this rule, the use of video depositions in court proceedings is governed by MCR 2.308.

(3) A party who seeks to use a video deposition at trial must provide the court with either

(a) a transcript of the deposition, which shall be used for ruling on any objections, or

(b) a stipulation by all parties that there are no objections to the deposition and that the recording (or an agreed portion of it) may be played.

(4) When a video deposition is used in a court proceeding, the court must indicate on the record what portions of the recording have been played. The court reporter or recorder need not make a record of the statements in the recording.

(G) **Custody of Video Deposition After Filing**. After filing, a video deposition shall remain in the custody of the court unless the court orders the recording stored elsewhere for technical reasons or because of special storage problems. The order directing the storage must direct the custodian to keep the recordings sealed until the further order of the court. Video depositions filed with the court shall have the same status as other depositions and documents filed with the court, and may be reproduced, preserved, destroyed, or salvaged as directed by order of the court.

(H) **Appeal**. On appeal the recording remains part of the record and shall be transmitted with it. A party may request that the appellate court view portions of the video deposition. If a transcript was not provided to the court under subrule (F)(3), the appellant must arrange and pay for the preparation of a transcript to be included in the record on appeal.

(I) **Costs**. The costs of taking a video deposition and the cost for its use in evidence may be taxed as costs as provided by MCR 2.625 in the same manner as depositions recorded in other ways.

Rule 2.316 Removal of Discovery Materials From File

(A) **Definition**. For the purpose of this rule, "discovery material" means deposition transcripts, audio or video recordings of depositions, interrogatories, and answers to interrogatories and requests to admit.

(B) **Removal from File**. In civil actions, discovery materials may be removed from files and destroyed in the manner provided in this rule.

(1) *By Stipulation*. If the parties stipulate to the removal of discovery materials from the file, the clerk may remove the materials and dispose of them in the manner provided in the stipulation.

(2) *By the Clerk*.

(a) The clerk may initiate the removal of discovery materials from the file in the following circumstances.

(i) If an appeal has not been taken, 18 months after entry of judgment on the merits or dismissal of the action.

(ii) If an appeal has been taken, 91 days after the appellate proceedings are concluded, unless the action is remanded for further proceedings in the trial court.

(b) The clerk shall notify the parties and counsel of record, when possible, that discovery materials will be removed from the file of the action and destroyed on a specified date at least 28 days after the notice is served unless within that time

(i) the party who filed the discovery materials retrieves them from the clerk's office, or

(ii) a party files a written objection to removal of discovery materials from the file.

If an objection to removal of discovery materials is filed, the discovery materials may not be removed unless the court so orders after notice and opportunity for the objecting party to be heard. The clerk shall schedule a hearing and give notice to the parties. The rules governing motion practice apply.

(3) *By Order*. On motion of a party, or on its own initiative after notice and hearing, the court may order discovery materials removed at any other time on a finding that the materials are no longer necessary. However, no discovery materials may be destroyed by court personnel or the clerk until the periods set forth in subrule (2)(a)(i) or (2)(a)(ii) have passed.

Subchapter 2.400 Pretrial Procedure; Alternative Dispute Resolution; Offers of Judgment; Settlements

Rule 2.401 Pretrial Procedures; Conferences; Scheduling Orders

(A) **Time; Discretion of Court**. At any time after the commencement of the action, on its own initiative or the request of a party, the court may direct that the attorneys for the parties, alone or with the parties, appear for a conference. The court shall give reasonable notice of the scheduling of a conference. More than one conference may be held in an action.

(B) **Early Scheduling Conference and Order**.

(1) *Early Scheduling Conference*. The court may direct that an early scheduling conference be held. In addition to those considerations enumerated in subrule (C)(1), during this conference the court should consider:

(a) whether jurisdiction and venue are proper or whether the case is frivolous,

(b) whether to refer the case to an alternative dispute resolution procedure under MCR 2.410,

(c) the complexity of a particular case and enter a scheduling order setting time limitations for the processing of the case and establishing dates when future actions should begin or be completed in the case, and

(d) discovery, preservation, and claims of privilege of electronically stored information.

(2) *Scheduling Order*.

(a) At an early scheduling conference under subrule (B)(1), a pretrial conference under subrule (C), or at such other time as the court concludes that such an order would facilitate the progress of the case, the court shall establish times for events the court deems appropriate, including

(i) the initiation or completion of an ADR process,

(ii) the amendment of pleadings, adding of parties, or filing of motions,

(iii) the completion of discovery,

(iv) the exchange of witness lists under subrule (I), and

(v) the scheduling of a pretrial conference, a settlement conference, or trial.

More than one such order may be entered in a case.

(b) The scheduling of events under this subrule shall take into consideration the nature and complexity of the case, including the issues involved, the number and location of parties and potential witnesses, including experts, the extent of expected and necessary discovery, and the availability of reasonably certain trial dates.

(c) The scheduling order also may include provisions concerning discovery of electronically stored information, any agreements the parties reach for asserting claims of privilege or of protection as trial-preparation material after production, preserving discoverable information, and the form in which electronically stored information shall be produced.

(d) Whenever reasonably practical, the scheduling of events under this subrule shall be made after meaningful consultation with all counsel of record.

(i) If a scheduling order is entered under this subrule in a manner that does not permit meaningful advance consultation with counsel, within 14 days after entry of the order, a party may file and serve a written request for amendment of the order detailing the reasons why the order should be amended.

(ii) Upon receiving such a written request, the court shall reconsider the order in light of the objections raised by the parties. Whether the reconsideration occurs at a conference or in some other manner, the court must either enter a new scheduling order or notify the parties in writing that the court declines to amend the order. The court must schedule a conference, enter the new order, or send the written notice, within 14 days after receiving the request.

(iii) The submission of a request pursuant to this subrule, or the failure to submit such a request, does not preclude a party from filing a motion to modify a scheduling order.

(C) **Pretrial Conference; Scope**.
(1) At a conference under this subrule, in addition to the matters listed in subrule (B)(1), the court and the attorneys for the parties may consider any matters that will facilitate the fair and expeditious disposition of the action, including:
(a) the simplification of the issues;
(b) the amount of time necessary for discovery;
(c) the necessity or desirability of amendments to the pleadings;
(d) the possibility of obtaining admissions of fact and of documents to avoid unnecessary proof;
(e) the limitation of the number of expert witnesses;
(f) the consolidation of actions for trial, the separation of issues, and the order of trial when some issues are to be tried by a jury and some by the court;
(g) the possibility of settlement;
(h) whether mediation, case evaluation, or some other form of alternative dispute resolution would be appropriate for the case, and what mechanisms are available to provide such services;
(i) the identity of the witnesses to testify at trial;
(j) the estimated length of trial;
(k) whether all claims arising out of the transaction or occurrence that is the subject matter of the action have been joined as required by MCR 2.203(A);
(l) other matters that may aid in the disposition of the action.
(2) Conference Order. If appropriate, the court shall enter an order incorporating agreements reached and decisions made at the conference.

(D) **Order for Trial Briefs**. The court may direct the attorneys to furnish trial briefs as to any or all of the issues involved in the action.

(E) **Appearance of Counsel**. The attorneys attending the conference shall be thoroughly familiar with the case and have the authority necessary to fully participate in the conference. The court may direct that the attorneys who intend to try the case attend the conference.

(F) **Presence of Parties at Conference**. If the court anticipates meaningful discussion of settlement, the court may direct that the parties to the action, agents of parties, representatives of lienholders, or representatives of insurance carriers, or other persons:
(1) be present at the conference or be immediately available at the time of the conference; and
(2) have information and authority adequate for responsible and effective participation in the conference for all purposes, including settlement.
The court's order may require the availability of a specified individual; provided, however, that the availability of a substitute who has the information and authority required by subrule (F)(2) shall constitute compliance with the order.
The court's order may specify whether the availability is to be in person or by telephone.
This subrule does not apply to an early scheduling conference held pursuant to subrule (B).

(G) **Failure to Attend or to Participate**.
(1) Failure of a party or the party's attorney or other representative to attend a scheduled conference or to have information and authority adequate for responsible and effective participation in the conference for all purposes, including settlement, as directed by the court, may constitute a default to which MCR 2.603 is applicable or a ground for dismissal under MCR 2.504(B).
(2) The court shall excuse a failure to attend a conference or to participate as directed by the court, and shall enter a just order other than one of default or dismissal, if the court finds that
(a) entry of an order of default or dismissal would cause manifest injustice; or
(b) the failure was not due to the culpable negligence of the party or the party's attorney.
The court may condition the order on the payment by the offending party or attorney of reasonable expenses as provided in MCR 2.313(B)(2).

(H) **Conference After Discovery**. If the court finds at a pretrial conference held after the completion of discovery that due to a lack of reasonable diligence by a party the action is not ready for trial, the court may enter an appropriate order to facilitate preparation of the action for trial and may require the offending party to pay the reasonable expenses, including attorney fees, caused by the lack of diligence.

(I) **Witness Lists**.
(1) No later than the time directed by the court under subrule (B)(2)(a), the parties shall file and serve witness lists. The witness list must include:
(a) the name of each witness, and the witness' address, if known; however, records custodians whose testimony would be limited to providing the foundation for the admission of records may be identified generally;
(b) whether the witness is an expert, and the field of expertise.
(2) The court may order that any witness not listed in accordance with this rule will be prohibited from testifying at trial except upon good cause shown.
(3) This subrule does not prevent a party from obtaining an earlier disclosure of witness information by other discovery means as provided in these rules.

Rule 2.402 Use of Communication Equipment

(A) **Definition**. "Communication equipment" means a conference telephone or other electronic device that permits all those appearing or participating to hear and speak to each other.

(B) **Use**. A court may, on its own initiative or on the written request of a party, direct that communication equipment be used for a motion hearing, pretrial conference, scheduling conference, or status conference. The court must give notice to the parties before directing on its own initiative that communication equipment be used. A party wanting to use communication equipment must submit a written request to the court at least 7 days before the day on which such equipment is sought to be used, and serve a copy on the other parties, unless good cause is shown to waive this requirement. The requesting party also must provide a copy of the request to the office of the judge to whom the request is directed. The court may, with the consent of all parties or for good cause, direct that the testimony of a witness be taken through communication equipment. A verbatim record of the proceeding must still be made.

(C) **Burden of Expense**. The party who initiates the use of communication equipment shall pay the cost for its use, unless the court otherwise directs. If the use of communication equipment is initiated by the court, the cost for its use is to be shared equally, unless the court otherwise directs.

Rule 2.403 Case Evaluation

(A) **Scope and Applicability of Rule**.

(1) A court may submit to case evaluation any civil action in which the relief sought is primarily money damages or division of property.

(2) Case evaluation of tort cases filed in circuit court is mandatory beginning with actions filed after the effective dates of Chapters 49 and 49A of the Revised Judicature Act, as added by 1986 PA 178.

(3) A court may exempt claims seeking equitable relief from case evaluation for good cause shown on motion or by stipulation of the parties if the court finds that case evaluation of such claims would be inappropriate.

(4) Cases filed in district court may be submitted to case evaluation under this rule. The time periods set forth in subrules (B)(1), (G)(1), (L)(1) and (L)(2) may be shortened at the discretion of the district judge to whom the case is assigned.

(B) **Selection of Cases**.

(1) The judge to whom an action is assigned or the chief judge may select it for case evaluation by written order after the filing of the answer

(a) on written stipulation by the parties,

(b) on written motion by a party, or

(c) on the judge's own initiative.

(2) Selection of an action for case evaluation has no effect on the normal progress of the action toward trial.

(C) **Objections to Case Evaluation**.

(1) To object to case evaluation, a party must file a written motion to remove from case evaluation and a notice of hearing of the motion and serve a copy on the attorneys of record and the ADR clerk within 14 days after notice of the order assigning the action to case evaluation. The motion must be set for hearing within 14 days after it is filed, unless the court orders otherwise.

(2) A timely motion must be heard before the case is submitted to case evaluation.

(D) **Case Evaluation Panel**.

(1) Case evaluation panels shall be composed of 3 persons.

(2) The procedure for selecting case evaluation panels is as provided in MCR 2.404.

(3) A judge may be selected as a member of a case evaluation panel, but may not preside at the trial of any action in which he or she served as a case evaluator.

(4) A case evaluator may not be called as a witness at trial.

(E) **Disqualification of Case Evaluators.** The rule for disqualification of a case evaluator is the same as that provided in MCR 2.003 for the disqualification of a judge.

(F) **ADR Clerk**. The court shall designate the ADR clerk specified under MCR 2.410, or some other person, to administer the case evaluation program. In this rule and MCR 2.404, "ADR clerk" refers to the person so designated.

(G) **Scheduling Case Evaluation Hearing**.

(1) The ADR clerk shall set a time and place for the hearing and send notice to the case evaluators and the attorneys at least 42 days before the date set.

(2) Adjournments may be granted only for good cause, in accordance with MCR 2.503.

(H) **Fees**.

(1) Each party must send a check for $75 made payable in the manner and within the time specified in the notice of the case evaluation hearing. However, if a judge is a member of the panel, the fee is $50. If the order for case evaluation directs that payment be made to the ADR clerk, the ADR clerk shall arrange payment to the case evaluators. Except by stipulation and court order, the parties may not make any other payment of fees or expenses to the case evaluators than that provided in this subrule.

(2) Only a single fee is required of each party, even where there are counterclaims, cross-claims, or third-party claims. A person entitled to a fee waiver under MCR 2.002 is entitled to a waiver of fees under this rule.

(3) If one claim is derivative of another (e.g., husband-wife, parent-child) they must be treated as a single claim, with one fee to be paid and a single award made by the case evaluators.

(4) Fees paid pursuant to subrule (H) shall be refunded to the parties if

(a) the court sets aside the order submitting the case to case evaluation or on its own initiative adjourns the case evaluation hearing, or

(b) the parties notify the ADR clerk in writing at least 14 days before the case evaluation hearing of the settlement, dismissal, or entry of judgment disposing of the action, or of an order of adjournment on stipulation or the motion of a party.

If case evaluation is rescheduled at a later time, the fee provisions of subrule (H) apply regardless of whether previously paid fees have been refunded.

(5) Fees paid pursuant to subrule (H) shall not be refunded to the parties if

(a) in the case of an adjournment, the adjournment order sets a new date for case evaluation and the fees are applied to the new date, or

(b) the request for and granting of adjournment is made within 14 days of the scheduled case evaluation, unless waived for good cause.

Penalties for late filing of papers under subrule (I)(2) are not to be refunded.

(I) **Submission of Summary and Supporting Documents**.

(1) Unless otherwise provided in the notice of hearing, at least 14 days before the hearing, each party shall

(a) serve a copy of the case evaluation summary and supporting documents in accordance with MCR 2.107, and

(b) file a proof of service and three copies of a case evaluation summary and supporting documents with the ADR clerk.

(2) Each failure to timely file and serve the materials identified in subrule (1) and each subsequent filing of supplemental materials within 14 days of the hearing, subjects the offending attorney or party to a $150 penalty to be paid in the manner specified in the notice of the case evaluation hearing. An offending attorney shall not charge the penalty to the client, unless the client agreed in writing to be responsible for the penalty.

(3) The case evaluation summary shall consist of a concise summary setting forth that party's factual and legal position on issues presented by the action. Except as permitted by the court, the summary shall not exceed 20 pages double spaced, exclusive of attachments. Quotations and footnotes may be single spaced. At least one inch margins must be used, and printing shall not be smaller than 12-point font.

(J) **Conduct of Hearing**.

(1) A party has the right, but is not required, to attend a case evaluation hearing. If scars, disfigurement, or other unusual conditions exist, they may be demonstrated to the panel by a personal appearance; however, no testimony will be taken or permitted of any party.

(2) The rules of evidence do not apply before the case evaluation panel. Factual information having a bearing on damages or liability must be supported by documentary evidence, if possible.

(3) Oral presentation shall be limited to 15 minutes per side unless multiple parties or unusual circumstances warrant additional time. Information on settlement negotiations not protected under MCR 2.412 and applicable insurance policy limits shall be disclosed at the request of the case evaluation panel.

(4) Statements by the attorneys and the briefs or summaries are not admissible in any court or evidentiary proceeding.

(5) Counsel or the parties may not engage in ex parte communications with the case evaluators concerning the action prior to the hearing. After the evaluation, the case evaluators need not respond to inquiries by the parties or counsel regarding the proceeding or the evaluation.

(K) **Decision**.

(1) Within 14 days after the hearing, the panel will make an evaluation and notify the attorney for each party of its evaluation in writing. If an award is not unanimous, the evaluation must so indicate.

(2) Except as provided in subrule (H)(3), the evaluation must include a separate award as to each plaintiff's claim against each defendant and as to each cross-claim, counterclaim, or third-party claim that has been filed in the action. For the purpose of this subrule, all such claims filed by any one party against any other party shall be treated as a single claim.

(3) The evaluation may not include a separate award on any claim for equitable relief, but the panel may consider such claims in determining the amount of an award.

(4) In a tort case to which MCL 600.4915(2) or MCL 600.4963(2) applies, if the panel unanimously finds that a party's action or defense as to any other party is frivolous, the panel shall so indicate on the evaluation. For the purpose of this rule, an action or defense is "frivolous" if, as to all of a plaintiff's claims or all of a defendant's defenses to liability, at least 1 of the following conditions is met:

(a) The party's primary purpose in initiating the action or asserting the defense was to harass, embarrass, or injure the opposing party.

(b) The party had no reasonable basis to believe that the facts underlying that party's legal position were in fact true.

(c) The party's legal position was devoid of arguable legal merit.

(5) In an action alleging medical malpractice to which MCL 600.4915 applies, the evaluation must include a specific finding that

(a) there has been a breach of the applicable standard of care,

(b) there has not been a breach of the applicable standard of care, or

(c) reasonable minds could differ as to whether there has been a breach of the applicable standard of care.

(L) **Acceptance or Rejection of Evaluation**.

(1) Each party shall file a written acceptance or rejection of the panel's evaluation with the ADR clerk within 28 days after service of the panel's evaluation. Even if there are separate awards on multiple claims, the party must either accept or reject the evaluation in its entirety as to a particular opposing party. The failure to file a written acceptance or rejection within 28 days constitutes rejection.

(2) There may be no disclosure of a party's acceptance or rejection of the panel's evaluation until the expiration of the 28-day period, at which time the ADR clerk shall send a notice indicating each party's acceptance or rejection of the panel's evaluation.

(3) In case evaluations involving multiple parties the following rules apply:

(a) Each party has the option of accepting all of the awards covering the claims by or against that party or of accepting some and rejecting others. However, as to any particular opposing party, the party must either accept or reject the evaluation in its entirety.

(b) A party who accepts all of the awards may specifically indicate that he or she intends the acceptance to be effective only if

(i) all opposing parties accept, and/or

(ii) the opposing parties accept as to specified coparties.

If such a limitation is not included in the acceptance, an accepting party is deemed to have agreed to entry of judgment, or dismissal as provided in subrule (M)(1), as to that party and those of the opposing parties who accept, with the action to continue between the accepting party and those opposing parties who reject.

(c) If a party makes a limited acceptance under subrule (L)(3)(b) and some of the opposing parties accept and others reject, for the purposes of the cost provisions of subrule (O) the party who made the limited acceptance is deemed to have rejected as to those opposing parties who accept.

(M) **Effect of Acceptance of Evaluation**.

(1) If all the parties accept the panel's evaluation, judgment will be entered in accordance with the evaluation, unless the amount of the award is paid within 28 days after notification of the acceptances, in which case the court shall dismiss the action with prejudice. The judgment or dismissal shall be deemed to dispose of all claims in the action and includes all fees, costs, and interest to the date it is entered, except for cases involving rights to personal protection insurance benefits under MCL 500.3101 et seq., for which judgment or dismissal shall not be deemed to dispose of claims that have not accrued as of the date of the case evaluation hearing.

(2) If only a part of an action has been submitted to case evaluation pursuant to subrule (A)(3) and all of the parties accept the panel's evaluation, the court shall enter an order disposing of only those claims.

(3) In a case involving multiple parties, judgment, or dismissal as provided in subrule (1), shall be entered as to those opposing parties who have accepted the portions of the evaluation that apply to them.

(N) **Proceedings After Rejection**.

(1) If all or part of the evaluation of the case evaluation panel is rejected, the action proceeds to trial in the normal fashion.

(2) If a party's claim or defense was found to be frivolous under subrule (K)(4), that party may request that the court review the panel's finding by filing a motion within 14 days after the ADR clerk sends notice of the rejection of the case evaluation award.

(a) The motion shall be submitted to the court on the case evaluation summaries and documents that were considered by the case evaluation panel. No other exhibits or testimony may be submitted. However, oral argument on the motion shall be permitted.

(b) After reviewing the materials submitted, the court shall determine whether the action or defense is frivolous.

(c) If the court agrees with the panel's determination, the provisions of subrule (N)(3) apply, except that the bond must be filed within 28 days after the entry of the court's order determining the action or defense to be frivolous.

(d) The judge who hears a motion under this subrule may not preside at a nonjury trial of the action.

(3) Except as provided in subrule (2), if a party's claim or defense was found to be frivolous under subrule (K)(4), that party shall post a cash or surety bond, pursuant to MCR 3.604, in the amount of $5,000 for each party against whom the action or defense was determined to be frivolous.

(a) The bond must be posted within 56 days after the case evaluation hearing or at least 14 days before trial, whichever is earlier.

(b) If a surety bond is filed, an insurance company that insures the defendant against a claim made in the action may not act as the surety.

(c) If the bond is not posted as required by this rule, the court shall dismiss a claim found to have been frivolous, and enter the default of a defendant whose defense was found to be frivolous. The action shall proceed to trial as to the remaining claims and parties, and as to the amount of damages against a defendant in default.

(d) If judgment is entered against the party who posted the bond, the bond shall be used to pay any costs awarded against that party by the court under any applicable law or court rule. MCR 3.604 applies to proceedings to enforce the bond.

(4) The ADR clerk shall place a copy of the case evaluation and the parties' acceptances and rejections in a sealed envelope for filing with the clerk of the court. In a nonjury action, the envelope may not be opened and the parties may not reveal the amount of the evaluation until the judge has rendered judgment.

(O) **Rejecting Party's Liability for Costs**.

(1) If a party has rejected an evaluation and the action proceeds to verdict, that party must pay the opposing party's actual costs unless the verdict is more favorable to the rejecting party than the case evaluation. However, if the opposing party has also rejected the evaluation, a party is entitled to costs only if the verdict is more favorable to that party than the case evaluation.

(2) For the purpose of this rule "verdict" includes,

(a) a jury verdict,

(b) a judgment by the court after a nonjury trial,

(c) a judgment entered as a result of a ruling on a motion after rejection of the case evaluation.

(3) For the purpose of subrule (O)(1), a verdict must be adjusted by adding to it assessable costs and interest on the amount of the verdict from the filing of the complaint to the date of the case evaluation, and, if applicable, by making the adjustment of future damages as provided by MCL 600.6306. After this adjustment, the verdict is considered more favorable to a defendant if it is more than 10 percent below the evaluation, and is considered more favorable to the plaintiff if it is more than 10 percent above the evaluation. If the evaluation was zero, a verdict finding that a defendant is not liable to the plaintiff shall be deemed more favorable to the defendant.

(4) In cases involving multiple parties, the following rules apply:

(a) Except as provided in subrule (O)(4)(b), in determining whether the verdict is more favorable to a party than the case evaluation, the court shall consider only the amount of the evaluation and verdict as to the particular pair of parties, rather than the aggregate evaluation or verdict as to all parties. However, costs may not be imposed on a plaintiff who obtains an aggregate verdict more favorable to the plaintiff than the aggregate evaluation.

(b) If the verdict against more than one defendant is based on their joint and several liability, the plaintiff may not recover costs unless the verdict is more favorable to the plaintiff than the total case evaluation as to those defendants, and a defendant may not recover costs unless the verdict is more favorable to that defendant than the case evaluation as to that defendant.

(c) Except as provided by subrule (O)(10), in a personal injury action, for the purpose of subrule (O)(1), the verdict against a particular defendant shall not be adjusted by applying that defendant's proportion of fault as determined under MCL 600.6304(1)-(2).

(5) If the verdict awards equitable relief, costs may be awarded if the court determines that

(a) taking into account both monetary relief (adjusted as provided in subrule [O][3]) and equitable relief, the verdict is not more favorable to the rejecting party than the evaluation, or, in situations where both parties have rejected the evaluation, the verdict in favor of the party seeking costs is more favorable than the case evaluation, and

(b) it is fair to award costs under all of the circumstances.

(6) For the purpose of this rule, actual costs are

(a) those costs taxable in any civil action, and

(b) a reasonable attorney fee based on a reasonable hourly or daily rate as determined by the trial judge for services necessitated by the rejection of the case evaluation.

For the purpose of determining taxable costs under this subrule and under MCR 2.625, the party entitled to recover actual costs under this rule shall be considered the prevailing party.

(7) Costs shall not be awarded if the case evaluation award was not unanimous. If case evaluation results in a nonunanimous award, a case may be ordered to a subsequent case evaluation hearing conducted without reference to the prior case evaluation award, or other alternative dispute resolution processes, at the expense of the parties, pursuant to MCR 2.410(C)(1).

(8) A request for costs under this subrule must be filed and served within 28 days after the entry of the judgment or entry of an order denying a timely motion

(i) for a new trial,

(ii) to set aside the judgment, or

(iii) for rehearing or reconsideration.

(9) In an action under MCL 436.1801, if the plaintiff rejects the award against the minor or alleged intoxicated person, or is deemed to have rejected such an award under subrule (L)(3)(c), the court shall not award costs against the plaintiff in favor of the minor or alleged intoxicated person unless it finds that the rejection was not motivated by the need to comply with MCL 436.1801(6).

(10) For the purpose of subrule (O)(1), in an action filed on or after March 28, 1996, and based on tort or another legal theory seeking damages for personal injury, property damage, or wrongful death, a verdict awarding damages shall be adjusted for relative fault as provided by MCL 600.6304.

(11) If the "verdict" is the result of a motion as provided by subrule (O)(2)(c), the court may, in the interest of justice, refuse to award actual costs.

Rule 2.404 Selection of Case Evaluation Panels

(A) **Case Evaluator Selection Plans.**

(1) *Requirement.* Each trial court that submits cases to case evaluation under MCR 2.403 shall adopt by local administrative order a plan to maintain a list of persons available to serve as case evaluators and to assign case evaluators from the list to panels. The plan must be in writing and available to the public in the ADR clerk's office.

(2) *Alternative Plans.*

(a) A plan adopted by a district or probate court may use the list of case evaluators and appointment procedure of the circuit court for the circuit in which the court is located.

(b) Courts in adjoining circuits or districts may jointly adopt and administer a case evaluation plan.

(c) If it is not feasible for a court to adopt its own plan because of the low volume of cases to be submitted or because of inadequate numbers of available case evaluators, the court may enter into an agreement with a neighboring court to refer cases for case evaluation under the other court's system. The agreement may provide for payment by the referring court to cover the cost of administering case evaluation. However, fees and costs may not be assessed against the parties to actions evaluated except as provided by MCR 2.403.

(d) Other alternative plans must be submitted as local court rules under MCR 8.112(A).

(B) **Lists of Case Evaluators.**

(1) *Application.* An eligible person desiring to serve as a case evaluator may apply to the ADR clerk to be placed on the list of case evaluators. Application forms shall be available in the office of the ADR clerk. The form shall include an optional section identifying the applicant's gender and racial/ethnic background. The form shall include a certification that

(a) the case evaluator meets the requirements for service under the court's selection plan, and

(b) the case evaluator will not discriminate against parties, attorneys, or other case evaluators on the basis of race, ethnic origin, gender, or other protected personal characteristic.

(2) *Eligibility.* To be eligible to serve as a case evaluator, a person must meet the qualifications provided by this subrule.

(a) The applicant must have been a practicing lawyer for at least 5 years and be a member in good standing of the State Bar of Michigan. The plan may not require membership in any other organization as a qualification for service as a case evaluator.

(b) An applicant must reside, maintain an office, or have an active practice in the jurisdiction for which the list of case evaluators is compiled.

(c) An applicant must demonstrate that a substantial portion of the applicant's practice for the last 5 years has been devoted to civil litigation matters, including investigation, discovery, motion practice, case evaluation, settlement, trial preparation, and/or trial.

(d) If separate sublists are maintained for specific types of cases, the applicant must have had an active practice in the practice area for which the case evaluator is listed for at least the last 3 years.

If there are insufficient numbers of potential case evaluators meeting the qualifications stated in this rule, the plan may provide for consideration of alternative qualifications.

(3) *Review of Applications.* The plan shall provide for a person or committee to review applications annually, or more frequently if appropriate, and compile one or more lists of qualified case evaluators. Persons meeting the qualifications

specified in this rule shall be placed on the list of approved case evaluators. Selections shall be made without regard to race, ethnic origin, or gender.

(a) If an individual performs this review function, the person must be an employee of the court.

(b) If a committee performs this review function, the following provisions apply.

(i) The committee must have at least three members.

(ii) The selection of committee members shall be designed to assure that the goals stated in subrule (D)(2) will be met.

(iii) A person may not serve on the committee more than 3 years in any 9 year period.

(c) Applicants who are not placed on the case evaluator list or lists shall be notified of that decision. The plan shall provide a procedure by which such an applicant may seek reconsideration of the decision by some other person or committee. The plan need not provide for a hearing of any kind as part of the reconsideration process. Documents considered in the initial review process shall be retained for at least the period of time during which the applicant can seek reconsideration of the original decision.

(4) *Specialized Lists.* If the number and qualifications of available case evaluators makes it practicable to do so, the ADR clerk shall maintain

(a) separate lists for various types of cases, and,

(b) where appropriate for the type of cases, separate sublists of case evaluators who primarily represent plaintiffs, primarily represent defendants, and neutral case evaluators whose practices are not identifiable as representing primarily plaintiffs or defendants.

(5) *Reapplication.* Persons shall be placed on the list of case evaluators for a fixed period of time, not to exceed seven years, and must reapply at the end of that time in the manner directed by the court.

(6) *Availability of Lists.* The list of case evaluators must be available to the public in the ADR clerk's office.

(7) *Removal from List.* The plan must include a procedure for removal from the list of case evaluators who have demonstrated incompetency, bias, made themselves consistently unavailable to serve as a case evaluator, or for other just cause.

(8) The court may require case evaluators to attend orientation or training sessions or provide written materials explaining the case evaluation process and the operation of the court's case evaluation program. However, case evaluators may not be charged any fees or costs for such programs or materials.

(C) **Assignments to Panels.**

(1) *Method of Assignment.* The ADR clerk shall assign case evaluators to panels in a random or rotating manner that assures as nearly as possible that each case evaluator on a list or sublist is assigned approximately the same number of cases over a period of time. If a substitute case evaluator must be assigned, the same or similar assignment procedure shall be used to select the substitute. The ADR clerk shall maintain records of service of case evaluators on panels and shall make those records available on request.

(2) *Assignment from Sublists.* If sublists of plaintiff, defense, and neutral case evaluators are maintained for a particular type of case, the panel shall include one case evaluator who primarily represents plaintiffs, one case evaluator who primarily represents defendants, and one neutral case evaluator. If a judge is assigned to a panel as permitted by MCR 2.403(D)(3), the judge shall serve as the neutral case evaluator if sublists are maintained for that class of cases.

(3) *Special Panels.* On stipulation of the parties, the court may appoint a panel selected by the parties. In such a case, the qualification requirements of subrule (B)(2) do not apply, and the parties may agree to modification of the procedures for conduct of case evaluation. Nothing in this rule or MCR 2.403 precludes parties from stipulating to other ADR procedures that may aid in resolution of the case.

(D) **Supervision of Selection Process.**

(1) The chief judge shall exercise general supervision over the implementation of this rule and shall review the operation of the court's case evaluation plan at least annually to assure compliance with this rule. In the event of noncompliance, the court shall take such action as is needed. This action may include recruiting persons to serve as case evaluators or changing the court's case evaluation plan.

(2) In implementing the selection plan, the court, court employees, and attorneys involved in the procedure shall take all steps necessary to assure that as far as reasonably possible the list of case evaluators fairly reflects the racial, ethnic, and gender diversity of the members of the state bar in the jurisdiction for which the list is compiled who are eligible to serve as case evaluators.

Rule 2.405 Offers to Stipulate to Entry of Judgment

(A) **Definitions**. As used in this rule:

(1) "Offer" means a written notification to an adverse party of the offeror's willingness to stipulate to the entry of a judgment in a sum certain, which is

deemed to include all costs and interest then accrued. If a party has made more than one offer, the most recent offer controls for the purposes of this rule.

(2) "Counteroffer" means a written reply to an offer, served within 21 days after service of the offer, in which a party rejects an offer of the adverse party and makes his or her own offer.

(3) "Average offer" means the sum of an offer and a counteroffer, divided by two. If no counteroffer is made, the offer shall be used as the average offer.

(4) "Verdict" includes,

(a) a jury verdict,

(b) a judgment by the court after a nonjury trial,

(c) a judgment entered as a result of a ruling on a motion after rejection of the offer of judgment.

(5) "Adjusted verdict" means the verdict plus interest and costs from the filing of the complaint through the date of the offer.

(6) "Actual costs" means the costs and fees taxable in a civil action and a reasonable attorney fee for services necessitated by the failure to stipulate to the entry of judgment.

(B) **Offer**. Until 28 days before trial, a party may serve on the adverse party a written offer to stipulate to the entry of a judgment for the whole or part of the claim, including interest and costs then accrued.

(C) **Acceptance or Rejection of Offer**.

(1) To accept, the adverse party, within 21 days after service of the offer, must serve on the other parties a written notice of agreement to stipulate to the entry of the judgment offered, and file the offer, the notice of acceptance, and proof of service of the notice with the court. The court shall enter a judgment according to the terms of the stipulation.

(2) An offer is rejected if the offeree

(a) expressly rejects it in writing, or

(b) does not accept it as provided by subrule (C)(1).

A rejection does not preclude a later offer by either party.

(3) A counteroffer may be accepted or rejected in the same manner as an offer.

(D) **Imposition of Costs Following Rejection of Offer**. If an offer is rejected, costs are payable as follows:

(1) If the adjusted verdict is more favorable to the offeror than the average offer, the offeree must pay to the offeror the offeror's actual costs incurred in the prosecution or defense of the action.

(2) If the adjusted verdict is more favorable to the offeree than the average offer, the offeror must pay to the offeree the offeree's actual costs incurred in the prosecution or defense of the action. However, an offeree who has not made a counteroffer may not recover actual costs unless the offer was made less than 42 days before trial.

(3) The court shall determine the actual costs incurred. The court may, in the interest of justice, refuse to award an attorney fee under this rule.

(4) Evidence of an offer is admissible only in a proceeding to determine costs.

(5) Proceedings under this rule do not affect a contract or relationship between a party and his or her attorney.

(6) A request for costs under this subrule must be filed and served within 28 days after the entry of the judgment or entry of an order denying a timely motion

(i) for a new trial,

(ii) too set aside the judgment, or

(iii) for rehearing or reconsideration.

(E) **Relationship to Case Evaluation**. Costs may not be awarded under this rule in a case that has been submitted to case evaluation under MCR 2.403 unless the case evaluation award was not unanimous.

Rule 2.406 Use of Facsimile Communication Equipment

(A) **Definition**. "Facsimile communication equipment" means a machine that transmits and reproduces graphic matter (as printing or still pictures) by means of signals sent over telephone lines.

(B) **Use**. Courts may permit the filing of pleadings, motions, affidavits, opinions, orders, or other documents by the use of facsimile communication equipment. Except as provided by MCR 2.002, a clerk shall not permit the filing of any document for which a filing fee is required unless the full amount of the filing fee is paid or deposited in advance with the clerk.

(C) **Paper**. All filings must be on good quality 8½ by 11-inch paper, and the print must be no smaller than 12-point type. These requirements do not apply to attachments and exhibits, but parties are encouraged to reduce or enlarge such documents to 8½ by 11 inches, if practical.

(D) **Fees**. In addition to fees required by statute, courts may impose fees for facsimile filings in accordance with the schedule that is established by the State Court Administrative Office for that purpose.

(E) **Number of Pages**. Courts may establish a maximum number of pages that may be sent at one time.

(F) **Hours**. Documents received during the regular business hours of the court will be deemed filed on that business day. Documents received after regular business hours and on weekends or designated court holidays will be deemed filed on the next business day. A document is considered filed if the transmission begins during regular business hours, as verified by the court, and the entire document is received.

(G) **Originals**. Documents filed by facsimile communication equipment shall be considered original documents. The filing party shall retain the documents that were transmitted by facsimile communication equipment.

(H) **Signature**. For purposes of MCR 2.114, a signature includes a signature transmitted by facsimile communication equipment.

Rule 2.407 Videoconferencing

(A) **Definitions**. In this subchapter:

(1) "Participants" include, but are not limited to, parties, counsel, and subpoenaed witnesses, but do not include the general public.

(2) "Videoconferencing" means the use of an interactive technology that sends video, voice, and data signals over a transmission circuit so that two or more individuals or groups can communicate with each other simultaneously using video codecs, monitors, cameras, audio microphones, and audio speakers.

(B) **Application**.

(1) Subject to standards published by the State Court Administrative Office and the criteria set forth in subsection (C), a court may, at the request of any participant, or sua sponte, allow the use of videoconferencing technology by any participant in any court-scheduled civil proceeding.

(2) Subject to State Court Administrative Office standards, courts may determine the manner and extent of the use of videoconferencing technology.

(3) This rule does not supersede a participant's ability to participate by telephonic means under MCR 2.402.

(C) **Criteria for Videoconferencing**. In determining in a particular case whether to permit the use of videoconferencing technology and the manner of proceeding with videoconferencing, the court shall consider the following factors:

(1) The capabilities of the court's videoconferencing equipment.

(2) Whether any undue prejudice would result.

(3) The convenience of the parties and the proposed witness, and the cost of producing the witness in person in relation to the importance of the offered testimony.

(4) Whether the procedure would allow for full and effective cross-examination, especially when the cross-examination would involve documents or other exhibits.

(5) Whether the dignity, solemnity, and decorum of the courtroom would tend to impress upon the witness the duty to testify truthfully.

(6) Whether a physical liberty or other fundamental interest is at stake in the proceeding.

(7) Whether the court is satisfied that it can sufficiently control the proceedings at the remote location so as to effectively extend the courtroom to the remote location.

(8) Whether the use of videoconferencing technology presents the person at a remote location in a diminished or distorted sense that negatively reflects upon the individual at the remote location to persons present in the courtroom.

(9) Whether the use of videoconferencing technology diminishes or detracts from the dignity, solemnity, and formality of the proceeding and undermines the integrity, fairness, or effectiveness of the proceeding.

(10) Whether the person appearing by videoconferencing technology presents a significant security risk to transport and be present physically in the courtroom.

(11) Whether the parties or witness(es) have waived personal appearance or stipulated to videoconferencing.

(12) The proximity of the videoconferencing request date to the proposed appearance date.

(13) Any other factors that the court may determine to be relevant.

(D) **Request for videoconferencing**.

(1) A participant who requests the use of videoconferencing technology shall ensure that the equipment available at the remote location meets the technical and operational standards established by the State Court Administrative Office.

(2) A participant who requests the use of videoconferencing technology must provide the court with the videoconference dialing information and the participant's contact information in advance of the court date when videoconferencing technology will be used.

(3) There is no motion fee for requests submitted under this rule.

(E) **Objections**. The court shall rule on an objection to the use of videoconferencing under the factors set forth under subsection C.

(F) **Mechanics of Videoconferencing**. The use of any videoconferencing technology must be conducted in accordance with standards published by the State Court Administrative Office. All proceedings at which videoconferencing technology is used must be recorded verbatim by the court with the exception of hearings that are not required to be recorded by law.

Rule 2.410 Alternative Dispute Resolution

(A) **Scope and Applicability of Rule; Definitions**.

(1) All civil cases are subject to alternative dispute resolution processes unless otherwise provided by statute or court rule.

(2) For the purposes of this rule, alternative dispute resolution (ADR) means any process designed to

resolve a legal dispute in the place of court adjudication, and includes settlement conferences ordered under MCR 2.401; case evaluation under MCR 2.403; mediation under MCR 2.411; domestic relations mediation under MCR 3.216; and other procedures provided by local court rule or ordered on stipulation of the parties.

(B) **ADR Plan.**

(1) Each trial court that submits cases to ADR processes under this rule shall adopt an ADR plan by local administrative order. The plan must be in writing and available to the public in the ADR clerk's office.

(2) At a minimum, the ADR plan must:

(a) designate an ADR clerk, who may be the clerk of the court, the court administrator, the assignment clerk, or some other person;

(b) if the court refers cases to mediation under MCR 2.411, specify how the list of persons available to serve as mediators will be maintained and the system by which mediators will be assigned from the list under MCR 2.411(B)(3);

(c) include provisions for disseminating information about the operation of the court's ADR program to litigants and the public; and

(d) specify how access to ADR processes will be provided for indigent persons. If a party qualifies for waiver of filing fees under MCR 2.002 or the court determines on other grounds that the party is unable to pay the full cost of an ADR provider's services, and free or low-cost dispute resolution services are not available, the court shall not order that party to participate in an ADR process.

(3) The plan may also provide for referral relationships with local dispute resolution centers, including those affiliated with the Community Dispute Resolution Program. In establishing a referral relationship with centers or programs, courts, at a minimum, shall take into consideration factors that include whether parties are represented by counsel, the number and complexity of issues in dispute, the jurisdictional amount of the cases to be referred, and the ability of the parties to pay for dispute resolution services. The plan must preserve the right of parties to stipulate to the selection of their own mediator under MCR 2.411(B)(1).

(4) Courts in adjoining circuits or districts may jointly adopt and administer an ADR plan.

(C) **Order for ADR.**

(1) At any time, after consultation with the parties, the court may order that a case be submitted to an appropriate ADR process. More than one such order may be entered in a case.

(2) Unless the specific rule under which the case is referred provides otherwise, in addition to other provisions the court considers appropriate, the order shall

(a) specify, or make provision for selection of, the ADR provider;

(b) provide time limits for initiation and completion of the ADR process; and

(c) make provision for the payment of the ADR provider.

(3) The order may require attendance at ADR proceedings as provided in subrule (D).

(D) **Attendance at ADR Proceedings.**

(1) *Appearance of Counsel.* The attorneys attending an ADR proceeding shall be thoroughly familiar with the case and have the authority necessary to fully participate in the proceeding. The court may direct that the attorneys who intend to try the case attend ADR proceedings.

(2) *Presence of Parties.* The court may direct that the parties to the action, agents of parties, representatives of lienholders, representatives of insurance carriers, or other persons:

(a) be present at the ADR proceeding or be immediately available at the time of the proceeding; and

(b) have information and authority adequate for responsible and effective participation in the conference for all purposes, including settlement.

The court's order may specify whether the availability is to be in person or by telephone.

(3) *Failure to Attend.*

(a) Failure of a party or the party's attorney or other representative to attend a scheduled ADR proceeding, as directed by the court, may constitute a default to which MCR 2.603 is applicable or a ground for dismissal under MCR 2.504(B).

(b) The court shall excuse a failure to attend an ADR proceeding, and shall enter a just order other than one of default or dismissal, if the court finds that

(i) entry of an order of default or dismissal would cause manifest injustice; or

(ii) the failure to attend was not due to the culpable negligence of the party or the party's attorney.

The court may condition the order on the payment by the offending party or attorney of reasonable expenses as provided in MCR 2.313(B)(2).

(E) **Objections to ADR.** Within 14 days after entry of an order referring a case to an ADR process, a party may move to set aside or modify the order. A timely motion must be decided before the case is submitted to the ADR process.

(F) **Supervision of ADR Plan**. The chief judge shall exercise general supervision over the implementation of this rule and shall review the operation of the court's ADR plan at least annually to assure compliance with this rule. In the event of noncompliance, the court shall take such action as is needed. This action may include recruiting persons to serve as ADR providers or changing the court's ADR plan.

Rule 2.411 Mediation

(A) **Scope and Applicability of Rule; Definitions**.

(1) This rule applies to cases that the court refers to mediation as provided in MCR 2.410. MCR 3.216 governs mediation of domestic relations cases.

(2) "Mediation" is a process in which a neutral third party facilitates communication between parties, assists in identifying issues, and helps explore solutions to promote a mutually acceptable settlement. A mediator has no authoritative decision-making power.

(B) **Selection of Mediator**.

(1) The parties may stipulate to the selection of a mediator. A mediator selected by agreement of the parties need not meet the qualifications set forth in subrule (F). The court must appoint a mediator stipulated to by the parties, provided the mediator is willing to serve within a period that would not interfere with the court's scheduling of the case for trial.

(2) If the order referring the case to mediation does not specify a mediator, the order shall set the date by which the parties are to have conferred on the selection of a mediator. If the parties do not advise the ADR clerk of the mediator agreed upon by that date, the court shall appoint one as provided in subrule (B)(3).

(3) The procedure for selecting a mediator from the approved list of mediators must be established by local ADR plan adopted under MCR 2.410(B). The ADR clerk shall assign mediators in a rotational manner that assures as nearly as possible that each mediator on the list is assigned approximately the same number of cases over a period of time. If a substitute mediator must be assigned, the same or similar assignment procedure shall be used to select the substitute.

(4) The court shall not appoint, recommend, direct, or otherwise influence a party's or attorney's selection of a mediator except as provided pursuant to this rule. The court may recommend or advise parties on the selection of a mediator only upon request of all parties by stipulation in writing or orally on the record.

(5) The rule for disqualification of a mediator is the same as that provided in MCR 2.003 for the disqualification of a judge. The mediator must promptly disclose any potential basis for disqualification.

(C) **Scheduling and Conduct of Mediation**.

(1) *Scheduling*. The order referring the case for mediation shall specify the time within which the mediation is to be completed. The ADR clerk shall send a copy of the order to each party and the mediator selected. Upon receipt of the court's order, the mediator shall promptly confer with the parties to schedule mediation in accordance with the order. Factors that may be considered in arranging the process may include the need for limited discovery before mediation, the number of parties and issues, and the necessity for multiple sessions. The mediator may direct the parties to submit in advance, or bring to the mediation, documents or summaries providing information about the case.

(2) *Conduct of Mediation*. The mediator shall meet with counsel and the parties, explain the mediation process, and then proceed with the process. The mediator shall discuss with the parties and counsel, if any, the facts and issues involved. The mediation will continue until a settlement is reached, the mediator determines that a settlement is not likely to be reached, the end of the first mediation session, or until a time agreed to by the parties. Additional sessions may be held as long as it appears that the process may result in settlement of the case.

(3) *Completion of Mediation*. Within 7 days after the completion of the ADR process, the mediator shall so advise the court, stating only the date of completion of the process, who participated in the mediation, whether settlement was reached, and whether further ADR proceedings are contemplated.

(4) *Settlement*. If the case is settled through mediation, within 21 days the attorneys shall prepare and submit to the court the appropriate documents to conclude the case.

(5) Confidentiality in the mediation process is governed by MCR 2.412.

(D) **Fees**.

(1) A mediator is entitled to reasonable compensation commensurate with the mediator's experience and usual charges for services performed.

(2) The costs of mediation shall be divided between the parties on a pro-rata basis unless otherwise agreed by the parties or ordered by the court. The mediator's fee shall be paid no later than

(a) 42 days after the mediation process is concluded, or

(b) the entry of judgment, or

(c) the dismissal of the action,

whichever occurs first.

(3) If acceptable to the mediator, the court may order an arrangement for the payment of the mediator's fee other than that provided in subrule (D)(2).

(4) The mediator's fee is deemed a cost of the action, and the court may make an appropriate order to enforce the payment of the fee.

(5) If a party objects to the total fee of the mediator, the matter may be scheduled before the trial judge for determination of the reasonableness of the fee.

(E) **List of Mediators.**

(1) *Application*. To appear on a roster, an applicant, which may be an individual or organization may apply to the ADR clerk to be placed on the court's list of mediators. Application forms shall be available in the office of the ADR clerk.

(a) The form shall include a certification that

(i) the applicant meets the requirements for service under the court's selection plan;

(ii) the applicant will not discriminate against parties or attorneys on the basis of race, ethnic origin, gender, or other protected personal characteristic; and

(iii) the applicant will comply with the court's ADR plan, orders of the court regarding cases submitted to mediation, and the standards of conduct adopted by the State Court Administrator under subrule (G).

(b) The applicant shall indicate on the form the applicant's rate for providing mediation services.

(c) The form shall include an optional section identifying the applicant's gender and racial/ethnic background.

(d) An applicant Community Dispute Resolution Program center must select only mediators who meet the qualifications of this rule or training requirements established by the State Court Administrator to mediate cases ordered by the court.

(2) *Review of Applications*. The court's ADR plan shall provide for a person or committee to review applications annually, or more frequently if appropriate, and compile a list of qualified mediators.

(a) Applicants meeting the qualifications specified in this rule shall be placed on the list of approved mediators. Approved mediators shall be placed on the list for a fixed period, not to exceed seven years, and must reapply at the end of that time in the manner directed by the court.

(b) Selections shall be made without regard to race, ethnic origin, or gender. Residency or principal place of business may not be a qualification.

(c) The approved list and the applications of approved mediators, except for the optional section identifying the applicant's gender and racial/ethnic background, shall be available to the public in the office of the ADR clerk.

(d) An applicant may attach a résumé or biographical information to the application.

(3) *Rejection; Reconsideration*. Applicants who are not placed on the list shall be notified of that decision. Within 21 days of notification of the decision to reject an application, the applicant may seek reconsideration of the ADR clerk's decision by the Chief Judge. The court does not need to provide a hearing. Documents considered in the initial review process shall be retained for at least the period during which the applicant can seek reconsideration of the original decision.

(4) *Removal from List*. The ADR clerk may remove from the list mediators who have demonstrated incompetence, bias, made themselves consistently unavailable to serve as a mediator, or for other just cause. Within 21 days of notification of the decision to remove a mediator from the list, the mediator may seek reconsideration of the ADR clerk's decision by the Chief Judge. The court does not need to provide a hearing.

(F) **Qualification of Mediators**.

(1) *Small Claims Mediation*. District courts may develop individual plans to establish qualifications for persons serving as mediators in small claims cases.

(2) *General Civil Mediation*. To be eligible to serve as a general civil mediator, a person must meet the following minimum qualifications:

(a) Complete a training program approved by the State Court Administrator providing the generally accepted components of mediation skills;

(b) Have one or more of the following:

(i) Juris doctor degree or graduate degree in conflict resolution; or

(ii) 40 hours of mediation experience over two years, including mediation, co-mediation, observation, and role-playing in the context of mediation.

(c) Upon completion of the training required under subrule (F)(2)(a), observe two general civil mediation proceedings conducted by an approved mediator, and conduct one general civil mediation to conclusion under the supervision and observation of an approved mediator.

(3) An applicant who has specialized experience or training, but does not meet the specific requirements of subrule (F)(2), may apply to the ADR clerk for special approval. The ADR clerk

shall make the determination on the basis of criteria provided by the State Court Administrator. Service as a case evaluator under MCR 2.403 does not constitute a qualification for serving as a mediator under this section.

(4) Approved mediators are required to obtain 8 hours of advanced mediation training during each 2-year period. Failure to submit documentation establishing compliance is ground for removal from the list under subrule(E)(4).

(5) Additional qualifications may not be imposed upon mediators.

(G) **Standards of Conduct for Mediators**. The State Court Administrator shall develop and approve standards of conduct for mediators designed to promote honesty, integrity, and impartiality in providing court-connected dispute resolution services. These standards shall be made a part of all training and educational requirements for court-connected programs, shall be provided to all mediators involved in court-connected programs, and shall be available to the public.

Rule 2.412 Mediation Communications; Confidentiality and Disclosure

(A) **Scope**. This rule applies to cases that the court refers to mediation as defined and conducted under MCR 2.411 and MCR 3.216.

(B) **Definitions**.

(1) "Mediator" means an individual who conducts a mediation.

(2) "Mediation communications" include statements whether oral or in a record, verbal or nonverbal, that occur during the mediation process or are made for purposes of retaining a mediator or for considering, initiating, preparing for, conducting, participating in, continuing, adjourning, concluding, or reconvening a mediation.

(3) "Mediation party" means a person who or entity that participates in a mediation and whose agreement is necessary to resolve the dispute.

(4) "Mediation participant" means a mediation party, a nonparty, an attorney for a party, or a mediator who participates in or is present at a mediation.

(5) "Protected individual" is used as defined in the Estates and Protected Individuals Code, MCL 700.1106(v).

(6) "Vulnerable" is used as defined in the Social Welfare Act, MCL 400.11(f).

(C) **Confidentiality**. Mediation communications are confidential. They are not subject to discovery, are not admissible in a proceeding, and may not be disclosed to anyone other than mediation participants except as provided in subrule (D).

(D) **Exceptions to Confidentiality**. Mediation communications may be disclosed under the following circumstances:

(1) All mediation parties agree in writing to disclosure.

(2) A statute or court rule requires disclosure.

(3) The mediation communication is in the mediator's report under MCR 2.411(C)(3) or MCR 3.216(H)(6).

(4) The disclosure is necessary for a court to resolve disputes about the mediator's fee.

(5) The disclosure is necessary for a court to consider issues about a party's failure to attend under MCR 2.410(D)(3).

(6) The disclosure is made during a mediation session that is open or is required by law to be open to the public.

(7) Court personnel reasonably require disclosure to administer and evaluate the mediation program.

(8) The mediation communication is

(a) a threat to inflict bodily injury or commit a crime,

(b) a statement of a plan to inflict bodily injury or commit a crime, or

(c) is used to plan a crime, attempt to commit or commit a crime, or conceal a crime.

(9) The disclosure

(a) Involves a claim of abuse or neglect of a child, a protected individual, or a vulnerable adult; and

(b) Is included in a report about such a claim or sought or offered to prove or disprove such a claim; and

(i) Is made to a governmental agency or law enforcement official responsible for the protection against such conduct, or

(ii) Is made in any subsequent or related proceeding based on the disclosure under subrule (D)(9)(b)(i).

(10) The disclosure is included in a report of professional misconduct filed against a mediation participant or is sought or offered to prove or disprove misconduct allegations in the attorney disciplinary process.

(11) The mediation communication occurs in a case out of which a claim of malpractice arises and the disclosure is sought or offered to prove or disprove a claim of malpractice against a mediation participant.

(12) The disclosure is in a proceeding to enforce, rescind, reform, or avoid liability on a document signed by the mediation parties or acknowledged by the parties on an audio or video recording that arose out of mediation, if the court finds, after an in camera hearing, that the party seeking discovery or the proponent of the evidence has shown

(a) that the evidence is not otherwise available, and
(b) that the need for the evidence substantially outweighs the interest in protecting confidentiality.

(E) **Scope of Disclosure When Permitted; Limitation on Confidentiality**.
(1) If a mediation communication may be disclosed under subrule (D), only that portion of the communication necessary for the application of the exception may be disclosed.
(2) Disclosure of a mediation communication under subrule (D) does not render the mediation communication subject to disclosure for another purpose.
(3) Evidence or information that is otherwise admissible or subject to discovery does not become inadmissible or protected from discovery solely by reason of its disclosure or use in a mediation.

Rule 2.420 Settlements and Judgments for Minors and Legally Incapacitated Individuals

(A) **Applicability**. This rule governs the procedure to be followed for the entry of a consent judgment, a settlement, or a dismissal pursuant to settlement in an action brought for a minor or a legally incapacitated individual person by a next friend, guardian, or conservator or where a minor or a legally incapacitated individual is to receive a distribution from a wrongful death claim. Before an action is commenced, the settlement of a claim on behalf of a minor or a legally incapacitated individual is governed by the Estates and Protected Individuals Code.

(B) **Procedure**. In actions covered by this rule, a proposed consent judgment, settlement, or dismissal pursuant to settlement must be brought before the judge to whom the action is assigned, and the judge shall pass on the fairness of the proposal.
(1) If the claim is for damages because of personal injury to the minor or legally incapacitated individual,
(a) the minor or legally incapacitated individual shall appear in court personally to allow the judge an opportunity to observe the nature of the injury unless, for good cause, the judge excuses the minor's or legally incapacitated individual presence, and
(b) the judge may require medical testimony, by deposition or in court, if not satisfied of the extent of the injury.
(2) If the next friend, guardian, or conservator is a person who has made a claim in the same action and will share in the settlement or judgment of the minor or legally incapacitated individual, then a guardian ad litem for the minor or legally incapacitated individual must be appointed by the judge before whom the action is pending to approve the settlement or judgment.
(3) If a guardian or conservator for the minor or legally incapacitated individual has been appointed by a probate court the terms of the proposed settlement or judgment may be approved by the court in which the action is pending upon a finding that the payment arrangement is in the best interests of the minor or legally incapacitated individual, but no judgment or dismissal may enter until the court receives written verification from the probate court, on a form substantially in the form approved by the state court administrator, that it has passed on the sufficiency of the bond and the bond, if any, has been filed with the probate court.
(4) The following additional provisions apply to settlements for minors.
(a) If the settlement or judgment requires payment of more than $5,000 to the minor either immediately, or if the settlement or judgment is payable in installments that exceed $5000 in any single year during minority, a conservator must be appointed by the probate court before the entry of the judgment or dismissal. The judgment or dismissal must require that payment be made payable to the minor’s conservator on behalf of the minor. The court shall not enter the judgment or dismissal until it receives written verification, on a form substantially in the form approved by the state court administrator, that the probate court has passed on the sufficiency of the bond of the conservator.
(b) If the settlement or judgment does not require payment of more than $5,000 to the minor in any single year, the money may be paid in accordance with the provisions of MCL 700.5102.
(5) If a settlement or judgment provides for the creation of a trust for the minor or legally incapacitated individual, the circuit court shall determine the amount to be paid to the trust, but the trust shall not be funded without prior approval of the trust by the probate court pursuant to notice to all interested persons and a hearing.

Subchapter 2.500 Trials; Subpoenas; Juries

Rule 2.501 Scheduling Trials; Court Calendars

(A) **Scheduling Conferences or Trial**.
(1) Unless the further processing of the action is already governed by a scheduling order under MCR 2.401(B)(2), the court shall

(a) schedule a pretrial conference under MCR 2.401,
(b) schedule the action for an alternative dispute resolution process,
(c) schedule the action for trial, or
(d) enter another appropriate order to facilitate preparation of the action for trial.

(2) A court may adopt a trial calendar or other method for scheduling trials without the request of a party.

(B) **Expedited Trials**.

(1) On its own initiative, the motion of a party, or the stipulations of all parties, the court may shorten the time in which an action will be scheduled for trial, subject to the notice provisions of subrule (C).

(2) In scheduling trials, the court shall give precedence to actions involving a contest over the custody of minor children and to other actions afforded precedence by statute or court rule.

(C) **Notice of Trial**. Attorneys and parties must be given 28 days' notice of trial assignments, unless

(1) a rule or statute provides otherwise as to a particular type of action,
(2) the adjournment is of a previously scheduled trial, or
(3) the court otherwise directs for good cause.

Notice may be given orally if the party is before the court when the matter is scheduled, or by mailing or delivering copies of the notice or calendar to attorneys of record and to any party who appears on his or her own behalf.

(D) **Attorney Scheduling Conflicts**.

(1) The court and counsel shall make every attempt to avoid conflicts in the scheduling of trials.

(2) When conflicts in scheduled trial dates do occur, it is the responsibility of counsel to notify the court as soon as the potential conflict becomes evident. In such cases, the courts and counsel involved shall make every attempt to resolve the conflict in an equitable manner, with due regard for the priorities and time constraints provided by statute and court rule. When counsel cannot resolve conflicts through consultation with the individual courts, the judges shall consult directly to resolve the conflict.

(3) Except where a statute, court rule, or other special circumstance dictates otherwise, priority for trial shall be given to the case in which the pending trial date was set first.

Rule 2.502 Dismissal for Lack of Progress

(A) **Notice of Proposed Dismissal**.

(1) On motion of a party or on its own initiative, the court may order that an action in which no steps or proceedings appear to have been taken within 91 days be dismissed for lack of progress unless the parties show that progress is being made or that the lack of progress is not attributable to the party seeking affirmative relief.

(2) A notice of proposed dismissal may not be sent with regard to a case

(a) in which a scheduling order has been entered under MCR 2.401(B)(2) and the times for completion of the scheduled events have not expired,
(b) which is set for a conference, an alternative dispute resolution process, hearing, or trial.

(3) The notice shall be given in the manner provided in MCR 2.501(C) for notice of trial.

(B) **Action by Court**.

(1) If a party does not make the required showing, the court may direct the clerk to dismiss the action for lack of progress. Such a dismissal is without prejudice unless the court specifies otherwise.

(2) If an action is not dismissed under this rule, the court shall enter orders to facilitate the prompt and just disposition of the action.

(C) **Reinstatement of Dismissed Action**. On motion for good cause, the court may reinstate an action dismissed for lack of progress on terms the court deems just. On reinstating an action, the court shall enter orders to facilitate the prompt and just disposition of the action.

Rule 2.503 Adjournments

(A) **Applicability**. This rule applies to adjournments of trials, alternative dispute resolution processes, pretrial conferences, and all motion hearings.

(B) **Motion or Stipulation for Adjournment**.

(1) Unless the court allows otherwise, a request for an adjournment must be by motion or stipulation made in writing or orally in open court and is based on good cause.

(2) A motion or stipulation for adjournment must state

(a) which party is requesting the adjournment,
(b) the reason for it, and
(c) whether other adjournments have been granted in the proceeding and, if so, the number granted.

(3) The entitlement of a motion or stipulation for adjournment must specify whether it is the first or a later request, e.g., "Plaintiff's Request for Third Adjournment."

(C) **Absence of Witness or Evidence**.

(1) A motion to adjourn a proceeding because of the unavailability of a witness or evidence must be made as soon as possible after ascertaining the facts.

(2) An adjournment may be granted on the ground of unavailability of a witness or evidence only if the court finds that the evidence is material and that diligent efforts have been made to produce the witness or evidence.

(3) If the testimony or the evidence would be admissible in the proceeding, and the adverse party stipulates in writing or on the record that it is to be considered as actually given in the proceeding, there may be no adjournment unless the court deems an adjournment necessary.

(D) **Order for Adjournment; Costs and Conditions.**

(1) In its discretion the court may grant an adjournment to promote the cause of justice. An adjournment may be entered by order of the court either in writing or on the record in open court, and the order must state the reason for the adjournment.

(2) In granting an adjournment, the court may impose costs and conditions. When an adjournment is granted conditioned on payment of costs, the costs may be taxed summarily to be paid on demand of the adverse party or the adverse party's attorney, and the adjournment may be vacated if nonpayment is shown by affidavit.

(E) **Rescheduling.**

(1) Except as provided in subrule (E)(2), at the time the proceeding is adjourned under this rule, or as soon thereafter as possible, the proceeding must be rescheduled for a specific date and time.

(2) A court may place the matter on a specified list of actions or other matters which will automatically reappear before the court on the first available date.

(F) **Death or Change of Status of Attorney**. If the court finds that an attorney

(1) has died or is physically or mentally unable to continue to act as an attorney for a party,

(2) has been disbarred,

(3) has been suspended,

(4) has been placed on inactive status, or

(5) has resigned from active membership in the bar,

the court shall adjourn a proceeding in which the attorney was acting for a party. The party is entitled to 28 days' notice that he or she must obtain a substitute attorney or advise the court in writing that the party intends to appear on his or her own behalf. See MCR 9.119.

Rule 2.504 Dismissal of Actions

(A) **Voluntary Dismissal; Effect.**

(1) *By Plaintiff; by Stipulation*. Subject to the provisions of MCR 2.420 and MCR 3.501(E), an action may be dismissed by the plaintiff without an order of the court and on the payment of costs

(a) by filing a notice of dismissal before service by the adverse party of an answer or of a motion under MCR 2.116, whichever first occurs; or

(b) by filing a stipulation of dismissal signed by all the parties.

Unless otherwise stated in the notice of dismissal or stipulation, the dismissal is without prejudice, except that a dismissal under subrule (A)(1)(a) operates as an adjudication on the merits when filed by a plaintiff who has previously dismissed an action in any court based on or including the same claim.

(2) *By Order of Court*. Except as provided in subrule (A)(1), an action may not be dismissed at the plaintiff's request except by order of the court on terms and conditions the court deems proper.

(a) If a defendant has pleaded a counterclaim before being served with the plaintiff's motion to dismiss, the court shall not dismiss the action over the defendant's objection unless the counterclaim can remain pending for independent adjudication by the court.

(b) Unless the order specifies otherwise, a dismissal under subrule (A)(2) is without prejudice.

(B) **Involuntary Dismissal; Effect.**

(1) If a party fails to comply with these rules or a court order, upon motion by an opposing party, or sua sponte, the court may enter a default against the noncomplying party or a dismissal of the noncomplying party's action or claims.

(2) In an action, claim, or hearing tried without a jury, after the presentation of the plaintiff's evidence, the court, on its own initiative, may dismiss, or the defendant, without waiving the defendant's right to offer evidence if the motion is not granted, may move for dismissal on the ground that on the facts and the law, the plaintiff has no right to relief. The court may then determine the facts and render judgment against the plaintiff, or may decline to render judgment until the close of all the evidence. If the court renders judgment on the merits against the plaintiff, the court shall make findings as provided in MCR 2.517.

(3) Unless the court otherwise specifies in its order for dismissal, a dismissal under this subrule or a dismissal not provided for in this rule, other than a dismissal for lack of jurisdiction or for failure to join a party under MCR 2.205, operates as an adjudication on the merits.

(C) **Dismissal of Counterclaim, Cross-Claim, or Third-Party Claim**. This rule applies to the dismissal of a counterclaim, cross-claim, or third-party claim. A voluntary dismissal by the claimant alone, pursuant to subrule (A)(1), must be made before service by the adverse party of a responsive pleading or a motion under MCR 2.116, or, if no pleading or motion is filed, before the introduction of evidence at the trial.

(D) **Costs of Previously Dismissed Action**. If a plaintiff who has once dismissed an action in any court commences an action based on or including the same claim against the same defendant, the court may order the payment of such costs of the action previously dismissed as it deems proper and may stay proceedings until the plaintiff has complied with the order.

(E) **Dismissal for Failure to Serve Defendant**. An action may be dismissed as to a defendant under MCR 2.102(E).

Rule 2.505 Consolidation; Separate Trials

(A) **Consolidation**. When actions involving a substantial and controlling common question of law or fact are pending before the court, it may
- (1) order a joint hearing or trial of any or all the matters in issue in the actions;
- (2) order the actions consolidated; and
- (3) enter orders concerning the proceedings to avoid unnecessary costs or delay.

(B) **Separate Trials**. For convenience or to avoid prejudice, or when separate trials will be conducive to expedition and economy, the court may order a separate trial of one or more claims, cross-claims, counterclaims, third-party claims, or issues.

Rule 2.506 Subpoena; Order to Attend

(A) **Attendance of Party or Witness**.
- (1) The court in which a matter is pending may by order or subpoena command a party or witness to appear for the purpose of testifying in open court on a date and time certain and from time to time and day to day thereafter until excused by the court, and to produce notes, records, documents, photographs, or other portable tangible things as specified.
- (2) A subpoena may specify the form or forms in which electronically stored information is to be produced, subject to objection. If the subpoena does not so specify, the person responding to the subpoena must produce the information in a form or forms in which the person ordinarily maintains it, or in a form or forms that are reasonably usable. A person producing electronically stored information need only produce the same information in one form.
- (3) A person responding to a subpoena need not provide discovery of electronically stored information from sources that the person identifies as not reasonably accessible because of undue burden or cost. In a hearing or submission under subrule (H), the person responding to the subpoena must show that the information sought is not reasonably accessible because of undue burden or cost. If that showing is made, the court may nonetheless order discovery from such sources if the requesting party shows good cause, considering the limitations of MCR 2.302(C). The court may specify conditions for such discovery.
- (4) The court may require a party and a representative of an insurance carrier for a party with information and authority adequate for responsible and effective participation in settlement discussions to be present or immediately available at trial.
- (5) A subpoena may be issued only in accordance with this rule or MCR 2.305, 2.621(C), 9.112(D), 9.115(I)(1), or 9.212.

(B) **Authorized Signatures**.
- (1) A subpoena signed by an attorney of record in the action or by the clerk of the court in which the matter is pending has the force and effect of an order signed by the judge of that court.
- (2) For the purpose of this subrule, an authorized signature includes but is not limited to signatures written by hand, printed, stamped, typewritten, engraved, photographed, or lithographed.

(C) **Notice to Witness of Required Attendance**.
- (1) The signer of a subpoena must issue it for service on the witness sufficiently in advance of the trial or hearing to give the witness reasonable notice of the date and time the witness is to appear. Unless the court orders otherwise, the subpoena must be served at least 2 days before the witness is to appear.
- (2) The party having the subpoena issued must take reasonable steps to keep the witness informed of adjournments of the scheduled trial or hearing.
- (3) If the served witness notifies the party that it is impossible for the witness to be present in court as directed, the party must either excuse the witness from attendance at that time or notify the witness that a special hearing may be held to adjudicate the issue.

(D) **Form of Subpoena**. A subpoena must:
- (1) be entitled in the name of the People of the State of Michigan;
- (2) be imprinted with the seal of the Supreme Court of Michigan;
- (3) have typed or printed on it the name of the court in which the matter is pending;
- (4) state the place where the trial or hearing is scheduled;
- (5) state the title of the action in which the person is expected to testify;
- (6) state the file designation assigned by the court; and
- (7) state that failure to obey the commands of the subpoena or reasonable directions of the signer as to time and place to appear may subject the person to whom it is directed to penalties for contempt of court.

  The state court administrator shall develop and approve a subpoena form for statewide use.

(E) **Refusal of Witness to Attend or to Testify; Contempt**.
- (1) If a person fails to comply with a subpoena served in accordance with this rule or with a notice under subrule (C)(2), the failure may be considered a

contempt of court by the court in which the action is pending.

(2) If a person refuses to be sworn or to testify regarding a matter not privileged after being ordered to do so by the court, the refusal may be considered a contempt of court.

(F) **Failure of Party to Attend**. If a party or an officer, director, or managing agent of a party fails to attend or produce documents or other tangible evidence pursuant to a subpoena or an order to attend, the court may:

(1) stay further proceedings until the order is obeyed;

(2) tax costs to the other party or parties to the action;

(3) strike all or a part of the pleadings of that party;

(4) refuse to allow that party to support or oppose designated claims and defenses;

(5) dismiss the action or any part of it; or

(6) enter judgment by default against that party.

(G) **Service of Subpoena and Order to Attend; Fees**.

(1) A subpoena may be served anywhere in Michigan in the manner provided by MCR 2.105. The fee for attendance and mileage provided by law must be tendered to the person on whom the subpoena is served at the time of service. Tender must be made in cash, by money order, by cashier's check, or by a check drawn on the account of an attorney of record in the action or the attorney's authorized agent.

(2) A subpoena may also be served by mailing to a witness a copy of the subpoena and a postage-paid card acknowledging service and addressed to the party requesting service. The fees for attendance and mileage provided by law are to be given to the witness after the witness appears at the court, and the acknowledgment card must so indicate. If the card is not returned, the subpoena must be served in the manner provided in subrule (G)(1).

(3) A subpoena or order to attend directed to a party, or to an officer, director, or managing agent of a party, may be served in the manner provided by MCR 2.107, and fees and mileage need not be paid.

(H) **Hearing on Subpoena or Order**.

(1) A person served with a subpoena or order to attend may appear before the court in person or by writing to explain why the person should not be compelled to comply with the subpoena, order to attend, or directions of the party having it issued.

(2) The court may direct that a special hearing be held to adjudicate the issue.

(3) For good cause with or without a hearing, the court may excuse a witness from compliance with a subpoena, the directions of the party having it issued, or an order to attend.

(4) A person must comply with the command of a subpoena unless relieved by order of the court or written direction of the person who had the subpoena issued.

(I) **Subpoena for Production of Hospital Medical Records**.

(1) Except as provided in subrule (I)(5), a hospital may comply with a subpoena calling for production of medical records belonging to the hospital in the manner provided in this subrule. This subrule does not apply to x-ray films or to other portions of a medical record that are not susceptible to photostatic reproduction.

(a) The hospital may deliver or mail to the clerk of the court in which the action is pending, without cost to the parties, a complete and accurate copy of the original record.

(b) The copy of the record must be accompanied by a sworn certificate, in the form approved by the state court administrator, signed by the medical record librarian or another authorized official of the hospital, verifying that it is a complete and accurate reproduction of the original record.

(c) The envelope or other container in which the record is delivered to the court shall be clearly marked to identify its contents. If the hospital wishes the record returned when it is no longer needed in the action, that fact must be stated on the container, and, with the record, the hospital must provide the clerk with a self-addressed, stamped envelope that the clerk may use to return the record.

(d) The hospital shall promptly notify the attorney for the party who caused the subpoena to be issued that the documents involved have been delivered or mailed to the court in accordance with subrule (I)(1).

(2) The clerk shall keep the copies sealed in the container in which they were supplied by the hospital. The container shall be clearly marked to identify the contents, the name of the patient, and the title and number of the action. The container shall not be opened except at the direction of the court.

(3) If the hospital has requested that the record be returned, the clerk shall return the record to the hospital when 42 days have passed after a final order terminating the action, unless an appeal has been taken. In the event of an appeal, the record shall be returned when 42 days have passed after a final order terminating the appeal. If the hospital did not request that the record be returned as provided in subrule (I)(1)(c), the clerk may destroy the record after the time provided in this subrule.

(4) The admissibility of the contents of medical records produced under this rule or under MCR 2.314 is not affected or altered by these procedures and remains subject to the same objections as if the original

records were personally produced by the custodian at the trial or hearing.

(5) A party may have a subpoena issued directing that an original record of a person be produced at the trial or hearing by the custodian of the record. The subpoena must specifically state that the original records, not copies, are required. A party may also require, by subpoena, the attendance of the custodian without the records.

Rule 2.507 Conduct of Trials

(A) **Opening Statements**. Before the introduction of evidence, the attorney for the party who is to commence the evidence must make a full and fair statement of that party's case and the facts the party intends to prove. Immediately thereafter or immediately before the introduction of evidence by the adverse party, the attorney for the adverse party must make a like statement. Opening statements may be waived with the consent of the court and the opposing attorney.

(B) **Opening the Evidence**. Unless otherwise ordered by the court, the plaintiff must first present the evidence in support of the plaintiff's case. However, the defendant must first present the evidence in support of his or her case, if

(1) the defendant's answer has admitted facts and allegations of the plaintiff's complaint to the extent that, in the absence of further statement on the defendant's behalf, judgment should be entered on the pleadings for the plaintiff, and

(2) the defendant has asserted a defense on which the defendant has the burden of proof, either as a counterclaim or as an affirmative defense.

(C) **Examination and Cross-Examination of Witnesses**. Unless otherwise ordered by the court, no more than one attorney for a party may examine or cross-examine a witness.

(D) **Court View**. On application of either party or on its own initiative, the court sitting as trier of fact without a jury may view property or a place where a material event occurred.

(E) **Final Arguments**. After the close of all the evidence, the parties may rest their cases with or without final arguments. The party who commenced the evidence is entitled to open the argument and, if the opposing party makes an argument, to make a rebuttal argument not beyond the issues raised in the preceding arguments.

(F) **Time Allowed for Opening Statements and Final Arguments**. The court may limit the time allowed each party for opening statements and final arguments. It shall give the parties adequate time for argument, having due regard for the complexity of the action, and may make separate time allowances for co-parties whose interests are adverse.

(G) **Agreements to be in Writing**. An agreement or consent between the parties or their attorneys respecting the proceedings in an action is not binding unless it was made in open court, or unless evidence of the agreement is in writing, subscribed by the party against whom the agreement is offered or by that party's attorney.

Rule 2.508 Jury Trial of Right

(A) **Right Preserved**. The right of trial by jury as declared by the constitution must be preserved to the parties inviolate.

(B) **Demand for Jury**.

(1) A party may demand a trial by jury of an issue as to which there is a right to trial by jury by filing a written demand for a jury trial within 28 days after the filing of the answer or a timely reply. A party may include the demand in a pleading if notice of the demand is included in the caption of the pleading. The jury fee provided by law must be paid at the time the demand is filed.

(2) If a party appealing to the circuit court from a municipal court desires a trial by jury of an issue triable of right, demand for jury must be included in the claim of appeal. If another party desires trial by jury of an issue triable of right, the demand must be included in the party's notice of appearance.

(3)

(a) If a case is entirely removed from circuit court to district court, or is entirely removed or transferred from district court to circuit court, a timely demand for a trial by jury in the court from which the case is removed or transferred remains effective in the court to which the case is removed or transferred. If a case is entirely removed or transferred from district court to circuit court, and if the amount paid to the district court for the jury fee is less than the circuit court jury fee, then the party requesting the jury shall pay the difference to the circuit court. If a case is entirely removed from circuit court to district court, no additional jury fee is to be paid to the district court nor is there to be a refund of any amount by which the circuit court jury fee exceeds the district court jury fee.

(b) If part of a case is removed from circuit court to district court, or part of a case is removed or transferred from district court to circuit court, but a portion of the case remains in the court from which the case is removed or transferred, then a demand for a trial by jury in the court from which the case is removed or transferred is not effective in the court to which the case is removed or transferred. A party who seeks a trial by jury in the court to which the case is partially removed or transferred must file a written demand for a trial by jury within 21 days of the removal or transfer order, and must pay the jury fee provided by law, even if the jury fee was paid in the court from which the case is removed or transferred.

(c) The absence of a timely demand for a trial by jury in the court from which a case is entirely or partially removed or transferred does not preclude filing a demand for a trial by jury in the court to which the case is removed or transferred. A party who seeks a trial by jury in the court to which the case is removed or transferred must file a written demand for a trial by jury within 21 days of the removal or transfer order, and must pay the jury fee provided by law.

(d) A party who is added to a case after it has been removed or transferred may demand trial by jury in accordance with paragraph (B)(1).

(C) **Specifications of Issues.**

(1) In a demand for jury trial, a party may specify the issues the party wishes so tried; otherwise, the party is deemed to have demanded trial by jury of all the issues so triable.

(2) If a party has demanded trial by jury of only some of the issues, another party, within 14 days after service of a copy of the demand or within less time as the court may order, may serve a demand for trial by jury of another or all the issues of fact in the action.

(D) **Waiver; Withdrawal.**

(1) A party who fails to file a demand or pay the jury fee as required by this rule waives trial by jury.

(2) Waiver of trial by jury is not revoked by an amendment of a pleading asserting only a claim or defense arising out of the conduct, transaction, or occurrence stated, or attempted to be stated, in the original pleading.

(3) A demand for trial by jury may not be withdrawn without the consent, expressed in writing or on the record, of the parties or their attorneys.

Rule 2.509 Trial by Jury or by Court

(A) **By Jury.** If a jury has been demanded as provided in MCR 2.508, the action or appeal must be designated in the court records as a jury action. The trial of all issues so demanded must be by jury unless

(1) the parties agree otherwise by stipulation in writing or on the record, or

(2) the court on motion or on its own initiative finds that there is no right to trial by jury of some or all of those issues.

(B) **By Court.** Issues for which a trial by jury has not been demanded as provided in MCR 2.508 will be tried by the court. In the absence of a demand for a jury trial of an issue as to which a jury demand might have been made of right, the court in its discretion may order a trial by jury of any or all issues.

(C) **Sequence of Trial.** In an action in which some issues are to be tried by jury and others by the court, or in which a number of claims, cross-claims, defenses, counterclaims, or third-party claims involve a common issue, the court may determine the sequence of trial of the issues, preserving the constitutional right to trial by jury according to the basic nature of every issue for which a demand for jury trial has been made under MCR 2.508.

(D) **Advisory Jury and Trial by Consent.** In appeals to circuit court from a municipal court and in actions involving issues not triable of right by a jury because of the basic nature of the issue, the court on motion or on its own initiative may

(1) try the issues with an advisory jury; or

(2) with the consent of all parties, order a trial with a jury whose verdict has the same effect as if trial by jury had been a matter of right.

Rule 2.510 Juror Personal History Questionnaire

(A) **Form.** The state court administrator shall adopt a juror personal history questionnaire.

(B) **Completion of Questionnaire.**

(1) The court clerk or the jury board, as directed by the chief judge, shall supply each juror drawn for jury service with a questionnaire in the form adopted pursuant to subrule (A). The court clerk or the jury board shall direct the juror to complete the questionnaire before the juror is called for service.

(2) Refusal to answer the questions on the questionnaire, or answering the questionnaire falsely, is contempt of court.

(C) **Return of the Questionnaire.**

(1) On completion, the questionnaire shall be returned to the court clerk or the jury board, as designated under subrule (B)(1). The only persons allowed to examine the questionnaire are:

(a) the judges of the court;

(b) the court clerk and deputy clerks;

(c) parties to actions in which the juror is called to serve and their attorneys; and

(d) persons authorized access by court rule or by court order.

(2) The attorneys must be given a reasonable opportunity to examine the questionnaires before being called on to challenge for cause.

(a) The state court administrator shall develop model procedures for providing attorneys and parties reasonable access to juror questionnaires.

(b) Each court shall select and implement one of these procedures by local administrative order adopted pursuant to MCR 8.112(B). If the state court administrator determines that, given the circumstances existing in an individual court, the procedure selected does not provide reasonable access, the state court administrator may direct the court to implement one of the other model procedures.

(c) If the procedure selected allows attorneys or parties to receive copies of juror questionnaires, an attorney or party may not release them to any person who would not be entitled to examine them under subrule (C)(1).

(3) The questionnaires must be maintained for 3 years from the time they are returned. They may be created and maintained in any medium authorized by court rules pursuant to MCR 1.109.

(D) **Summoning Jurors for Court Attendance**. The court clerk, the court administrator, the sheriff, or the jury board, as designated by the chief judge, shall summon jurors for court attendance at the time and in the manner directed by the chief judge. For a juror's first required court appearance, service must be by written notice addressed to the juror at the juror's residence as shown by the records of the clerk or jury board. The notice may be by ordinary mail or by personal service. For later service, notice may be in the manner directed by the court. The person giving notice to jurors shall keep a record of the notice and make a return if directed by the court. The return is presumptive evidence of the fact of service.

(E) **Special Provision Pursuant to MCL 600.1324**. If a city located in more than one county is entirely within a single district of the district court, jurors shall be selected for court attendance at that district from a list that includes the names and addresses of jurors from the entire city, regardless of the county where the juror resides or the county where the cause of action arose.

Rule 2.511 Impaneling the Jury

(A) **Selection of Jurors**.

(1) Persons who have not been discharged or excused as prospective jurors by the court are subject to selection for the action or actions to be tried during their term of service as provided by law.

(2) In an action that is to be tried before a jury, the names or corresponding numbers of the prospective jurors shall be deposited in a container, and the prospective jurors must be selected for examination by a random blind draw from the container.

(3) The court may provide for random selection of prospective jurors for examination from less than all of the prospective jurors not discharged or excused.

(4) Prospective jurors may be selected by any other fair and impartial method directed by the court or agreed to by the parties.

(B) **Alternate Jurors**. The court may direct that 7 or more jurors be impaneled to sit. After the instructions to the jury have been given and the action is ready to be submitted, unless the parties have stipulated that all the jurors may deliberate, the names of the jurors must be placed in a container and names drawn to reduce the number of jurors to 6, who shall constitute the jury. The court may retain the alternate jurors during deliberations. If the court does so, it shall instruct the alternate jurors not to discuss the case with any other person until the jury completes its deliberations and is discharged. If an alternate juror replaces a juror after the jury retires to consider its verdict, the court shall instruct the jury to begin its deliberations anew.

(C) **Examination of Jurors; Discharge of Unqualified Juror**. The court may conduct the examination of prospective jurors or may permit the attorneys to do so. When the court finds that a person in attendance at court as a juror is not qualified to serve as a juror, the court shall discharge him or her from further attendance and service as a juror.

(D) **Challenges for Cause**. The parties may challenge jurors for cause, and the court shall rule on each challenge. A juror challenged for cause may be directed to answer questions pertinent to the inquiry. It is grounds for a challenge for cause that the person:

(1) is not qualified to be a juror;

(2) is biased for or against a party or attorney;

(3) shows a state of mind that will prevent the person from rendering a just verdict, or has formed a positive opinion on the facts of the case or on what the outcome should be;

(4) has opinions or conscientious scruples that would improperly influence the person's verdict;

(5) has been subpoenaed as a witness in the action;

(6) has already sat on a trial of the same issue;

(7) has served as a grand or petit juror in a criminal case based on the same transaction;

(8) is related within the ninth degree (civil law) of consanguinity or affinity to one of the parties or attorneys;

(9) is the guardian, conservator, ward, landlord, tenant, employer, employee, partner, or client of a party or attorney;

(10) is or has been a party adverse to the challenging party or attorney in a civil action, or has complained of or has been accused by that party in a criminal prosecution;

(11) has a financial interest other than that of a taxpayer in the outcome of the action;

(12) is interested in a question like the issue to be tried.

Exemption from jury service is the privilege of the person exempt, not a ground for challenge.

(E) **Peremptory Challenges.**

(1) A juror peremptorily challenged is excused without cause.

(2) Each party may peremptorily challenge three jurors. Two or more parties on the same side are considered a single party for purposes of peremptory challenges. However, when multiple parties having adverse interests are aligned on the same side, three peremptory challenges are allowed to each party represented by a different attorney, and the court may allow the opposite side a total number of peremptory challenges not exceeding the total number of peremptory challenges allowed to the multiple parties.

(3) Peremptory challenges must be exercised in the following manner:

(a) First the plaintiff and then the defendant may exercise one or more peremptory challenges until each party successively waives further peremptory challenges or all the challenges have been exercised, at which point jury selection is complete.

(b) A "pass" is not counted as a challenge but is a waiver of further challenge to the panel as constituted at that time.

(c) If a party has exhausted all peremptory challenges and another party has remaining challenges, that party may continue to exercise their remaining peremptory challenges until such challenges are exhausted.

(F) **Discrimination in the Selection Process.**

(1) No person shall be subjected to discrimination during voir dire on the basis of race, color, religion, national origin, or sex.

(2) Discrimination during voir dire on the basis of race, color, religion, national origin, or sex for the purpose of achieving what the court believes to be a balanced, proportionate, or representative jury in terms of these characteristics shall not constitute an excuse or justification for a violation of this subsection.

(G) **Replacement of Challenged Jurors**. After the jurors have been seated in the jurors' box and a challenge for cause is sustained or a peremptory challenge or challenges exercised, another juror or other jurors must be selected and examined. Such jurors are subject to challenge as are previously seated jurors.

(H) **Oath of Jurors; Instruction regarding prohibited actions.**

(1) The jury must be sworn by the clerk substantially as follows: "Each of you do solemnly swear (or affirm) that, in this action now before the court, you will justly decide the questions submitted to you, that, unless you are discharged by the court from further deliberation, you will render a true verdict, and that you will render your verdict only on the evidence introduced and in accordance with the instructions of the court, so help you God."

(2) The court shall instruct the jurors that until their jury service is concluded, they shall not

(a) discuss the case with others, including other jurors, except as otherwise authorized by the court;

(b) read or listen to any news reports about the case;

(c) use a computer, cellular phone, or other electronic device with communication capabilities while in attendance at trial or during deliberation. These devices may be used during breaks or recesses but may not be used to obtain or disclose information prohibited in subsection (d) below;

(d) use a computer, cellular phone, or other electronic device with communication capabilities, or any other method, to obtain or disclose information about the case when they are not in court. As used in this subsection, information about the case includes, but is not limited to, the following:

(i) information about a party, witness, attorney, or court officer;

(ii) news accounts of the case;

(iii) information collected through juror research on any topics raised or testimony offered by any witness;

(iv) information collected through juror research on any other topic the juror might think would be helpful in deciding the case.

Rule 2.512 Instructions to Jury

(A) **Request for Instructions.**

(1) At a time the court reasonably directs, the parties must file written requests that the court instruct the jury on the law as stated in the requests. In the absence of a direction from the court, a party may file a written request for jury instructions at or before the close of the evidence.

(2) In addition to requests for instructions submitted under subrule (A)(1), after the close of the evidence, each party shall submit in writing to the court a statement of the issues and may submit the party's theory of the case regarding each issue. The statement must be concise, be narrative in form, and set forth as issues only those disputed propositions of fact that are supported by the evidence. The theory may include those claims supported by the evidence or admitted.

(3) A copy of the requested instructions must be served on the adverse parties in accordance with MCR 2.107.

(4) The court shall inform the attorneys of its proposed action on the requests before their arguments to the jury.

(5) The court need not give the statements of issues or theories of the case in the form submitted if the court presents to the jury the material substance of the issues and theories of each party.

(B) **Instructing the Jury**.

(1) At any time during the trial, the court may, with or without request, instruct the jury on a point of law if the instruction will materially aid the jury in understanding the proceedings and arriving at a just verdict.

(2) Before or after arguments or at both times, as the court elects, the court shall instruct the jury on the applicable law, the issues presented by the case, and, if a party requests as provided in subrule (A)(2), that party's theory of the case.

(C) **Objections**. A party may assign as error the giving of or the failure to give an instruction only if the party objects on the record before the jury retires to consider the verdict (or, in the case of instructions given after deliberations have begun, before the jury resumes deliberations), stating specifically the matter to which the party objects and the grounds for the objection. Opportunity must be given to make the objection out of the hearing of the jury.

(D) **Model Civil Jury Instructions**.

(1) The Committee on Model Civil Jury Instructions appointed by the Supreme Court has the authority to adopt model civil jury instructions (M Civ JI) and to amend or repeal those instructions approved by the predecessor committee. Before adopting, amending, or repealing an instruction, the committee shall publish notice of the committee's intent, together with the text of the instruction to be adopted, or the amendment to be made, or a reference to the instruction to be repealed, in the manner provided in MCR 1.201. The notice shall specify the time and manner for commenting on the proposal. The committee shall thereafter publish notice of its final action on the proposed change, including, if appropriate, the effective date of the adoption, amendment, or repeal. A model civil jury instruction does not have the force and effect of a court rule.

(2) Pertinent portions of the instructions approved by the Committee on Model Civil Jury Instructions or its predecessor committee must be given in each action in which jury instructions are given if

(a) they are applicable,

(b) they accurately state the applicable law, and

(c) they are requested by a party.

(3) Whenever the committee recommends that no instruction be given on a particular matter, the court shall not give an instruction unless it specifically finds for reasons stated on the record that

(a) the instruction is necessary to state the applicable law accurately, and

(b) the matter is not adequately covered by other pertinent model civil jury instructions.

(4) This subrule does not limit the power of the court to give additional instructions on applicable law not covered by the model instructions. Additional instructions, when given, must be patterned as nearly as practicable after the style of the model instructions and must be concise, understandable, conversational, unslanted, and nonargumentative.

Rule 2.513 Conduct of Jury Trial

(A) **Preliminary Instructions**. After the jury is sworn and before evidence is taken, the court shall provide the jury with pretrial instructions reasonably likely to assist in its consideration of the case. Such instructions, at a minimum, shall communicate the duties of the jury, trial procedure, and the law applicable to the case as are reasonably necessary to enable the jury to understand the proceedings and the evidence. The jury also shall be instructed about the elements of all civil claims or all charged offenses, as well as the legal presumptions and burdens of proof. The court shall provide each juror with a copy of such instructions. MCR 2.512(D)(2) does not apply to such preliminary instructions.

(B) **Court's Responsibility**. The trial court must control the proceedings during trial, limit the evidence and arguments to relevant and proper matters, and take appropriate steps to ensure that the jurors will not be exposed to information or influences that might affect their ability to render an impartial verdict on the evidence presented in court. The court may not communicate with the jury or any juror pertaining to the case without notifying the parties and permitting them to be present. The court must ensure that all communications pertaining to the case between the court and the jury or any juror are made a part of the record.

(C) **Opening Statements**. Unless the parties and the court agree otherwise, the plaintiff or the prosecutor, before presenting evidence, must make a full and fair statement of the case and the facts the plaintiff or the prosecutor intends to prove. Immediately thereafter, or immediately before presenting evidence, the defendant may make a similar statement. The court may impose reasonable time limits on the opening statements.

(D) **Interim Commentary**. Each party may, in the court's discretion, present interim commentary at appropriate junctures of the trial.

(E) **Reference Documents**. The court may authorize or require counsel in civil and criminal cases to provide the jurors with a reference document or notebook, the contents of which should include, but which is not limited to, a list of witnesses, relevant statutory provisions, and, in cases where the interpretation of a document is at issue, copies of the relevant document. The court and the parties may supplement the reference document during trial with copies of the preliminary jury instructions, admitted exhibits, and other admissible information to assist jurors in their deliberations.

(F) **Deposition Summaries**. Where it appears likely that the contents of a deposition will be read to the jury, the court should encourage the parties to prepare concise, written summaries of depositions for reading at trial in lieu of the full deposition. Where a summary is prepared, the opposing party shall have the opportunity to object to its contents. Copies of the summaries should be provided to the jurors before they are read.

(G) **Scheduling Expert Testimony**. In a civil action, the court may, in its discretion, craft a procedure for the presentation of all expert testimony to assist the jurors in performing their duties. Such procedures may include, but are not limited to:

(1) Scheduling the presentation of the parties' expert witnesses sequentially; or

(2) allowing the opposing experts to be present during the other's testimony and to aid counsel in formulating questions to be asked of the testifying expert on cross-examination.

(H) **Note Taking by Jurors**. The court may permit the jurors to take notes regarding the evidence presented in court. If the court permits note taking, it must instruct the jurors that they need not take notes, and they should not permit note taking to interfere with their attentiveness. If the court allows jurors to take notes, jurors must be allowed to refer to their notes during deliberations, but the court must instruct the jurors to keep their notes confidential except as to other jurors during deliberations. The court shall ensure that all juror notes are collected and destroyed when the trial is concluded.

(I) **Juror Questions**. The court may permit the jurors to ask questions of witnesses. If the court permits jurors to ask questions, it must employ a procedure that ensures that such questions are addressed to the witnesses by the court itself, that inappropriate questions are not asked, and that the parties have an opportunity outside the hearing of the jury to object to the questions. The court shall inform the jurors of the procedures to be followed for submitting questions to witnesses.

(J) **Jury View**. On motion of either party, on its own initiative, or at the request of the jury, the court may order a jury view of property or of a place where a material event occurred. The parties are entitled to be present at the jury view, provided, however, that in a criminal case, the court may preclude a defendant from attending a jury view in the interests of safety and security. During the view, no person, other than an officer designated by the court, may speak to the jury concerning the subject connected with the trial. Any such communication must be recorded in some fashion.

(K) **Juror Discussion**. In a civil case, after informing the jurors that they are not to decide the case until they have heard all the evidence, instructions of law, and arguments of counsel, the court may instruct the jurors that they are permitted to discuss the evidence among themselves in the jury room during trial recesses. The jurors should be instructed that such discussions may only take place when all jurors are present and that such discussions must be clearly understood as tentative pending final presentation of all evidence, instructions, and argument.

(L) **Closing Arguments**. After the close of all the evidence, the parties may make closing arguments. The plaintiff or the prosecutor is entitled to make the first closing argument. If the defendant makes an argument, the plaintiff or the prosecutor may offer a rebuttal limited to the issues raised in the defendant's argument. The court may impose reasonable time limits on the closing arguments.

(M) **Summing up the Evidence**. After the close of the evidence and arguments of counsel, the court may fairly and impartially sum up the evidence if it also instructs the jury that it is to determine for itself the weight of the evidence and the credit to be given to the witnesses and that jurors are not bound by the court's summation. The court shall not comment on the credibility of witnesses or state a conclusion on the ultimate issue of fact before the jury.

(N) **Final Instructions to the Jury**.

(1) Before closing arguments, the court must give the parties a reasonable opportunity to submit written requests for jury instructions. Each party must serve a copy of the written requests on all other parties. The court must inform the parties of its proposed action on the requests before their closing arguments. After closing arguments are made or waived, the court must instruct the jury as required and appropriate, but at the discretion of the court, and on notice to the parties, the court may instruct the jury before the parties make closing arguments. After jury deliberations begin, the court may give additional instructions that are appropriate.

(2) Solicit Questions about Final Instructions. As part of the final jury instructions, the court shall advise the jury that it may submit in a sealed envelope given to the bailiff any written questions about the jury instructions that arise during deliberations. Upon concluding the final instructions, the court shall invite the jurors to ask any questions in order

to clarify the instructions before they retire to deliberate.

If questions arise, the court and the parties shall convene, in the courtroom or by other agreed-upon means. The question shall be read into the record, and the attorneys shall offer comments on an appropriate response. The court may, in its discretion, provide the jury with a specific response to the jury's question, but the court shall respond to all questions asked, even if the response consists of a directive for the jury to continue its deliberations.

(3) Copies of Final Instructions. The court shall provide a written copy of the final jury instructions to take into the jury room for deliberation. Upon request by any juror, the court may provide additional copies as necessary. The court, in its discretion, also may provide the jury with a copy of electronically recorded instructions.

(4) Clarifying or Amplifying Final Instructions. When it appears that a deliberating jury has reached an impasse, or is otherwise in need of assistance, the court may invite the jurors to list the issues that divide or confuse them in the event that the judge can be of assistance in clarifying or amplifying the final instructions.

(O) **Materials in the Jury Room**. The court shall permit the jurors, on retiring to deliberate, to take into the jury room their notes and final instructions. The court may permit the jurors to take into the jury room the reference document, if one has been prepared, as well as any exhibits and writings admitted into evidence.

(P) **Provide Testimony or Evidence**. If, after beginning deliberation, the jury requests a review of certain testimony or evidence that has not been allowed into the jury room under subrule (O), the court must exercise its discretion to ensure fairness and to refuse unreasonable requests, but it may not refuse a reasonable request. The court may make a video or audio recording of witness testimony, or prepare an immediate transcript of such testimony, and such tape or transcript, or other testimony or evidence, may be made available to the jury for its consideration. The court may order the jury to deliberate further without the requested review, as long as the possibility of having the testimony or evidence reviewed at a later time is not foreclosed.

Rule 2.514 Rendering Verdict

(A) **Majority Verdict; Stipulations Regarding Number of Jurors and Verdict**. The parties may stipulate in writing or on the record that

(1) the jury will consist of any number less than 6,

(2) a verdict or a finding of a stated majority of the jurors will be taken as the verdict or finding of the jury, or

(3) if more than 6 jurors were impaneled, all the jurors may deliberate.

Except as provided in MCR 5.740(C), in the absence of such stipulation, a verdict in a civil action tried by 6 jurors will be received when 5 jurors agree.

(B) **Return; Poll**.

(1) The jury must return its verdict in open court.

(2) A party may require a poll to be taken by the court asking each juror if it is his or her verdict.

(3) If the number of jurors agreeing is less than required, the jury must be sent back for further deliberation; otherwise, the verdict is complete, and the court shall discharge the jury.

(C) **Discharge From Action; New Jury**. The court may discharge a jury from the action:

(1) because of an accident or calamity requiring it;

(2) by consent of all the parties;

(3) whenever an adjournment or mistrial is declared;

(4) whenever the jurors have deliberated and it appears that they cannot agree.

The court may order another jury to be drawn, and the same proceedings may be had before the new jury as might have been had before the jury that was discharged.

(D) **Responsibility of Officers**.

(1) All court officers, including trial attorneys, must attend during the trial of an action until the verdict of the jury is announced.

(2) A trial attorney may, on request, be released by the court from further attendance, or the attorney may designate an associate or other attorney to act for him or her during the deliberations of the jury.

Rule 2.515 Special Verdicts

(A) **Use of Special Verdicts; Form**. The court may require the jury to return a special verdict in the form of a written finding on each issue of fact, rather than a general verdict. If a special verdict is required, the court shall, in advance of argument and in the absence of the jury, advise the attorneys of this fact and, on the record or in writing, settle the form of the verdict. The court may submit to the jury:

(1) written questions that may be answered categorically and briefly;

(2) written forms of the several special findings that might properly be made under the pleadings and evidence; or

(3) the issues by another method, and require the written findings it deems most appropriate.

The court shall give to the jury the necessary explanation and instruction concerning the matter submitted to enable the jury to make its findings on each issue.

(B) **Judgment**. After a special verdict is returned, the court shall enter judgment in accordance with the jury's findings.

(C) **Failure to Submit Question; Waiver; Findings by Court**. If the court omits from the special verdict form an issue of fact raised by the pleadings or the evidence, a party waives the right to a trial by jury of the issue omitted unless the party demands its submission to the jury before it retires for deliberations. The court may make a finding with respect to an issue omitted without a demand. If the court fails to do so, it is deemed to have made a finding in accord with the judgment on the special verdict.

Rule 2.516 Motion for Directed Verdict

A party may move for a directed verdict at the close of the evidence offered by an opponent. The motion must state specific grounds in support of the motion. If the motion is not granted, the moving party may offer evidence without having reserved the right to do so, as if the motion had not been made. A motion for a directed verdict that is not granted is not a waiver of trial by jury, even though all parties to the action have moved for directed verdicts.

Rule 2.517 Findings by Court

(A) **Requirements**.

(1) In actions tried on the facts without a jury or with an advisory jury, the court shall find the facts specially, state separately its conclusions of law, and direct entry of the appropriate judgment.

(2) Brief, definite, and pertinent findings and conclusions on the contested matters are sufficient, without over elaboration of detail or particularization of facts.

(3) The court may state the findings and conclusions on the record or include them in a written opinion.

(4) Findings of fact and conclusions of law are unnecessary in decisions on motions unless findings are required by a particular rule. See, e.g., MCR 2.504(B).

(5) The clerk shall notify the attorneys for the parties of the findings of the court.

(6) Requests for findings are not necessary for purposes of review.

(7) No exception need be taken to a finding or decision.

(B) **Amendment**. On motion of a party made within 21 days after entry of judgment, the court may amend its findings or make additional findings, and may amend the judgment accordingly. The motion may be made with a motion for new trial pursuant to MCR 2.611. When findings of fact are made in an action tried by the court without a jury, the question of the sufficiency of the evidence to support the findings may thereafter be raised whether the party raising the question has objected to the findings or has moved to amend them or for judgment.

Rule 2.518 Receipt and Return or Disposal of Exhibits

(A) **Receipt of Exhibits**. Except as otherwise required by statute or court rule, materials that are intended to be used as evidence at or during a trial shall not be filed with the clerk of the court, but shall be submitted to the judge for introduction into evidence as exhibits. Exhibits introduced into evidence at or during court proceedings shall be received and maintained as provided by Michigan Supreme Court trial court case file management standards. As defined in MCR 1.109, exhibits received and accepted into evidence under this rule are not court records.

(B) **Return or Disposal of Exhibits**. At the conclusion of a trial or hearing, the court shall direct the parties to retrieve the exhibits submitted by them except that any weapons and drugs shall be returned to the confiscating agency for proper disposition. If the exhibits are not retrieved by the parties as directed within 56 days after conclusion of the trial or hearing, the court may properly dispose of the exhibits without notice to the parties.

(C) **Confidentiality**. If the court retains discovery materials filed pursuant to MCR 1.109(C) or an exhibit submitted pursuant to this rule after a hearing or trial and the material is confidential as provided by law, court rule, or court order pursuant to MCR 8.119(I), the court must continue to maintain the material in a confidential manner.

Subchapter 2.600 Judgments and Orders; Postjudgment Proceedings

Rule 2.601 Judgments

(A) **Relief Available**. Except as provided in subrule (B), every final judgment may grant the relief to which the party in whose favor it is rendered is entitled, even if the party has not demanded that relief in his or her pleadings.

(B) **Default Judgment**. A judgment by default may not be different in kind from, nor exceed in amount, the relief demanded in the pleading, unless notice has been given pursuant to MCR 2.603(B)(1).

Rule 2.602 Entry of Judgments and Orders

(A) **Signing; Statement; Date of Entry**.

(1) Except as provided in this rule and in MCR 2.603, all judgments and orders must be in writing, signed by the court and dated with the date they are signed.

(2) The date of signing an order or judgment is the date of entry.

(3) Each judgment must state, immediately preceding the judge's signature, whether it resolves the last pending claim and closes the case. Such a statement must also appear on any other order that disposes of the last pending claim and closes the case.

(B) **Procedure of Entry of Judgments and Orders**. An order or judgment shall be entered by one of the following methods:

(1) The court may sign the judgment or order at the time it grants the relief provided by the judgment or order.

(2) The court shall sign the judgment or order when its form is approved by all the parties and if, in the court's determination, it comports with the court's decision.

(3) Within 7 days after the granting of the judgment or order, or later if the court allows, a party may serve a copy of the proposed judgment or order on the other parties, with a notice to them that it will be submitted to the court for signing if no written objections to its accuracy or completeness are filed with the court clerk within 7 days after service of the notice. The party must file with the court clerk the original of the proposed judgment or order and proof of its service on the other parties.

(a) If no written objections are filed within 7 days, the clerk shall submit the judgment or order to the court, and the court shall then sign it if, in the court's determination, it comports with the court's decision. If the proposed judgment or order does not comport with the decision, the court shall direct the clerk to notify the parties to appear before the court on a specified date for settlement of the matter.

(b) Objections regarding the accuracy or completeness of the judgment or order must state with specificity the inaccuracy or omission.

(c) The party filing the objections must serve them on all parties as required by MCR 2.107, together with a notice of hearing and an alternative proposed judgment or order.

(4) A party may prepare a proposed judgment or order and notice it for settlement before the court.

(C) **Filing**. The original of the judgment or order must be placed in the file.

(D) **Service**.

(1) The party securing the signing of the judgment or order shall serve a copy, within 7 days after it has been signed, on all other parties, and file proof of service with the court clerk.

(2) If a judgment for reimbursement to the state for the value of game or protected animals is entered pursuant to MCL 324.40119 or for the value of fish is entered pursuant to MCL 324.48740, the clerk shall provide a copy of the judgment to the Department of Natural Resources. The judgment may be enforced as a civil judgment.

Rule 2.603 Default and Default Judgment

(A) **Entry of Default; Notice; Effect**.

(1) If a party against whom a judgment for affirmative relief is sought has failed to plead or otherwise defend as provided by these rules, and that fact is made to appear by affidavit or otherwise, the clerk must enter the default of that party.

(2) Notice that the default has been entered must be sent to all parties who have appeared and to the defaulted party. If the defaulted party has not appeared, the notice to the defaulted party may be served by personal service, by ordinary first-class mail at his or her last known address or the place of service, or as otherwise directed by the court.

(a) In the district court, the court clerk shall send the notice.

(b) In all other courts, the notice must be sent by the party who sought entry of the default. Proof of service and a copy of the notice must be filed with the court.

(3) Once the default of a party has been entered, that party may not proceed with the action until the default has been set aside by the court in accordance with subrule (D) or MCR 2.612.

(B) **Default Judgment**.

(1) *Notice of Request for Default Judgment*.

(a) A party requesting a default judgment must give notice of the request to the defaulted party, if

(i) the party against whom the default judgment is sought has appeared in the action;

(ii) the request for entry of a default judgment seeks relief different in kind from, or greater in amount than, that stated in the pleadings; or

(iii) the pleadings do not state a specific amount demanded.

(b) The notice required by this subrule must be served at least 7 days before entry of the requested default judgment.

(c) If the defaulted party has appeared, the notice may be given in the manner provided by MCR 2.107. If the defaulted party has not appeared, the notice may be served by personal service, by ordinary first-class mail at the defaulted party's last known address or the place of service, or as otherwise directed by the court.

(d) If the default is entered for failure to appear for a scheduled trial, notice under this subrule is not required.

(2) *Default Judgment Entered by Clerk*. On request of the plaintiff supported by an affidavit as to the amount due, the clerk may sign and enter a default judgment for that amount and costs against the defendant, if
(a) the plaintiff's claim against a defendant is for a sum certain or for a sum that can by computation be made certain;
(b) the default was entered because the defendant failed to appear; and
(c) the defaulted defendant is not an infant or incompetent person and
(d) the damages amount requested is not greater than the amount stated in the complaint.
(3) *Default Judgment Entered by Court*. In all other cases, the party entitled to a default judgment must file a motion that asks the court to enter the default judgment.
(a) A default judgment may not be entered against a minor or an incompetent person unless the person is represented in the action by a conservator, guardian ad litem, or other representative.
(b) If, in order for the court to enter a default judgment or to carry it into effect, it is necessary to
(i) take an account,
(ii) determine the amount of damages,
(iii) establish the truth of an allegation by evidence, or
(iv) investigate any other matter,
the court may conduct hearings or order references it deems necessary and proper, and shall accord a right of trial by jury to the parties to the extent required by the constitution.
(4) *Notice of Entry of Default Judgment*. The court clerk must promptly mail notice of entry of a default judgment to all parties. The notice to the defendant shall be mailed to the defendant's last known address or the address of the place of service. The clerk must keep a record that notice was given.
(C) **Nonmilitary Affidavit**. Nonmilitary affidavits required by law must be filed before judgment is entered in actions in which the defendant has failed to appear.
(D) **Setting Aside Default or Default Judgment**.
(1) A motion to set aside a default or a default judgment, except when grounded on lack of jurisdiction over the defendant, shall be granted only if good cause is shown and an affidavit of facts showing a meritorious defense is filed.
(2) Except as provided in MCR 2.612, if personal service was made on the party against whom the default was taken, the default, and default judgment if one has been entered, may be set aside only if the motion is filed
(a) before entry of a default judgment, or
(b) if a default judgment has been entered, within 21 days after the default judgment was entered.
(3) In addition, the court may set aside a default and a default judgment in accordance with MCR 2.612.
(4) An order setting aside the default or default judgment must be conditioned on the defaulted party paying the taxable costs incurred by the other party in reliance on the default or default judgment, except as prescribed in MCR 2.625(D). The order may also impose other conditions the court deems proper, including a reasonable attorney fee.
(E) **Application to Parties Other Than Plaintiff**. The provisions of this rule apply whether the party entitled to the default judgment is a plaintiff or a party who pleaded a cross-claim or counterclaim. In all cases a default judgment is subject to the limitations of MCR 2.601(B).

Rule 2.604 Judgment in Actions Involving Multiple Claims or Multiple Parties

(A) Except as provided in subrule (B), an order or other form of decision adjudicating fewer than all the claims, or the rights and liabilities of fewer than all the parties, does not terminate the action as to any of the claims or parties, and the order is subject to revision before entry of final judgment adjudicating all the claims and the rights and liabilities of all the parties. Such an order or other form of decision is not appealable as of right before entry of final judgment. A party may file an application for leave to appeal from such an order.
(B) In receivership and similar actions, the court may direct that an order entered before adjudication of all of the claims and rights and liabilities of all the parties constitutes a final order on an express determination that there is no just reason for delay.

Rule 2.605 Declaratory Judgments

(A) **Power to Enter Declaratory Judgment**.
(1) In a case of actual controversy within its jurisdiction, a Michigan court of record may declare the rights and other legal relations of an interested party seeking a declaratory judgment, whether or not other relief is or could be sought or granted.
(2) For the purpose of this rule, an action is considered within the jurisdiction of a court if the court would have jurisdiction of an action on the same claim or claims in which the plaintiff sought relief other than a declaratory judgment.
(B) **Procedure**. The procedure for obtaining declaratory relief is in accordance with these rules, and the right to trial by jury may be demanded under the circumstances and in the manner provided in the constitution, statutes, and court rules of the State of Michigan.

(C) **Other Adequate Remedy**. The existence of another adequate remedy does not preclude a judgment for declaratory relief in an appropriate case.

(D) **Hearing**. The court may order a speedy hearing of an action for declaratory relief and may advance it on the calendar.

(E) **Effect; Review**. Declaratory judgments have the force and effect of, and are reviewable as, final judgments.

(F) **Other Relief**. Further necessary or proper relief based on a declaratory judgment may be granted, after reasonable notice and hearing, against a party whose rights have been determined by the declaratory judgment.

Rule 2.610 Motion for Judgment Notwithstanding the Verdict

(A) **Motion**.

(1) Within 21 days after entry of judgment, a party may move to have the verdict and judgment set aside, and to have judgment entered in the moving party's favor. The motion may be joined with a motion for a new trial, or a new trial may be requested in the alternative.

(2) If a verdict was not returned, a party may move for judgment within 21 days after the jury is discharged.

(3) A motion to set aside or otherwise nullify a verdict or a motion for a new trial is deemed to include a motion for judgment notwithstanding the verdict as an alternative.

(B) **Ruling**.

(1) If a verdict was returned, the court may allow the judgment to stand or may reopen the judgment and either order a new trial or direct the entry of judgment as requested in the motion.

(2) If a verdict was not returned, the court may direct the entry of judgment as requested in the motion or order a new trial.

(3) In ruling on a motion under this rule, the court must give a concise statement of the reasons for the ruling, either in a signed order or opinion filed in the action, or on the record.

(C) **Conditional Ruling on Motion for New Trial**.

(1) If the motion for judgment notwithstanding the verdict under subrule (A) is granted, the court shall also conditionally rule on any motion for a new trial, determining whether it should be granted if the judgment is vacated or reversed, and shall specify the grounds for granting or denying the motion for a new trial.

(2) A conditional ruling under this subrule has the following effects:

(a) If the motion for a new trial is conditionally granted, that ruling does not affect the finality of the judgment.

(b) If the motion for a new trial is conditionally granted and the judgment is reversed on appeal, the new trial proceeds unless the appellate court orders otherwise.

(c) If the motion for a new trial is conditionally denied, on appeal the appellee may assert error in that denial. If the judgment is reversed on appeal, subsequent proceedings are in accordance with the order of the appellate court.

(D) **Motion for New Trial After Ruling**. The party whose verdict has been set aside on a motion for judgment notwithstanding the verdict may serve and file a motion for a new trial pursuant to MCR 2.611 within 14 days after entry of judgment. A party who fails to move for a new trial as provided in this subrule has waived the right to move for a new trial.

(E) **Appeal After Denial of Motion**.

(1) If the motion for judgment notwithstanding the verdict is denied, the party who prevailed on that motion may, as appellee, assert grounds entitling that party to a new trial if the appellate court concludes that the trial court erred in denying the motion for judgment notwithstanding the verdict.

(2) If the appellate court reverses the judgment, nothing in this rule precludes it from determining that the appellee is entitled to a new trial, or from directing the trial court to determine whether a new trial should be granted.

Rule 2.611 New Trials; Amendment of Judgments

(A) **Grounds**.

(1) A new trial may be granted to all or some of the parties, on all or some of the issues, whenever their substantial rights are materially affected, for any of the following reasons:

(a) Irregularity in the proceedings of the court, jury, or prevailing party, or an order of the court or abuse of discretion which denied the moving party a fair trial.

(b) Misconduct of the jury or of the prevailing party.

(c) Excessive or inadequate damages appearing to have been influenced by passion or prejudice.

(d) A verdict clearly or grossly inadequate or excessive.

(e) A verdict or decision against the great weight of the evidence or contrary to law.

(f) Material evidence, newly discovered, which could not with reasonable diligence have been discovered and produced at trial.

(g) Error of law occurring in the proceedings, or mistake of fact by the court.

(h) A ground listed in MCR 2.612 warranting a new trial.

(2) On a motion for a new trial in an action tried without a jury, the court may
   (a) set aside the judgment if one has been entered,
   (b) take additional testimony,
   (c) amend findings of fact and conclusions of law, or
   (d) make new findings and conclusions and direct the entry of a new judgment.

(B) **Time for Motion**. A motion for a new trial made under this rule or a motion to alter or amend a judgment must be filed and served within 21 days after entry of the judgment.

(C) **On Initiative of Court**. Within 21 days after entry of a judgment, the court on its own initiative may order a new trial for a reason for which it might have granted a new trial on motion of a party. The order must specify the grounds on which it is based.

(D) **Affidavits**.
   (1) If the facts stated in the motion for a new trial or to amend the judgment do not appear on the record of the action, the motion must be supported by affidavit, which must be filed and served with the motion.
   (2) The opposing party has 21 days after service within which to file and serve opposing affidavits. The period may be extended by the parties by written stipulation for 21 additional days, or may be extended or shortened by the court for good cause shown.
   (3) The court may permit reply affidavits and may call and examine witnesses.

(E) **Remittitur and Additur**.
   (1) If the court finds that the only error in the trial is the inadequacy or excessiveness of the verdict, it may deny a motion for new trial on condition that within 14 days the nonmoving party consent in writing to the entry of judgment in an amount found by the court to be the lowest (if the verdict was inadequate) or highest (if the verdict was excessive) amount the evidence will support.
   (2) If the moving party appeals, the agreement in no way prejudices the nonmoving party's argument on appeal that the original verdict was correct. If the nonmoving party prevails, the original verdict may be reinstated by the appellate court.

(F) **Ruling on Motion**. In ruling on a motion for a new trial or a motion to amend the judgment, the court shall give a concise statement of the reasons for the ruling, either in an order or opinion filed in the action or on the record.

(G) **Notice of Decision**. The clerk must notify the parties of the decision on the motion for a new trial, unless the decision is made on the record while the parties are present.

Rule 2.612 Relief From Judgment or Order

(A) **Clerical Mistakes**.
   (1) Clerical mistakes in judgments, orders, or other parts of the record and errors arising from oversight or omission may be corrected by the court at any time on its own initiative or on motion of a party and after notice, if the court orders it.
   (2) If a claim of appeal is filed or an appellate court grants leave to appeal, the trial court may correct errors as provided in MCR 7.208(A) and (C).

(B) **Defendant Not Personally Notified**. A defendant over whom personal jurisdiction was necessary and acquired, but who did not in fact have knowledge of the pendency of the action, may enter an appearance within 1 year after final judgment, and if the defendant shows reason justifying relief from the judgment and innocent third persons will not be prejudiced, the court may relieve the defendant from the judgment, order, or proceedings for which personal jurisdiction was necessary, on payment of costs or on conditions the court deems just.

(C) **Grounds for Relief From Judgment**.
   (1) On motion and on just terms, the court may relieve a party or the legal representative of a party from a final judgment, order, or proceeding on the following grounds:
      (a) Mistake, inadvertence, surprise, or excusable neglect.
      (b) Newly discovered evidence which by due diligence could not have been discovered in time to move for a new trial under MCR 2.611(B).
      (c) Fraud (intrinsic or extrinsic), misrepresentation, or other misconduct of an adverse party.
      (d) The judgment is void.
      (e) The judgment has been satisfied, released, or discharged; a prior judgment on which it is based has been reversed or otherwise vacated; or it is no longer equitable that the judgment should have prospective application.
      (f) Any other reason justifying relief from the operation of the judgment.
   (2) The motion must be made within a reasonable time, and, for the grounds stated in subrules (C)(1)(a), (b), and (c), within one year after the judgment, order, or proceeding was entered or taken. Except as provided in MCR 2.614(A)(1), a motion under this subrule does not affect the finality of a judgment or suspend its operation.
   (3) This subrule does not limit the power of a court to entertain an independent action to relieve a party from a judgment, order, or proceeding; to grant relief to a defendant not actually personally notified as provided in subrule (B); or to set aside a judgment for fraud on the court.

Rule 2.613 Limitations on Corrections of Error

(A) **Harmless Error**. An error in the admission or the exclusion of evidence, an error in a ruling or order, or an error or defect in anything done or omitted by the court or by the parties is not ground for granting a new trial, for setting aside a verdict, or for vacating, modifying, or otherwise disturbing a judgment or order, unless refusal to take this action appears to the court inconsistent with substantial justice.

(B) **Correction of Error by Other Judges**. A judgment or order may be set aside or vacated, and a proceeding under a judgment or order may be stayed, only by the judge who entered the judgment or order, unless that judge is absent or unable to act. If the judge who entered the judgment or order is absent or unable to act, an order vacating or setting aside the judgment or order or staying proceedings under the judgment or order may be entered by a judge otherwise empowered to rule in the matter.

(C) **Review of Findings by Trial Court**. Findings of fact by the trial court may not be set aside unless clearly erroneous. In the application of this principle, regard shall be given to the special opportunity of the trial court to judge the credibility of the witnesses who appeared before it.

Rule 2.614 Stay of Proceedings to Enforce Judgment

(A) **Automatic Stay; Exceptions: Injunctions, Receiverships, and Family Litigation**.

(1) Except as provided in this rule, execution may not issue on a judgment and proceedings may not be taken for its enforcement until the expiration of 21 days after its entry. If a motion for new trial, a motion for rehearing or reconsideration, or a motion for other relief from judgment is filed and served within 21 days after entry of the judgment or within further time the trial court has allowed for good cause during that 21-day period, execution may not issue on the judgment and proceedings may not be taken for its enforcement until the expiration of 21 days after the entry of the order deciding the motion, unless otherwise ordered by the court on motion for good cause. Nothing in this rule prohibits the court from enjoining the transfer or disposition of property during the 21-day period.

(2) The following orders may be enforced immediately after entry unless the court orders otherwise on motion for good cause:

(a) A temporary restraining order.

(b) A preliminary injunction.

(c) Injunctive relief included in a final judgment.

(d) An interlocutory order in a receivership action.

(e) In a domestic relations action, an order before judgment concerning the custody, control, and management of property; for temporary alimony; or for support or custody of minor children and expenses.

(3) Subrule (C) governs the suspending, modifying, restoring, or granting of an injunction during the pendency of an appeal.

(B) **Stay on Motion for Relief From Judgment**. In its discretion and on proper conditions for the security of the adverse party, the court may stay the execution of, or proceedings to enforce, a judgment pending the disposition of a motion for relief from a judgment or order under MCR 2.612.

(C) **Injunction Pending Appeal**. If an appeal is taken from an interlocutory or final judgment granting, dissolving, or denying an injunction, the court may suspend, modify, restore, or grant an injunction during the pendency of the appeal on terms as to bond or otherwise that are proper for the security of the adverse party's rights.

(D) **Stay on Appeal**. Stay on appeal is governed by MCR 7.101(H), 7.209, and 7.302(I). If a party appeals a trial court’s denial of the party’s claim of governmental immunity, the party’s appeal operates as an automatic stay of any and all proceedings in the case until the issue of the party’s status is finally decided.

(E) **Stay in Favor of Governmental Party**. In an action or proceeding in which the state, an authorized state officer, a corporate body in charge of a state institution, or a municipal corporation, is a party, bond may not be required of that party as a prerequisite to taking an appeal or making an order staying proceedings.

(F) **Power of Appellate Court Not Limited**. This rule does not limit the power of the Court of Appeals or the Supreme Court to

(1) stay proceedings during the pendency of an appeal before them;

(2) suspend, modify, restore, or grant an injunction during the pendency of the appeal; or

(3) enter an order appropriate to preserve the status quo or effectiveness of the judgment to be entered.

(G) **Stay of Judgment on Multiple Claims**. When a court has ordered a final judgment on some, but not all, of the claims presented in the action under the conditions stated in MCR 2.604(B), the court may

(1) stay enforcement of the judgment until the entry of a later judgment or judgments, and

(2) prescribe conditions necessary to secure the benefit of the judgment to the party in whose favor it was entered.

Rule 2.615 Enforcement of Tribal Judgments

(A) The judgments, decrees, orders, warrants, subpoenas, records, and other judicial acts of a tribal court of a federally recognized Indian tribe are recognized, and have the same effect and are subject to the same procedures, defenses, and proceedings as judgments, decrees, orders, warrants, subpoenas, records, and other judicial acts of any court of record in this state, subject to the provisions of this rule.

(B) The recognition described in subrule (A) applies only if the tribe or tribal court

(1) enacts an ordinance, court rule, or other binding measure that obligates the tribal court to enforce the judgments, decrees, orders, warrants, subpoenas, records, and judicial acts of the courts of this state, and

(2) transmits the ordinance, court rule or other measure to the State Court Administrative Office. The State Court Administrative Office shall make available to state courts the material received pursuant to paragraph (B)(1).

(C) A judgment, decree, order, warrant, subpoena, record, or other judicial act of a tribal court of a federally recognized Indian tribe that has taken the actions described in subrule (B) is presumed to be valid. To overcome that presumption, an objecting party must demonstrate that

(1) the tribal court lacked personal or subject-matter jurisdiction, or

(2) the judgment, decree, order, warrant, subpoena, record, or other judicial act of the tribal court

(a) was obtained by fraud, duress, or coercion,

(b) was obtained without fair notice or a fair hearing,

(c) is repugnant to the public policy of the State of Michigan, or

(d) is not final under the laws and procedures of the tribal court.

(D) This rule does not apply to judgments or orders that federal law requires be given full faith and credit.

Rule 2.620 Satisfaction of Judgment

A judgment may be shown satisfied of record in whole or in part by:

(1) filing with the clerk a satisfaction signed and acknowledged by the party or parties in whose favor the judgment was rendered, or their attorneys of record;

(2) payment to the clerk of the judgment, interest, and costs, if it is a money judgment only; or

(3) filing a motion for entry of an order that the judgment has been satisfied.

The court shall hear proofs to determine whether the order should be entered.

The clerk must, in each instance, indicate in the court records that the judgment is satisfied in whole or in part.

Rule 2.621 Proceedings Supplementary to Judgment

(A) **Relief Under These Rules**. When a party to a civil action obtains a money judgment, that party may, by motion in that action or by a separate civil action:

(1) obtain the relief formerly obtainable by a creditor's bill;

(2) obtain relief supplementary to judgment under MCL 600.6101-600.6143 and

(3) obtain other relief in aid of execution authorized by statute or court rule.

(B) **Pleading.**

(1) If the motion or complaint seeks to reach an equitable interest of a debtor, it must be verified, and

(a) state the amount due the creditor on the judgment, over and above all just claims of the debtor by way of setoff or otherwise, and

(b) show that the debtor has equitable interests exceeding $100 in value.

(2) The judgment creditor may obtain relief under MCL 600.6110, and discovery under subchapter 2.300 of these rules.

(C) **Subpoenas and Orders**. A subpoena or order to enjoin the transfer of assets pursuant to MCL 600.6119 must be served under MCR 2.105. The subpoena must specify the amount claimed by the judgment creditor. The court shall endorse its approval of the issuance of the subpoena on the original subpoena, which must be filed in the action. The subrule does not apply to subpoenas for ordinary witnesses.

(D) **Order Directing Delivery of Property or Money**.

(1) When a court orders the payment of money or delivery of personal property to an officer who has possession of the writ of execution, the order may be entered on notice the court deems just, or without notice.

(2) If a receiver has been appointed, or a receivership has been extended to the supplementary proceeding, the order may direct the payment of money or delivery of property to the receiver.

(E) **Receivers**. When necessary to protect the rights of a judgment creditor, the court may, under MCR 2.622, appoint a receiver in a proceeding under subrule (A)(2), pending the determination of the proceeding.

(F) **Violation of Injunction**. The court may punish for contempt a person who violates the restraining provision of an order or subpoena or, if the person is not the judgment debtor, may enter judgment against the person in the amount of the unpaid portion of the judgment and costs allowed by law or these rules or in the amount of the value of the property transferred, whichever is less.

(G) **New Proceeding**. If there has been a prior supplementary proceeding with respect to the same judgment against the party, whether the judgment debtor or another person, further proceedings may be commenced against that party only by leave of court. Leave may be granted on ex parte motion of the judgment creditor, but only on a finding by the court, based on affidavit of the judgment creditor or another person having personal knowledge of the facts, other than the attorney of the judgment creditor. The affidavit must state that

(1) there is reason to believe that the party against whom the proceeding is sought to be commenced has property or income the creditor is entitled to reach, or, if a third party, is indebted to the judgment debtor;

(2) the existence of the property, income, or indebtedness was not known to the judgment creditor during the pendency of a prior supplementary proceeding; and

(3) the additional supplementary proceeding is sought in good faith to discover assets and not to harass the judgment debtor or third party.

(H) **Appeal; Procedure; Bonds**. A final order entered in a supplementary proceeding may be appealed in the usual manner. The appeal is governed by the provisions of chapter 7 of these rules except as modified by this subrule.

(1) The appellant must give a bond to the effect that he or she will pay all costs and damages that may be awarded against him or her on the appeal. If the appeal is by the judgment creditor, the amount of the bond may not exceed $200, and subrules (H)(2)-(4) do not apply. If the appeal is by a party other than the judgment creditor, subrules (H)(2)-(4) apply.

(2) If the order appealed from is for the payment of money or the delivery of property, the bond of the appellant must be in an amount at least double the amount of the money or property ordered to be paid or delivered. The bond must be on the condition that if the order appealed from is affirmed in whole or in part the appellant will

(a) pay the amount directed to be paid or deliver the property in as good condition as it is at the time of the appeal, and

(b) pay all damages and costs that may be awarded against the appellant.

(3) If the order appealed from directs the assignment or delivery of papers or documents by the appellant, the papers must be delivered to the clerk of the court in which the proceeding is pending or placed in the hands of an officer or receiver, as the judge who entered the order directs, to await the appeal, subject to the order of the appellate courts.

(4) If the order appealed from directs the sale of real estate of the appellant or delivery of possession by the appellant, the appeal bond must also provide that during the possession of the property by the appellant, or any person holding under the appellant, he or she will not commit or suffer any waste of the property, and that if the order is affirmed he or she will pay the value of the use of the property from the time of appeal until the delivery of possession.

Rule 2.622 Receivers

(A) **Appointment of Receiver**. Upon the motion of a party or on its own initiative, and for good cause shown, the court may appoint a receiver as provided by law. A receiver appointed under this section is a fiduciary for the benefit of all persons appearing in the action or proceeding. For purposes of this rule, "receivership estate" means the entity, person, or property subject to the receivership.

(B) **Selection of Receiver**. If the court determines there is good cause to appoint a receiver, the court shall select the receiver in accordance with this subrule. Every receiver selected by the court must have sufficient competence, qualifications, and experience to administer the receivership estate.

(1) *Stipulated Receiver or No Objection Raised*. The moving party may request, or the parties may stipulate to, the selection of a receiver. The moving party shall describe how the nominated receiver meets the requirement in subsection (B) that a receiver selected by the court have sufficient competence, qualifications, and experience to administer the receivership estate, considering the factors listed in subsection (B)(5). If the nonmoving party does not file an objection to the moving party's nominated receiver within 14 days after the petition or motion is served, or if the parties stipulate to the selection of a receiver, the court shall appoint the receiver nominated by the party or parties, unless the court finds that a different receiver should be appointed.

(2) *Receiver Appointed Sua Sponte*. If the court appoints a receiver on its own initiative, any party may file objection to the selected receiver and submit an alternative nominee for appointment as receiver within 14 days after the order appointing the receiver is served. The objecting party shall describe how the alternative nominee meets the requirement in subsection (B) that a receiver selected by the court have sufficient competence, qualifications, and experience to administer the receivership estate, considering the factors listed in subsection (B)(5).

(3) *Reduction in Time to Object*. The court, for good cause shown, may in its discretion, with or without motion or notice, order the period for objection to the selected receiver reduced.

(4) *Objections*. The party filing an objection must serve it on all parties as required by MCR 2.107, together with a notice of hearing.

(5) If a party objects under subsection (B)(2) or the court makes an initial determination that a different receiver should be appointed than the receiver nominated by a party under subsection (B)(1), the court shall state its rationale for selecting a particular receiver after considering the following factors:

(a) experience in the operation and/or liquidation of the type of assets to be administered;

(b) relevant business, legal and receivership knowledge, if any;

(c) ability to obtain the required bonding if more than a nominal bond is required;

(d) any objections to any receiver considered for appointment;

(e) whether the receiver considered for appointment is disqualified under subrule (B)(6); and

(f) any other factor the court deems appropriate.

(6) Except as otherwise provided by law or by subrule (B)(7), a person or entity may not serve as a receiver or in any other professional capacity representing or assisting the receiver, if such person or entity:

(a) is a creditor or a holder of an equity security of the receivership estate:

(b) is or was an investment banker for any outstanding security of the receivership estate;

(c) has been, within three years before the date of the appointment of a receiver, an investment banker for a security of the receivership estate, or an attorney for such an investment banker, in connection with the offer, sale, or issuance of a security of the receivership estate;

(d) is or was, within two years before the date of the appointment of a receiver, a director, an officer, or an employee of the receivership estate or of an investment banker specified in subrule (b) or (c) of this section, unless the court finds the appointment is in the best interest of the receivership estate and that there is no actual conflict of interest by reason of the employment;

(e) has an interest materially adverse to the interest of any class of creditors or equity security holders by reason of any direct or indirect relationship to, connection with, or interest in the receivership estate or an investment banker specified in subrule (b) or (c) of this section, or for any other reason;

(f) has or represents an interest adverse to the receivership estate or stands in any relation to the subject of the action or proceeding that would tend to interfere with the impartial discharge of duties as an officer of the court.

(g) has, at any time within five years before the date of the appointment of a receiver, represented or been employed by the receivership estate or any secured creditor of the receivership estate as an attorney, accountant, appraiser, or in any other professional capacity and the court finds an actual conflict of interest by reason of the representation or employment;

(h) is an "insider" as defined by MCL 566.31(g);

(i) represents or is employed by a creditor of the receivership estate and, on objection of an interested party, the court finds an actual conflict of interest by reason of the representation or employment; or

(j) has a relationship to the action or proceeding that will interfere with the impartial discharge of the receiver's duties.

(7) Any person who has represented or has been employed by the receivership estate is eligible to serve for a specified limited purpose, if the court determines such employment or appointment is in the best interest of the receivership estate and if such professional does not represent or hold an interest materially adverse to the receivership estate.

(C) **Order of Appointment**. The order of appointment shall include provisions related to the following:

(1) bonding amounts and requirements as provided in subrule (G);

(2) identification of real and personal property of the receivership estate;

(3) procedures and standards related to the reasonable compensation of the receiver as provided in subrule (F);

(4) reports required to be produced and filed by the receiver, including the final report and accounting;

(5) a description of the duties, authority and powers of the receiver;

(6) a listing of property to be surrendered to the receiver; and

(7) any other provision the court deems appropriate.

(D) **Duties**.

(1) Within 7 days after entry of the order of appointment, the receiver shall file an acceptance of receivership with the court. The acceptance shall be served on all parties to the action.

(2) Unless otherwise ordered, within 28 days after the filing of the acceptance of appointment, the receiver shall provide notice of entry of the order of appointment to any person or entity having a recorded interest in all or any part of the receivership estate.

(3) The receiver shall file with the court an inventory of the property of the receivership estate within 35 days after entry of the order of appointment, unless an inventory has already been filed.
(4) The receiver shall account for all receipts, disbursements and distributions of money and property of the receivership estate.
(5) If there are sufficient funds to make a distribution to a class of creditors, the receiver may request that each creditor in the class of all creditors file a written proof of claim with the court. The receiver may contest the allowance of any claim.
(6) The receiver shall furnish information concerning the receivership estate and its administration as reasonably requested by any party to the action or proceeding.
(7) The receiver shall file with the court a final written report and final accounting of the administration of the receivership estate.

(E) **Powers.**
(1) Except as otherwise provided by law or by the order of appointment, a receiver has general power to sue for and collect all debts, demands, and rents of the receivership estate, and to compromise or settle claims.
(2) A receiver may liquidate the personal property of the receivership estate into money. By separate order of the court, a receiver may sell real property of the receivership estate.
(3) A receiver may pay the ordinary expenses of the receivership but may not distribute the funds in the receivership estate to a party to the action without an order of the court.
(4) A receiver may only be discharged on order of the court.

(F) **Compensation and Expenses of Receiver.**
(1) A receiver shall be entitled to reasonable compensation for services rendered to the receivership estate.
(2) The order appointing a receiver shall specify:
(a) the source and method of compensation of the receiver;
(b) that interim compensation may be paid to the receiver after notice to all parties to the action or proceeding and opportunity to object as provided in subsection (5);
(c) that all compensation of the receiver is subject to final review and approval of the court.
(3) All approved fees and expenses incurred by a receiver, including fees and expenses for persons or entities retained by the receiver, shall be paid or reimbursed as provided in the order appointing the receiver.
(4) The receiver shall file with the court an application for payment of fees and the original notice of the request. The notice shall provide that fees and expenses will be deemed approved if no written objection is filed with the court within 7 days after service of the notice. The receiver shall serve the notice and a copy of the application on all parties to the action or proceedings, and file a proof of service with the court.
(5) The application by a receiver, for interim or final payment of fees and expenses, shall include:
(a) A description in reasonable detail of the services rendered, time expended, and expenses incurred;
(b) The amount of compensation and expenses requested;
(c) The amount of any compensation and expenses previously paid to the receiver;
(d) The amount of any compensation and expenses received by the receiver from or to be paid by any source other than the receivership estate;
(e) A description in reasonable detail of any agreement or understanding for a division or sharing of compensation between the person rendering the services and any other person except as permitted in subpart (6).

If written objections are filed or if, in the court's determination, the application for compensation requires a hearing, the court shall schedule a hearing and notify all parties of the scheduled hearing.
(6) A receiver or person performing services for a receiver shall not, in any form or manner, share or agree to share compensation for services rendered to the receivership estate with any person other than a firm member, partner, employer, or regular associate of the person rendering the services except as authorized by order of the court.

(G) **Bond**. In setting an appropriate bond for the receiver, the court may consider factors including but not limited to:
(1) The value of the receivership estate, if known;
(2) The amount of cash or cash equivalents expected to be received into the receivership estate;
(3) The amount of assets in the receivership estate on deposit in insured financial institutions or invested in U.S. Treasury obligations;
(4) Whether the assets in the receivership estate cannot be sold without further order of the court;
(5) If the receiver is an entity, whether the receiver has sufficient assets or acceptable errors and omissions insurance to cover any potential losses or liabilities of the receivership estate;
(6) The extent to which any secured creditor is undersecured;
(7) Whether the receivership estate is a single parcel of real estate involving few trade creditors; and
(8) Whether the parties have agreed to a nominal bond.

(H) **Intervention**. An interested person or entity may move to intervene. Any motion to intervene shall comply with MCR 2.209.

(I) **Removal of Receiver**. After notice and hearing, the court may remove any receiver for good cause shown.

Rule 2.625 Taxation of Costs

(A) **Right to Costs**.

(1) *In General*. Costs will be allowed to the prevailing party in an action, unless prohibited by statute or by these rules or unless the court directs otherwise, for reasons stated in writing and filed in the action.

(2) *Frivolous Claims and Defenses*. In an action filed on or after October 1, 1986, if the court finds on motion of a party that an action or defense was frivolous, costs shall be awarded as provided by MCL 600.2591.

(B) **Rules for Determining Prevailing Party**.

(1) *Actions With Several Judgments*. If separate judgments are entered under MCR 2.116 or 2.505(A) and the plaintiff prevails in one judgment in an amount and under circumstances which would entitle the plaintiff to costs, he or she is deemed the prevailing party. Costs common to more than one judgment may be allowed only once.

(2) *Actions With Several Issues or Counts*. In an action involving several issues or counts that state different causes of action or different defenses, the party prevailing on each issue or count may be allowed costs for that issue or count. If there is a single cause of action alleged, the party who prevails on the entire record is deemed the prevailing party.

(3) *Actions With Several Defendants*. If there are several defendants in one action, and judgment for or dismissal of one or more of them is entered, those defendants are deemed prevailing parties, even though the plaintiff ultimately prevails over the remaining defendants.

(4) *Costs on Review in Circuit Court*. An appellant in the circuit court who improves his or her position on appeal is deemed the prevailing party.

(C) **Costs in Certain Trivial Actions**. In an action brought for damages in contract or tort in which the plaintiff recovers less than $100 (unless the recovery is reduced below $100 by a counterclaim), the plaintiff may recover costs no greater than the amount of damages.

(D) **Costs When Default or Default Judgment Set Aside**. The following provisions apply to an order setting aside a default or a default judgment:

(1) If personal jurisdiction was acquired over the defendant, the order must be conditioned on the defendant's paying or securing payment to the party seeking affirmative relief the taxable costs incurred in procuring the default or the default judgment and acting in reliance on it;

(2) If jurisdiction was acquired by publication, the order may be conditioned on the defendant's paying or securing payment to the party seeking affirmative relief all or a part of the costs as the court may direct;

(3) If jurisdiction was in fact not acquired, costs may not be imposed.

(E) **Costs in Garnishment Proceedings**. Costs in garnishment proceedings are allowed as in civil actions. Costs may be awarded to the garnishee defendant as follows:

(1) The court may award the garnishee defendant as costs against the plaintiff reasonable attorney fees and other necessary expenses the garnishee defendant incurred in filing the disclosure, if the issue of the garnishee defendant's liability to the principal defendant is not brought to trial.

(2) The court may award the garnishee defendant, against the plaintiff, the total costs of the garnishee defendant's defense, including all necessary expenses and reasonable attorney fees, if the issue of the garnishee defendant's liability to the principal defendant is tried and

(a) the garnishee defendant is held liable in a sum no greater than that admitted in disclosure, or

(b) the plaintiff fails to recover judgment against the principal defendant.

In either (a) or (b), the garnishee defendant may withhold from the amount due the principal defendant the sum awarded for costs, and is chargeable only for the balance.

(F) **Procedure for Taxing Costs**.

(1) Costs may be taxed by the court on signing the judgment, or may be taxed by the clerk as provided in this subrule.

(2) When costs are to be taxed by the clerk, the party entitled to costs must present to the clerk, within 28 days after the judgment is signed, or within 28 days after entry of an order denying a motion for new trial, a motion to set aside the judgment, a motion for rehearing or reconsideration, or a motion for other postjudgment relief except a motion under MCR 2.612(C),

(a) a bill of costs conforming to subrule (G),

(b) a copy of the bill of costs for each other party, and

(c) a list of the names and addresses of the attorneys for each party or of parties not represented by attorneys.

In addition, the party presenting the bill of costs shall immediately serve a copy of the bill and any accompanying affidavits on the other parties. Failure to present a bill of costs within the time prescribed constitutes a waiver of the right to costs.

(3) Within 14 days after service of the bill of costs, another party may file objections to it, accompanied by affidavits if appropriate. After the time for filing objections, the clerk must promptly examine the bill and any objections or affidavits submitted and allow only those items that appear to be correct, striking all charges for services that in the clerk's judgment were not necessary. The clerk shall notify the parties in the manner provided in MCR 2.107.

(4) The action of the clerk is reviewable by the court on motion of any affected party filed within 7 days from the date that notice of the taxing of costs was sent, but on review only those affidavits or objections that were presented to the clerk may be considered by the court.

(G) **Bill of Costs; Supporting Affidavits**.

(1) Each item claimed in the bill of costs, except fees of officers for services rendered, must be specified particularly.

(2) The bill of costs must be verified and must contain a statement that

(a) each item of cost or disbursement claimed is correct and has been necessarily incurred in the action, and

(b) the services for which fees have been charged were actually performed.

(3) If witness fees are claimed, an affidavit in support of the bill of costs must state the distance traveled and the days actually attended. If fees are claimed for a party as a witness, the affidavit must state that the party actually testified as a witness on the days listed.

(H) **Taxation of Fees on Settlement**. Unless otherwise specified a settlement is deemed to include the payment of any costs that might have been taxable.

(I) **Special Costs or Damages**.

(1) In an action in which the plaintiff's claim is reduced by a counterclaim, or another fact appears that would entitle either party to costs, to multiple costs, or to special damages for delay or otherwise, the court shall, on the application of either party, have that fact entered in the records of the court. A taxing officer may receive no evidence of the matter other than a certified copy of the court records or the certificate of the judge who entered the judgment.

(2) Whenever multiple costs are awarded to a party, they belong to the party. Officers, witnesses, jurors, or other persons claiming fees for services rendered in the action are entitled only to the amount prescribed by law.

(3) A judgment for multiple damages under a statute entitles the prevailing party to single costs only, except as otherwise specially provided by statute or by these rules.

(J) **Costs in Headlee Amendment Suits**. A plaintiff who prevails in an action brought pursuant to Const 1963, art 9, § 32 shall receive from the defendant the costs incurred by the plaintiff in maintaining the action as authorized by MCL 600.308a(1) and (6). Costs include a reasonable attorney fee.

Rule 2.626 Attorney Fees

An award of attorney fees may include an award for the time and labor of any legal assistant who contributed nonclerical, legal support under the supervision of an attorney, provided the legal assistant meets the criteria set forth in Article 1, § 6 of the Bylaws of the State Bar of Michigan.

Rule 2.630 Disability of Judge

If, after a verdict is returned or findings of fact and conclusions of law are filed, the judge before whom an action has been tried is unable to perform the duties prescribed by these rules because of death, illness, or other disability, another judge regularly sitting in or assigned to the court in which the action was tried may perform those duties. However, if the substitute judge is not satisfied that he or she can do so, the substitute judge may grant a new trial.

CHAPTER 3. SPECIAL PROCEEDINGS AND ACTIONS

Subchapter 3.000 General Provisions

Rule 3.001 Applicability and Scope

The rules in this chapter apply in circuit court and in other courts as provided by law or by these rules. Except as otherwise provided in this chapter and law, proceedings under this chapter are governed by the Michigan Court Rules.

Rule 3.002 Indian Children

For purposes of applying the Indian Child Welfare Act, 25 USC 1901 et seq., and the Michigan Indian Family Preservation Act, MCL 712B.1 et seq. to proceedings under the Juvenile Code, the Adoption Code, and the Estates and Protected Individuals Code, the following definitions taken from MCL 712B.3 and MCL 712B.7 shall apply.

(1) "Active efforts" means actions to provide remedial services and rehabilitative programs designed to prevent the breakup of the Indian family and to reunify the child with the Indian family. Active efforts require more than a referral to a service without actively engaging the Indian child and family. Active efforts include reasonable efforts as required by title IV-E of the social security act, 42 USC 670 to 679c, and also include doing or addressing all of the following:

(a) Engaging the Indian child, child's parents, tribe, extended family members, and individual Indian caregivers through the utilization of culturally appropriate services and in collaboration with the parent or child's Indian tribes and Indian social services agencies.

(b) Identifying appropriate services and helping the parents to overcome barriers to compliance with those services.

(c) Conducting or causing to be conducted a diligent search for extended family members for placement.

(d) Requesting representatives designated by the Indian child's tribe with substantial knowledge of the prevailing social and cultural standards and child rearing practice within the tribal community to evaluate the circumstances of the Indian child's family and to assist in developing a case plan that uses the resources of the Indian tribe and Indian community, including traditional and customary support, actions, and services, to address those circumstances.

(e) Completing a comprehensive assessment of the situation of the Indian child's family, including a determination of the likelihood of protecting the Indian child's health, safety, and welfare effectively in the Indian child's home.

(f) Identifying, notifying, and inviting representatives of the Indian child's tribe to participate in all aspects of the Indian child custody proceeding at the earliest possible point in the proceeding and actively soliciting the tribe's advice throughout the proceeding.

(g) Notifying and consulting with extended family members of the Indian child, including extended family members who were identified by the Indian child's tribe or parents, to identify and to provide family structure and support for the Indian child, to assure cultural connections, and to serve as placement resources for the Indian child.

(h) Making arrangements to provide natural and family interaction in the most natural setting that can ensure the Indian child's safety, as appropriate to the goals of the Indian child's permanency plan, including, when requested by the tribe, arrangements for transportation and other assistance to enable family members to participate in that interaction.

(i) Offering and employing all available family preservation strategies and requesting the involvement of the Indian child's tribe to identify those strategies and to ensure that those strategies are culturally appropriate to the Indian child's tribe.

(j) Identifying community resources offering housing, financial, and transportation assistance and in-home support services, in-home intensive treatment services, community support services, and specialized services for members of the Indian child's family with special needs, and providing information about those resources to the Indian child's family, and actively assisting the Indian child's family or offering active assistance in accessing those resources.

(k) Monitoring client progress and client participation in services.

(l) Providing a consideration of alternative ways of addressing the needs of the Indian child's family, if services do not exist or if existing services are not available to the family.

(2) "Child custody proceeding" shall mean and include

(a) "foster-care placement," which shall mean any action removing an Indian child from his or her parent or Indian custodian for temporary placement in a foster home or institution or the home of a guardian or conservator where the parent or Indian custodian cannot have the child returned upon demand, but where parental rights have not been terminated,

(b) "termination of parental rights," which shall mean any action resulting in the termination of the parent-child relationship,
(c) "preadoptive placement," which shall mean the temporary placement of an Indian child in a foster home or institution after the termination of parental rights, but before or in lieu of adoptive placement, and
(d) "adoptive placement," which shall mean the permanent placement of an Indian child for adoption, including any action resulting in a final decree of adoption.

Such term or terms shall not include a placement based upon an act that, if committed by an adult, would be deemed a crime or upon an award, in a divorce proceeding, of custody to one of the parents.

(3) "Court" means the family division of circuit court or the probate court.

(4) "Culturally appropriate services" means services that enhance an Indian child's and family's relationship to, identification, and connection with the Indian child's tribe. Culturally appropriate services should provide the opportunity to practice the teachings, beliefs, customs, and ceremonies of the Indian child's tribe so those may be incorporated into the Indian child's daily life, as well as services that address the issues that have brought the child and family to the attention of the department that are consistent with the tribe's beliefs about child rearing, child development, and family wellness. Culturally appropriate services may involve tribal representatives, extended family members, tribal elders, spiritual and cultural advisors, tribal social services, individual Indian caregivers, medicine men or women, and natural healers. If the Indian child's tribe establishes a different definition of culturally appropriate services, the court shall follow the tribe's definition.

(5) "Department" means the department of human services or any successor department or agency.

(6) "Exclusive jurisdiction" shall mean that an Indian tribe has jurisdiction exclusive as to any state over any child custody proceeding as defined above involving an Indian child who resides or is domiciled within the reservation of such tribe, except where such jurisdiction is otherwise vested in the state by existing federal law. Where an Indian child is a ward of a tribal court, the Indian tribe retains exclusive jurisdiction, regardless of the residence or domicile or subsequent change in his or her residence or domicile.

(7) "Extended family member" shall be as defined by the law or custom of the Indian child's tribe or, in the absence of such law or custom, shall be a person who has reached the age of 18 years and who is the Indian child's grandparent, aunt or uncle, brother or sister, brother-in-law or sister-in-law, niece or nephew, first or second cousin, or stepparent and includes the term "relative" as that term is defined in MCL 712A.13a(j).

(8) "Foster home or institution" means a child caring institution as that term is defined in section 1 of 1973 PA 116, MCL 722.111.

(9) "Guardian" means a person who has qualified as a guardian of a minor under a parental or spousal nomination or a court order issued under section 19a or 19c of chapter XIIA, section 5204 or 5205 of the estates and protected individuals code, 1998 PA 386, MCL 700.5204 and 700.5205, or sections 600 to 644 of the mental health code, 1974 PA 258, MCL 330.1600 to 330.1644. Guardian may also include a person appointed by a tribal court under tribal code or custom. Guardian does not include a guardian ad litem.

(10) "Guardian ad litem" means an individual whom the court appoints to assist the court in determining the child's best interests. A guardian ad litem does not need to be an attorney.

(11) "Indian" means any member of any Indian tribe, band, nation, or other organized group or community of Indians recognized as eligible for the services provided to Indians by the secretary because of their status as Indians, including any Alaska native village as defined in section 1602(c) of the Alaska native claims settlement act, 43 USC 1602.

(12) "Indian child" means any unmarried person who is under age 18 and is either
(a) a member of an Indian tribe, or
(b) is eligible for membership in an Indian tribe as determined by that Indian tribe.

(13) "Indian child's tribe" means
(a) the Indian tribe in which an Indian child is a member or eligible for membership, or
(b) in the case of an Indian child who is a member of or eligible for membership in more than one tribe, the Indian tribe with which the Indian child has the most significant contacts.

(14) "Indian child welfare act" means the Indian child welfare act of 1978, 25 USC 1901 to 1963.

(15) "Indian custodian" means any Indian person who has custody of an Indian child under tribal law or custom or under state law, or to whom temporary physical care, custody, and control have been transferred by the child's parent.

(16) "Indian organization" means any group, association, partnership, corporation, or other legal entity owned or controlled by Indians, or a majority of whose members are Indians.

(17) "Indian tribe" means any Indian tribe, band, nation, or other organized group or community of Indians recognized as eligible for the services provided to Indians by the Secretary because of their status as Indians, including any Alaska Native village as defined in section 43 USC 1602(c).

(18) "Lawyer-guardian ad litem" means an attorney appointed under MCL 712B.21 to represent the child with the powers and duties as set forth in MCL 712A.17d. The provisions of MCL 712A.17d also apply to a lawyer-guardian ad litem appointed for the purposes of MIFPA under each of the following:

(a) MCL 700.5213 and 700.5219,

(b) MCL 722.24, and

(c) MCL 722.630.

(19) "Official tribal representative" means an individual who is designated by the Indian child's tribe to represent the tribe in a court overseeing a child custody proceeding. An official tribal representative does not need to be an attorney.

(20) "Parent" means any biological parent or parents of an Indian child or any Indian person who has lawfully adopted an Indian child, including adoptions under tribal law or custom. It does not include the putative father if paternity has not been acknowledged or established.

(21) "Reservation" means Indian country as defined in section 18 USC 1151 and any lands not covered under such section, for which title is either held by the United States in trust for the benefit of any Indian tribe or individual or held by any Indian tribe or individual subject to a restriction by the United States against alienation.

(22) "Secretary" means the Secretary of the Interior.

(23) "Tribal court" means a court with jurisdiction over child custody proceedings and that is either a Court of Indian Offenses, a court established and operated under the code or custom of an Indian tribe, or any other administrative body of a tribe that is vested with authority over child custody proceedings.

(24) "Ward of tribal court" means a child over whom an Indian tribe exercises authority by official action in tribal court or by the governing body of the tribe.

Subchapter 3.100 Debtor-Creditor

Rule 3.101 Garnishment After Judgment

(A) **Definitions**. In this rule,

(1) "plaintiff" refers to any judgment creditor,

(2) "defendant" refers to any judgment debtor,

(3) "garnishee" refers to the garnishee defendant,

(4) "periodic payments" includes but is not limited to, wages, salary, commissions, bonuses, and other income paid to the defendant during the period of the writ; land contract payments; rent; and other periodic debt or contract payments. Interest payments and other payments listed in MCL 600.4012(4)(a)-(d) are not periodic payments.

(B) **Postjudgment Garnishments**.

(1) Periodic garnishments are garnishments of periodic payments, as provided in this rule.

(a) Unless otherwise ordered by the court, a writ of periodic garnishment served on a garnishee who is obligated to make periodic payments to the defendant is effective until the first to occur of the following events:

(i) the amount withheld pursuant to the writ equals the amount of the unpaid judgment, interest, and costs stated in the verified statement in support of the writ;

(ii) the expiration of 182 days after the date the writ was issued;

(iii) the plaintiff files and serves on the defendant and the garnishee a notice that the amount withheld exceeds the remaining unpaid judgment, interest, and costs, or that the judgment has otherwise been satisfied.

(b) The plaintiff may not obtain the issuance of a second writ of garnishment on a garnishee who is obligated to make periodic payments to the defendant while a prior writ served on that garnishee remains in effect relating to the same judgment. The plaintiff may seek a second writ after the first writ expires under subrule (B)(1)(a).

(c) If a writ of periodic garnishment is served on a garnishee who is obligated to make periodic payments to the defendant while another order that has priority under MCL 600.4012(2) is in effect, or if a writ or order with higher priority is served on the garnishee while another writ is in effect, the garnishee is not obligated to withhold payments pursuant to the lower priority writ until the expiration of the higher priority one. However, in the case of garnishment of earnings, the garnishee shall withhold pursuant to the lower priority writ to the extent that the amount being withheld pursuant to the higher priority order is less than the maximum that could be withheld by law pursuant to the lower priority writ (see, e.g., 15 USC 1673). Upon the expiration of the higher priority writ, the lower priority one becomes effective until it would otherwise have expired under subrule (B)(1)(a). The garnishee shall notify the plaintiff of receipt of any higher priority writ or order and provide the information required by subrule (H)(2)(c).

(2) Nonperiodic garnishments are garnishments of property or obligations other than periodic payments.

(C) **Forms**. The state court administrator shall publish approved forms for use in garnishment proceedings. Separate forms shall be used for periodic and nonperiodic garnishments. The verified statement, writ, and disclosure filed in garnishment proceedings must be substantially in the form approved by the state court administrator.

(D) **Request for and Issuance of Writ**. The clerk of the court that entered the judgment shall review the request. The clerk shall issue a writ of garnishment if the writ appears to be correct, complies with these rules and the Michigan statutes, and if the plaintiff, or someone on the plaintiff's behalf, makes and files a statement verified in the manner provided in MCR 2.114(A) stating:

(1) that a judgment has been entered against the defendant and remains unsatisfied;

(2) the amount of the judgment; the total amount of the postjudgment interest accrued to date; the total amount of the postjudgment costs accrued to date; the total amount of the postjudgment payments made to date, and the amount of the unsatisfied judgment now due (including interest and costs);

(3) that the person signing the verified statement knows or has good reason to believe that

(a) a named person has control of property belonging to the defendant,

(b) a named person is indebted to the defendant, or

(c) a named person is obligated to make periodic payments to the defendant.

(E) **Writ of Garnishment**.

(1) The writ of garnishment must have attached or must include a copy of the verified statement requesting issuance of the writ, and must include information that will permit the garnishee to identify the defendant, such as the defendant's address, social security number, employee identification number, federal tax identification number, employer number, or account number, if known.

(2) Upon issuance of the writ, it shall be served upon the garnishee as provided in subrule (F)(1). The writ shall include the date on which it was issued and the last day by which it must be served to be valid, which is 182 days after it was issued.

(3) The writ shall direct the garnishee to:

(a) serve a copy of the writ on the defendant as provided in subrule (F)(2);

(b) within 14 days after the service of the writ, file with the court clerk a verified disclosure indicating the garnishee's liability (as specified in subrule [G][1]) to the defendant and mail or deliver a copy to the plaintiff and the defendant;

(c) deliver no tangible or intangible property to the defendant, unless allowed by statute or court rule;

(d) pay no obligation to the defendant, unless allowed by statute or court rule; and

(e) in the discretion of the court and in accordance with subrule (J), order the garnishee either to

(i) make all payments directly to the plaintiff or

(ii) send the funds to the court in the manner specified in the writ.

(4) The writ shall direct the defendant to refrain from disposing of

[A] any negotiable instrument representing a debt of the garnishee (except the earnings of the defendant), or

[B] any negotiable instrument of title representing property in which the defendant claims an interest held in the possession or control of the garnishee.

(5) The writ shall inform the defendant that unless the defendant files objections within 14 days after the service of the writ on the defendant,

(a) without further notice the property or debt held pursuant to the garnishment may be applied to the satisfaction of the plaintiff's judgment, and

(b) periodic payments due to the defendant may be withheld until the expiration of the writ and in the discretion of the court paid directly to the plaintiff.

(6) The writ shall direct the plaintiff to serve the garnishee as provided in subrule (F)(1), and to file a proof of service.

(F) **Service of Writ**.

(1) The plaintiff shall serve the writ of garnishment, a copy of the writ for the defendant, the disclosure form, and any applicable fees, on the garnishee within 182 days after the date the writ was issued in the manner provided for the service of a summons and complaint in MCR 2.105.

(2) The garnishee shall within 7 days after being served with the writ deliver a copy of the writ to the defendant or mail a copy to the defendant at the defendant's last known address by first class mail.

(G) **Liability of Garnishee**.

(1) Subject to the provisions of the garnishment statute and any setoff permitted by law or these rules, the garnishee is liable for

(a) all tangible or intangible property belonging to the defendant in the garnishee's possession or control when the writ is served on the garnishee, unless the property is represented by a negotiable document of title held by a bona fide purchaser for value other than the defendant;

(b) all negotiable documents of title and all goods represented by negotiable documents of title belonging to the defendant if the documents of title are in the garnishee's possession when the writ is served on the garnishee;

(c) all corporate share certificates belonging to the defendant in the garnishee's possession or control when the writ is served on the garnishee;

(d) all debts, whether or not due, owing by the garnishee to the defendant when the writ is served on the garnishee, except for debts evidenced by negotiable instruments or representing the earnings of the defendant;

(e) all debts owing by the garnishee evidenced by negotiable instruments held or owned by the defendant when the writ of garnishment is served on the defendant, as long as the instruments are brought before the court before their negotiation to a bona fide purchaser for value;

(f) the portion of the defendant's earnings that are not protected from garnishment by law (see, e.g., 15 USC 1673) as provided in subrule (B);

(g) all judgments in favor of the defendant against the garnishee in force when the writ is served on the garnishee;

(h) all tangible or intangible property of the defendant that, when the writ is served on the garnishee, the garnishee holds by conveyance, transfer, or title that is void as to creditors of the defendant, whether or not the defendant could maintain an action against the garnishee to recover the property; and

(i) the value of all tangible or intangible property of the defendant that, before the writ is served on the garnishee, the garnishee received or held by conveyance, transfer, or title that was void as to creditors of the defendant, but that the garnishee no longer held at the time the writ was served, whether or not the defendant could maintain an action against the garnishee for the value of the property.

(2) The garnishee is liable for no more than the amount of the unpaid judgment, interest, and costs as stated in the verified statement requesting the writ of garnishment. Property or debts exceeding that amount may be delivered or paid to the defendant notwithstanding the garnishment.

(H) **Disclosure**. The garnishee shall mail or deliver to the court, the plaintiff, and the defendant, a verified disclosure within 14 days after being served with the writ.

(1) *Nonperiodic Garnishments.*

(a) If indebted to the defendant, the garnishee shall file a disclosure revealing the garnishee's liability to the defendant as specified in subrule (G)(1) and claiming any setoff that the garnishee would have against the defendant, except for claims for unliquidated damages for wrongs or injuries.

(b) If not indebted to the defendant, the garnishee shall file a disclosure so indicating.

(c) If the garnishee is indebted to the defendant, but claims that withholding is exempt under MCR 3.101(I)(6), the garnishee shall indicate on the disclosure the specific exemption. If the garnishee is indebted, but claims that withholding is exempt for some reason other than those set forth in MCR 3.101(I)(6), the garnishee shall indicate on the disclosure the basis for its claim of exemption and cite the legal authority for the exemption.

(2) *Periodic Garnishments.*

(a) If not obligated to make periodic payments to the defendant, the disclosure shall so indicate, and the garnishment shall be considered to have expired.

(b) If obligated to make periodic payments to the defendant, the disclosure shall indicate the nature and frequency of the garnishee's obligation. The information must be disclosed even if money is not owing at the time of the service of the writ.

(c) If a writ or order with a higher priority is in effect, in the disclosure the garnishee shall specify the court that issued the writ or order, the file number of the case in which it was issued, the date it was issued, and the date it was served.

(I) **Withholding**. This subrule applies only if the garnishee is indebted to or obligated to make periodic payments to the defendant.

(1) Except as otherwise provided in this subrule, the writ shall be effective as to obligations owed and property held by the garnishee as of the time the writ is served on the garnishee.

(2) In the case of periodic earnings, withholding shall commence according to the following provisions:

(a) For garnishees with weekly, biweekly, or semimonthly pay periods, withholding shall commence with the first full pay period after the writ was served.

(b) For garnishees with monthly pay periods, if the writ is served on the garnishee within the first 14 days of the pay period, withholding shall commence on the date the writ is served. If the writ is served on the garnishee on or after the 15th day of the pay period, withholding shall commence the first full pay period after the writ was served.

(3) In the case of periodic earnings, withholding shall cease according to the following provisions:
   (a) For garnishees with weekly, biweekly, or semimonthly pay periods, withholding shall cease upon the end of the last full pay period prior to the expiration of the writ.
   (b) For garnishees with monthly pay periods, withholding shall continue until the writ expires.

(4) At the time that a periodic payment is withheld, the garnishee shall provide the following information to the plaintiff and defendant:
   (a) the name of the parties;
   (b) the case number;
   (c) the date and amount withheld;
   (d) the balance due on the writ.

   The information shall also be provided to the court if funds are sent to the court.

(5) If funds have not been withheld because a higher priority writ or order was in effect, and the higher priority writ ceases to be effective before expiration of the lower priority one, the garnishee shall begin withholding pursuant to the lower priority writ as of the date of the expiration of the higher priority writ.

(6) A bank or other financial institution, as garnishee, shall not withhold exempt funds of the debtor from an account into which only exempt funds are directly deposited and where such funds are clearly identifiable upon deposit as exempt Social Security benefits, Supplemental Security Income benefits, Railroad Retirement benefits, Black Lung benefits, or Veterans Assistance benefits.

(J) **Payment**.

(1) After 28 days from the date of the service of the writ on the garnishee, the garnishee shall transmit all withheld funds to the plaintiff or the court as directed by the court pursuant to subrule (E)(3)(e) unless notified that objections have been filed.

(2) For periodic garnishments, all future payments shall be paid as they become due as directed by the court pursuant to subrule (E)(3)(e) until expiration of the garnishment.

(3) Upon receipt of proceeds from the writ, the court shall forward such proceeds to the plaintiff.

(4) Payment to the plaintiff may not exceed the amount of the unpaid judgment, interest, and costs stated in the verified statement requesting the writ of garnishment. If the plaintiff claims to be entitled to a larger amount, the plaintiff must proceed by motion with notice to the defendant.

(5) In the case of earnings, the garnishee shall maintain a record of all payment calculations and shall make such information available for review by the plaintiff, the defendant, or the court, upon request.

(6) For periodic garnishments, within 14 days after the expiration of the writ or after the garnishee is no longer obligated to make periodic payments, the garnishee shall file with the court and mail or deliver to the plaintiff and the defendant, a final statement of the total amount paid on the writ. If the garnishee is the defendant's employer, the statement is to be filed within 14 days after the expiration of the writ, regardless of changes in employment status during the time that the writ was in effect. The statement shall include the following information:
   (a) the names of the parties and the court in which the case is pending;
   (b) the case number;
   (c) the date of the statement;
   (d) the total amount withheld;
   (e) the difference between the amount stated in the verified statement requesting the writ and the amount withheld.

(7) If the disclosure states that the garnishee holds property other than money belonging to the defendant, the plaintiff must proceed by motion (with notice to the defendant and the garnishee) to seek an appropriate order regarding application of the property to satisfaction of the judgment. If there are no pending objections to the garnishment, and the plaintiff has not filed such a motion within 56 days after the filing of the disclosure, the garnishment is dissolved and the garnishee may release the property to the defendant.

(K) **Objections**.

(1) Objections shall be filed with the court within 14 days of the date of service of the writ on the defendant. Objections may be filed after the time provided in this subrule but do not suspend payment pursuant to subrule (J) unless ordered by the court. Objections may only be based on defects in or the invalidity of the garnishment proceeding itself, and may not be used to challenge the validity of the judgment previously entered.

(2) Objections shall be based on one or more of the following:
   (a) the funds or property are exempt from garnishment by law;
   (b) garnishment is precluded by the pendency of bankruptcy proceedings;
   (c) garnishment is barred by an installment payment order;
   (d) garnishment is precluded because the maximum amount permitted by law is being withheld pursuant to a higher priority garnishment or order;
   (e) the judgment has been paid;
   (f) the garnishment was not properly issued or is otherwise invalid.

(3) Within 7 days of the filing of objections, notice of the date of hearing on the objections shall be sent to the plaintiff, the defendant, and the garnishee. The hearing date shall be within 21 days of the date the objections are filed. In district court, notice shall be sent by the court. In circuit and probate court, notice shall be sent by the objecting party.

(4) The court shall notify the plaintiff, the defendant, and the garnishee of the court's decision.

(L) **Steps After Disclosure; Third Parties; Interpleader; Discovery.**

(1) Within 14 days after service of the disclosure, the plaintiff may serve the garnishee with written interrogatories or notice the deposition of the garnishee. The answers to the interrogatories or the deposition testimony becomes part of the disclosure.

(2) If the garnishee's disclosure declares that a named person other than the defendant and the plaintiff claims all or part of the disclosed indebtedness or property, the court may order that the claimant be added as a defendant in the garnishment action under MCR 2.207. The garnishee may proceed under MCR 3.603 as in interpleader actions, and other claimants may move to intervene under MCR 2.209.

(3) The discovery rules apply to garnishment proceedings.

(4) The filing of a disclosure, the filing of answers to interrogatories, or the personal appearance by or on behalf of the garnishee at a deposition does not waive the garnishee's right to question the court's jurisdiction, the validity of the proceeding, or the plaintiff's right to judgment.

(M) **Determination of Garnishee's Liability**.

(1) If there is a dispute regarding the garnishee's liability or if another person claims an interest in the garnishee's property or obligation, the issue shall be tried in the same manner as other civil actions.

(2) The verified statement acts as the plaintiff's complaint against the garnishee, and the disclosure serves as the answer. The facts stated in the disclosure must be accepted as true unless the plaintiff has served interrogatories or noticed a deposition within the time allowed by subrule (L)(1) or another party has filed a pleading or motion denying the accuracy of the disclosure. Except as the facts stated in the verified statement are admitted by the disclosure, they are denied. Admissions have the effect of admissions in responsive pleadings. The defendant and other claimants added under subrule (L)(2) may plead their claims and defenses as in other civil actions. The garnishee's liability to the plaintiff shall be tried on the issues thus framed.

(3) Even if the amount of the garnishee's liability is disputed, the plaintiff may move for judgment against the garnishee to the extent of the admissions in the disclosure. The general motion practice rules govern notice (including notice to the garnishee and the defendant) and hearing on the motion.

(4) The issues between the plaintiff and the garnishee will be tried by the court unless a party files a demand for a jury trial within 7 days after the filing of the disclosure, answers to interrogatories, or deposition transcript, whichever is filed last. The defendant or a third party waives any right to a jury trial unless a demand for a jury is filed with the pleading stating the claim.

(5) On the trial of the garnishee's liability, the plaintiff may offer the record of the garnishment proceeding and other evidence. The garnishee may offer evidence not controverting the disclosure, or in the discretion of the court, may show error or mistakes in the disclosure.

(6) If the court determines that the garnishee is indebted to the defendant, but the time for payment has not arrived, a judgment may not be entered until after the time of maturity stated in the verdict or finding.

(N) **Orders for Installment Payments**.

(1) An order for installment payments under MCL 600.6201 et eq. suspends the effectiveness of a writ of garnishment of periodic payments for work and labor performed by the defendant from the time the order is served on the garnishee. An order for installment payments does not suspend the effectiveness of a writ of garnishment of nonperiodic payments or of an income tax refund or credit.

(2) If an order terminating the installment payment order is entered and served on the garnishee, the writ again becomes effective and remains in force until it would have expired if the installment payment order had never been entered.

(O) **Judgment and Execution**.

(1) Judgment may be entered against the garnishee for the payment of money or the delivery of specific property as the facts warrant. A money judgment against the garnishee may not be entered in an amount greater than the amount of the unpaid judgment, interest, and costs as stated in the verified statement requesting the writ of garnishment. Judgment for specific property may be enforced only to the extent necessary to satisfy the judgment against the defendant.

(2) The judgment against the garnishee discharges the garnishee from all demands by the defendant for the money paid or property delivered in satisfaction of the judgment. If the garnishee is sued by the defendant for anything done under the provisions of

these garnishment rules, the garnishee may introduce as evidence the judgment and the satisfaction.

(3) If the garnishee is chargeable for specific property that the garnishee holds for or is bound to deliver to the defendant, judgment may be entered and execution issued against the interest of the defendant in the property for no more than is necessary to satisfy the judgment against the defendant. The garnishee must deliver the property to the officer serving the execution, who shall sell, apply, and account as in other executions.

(4) If the garnishee is found to be under contract for the delivery of specific property to the defendant, judgment may be entered and execution issued against the interest of the defendant in the property for no more than is necessary to satisfy the judgment against the defendant. The garnishee must deliver the property to the officer serving the execution according to the terms of the contract. The officer shall sell, apply, and account as in ordinary execution.

(5) If the garnishee is chargeable for specific property and refuses to expose it so that execution may be levied on it, the court may order the garnishee to show cause why general execution should not issue against the garnishee. Unless sufficient cause is shown to the contrary, the court may order that an execution be issued against the garnishee in an amount not to exceed twice the value of the specifically chargeable property.

(6) The court may issue execution against the defendant for the full amount due the plaintiff on the judgment against the defendant. Execution against the garnishee may not be ordered by separate writ, but must always be ordered by endorsement on or by incorporation within the writ of execution against the defendant. The court may order additional execution to satisfy the plaintiff's judgment as justice requires.

(7) Satisfaction of all or part of the judgment against the garnishee constitutes satisfaction of a judgment to the same extent against the defendant.

(P) **Appeals**. A judgment or order in a garnishment proceeding may be set aside or appealed in the same manner and with the same effect as judgments or orders in other civil actions.

(Q) **Receivership**.

(1) If on disclosure or trial of a garnishee's liability, it appears that when the writ was served the garnishee possessed,

(a) a written promise for the payment of money or the delivery of property belonging to the defendant, or

(b) personal property belonging to the defendant, the court may order the garnishee to deliver it to a person appointed as receiver.

(2) The receiver must

(a) collect the written promise for payment of money or for the delivery of property and apply the proceeds on any judgment in favor of the plaintiff against the garnishee and pay any surplus to the garnishee, and

(b) dispose of the property in an amount greater than any encumbrance on it can be obtained, and after paying the amount of the encumbrance, apply the balance to the plaintiff's judgment against the garnishee and pay any surplus to the garnishee.

(3) If the garnishee refuses to comply with the delivery order, the garnishee is liable for the amount of the written promise for the payment of money, the value of the promise for the delivery of property, or the value of the defendant's interest in the encumbered personal property. The facts of the refusal and the valuation must be included in the receiver's report to the court.

(4) The receiver shall report all actions pertaining to the promise or property to the court. The report must include a description and valuation of any property, with the valuation to be ascertained by appraisal on oath or in a manner the court may direct.

(R) **Costs and Fees**.

(1) Costs and fees are as provided by law or these rules.

(2) If the garnishee is not indebted to the defendant, does not hold any property subject to garnishment, and is not the defendant's employer, the plaintiff is not entitled to recover the costs of that garnishment.

(S) **Failure to Disclose or to Do Other Acts; Default; Contempt**.

(1) If the garnishee fails to disclose or do a required act within the time limit imposed, a default may be taken as in other civil actions. A default judgment against a garnishee may not exceed the amount of the garnishee's liability as provided in subrule (G)(2).

(2) If the garnishee fails to comply with the court order, the garnishee may be adjudged in contempt of court.

(3) In addition to other actions permitted by law or these rules, the court may impose costs on a garnishee whose default or contempt results in expense to other parties. Costs imposed shall include reasonable attorney fees and shall not be less than $100.

(T) **Judicial Discretion**. On motion the court may by order extend the time for:

(1) the garnishee's disclosure;

(2) the plaintiff's filing of written interrogatories;

(3) the plaintiff's filing of a demand for oral examination of the garnishee;
(4) the garnishee's answer to written interrogatories;
(5) the garnishee's appearance for oral examination; and
(6) the demand for jury trial.
The order must be filed with the court and served on the other parties.

Rule 3.102 Garnishment Before Judgment

(A) **Availability of Prejudgment Garnishment.**
(1) After commencing an action on a contract, the plaintiff may obtain a prejudgment writ of garnishment under the circumstances and by the procedures provided in this rule.
(2) Except as provided in subrule (A)(3), a prejudgment garnishment may not be used
(a) unless the defendant is subject to the jurisdiction of the court under chapter 7 of the Revised Judicature Act, MCL 600.701 et seq.;
(b) to garnish a defendant's earnings; or
(c) to garnish property held or an obligation owed by the state or a governmental unit of the state.
(3) This rule also applies to a prejudgment garnishment in an action brought to enforce a foreign judgment. However, the following provisions apply:
(a) The defendant need not be subject to the court's jurisdiction;
(b) The request for garnishment must show that
(i) the defendant is indebted to the plaintiff on a foreign judgment in a stated amount in excess of all setoffs;
(ii) the defendant is not subject to the jurisdiction of the state, or that after diligent effort the plaintiff cannot serve the defendant with process; and
(iii) the person making the request knows or has good reason to believe that a named person
[A] has control of property belonging to the defendant, or
[B] is indebted to the defendant.
(c) Subrule (H) does not apply.

(B) **Request for Garnishment**. After commencing an action, the plaintiff may seek a writ of garnishment by filing an ex parte motion supported by a verified statement setting forth specific facts showing that:
(1) the defendant is indebted to the plaintiff on a contract in a stated amount in excess of all setoffs;
(2) the defendant is subject to the jurisdiction of the state;
(3) after diligent effort the plaintiff cannot serve the defendant with process; and
(4) the person signing the statement knows or has good reason to believe that a named person
(a) has control of property belonging to the defendant, or
(b) is indebted to the defendant.
On a finding that the writ is available under this rule and that the verified statement states a sufficient basis for issuance of the writ, the judge to whom the action is assigned may issue the writ.

(C) **Writ of Garnishment**. The writ of garnishment must have attached or include a copy of the verified statement, and must:
(1) direct the garnishee to:
(a) file with the court clerk within 14 days after the service of the writ on him or her a verified disclosure indicating his or her liability (as specified in subrule [E]) to the defendant;
(b) deliver no tangible or intangible property to the defendant, unless allowed by statute or court rule;
(c) pay no obligation to the defendant, unless allowed by statute or court rule; and
(d) promptly provide the defendant with a copy of the writ and verified statement by personal delivery or by first class mail directed to the defendant's last known address;
(2) direct the defendant to refrain from disposing of any negotiable instrument representing a debt of the garnishee or of any negotiable instrument of titlerepresenting property in which he or she claims an interest held in the possession or control of the garnishee;
(3) inform the defendant that unless the defendant files objections within 14 days after service of the writ on the defendant, or appears and submits to the jurisdiction of the court, an order may enter requiring the garnishee to deliver the garnished property or pay the obligation to be applied to the satisfaction of the plaintiff's claim; and
(4) command the process server to serve the writ and to file a proof of service.

(D) **Service of Writ**. MCR 3.101(F) applies to prejudgment garnishment.

(E) **Liability of Garnishee**. MCR 3.101(G) applies to prejudgment garnishment except that the earnings of the defendant may not be garnished before judgment.

(F) **Disclosure**. The garnishee shall file and serve a disclosure as provided in MCR 3.101(H).

(G) **Payment or Deposit Into Court**. MCR 3.101(I) and (J) apply to prejudgment garnishment, except that payment may not be made to the plaintiff until after entry of judgment, as provided in subrule (I).

(H) **Objection; Dissolution of Prejudgment Garnishment**. Objections to and dissolution of a prejudgment garnishment are governed by MCR 3.101(K) and MCR 3.103(H).

(I) **Proceedings After Judgment.**
  (1) If the garnishment remains in effect until entry of judgment in favor of the plaintiff against the defendant, the garnished property or obligation may be applied to the satisfaction of the judgment in the manner provided in MCR 3.101(I), (J), (M), and (O).
  (2) MCR 3.101(P) and (Q) and MCR 3.103(I)(2) apply to prejudgment garnishment.

(J) **Costs and Fees; Default; Contempt; Judicial Discretion**. MCR 3.101(R), (S), and (T) apply to prejudgment garnishment.

Rule 3.103 Attachment

(A) **Availability of Writ**. After commencing an action, the plaintiff may obtain a writ of attachment under the circumstances and by the procedures provided in this rule. Except in an action brought on a foreign judgment, attachment may not be used unless the defendant is subject to the jurisdiction of the court under chapter 7 of the Revised Judicature Act. MCL 600.701 et seq.

(B) **Motion for Writ.**
  (1) The plaintiff may seek a writ of attachment by filing an ex parte motion supported by an affidavit setting forth specific facts showing that
    (a) at the time of the execution of the affidavit the defendant is indebted to the plaintiff in a stated amount on a contract in excess of all setoffs,
    (b) the defendant is subject to the judicial jurisdiction of the state, and
    (c) after diligent effort the plaintiff cannot serve the defendant with process.

  In an action brought on a tort claim or a foreign judgment, subrules (B)(2) and (3), respectively, apply.
  (2) In a tort action the following provisions apply:
    (a) Instead of the allegations required by subrule (B)(1)(a), the affidavit in support of the motion must describe the injury claimed and state that the affiant in good faith believes that the defendant is liable to the plaintiff in a stated amount. The other requirements of subrule (B)(1) apply.
    (b) If the writ is issued the court shall specify the amount or value of property to be attached.
  (3) In an action brought on a foreign judgment, instead of the allegations required by subrule (B)(1), the affidavit in support of the motion must show that
    (a) the defendant is indebted to the plaintiff on a foreign judgment in a stated amount in excess of all setoffs,
    (b) the defendant is not subject to the jurisdiction of the state or that after diligent effort the plaintiff cannot serve the defendant with process.

(C) **Issuance of Writ.**
  (1) On a finding that the writ is available under this rule and that the affidavit states a sufficient basis for issuance of the writ, the judge to whom the action is assigned may issue the writ.
  (2) The judge's order shall specify what further steps, if any, must be taken by the plaintiff to notify the defendant of the action and the attachment.

(D) **Contents of Writ**. The writ of attachment must command the sheriff or other officer to whom it is directed
  (1) to attach so much of the defendant's real and personal property not exempt from execution as is necessary to satisfy the plaintiff's demand and costs, and
  (2) to keep the property in a secure place to satisfy any judgment that may be recovered by the plaintiff in the action until further order of the court.

(E) **Execution of Writ; Subsequent Attachments.**
  (1) The sheriff or other officer to whom a writ of attachment is directed shall execute the writ by seizing and holding so much of the defendant's property not exempt from execution, wherever found within the county, as is necessary to satisfy the plaintiff's demand and costs. If insufficient property is seized, then the officer shall seize other property of the defendant not exempt from execution, wherever found within Michigan, as is necessary when added to that already seized, to satisfy the plaintiff's demand and costs. The property seized must be inventoried by the officer and appraised by two disinterested residents of the county in which the property was seized. After being sworn under oath to make a true appraisal, the appraisers shall make and sign an appraisal. The inventory and appraisal must be filed and a copy served on the parties under MCR 2.107.
  (2) In subsequent attachments of the same property while in the hands of the officer, the original inventory and appraisal satisfy the requirement of subrule (E)(1).

(F) **Attachment of Realty; Stock.**
  (1) The officer may seize an interest in real estate by depositing a certified copy of the writ of attachment, including a description of the land affected, with the register of deeds for the county in which the land is located. It is not necessary that the officer enter on the land or be within view of it.
  (2) Shares of stock or the interest of a stockholder in a domestic corporation must be seized in the manner provided for the seizure of that property on execution.

(G) **Animals or Perishable Property; Sale; Distribution of Proceeds.**
  (1) When any of the property attached consists of animals or perishable property, the court may order

the property sold and the money from the sale brought into court, to await the order of the court.

(2) After the order for a sale is entered, the officer having the property shall advertise and sell it in the manner that personal property of like character is required to be advertised and sold on execution. The officer shall deposit the proceeds with the clerk of the court in which the action is pending.

(3) If the plaintiff recovers judgment, the court may order the money paid to the plaintiff. If the judgment is entered against the plaintiff or the suit is dismissed or the attachment is dissolved, the court shall order the money paid to the defendant or other person entitled to it.

(H) **Dissolution of Attachment.**

(1) Except in an action brought on a foreign judgment, if the defendant submits to the jurisdiction of the court, the court shall dissolve the attachment.

(2) A person who owns, possesses, or has an interest in attached property may move at any time to dissolve the attachment. The defendant may move to dissolve the attachment without submitting to the jurisdiction of the court.

(a) When a motion for dissolution of attachment is filed, the court shall enter an order setting a time and place for hearing the motion, and may issue subpoenas to compel witnesses to attend.

(b) The plaintiff must be served with notice under MCR 2.107 at least 3 days before the hearing unless the court's order prescribes a different notice requirement.

(c) At the hearing, the proofs are heard in the same manner as in a nonjury trial. If the court decides that the defendant was not subject to the jurisdiction of the state or that the property was not subject to or was exempt from attachment, it shall dissolve the attachment and restore the property to the defendant, and the attachment may be dissolved for any other sufficient reason. The court may order the losing party to pay the costs of the dissolution proceeding.

(3) If the action is dismissed or judgment is entered for the defendant, the attachment is dissolved.

(I) **Satisfaction of Judgment.**

(1) If the attachment remains in effect until the entry of judgment against the defendant, the attached property may be applied to the satisfaction of the judgment, including interest and costs, in the same manner as in the case of an execution.

(2) If the court does not acquire personal jurisdiction over the defendant, either by service or by the defendant's appearance, a judgment against the defendant is not binding beyond the value of the attached property.

Rule 3.104 Installment Payment Orders

(A) **Motion for Installment Payment Order**. A party against whom a money judgment has been entered may move for entry of an order permitting the judgment to be paid in installments in accordance with MCL 600.6201 et seq. A copy of the motion must be served on the plaintiff, by the clerk of the court in district court and by the party who filed the objection in circuit or probate court.

(B) **Consideration of Motion**. The motion will be granted without further hearing unless the plaintiff files, and serves on the defendant, written objections within 14 days after the service date of the defendant's motion. If objections are filed, the clerk must promptly present the motion and objections to the court. The court will decide the motion based on the papers filed or notify the parties that a hearing will be required. Unless the court schedules the hearing, the moving party is responsible for noticing the motion for hearing.

(C) **Failure to Comply with Installment Order**. If the defendant fails to make payments pursuant to the order for installment payments, the plaintiff may file and serve on the defendant a motion to set aside the order for installment payments. Unless a hearing is requested within 14 days after service of the motion, the order to set aside the order for installment payments will be entered.

(D) **Request After Failure to Comply with Previous Order**. If the defendant moves for an order for installment payments within 91 days after a previous installment order has been set aside, unless good cause is shown the court shall assess costs against the defendant as a condition of entry of the new order.

Rule 3.105 Claim and Delivery

(A) **Nature of Action; Replevin**. Claim and delivery is a civil action to recover

(1) possession of goods or chattels which have been unlawfully taken or unlawfully detained, and

(2) damages sustained by the unlawful taking or unlawful detention.

A statutory reference to the action of replevin is to be construed as a reference to the action of claim and delivery.

(B) **Rules Applicable**. A claim and delivery action is governed by the rules applicable to other civil actions, except as provided in MCL 600.2920, and this rule.

(C) **Complaint; Joinder of Claims; Interim Payments**. A claim and delivery complaint must:

(1) specifically describe the property claimed;

(2) state the value of the property claimed (which will be used only to set the amount of bond and not as an admission of value);

(3) state if the property claimed is an independent piece of property or a portion of divisible property of uniform kind, quality, and value; and

(4) specifically describe the nature of the claim and the basis for the judgment requested.

If the action is based on a security agreement, a claim for the debt may be joined as a separate count in the complaint. If the plaintiff, while the action is pending, receives interim payments equal to the amount originally claimed, the action must be dismissed.

(D) **Answer**. An answer to a claim and delivery complaint may concede the claim for possession and yet contest any other claim.

(E) **Possession Pending Final Judgment**.

(1) *Motion for Possession Pending Final Judgment.* After the complaint is filed, the plaintiff may file a verified motion requesting possession pending final judgment. The motion must

(a) describe the property to be seized, and

(b) state sufficient facts to show that the property described will be damaged, destroyed, concealed, disposed of, or used so as to substantially impair its value, before final judgment unless the property is taken into custody by court order.

(2) *Court Order Pending Hearing.* After a motion for possession pending final judgment is filed, the court, if good cause is shown, must order the defendant to

(a) refrain from damaging, destroying, concealing, disposing of, or using so as to substantially impair its value, the property until further order of the court; and

(b) appear before the court at a specified time to answer the motion.

(3) *Hearing on Motion for Possession Pending Final Judgment.*

(a) At least 7 days before a hearing on a motion filed under this subrule, the defendant must be served with

(i) a copy of the motion; and

(ii) an order entered under subrule (E)(2).

(b) At the hearing, each party may present proofs. To obtain possession before judgment, the plaintiff must establish

(i) that the plaintiff's right to possession is probably valid; and

(ii) that the property will be damaged, destroyed, concealed, disposed of, or used so as to substantially impair its value, before trial.

(c) Adjournment. A court may not

(i) grant an adjournment of this hearing on the basis that a defendant has not yet answered the complaint or the motion filed under this subrule; or

(ii) allow a hearing on this motion if the hearing date has been adjourned more than 56 days with the assent of the plaintiff, unless the plaintiff files a new motion which includes recitations of any payments made by the defendant after the original motion was filed.

(4) *Order for Custody Pending Final Judgment.* After proofs have been taken on the plaintiff's motion for possession pending final judgment, the court may order whatever relief the evidence requires. This includes:

(a) denying the motion;

(b) leaving the defendant in possession of the property and restraining the defendant from damaging, destroying, concealing, or disposing of the property. The court may condition the defendant's continued possession by requiring the defendant to

(i) furnish a penalty bond, payable to the plaintiff, of not less than $100 and at least twice the value of the property stated in the complaint; and

(ii) agree that he or she will surrender the property to the person adjudged entitled to possession and will pay any money that may be recovered against him or her in the action;

(c) ordering the sheriff or court officer to seize the property within 21 days and either hold it or deliver it to the plaintiff. The court may condition the plaintiff's possession by requiring the plaintiff to

(i) furnish a penalty bond payable to the defendant, and to the sheriff or court officer, of not less than $100 and at least twice the value of the property stated in the complaint; and

(ii) agree that he or she will surrender the property to the person adjudged entitled to possession, diligently prosecute the suit to final judgment, and pay any money that may be recovered against him or her in the action.

A bond required in a claim and delivery action must be approved by and filed with the court within the time the order provides.

(F) **Seizure**. A copy of an order issued under subrule (E)(4)(c) must be delivered to the sheriff or court officer, who must

(1) seize the property described in the order;

(2) serve a copy of the order on the defendant, under MCR 2.107; and

(3) file a return with the court showing seizure and service.

(G) **Custody; Delivery**. After seizing the property, the sheriff or court officer shall keep it in a secure place and deliver it in accordance with the court order. The sheriff or court officer is entitled to receive the lawful fees for seizing the property and the necessary expenses for seizing and keeping it.

(H) **Judgment**.

(1) The judgment must determine

(a) the party entitled to possession of the property,

(b) the value of the property,

(c) the amount of any unpaid debt, and

(d) any damages to be awarded.

(2) If the property is not in the possession of the party who is entitled to possession, a judgment must order the property to be immediately delivered to that party.

(3) If the action is tried on the merits, the value of the property and the damages are determined by the trier of fact.

(4) If the defendant has been deprived of the property by a prejudgment order and the main action is dismissed, the defendant may apply to the court for default judgment under MCR 2.603.

(5) If the plaintiff takes a default judgment, the value of the property and the damages are determined under MCR 2.603. A defendant who appeared at a show-cause proceeding is deemed to have filed an appearance.

(6) The party adjudged entitled to possession of the property described may elect to take judgment for the value of the property instead of possession. The judgment value may not exceed the unpaid debt, if any, secured by such property.

(7) The liability of a surety on a bond given under this rule may be determined on motion under MCR 3.604.

(I) **Costs**. Costs may be taxed in the discretion of the court. Costs may include the cost of a bond required by the court, and the costs of seizing and keeping the property.

(J) **Execution**.

(1) The execution issued on a judgment in a claim and delivery action must command the sheriff or court officer

(a) to levy the prevailing party's damages and costs on the property of the opposite party, as in other executions against property; and

(b) if the property described in the judgment is found in the possession of the defendant, to seize the property described in the judgment and deliver it to the prevailing party; or, if the property is not found in the possession of the defendant, to levy the value of it. The value may not exceed the total of the unpaid debt, costs, and damages.

(2) Execution may not issue on a judgment in a claim and delivery action if more than 28 days have passed from the signing of the judgment, unless

(a) the plaintiff files a motion for execution which must include, if money has been paid on the judgment, the amount paid and the conditions under which it was accepted; and

(b) a hearing is held after the defendant has been given notice and an opportunity to appear.

Rule 3.106 Procedures Regarding Orders for the Seizure of Property and Orders of Eviction

(A) **Scope of Rule**. This rule applies to orders for the seizure of property and orders of eviction.

(B) **Persons Who May Seize Property or Conduct Evictions**. The persons who may seize property or conduct evictions are those persons named in MCR 2.103(B), and they are subject to the provisions of this rule unless a provision or a statute specifies otherwise.

(1) A court may provide that property shall be seized and evictions conducted only by

(a) court officers and bailiffs serving that court;

(b) sheriffs and deputy sheriffs;

(c) officers of the Department of State Police in an action in which the state is a party; and

(d) police officers of an incorporated city or village in an action in which the city or village is a party.

(2) Each court must post, in a public place at the court, a list of those persons who are serving as court officers or bailiffs. The court must provide the State Court Administrative Office with a copy of the list, and must notify the State Court Administrative Office of any changes.

(C) **Appointment of Court Officers**. Court officers may be appointed by a court for a term not to exceed 2 years.

(1) The appointment shall be made by the chief judge. Two or more chief judges may jointly appoint court officers for their respective courts.

(2) The appointing court must specify the nature of the court officer's employment relationship at the time of appointment.

(3) The appointing court must maintain a copy of each court officer's application, as required by the State Court Administrative Office.

(4) The State Court Administrative Office shall develop a procedure for the appointment and supervision of court officers, including a model application form. Considerations shall include, but are not limited to, an applicant's character, experience, and references.

(D) **Conditions of Service as a Court Officer or Bailiff**. Court officers and bailiffs must

(1) post a surety bond pursuant to MCR 8.204;

(2) provide the names and addresses of all financial institutions in which they deposit funds obtained

under this rule, and the respective account numbers; and

(3) provide the names and addresses of those persons who regularly provide services to them in the seizure of property or evictions.

(E) **Forms**. The State Court Administrative Office shall publish forms approved for use with regard to the procedures described in this rule.

(F) **Procedures Generally**.

(1) All persons specified in MCR 2.103(B) must carry and display identification authorized by the court or the agency that they serve.

(2) A copy of the order for seizure of property or eviction shall be served on the defendant or the defendant's agent, or left or posted on the premises in a conspicuous place. If property is seized from any other location, a copy of the order shall be mailed to the defendant's last known address.

(G) **Procedures Regarding Orders for Seizure of Property**.

(1) Orders for seizure of property shall be issued pursuant to statute and endorsed upon receipt.

(2) No funds may be collected pursuant to an order for seizure of property prior to service under subrule (F)(2).

(3) An inventory and receipt shall be prepared upon seizure of property or payment of funds.

(a) The original shall be filed with the court within 7 days of the seizure or payment.

(b) A copy shall be

(i) provided to the parties or their respective attorneys or agents and posted on the premises in a conspicuous place; if the property is seized from any other location, a copy shall be mailed to the nonprevailing party's last known address, and

(ii) retained by the person who seized the property.

(4) Property seized shall be disposed of according to law.

(5) Within 21 days, and as directed by the court, any money that is received shall be paid to the court or deposited in a trust account for payment to the prevailing party or that party's attorney.

(6) Costs allowed by statute shall be paid according to law.

(a) Copies of all bills and receipts for service shall be retained for one year by the person serving the order.

(b) Statutory collection fees shall be paid in proportion to the amount received.

(c) There shall be no payment except as provided by law.

(7) Within 14 days after the expiration of the order or satisfaction of judgment, whichever is first, the following shall be filed with the court and a copy provided to the prevailing party or that party's attorney:

(a) a report summarizing collection activities, including an accounting of all money or property collected,

(b) a report that collection activities will continue pursuant to statute, if applicable, or

(c) a report that no collection activity occurred.

(H) **Procedures Regarding Orders of Eviction**. Copies of all bills and receipts for services shall be retained by the person serving the order for one year.

Rule 3.110 Stockholders' Liability Proceedings

(A) **Scope of Rule**. This rule applies to actions brought under MCL 600.2909.

(B) **When Action May Be Brought**. An action against stockholders in which it is claimed that they are individually liable for debts of a corporation may not be brought until:

(1) a judgment has been recovered against the corporation for the indebtedness;

(2) an execution on the judgment has been issued to the county in which the corporation has its principal office or carries on its business; and

(3) the execution has been returned unsatisfied in whole or in part.

(C) **Order for List of Stockholders**. When the conditions set out in subrule (B) are met, the plaintiff may apply to the court that entered the judgment to order a list of stockholders. The court shall enter an order to be served on the secretary or other proper officer of the corporation, requiring the officer, within the time provided in the order, to file a statement under oath listing the names and addresses of all persons who appear by the corporation books to have been, or who the officer has reason to believe were, stockholders when the debt accrued, and the amount of stock held by each of them.

(D) **Commencement of Action; Complaint**. An action against the stockholders to impose personal liability on them for the debt of the corporation may be commenced and carried on as other civil actions under these rules. The complaint must, among other things, state:

(1) that the plaintiff has obtained a judgment against the corporation and the amount;

(2) that execution has been issued and returned unsatisfied in whole or in part, and the amount remaining unpaid;

(3) that the persons named as defendants are the persons listed in the statement filed by the officer of the corporation under subrule (C);

(4) the amount of stock held by each defendant, or that the plaintiff could not, with reasonable diligence, ascertain the amounts;

(5) the consideration received by the corporation for the debt on which judgment was rendered;

(6) a request for judgment against the stockholders in favor of the plaintiff for the amount alleged to be due from the corporation.

(E) **Judgment Against Corporation As Evidence**. At the trial the judgment against the corporation and the amount remaining unpaid are prima facie evidence of the amount due to the plaintiff but are not evidence that the debt on which the judgment was rendered is one for which the defendants are personally liable.

(F) **Entry of Judgment Against Defendant**. If a defendant admits the facts set forth in the complaint or defaults by failing to answer, or if the issues are determined against the defendant, judgment may be entered against him or her for the amount of the judgment against the corporation remaining unpaid, on proof that the debt is one for which that defendant is personally liable as a stockholder.

(G) **Order of Apportionment; Execution**. After judgment has been entered against all or some of the defendants, the court may apportion among these defendants the sum for which they have been adjudged liable pro rata according to the stock held by each. If any defendant fails to pay the amount apportioned against that defendant within 21 days, execution may issue as in other civil actions.

(H) **Reapportionment**. If execution is returned unsatisfied in whole or in part against any of the defendants as to whom apportionment has been made, the court has the power and the duty on application by the plaintiff to reapportion the sum remaining uncollected on the basis of subrule (G) among the remaining defendants adjudged liable. Execution may issue for the collection of these amounts.

(I) **Contribution Among Stockholders**. A stockholder who has been compelled to pay more than his or her pro rata share of the debts of the corporation, according to the amount of stock held, is entitled to contribution from other stockholders who are also liable for the debt and who have not paid their portions.

Subchapter 3.200 Domestic Relations Actions

Rule 3.201 Applicability of Rules

(A) Subchapter 3.200 applies to
  (1) actions for divorce, separate maintenance, the annulment of marriage, the affirmation of marriage, paternity, family support under MCL 552.451 et seq., the custody of minors under MCL 722.21 et seq., and visitation with minors under MCL 722.27b, and to
  (2) proceedings that are ancillary or subsequent to the actions listed in subrule (A)(1) and that relate to
    (a) the custody of minors,
    (b) visitation with minors, or
    (c) the support of minors and spouses or former spouses.

(B) As used in this subchapter with regard to child support, the terms "minor" or "child" may include children who have reached the age of majority, in the circumstances where the legislature has so provided.

(C) Except as otherwise provided in this subchapter, practice and procedure in domestic relations actions is governed by other applicable provisions of the Michigan Court Rules.

(D) When used in this subchapter, unless the context otherwise indicates:
  (1) "Case" means an action initiated in the family division of the circuit court by:
    (a) submission of an original complaint, petition, or citation;
    (b) acceptance of transfer of an action from another court or tribunal; or
    (c) filing or registration of a foreign judgment or order.
  (2) "File" means the repository for collection of the pleadings and other documents and materials related to a case. A file may include more than one case involving a family.
  (3) "Jurisdiction" means the authority of the court to hear cases and make decisions and enter orders on cases.

Rule 3.202 Capacity to Sue

(A) **Minors and Incompetent Persons**. Except as provided in subrule (B), minors and incompetent persons may sue and be sued as provided in MCR 2.201.

(B) **Emancipated Minors**. An emancipated minor may sue and be sued in the minor's own name, as provided in MCL 722.4e(1)(b).

Rule 3.203 Service of Notice and Court Papers in Domestic Relations Cases

(A) **Manner of Service**. Unless otherwise required by court rule or statute, the summons and complaint must be served pursuant to MCR 2.105. In cases in which the court retains jurisdiction
  (1) notice must be provided as set forth in the statute requiring the notice. Unless otherwise required by court rule or statute, service by mail shall be to a party's last known mailing address, and
  (2) court papers and notice for which the statute or court rule does not specify the manner of service must be served as provided in MCR 2.107, except that service by mail shall be to a party's last known mailing address.

(B) **Place of Service; After Entry of Judgment or Order**. When a domestic relations judgment or order requires the parties to inform the friend of the court office of any changes in their mailing address, a party's last known mailing address means the most recent address

(1) that the party provided in writing to the friend of the court office, or
(2) set forth in the most recent judgment or order entered in the case, or
(3) the address established by the friend of the court office pursuant to subrule (D).

(C) **Place of Service; Before Entry of Judgment or Order**. After a summons and complaint has been filed and served on a party, but before entry of a judgment or order that requires the parties to inform the friend of the court of any changes in their mailing address, the last known mailing address is the most recent address
(1) set forth in the pleadings, or
(2) that a party provides in writing to the friend of the court office.

(D) **Administrative Change of Address**. The friend of the court office shall change a party's address administratively pursuant to the policy established by the state court administrator for that purpose when:
(1) a party's address changes in another friend of the court office pursuant to these rules, or
(2) notices and court papers are returned to the friend of the court office as undeliverable.

(E) **Service on Nonparties**. Notice to a nonparty must be provided as set forth in the statute requiring the notice. Absent statutory direction, the notice may be provided by regular mail. Absent statutory direction, court papers initiating an action against nonparties to enforce a notice must be served in the same manner as a summons and complaint pursuant to MCR 2.105.

(F) **Confidential Addresses**. When a court order makes a party's address confidential, the party shall provide an alternative address for service of notice and court papers.

(G) **Notice to Friend of the Court**. If a child of the parties or a child born during the marriage is under the age of 18, or if a party is pregnant, or if child support or spousal support is requested, the parties must provide the friend of the court with a copy of all pleadings and other papers filed in the action. The copy must be marked "friend of the court" and submitted to the court clerk at the time of filing. The court clerk must send the copy to the friend of the court.

(H) **Notice to Prosecuting Attorney**. In an action for divorce or separate maintenance in which a child of the parties or a child born during the marriage is under the age of 18, or if a party is pregnant, the plaintiff must serve a copy of the summons and complaint on the prosecuting attorney when required by law. Service must be made at the time of filling by providing the court clerk with an additional copy marked "prosecuting attorney". The court clerk must send the copy to the prosecuting attorney.

(I) **Service of Informational Pamphlet**. If a child of the parties or a child born during the marriage is under the age of 18, or if a party is pregnant, or if child support or spousal support is requested, the plaintiff must serve with the complaint a copy of the friend of the court informational pamphlet required by MCL 552.505(a). The proof of service must state that service of the informational pamphlet has been made.

Rule 3.204 Proceedings Affecting Children

(A) Unless the court orders otherwise for good cause, if a circuit court action involving child support, custody, or parenting time is pending, or if the circuit court has continuing jurisdiction over such matters because of a prior action:
(1) A new action concerning support, custody or parenting time of the same child must be filed as a motion in the earlier action if the relief sought would have been available in the original cause of action. If the relief sought was not available in the original action, the new action must be filed as a new complaint.
(2) A new action for the support, custody, or parenting time of a different child of the same parents must be filed in the same county as the prior action if the circuit court for that county has jurisdiction over the new action and the new case must be assigned to the same judge to whom the previous action was assigned.
(3) Whenever possible, all actions involving the custody, parenting time, and support of children of the same parents shall be administered together. Unless the court finds that good cause exists not to do so, when the court enters a final order in a new action involving a new child of those parents, the order shall consolidate the provisions for custody, parenting time, and support for both that child and any children named in previous actions over which the court has jurisdiction involving the same parents. The order must reference the other cases and state that it supersedes the custody, parenting time, and support provisions of the orders entered previously in those cases. In the new action, the court may modify custody, parenting time, and support provisions in preexisting orders involving another child or children of the same parents, provided that the modification is supported by evidence presented in the new case and both parents have had an opportunity to be heard concerning the proposed modifications.

(B) When more than one circuit court action involving support, custody, or parenting time of a child is pending, or more than one circuit court has continuing jurisdiction over those matters because of prior actions, a complaint for the support, custody, or parenting time of a different child of the same parents must be filed in whichever circuit court has jurisdiction to decide the new action. If more than one of the previously involved circuit courts would have jurisdiction to decide the new action, or if the action might be filed in more than one county within a circuit:

(1) The new action must be filed in the same county as a prior action involving the parents' separate maintenance, divorce, or annulment.

(2) If no prior action involves separate maintenance, divorce, or annulment, the new action must be filed:

(a) in the county of the circuit court that has issued a judgment affecting the majority of the parents' children in common, or

(b) if no circuit court for a county has issued a judgment affecting a majority of the parents' children in common, then in the county of the circuit court that has issued the most recent judgment affecting a child of the same parents.

(C) The court may enter an order that consolidates the custody, parenting time, and support provisions of multiple orders administratively when:

(1) the cases involve different children of the same parents but all other parties are the same, or

(2) more than one action involves the same child and parents.

The order must reference the other cases and state that it supersedes the custody, parenting time, and support provisions of the orders in those cases.

(D) In a case involving a dispute regarding the custody of a minor child, the court may, on motion of a party or on its own initiative, for good cause shown, appoint a guardian ad litem to represent the child and assess the costs and reasonable fees against the parties involved in full or in part.

Rule 3.205 Prior and Subsequent Orders and Judgments Affecting Minors

(A) **Jurisdiction**. If an order or judgment has provided for continuing jurisdiction of a minor and proceedings are commenced in another Michigan court having separate jurisdictional grounds for an action affecting that minor, a waiver or transfer of jurisdiction is not required for the full and valid exercise of jurisdiction by the subsequent court.

(B) **Notice to Prior Court, Friend of the Court, Juvenile Officer, and Prosecuting Attorney**.

(1) As used in this rule, "appropriate official" means the friend of the court, juvenile officer, or prosecuting attorney, depending on the nature of the prior or subsequent court action and the court involved.

(2) If a minor is known to be subject to the prior continuing jurisdiction of a Michigan court, the plaintiff or other initiating party must mail written notice of proceedings in the subsequent court to the attention of

(a) the clerk or register of the prior court, and

(b) the appropriate official of the prior court.

(3) The notice must be mailed at least 21 days before the date set for hearing. If the fact of continuing jurisdiction is not then known, notice must be given immediately when it becomes known.

(4) The notice requirement of this subrule is not jurisdictional and does not preclude the subsequent court from entering interim orders before the expiration of the 21-day period, if required by the best interests of the minor.

(C) **Prior Orders**.

(1) Each provision of a prior order remains in effect until the provision is superseded, changed, or terminated by a subsequent order.

(2) A subsequent court must give due consideration to prior continuing orders of other courts, and may not enter orders contrary to or inconsistent with such orders, except as provided by law.

(D) **Duties of Officials of Prior and Subsequent Courts**.

(1) Upon receipt of the notice required by subrule (B), the appropriate official of the prior court

(a) must provide the subsequent court with copies of all relevant orders then in effect and copies of relevant records and reports, and

(b) may appear in person at proceedings in the subsequent court, as the welfare of the minor and the interests of justice require.

(2) Upon request of the prior court, the appropriate official of the subsequent court

(a) must notify the appropriate official of the prior court of all proceedings in the subsequent court, and

(b) must send copies of all orders entered in the subsequent court to the attention of the clerk or register and the appropriate official of the prior court.

(3) If a circuit court awards custody of a minor pursuant to MCL 722.26b, the clerk of the circuit court must send a copy of the judgment or order of disposition to the probate court that has prior or continuing jurisdiction of the minor as a result of the guardianship proceedings, regardless whether there is a request.

(4) Upon receipt of an order from the subsequent court, the appropriate official of the prior court must take the steps necessary to implement the order in the prior court.

Rule 3.206 Pleading

(A) **Information in Complaint**.

(1) Except for matters considered confidential by statute or court rule, in all domestic relations actions, the complaint must state

(a) the allegations required by applicable statutes;

(b) the residence information required by statute;

(c) the complete names of all parties; and

(d) the complete names and dates of birth of any minors involved in the action, including all minor children of the parties and all minor children born during the marriage.

(2) In a case that involves a minor, or if child support is requested, the complaint also must state whether any Michigan court has prior continuing jurisdiction of the minor. If so, the complaint must specify the court and the file number.

(3) In a case in which the custody of a minor is to be determined, the complaint or an affidavit attached to the complaint also must state the information required by MCL 722.1209.

(4) The caption of the complaint must also contain either (a) or (b) as a statement of the attorney for the plaintiff or petitioner, or of a plaintiff or petitioner appearing without an attorney:

(a) There is no other pending or resolved action within the jurisdiction of the family division of the circuit court involving the family or family members of the person[s] who [is/are] the subject of the complaint or petition.

(b) An action within the jurisdiction of the family division of the circuit court involving the family or family members of the person[s] who [is/are] the subject of the complaint or petition has been previously filed in [this court]/[______Court], where it was given docket number ______ and was assigned to Judge ________. The action [remains]/[is no longer] pending.

(5) In an action for divorce, separate maintenance, annulment of marriage, or affirmation of marriage, regardless of the contentions of the parties with respect to the existence or validity of the marriage, the complaint also must state

(a) the names of the parties before the marriage;

(b) whether there are minor children of the parties or minor children born during the marriage;

(c) whether a party is pregnant;

(d) the factual grounds for the action, except that in an action for divorce or separate maintenance the grounds must be stated in the statutory language, without further particulars; and

(e) whether there is property to be divided.

(6) A party who requests spousal support in an action for divorce, separate maintenance, annulment, affirmation of marriage, or spousal support, must allege facts sufficient to show a need for such support and that the other party is able to pay.

(7) A party who requests an order for personal protection or for the protection of property, including but not limited to restraining orders and injunctions against domestic violence, must allege facts sufficient to support the relief requested.

(B) **Verified Statement**.

(1) In an action involving a minor, or if child support or spousal support is requested, the party seeking relief must attach a verified statement to the copies of the papers served on the other party and provided to the friend of the court, stating

(a) the last known telephone number, post office address, residence address, and business address of each party;

(b) the social security number and occupation of each party;

(c) the name and address of each party's employer;

(d) the estimated weekly gross income of each party;

(e) the driver's license number and physical description of each party, including eye color, hair color, height, weight, race, gender, and identifying marks;

(f) any other names by which the parties are or have been known;

(g) the name, age, birth date, social security number, and residence address of each minor involved in the action, as well as of any other minor child of either party;

(h) the name and address of any person, other than the parties, who may have custody of a minor during the pendency of the action;

(i) the kind of public assistance, if any, that has been applied for or is being received by either party or on behalf of a minor, and the AFDC and recipient identification numbers; if public assistance has not been requested or received, that fact must be stated; and

(j) the health care coverage, if any, that is available for each minor child; the name of the policyholder; the name of the insurance company, health care organization, or health maintenance organization; and the policy, certificate, or contract number.

(2) The information in the verified statement is confidential, and is not to be released other than to the court, the parties, or the attorneys for the parties, except on court order. For good cause, the addresses of a party and minors may be omitted from the copy of the statement that is served on the other party.

(3) If any of the information required to be in the verified statement is omitted, the party seeking relief must explain the omission in a sworn affidavit, to be filed with the court.

(C) **Attorney Fees and Expenses**.

(1) A party may, at any time, request that the court order the other party to pay all or part of the attorney fees and expenses related to the action or a specific proceeding, including a post-judgment proceeding.

(2) A party who requests attorney fees and expenses must allege facts sufficient to show that
   (a) the party is unable to bear the expense of the action, and that the other party is able to pay, or
   (b) the attorney fees and expenses were incurred because the other party refused to comply with a previous court order, despite having the ability to comply.

Rule 3.207 Ex Parte, Temporary, and Protective Orders

(A) **Scope of Relief**. The court may issue ex parte and temporary orders with regard to any matter within its jurisdiction, and may issue protective orders against domestic violence as provided in subchapter 3.700.

(B) **Ex Parte Orders**.
   (1) Pending the entry of a temporary order, the court may enter an ex parte order if the court is satisfied by specific facts set forth in an affidavit or verified pleading that irreparable injury, loss, or damage will result from the delay required to effect notice, or that notice itself will precipitate adverse action before an order can be issued.
   (2) The moving party must arrange for the service of true copies of the ex parte order on the friend of the court and the other party.
   (3) An ex parte order is effective upon entry and enforceable upon service.
   (4) An ex parte order remains in effect until modified or superseded by a temporary or final order.
   (5) An ex parte order providing for child support, custody, or visitation pursuant to MCL 722.27a, must include the following notice:
   "Notice:
   "1. You may file a written objection to this order or a motion to modify or rescind this order. You must file the written objection or motion with the clerk of the court within 14 days after you were served with this order. You must serve a true copy of the objection or motion on the friend of the court and the party who obtained the order.
   "2. If you file a written objection, the friend of the court must try to resolve the dispute. If the friend of the court cannot resolve the dispute and if you wish to bring the matter before the court without the assistance of counsel, the friend of the court must provide you with form pleadings and written instructions and must schedule a hearing with the court.
   "3. The ex parte order will automatically become a temporary order if you do not file a written objection or motion to modify or rescind the ex parte order and a request for a hearing. Even if an objection is filed, the ex parte order will remain in effect and must be obeyed unless changed by a later court order."
   (6) In all other cases, the ex parte order must state that it will automatically become a temporary order if the other party does not file a written objection or motion to modify or rescind the ex parte order and a request for a hearing. The written objection or motion and the request for a hearing must be filed with the clerk of the court, and a true copy provided to the friend of the court and the other party, within 14 days after the order is served.
      (a) If there is a timely objection or motion and a request for a hearing, the hearing must be held within 21 days after the objection or motion and request are filed.
      (b) A change that occurs after the hearing may be made retroactive to the date the ex parte order was entered.
   (7) The provisions of MCR 3.310 apply to temporary restraining orders in domestic relations cases.

(C) **Temporary Orders**.
   (1) A request for a temporary order may be made at any time during the pendency of the case by filing a verified motion that sets forth facts sufficient to support the relief requested.
   (2) A temporary order may not be issued without a hearing, unless the parties agree otherwise or fail to file a written objection or motion as provided in subrules (B)(5) and (6).
   (3) A temporary order may be modified at any time during the pendency of the case, following a hearing and upon a showing of good cause.
   (4) A temporary order must state its effective date and whether its provisions may be modified retroactively by a subsequent order.
   (5) A temporary order remains in effect until modified or until the entry of the final judgment or order.
   (6) A temporary order not yet satisfied is vacated by the entry of the final judgment or order, unless specifically continued or preserved. This does not apply to support arrearages that have been assigned to the state, which are preserved unless specifically waived or reduced by the final judgment or order.

Rule 3.208 Friend of the Court

(A) **General**. The friend of the court has the powers and duties prescribed by statute, including those duties in the Friend of the Court Act, MCL 552.501 et seq., and the Support and Visitation Enforcement Act, MCL 552.601 et seq.

(B) **Enforcement**. The friend of the court is responsible for initiating proceedings to enforce an order or judgment for support, visitation, or custody.
   (1) If a party has failed to comply with an order or judgment, the friend of the court may petition for

an order to show cause why the party should not be held in contempt.

(2) The order to show cause must be served personally or by ordinary mail at the party's last known address.

(3) The hearing on the order to show cause may be held no sooner than seven days after the order is served on the party. If service is by ordinary mail, the hearing may be held no sooner than nine days after the order is mailed.

(4) If the party fails to appear in response to the order to show cause, the court may issue an order for arrest.

(5) The relief available under this rule is in addition to any other relief available by statute.

(6) The friend of the court may petition for an order of arrest at any time, if immediate action is necessary.

(C) **Allocation and Distribution of Payments**.

(1) Except as otherwise provided in this subrule, all payments shall be allocated and distributed as required by the guidelines established by the state court administrator for that purpose.

(2) If the court determines that following the guidelines established by the state court administrator would produce an unjust result in a particular case, the court may order that payments be made in a different manner. The order must include specific findings of fact that set forth the basis for the court's decision, and must direct the payer to designate with each payment the name of the payer and the payee, the case number, the amount, and the date of the order that allows the special payment.

(3) If a payer with multiple cases makes a payment directly to the friend of the court rather than through income withholding, the payment shall be allocated among all the cases unless the payer requests a different allocation in writing at the time of payment and provides the following information about each case for which payment is intended:

(a) the name of the payer,

(b) the name of the payee,

(c) the case number, and

(d) the amount designated for that case.

(4) A notice of income withholding may not be used by the friend of the court or the state disbursement unit to determine the specific allocation or distribution of payments.

(D) **Notice to Attorneys**.

(1) Copies of notices required to be given to the parties also must be sent to the attorneys of record.

(2) The notice requirement of this subrule remains in effect until 21 days after judgment is entered or until postjudgment matters are concluded, whichever is later.

Rule 3.209 Suspension of Enforcement and Dismissal

(A) **Suspension of Enforcement**.

(1) Because of a reconciliation or for any other reason, a party may file a motion to suspend the automatic enforcement of a support obligation by the friend of the court. Such a motion may be filed before or after the entry of a judgment.

(2) A support obligation cannot be suspended except by court order.

(B) **Dismissal**. Unless the order of dismissal specifies otherwise, dismissal of an action under MCR 2.502 or MCR 2.504 cancels past-due child support, except for that owed to the State of Michigan.

Rule 3.210 Hearings and Trials

(A) **In General**.

(1) Proofs or testimony may not be taken in an action for divorce or separate maintenance until the expiration of the time prescribed by the applicable statute, except as otherwise provided by this rule.

(2) In cases of unusual hardship or compelling necessity, the court may, upon motion and proper showing, take testimony and render judgment at any time 60 days after the filing of the complaint.

(3) Testimony may be taken conditionally at any time for the purpose of perpetuating it.

(4) Testimony must be taken in person, except that the court may allow testimony to be taken by telephone, in extraordinary circumstances, or under MCR 2.407.

(B) **Default Cases**.

(1) This subrule applies to the entry of a default and a default judgment in all cases governed by this subchapter.

(2) *Entry of Default.*

(a) A party may request the entry of a default of another party for failure to plead or otherwise defend. Upon presentation of an affidavit by a party asserting facts setting forth proof of service and failure to plead or otherwise defend, the clerk must enter a default of the party.

(b) The party who requested entry of the default must provide prompt notice, as provided by MCR 3.203, to the defaulted party and all other parties and persons entitled to notice that the default has been entered, and file a proof of service.

(c) Except as provided under subrule (B)(2)(d), after the default of a party has been entered, that party may not proceed with the action until the default has been set aside by the court under subrule (B)(3).

(d) The court may permit a party in default to participate in discovery as provided in Subchapter 2.300, file motions, and participate in court proceedings, referee hearings, mediations, arbitrations, and other alternative dispute resolution proceedings. The court may impose conditions or limitations on the defaulted party's participation.

(e) A party in default must be service with the notice of default and a copy of every paper later filed in the case as provided by MCR 3.203, and the person serving the notice or other paper must file a proof of service with the court.

(3) *Setting Aside Default Before Entry of Default Judgment.* A motion to set aside a default, except when grounded on lack of jurisdiction over the defendant or subject matter, shall be granted only upon verified motion of the defaulted party showing good cause.

(4) *Notice of Hearing and Motion for Entry of Default Judgment.*

(a) A party moving for default judgment must schedule a hearing and serve the motion, notice of hearing, and a copy of the proposed judgment upon the defaulted party at least 14 days before the hearing on entry of the default judgment, and promptly file a proof of service when:

(i) the action involves entry of judgment of divorce, separate maintenance, or annulment under subrule (B)(5)(a);

(ii) the proposed judgment involves a request for relief that is different from the relief requested in the complaint; or

(iii) the moving party does not have sufficient facts to complete the judgment or order without a judicial determination of the relief to which the party is entitled.

(b) If the action does not require a hearing under subrule (B)(4)(a) and if the relief can be determined based on information available to the moving party that is stated in or attached to the motion or complaint, the moving party for default judgment may either:

(i) schedule a hearing and serve the motion, notice of hearing, and a copy of the proposed judgment upon the defaulted party at least 14 days before the hearing on entry of the default judgment, and promptly file a proof of service, or

(ii) serve a verified motion for default judgment supporting the relief requested and a copy of the proposed judgment upon the defaulted party, along with a notice that it will be submitted to the court for signing if no written objections are filed with the court clerk within 14 days. If no written objections are filed within 14 days after filing, the moving party shall submit the judgment or order to the court for entry. If objections are filed, the moving party shall notice the entry of default judgment for hearing.

(c) Service under this subrule shall be made in the manner provided by MCR 3.203 or, as permitted by the court, in any manner reasonably calculated to give the defaulted party actual notice of the proceedings and an opportunity to be heard.

(d) If the default is entered for failure to appear for a scheduled trial or hearing, notice under this subrule is not required.

(5) *Entry of Default Judgment.*

(a) A judgment of divorce, separate maintenance, or annulment may not be entered as a matter of course on the default of a party because of failure to appear at the hearing or by consent, and the case must be heard in open court on proofs taken, except as otherwise provided by statute or court rule.

(b) Proofs for a default judgment may not be taken unless the judgment fee has been deposited with the court clerk and the proposed judgment has been given to the court. Nonmilitary affidavits required by law must be filed before a default judgment is entered in cases in which the defendant has failed to appear. A default judgment may not be entered against a minor or an incompetent person unless the person is represented in the action by a conservator or other representative, except as otherwise provided by law.

(c) The moving party may be required to present evidence sufficient to satisfy the court that the terms of the proposed judgment are in accordance with law. The court may consider relevant and material affidavits, testimony, documents, exhibits, or other evidence.

(d) In cases involving minor children, the court may take testimony and receive or consider relevant and material affidavits, testimony, documents, exhibits, or other evidence, as necessary, to make findings concerning the award of custody, parenting time, and support of the children.

(e) If the court does not approve the proposed judgment, the party who prepared it must, within 14 days, submit a modified judgment under MCR 2.602(B)(3), in conformity with the court's ruling, or as otherwise directed by the court.

(f) Upon entry of a default judgment and as provided by MCR 3.203, the moving party must serve a copy of the judgment as entered by the court on the defaulted party within 7 days after it has been entered, and promptly file a proof of service.

(6) *Setting Aside Default Judgment.*

(a) A motion to set aside a default judgment, except when grounded on lack of jurisdiction over the defendant, lack of subject matter jurisdiction, failure to serve the notice of default as required by subrule (B)(2)(b), or failure to serve the proposed default judgment and notice of hearing for the entry of the judgment under subrule (B)(4), shall be granted only if the motion is filed within 21 days after the default judgment was entered and if good cause is shown.

(b) In addition, the court may set aside a default judgment or modify the terms of the judgment in accordance with statute or MCR 2.612.

(7) *Costs.* An order setting aside the default or default judgment must be conditioned on the defaulted party paying the taxable costs incurred by the other party in reliance on the default or default judgment, except as prescribed in MCR 2.625(D). The order may also impose other conditions, including imposition of a reasonable attorney fee.

(C) **Custody of a Minor.**

(1) When the custody of a minor is contested, a hearing on the matter must be held within 56 days

(a) after the court orders, or

(b) after the filing of notice that a custody hearing is requested,

unless both parties agree to mediation under MCL 552.513 and mediation is unsuccessful, in which event the hearing must be held within 56 days after the final mediation session.

(2) If a custody action is assigned to a probate judge pursuant to MCL 722.26b, a hearing on the matter must be held by the probate judge within 56 days after the case is assigned.

(3) The court must enter a decision within 28 days after the hearing.

(4) The notice required by this subrule may be filed as a separate document, or may be included in another paper filed in the action if the notice is mentioned in the caption.

(5) The court may interview the child privately to determine if the child is of sufficient age to express a preference regarding custody, and, if so, the reasonable preference of the child. The court shall focus the interview on these determinations, and the information received shall be applied only to the reasonable preference factor.

(6) If a report has been submitted by the friend of the court, the court must give the parties an opportunity to review the report and to file objections before a decision is entered.

(7) The court may extend for good cause the time within which a hearing must be held and a decision rendered under this subrule.

(8) In deciding whether an evidentiary hearing is necessary with regard to a postjudgment motion to change custody, the court must determine, by requiring an offer of proof or otherwise, whether there are contested factual issues that must be resolved in order for the court to make an informed decision on the motion.

(D) The court must make findings of fact as provided in MCR 2.517, except that

(1) findings of fact and conclusions of law are required on contested postjudgment motions to modify a final judgment or order, and

(2) the court may distribute pension, retirement, and other deferred compensation rights with a qualified domestic relations order, without first making a finding with regard to the value of those rights.

(E) **Consent Judgment.**

(1) At a hearing that involves entry of a judgment of divorce, separate maintenance, or annulment under subrule (B)(5)(a), or at any time for all other actions, any party may present to the court for entry a judgment approved as to form and content and signed by all parties and their attorneys of record.

(2) If the court determines that the proposed consent judgment is not in accordance with law, the parties shall submit a modified consent judgment in conformity with the court's ruling within 14 days, or as otherwise directed by the court.

(3) Upon entry of a consent judgment and as provided by MCR 3.203, the moving party must serve a copy of the judgment as entered by the court on all other parties within 7 days after it has been entered and promptly file a proof of service.

Rule 3.211 Judgments and Orders

(A) Each separate subject in a judgment or order must be set forth in a separate paragraph that is prefaced by an appropriate heading.

(B) A judgment of divorce, separate maintenance, or annulment must include

(1) the insurance and dower provisions required by MCL 552.101;

(2) a determination of the rights of the parties in pension, annuity, and retirement benefits, as required by MCL 552.101(4);

(3) a determination of the property rights of the parties; and

(4) a provision reserving or denying spousal support, if spousal support is not granted; a judgment silent with regard to spousal support reserves it.

(C) A judgment or order awarding custody of a minor must provide that

(1) the domicile or residence of the minor may not be moved from Michigan without the approval of the judge who awarded custody or the judge's successor,

(2) the person awarded custody must promptly notify the friend of the court in writing when the minor is moved to another address, and

(3) a parent whose custody or parenting time of a child is governed by the order shall not change the legal residence of the child except in compliance with section 11 of the Child Custody Act, MCL 722.31.

(D) Uniform Support Orders

(1) Any provisions regarding child support or spousal support must be prepared on the latest version of the Uniform Support Order approved by the state court administrative office. This order must accompany any judgment or order affecting child support or spousal support, and both documents must be signed by the judge. If only child support or spousal support is ordered, then only the Uniform Support Order must be submitted to the court for entry. The Uniform Support Order shall govern if the terms of the judgment or order conflict with the Uniform Support Order.

(2) No judgment or order concerning a minor or a spouse shall be entered unless either:

(a) the final judgment or order incorporates by reference a Uniform Support Order, or

(b) the final judgment or order states that no Uniform Support Order is required because support is reserved or spousal support is not ordered.

(3) The clerk shall charge a single judgment entry fee when a Uniform Support Order is submitted for entry along with a judgment or order that incorporates it by reference.

(E) Unless otherwise ordered, all support arrearages owing to the state are preserved upon entry of a final order or judgment. Upon a showing of good cause and notice to the friend of the court, the prosecuting attorney, and other interested parties, the court may waive or reduce such arrearages.

(F) Entry of Judgment or Order

(1) Within 21 days after the court renders an opinion or the settlement agreement is placed on the record, the moving party must submit a judgment, order, or a motion to settle the judgment or order, unless the court has granted an extension.

(2) The party submitting the first temporary order awarding child custody, parenting time, or support and the party submitting any final proposed judgment awarding child custody, parenting time, or support must:

(a) serve the friend of the court office and, unless the court orders otherwise, all other parties, with a completed copy of the latest version of the state court administrative office's domestic relations Judgment Information Form, and

(b) file a proof of service certifying that the Judgment Information Form has been provided to the friend of the court office and, unless the court orders otherwise, to all other parties.

(3) If the court modifies the proposed judgment or order before signing it, the party submitting the judgment or order must, within 7 days, submit a new Judgment Information Form if any of the information previously submitted changes as a result of the modification.

(4) Before it signs a judgment or order awarding child support or spousal support, the court must determine that:

(a) the party submitting the judgment or order has certified that the Judgment Information Form in subrule (F)(2) has been submitted to the friend of the court, and

(b) pursuant to subrule (D)(2) any judgment or order concerning a minor or a spouse is accompanied by a Uniform Support Order or explains why a Uniform Support Order is unnecessary.

(5) The Judgment Information Form must be filed in addition to the verified statement that is required by MCR 3.206.

(G) Friend of the Court Review. For all judgments and orders containing provisions identified in subrules (C), (D), (E), and (F), the court may require that the judgment or order be submitted to the friend of the court for review.

(H) Service of Judgment or Order.

(1) When a judgment or order is obtained for temporary or permanent spousal support, child support, or separate maintenance, the prevailing party must immediately deliver one copy to the court clerk. The court clerk must write or stamp "true copy" on the order or judgment and file it with the friend of the court.

(2) The party securing entry of a judgment or order that provides for child support or spousal support must serve a copy on the party ordered to pay the support, as provided in MCR 2.602(D)(1), even if that party is in default.

(3) The record of divorce and annulment required by MCL 333.2864 must be filed at the time of the filing of the judgment.

Rule 3.212 Postjudgment Transfer of Domestic Relations Cases

(A) **Motion**.

(1) A party, court-ordered custodian, or friend of the court may move for the postjudgment transfer of a domestic relations action in accordance with this rule, or the court may transfer such an action on its own motion. A transfer includes a change of venue and a transfer of all friend of the court responsibilities. The court may enter a consent order transferring a postjudgment domestic relations action, provided the conditions under subrule (B) are met.

(2) The postjudgment transfer of an action initiated pursuant to MCL 780.151 et seq., is controlled by MCR 3.214.

(B) **Conditions**.

(1) A motion filed by a party or court-ordered custodian may be granted only if all of the following conditions are met:

(a) the transfer of the action is requested on the basis of the residence and convenience of the parties, or other good cause consistent with the best interests of the child;

(b) neither party nor the court-ordered custodian has resided in the county of current jurisdiction for at least 6 months prior to the filing of the motion;

(c) at least one party or the court-ordered custodian has resided in the county to which the transfer is requested for at least 6 months prior to the filing of the motion; and

(d) the county to which the transfer is requested is not contiguous to the county of current jurisdiction.

(2) When the court or the friend of the court initiates a transfer, the conditions stated in subrule (B)(1) do not apply.

(C) Unless the court orders otherwise for good cause, if a friend of the court becomes aware of a more recent final judgment involving the same parties issued in a different county, the friend of the court must initiate a transfer of the older case to the county in which the new judgment was entered if neither of the parents, any of their children who are affected by the judgment in the older case, nor another party resides in the county in which the older case was filed.

(D) **Transfer Order**.

(1) The court ordering a postjudgment transfer must enter all necessary orders pertaining to the certification and transfer of the action. The transferring court must send to the receiving court all court files and friend of the court files, ledgers, records, and documents that pertain to the action. Such materials may be used in the receiving jurisdiction in the same manner as in the transferring jurisdiction.

(2) The court may order that any past-due fees and costs be paid to the transferring friend of the court office at the time of transfer.

(3) The court may order that one or both of the parties or the court-ordered custodian pay the cost of the transfer.

(E) **Filing Fee**. An order transferring a case under this rule must provide that the party who moved for the transfer pay the statutory filing fee applicable to the court to which the action is transferred, except where MCR 2.002 applies. If the parties stipulate to the transfer of a case, they must share equally the cost of transfer unless the court orders otherwise. In either event, the transferring court must submit the filing fee to the court to which the action is transferred, at the time of transfer. If the court or the friend of the court initiates the transfer, the statutory filing fee is waived.

(F) **Physical Transfer of Files**. Court and friend of the court files must be transferred by registered or certified mail, return receipt requested, or by another secure method of transfer.

(G) Upon completion of the transfer, the transferee friend of the court must review the case and determine whether the case contains orders specific to the transferring court or county. The friend of the court must take such action as is necessary, which may include obtaining ex parte orders to transfer court- or county-specific actions to the transferee court.

Rule 3.213 Postjudgment Motions and Enforcement

Postjudgment motions in domestic relations actions are governed by MCR 2.119.

Rule 3.214 Actions Under Uniform Acts

(A) **Governing Rules**. Actions under the Revised Uniform Reciprocal Enforcement of Support Act (RURESA), MCL 780.151 et seq., the Uniform Interstate Family Support Act (UIFSA), MCL 552.1101 et seq., and the Uniform Child-Custody Jurisdiction and Enforcement Act (UCCJEA), MCL 722.1101 et seq., are governed by the rules applicable to other civil actions, except as otherwise provided by those acts and this rule.

(B) **RURESA Actions**.

(1) *Definition*. As used in this subrule, “support order” is defined by MCL 780.153b(8).

(2) *Transfer; Initiating and Responding RURESA Cases*.

(a) If a Michigan court initiates a RURESA action and there exists in another Michigan court a prior valid support order, the initiating court must transfer to that other court any RURESA order entered in a responding state. The initiating court must inform the responding court of the transfer.

(b) If a court in another state initiates a RURESA action and there exists in Michigan a prior valid support order, the responsive proceeding should be commenced in the court that issued the prior valid support order. If the responsive proceeding is commenced erroneously in any other Michigan court and a RURESA order enters, that court, upon learning of the error, must transfer the RURESA order to the court that issued the prior valid support order. The transferring court must inform the initiating court of the transfer.

(c) A court ordering a transfer must send to the court that issued the prior valid support order all pertinent papers, including all court files and friend of the court files, ledgers, records, and documents.

(d) Court files and friend of the court files must be transferred by registered or certified mail, return receipt requested, or by other secure method.

(e) The friend of the court office that issued the prior valid support order must receive and disburse immediately all payments made by the obligor or sent by a responding state.

(C) **Sending Notices in UIFSA cases**. The friend of the court office shall send all notices and copies of orders required to be sent by the tribunal under MCL 552.1101 et seq.

(D) **Registration of Child Custody Determinations Under UCCJEA**. The procedure for registration and enforcement of a child custody determination by the court of another state is as provided in MCL 722.1304. There is no fee for the registration of such a determination.

Rule 3.215 Domestic Relations Referees

(A) **Qualifications of Referees**. A referee appointed pursuant to MCL 552.507(1) must be a member in good standing of the State Bar of Michigan. A non-attorney friend of the court who was serving as a referee when this rule took effect on May 1, 1993, may continue to serve.

(B) **Referrals to the Referee**.

(1) The chief judge may, by administrative order, direct that specified types of domestic relations motions be heard initially by a referee.

(2) To the extent allowed by law, the judge to whom a domestic relations action is assigned may refer other motions in that action to a referee

(a) on written stipulation of the parties,

(b) on a party's motion, or

(c) on the judge's own initiative.

(3) In domestic relations matters, the judge to whom an action is assigned, or the chief judge by administrative order, may authorize referees to conduct settlement conferences and, subject to judicial review, scheduling conferences.

(C) **Scheduling of the Referee Hearing**.

(1) Within 14 days after receiving a motion referred under subrule (B)(1) or (B)(2), the referee must arrange for service of a notice scheduling a referee hearing on the attorneys for the parties, or on the parties if they are not represented by counsel. The notice of hearing must clearly state that the matter will be heard by a referee

(2) The referee may adjourn a hearing for good cause without preparing a recommendation for an order, except that if the adjournment is subject to any terms or conditions, the referee may only prepare a recommendation for an adjournment order to be signed by a judge.

(D) **Conduct of Referee Hearings**.

(1) The Michigan Rules of Evidence apply to referee hearings.

(2) A referee must provide the parties with notice of the right to request a judicial hearing by giving

(a) oral notice during the hearing, and

(b) written notice in the recommendation for an order.

(3) Testimony must be taken in person, except that, a referee may allow testimony to be taken by telephone for good cause, or under MCR 2.407.

(4) An electronic or stenographic record must be kept of all hearings.

(a) The parties must be allowed to make contemporaneous copies of the record if the referee's recording equipment can make multiple copies simultaneously and if the parties supply the recording media. A recording made under this rule may be used solely to assist the parties during the proceeding recorded or, at the discretion of the trial judge, in any judicial hearing following an objection to the referee's recommended order; it may not be used publicly.

(b) If ordered by the court, or if stipulated by the parties, the referee must provide a transcript, verified by oath, of each hearing held. The cost of preparing a transcript must be apportioned equally between the parties, unless otherwise ordered by the court.

(c) At least 7 days before the judicial hearing, a party who intends to offer evidence from the record of the referee hearing must provide notice to the court and each other party. If a stenographic transcript is necessary, except as provided in subrule (4)(b), the party offering the evidence must pay for the transcript.

(d) If the court on its own motion uses the record of the referee hearing to limit the judicial hearing under subrule (F), the court must make the record available to the parties and must allow the parties to file supplemental objections within 7 days of the date the record is provided to the parties. Following the judicial hearing, the court may assess the costs of preparing a transcript of the referee hearing to one or more of the parties. This subrule does not apply when a party requests the court to limit the judicial hearing under subrule (F) or when the court orders a transcript to resolve a dispute concerning what occurred at the referee hearing.

(E) **Posthearing Procedures**.

(1) Within 21 days after a hearing, the referee must either make a statement of findings on the record or submit a written, signed report containing a summary of testimony and a statement of findings. In either event, the referee must make a recommendation for an order and arrange for it to be submitted to the court and the attorneys for the parties, or the parties if they are not represented by counsel. A proof of service must be filed with the court.

(a) The referee must find facts specially and state separately the law the referee applied. Brief, definite, and pertinent findings and conclusions on the contested matters are sufficient, without overelaboration of detail or particularization of facts.

(b) The referee's recommended order must include:

(i) a signature line for the court to indicate its approval of the referee's recommended order;

(ii) notice that if the recommended order is approved by the court and no written objection is filed with the court clerk within 21 days after the recommended order is served, the recommended order will become the final order;

(iii) notice advising the parties of any interim effect the recommended order may have; and

(iv) prominent notice of all available methods for obtaining a judicial hearing.

(c) If the court approves the referee's recommended order, the recommended order must be served within 7 days of approval, or within 3 days of approval if the recommended order is given interim effect, and a proof of service must be filed with the court. If the recommendation is approved by the court and no written objection is filed with the court clerk within 21 days after service, the recommended order will become a final order.

(2) If the hearing concerns income withholding, the referee must arrange for a recommended order to be submitted to the court forthwith. If the recommended order is approved by the court, it must be given immediate effect pursuant to MCL 552.607(4).

(3) The recommended order may be prepared using any of the following methods:

(a) the referee may draft a recommended order;

(b) the referee may approve a proposed recommended order prepared by a party and submitted to the referee at the conclusion of the referee hearing;

(c) within 7 days of the date of the referee's findings, a party may draft a proposed recommended order and have it approved by all the parties and the referee; or

(d) within 7 days after the conclusion of the referee hearing, a party may serve a copy of a proposed recommended order on all other parties with a notice to them that it will be submitted to the referee for approval if no written objections to its accuracy or completeness are filed with the court clerk within 7 days after service of the notice. The party must file with the court clerk the original of the proposed recommended order and proof of its service on the other parties.

(i) If no written objections are filed within 7 days, the clerk shall submit the proposed recommended order to the referee for approval. If the referee does not approve the proposed recommended order, the referee may notify the parties to appear on a specified date for settlement of the matter.

(ii) To object to the accuracy or completeness of a proposed recommended order, the party must within 7 days after service of the proposed order, file written objections with the court clerk that state with specificity the inaccuracy or omission in the proposed recommended order, and serve the objections on all parties as required by MCR 2.107, together with a notice of hearing and an alternative proposed recommended order. Upon conclusion of the hearing, the referee shall sign the appropriate recommended order.

(4) A party may obtain a judicial hearing on any matter that has been the subject of a referee hearing and that resulted in a statement of findings and a recommended order by filing a written objection and notice of hearing within 21 days after the

referee's recommendation for an order is served on the attorneys for the parties, or the parties if they are not represented by counsel. The objection must include a clear and concise statement of the specific findings or application of law to which an objection is made. Objections regarding the accuracy or completeness of the recommendation must state with specificity the inaccuracy or omission.

(5) The party who requests a judicial hearing must serve the objection and notice of hearing on the opposing party or counsel in the manner provided in MCR 2.119(C).

(6) A circuit court may, by local administrative order, establish additional methods for obtaining a judicial hearing.

(7) The court may hear a party's objection to the referee's recommendation for an order on the same day as the referee hearing, provided that the notice scheduling the referee hearing advises the parties that a same-day judicial hearing will be available and the parties have the option of refusing a same-day hearing if they have not yet decided whether they will object to the referee's recommendation for an order.

(8) The parties may waive their right to object to the referee's recommendation for an order by consenting in writing to the immediate entry of the recommended order.

(F) **Judicial Hearings.**

(1) The judicial hearing must be held within 21 days after the written objection is filed, unless the time is extended by the court for good cause.

(2) To the extent allowed by law, the court may conduct the judicial hearing by review of the record of the referee hearing, but the court must allow the parties to present live evidence at the judicial hearing. The court may, in its discretion:

(a) prohibit a party from presenting evidence on findings of fact to which no objection was filed;

(b) determine that the referee's finding was conclusive as to a fact to which no objection was filed;

(c) prohibit a party from introducing new evidence or calling new witnesses unless there is an adequate showing that the evidence was not available at the referee hearing;

(d) impose any other reasonable restrictions and conditions to conserve the resources of the parties and the court.

(3) If the court determines that an objection is frivolous or has been interposed for the purpose of delay, the court may assess reasonable costs and attorney fees.

(G) **Interim Effect for Referee's Recommendation for an Order.**

(1) Except as limited by subrules (G)(2) and (G)(3), the court may, by an administrative order or by an order in the case, provide that the referee's recommended order will take effect on an interim basis pending a judicial hearing. The court must provide notice that the referee's recommended order will be an interim order by including that notice under a separate heading in the referee's recommended order, or by an order adopting the referee's recommended order as an interim order.

(2) The court may not give interim effect to a referee's recommendation for any of the following orders:

(a) An order for incarceration;

(b) An order for forfeiture of any property;

(c) An order imposing costs, fines, or other sanctions.

(3) The court may not, by administrative order, give interim effect to a referee's recommendation for the following types of orders:

(a) An order under subrule (G)(2);

(b) An order that changes a child's custody;

(c) An order that changes a child's domicile;

(d) An order that would render subsequent judicial consideration of the matter moot.

Rule 3.216 Domestic Relations Mediation

(A) **Scope and Applicability of Rule, Definitions.**

(1) All domestic relations cases, as defined in MCL 552.502(m), and actions for divorce and separate maintenance that involve the distribution of property are subject to mediation under this rule, unless otherwise provided by statute or court rule.

(2) Domestic relations mediation is a nonbinding process in which a neutral third party facilitates communication between parties to promote settlement. If the parties so request, and the mediator agrees to do so, the mediator may provide a written recommendation for settlement of any issues that remain unresolved at the conclusion of a mediation proceeding. This procedure, known as evaluative mediation, is governed by subrule (I).

(3) This rule does not restrict the Friend of the Court from enforcing custody, parenting time, and support orders.

(4) The court may order, on stipulation of the parties, the use of other settlement procedures.

(B) **Mediation Plan.** Each trial court that submits domestic relations cases to mediation under this rule shall include in its alternative dispute resolution plan adopted under MCR 2.410(B) provisions governing selection of domestic relations mediators, and for providing parties with information about mediation in the family division as soon as reasonably practical.

(C) **Referral to Mediation**.

(1) On written stipulation of the parties, on written motion of a party, or on the court's initiative, the court may submit to mediation by written order any contested issue in a domestic relations case, including postjudgment matters.

(2) The court may not submit contested issues to evaluative mediation unless all parties so request.

(3) Parties who are subject to a personal protection order or who are involved in a child abuse and neglect proceeding may not be referred to mediation without a hearing to determine whether mediation is appropriate.

(D) **Objections to Referral to Mediation**.

(1) To object to mediation, a party must file a written motion to remove the case from mediation and a notice of hearing of the motion, and serve a copy on the attorneys of record within 14 days after receiving notice of the order assigning the action to mediation. The motion must be set for hearing within 14 days after it is filed, unless the hearing is adjourned by agreement of counsel or unless the court orders otherwise.

(2) A timely motion must be heard before the case is mediated.

(3) Cases may be exempt from mediation on the basis of the following:

(a) child abuse or neglect;

(b) domestic abuse, unless attorneys for both parties will be present at the mediation session;

(c) inability of one or both parties to negotiate for themselves at the mediation, unless attorneys for both parties will be present at the mediation session;

(d) reason to believe that one or both parties' health or safety would be endangered by mediation; or

(e) for other good cause shown.

(E) **Selection of Mediator**.

(1) Domestic relations mediation will be conducted by a mediator selected as provided in this subrule.

(2) The parties may stipulate to the selection of a mediator. A mediator selected by agreement of the parties need not meet the qualifications set forth in subrule (G). The court must appoint a mediator stipulated to by the parties, provided the mediator is willing to serve within a period that would not interfere with the court's scheduling of the case for trial.

(3) If the parties have not stipulated to a mediator:

(a) the parties must indicate whether they prefer a mediator who is willing to conduct evaluative mediation. Failure to indicate a preference will be treated as not requesting evaluative mediation.

(b) the ADR clerk will assign a mediator from the list of qualified mediators maintained under subrule (F). The assignment shall be made on a rotational basis, except that if the parties have requested evaluative mediation, only a mediator who is willing to provide an evaluation may be assigned.

(4) The court shall not appoint, recommend, direct, or otherwise influence a party's or attorney's selection of a mediator except as provided pursuant to this rule. The court may recommend or advise parties on the selection of a mediator only upon request of all parties by stipulation in writing or orally on the record.

(5) The rule for disqualification of a mediator is the same as that provided in MCR 2.003 for the disqualification of a judge. The mediator must promptly disclose any potential basis for disqualification.

(F) **List of Mediators**.

(1) *Application*. To appear on a roster, an applicant, which may be an individual or organization, may apply to the ADR clerk to be placed on the court's list of mediators. Application forms shall be available in the office of the ADR clerk.

(a) The form shall include a certification that

(i) the applicant meets the requirements for service under the court's selection plan;

(ii) the applicant will not discriminate against parties or attorneys on the basis of race, ethnic origin, gender, or other protected personal characteristic; and

(iii) the applicant will comply with the court's ADR plan, orders of the court regarding cases submitted to mediation, and the standards of conduct adopted by the State Court Administrator under subrule (K).

(b) The applicant shall indicate on the form whether the applicant is willing to offer evaluative mediation, and the applicant's rate for providing mediation services.

(c) The form shall include an optional section identifying the applicant's gender and racial/ethnic background; however, this section shall not be made available to the public.

(2) *Review of Applications*. The court's ADR plan shall provide for a person or committee to review applications annually, or more frequently if appropriate, and compile a list of qualified mediators.

(a) Applicants meeting the qualifications specified in this rule shall be placed on the list of approved mediators. Approved mediators shall be placed on the list for a fixed period of time, not to exceed seven years, and must reapply at the end of that time in the manner directed by the court.

(b) Selections shall be made without regard to race, ethnic origin, or gender. Residency or principal place of business may not be a qualification.

(c) The approved list and the applications of approved mediators, except for the optional section identifying the applicant's gender and racial/ethnic background, shall be available to the public in the office of the ADR clerk.

(d) An applicant may attach a résumé or biographical information to the application.

(e) An applicant Community Dispute Resolution Program center must select only mediators who meet the qualifications of this rule or training requirements established by the State Court Administrator to mediate cases ordered by the court.

(3) *Rejection; Reconsideration*. Applicants who are not placed on the list shall be notified of that decision. Within 21 days of notification of the decision to reject an application, the applicant may seek reconsideration of the ADR clerk's decision by the presiding judge of the family division. The court does not need to provide a hearing. Documents considered in the initial review process shall be retained for at least the period during which the applicant can seek reconsideration of the original decision.

(4) *Removal from List*. The ADR clerk may remove from the list mediators who have demonstrated incompetence, bias, made themselves consistently unavailable to serve as a mediator, or for other just cause. Within 21 days of notification of the decision to remove a mediator from the list, the mediator may seek reconsideration of the ADR clerk's decision by the presiding judge of the family division. The court does not need to provide a hearing.

(G) **Qualification of Mediators**.

(1) To be eligible to serve as a domestic relations mediator under this rule, an applicant must meet the following minimum qualifications:

(a) The applicant must

(i) be a licensed attorney, a licensed or limited licensed psychologist, a licensed professional counselor, or a licensed marriage and family therapist;

(ii) have a masters degree in counseling, social work, or marriage and family therapy;

(iii) have a graduate degree in a behavioral science; or

(iv) have 5 years experience in family counseling.

(b) The applicant must have completed a training program approved by the State Court Administrator providing the generally accepted components of domestic relations mediation skills.

(c) Upon completion of the training required under subrule (G)(1)(b), the applicant must observe two domestic relations mediation proceedings conducted by an approved mediator, and conduct one domestic relations mediation to conclusion under the supervision and observation of an approved mediator.

(2) An applicant who has specialized experience or training, but does not meet the specific requirements of subrule (G)(1), may apply to the ADR clerk for special approval. The ADR clerk shall make the determination on the basis of criteria provided by the State Court Administrator.

(3) Approved mediators are required to obtain 8 hours of advanced mediation training during each 2-year period. Failure to submit documentation establishing compliance is grounds for removal from the list under subrule(F)(4).

(4) Additional qualifications may not be imposed upon mediators.

(H) **Mediation Procedure**.

(1) The mediator must schedule a mediation session within a reasonable time at a location accessible by the parties.

(2) A mediator may require that no later than 3 business days before the mediation session, each party submit to the mediator, and serve on the opposing party, a mediation summary that provides the following information, where relevant:

(a) the facts and circumstances of the case;

(b) the issues in dispute;

(c) a description of the marital assets and their estimated value, where such information is appropriate and reasonably ascertainable;

(d) the income and expenses of the parties;

(e) a proposed settlement; and

(f) such documentary evidence as may be available to substantiate information contained in the summary.

Failure to submit these materials to the mediator within the designated time may subject the offending party to sanctions imposed by the court.

(3) The parties must attend the mediation session in person unless excused by the mediator.

(4) Except for legal counsel, the parties may not bring other persons to the mediation session, whether expert or lay witnesses, unless permission is first obtained from the mediator, after notice to opposing counsel. If the mediator believes it would be helpful to the settlement of the case, the mediator may request information or assistance

from third persons at the time of the mediation session.

(5) The mediator shall discuss with the parties and counsel, if any, the facts and issues involved. The mediation will continue until a settlement is reached, the mediator determines that a settlement is not likely to be reached, the end of the first mediation session, or until a time agreed to by the parties.

(6) Within 7 days of the completion of mediation, the mediator shall so advise the court, stating only the date of completion of the process, who participated in the mediation, whether settlement was reached, and whether further ADR proceedings are contemplated. If an evaluation will be made under subrule (I), the mediator may delay reporting to the court until completion of the evaluation process.

(7) If a settlement is reached as a result of the mediation, to be binding, the terms of that settlement must be reduced to a signed writing by the parties or acknowledged by the parties on an audio or video recording. After a settlement has been reached, the parties shall take steps necessary to enter judgment as in the case of other settlements.

(8) Confidentiality in the mediation process is governed by MCR 2.412.

(I) **Evaluative Mediation.**

(1) This subrule applies if the parties requested evaluative mediation, or if they do so at the conclusion of mediation and the mediator is willing to provide an evaluation.

(2) If a settlement is not reached during mediation, the mediator, within a reasonable period after the conclusion of mediation shall prepare a written report to the parties setting forth the mediator's proposed recommendation for settlement purposes only. The mediator's recommendation shall be submitted to the parties of record only and may not be submitted or made available to the court.

(3) If both parties accept the mediator's recommendation in full, the attorneys shall proceed to have a judgment entered in conformity with the recommendation.

(4) If the mediator's recommendation is not accepted in full by both parties and the parties are unable to reach an agreement as to the remaining contested issues, mediator shall report to the court under subrule (H)(6), and the case shall proceed toward trial.

(5) A court may not impose sanctions against either party for rejecting the mediator's recommendation. The court may not inquire and neither the parties nor the mediator may inform the court of the identity of the party or parties who rejected the mediator's recommendation.

(6) The mediator's report and recommendation may not be read by the court and may not be admitted into evidence or relied upon by the court as evidence of any of the information contained in it without the consent of both parties. The court shall not request the parties' consent to read the mediator's recommendation.

(J) **Fees.**

(1) A mediator is entitled to reasonable compensation based on an hourly rate commensurate with the mediator's experience and usual charges for services performed.

(2) Before mediation, the parties shall agree in writing that each shall pay one-half of the mediator's fee no later than:

(a) 42 days after the mediation process is concluded or the service of the mediator's report and recommendation under subrule (I)(2), or

(b) the entry of judgment, or

(c) the dismissal of the action,

whichever occurs first. If the court finds that some other allocation of fees is appropriate, given the economic circumstances of the parties, the court may order that one of the parties pay more than one-half of the fee.

(3) If acceptable to the mediator, the court may order an arrangement for the payment of the mediator's fee other than that provided in subrule (J)(2).

(4) The mediator's fee is deemed a cost of the action, and the court may make an appropriate judgment under MCL 552.13(1) to enforce the payment of the fee.

(5) In the event either party objects to the total fee of the mediator, the matter may be scheduled before the trial judge for determination of the reasonableness of the fee.

(K) **Standards of Conduct.** The State Court Administrator shall develop and approve standards of conduct for domestic relations mediators designed to promote honesty, integrity, and impartiality in providing court-connected dispute resolution services. These standards shall be made a part of all training and educational requirements for court-connected programs, shall be provided to all mediators involved in court-connected programs, and shall be available to the public.

Rule 3.217 Actions Under the Paternity Act

(A) **Governing Law.** Procedure in actions under the Paternity Act, MCL 722.711 et seq. is governed by the rules applicable to other civil actions except as otherwise provided by this rule and the act.

(B) **Blood or Tissue Typing Tests.** A petition for blood or tissue typing tests under MCL 722.716 must be filed at or before the pretrial conference or, if a pretrial conference is not held, within the time specified by the court. Failure to timely petition waives the right to such tests, unless the court, in the interest of justice, permits a petition at a later time.

(C) **Advice Regarding Right to an Attorney**.

(1) The summons issued under MCL 722.714 must include a form advising the alleged father of the right to an attorney as described in subrule (C)(2), and the procedure for requesting the appointment of an attorney. The form must be served with the summons and the complaint, and the proof of service must so indicate.

(2) If the alleged father appears in court following the issuance of a summons under MCL 722.714, the court must personally advise him that he is entitled to the assistance of an attorney, and that the court will appoint an attorney at public expense, at his request, if he is financially unable to retain an attorney of his choice.

(3) If the alleged father indicates that he wants to proceed without an attorney, the record must affirmatively show that he was given the advice required by subrule (C)(2) and that he waived the right to counsel.

(4) If the alleged father does not appear in court following the issuance of a summons under MCL 722.714, subrule (C)(3) does not apply.

(D) **Visitation Rights of Noncustodial Parent**.

(1) On the petition of either party, the court may provide in the order of filiation for such reasonable visitation by the noncustodial parent as the court deems justified and in the best interests of the child.

(2) Absent a petition from either party, the right of reasonable visitation is reserved.

Rule 3.218 Friend of the Court Records; Access

(A) **General**. Friend of the court records are not subject to a subpoena issued under these Michigan Court Rules. Unless another rule specifically provides for the protection or release of friend of the court records, this rule governs. When used in this subrule, unless the context indicates otherwise,

(1) "records" means any case-specific information the friend of the court office maintains in any media;

(2) "access" means inspection of records, obtaining copies of records upon receipt of payment for costs of reproduction, and oral transmission by staff of information contained in friend of the court records;

(3) "confidential information" means

(a) staff notes;

(b) any confidential information from the Department of Human Services child protective services unit or information included in any reports to protective services from a friend of the court office;

(c) records from alternative dispute resolution processes, including the confidentiality of mediation records as defined in MCR 2.412;

(d) communications from minors;

(e) friend of the court grievances filed by the opposing party and the responses;

(f) any information when a court order prohibits its releaser;

(g) except as provided in MCR 3.219, any information for which a privilege could be claimed, or that was provided by a governmental agency subject to the express written condition that it remain confidential; and

(h) all information classified as confidential by the laws and regulations of title IV, part D of the Social Security Act, 42 USC 651 et seq.

(4) Reference to an agency, office, officer, or capacity includes an employee or contractor working within that agency or office, or an employee or caseworker acting on behalf of that office or working in the capacity referred to.

(5) "Governmental agency" means any entity exercising constitutional, legislative, executive, or judicial authority, when providing benefits or services.

(B) A friend of the court office must provide access to nonconfidential records to the following:

(1) A party; third-party custodian; guardian or conservator; guardian ad litem or counsel for a minor; lawyer-guardian ad litem; an attorney of record; and the personal representative of the estate of a party.

The friend of the court may honor a request from a person identified in this paragraph to release information to a governmental agency providing services to that individual, or before which an application for services is pending.

(2) An officer in the Judge Advocate General's office in any branch of the United States military, if the request is made on behalf of a service member on active duty otherwise identified in this subrule.

(C) Unless the release is otherwise prohibited by law, a friend of the court office must provide access to all nonconfidential and confidential records to the following:

(1) Other agencies and individuals as necessary for the friend of the court to implement the state's plan under Title IV, Part D of the Social Security Act, 42 USC 651 et seq. or as required by the court, state law, or regulation that is consistent with this state's IV-D plan.

(2) The Department of Human Services, as necessary to report suspected abuse or neglect or to allow the Department of Human Services to investigate or provide services to a party or child in the case.

(3) Other agencies that provide services under Title IV, part D of the Social Security Act, 42 USC 651 et seq.
(4) Auditors from state and federal agencies, as required to perform their audit functions with respect to a friend of the court matter.
(5) Corrections, parole, or probation officers, when, in the opinion of the friend of the court, access would assist the office in enforcing a provision of a custody, parenting time, or support order.
(6) Michigan law enforcement personnel who are conducting a civil or criminal investigation related directly to a friend of the court matter, and to federal law enforcement officers pursuant to a federal subpoena in a criminal or civil investigation.

(D) A citizen advisory committee established under the Friend of the Court Act, MCL 552.501 et seq.
(1) shall be given access to a grievance filed with the friend of the court, and to information related to the case, other than confidential information.
(2) may be given access to confidential information related to a grievance if the court so orders, upon demonstration by the committee that the information is necessary to the performance of its duties and that the release will not impair the rights of a party or the well-being of a child involved in the case.
When a citizen advisory committee requests information that may be confidential, the friend of the court shall notify the parties of the request and that they have 14 days from the date the notice was mailed to file a written response with the court.
If the court grants access to the information, it may impose such terms and conditions as it determines are appropriate to protect the rights of a party of the well-being of a child.

(E) A friend of the court office may refuse to provide access to a record in the friend of the court file if the friend of the court did not create or author the record. On those occasions, the requestor may request access from the person or entity that created the record.

(F) Any person who is denied access to friend of the court records or confidential information may file a motion for an order of access with the judge assigned to the case or, if none, the chief judge.

(G) A court, by administrative order adopted pursuant to MCR 8.112(B), may make reasonable regulations necessary to protect friend of the court records and to prevent excessive and unreasonable interference with the discharge of friend of the court functions.

Rule 3.219 Dissemination of a Professional Report

If there is a dispute involving custody, visitation, or change of domicile, and the court uses a community resource to assist its determination, the court must assure that copies of the written findings and recommendations of the resource are provided to the friend of the court and to the attorneys of record for the parties, or the parties if they are not represented by counsel. The attorneys for the parties, or the parties if they are not represented by counsel, may file objections to the report before a decision is made.

Rule 3.221 Hearings on Support and Parenting Time Enforcement Act Bench Warrants

(A) **Definitions.**
(1) Unless the context indicates otherwise, the term "bond" means the performance bond required by MCL 552.631.
(2) The term "cash" means money or the equivalent of money, such as a money order, cashier's check, or negotiable check or a payment by debit or credit card, which equivalent is accepted as cash by the agency accepting the payment.
(3) Unless the context indicates otherwise, the term "person," when used in this rule, means a party who has been arrested on a bench warrant issued pursuant to MCL 552.631.

(B) **Hearing on the Merits**. The court shall hold a hearing in connection with the matter in which the warrant was issued within 21 days of the date of arrest. Except as provided in this rule, a person who does not post a bond, within 48 hours of arrest excluding weekends and holidays, shall be brought before the court that issued the warrant for further proceedings on the matter in which the warrant was issued. The hearing may be adjourned when necessary to give notice of the proceedings to another party or to receive additional evidence. In the event the hearing is adjourned, the court shall set terms of release under subrule (F). Failure to hold a hearing within 21 days will not deprive the court of jurisdiction to proceed.

(C) **Bond Review Hearing**. A person who has not posted a bond, and whose case cannot be heard as provided in subrule (B), must without unnecessary delay be brought before a judge or referee for a review of the bond.

(D) **Place of Bond Review Hearing**. Except as otherwise provided in this subrule, a bond review hearing under subrule (E) must be held in the circuit court specified in the warrant. If a person is arrested in a circuit other than the one specified in the warrant, the arresting agency must make arrangements to assure that the person is promptly transported to the court specified in the warrant for a hearing in accordance with the provisions of this rule. If prompt transportation cannot be arranged, the bond review hearing must be held in the jurisdiction in which the individual is being held.

(E) **Conduct of Bond Review Hearing**. At the bond review hearing, the person must be advised of the purpose of the hearing on the merits and a determination must be made of what form of prehearing release is appropriate. A verbatim record must be made of the bond review hearing. Pending the hearing required under subrule (B), the person must be released on conditions under subrule (F).

(F) **Conditional Release.** The person must be released on condition that the person will appear for a hearing under subrule (B) and any other conditions that are appropriate to ensure that the person will appear as required for a hearing under subrule (B), including requiring the person to:

(1) make reports to a court agency as required by the court or the agency;

(2) comply with restrictions on personal associations, place of residence, place of employment, or travel;

(3) surrender driver's license or passport;

(4) comply with a specified curfew;

(5) continue or seek employment or participate in a work program;

(6) continue or begin an educational program;

(7) remain in the custody of a responsible member of the community who agrees to monitor the person and report any violation of any release condition to the court;

(8) post a bond as described in subrule (G).

In the event the person cannot satisfy a condition of release, the arresting agency must make arrangements with the authorities in the county of the court specified in the warrant to have the person promptly transported to that county for a hearing in accordance with the provisions of this rule.

(G) **Performance Bond Modification.** If it is determined for reasons stated on the record that the person's appearance cannot otherwise be assured, the person, in addition to any conditions described in subrule (F), may be required to post a bond at the person's option, executed:

(1) by the person, or by another who is not a licensed surety, and secured by a cash deposit for the full bond amount, or

(2) by a surety approved by the court.

(H) **Decision; Statement of Reasons.**

(1) In deciding what terms and conditions to impose under subrule (F), relevant information, including the following shall be considered:

(a) the person's record for reporting information to the friend of the court and complying with court orders;

(b) the person's record of appearance or nonappearance at court proceedings;

(c) the person's history of substance abuse or addiction;

(d) the amount of support owed;

(e) the person's employment status and history and financial history insofar as these factors relate to the ability to post bond;

(f) the availability of responsible members of the community who would vouch for or monitor the person;

(g) facts indicating the person's ties to the community, including family ties and relationships, and length of residence; and

(h) any other facts bearing on the risk of nonappearance.

(2) The reasons for requiring a bond under subrule (F), must be stated on the record. A finding on each of the enumerated factors is not necessary.

(3) Nothing in this rule may be construed to sanction the determination of prehearing release on the basis of race, religion, gender, economic status, or other impermissible criteria.

(I) **Review; Modification of Release Decision.**

(1) *Review.* A party seeking review of a release decision may file a motion in the court having appellate jurisdiction over the decision maker. If the decision was made by a referee, a party is entitled to a new hearing. Otherwise, the reviewing court may not stay, vacate, modify, or reverse the release decision except on finding an abuse of discretion.

(2) *Emergency Release.* If a person is ordered released from custody as a result of a court order or law requiring the release of prisoners to relieve jail conditions, the court ordering the release shall impose conditions of release in accordance with this rule to ensure the appearance of the individual as required. If such conditions of release are imposed, the court must inform the person of the conditions on the record or by furnishing to the person or the person's lawyer a copy of the release order setting forth the conditions.

(J) **Termination of Release Order.**

(1) After a bond is set pursuant to subrule (G), if the person appears for the hearing in subrule (B) the court must vacate the release order, discharge a third party who has posted the bond, and return the cash posted in the full amount of a bond. At the court's discretion, an arrested person who has deposited money with the court may be required to forfeit all or a portion of the amount to pay support, fines, fees, costs, and sanctions.

(2) If the person fails to comply with any conditions of release, the court that issued the original bench warrant may issue a new bench warrant for the person's arrest and enter an order revoking the release order and declaring the bond, if any, forfeited.

(a) The court must mail notice of any revocation order immediately to the person at the person's last known address and, if forfeiture of bond has been ordered, to anyone who posted bond.

(b) If the person does not appear and surrender to the court within 28 days after the revocation date or does not within the period satisfy the court that there was compliance with the conditions of release or that compliance was impossible through no fault of the person, the court may continue the revocation order and enter judgment forfeiting the bond against the individual and anyone who posted bond for the entire amount of the bond and costs of the court proceedings and costs associated with the arrest.

(K) **Plan for Remote Bond Review Hearings**. In each county, the court with trial jurisdiction over friend of the court cases must adopt and file with the State Court Administrator a plan for conducting bond review hearings on bench warrants issued as a result of a show cause hearing when the person is arrested in another county and cannot be transported immediately. The plan shall provide for the use of available technology for a person's appearance and the transmission and presentation of evidence in hearings under this rule.

Subchapter 3.300 Extraordinary Writs

Rule 3.301 Extraordinary Writs in General

(A) **Applicability and Scope of Rules.**
(1) A civil action or appropriate motion in a pending action may be brought to obtain
(a) superintending control,
(b) habeas corpus,
(c) mandamus, or
(d) quo warranto.
Unless a particular rule or statute specifically provides otherwise, an original action may not be commenced in the Supreme Court or the Court of Appeals if the circuit court would have jurisdiction of an action seeking that relief.
(2) These special rules govern the procedure for seeking the writs or relief formerly obtained by the writs, whether the right to relief is created by statute or common law. If the right to relief is created by statute, the limitations on relief in the statute apply, as well as the limitations on relief in these rules.
(3) The general rules of procedure apply except as otherwise provided in this subchapter.

(B) **Joinder of Claims**. More than one kind of writ may be sought in an action either as an independent claim or as an alternative claim. Subject to MCR 2.203, other claims may be joined in an action for a writ or writs.

(C) **Process; Service of Writs**. Process must be issued and served as in other civil actions. However, if a writ, order, or order to show cause is issued before service of process, then service of the writ, order, or order to show cause in the manner prescribed in MCR 2.105, accompanied by a copy of the complaint, makes service of other process unnecessary.

(D) **Assignment for Trial**. Actions brought under these special rules may be given precedence under MCR 2.501(B).

(E) **Records**. The action taken on applications for writs or orders to show cause must be noted in court records in the same manner as actions taken in other civil actions.

(F) **No Automatic Stay**. The automatic stay provisions of MCR 2.614(A) do not apply to judgments in actions brought under this subchapter.

(G) **Procedure Where Relief Is Sought in Supreme Court or Court of Appeals.**
(1) MCR 7.304 applies to original proceedings brought in the Supreme Court to obtain relief under this subchapter.
(2) MCR 7.206 applies to original proceedings brought in the Court of Appeals to obtain relief under this subchapter.

Rule 3.302 Superintending Control

(A) **Scope**. A superintending control order enforces the superintending control power of a court over lower courts or tribunals.

(B) **Policy Concerning Use**. If another adequate remedy is available to the party seeking the order, a complaint for superintending control may not be filed. See subrule (D)(2), and MCR 7.101(A)(2), and 7.304(A).

(C) **Writs Superseded**. A superintending control order replaces the writs of certiorari and prohibition and the writ of mandamus when directed to a lower court or tribunal.

(D) **Jurisdiction.**
(1) The Supreme Court, the Court of Appeals, and the circuit court have jurisdiction to issue superintending control orders to lower courts or tribunals.
(2) When an appeal in the Supreme Court, the Court of Appeals, or the circuit court, is available, that method of review must be used. If superintending control is sought and an appeal is available, the complaint for superintending control must be dismissed.

(E) **Procedure for Superintending Control in Circuit Court.**
(1) Complaint. A person seeking superintending control in the circuit court must file a complaint with the court. Only the plaintiff's name may appear in the title of the action (for example, In re Smith). The plaintiff must serve a copy of the complaint on the court or tribunal over which superintending control is sought. If the superintending control action arises out of a particular action, a copy of the complaint must also be served on each other party to the proceeding in that court or tribunal.

(2) Answer. Anyone served under subrule (E)(1) may file an answer within 21 days after the complaint is served.
(3) Issuance of Order; Dismissal.
(a) After the filing of a complaint and answer or, if no answer is filed, after expiration of the time for filing an answer, the court may
(i) issue an order to show cause why the order requested should not be issued,
(ii) issue the order requested, or
(iii) dismiss the complaint.
(b) If a need for immediate action is shown, the court may enter an order before an answer is filed.
(c) The court may require in an order to show cause that additional records and papers be filed.
(d) An order to show cause must specify the date for hearing the complaint.

Rule 3.303 Habeas Corpus to Inquire Into Cause of Detention

(A) **Jurisdiction and Venue; Persons Detained on Criminal Charges**.
(1) An action for habeas corpus to inquire into the cause of detention of a person may be brought in any court of record except the probate court.
(2) The action must be brought in the county in which the prisoner is detained. If it is shown that there is no judge in that county empowered and available to issue the writ or that the judicial circuit for that county has refused to issue the writ, the action may be brought in the Court of Appeals.
(3) A prisoner detained in a county jail for a criminal charge, who has not been sentenced to detention by a court of competent jurisdiction, may be removed from detention by a writ of habeas corpus to inquire into the cause of detention only if the writ is issued by the court in which the prisoner would next appear if the criminal process against the prisoner continued, or by the judicial circuit for the county in which the prisoner is detained. This subrule does not limit the power of the Court of Appeals or Supreme Court to issue the writ.

(B) **Who May Bring**. An action for habeas corpus may be brought by the prisoner or by another person on the prisoner's behalf.

(C) **Complaint**. The complaint must state:
(1) that the person on whose behalf the writ is applied for (the prisoner) is restrained of his or her liberty;
(2) the name, if known, or the description of the prisoner;
(3) the name, if known, or the description of the officer or person by whom the prisoner is restrained;
(4) the place of restraint, if known;
(5) that the action for habeas corpus by or on behalf of the prisoner is not prohibited;
(6) the cause or pretense of the restraint, according to the plaintiff's best knowledge and belief; and
(7) why the restraint is illegal.

(D) **Issuance of the Writ or Order to Show Cause**.
(1) On the filing of the complaint, the court may issue
(a) a writ of habeas corpus directed to the person having custody of the prisoner, or that person's superior, ordering him or her to bring the prisoner before the court forthwith; or
(b) an order to show cause why the writ should not be issued, unless it appears that the prisoner is not entitled to relief.
(2) On the showing required by MCL 600.4337, the court may issue a warrant in lieu of habeas corpus.
(3) Duplicate original writs may be issued.

(E) **Certification of Record**. When proceedings in another court or agency are pertinent to a determination of the issue raised in a habeas corpus action, the court may order the transcript of the record and proceedings certified to the court within a specified time. The order must identify the records to be certified with sufficient specificity to allow them to be located.

(F) **Issuance Without Application or Before Filing**.
(1) A judge of a court of record, except the probate court, may issue a writ of habeas corpus or order to show cause if
(a) the judge learns that a person within the judge's jurisdiction is illegally restrained, or
(b) an application is presented to the judge before or after normal court hours.
(2) If the prisoner is being held on criminal charges, the writ or order may only be issued by a judge of a court authorized to issue a writ of habeas corpus under subrule (A)(3).
(3) If a complaint is presented to a judge under the provisions of subrule (F)(1)(b), it need not be filed with the court before the issuance of a writ of habeas corpus. The complaint must subsequently be filed with the court whether or not the writ is granted.

(G) **Endorsement of Allowance of Writ**. Every writ issued must be endorsed with a certificate of its allowance and the date of the allowance. The endorsement must be signed by the judge issuing the writ, or, if the writ is issued by a panel of more than 1 judge, by a judge of the court.

(H) **Form of Writ**. A writ of habeas corpus must be substantially in the form approved by the state court administrator.

(I) **Service of Writ**.
(1) *Person to be Served*. The writ or order to show cause must be served on the defendant in the manner prescribed in MCR 2.105. If the defendant cannot be found, or if the defendant does not have

the prisoner in custody, the writ or order to show cause may be served on anyone having the prisoner in custody or that person's superior, in the manner and with the same effect as if that person had been made a defendant in the action.

(2) *Tender of Fees*. If the Attorney General or a prosecuting attorney brings the action, or if a judge issues the writ on his or her own initiative, there is no fee. In other actions, to make the service of a writ of habeas corpus effective, the person making service must give the fee provided by law or this rule to the person having custody of the prisoner or to that person's superior.

(a) If the prisoner is in the custody of a sheriff, coroner, constable, or marshal, the fee is that allowed by law to a sheriff for bringing up a prisoner.

(b) If the prisoner is in the custody of another person, the fee is that, if any, allowed by the court issuing the writ, not exceeding the fee allowed by law to a sheriff for similar services.

(J) **Sufficiency of Writ**. The writ or order to show cause may not be disobeyed because of a defect in form. The writ or order to show cause is sufficient if the prisoner is designated by name, if known, or by a description sufficient to permit identification. The writ or order may designate the person to whom it is directed as the person having custody of the prisoner. Anyone served with the writ or order is deemed the person to whom it is directed and is considered a defendant in the action.

(K) **Time for Answer and Hearing**.

(1) If the writ is to be answered and the hearing held on a specified day and hour, the answer must be made and the prisoner produced at the time and place specified in the writ.

(2) If an order to show cause is issued, it must be answered as provided in subrule (N), and the hearing must be held at the time and place specified in the order.

(L) **Notice of Hearing Before Discharge**.

(1) When the answer states that the prisoner is in custody on process under which another person has an interest in continuing the custody, an order of discharge may not be issued unless the interested person or that person's attorney has had at least 4 days' notice of the time and place of the hearing.

(2) When the answer states that the prisoner is detained on a criminal charge, the prisoner may not be discharged until sufficient notice of the time and place of the hearing is given to the prosecuting attorney of the county within which the prisoner is detained or, if there is no prosecuting attorney within the county, to the Attorney General.

(M) **Habeas Corpus to Obtain Custody of Child**.

(1) A complaint seeking a writ of habeas corpus to inquire into a child's custody must be presented to the judicial circuit for the county in which the child resides or is found.

(2) An order to show cause, not a writ of habeas corpus, must be issued initially if the action is brought by a parent, foster parent, or other relative of the child, to obtain custody of a child under the age of 16 years from a parent, foster parent, or other relative of the child. The court may direct the friend of the court to investigate the circumstances of the child's custody.

(N) **Answer**.

(1) *Contents of Answer; Contempt*. The defendant or person served must obey the writ or order to show cause or show good cause for not doing so, and must answer the writ or order to show cause within the time allowed. Failure to file an answer is contempt. The answer must state plainly and unequivocally

(a) whether the defendant then has, or at any time has had, the prisoner under his or her control and, if so, the reason; and

(b) if the prisoner has been transferred, to whom, when the transfer was made, and the reason or authority for the transfer.

(2) *Exhibits*. If the prisoner is detained because of a writ, warrant, or other written authority, a copy must be attached to the answer as an exhibit, and the original must be produced at the hearing. If an order under subrule (E) requires it, the answer must be accompanied by the certified transcript of the record and proceedings.

(3) *Verification*. The answer must be signed by the person answering, and, except when the person is a sworn public officer and answers in his or her official capacity, it must be verified by oath.

(O) **Answer May Be Controverted**. In a reply or at a hearing, the plaintiff or the prisoner may controvert the answer under oath, to show either that the restraint is unlawful or that the prisoner is entitled to discharge.

(P) **Prisoner; When Bailed**. Because a habeas corpus action must be decided promptly with no more than the brief delay provided by subrule (Q)(2), release of a prisoner on bail will not normally be considered until after determination that legal cause exists for the detention. Thereafter, if the prisoner is entitled to bail, the court issuing the writ or order may set bail.

(Q) **Hearing and Judgment**.

(1) The court shall proceed promptly to hear the matter in a summary manner and enter judgment.

(2) In response to the writ of habeas corpus or order to show cause, the defendant may request adjournment of the hearing. Adjournment may be granted only for the brief delay necessary to permit the defendant

(a) to prepare a written answer (unless waived by the plaintiff); or

(b) to present to the court or judge issuing the writ or order testimonial or documentary evidence to establish the cause of detention at the time for answer.

(3) In the defendant's presence, the court shall inform the prisoner that he or she has the right to an attorney and the right to remain silent.

(4) From the time the prisoner is produced in response to the writ or order until judgment is entered, the judge who issued the writ or order has custody of the prisoner and shall make certain that the prisoner's full constitutional rights are protected.

(5) The hearing on the return to a writ of habeas corpus or an order to show cause must be recorded verbatim, unless a court reporter or recorder is not available. If the hearing is conducted without a verbatim record being made, as soon as possible the judge shall prepare and certify a narrative written report. The original report is part of the official record in the action, and copies must be sent forthwith to the parties or their attorneys.

(6) If the prisoner is restrained because of mental disease, the court shall consider the question of the prisoner's mental condition at the time of the hearing, rather than merely the legality of the original detention.

Rule 3.304 Habeas Corpus to Bring Prisoner to Testify or for Prosecution

(A) **Jurisdiction; When Available**. A court of record may issue a writ of habeas corpus directing that a prisoner in a jail or prison in Michigan be brought to testify

(1) on the court's own initiative; or

(2) on the ex parte motion of a party in an action before a court or an officer or body authorized to examine witnesses.

A writ of habeas corpus may also be issued to bring a prisoner to court for prosecution. Subrules (C)-(G) apply to such a writ.

(B) **Contents of Motion**. The motion must be verified by the party and must state

(1) the title and nature of the action in which the testimony of the prisoner is desired; and

(2) that the testimony of the prisoner is relevant and necessary to the party in that proceeding.

(C) **Direction to Surrender Custody for Transportation**. The writ may direct that the prisoner be placed in the custody of a designated officer for transportation to the place where the hearing or trial is to be held, rather than requiring the custodian to bring the prisoner to that place.

(D) **Form of Writ**. A writ of habeas corpus to produce a prisoner to testify or for prosecution must be substantially in the form approved by the state court administrator.

(E) **Answer and Hearing**. If the prisoner is produced or delivered to the custody of a designated officer as ordered, the person served with the writ need not answer the writ, and a hearing on the writ is unnecessary.

(F) **Remand**. When a prisoner is brought on a writ of habeas corpus to testify or for prosecution, the prisoner must be returned to the original custodian after testifying or prosecution.

(G) **Applicability of Other Rules**. MCR 3.303(G), (I), (J), and (K)(1) apply to habeas corpus to produce a prisoner to testify or for prosecution.

Rule 3.305 Mandamus

(A) **Jurisdiction.**

(1) An action for mandamus against a state officer may be brought in the Court of Appeals or the circuit court.

(2) All other actions for mandamus must be brought in the circuit court unless a statute or rule requires or allows the action to be brought in another court.

(B) **Venue.**

(1) The general venue statutes and rules apply to actions for mandamus unless a specific statute or rule contains a special venue provision.

(2) In addition to any other county in which venue is proper, an action for mandamus against a state officer may be brought in Ingham County.

(C) **Order to Show Cause**. On ex parte motion and a showing of the necessity for immediate action, the court may issue an order to show cause. The motion may be made in the complaint. The court shall indicate in the order when the defendant must answer the order.

(D) **Answer**. If necessity for immediate action is not shown, and the action is not dismissed, the defendant must answer the complaint as in an ordinary civil action.

(E) **Exhibits**. A party may attach to the pleadings, as exhibits, certified or authenticated copies of record evidence on which the party relies.

(F) **Hearings in Circuit Court**. The court may hear the matter or may allow the issues to be tried by a jury.

(G) **Writ Contained in Judgment**. If the judgment awards a writ of mandamus, the writ may be contained in the judgment in the form of an order, and a separate writ need not be issued or served.

Rule 3.306 Quo Warranto

(A) **Jurisdiction.**

(1) An action for quo warranto against a person who usurps, intrudes into, or unlawfully holds or exercises a state office, or against a state officer who does or suffers an act that by law works a forfeiture of the office, must be brought in the Court of Appeals.

(2) All other actions for quo warranto must be brought in the circuit court.

(B) **Parties**.

(1) *Actions by Attorney General*. An action for quo warranto is to be brought by the Attorney General when the action is against:

(a) a person specified in subrule (A)(1);

(b) a person who usurps, intrudes into, or wrongfully holds or exercises an office in a public corporation created by this state's authority;

(c) an association, or number of persons, acting as a corporation in Michigan without being legally incorporated;

(d) a corporation that is in violation of a provision of the act or acts creating, offering, or renewing the corporation;

(e) a corporation that has violated the provisions of a law under which the corporation forfeits its charter by misuse;

(f) a corporation that has forfeited its privileges and franchises by nonuse;

(g) a corporation that has committed or omitted acts that amount to a surrender of its corporate rights, privileges, and franchises, or has exercised a franchise or privilege not conferred on it by law.

(2) *Actions by Prosecutor or Citizen*. Other actions for quo warranto may be brought by the prosecuting attorney of the proper county, without leave of court, or by a citizen of the county by special leave of the court.

(3) *Application to Attorney General*.

(a) A person may apply to the Attorney General to have the Attorney General bring an action specified in subrule (B)(1). The Attorney General may require the person to give security to indemnify the state against all costs and expenses of the action. The person making the application, and any other person having the proper interest, may be joined as parties plaintiff.

(b) If, on proper application and offer of security, the Attorney General refuses to bring the action, the person may apply to the appropriate court for leave to bring the action himself or herself.

(C) **Person Alleged to be Entitled to Office**. If the action is brought against the defendant for usurping an office, the complaint may name the person rightfully entitled to the office, with an allegation of his or her right to it, and that person may be made a party.

(D) **Venue**. The general venue statutes and rules apply to actions for quo warranto, unless a specific statute or rule contains a special venue provision applicable to an action for quo warranto.

(E) **Hearing**. The court may hear the matter or may allow the issues to be tried by a jury.

Rule 3.310 Injunctions

(A) **Preliminary Injunctions**.

(1) Except as otherwise provided by statute or these rules, an injunction may not be granted before a hearing on a motion for a preliminary injunction or on an order to show cause why a preliminary injunction should not be issued.

(2) Before or after the commencement of the hearing on a motion for a preliminary injunction, the court may order the trial of the action on the merits to be advanced and consolidated with the hearing on the motion. Even when consolidation is not ordered, evidence received at the hearing for a preliminary injunction that would be admissible at the trial on the merits becomes part of the trial record and need not be repeated at the trial. This provision may not be used to deny the parties any rights they may have to trial by jury.

(3) A motion for a preliminary injunction must be filed and noticed for hearing in compliance with the rules governing other motions unless the court orders otherwise on a showing of good cause.

(4) At the hearing on an order to show cause why a preliminary injunction should not issue, the party seeking injunctive relief has the burden of establishing that a preliminary injunction should be issued, whether or not a temporary restraining order has been issued.

(5) If a preliminary injunction is granted, the court shall promptly schedule a pretrial conference. The trial of the action on the merits must be held within 6 months after the injunction is granted, unless good cause is shown or the parties stipulate to a longer period. The court shall issue its decision on the merits within 56 days after the trial is completed.

(B) **Temporary Restraining Orders**.

(1) A temporary restraining order may be granted without written or oral notice to the adverse party or the adverse party's attorney only if

(a) it clearly appears from specific facts shown by affidavit or by a verified complaint that immediate and irreparable injury, loss, or damage will result to the applicant from the delay required to effect notice or from the risk that notice will itself precipitate adverse action before an order can be issued;

(b) the applicant's attorney certifies to the court in writing the efforts, if any, that have been made to give the notice and the reasons supporting the claim that notice should not be required; and

(c) a permanent record or memorandum is made of any nonwritten evidence, argument, or other representations made in support of the application.

(2) A temporary restraining order granted without notice must:
   (a) be endorsed with the date and time of issuance;
   (b) describe the injury and state why it is irreparable and why the order was granted without notice;
   (c) except in domestic relations actions, set a date for hearing at the earliest possible time on the motion for a preliminary injunction or order to show cause why a preliminary injunction should not be issued.

(3) Except in domestic relations actions, a temporary restraining order granted without notice expires by its terms within such time after entry, not to exceed 14 days, as the court sets unless within the time so fixed the order, for good cause shown, is extended for a like period or unless the party against whom the order is directed consents that it may be extended for a longer period. The reasons for the extension must be stated on the record or in a document filed in the action.

(4) A temporary restraining order granted without notice must be filed forthwith in the clerk's office and entered in the court records.

(5) A motion to dissolve a temporary restraining order granted without notice takes precedence over all matters except older matters of the same character, and may be heard on 24 hours' notice. For good cause shown, the court may order the motion heard on shorter notice. The court may set the time for the hearing at the time the restraining order is granted, without waiting for the filing of a motion to dissolve it, and may order that the hearing on a motion to dissolve a restraining order granted without notice be consolidated with the hearing on a motion for a preliminary injunction or an order to show cause why a preliminary injunction should not be issued. At a hearing on a motion to dissolve a restraining order granted without notice, the burden of justifying continuation of the order is on the applicant for the restraining order whether or not the hearing has been consolidated with a hearing on a motion for a preliminary injunction or an order to show cause.

(C) **Form and Scope of Injunction**. An order granting an injunction or restraining order
   (1) must set forth the reasons for its issuance;
   (2) must be specific in terms;
   (3) must describe in reasonable detail, and not by reference to the complaint or other document, the acts restrained; and
   (4) is binding only on the parties to the action, their officers, agents, servants, employees, and attorneys, and on those persons in active concert or participation with them who receive actual notice of the order by personal service or otherwise.

(D) **Security**.
   (1) Before granting a preliminary injunction or temporary restraining order, the court may require the applicant to give security, in the amount the court deems proper, for the payment of costs and damages that may be incurred or suffered by a party who is found to have been wrongfully enjoined or restrained.
   (2) Security is not required of the state or of a Michigan county or municipal corporation or its officer or agency acting in an official capacity. As to other parties, if security is not required the order must state the reason.
   (3) If the party enjoined deems the security insufficient and has had no prior opportunity to be heard, the party may object to the sufficiency of the surety in the manner provided in MCR 3.604(E). The procedures provided in MCR 3.604(F) apply to the objection.
   (4) When a bond is required before the issuance of an injunction or temporary restraining order, the bond must be filed with the clerk before the sealing and delivery of the injunction or restraining order.

(E) **Stay of Action**. An injunction or temporary restraining order may not be granted in one action to stay proceedings in another action pending in another court if the relief requested could be sought in the other pending action.

(F) **Denial of Application**. When an application for a preliminary injunction or temporary restraining order is denied, but an order is not signed, an endorsement of the denial must be made on the complaint or affidavit, and the complaint or affidavit filed.

(G) **Later Application After Denial of Injunction**.
   (1) If a circuit judge has denied an application for an injunction or temporary restraining order, in whole or in part, or has granted it conditionally or on terms, later application for the same purpose and in relation to the same matter may not be made to another circuit judge.
   (2) If an order is entered on an application in violation of subrule (G)(1), it is void and must be revoked by the judge who entered it, on due proof of the facts. A person making the later application contrary to this rule is subject to punishment for contempt.

(H) **Motion for Injunction in Pending Actions**. An injunction may also be granted before or in connection with final judgment on a motion filed after an action is commenced.

(I) **Application to Special Actions**. This rule applies to a special statutory action for an injunction only to the extent that it does not conflict with special procedures prescribed by the statute or the rules governing the special action.

Subchapter 3.400 Proceedings Involving Real Property

Rule 3.401 Partition

(A) **Matters to be Determined by Court**. On the hearing of an action or proceeding for partition, the court shall determine

(1) whether the premises can be partitioned without great prejudice to the parties;

(2) the value of the use of the premises and of improvements made to the premises; and

(3) other matters the court considers pertinent.

(B) **Partition or Sale in Lieu of Partition**. If the court determines that the premises can be partitioned, MCR 3.402 governs further proceedings. If the court determines that the premises cannot be partitioned without undue prejudice to the owners, it may order the premises sold in lieu of partition under MCR 3.403.

(C) **Joinder of Lienholders**. A creditor having a lien on all or part of the premises, by judgment, mortgage, or otherwise, need not be made a party to the partition proceedings. However, the plaintiff may join every creditor having a specific lien on the undivided interest or estate of a party. If the creditors are made parties, the complaint must state the nature of every lien or encumbrance.

Rule 3.402 Partition Procedure

(A) **Determination of Parties' Interests**. In ordering partition the court shall determine the rights and interests of the parties in the premises, and describe parts or shares that are to remain undivided for owners whose interests are unknown or not ascertained.

(B) **Appointment of Partition Commissioner**.

(1) The court shall appoint a disinterested person as partition commissioner to make the partition according to the court's determination of the rights and interests of the parties. If the parties agree, three commissioners may be appointed who shall meet together to perform their duties and act by majority vote.

(2) The partition commissioner must be sworn before an officer authorized to administer oaths to honestly and impartially partition the property as directed by the court. The oath must be filed with the clerk of the court.

(3) If the partition commissioner dies, resigns, or neglects to serve, the court may appoint a replacement.

(C) **Proceedings Before Partition Commissioner**.

(1) The partition commissioner

(a) may apply to the court for instructions;

(b) must give notice of the meeting to consider the problems of the partition to the parties so that they may be heard if they wish to be; and

(c) may take evidence at the meeting concerning the problems of partition.

(2) The partition commissioner shall divide the premises and allot the respective shares according to the terms in the court's judgment or separate order, and shall designate the several shares and portions by reference to a plat or survey prepared by a land surveyor or engineer licensed by the state.

(3) The partition commissioner must report to the court, specifying the procedures followed, describing the land divided and the shares allotted to each party, and listing the commissioner's charges. The parties shall not be present during the preparation of the report or during the deliberations of a panel of three commissioners. A copy of the report must be sent to each party who has appeared in the action.

(D) **Setting Aside, Modification, or Confirmation of Partition Commissioner's Report.**

(1) The court may modify or set aside the report and may refer the action to either the same or a newly appointed partition commissioner as often as necessary.

(2) On confirming the report, the court shall enter a judgment binding and conclusive on:

(a) all parties named in the action who

(i) have an interest in the partitioned premises as owners in fee or tenants for years,

(ii) are entitled to the reversion, remainder, or inheritance of the premises after the termination of a particular estate in the premises,

(iii) are or will become entitled to a beneficial interest in the premises, or

(iv) have an interest in an undivided share of the premises as tenants for years, for life, or in dower;

(b) the legal representatives of the parties listed in subrule (D)(2)(a);

(c) all persons interested in the premises who were unknown at the time the action was commenced and were given sufficient notice either by publication or personally; and

(d) all other persons claiming from any of the above parties or persons.

(3) The judgment and partition do not affect persons who have claims as tenants in dower or for life to the entire premises subject to the partition; nor do they preclude a person, except those specified in subrule (D)(2), from claiming title to the premises in question or from controverting the title or interest of the parties among whom the partition was made.

(4) An authenticated copy of the report, the judgment confirming it, and any incorporated surveys may be recorded with the register of deeds of the county in

which the land is located. Copies of subdivision plats already of record need not be recorded.

(E) **Expenses and Costs**. The court may order that the expenses and costs, including attorney fees, be paid by the parties in accordance with their respective rights and equities in the premises. An order requiring a party to pay expenses and costs may be enforced in the same manner as a judgment.

(F) **Setting Off of Interests in Special Cases.**

(1) The court may by order set off the interest that belonged to a deceased party, without subdivision, to those claiming under that party when it is expedient to do so. Those legally entitled under or through the deceased party must be mentioned by name in the judgment.

(2) If the original parties in interest were fully known, but death, legal proceedings, or other operation of law has caused uncertainty about the identity of the present parties in interest, the interests originally owned by known parties but now owned by unknown persons may be separated as provided in this rule, instead of being left undivided. The division and judgment operate to convey the title to the persons claiming under the known party, according to their legal rights.

(3) If an interest in the premises belongs to known or unknown parties who have not appeared in the action, the court shall order partition of the ascertained interests of the known parties who have appeared in the action. The residue of the premises remains for the parties whose interests have not been ascertained, subject to future division.

Rule 3.403 Sale of Premises and Division of Proceeds as Substitute for Partition

(A) **Order of Sale**.

(1) If a party has a dower interest or life estate in all or a part of the premises at the time of the order for sale, the court shall determine whether, under all the circumstances and with regard for the interests of all the parties, that interest should be excepted from the sale or be sold with the premises. If the court orders that the sale include that party's interest, the sale conveys that interest.

(2) In the order of sale the court shall designate:

(a) which premises are to be sold;

(b) whether the premises are to be sold in separate parcels or together;

(c) whether there is a minimum price at which the premises may be sold;

(d) the terms of credit to be allowed and the security to be required; and

(e) how much of the proceeds will be invested, as required by this rule, for the benefit of unknown owners, infants, parties outside Michigan, and parties who have dower interests or life estates.

(B) **Specific Procedures and Requirements of Sale**.

(1) The person appointed by the court to conduct the sale shall give notice of the sale, including the terms. Notice must be given in the same manner as required by MCL 600.6052.

(2) Neither the person conducting the sale nor anyone acting in his or her behalf may directly or indirectly purchase or be interested in the purchase of the premises sold. The conservator of a minor or legally incapacitated individual may not purchase or be interested in the purchase of lands that are the subject of the proceedings, except for the benefit of the ward. Sales made contrary to this provision are voidable, except as provided by MCL 700.5421.

(3) The part of the price for which credit is allowed must be secured at interest by a mortgage of the premises sold, a note of the purchaser, and other security the court prescribes.

(a) The person conducting the sale may take separate mortgages and other securities in the name of the clerk of the court and the clerk's successors for the shares of the purchase money the court directs to be invested, and in the name of a known owner, 18 years of age or older, who desires to have his or her share so invested.

(b) When the sale is confirmed, the person conducting the sale must deliver the mortgages and other securities to the clerk of the court, or to the known owners whose shares are invested.

(4) After completing the sale, the person conducting the sale shall file a report with the court, stating

(a) the name of each purchaser,

(b) a description of the parcels of land sold to each purchaser, and

(c) the price paid for each parcel.

A copy of the report must be sent to each party who has appeared in the action.

(5) If the court confirms the sale, it shall enter an order authorizing and directing the person conducting the sale to execute conveyances pursuant to the sale.

(6) Conveyances executed according to these rules shall be recorded in the county where the land is located. These conveyances are a bar against

(a) all interested persons who were made parties to the proceedings;

(b) all unknown parties who were ordered to appear and answer by proper publication or personal service of notice;

(c) all persons claiming through parties listed in subrules (B)(6)(a) and (b);

(d) all persons who have specific liens on an undivided share or interest in the premises, if they were made parties to the proceedings.

(7) If the court confirms the sale, and the successful bidder fails to purchase under the terms of the sale, the court may order that the premises be resold at that bidder's risk. That bidder is liable to pay the amount of his or her bid minus the amount received on resale.

(C) **Costs and Expenses of the Proceeding**. The person conducting the sale shall deduct the costs and expenses of the proceeding, including the plaintiff's reasonable attorney fees as determined by the court, from the proceeds of the sale and pay them to the plaintiff or the plaintiff's attorney.

(D) **Distribution of Proceeds of Sale**.

(1) When premises that include a dower interest or life estate are sold, the owner of the dower interest or life estate shall be compensated as provided in this subrule.

(a) Unless the owner consents to the alternative compensation provided in subrule (D)(1)(b), the court shall order that the following amount be invested in interest-bearing accounts insured by an agency of the United States government, with the interest paid annually for life to the owner of the dower interest or life estate:

(i) in the case of a dower interest, one-third of the proceeds of the sale of the premises or of the undivided share of the premises on which the claim of dower existed, after deduction of the owner's share of the expenses of the proceeding;

(ii) in the case of a life estate, the entire proceeds of the sale of the premises, or undivided share of the premises in which the life estate existed, after deduction of the proportion of the owner's share of the expenses of the proceeding.

If the owner of the dower interest or life estate is unknown, the court shall order the protection of the person's rights in the same manner, as far as possible, as if he or she were known and had appeared.

(b) If, before the person conducting the sale files the report of sale, the owner of the dower interest or life estate consents, the court shall direct that the owner be paid an amount that, on the principles of law applicable to annuities, is reasonable compensation for the interest or estate. To be effective the consent must be by a written instrument witnessed and acknowledged in the manner required to make a deed eligible for recording.

(2) If there are encumbrances on the estate or interest in the premises of a party to the proceeding, the person conducting the sale must pay to the clerk the portion of the proceeds attributable to the sale of that estate or interest, after deducting the share of the costs, charges, and expenses for which it is liable. The party who owned that estate or interest may apply to the court for payment of his or her claim out of these proceeds. The application must be accompanied by

(a) an affidavit stating the amount due on each encumbrance and the name and address of the owner of each encumbrance, as far as known; and

(b) proof by affidavit that notice was served on each owner of an encumbrance, in the manner prescribed in MCR 2.107.

The court shall hear the proofs, determine the rights of the parties, and direct who must pay the costs of the trial.

After ascertaining the amount of existing encumbrances, the court shall order the distribution of the money held by the clerk among the creditors having encumbrances, according to their priority. When paying an encumbrance the clerk must procure satisfaction of the encumbrance, acknowledged in the form required by law, and must record the satisfaction of the encumbrance. The clerk may pay the expenses of these services out of the portion of the money in court that belongs to the party by whom the encumbrance was payable.

The proceedings under this subrule to ascertain and settle the amounts of encumbrances do not affect other parties to the proceedings for partition and do not delay the payment to a party whose estate in the premises is not subject to an encumbrance or the investing of the money for the benefit of such a person.

(3) The proceeds of a sale, after deducting the costs, must be divided among the parties whose rights and interests have been sold, in proportion to their respective rights in the premises.

(a) The shares of the parties who are 18 years of age or older must be paid to them or to their legal representatives (or brought into court for their use) by the person conducting the sale.

(b) The court may direct that the share of a minor or a legally incapacitated individual be paid to his or her conservator or be invested in interest-bearing accounts insured by an agency of the United States government in the name and for the benefit of the minor or legally incapacitated individual.

(c) If a party whose interest has been sold is absent from the state and has no legal representative in the state or is not known or named in the proceedings, the court shall direct that his or her share be invested in interest-bearing accounts insured by the United States government for the party's benefit until claimed.

(4) The court may require that before receiving a share of the proceeds of a sale a party give a note to secure refund of the share, with interest, if the party is later found not entitled to it.

(5) When the court directs that security be given or investments be made, or the person conducting the sale takes security on the sale of real estate, the bonds, notes, and investments must be taken in the name of the clerk of the court and the clerk's successors in office, unless provision is made to take them in the name of a known owner.

The clerk must hold them and deliver them to his or her successor, and must receive the interest and principal as they become due and apply or reinvest them, as the court directs. The clerk shall annually give to the court a written, sworn account of the money received and the disposition of it.

A security, bond, note, mortgage, or other evidence of the investment may not be discharged, transferred, or impaired by an act of the clerk without the order of the court. A person interested in an investment, with the leave of the court, may prosecute it in the name of the existing clerk, and an action is not abated by the death, removal from office, or resignation of the clerk to whom the instruments were executed or the clerk's successors.

Rule 3.410 Foreclosure of Mortgages and Land Contracts

(A) **Rules Applicable**. Except as prescribed in this rule, the general rules of procedure apply to actions to foreclose mortgages and land contracts.

(B) **Pleading**.

(1) A plaintiff seeking foreclosure or satisfaction of a mortgage on real estate or a land contract must state in the complaint whether an action has ever been brought to recover all or part of the debt secured by the mortgage or land contract and whether part of the debt has been collected or paid.

(2) In a complaint for foreclosure or satisfaction of a mortgage or a land contract, it is not necessary to set out in detail the rights and interests of the defendants who are purchasers of, or who have liens on, the premises, subsequent to the recording of the mortgage or land contract. It is sufficient for the plaintiff, after setting out his or her own interest in the premises, to state generally that the defendants have or claim some interest in the premises as subsequent purchasers, encumbrancers, or otherwise.

(C) **Time for Sale**. A sale under a judgment of foreclosure may not be ordered on less than 42 days' notice. Publication may not begin until the time set by the judgment for payment has expired, and

(1) until 6 months after an action to foreclose a mortgage is begun;

(2) until 3 months after an action to foreclose a land contract is begun.

(D) **Disposition of Surplus**. When there is money remaining from a foreclosure sale after paying the amount due the plaintiff, a party to the action may move for the disposition of the surplus in accordance with the rights of the parties entitled to it.

(E) **Administration of Mortgage Trusts in Equity**.

(1) Proceedings of the kind described in MCL 600.3170 are governed by the procedures prescribed by MCL 451.401-451.405, except as modified by this subrule.

(2) A bond, other obligation, or beneficial interest held by or for the benefit of the mortgagor or the mortgagor's successor in estate, or subject to an agreement or option by which the mortgagor or the mortgagor's successor in estate may acquire it or an interest in it, may not be considered in determining a majority of such obligations or beneficial interests, either as part of the majority or as part of the whole number of which the majority is required.

Rule 3.411 Civil Action to Determine Interests in Land

(A) This rule applies to actions to determine interests in land under MCL 600.2932. It does not apply to summary proceedings to recover possession of premises under MCL 600.5701-600.5759.

(B) **Complaint**.

(1) The complaint must describe the land in question with reasonable certainty by stating

(a) the section, township, and range of the premises;

(b) the number of the block and lot of the premises; or

(c) another description of the premises sufficiently clear so that the premises may be identified.

(2) The complaint must allege

(a) the interest the plaintiff claims in the premises;

(b) the interest the defendant claims in the premises; and

(c) the facts establishing the superiority of the plaintiff's claim.

(C) **Written Evidence of Title to be Referred to in Pleadings**.

(1) Written evidence of title may not be introduced at trial unless it has been sufficiently referred to in the pleadings in accordance with this rule.

(2) The plaintiff must attach to the complaint, and the defendant must attach to the answer, a statement of the title on which the pleader relies, showing from

whom the title was obtained and the page and book where it appears of record.

(3) Within a reasonable time after demand for it, a party must furnish to the adverse party a copy of an unrecorded conveyance on which he or she relies or give a satisfactory reason for not doing so.

(4) References to title may be amended or made more specific in accordance with the general rules regarding amendments and motions for more definite statement.

(D) **Findings As to Rights in and Title to Premises.**

(1) After evidence has been taken, the court shall make findings determining the disputed rights in and title to the premises.

(2) If a party not in possession of the premises is found to have had a right to possession at the time the action was commenced, but that right expired before the trial, that party must prove the damages sustained because the premises were wrongfully withheld, and the court shall enter judgment in the amount proved.

(E) **Claim for Reasonable Value of Use of Premises.**

(1) Within 28 days after the finding of title, the party found to have title to the premises may file a claim against the party who withheld possession of the premises for the reasonable value of the use of the premises during the period the premises were withheld, beginning 6 years before the action was commenced.

(2) The court shall hear evidence and make findings, determining the value of the use of the premises.

(a) The findings must be based on the value of the use of the premises in their condition at the time the withholding party, or those through whom that party claims, first went into possession. The use of the buildings or improvements put on the land by the party who withheld possession may not be considered.

(b) The findings must be based on the general value of the use of the premises, not on a peculiar value the use of the premises had to the party who withheld possession or might have had to the party who had title.

(F) **Claim for Value of Buildings Erected and Improvements Made on Premises.**

(1) Within 28 days after the finding of title, a party may file a claim against the party found to have title to the premises for the amount that the present value of the premises has been increased by the erection of buildings or the making of improvements by the party making the claim or those through whom he or she claims.

(2) The court shall hear evidence as to the value of the buildings erected and the improvements made on the premises, and the value the premises would have if they had not been improved or built upon. The court shall determine the amount the premises would be worth at the time of the claim had the premises not been improved, and the amount the value of the premises was increased at the time of the claim by the buildings erected and improvements made.

(3) The party claiming the value of the improvements may not recover their value if they were made in bad faith.

(G) **Election by Party in Title.**

(1) The person found to have title to the premises may elect to abandon them to the party claiming the value of the improvements and to take a judgment against that party for the value the premises would have had at the time of the trial if they had not been improved. The election must be filed with the court within 28 days after the findings on the claim for improvements. The judgment for the value of the premises is a lien against the premises.

(2) If the person found to have title does not elect to abandon the premises under subrule (G)(1), the judgment will provide that he or she recover the premises and pay the value of the improvements to the clerk of the court within the time set in the judgment.

(a) The person found to have title must pay the amount, plus accrued interest, before taking possession of the premises under the judgment, if that person is not already in possession.

(b) If the person found to have title fails to pay the amount of the judgment and the accrued interest within the time set in the judgment, he or she is deemed to have abandoned all claim of title to the premises to the parties in whose favor the judgment for the value of the improvements runs.

(H) **Judgment Binding Only on Parties to Action.** Except for title acquired by adverse possession, the judgment determining a claim to title, equitable title, right to possession, or other interests in lands under this rule, determines only the rights and interests of the known and unknown persons who are parties to the action, and of persons claiming through those parties by title accruing after the commencement of the action.

(I) Possession Under Judgment Not to be Affected by Vacation of Judgment Alone. When the judgment in an action under these rules determines that a party is entitled to possession of the premises in dispute, that party's right to possession is not affected by vacation of the judgment and the granting of a new trial, until a contrary judgment is rendered as a result of the new trial.

Rule 3.412 Construction Liens

In an action to enforce a lien under MCL 570.1101 et seq., or other similar law, if the plaintiff has joined others holding liens or others have filed notice of intention to claim liens against the same property, it is not necessary for the plaintiff to answer the counterclaim or cross-claim of another lien claimant, nor for the other lien claimants to answer the plaintiff's complaint or the cross-claim of another lien claimant, unless one of them disputes the validity or amount of the lien sought to be enforced. If no issue has been raised between lien claimants as to the validity or amount of a lien, the action is ready for hearing when at issue between the lien claimants and the owners, part owners, or lessees of the property.

Subchapter 3.500 Representative Actions

Rule 3.501 Class Actions

(A) **Nature of Class Action.**

(1) One or more members of a class may sue or be sued as representative parties on behalf of all members in a class action only if:

(a) the class is so numerous that joinder of all members is impracticable;

(b) there are questions of law or fact common to the members of the class that predominate over questions affecting only individual members;

(c) the claims or defenses of the representative parties are typical of the claims or defenses of the class;

(d) the representative parties will fairly and adequately assert and protect the interests of the class; and

(e) the maintenance of the action as a class action will be superior to other available methods of adjudication in promoting the convenient administration of justice.

(2) In determining whether the maintenance of the action as a class action will be superior to other available methods of adjudication in promoting the convenient administration of justice, the court shall consider among other matters the following factors:

(a) whether the prosecution of separate actions by or against individual members of the class would create a risk of

(i) inconsistent or varying adjudications with respect to individual members of the class that would confront the party opposing the class with incompatible standards of conduct; or

(ii) adjudications with respect to individual members of the class that would as a practical matter be dispositive of the interests of other members not parties to the adjudications or substantially impair or impede their ability to protect their interests;

(b) whether final equitable or declaratory relief might be appropriate with respect to the class;

(c) whether the action will be manageable as a class action;

(d) whether in view of the complexity of the issues or the expense of litigation the separate claims of individual class members are insufficient in amount to support separate actions;

(e) whether it is probable that the amount which may be recovered by individual class members will be large enough in relation to the expense and effort of administering the action to justify a class action; and

(f) whether members of the class have a significant interest in controlling the prosecution or defense of separate actions.

(3) Class members shall have the right to be excluded from the action in the manner provided in this rule, subject to the authority of the court to order them made parties to the action pursuant to other applicable court rules.

(4) Class members have the right to intervene in the action, subject to the authority of the court to regulate the orderly course of the action.

(5) An action for a penalty or minimum amount of recovery without regard to actual damages imposed or authorized by statute may not be maintained as a class action unless the statute specifically authorizes its recovery in a class action.

(B) **Procedure for Certification of Class Action.**

(1) *Motion.*

(a) Within 91 days after the filing of a complaint that includes class action allegations, the plaintiff must move for certification that the action may be maintained as a class action.

(b) The time for filing the motion may be extended by order on stipulation of the parties or on motion for cause shown.

(2) *Effect of Failure to File Motion.* If the plaintiff fails to file a certification motion within the time allowed by subrule (B)(1), the defendant may file a notice of the failure. On the filing of such a notice, the class action allegations are deemed stricken, and the action continues by or against the named parties alone. The class action allegations may be reinstated only if the plaintiff shows that the failure was due to excusable neglect.

(3) *Action by Court.*

(a) Except on motion for good cause, the court shall not proceed with consideration of the motion to certify until service of the summons and complaint on all named defendants or until the expiration of any unserved summons under MCR 2.102(D).

(b) The court may allow the action to be maintained as a class action, may deny the motion, or may order that a ruling be postponed pending discovery or other preliminary procedures.

(c) In an order certifying a class action, the court shall set forth a description of the class.

(d) When appropriate the court may order that

(i) the action be maintained as a class action limited to particular issues or forms of relief, or

(ii) a proposed class be divided into separate classes with each treated as a class for purposes of certifying, denying certification, or revoking a certification.

(e) If certification is denied or revoked, the action shall continue by or against the named parties alone.

(C) **Notice to Class Members**.

(1) *Notice Requirement.* Notice shall be given as provided in this subrule to persons who are included in a class action by certification or amendment of a prior certification, and to persons who were included in a class action by a prior certification but who are to be excluded from the class by amendment or revocation of the certification.

(2) *Proposals Regarding Notice.* The plaintiff shall include in the motion for certification a proposal regarding notice covering the matters that must be determined by the court under subrule (C)(3). In lieu of such a proposal, the plaintiff may state reasons why a determination of these matters cannot then be made and offer a proposal as to when such a determination should be made. Such a proposal must also be included in a motion to revoke or amend certification.

(3) *Action by Court.* As soon as practicable, the court shall determine how, when, by whom, and to whom the notice shall be given; the content of the notice; and to whom the response to the notice is to be sent. The court may postpone the notice determination until after the parties have had an opportunity for discovery, which the court may limit to matters relevant to the notice determination.

(4) *Manner of Giving Notice.*

(a) Reasonable notice of the action shall be given to the class in such manner as the court directs.

(b) The court may require individual written notice to all members who can be identified with reasonable effort. In lieu of or in addition to individual notice, the court may require notice to be given through another method reasonably calculated to reach the members of the class. Such methods may include using publication in a newspaper or magazine; broadcasting on television or radio; posting; or distribution through a trade or professional association, union, or public interest group.

(c) In determining the manner of notice, the court shall consider, among other factors,

(i) the extent and nature of the class,

(ii) the relief requested,

(iii) the cost of notifying the members,

(iv) the resources of the plaintiff, and

(v) the possible prejudice to be suffered by members of the class or by others if notice is not received.

(5) *Content of Notice.* The notice shall include:

(a) a general description of the action, including the relief sought, and the names and addresses of the representative parties;

(b) a statement of the right of a member of the class to be excluded from the action by submitting an election to be excluded, including the manner and time for exercising the election;

(c) a description of possible financial consequences for the class;

(d) a general description of any counterclaim or notice of intent to assert a counterclaim by or against members of the class, including the relief sought;

(e) a statement that the judgment, whether favorable or not, will bind all members of the class who are not excluded from the action;

(f) a statement that any member of the class may intervene in the action;

(g) the address of counsel to whom inquiries may be directed; and

(h) other information the court deems appropriate.

(6) *Cost of Notice.*

(a) The plaintiff shall bear the expense of the notification required by subrule (C)(1). The court may require the defendant to cooperate in the notice process, but any additional costs incurred by the defendant in doing so shall be paid by the plaintiff.

(b) Upon termination of the action, the court may allow as taxable costs the expenses of notification incurred by the prevailing party.

(c) Subrules (C)(6)(a) and (b) shall not apply when a statute provides for a different allocation of the cost of notice in a particular class of actions.

(7) *Additional Notices.* In addition to the notice required by subrule (C)(1), during the course of the action the court may require that notice of any other matter be given in such manner as the court directs to some or all of the members of the class.

(D) **Judgment**.

(1) The judgment shall describe the parties bound.

(2) A judgment entered before certification of a class binds only the named parties.

(3) A motion for judgment (including partial judgment) under MCR 2.116 may be filed and decided before the decision on the question of class certification. A judgment entered before certification in favor of a named party does not preclude that party from representing the class in the action if that is otherwise appropriate.

(4) A complaint that does not include class action allegations may not be amended to include such allegations after the granting of judgment or partial judgment under MCR 2.116.

(5) A judgment entered in an action certified as a class action binds all members of the class who have not submitted an election to be excluded, except as otherwise directed by the court.

(E) **Dismissal or Compromise**. An action certified as a class action may not be dismissed or compromised without the approval of the court, and notice of the proposed dismissal or compromise shall be given to the class in such manner as the court directs.

(F) **Statute of Limitations**.

(1) The statute of limitations is tolled as to all persons within the class described in the complaint on the commencement of an action asserting a class action.

(2) The statute of limitations resumes running against class members other than representative parties and intervenors:

(a) on the filing of a notice of the plaintiff's failure to move for class certification under subrule (B)(2);

(b) 28 days after notice has been made under subrule (C)(1) of the entry, amendment, or revocation of an order of certification eliminating the person from the class;

(c) on entry of an order denying certification of the action as a class action;

(d) on submission of an election to be excluded;

(e) on final disposition of the action.

(3) If the circumstance that brought about the resumption of the running of the statute is superseded by a further order of the trial court, by reversal on appeal, or otherwise, the statute of limitations shall be deemed to have been tolled continuously from the commencement of the action.

(G) **Discovery**. Representative parties and intervenors are subject to discovery in the same manner as parties in other civil actions. Other class members are subject to discovery in the same manner as persons who are not parties, and may be required to submit to discovery procedures applicable to parties to the extent ordered by the court.

(H) **Counterclaims**.

(1) *Right to File Counterclaims*. A party to a class action may file counterclaims as in any other action, including counterclaims by or against a class or an individual class member.

(2) *Notice of Intent to File Counterclaims*. The defendant may file notice of intent to assert counterclaims against absent class members before notice of certification is given under subrule (C)(1), identifying or describing the persons against whom counterclaims may be filed and describing the nature of the counterclaims.

(3) *Time to File*. A counterclaim against a class member other than a representative party must be filed and served within 56 days after the class member intervenes or submits a claim for distribution of a share of any award recovered in the action, whichever is earlier, or within such further time as the court allows.

(4) *Notice to Class Members*. If the notice of certification given under subrule (C)(1) did not notify potential class members of the counterclaim, each class member against whom a counterclaim is asserted shall be permitted to elect to be excluded from the action. Notice of this right shall be served with the counterclaim.

(5) *Control of Action*. The court shall take such steps as are necessary to prevent the pendency of counterclaims from making the action unmanageable as a class action. Such steps include but are not limited to severing counterclaims for separate trial under MCR 2.505(B) or ordering that consideration of the counterclaims be deferred until after determination of the issue of the defendant's liability, at which time the court may hear the counterclaims, remove them to a lower court, change venue, dismiss them without prejudice, or take other appropriate action.

(I) **Defendant Classes**.

(1) An action that seeks to recover money from individual members of a defendant class may not be maintained as a class action.

(2) A representative of a defendant class, other than a public body or a public officer, may decline to defend the action in a representative capacity unless the court finds that the convenient administration of justice otherwise requires.

Rule 3.502 Secondary Action by Shareholders

(A) **Pleading**. In an action brought by one or more shareholders in an incorporated or unincorporated association because the association has refused or failed to enforce rights which may properly be asserted by it, the complaint shall set forth under oath and with particularity the efforts of the plaintiff to secure from the managing directors or trustees the action the plaintiff desires and the reasons for the failure to obtain such action, or the reasons for not making such an effort.

(B) **Security**. At any stage of an action under this subrule the court may require such security and impose such terms as shall fairly and adequately protect the interests of the class or association in whose behalf the action is brought or defended.

(C) **Notice**. The court may order that notice be given, in the manner and to the persons it directs,
   (1) of the right of absent persons to appear and present claims and defenses;
   (2) of the pendency of the action;
   (3) of a proposed settlement;
   (4) of entry of judgment; or
   (5) of any other proceedings in the action.

(D) **Inadequate Representation**. Whenever the representation appears to the court inadequate to protect the interests of absent persons who may be bound by the judgment, the court may at any time prior to judgment order an amendment of the pleadings to eliminate references to representation of absent persons, and the court shall enter judgment in such form as to affect only the parties to the action and those adequately represented.

Rule 3.503 Action by Fiduciary

(A) **Court Order**. When a proceeding is instituted by a fiduciary seeking instruction or authorization with respect to fiduciary duties or the trust property, and it appears that it is impracticable to bring all of the beneficiaries before the court, the court shall enter an order:
   (1) setting forth the form of and manner for giving notice of the proceedings to the beneficiaries, and
   (2) selecting representatives of the beneficiaries to act as representatives of the class.

(B) **Notice**. The contents of the notice shall fairly state the purpose of the proceedings and shall specify the time and place of hearing. Where an applicable statute provides for notice, the court may dispense with other notice.

Subchapter 3.600 Miscellaneous Proceedings

Rule 3.601 Public Nuisances

(A) **Procedure to Abate Public Nuisance**. Actions to abate public nuisances are governed by the general rules of procedure and evidence applicable to nonjury actions, except as provided by the statutes covering public nuisances and by this rule.

(B) **Default; Hearing; Notice and Time**. If a defendant fails to answer within the time provided, his or her default may be taken. On answer of a defendant or entry of a defendant's default, a party other than a defendant in default may notice the action for hearing on 7 days' notice. Hearings in actions under this rule take precedence over actions that are not entitled to priority by statute or rule and may be held at the time they are noticed without further pretrial proceedings.

(C) **Motions; Hearing**. Motions by the defendant filed and served with the answer are heard on the day of the hearing of the action.

(D) **Entry of Order or Judgment; Preliminary Injunction**.
   (1) On the day noticed for hearing, the court shall hear and determine the disputed issues and enter a proper order and judgment.
   (2) If the hearing is adjourned at the defendant's request, and the court is satisfied by affidavit or otherwise that the allegations in the complaint are true and that the plaintiff is entitled to relief, an injunction as requested may be granted, to be binding until further order.
   (3) If service is not obtained on all of the defendants named in the complaint, the court has jurisdiction to hear the action and enter a proper order of abatement and judgment against those defendants who have been served. The order and judgment may not adversely affect the interests of the defendants who have not been served.

(E) **Temporary Restraining Order**. If a preliminary injunction is requested in the complaint and the court is satisfied by affidavit or otherwise that the material allegations are true, and that the plaintiff is entitled to relief, it may issue a temporary restraining order in accordance with MCR 3.310(B), restraining the defendant from conducting, maintaining, and permitting the continuance of the nuisance and from removing or permitting the removal of the liquor, furniture, fixtures, vehicles, or other things used in the maintenance of the nuisance, until the final hearing and determination on the complaint or further order.

(F) **Substitution for Complaining Party**. The court may substitute the Attorney General or prosecuting attorney for the complaining party and direct the substituted officer to prosecute the action to judgment.

(G) **Further Orders of Court**. The court may enter other orders consistent with equity and not inconsistent with the provisions of the statute and this rule.

Rule 3.602 Arbitration

(A) **Applicability of Rule**. Courts shall have all powers described in MCL 691.1681 *et seq.*, or reasonably related thereto, for arbitrations governed by that statute. The remainder of this rule applies to all other forms of arbitration, in the absence of contradictory provisions in the arbitration agreement or limitations imposed by statute, including MCL 691.1683(2).

(B) **Proceedings Regarding Arbitration**.
   (1) A request for an order to compel or to stay arbitration or for another order under this rule must be by motion, which shall be heard in the manner and on the notice provided by these rules for

motions. If there is not a pending action between the parties, the party seeking the requested relief must first file a complaint as in other civil actions.

(2) On motion of a party showing an agreement to arbitrate, and the opposing party's refusal to arbitrate, the court may order the parties to proceed with arbitration and to take other steps necessary to carry out the arbitration agreement. If the opposing party denies the existence of an agreement to arbitrate, the court shall summarily determine the issues and may order arbitration or deny the motion.

(3) On motion, the court may stay an arbitration proceeding commenced or threatened on a showing that there is no agreement to arbitrate. If there is a substantial and good-faith dispute, the court shall summarily try the issue and may enter a stay or direct the parties to proceed to arbitration.

(4) A motion to compel arbitration may not be denied on the ground that the claim sought to be arbitrated lacks merit or is not filed in good faith, or because fault or grounds for the claim have not been shown.

(C) **Action Involving Issues Subject to Arbitration; Stay**. Subject to MCR 3.310(E), an action or proceeding involving an issue subject to arbitration must be stayed if an order for arbitration or motion for such an order has been made under this rule. If the issue subject to arbitration is severable, the stay may be limited to that issue. If a motion for an order compelling arbitration is made in the action or proceeding in which the issue is raised, an order for arbitration must include a stay.

(D) **Hearing; Time; Place; Adjournment**.

(1) The arbitrator shall set the time and place for the hearing, and may adjourn it as necessary.

(2) On a party's request for good cause, the arbitrator may postpone the hearing to a time not later than the day set for rendering the award.

(E) **Oath of Arbitrator and Witnesses**.

(1) Before hearing testimony, the arbitrator must be sworn to hear and fairly consider the matters submitted and to make a just award according to his or her best understanding.

(2) The arbitrator has the power to administer oaths to the witnesses.

(F) **Discovery and Subpoenas**.

(1) The court may enforce a subpoena or discovery-related order for the attendance of a witness in this state and for the production of records and other evidence issued by an arbitrator in connection with an arbitration proceeding in another state on conditions determined by the court so as to make the arbitration proceeding fair, expeditious, and cost effective.

(2) A subpoena or discovery-related order issued by an arbitrator in another state shall be served in the manner provided by law for service of subpoenas in a civil action in this state and, on motion to the court by a party to the arbitration proceeding or the arbitrator, enforced in the manner provided by law for enforcement of subpoenas in a civil action in this state.

(3) On a party's request, the arbitrator may permit the taking of a deposition, for use as evidence, of a witness who cannot be subpoenaed or is unable to attend the hearing. The arbitrator may designate the manner of and the terms for taking the deposition.

(G) **Representation by Attorney**. A party has the right to be represented by an attorney at a proceeding or hearing under this rule. A waiver of the right before the proceeding or hearing is ineffective.

(H) **Award by Majority; Absence of Arbitrator**. If the arbitration is by a panel of arbitrators, the hearing shall be conducted by all of them, but a majority may decide any question and render a final award unless the concurrence of all of the arbitrators is expressly required by the agreement to submit to arbitration. If, during the course of the hearing, an arbitrator ceases to act for any reason, the remaining arbitrator or arbitrators may continue with the hearing and determine the controversy.

(I) **Award; Confirmation by Court**. A party may move for confirmation of an arbitration award within one year after the award was rendered. The court may confirm the award, unless it is vacated, corrected, or modified, or a decision is postponed, as provided in this rule.

(J) **Vacating Award**.

(1) A request for an order to vacate an arbitration award under this rule must be made by motion. If there is not a pending action between the parties, the party seeking the requested relief must first file a complaint as in other civil actions. A complaint or motion to vacate an arbitration award must be filed no later than 21 days after the date of the arbitration award.

(2) On motion of a party, the court shall vacate an award if:

(a) the award was procured by corruption, fraud, or other undue means;

(b) there was evident partiality by an arbitrator appointed as a neutral, corruption of an arbitrator, or misconduct prejudicing a party's rights;

(c) the arbitrator exceeded his or her powers; or

(d) the arbitrator refused to postpone the hearing on a showing of sufficient cause, refused to hear evidence material to the controversy, or otherwise conducted the hearing to prejudice substantially a party's rights.

The fact that the relief could not or would not be granted by a court of law or equity is not ground for vacating or refusing to confirm the award.

(3) A motion to vacate an award must be filed within 91 days after the date of the award. However, if the motion is predicated on corruption, fraud, or other undue means, it must be filed within 21 days after the grounds are known or should have been known. A motion to vacate an award in a domestic relations case must be filed within 21 days after the date of the award.

(4) In vacating the award, the court may order a rehearing before a new arbitrator chosen as provided in the agreement, or, if there is no such provision, by the court. If the award is vacated on grounds stated in subrule (J)(1)(c) or (d), the court may order a rehearing before the arbitrator who made the award. The time within which the agreement requires the award to be made is applicable to the rehearing and commences from the date of the order.

(5) If the motion to vacate is denied and there is no motion to modify or correct the award pending, the court shall confirm the award.

(K) **Modification or Correction of Award**.

(1) A request for an order to modify or correct an arbitration award under this rule must be made by motion. If there is not a pending action between the parties, the party seeking the requested relief must first file a complaint as in other civil actions. A complaint to correct or modify an arbitration award must be filed no later than 21 days after the date of the arbitration award.

(2) On motion made within 91 days after the date of the award, the court shall modify or correct the award if:

(a) there is an evident miscalculation of figures or an evident mistake in the description of a person, a thing, or property referred to in the award;

(b) the arbitrator has awarded on a matter not submitted to the arbitrator, and the award may be corrected without affecting the merits of the decision on the issues submitted; or

(c) the award is imperfect in a matter of form, not affecting the merits of the controversy.

(3) If the motion is granted, the court shall modify and correct the award to effect its intent and shall confirm the award as modified and corrected. Otherwise, the court shall confirm the award as made.

(4) A motion to modify or correct an award may be joined in the alternative with a motion to vacate the award.

(L) **Judgment**. The court shall render judgment giving effect to the award as corrected, confirmed, or modified. The judgment has the same force and effect, and may be enforced in the same manner, as other judgments.

(M) **Costs**. The costs of the proceedings may be taxed as in civil actions, and, if provision for the fees and expenses of the arbitrator has not been made in the award, the court may allow compensation for the arbitrator's services as it deems just. The arbitrator's compensation is a taxable cost in the action.

(N) **Appeals**. Appeals may be taken as from orders or judgments in other civil actions.

Rule 3.603 Interpleader

(A) **Availability**.

(1) Persons having claims against the plaintiff may be joined as defendants and required to interplead when their claims are such that the plaintiff is or may be exposed to double or multiple liability. It is not a ground for objection to the joinder that the claims of the several claimants or the titles on which their claims depend do not have a common origin or are not identical, but are adverse to and independent of one another, or that the plaintiff denies liability to any or all of the claimants in whole or in part.

(2) A defendant exposed to liability as described in subrule (A)(1), may obtain interpleader by counterclaim or cross-claim. A claimant not already before the court may be joined as defendant, as provided in MCR 2.207 or MCR 2.209.

(3) If one or more actions concerning the subject matter of the interpleader action have already been filed, the interpleader action must be filed in the court where the first action was filed.

(B) **Procedure**.

(1) The court may order the property or the amount of money as to which the plaintiff admits liability to be deposited with the court or otherwise preserved, or to be secured by a bond in an amount sufficient to assure payment of the liability admitted.

(2) The court may thereafter enjoin the parties before it from commencing or prosecuting another action regarding the subject matter of the interpleader action.

(3) On hearing, the court may order the plaintiff discharged from liability as to property deposited or secured before determining the rights of the claimants.

(C) **Rule Not Exclusive**. The provisions of this rule supplement and do not in any way limit the joinder of parties permitted by MCR 2.206.

(D) **Disposition of Earlier Action**. If another action concerning the subject matter of the interpleader action has previously been filed, the court in which the earlier action was filed may:

(1) transfer the action, entirely or in part, to the court in which the interpleader action is pending,

(2) hold the action entirely or partially in abeyance, pending resolution of the interpleader action,

(3) dismiss the action, entirely or in part, or
(4) upon a showing of good cause, proceed with the action, explaining on the record the basis of the decision to proceed.

(E) **Actual Costs**. The court may award actual costs to an interpleader plaintiff. For the purposes of this rule, actual costs are those costs taxable in any civil action, and a reasonable attorney fee as determined by the trial court.
(1) The court may order that the plaintiff's actual costs of filing the interpleader request, tendering the disputed property to the court, and participating in the case as a disinterested stakeholder be paid from the disputed property or by another party.
(2) If the plaintiff incurs actual costs other than those described in subrule (1) due to another party's unreasonable litigation posture, the court may order that the other party pay those additional actual costs.
(3) An award made pursuant to this rule may not include reimbursement for the actual costs of asserting the plaintiff's own claim to the disputed property, or of supporting or opposing another party's claim.

Rule 3.604 Bonds

(A) **Scope of Rule**. This rule applies to bonds given under the Michigan Court Rules and the Revised Judicature Act, unless a rule or statute clearly indicates that a different procedure is to be followed.

(B) **Submission to Jurisdiction of Court by Surety**. A surety on a bond or undertaking given under the Michigan Court Rules or the Revised Judicature Act submits to the jurisdiction of the court and consents that further proceedings affecting the surety's liability on the bond or undertaking may be conducted under this rule.

(C) **Death of Party; Substitution of Surety**. If the only plaintiff or the only defendant dies during the pendency of an action, in addition to the parties substituted under MCR 2.202, each surety on a bond given by the deceased party shall be made a party to the action, on notice to the surety in the manner prescribed in MCR 2.107.

(D) **Affidavit of Surety; Notice of Bond**.
(1) A surety on a bond, except for a surety company authorized to do business in Michigan, must execute an affidavit that he or she has pecuniary responsibility and attach the affidavit to the bond.
(2) In alleging pecuniary responsibility, a surety must affirm that he or she owns assets not exempt from execution having a fair market value exceeding his or her liabilities by at least twice the amount of the bond.
(3) A copy of a bond and the accompanying affidavit must be promptly served on the party for whose benefit it is given in the manner prescribed in MCR 2.107. Proof of service must be filed promptly with the court in which the bond has been filed.
(4) In an action alleging medical malpractice filed on or after October 1, 1986, notice of the filing of security for costs or the affidavit in lieu of such security, required by MCL 600.2912d, 600.2912e, shall be given as provided in MCR 2.109(B).

(E) **Objections to Surety**. A party for whose benefit a bond is given may, within 7 days after receipt of a copy of the bond, serve on the officer taking the bond and the party giving the bond a notice that the party objects to the sufficiency of the surety. Failure to do so waives all objections to the surety.

(F) **Hearing on Objections to Surety**. Notice of objection to a surety must be filed as a motion for hearing on objections to the bond.
(1) On demand of the objecting party, the surety must appear at the hearing of the motion and be subject to examination as to the surety's pecuniary responsibility or the validity of the execution of the bond.
(2) After the hearing, the court may approve or reject the bond as filed or require an amended, substitute, or additional bond, as the circumstances warrant.
(3) In an appeal to the circuit court from a lower court or tribunal, an objection to the surety is heard in the circuit court.

(G) **Surety Company Bond**. A surety company certified by the Commissioner of Insurance as authorized to do business in Michigan may act as surety on a bond.

(H) **Assignment or Delivery of Bond**. If the condition of a bond is broken, or the circumstances require, the court shall direct the delivery or assignment of the bond for prosecution to the person for whose benefit it was given. Proceedings to enforce the bond may be taken in the action pursuant to subrule (I).

(I) **Judgment Against Surety**.
(1) Judgment on Motion. In an action in which a bond or other security has been posted, judgment may be entered directly against the surety or the security on motion without the necessity of an independent action on a showing that the condition has occurred giving rise to the liability on the bond or to the forfeiture of the security.
(2) Notice. Notice of the hearing on the motion for judgment must be given to the surety or the owner of the security in the manner prescribed in MCR 2.107. The notice may be mailed to the address stated in the bond or stated when the security was furnished unless the surety or owner has given notice of a change of address.
(3) Restitution. If in later proceedings in the action, on appeal or otherwise, it is determined that the surety is not liable or that the security should not have been forfeited, the court may order restitution of money paid or security forfeited.

(J) **Application to Another Judge After Supersedeas Refused.**
   (1) If a circuit judge has denied an application for supersedeas in whole or in part, or has granted it conditionally or on terms, a later application for the same purpose and in the same matter may not be made to another circuit judge if the first judge is available.
   (2) If an order is entered contrary to the provisions of subrule (J)(1), it is void and must be revoked by the judge who entered it, on proof of the facts. A person making a later application contrary to this rule is subject to punishment for contempt.

(K) **Cash or Securities Bond**. The furnishing of a cash or securities bond under MCL 600.2631 is deemed compliance with these rules.

(L) **Stay of Proceedings Without Bond**. If a party required to give a bond under these rules for supersedeas, appeal, or otherwise is unable to give the bond by reason of poverty, the court may, on proof of the inability, limit or eliminate the requirement for surety on the bond on appropriate conditions and for a reasonable time.

Rule 3.605 Collection of Penalties, Fines, Forfeitures, and Forfeited Recognizances

(A) **Definition**. The term "penalty," as used in this rule, includes fines, forfeitures, and forfeited recognizances, unless otherwise provided in this rule.

(B) **Parties**. The civil action for a pecuniary penalty incurred for the violation of an ordinance of a city or village must be brought in the name of the city or village. Other actions to recover penalties must be brought in the name of the people of the State of Michigan.

(C) **Judgment on Penalty**. In an action against a party liable for a penalty, judgment may be rendered directly against the party and in favor of the other party on motion and showing that the condition has occurred giving rise to the penalty. This subrule does not apply to forfeited civil recognizances under MCR 3.604 or to forfeited criminal recognizances under MCL 765.28.

(D) **Remission of Penalty**. An application for the remission of a penalty, including a bond forfeiture, may be made to the judge who imposed the penalty or ordered the forfeiture. The application may not be heard until reasonable notice has been given to the prosecuting attorney (or municipal attorney) and he or she has had an opportunity to examine the matter and prepare to resist the application. The application may not be granted without payment of the costs and expenses incurred in the proceedings for the collection of the penalty.

(E) **Duty of Clerk When Fine Without Order for Commitment; Duty of Prosecutor**. When a fine is imposed by a court on a person, without an order for the immediate commitment of the person until the fine is paid, the clerk of the court shall deliver a copy of the order imposing the fine to the prosecuting attorney of the county in which the court is held, or the municipal attorney in the case of a fine that is payable to a municipality. The prosecuting attorney (or municipal attorney) shall obtain execution to collect the fine.

Rule 3.606 Contempts Outside Immediate Presence of Court

(A) **Initiation of Proceeding**. For a contempt committed outside the immediate view and presence of the court, on a proper showing on ex parte motion supported by affidavits, the court shall either
   (1) order the accused person to show cause, at a reasonable time specified in the order, why that person should not be punished for the alleged misconduct; or
   (2) issue a bench warrant for the arrest of the person.

(B) **Writ of Habeas Corpus**. A writ of habeas corpus to bring up a prisoner to testify may be used to bring before the court a person charged with misconduct under this rule. The court may enter an appropriate order for the disposition of the person.

(C) **Bond for Appearance**.
   (1) The court may allow the giving of a bond in lieu of arrest, prescribing in the bench warrant the penalty of the bond and the return day for the defendant.
   (2) The defendant is discharged from arrest on executing and delivering to the arresting officer a bond
      (a) in the penalty endorsed on the bench warrant to the officer and the officer's successors,
      (b) with two sufficient sureties, and
      (c) with a condition that the defendant appear on the return day and await the order and judgment of the court.
   (3) Return of Bond. On returning a bench warrant, the officer executing it must return the bond of the defendant, if one was taken. The bond must be filed with the bench warrant.

(D) **Assignment of Bond; Damages**. The court may order assignment of the bond to an aggrieved party who is authorized by the court to prosecute the bond under MCR 3.604(H). The measure of the damages to be assessed in an action on the bond is the extent of the loss or injury sustained by the aggrieved party because of the misconduct for which the order for arrest was issued, and that party's costs and expenses in securing the order. The remainder of the penalty of the bond is paid into the treasury of the county in which the bond was taken, to the credit of the general fund.

(E) **Prosecution on Bond by Attorney General or Prosecutor**. If the court does not order an assignment as provided in (D), it shall order the breach prosecuted by the Attorney General or by the prosecuting attorney for the county in which the bond was taken, under MCR

3.604. The penalty recovered is to be paid into the treasury of the county in which the bond was taken, to the credit of the general fund.

Rule 3.607 Proceedings to Restore Lost Records or Papers in Courts of Record

(A) **Application for Order**. When a record or paper relating to an action or proceeding pending or determined in a Michigan court of record is lost, a person having an interest in its recovery may apply to the court having jurisdiction of the action or the record for an order that a duplicate of the lost record or paper be prepared and filed in the court.

(B) **Manner of Proceeding; Notice to Interested Parties.** The party making the application must show to the satisfaction of the court that the record or paper once existed and has been lost, without the fault or connivance, directly or indirectly, of the applicant. On that showing, the court shall direct the manner of proceeding to replace the lost item, and the notice to be given to parties interested in the application.

(C) **Witnesses; Interrogatories**. The court before which the application is pending may issue subpoenas for and compel the attendance of witnesses, or may compel witnesses to submit to examination on interrogatories and to establish facts relevant to the proceeding.

(D) **Order; Effect of Duplicate**. If the court is satisfied that the record or paper proposed as a substitute for the lost one exhibits all the material facts of the original, the court shall enter an order providing that the substitute record or paper be filed or recorded with the officer who had custody of the original. During the continuance of the loss, the substituted record or paper has the same effect in all respects and in all places as the original.

Rule 3.611 Voluntary Dissolution of Corporations

(A) **Scope; Rules Applicable.** This rule governs actions to dissolve corporations brought under MCL 600.3501. The general rules of procedure apply to these actions, except as provided in this rule and in MCL 600.3501-600.3515.

(B) **Contents of Complaint; Statements Attached.** A complaint seeking voluntary dissolution of a corporation must state why the plaintiff desires a dissolution of the corporation, and there must be attached:
  (1) an inventory of all the corporation's property;
  (2) a statement of all encumbrances on the corporation's property;
  (3) an account of the corporation's capital stock, specifying the names of the stockholders, their addresses, if known, the number of shares belonging to each, the amount paid in on the shares, and the amount still due on them;
  (4) an account of all the corporation's creditors and the contracts entered into by the corporation that may not have been fully satisfied and canceled, specifying:
    (a) the address of each creditor and of every known person with whom the contracts were made, if known, and if not known, that fact to be stated;
    (b) the amount owing to each creditor;
    (c) the nature of each debt, demand, or obligation; and
    (d) the basis of and consideration for each debt, demand, or obligation; and
  (5) the affidavit of the plaintiff that the facts stated in the complaint, accounts, inventories, and statements are complete and true, so far as the plaintiff knows or has the means of knowing.

(C) **Notice of Action**. Process may be served as in other actions, or, on the filing of the complaint, the court may order all persons interested in the corporation to show cause why the corporation should not be dissolved, at a time and place to be specified in the order, but at least 28 days after the date of the order. Notice of the contents of the order must be served by mail on all creditors and stockholders at least 28 days before the hearing date, and must be published once each week for 3 successive weeks in a newspaper designated by the court.

(D) **Hearing.** At a hearing ordered under subrule (C), the court shall hear the allegations and proofs of the parties and take testimony relating to the property, debts, credits, engagements, and condition of the corporation. After the hearing, the court may dismiss the action, order the corporation dissolved, appoint a receiver, schedule further proceedings, or enter another appropriate order.

(E) **Suits by Receiver**. An action may be brought by the receiver in his or her own name and may be continued by the receiver's successor or co-receiver. An action commenced by or against the corporation before the filing of the complaint for dissolution is not abated by the complaint or by the judgment of dissolution, but may be prosecuted or defended by the receiver. The court in which an action is pending may on motion order substitution of parties or enter another necessary order.

Rule 3.612 Winding Up of Corporation Whose Term or Charter Has Expired

(A) **Scope; Rules Applicable**. This rule applies to actions under MCL 450.1801 et seq. The general rules of procedure apply to these actions, except as provided in this rule and in MCL 450.1801 et seq.

(B) **Contents of Complaint**. The complaint must include:
  (1) the nature of the plaintiff's interest in the corporation or its property, the date of organization of the corporation, the title and the date of approval of the special act under which the corporation is

organized, if appropriate, and the term of corporate existence;

(2) whether any of the corporation's stockholders are unknown to the plaintiff;

(3) that the complaint is filed on behalf of the plaintiff and all other persons interested in the property of the corporation as stockholders, creditors, or otherwise who may choose to join as parties plaintiff and share the expense of the action;

(4) an incorporation by reference of the statements required by subrule (C);

(5) other appropriate allegations; and

(6) a demand for appropriate relief, which may include that the affairs of the corporation be wound up and its assets disposed of and distributed and that a receiver of its property be appointed.

(C) **Statements Attached to Complaint**. The complaint must have attached:

(1) a copy of the corporation's articles of incorporation, if they are on file with the Department of Commerce, and, if the corporation is organized by special act, a copy of the act;

(2) a statement of the corporation's assets, so far as known to the plaintiff;

(3) a statement of the amount of capital stock and of the amount paid in, as far as known, from the last report of the corporation on file with the Department of Commerce or, if none has been filed, from the articles of incorporation on file with the Department of Commerce, or the special legislative act organizing the corporation;

(4) if the corporation's stock records are accessible to the plaintiff, a list of the stockholders' names and addresses and the number of shares held by each, insofar as shown in the records;

(5) a statement of all encumbrances on the corporation's property, and all claims against the corporation, and the names and addresses of the encumbrancers and claimants, so far as known to the plaintiff; and

(6) a statement of the corporation's debts, the names and addresses of the creditors, and the nature of the consideration for each debt, so far as known to the plaintiff.

(D) **Parties Defendant**. The corporation must be made a defendant. All persons claiming encumbrances on the property may be made defendants. It is not necessary to make a stockholder or creditor of the corporation a defendant.

(E) **Process and Order for Appearance; Publication**.

(1) Process must be issued and served as in other civil actions or, on the filing of the complaint, the court may order the appearance and answer of the corporation, its stockholders, and creditors at least 28 days after the date of the order.

(2) The order for appearance must be published in the manner prescribed in MCR 2.106.

(3) When proof of the publication is filed and the time specified in the order for the appearance of the corporation, stockholders, and creditors has expired, an order may be entered taking the complaint as confessed by those who have not appeared.

(F) **Appearance by Defendants**.

(1) Within the time the order for appearance sets, the following persons may appear and defend the suit as the corporation might have:

(a) a stockholder in the corporation while it existed and who still retains rights in its property by owning stock;

(b) an assignee, purchaser, heir, devisee, or personal representative of a stockholder; or

(c) a creditor of the corporation, whose claim is not barred by the statute of limitations.

(2) All persons so appearing must defend in the name of the corporation.

(3) If a person other than the corporation has been named as a defendant in the complaint, that person must be served with process as in other civil actions.

(G) **Subsequent Proceedings**. So far as applicable, the procedures established in MCR 3.611 govern hearings and later proceedings in an action under this rule.

(H) **Continuation of Proceeding for Benefit of Stockholder or Creditor**. If the plaintiff fails to establish that he or she is a stockholder or creditor of the corporation, the action may be continued by another stockholder or creditor who has appeared in the action.

Rule 3.613 Change of Name

(A) **Published Notice, Contents**. A published notice of a proceeding to change a name shall include the name of the petitioner; the current name of the subject of the petitioner; the proposed name; and the time, date and place of the hearing.

(B) **Minor's Signature**. A petition for a change of name by a minor need not be signed in the presence of a judge.

(C) **Notice to Noncustodial Parent**. Service on a noncustodial parent of a minor who is the subject of a petition for change of name shall be made in the following manner.

(1) *Address Known*. If the noncustodial parent's address or whereabouts is known, that parent shall be served with a copy of the petition and a notice of hearing.

(2) *Address Unknown*. If the noncustodial parent's address or whereabouts is not known and cannot be ascertained after diligent inquiry, that parent shall be served with a notice of hearing by publishing in a newspaper and filing a proof of service as provided by MCR 2.106(F) and (G). The notice

must be published one time at least 14 days before the date of the hearing, must include the name of the noncustodial parent and a statement that the result of the hearing may be to bar or affect the noncustodial parent's interest in the matter, and that publication must be in the county where the court is located unless a different county is specified by statute, court rule, or order of the court. A notice published under this subrule need not set out the contents of the petition if it contains the information required under subrule (A). A single publication may be used to notify the general public and the noncustodial parent whose address cannot be ascertained if the notice contains the noncustodial parent's name.

(D) **Consultation with Minor, Presumption**. A child 7 years of age and under is presumed not of sufficient age to be consulted concerning a preference on change of name.

(E) **Confidential Records**. In cases where the court orders that records are to be confidential and that no publication is to take place, records are to be maintained in a sealed envelope marked confidential and placed in a private file. Except as otherwise ordered by the court, only the original petitioner may gain access to confidential files, and no information relating to a confidential record, including whether the record exists, shall be accessible to the general public.

Rule 3.614 Health Threats to Others

(A) **Public Health Code, Application**. Except as modified by this rule, proceedings relating to carriers of contagious diseases who pose threats to the health of others under part 52 of the public health code are governed by the rules generally applicable to civil proceedings.

(B) **Service of Papers**. The moving party is responsible for service when service is required.

(C) **Interested Parties**. The interested parties in a petition for treatment of infectious disease are the petitioner and the respondent.

(D) **Commitment Review Panel**.

(1) *Appointment*. On receipt of a petition for treatment of infectious disease which requests that the individual be committed to an appropriate facility, the Court shall forthwith appoint a Commitment Review Panel from a list of physicans prepared by the Department of Public health.

(2) *Respondent's Choice of Physican*. On motion of the respondent requesting that a specific physician be appointed to the Commitment Review Panel, the Court shall appoint the physician so requested, unless the physician refuses. If the individual is unable to pay such physician , the court shall pay such physician a reasonable fee comparable with fees paid to other court appointed experts. On appointment of the requested physician, the Court shall discharge one of the initially appointed physicians.

(3) The Commitment Review Panel shall make written recommendations to the Court prior to the date of hearing on the petition. The recommendations shall be substantially in a form approved by the State Court Administrator.

(E) **Commitment to Facility**.

(1) *Renewal of Order of Commitment*. A motion for continuing commitment shall be filed at least 14 days prior to the expiration of the order of commitment. The motion shall be made by the director of the commitment facility or the director's designee. The court shall conduct a hearing on the motion prior to the expiration of the existing order of commitment. Notice shall be given as on the initial petition and to the local department of public health. The court shall reconvene the respondent's Commitment Review Panel. At the hearing, the petitioner must show good cause for continued commitment in the facility. No order of commitment shall exceed 6 months in length.

(2) *Reevaluation at Request of Respondent*. Once within any six-month period or more often by leave of the court, an individual committed to a facility for treatment of an infectious disease may file in the court a petition for a new Commitment Review Panel recommendation on whether the patient's commitment should be terminated. Within 14 days after receipt of the report of the reconvened Commitment Review Panel, the court shall review the panel's report and enter an order. The court may modify, continue or terminate its order of commitment without a hearing.

Rule 3.615 Parental Rights Restoration Act Proceedings

(A) **Applicable Rules**. A proceeding by a minor to obtain a waiver of parental consent for an abortion shall be governed by the rules applicable to civil proceedings except as modified by this rule.

(B) **Confidentiality, Use of Initials, Private File, Reopening**.

(1) The court shall assure the confidentiality of the file, the assistance given the minor by court personnel, and the proceedings.

(2) If requested by the minor, the title of the proceeding shall be by initials or some other means of assuring confidentiality. At the time the petition is filed, the minor shall file a Confidential Information Sheet listing the minor's name, date of birth, permanent residence, title to be used in the proceeding and the method by which the minor may be reached during the pendency of the proceeding. The Confidential Information Sheet

and all other documents containing identifying information shall be sealed in an envelope marked confidential on which the case number has been written and placed in a private file. Confidential information shall not be entered into a computer file.

(3) The court shall maintain only one file of all papers for each case. The file shall be inspected only by the judge, specifically authorized court personnel, the minor, her attorney, her next friend, the guardian ad litem, and any other person authorized by the minor. After the proceedings are completed, the file may be opened only by order of the court for good cause shown and only for a purpose specified in the order of the court.

(4) The file of a completed case shall not be destroyed until two years after the minor has reached the age of majority. The court shall not microfilm or otherwise copy the file.

(C) **Advice of Rights, Method of Contact**.

(1) If a minor seeking a waiver of parental consent makes first contact with the court by personal visit to the court, the court shall provide a written notice of rights and forms for a petition for waiver of parental consent, a confidential information sheet, and a request for appointment of an attorney, each substantially in the form approved by the state court administrator.

(2) If a minor seeking a waiver of parental consent makes first contact with the court by telephone, the court shall tell the minor that she can receive a notice of rights and forms for a petition, a confidential information sheet, and a request for appointment of an attorney by coming to the court or that the court will mail such forms to the minor. If the minor requests that the court mail the forms, the court shall mail the forms within 24 hours of the telephone contact to an address specified by the minor.

(3) Any person on personal visit to the court shall be given, on request, a copy of the notice of rights or any other form.

(D) **Assistance with Preparation of Petition**. On request of the minor or next friend, the court shall provide the minor with assistance in preparing and filing of a petition, confidential information sheet and request for appointment of an attorney, each substantially in the form approved by the state court administrator.

(E) **Next Friend**. If the minor proceeds through a next friend, the petitioner shall certify that the next friend is not disqualified by statute and that the next friend is an adult. The next friend may act on behalf of the minor without prior appointment of the court and is not responsible for the costs of the action.

(F) **Attorney, Request, Appointment, Duties**.

(1) At the request of the minor or next friend before or after filing the petition, the court shall immediately appoint an attorney to represent the minor. The request shall be in writing in substantially the form approved by the state court administrator. Except for good cause stated on the record, the court shall appoint an attorney selected by the minor if the minor has secured the attorney's agreement to represent her or the attorney has previously indicated to the court a willingness to be appointed.

(2) If it deems necessary, the court may appoint an attorney to represent the minor at any time.

(3) The minor shall contact the court appointed attorney within 24 hours of such appointment. The court shall advise the minor of this requirement.

(4) If an attorney is appointed to represent a minor prior to filing a petition, the attorney shall consult with the minor within 48 hours of appointment.

(G) **Guardian Ad Litem, Appointment, Duties**.

(1) *Request of Minor*. The court shall immediately appoint a guardian ad litem to represent the minor at the request of the minor or next friend before or after filing the petition.

(2) *Appointment on Court's Motion*.

(a) At any time if it deems necessary, the court may appoint a guardian ad litem to assist the court.

(b) The guardian ad litem may obtain information by contacting the minor and other persons with the consent of the minor, provided the confidentiality of the proceedings is not violated.

(H) **Filing Petition, Setting Hearing, Notice of Hearing**.

(1) The petition shall be filed in person by the minor, attorney or next friend.

(2) The court shall set a time and place for a hearing and notify the filer at the time the petition is filed. The court shall give notice of the hearing only to the minor, the minor's attorney, next friend and guardian ad litem. Notice of hearing may be oral or written and may be given at any time prior to the hearing. The hearing may be scheduled to commence immediately if the minor and her attorney, if any, are ready to proceed.

(3) Insofar as practical, at the minor's request the hearing shall be scheduled at a time and place that will not interfere with the minor's school attendance.

(I) **Venue, Transfer**. Venue is in the county of the minor's residence or where the minor is found at the time of the filing of the petition. Transfer of venue properly laid shall not be made without consent of the minor.

(J) **Hearing**.

(1) *Burden and Standard of Proof.* The petitioner has the burden of proof by preponderance of the

evidence and must establish the statutory criteria at a hearing.

(2) *Closed Hearing*. The hearing shall be closed to the public. The court shall limit attendance at the hearing to the minor, the minor's attorney, the next friend, the guardian ad litem, persons who are called to testify by the minor or with the minor's consent, necessary court personnel and one support person who would not be disqualified as a next friend by MCL 722.902(d).

(3) All relevant and material evidence may be received.

(4) The hearing may be conducted informally in the chambers of a judge.

(5) The hearing shall commence and be concluded within 72 hours, excluding Sundays and holidays, of the filing of the petition, unless the minor consents to an adjournment. The order of the court shall be issued within 48 hours, excluding Sundays and holidays, of the conclusion of the hearing.

(K) **Order**.

(1) *Order Granting Waiver, Duration, Effect*. If the petition is granted, the court immediately shall provide the minor with two certified copies of the order granting waiver of parental consent. The order shall be valid for 90 days from the date of entry. Nothing in the order shall require or permit an abortion that is otherwise prohibited by law.

(2) *Order Denying Waiver, Notice of Appeal, Appointment of Counsel, Preparation of Transcript*. If the order denies relief, the court shall endorse the time and date on the order. The order shall be served on the minor's attorney or, if none, the minor along with

(a) a unified appellate document substantially in the form approved by the state court administrator which may be used as notice of appeal, claim of appeal, request for appointment of an attorney and order of transcript, and

(b) a notice that, if the minor desires to appeal, the minor must file the notice of appeal with the court within 24 hours.

(3) *Appeal*.

(a) Upon receipt of a timely notice of appeal, the court must appoint counsel and order that the transcript be prepared immediately and two copies filed within 72 hours. If the minor was represented by counsel in the court proceedings, the court must reappoint the same attorney unless there is good cause for a different appointment. As soon as the transcript is filed, the court shall forward the file to the Court of Appeals.

(b) Time for filing notice.

(i) If the order was entered at the conclusion of the hearing or at any other time when the minor's attorney or, if none, the minor was in attendance at court, the minor must file the notice of appeal within 24 hours of the date and time stamped on the order, or

(ii) If the order was entered at any other time, the minor must file the notice of appeal within 24 hours of the time when the order was received by the minor's attorney or, if none, the minor.

(c) If a court in which a document is to be filed is closed for business at the end of a filing period, the document will be filed on a timely basis if filed during the morning of the next day when the court is open for business.

(d) Perfection of Appeal. The minor's attorney must perfect the appeal by filing in the Court of Appeals a claim of appeal and a copy of the order denying waiver. The appeal must be perfected within 72 hours, excluding Sundays and holidays, of the filing of the notice of appeal.

(e) Brief. The minor's attorney shall file at the time of perfecting appeal five copies of the brief on appeal. The brief need not contain citations to the transcript.

(f) Oral Argument. There will be no oral argument, unless ordered by the Court of Appeals.

Rule 3.616. Proceeding to Determine Continuation of Voluntary Foster Care Services.

(A) **Scope of Rule**. This rule governs review of all voluntary foster care agreements made pursuant to article II of the Young Adult Voluntary Foster Care Act, MCL 400.645 through MCL 400.663.

(B) **Jurisdiction**. Upon the filing of a petition under this rule, the family division of the circuit court has jurisdiction to review an agreement for the voluntary extension of foster care services after age 18.

(C) **Court File**. Upon the filing of a petition under subrule (E), the court shall open a file using the appropriate case classification code from MCR 8.117(A)(9). The file shall be closed following the issuance of the court's determination under subrule (F).

(D) **Form**. The petition and the judicial determination shall be prepared on forms approved by the state court administrator.

(E) **Ex Parte Petition; Filing, Contents, Service**. Within 150 days after the signing of a voluntary foster care agreement, the Department of Human Services shall file with the family division of the circuit court, in the county where the youth resides, an ex parte petition requesting the court's determination that continuing in voluntary foster care is in the youth's best interests.

(1) *Contents of Petition*. The petition shall contain

(a) the youth's name, date of birth, race, gender, and current address;
(b) the name, date of birth, and residence address of the youth's parents or legal custodian (if parental rights have not been terminated);
(c) the name and address of the youth's foster parent or parents;
(d) a statement that the youth has been notified of the right to request a hearing regarding continuing in foster care;
(e) a showing that jurisdiction of a court over the youth's child protective proceeding has been terminated, including the name of the court and the date jurisdiction was terminated; and
(f) any other information the Department of Human Services, parent or legal custodian, youth, or foster parent wants the court to consider.

(2) *Supporting Documents*. The petition shall be accompanied by a written report prepared pursuant to MCL 400.655 and a copy of the signed voluntary foster care agreement.

(3) *Service*. The Department of Human Services shall serve the petition on
(a) the youth; and
(b) the foster parent or parents, if any.

(F) **Judicial Determination**. The court shall review the petition, report, and voluntary foster care agreement filed pursuant to subrule (E), and then make a determination whether continuing in voluntary foster care is in the best interests of the youth.

(1) *Written Order; Time*. The court shall issue an order that includes its determination and individualized findings that support its determination. The findings shall be based on the Department of Human Services' written report and other information filed with the court. The order must be signed and dated within 21 days of the filing of the petition.

(2) *Service*. The court shall serve the order on
(a) the Department of Human Services;
(b) the youth; and
(c) the foster parent or parents, if any.

(G) **Confidential File**. The Department of Human Services and the youth are entitled to access to the records contained in the file, but otherwise, the file is confidential.

Subchapter 3.700 Personal Protection Proceedings

Rule 3.701 Applicability of Rules; Forms

(A) **Scope**. Except as provided by this subchapter and the provisions of MCL 600.2950 and 600.2950a, actions for personal protection for relief against domestic violence or stalking are governed by the Michigan Court Rules. Procedure related to personal protection orders against adults is governed by this subchapter. Procedure related to personal protection orders against minors is governed by subchapter 3.900, except as provided in MCR 3.981.

(B) **Forms**. The state court administrator shall approve forms for use in personal protection act proceedings. The forms shall be made available for public distribution by the clerk of the circuit court.

Rule 3.702 Definitions

When used in this subchapter, unless the context otherwise indicates:

(1) "personal protection order" means a protection order as described under MCL 600.2950 and 600.2950a;
(2) "petition" refers to a pleading for commencing an independent action for personal protection and is not considered a motion as defined in MCR 2.119;
(3) "petitioner" refers to the party seeking protection;
(4) "respondent" refers to the party to be restrained;
(5) "existing action" means an action in this court or any other court in which both the petitioner and the respondent are parties; existing actions include, but are not limited to, pending and completed domestic relations actions, criminal actions, other actions for personal protection orders.
(6) "minor" means a person under the age of 18.
(7) "minor personal protection order" means a personal protection order issued by a court against a minor and under jurisdiction granted by MCL 712A.2(h).

Rule 3.703 Commencing a Personal Protection Action

(A) **Filing**. A personal protection action is an independent action commenced by filing a petition with a court. There are no fees for filing a personal protection action and no summons is issued. A personal protection action may not be commenced by filing a motion in an existing case or by joining a claim to an action.

(B) **Petition in General**. The petition must
(1) be in writing;
(2) state with particularity the facts on which it is based;
(3) state the relief sought and the conduct to be restrained;
(4) state whether an ex parte order is being sought;
(5) state whether a personal protection order action involving the same parties has been commenced in another jurisdiction; and
(6) be signed by the party or attorney as provided in MCR 2.114. The petitioner may omit his or her residence address from the documents filed with the court, but must provide the court with a mailing address.

(C) **Petition Against a Minor**. In addition to the requirements outlined in (B), a petition against a minor must list:

(1) the minor's name, address, and either age or date of birth; and
(2) if known or can be easily ascertained, the names and addresses of the minor's parent or parents, guardian, or custodian.

(D) **Other Pending Actions; Order, Judgments**.
(1) The petition must specify whether there are any other pending actions in this or any other court, or orders or judgments already entered by this or any other court affecting the parties, including the name of the court and the case number, if known.
(a) If the petition is filed in the same court as a pending action or where an order or judgment has already been entered by that court affecting the parties, it shall be assigned to the same judge.
(b) If there are pending actions in another court or orders or judgments already entered by another court affecting the parties, the court should contact the court where the pending actions were filed or orders or judgments were entered, if practicable, to determine any relevant information.
(2) If the prior action resulted in an order providing for continuing jurisdiction of a minor, and the new action requests relief with regard to the minor, the court must comply with MCR 3.205.

(E) **Venue**.
(1) If the respondent is an adult, the petitioner may file a personal protection action in any county in Michigan regardless of residency.
(2) If the respondent is a minor, the petitioner may file a personal protection order in either the petitioner's or respondent's county of residence. If the respondent does not live in this state, venue for the action is proper in the petitioner's county of residence.

(F) **Minor or Legally Incapacitated Individual as Petitioner**.
(1) If the petitioner is a minor or a legally incapacitated individual, the petitioner shall proceed through a next friend. The petitioner shall certify that the next friend is not disqualified by statute and that the next friend is an adult.
(2) Unless the court determines appointment is necessary, the next friend may act on behalf of the minor or legally incapacitated person without appointment. However, the court shall appoint a next friend if the minor is less than 14 years of age. The next friend is not responsible for the costs of the action.

(G) **Request for Ex Parte Order**. If the petition requests an ex parte order, the petition must set forth specific facts showing that immediate and irreparable injury, loss, or damage will result to the petitioner from the delay required to effect notice or from the risk that notice will itself precipitate adverse action before an order can be issued.

Rule 3.704 Dismissal

Except as specified in MCR 3.705(A)(5) and (B), an action for a personal protection order may only be dismissed upon motion by the petitioner prior to the issuance of an order. There is no fee for such a motion.

Rule 3.705 Issuance of Personal Protection Orders

(A) **Ex Parte Orders**.
(1) The court must rule on a request for an ex parte order within 24 hours of the filing of the petition.
(2) If it clearly appears from specific facts shown by verified complaint, written petition, or affidavit that the petitioner is entitled to the relief sought, an ex parte order shall be granted if immediate and irreparable injury, loss, or damage will result from the delay required to effectuate notice or that the notice will itself precipitate adverse action before a personal protection order can be issued. In a proceeding under MCL 600.2950a, the court must state in writing the specific reasons for issuance of the order. A permanent record or memorandum must be made of any nonwritten evidence, argument or other representations made in support of issuance of an ex parte order.
(3) An ex parte order is valid for not less than 182 days, and must state its expiration date.
(4) If an ex parte order is entered, the petitioner shall serve the petition and order as provided in MCR 3.706(D). However, failure to make service does not affect the order's validity or effectiveness.
(5) If the court refuses to grant an ex parte order, it shall state the reasons in writing and shall advise the petitioner of the right to request a hearing as provided in subrule (B). If the petitioner does not request a hearing within 21 days of entry of the order, the order denying the petition is final. The court shall not be required to give such notice if the court determines after interviewing the petitioner that the petitioner's claims are sufficiently without merit that the action should be dismissed without a hearing.

(B) **Hearings**.
(1) The court shall schedule a hearing as soon as possible in the following instances, unless it determines after interviewing the petitioner that the claims are sufficiently without merit that the action should be dismissed without a hearing:
(a) the petition does not request an ex parte order; or
(b) the court refuses to enter an ex parte order and the petitioner subsequently requests a hearing.

(2) The petitioner shall serve on the respondent notice of the hearing along with the petition as provided in MCR 2.105(A). If the respondent is a minor, and the where-abouts of the respondent's parent or parents, guardian, or custodian is known, the petitioner shall also in the same manner serve notice of the hearing and the petition on the respondent's parent or parents, guardian, or custodian. One day before the hearing on a petition seeking a PPO under MCL 600.2950 or MCL 600.2950a(1) is deemed sufficient notice. Two days before the hearing on a petition seeking a PPO under MCL 600.2950a(2) is deemed sufficient notice.

(3) The hearing shall be held on the record.

(4) The petitioner must attend the hearing. If the petitioner fails to attend the hearing, the court may adjourn and reschedule the hearing or dismiss the petition.

(5) If the respondent fails to appear at a hearing on the petition and the court determines the petitioner made diligent attempts to serve the respondent, whether the respondent was served or not, the order may be entered without further notice to the respondent if the court determines that the petitioner is entitled to relief.

(6) At the conclusion of the hearing the court must state the reasons for granting or denying a personal protection order on the record and enter an appropriate order. In addition, the court must state the reasons for denying a personal protection order in writing, and, in a proceeding under MCL 600.2950a, the court must state in writing the specific reasons for issuance of the order.

(C) Pursuant to 18 USC 2265(d)(3), a court is prohibited from making available to the public on the Internet any information regarding the registration of, filing of a petition for, or issuance of an order under this rule if such publication would be likely to publicly reveal the identity or location of the party protected under the order.

Rule 3.706 Orders

(A) **Form and Scope of Order**. An order granting a personal protection order must include the following:

(1) A statement that the personal protection order has been entered, listing the type or types of conduct enjoined.

(2) A statement that the personal protection order is effective when signed by the judge and is immediately enforceable anywhere in Michigan, and that, after service, the personal protecion order may be enforced by another state, an Indian tribe, or a territory of the United States.

(3) A statement that violation of the personal protection order will subject the individual restrained or enjoined to either of the following:

(a) If the respondent is 17 years of age or more, immediate arrest and, if the respondent is found guilty of criminal contempt, imprisonment for not more than 93 days and may be fined not more than $500; or

(b) If the respondent is less than 17 years of age, immediate apprehension and, if the respondent is found in contempt, the dispositional alternatives listed in MCL 712A.18.

(4) An expiration date stated clearly on the face of the order.

(5) A statement that the personal protection order is enforceable anywhere in Michigan by any law enforcement agency, and that if the respondent violates the personal protection order in another jurisdiction, the respondent is subject to the enforcement procedures and penalties of the jurisdiction in which the violation occurred.

(6) Identification of the law enforcement agency, designated by the court to enter the personal protection order into the law enforcement information network.

(7) For ex parte orders, a statement that, within 14 days after being served with or receiving actual notice of the order, the individual restrained or enjoined may file a motion to modify or terminate the personal protection order and a request for a hearing, and that motion forms and filing instructions are available from the clerk of the court.

(B) **Mutual Orders Prohibited**. A personal protection order may not be made mutual.

(C) **Existing Custody and Parenting Time Orders**.

(1) Contact With Court Having Prior Jurisdiction. The court issuing a personal protection order must contact the court having jurisdiction over the parenting time or custody matter as provided in MCR 3.205, and where practicable, the judge should consult with that court, as contemplated in MCR 3.205(C)(2), regarding the impact upon custody and parenting time rights before issuing the personal protection order.

(2) Conditions Modifying Custody and Parenting Time Provisions. If the respondent's custody or parenting time rights will be adversely affected by the personal protection order, the issuing court shall determine whether conditions should be specified in the order which would accommodate the respondent's rights or whether the situation is such that the safety of the petitioner and minor children would be compromised by such conditions.

(3) Effect of Personal Protection Order. A personal protection order takes precedence over any existing custody or parenting time order until the personal

protection order has expired, or the court having jurisdiction over the custody or parenting time order modifies the custody or parenting time order to accommodate the conditions of the personal protection order.

(a) If the respondent or petitioner wants the existing custody or parenting time order modified, the respondent or petitioner must file a motion with the court having jurisdiction of the custody or parenting time order and request a hearing. The hearing must be held within 21 days after the motion is filed.

(b) Proceedings to modify custody and parenting time orders are subject to subchapter 3.200.

(D) **Service**. The petitioner shall serve the order on the respondent as provided in MCR 2.105(A). If the respondent is a minor, and the whereabouts of the respondent's parent or parents, guardian, or custodian is known, the petitioner shall also in the same manner serve the order on the respondent's parent or parents, guardian, or custodian. On an appropriate showing, the court may allow service in another manner as provided in MCR 2.105(I). Failure to serve the order does not affect its validity or effectiveness.

(E) **Oral Notice**. If oral notice of the order is made by a law enforcement officer as described in MCL 600.2950(22) or 600.2950a(19), proof of the notification must be filed with the court by the law enforcement officer.

Rule 3.707 Modification, Termination, or Extension of Order

(A) **Modification or Termination**.

(1) *Time for Filing and Service*.

(a) The petitioner may file a motion to modify or terminate the personal protection order and request a hearing at any time after the personal protection order is issued.

(b) The respondent may file a motion to modify or terminate an ex parte personal protection order or an ex parte order extending a personal protection order and request a hearing within 14 days after being served with, or receiving actual notice of, the order. Any motion otherwise to modify or terminate a personal protection order by the respondent requires a showing of good cause.

(c) The moving party shall serve the motion to modify or terminate the order and the notice of hearing at least 7 days before the hearing date as provided in MCR 2.105(A)(2) at the mailing address or addresses provided to the court. On an appropriate showing, the court may allow service in another manner as provided in MCR 2.105(I). If the moving party is a respondent who is issued a license to carry a concealed weapon and is required to carry a weapon as a condition of employment, a police officer certified by the Michigan law enforcement training council act of 1965, 1965 PA 203, MCL 28.601 to 28.616, a sheriff, a deputy sheriff or a member of the Michigan department of state police, a local corrections officer, department of corrections employee, or a federal law enforcement officer who carries a firearm during the normal course of employment, providing notice one day before the hearing is deemed as sufficient notice to the petitioner.

(2) *Hearing on the Motion*. The court must schedule and hold a hearing on a motion to modify or terminate a personal protection order within 14 days of the filing of the motion, except that if the respondent is a person described in MCL 600.2950(2) or 600.2950a(2), the court shall schedule the hearing on the motion within 5 days after the filing of the motion.

(3) *Notice of Modification or Termination*. If a personal protection order is modified or terminated, the clerk must immediately notify the law enforcement agency specified in the personal protection order of the change. A modified or terminated order must be served as provided in MCR 2.107.

(B) **Extension of Order**.

(1) *Time for Filing*. The petitioner may file an ex parte motion to extend the effectiveness of the order, without hearing, by requesting a new expiration date. The motion must be filed with the court that issued the personal protection order no later than 3 days before the order is to expire. The court must act on the motion within 3 days after it is filed. Failure to timely file a motion to extend the effectiveness of the order does not preclude the petitioner from commencing a new personal protection action regarding the same respondent, as provided in MCR 3.703.

(2) *Notice of Extension*. If the expiration date on a personal protection order is extended, an amended order must be entered. The clerk must immediately notify the law enforcement agency specified in the personal protection order of the change. The order must be served on the respondent as provided in MCR 2.107.

(C) **Minors and Legally Incapacitated Individuals**. Petitioners or respondents who are minors or legally incapacitated individuals must proceed through a next friend, as provided in MCR 3.703(F).

(D) **Fees**. There are no motion fees for modifying, terminating, or extending a personal protection order.

Rule 3.708 Contempt Proceedings for Violation of Personal Protection Orders

(A) **In General**.

(1) A personal protection order is enforceable under MCL 600.2950(23), (25), 600.2950a(20), (22), 764.15b, and 600.1701 et seq. For the purpose of this rule, "personal protection order" includes a foreign protection order enforceable in Michigan under MCL 600.29501.

(2) Proceedings to enforce a minor personal protection order where the respondent is under 18 are governed by subchapter 3.900. Proceedings to enforce a personal protection order issued against an adult, or to enforce a minor personal protection order still in effect when the respondent is 18 or older, are governed by this rule.

(B) **Motion to Show Cause**.

(1) *Filing*. If the respondent violates the personal protection order, the petitioner may file a motion, supported by appropriate affidavit, to have the respondent found in contempt. There is no fee for such a motion. If the petitioner's motion and affidavit establish a basis for a finding of contempt, the court shall either:

(a) order the respondent to appear at a specified time to answer the contempt charge; or

(b) issue a bench warrant for the arrest of the respondent.

(2) *Service*. The petitioner shall serve the motion to show cause and the order on the respondent by personal service at least 7 days before the show cause hearing.

(C) **Arrest**.

(1) If the respondent is arrested for violation of a personal protection order as provided in MCL 764.15b(1), the court in the county where the arrest is made shall proceed as provided in MCL 764.15b(2)-(5), except as provided in this rule.

(2) A contempt proceeding brought in a court other than the one that issued the personal protection order shall be entitled "In the Matter of Contempt of [Respondent]." The clerk shall provide a copy of any documents pertaining to the contempt proceeding to the court that issued the personal protection order.

(3) If it appears that a circuit judge will not be available within 24 hours after arrest, the respondent shall be taken, within that time, before a district court, which shall set bond and order the respondent to appear for arraignment before the family division of the circuit court in that county.

(D) **Appearance or Arraignment; Advice to Respondent**. At the respondent's first appearance before the circuit court, whether for arraignment under MCL 764.15b, enforcement under MCL 600.2950, 600.2950a, or 600.1701, or otherwise, the court must:

(1) advise the respondent of the alleged violation,

(2) advise the respondent of the right to contest the charge at a contempt hearing,

(3) advise the respondent that he or she is entitled to a lawyer's assistance at the hearing and, if the court determines it might sentence the respondent to jail, that the court will appoint a lawyer at public expense if the individual wants one and is financially unable to retain one,

(4) if requested and appropriate, appoint a lawyer,

(5) set a reasonable bond pending a hearing of the alleged violation,

(6) take a guilty plea as provided in subrule (E) or schedule a hearing as provided in subrule (F).

(E) **Pleas of Guilty**. The respondent may plead guilty to the violation. Before accepting a guilty plea, the court, speaking directly to the respondent and receiving the respondent's response, must

(1) advise the respondent that by pleading guilty the respondent is giving up the right to a contested hearing and, if the respondent is proceeding without legal representation, the right to a lawyer's assistance as set forth in subrule (D)(3),

(2) advise the respondent of the maximum possible jail sentence for the violation,

(3) ascertain that the plea is understandingly, voluntarily, and knowingly made, and

(4) establish factual support for a finding that the respondent is guilty of the alleged violation.

(F) **Scheduling or Postponing Hearing**. Following the respondent's appearance or arraignment, the court shall do the following:

(1) Set a date for the hearing at the earliest practicable time except as required under MCL 764.15b.

(a) The hearing of a respondent being held in custody for an alleged violation of a personal protection order must be held within 72 hours after the arrest, unless extended by the court on the motion of the arrested individual or the prosecuting attorney. The court must set a reasonable bond pending the hearing unless the court determines that release will not reasonably ensure the safety of the individuals named in the personal protection order.

(b) If a respondent is released on bond pending the hearing, the bond may include any condition specified in MCR 6.106(D) necessary to reasonably ensure the safety of the individuals named in the personal protection order, including continued compliance with the personal protection order. The release order shall also comply with MCL 765.6b.

(c) If the alleged violation is based on a criminal offense that is a basis for a separate criminal prosecution, upon motion of the prosecutor, the court may postpone the hearing for the outcome of that prosecution.

(2) Notify the prosecuting attorney of a criminal contempt proceeding.

(3) Notify the petitioner and his or her attorney, if any, of the contempt proceeding and direct the party to appear at the hearing and give evidence on the charge of contempt.

(G) **Prosecution After Arrest**. In a criminal contempt proceeding commenced under MCL 764.15b, the prosecuting attorney shall prosecute the proceeding unless the petitioner retains his or her own attorney for the criminal contempt proceeding.

(H) **The Violation Hearing**.

(1) *Jury*. There is no right to a jury trial.

(2) *Conduct of the Hearing*. The respondent has the right to be present at the hearing, to present evidence, and to examine and cross-examine witnesses.

(3) *Evidence; Burden of Proof*. The rules of evidence apply to both criminal and civil contempt proceedings. The petitioner or the prosecuting attorney has the burden of proving the respondent's guilt of criminal contempt beyond a reasonable doubt and the respondent's guilt of civil contempt by clear and convincing evidence.

(4) *Judicial Findings*. At the conclusion of the hearing, the court must find the facts specially, state separately its conclusions of law, and direct entry of the appropriate judgment. The court must state its findings and conclusions on the record or in a written opinion made a part of the record.

(5) *Sentencing*.

(a) If the respondent pleads or is found guilty of criminal contempt, the court shall impose a sentence of incarceration for no more than 93 days and may impose a fine of not more than $500.00.

(b) If the respondent pleads or is found guilty of civil contempt, the court shall impose a fine or imprisonment as specified in MCL 600.1715 and 600.1721.

In addition to such a sentence, the court may impose other conditions to the personal protection order.

Rule 3.709 Appeals

(A) **Rules Applicable**. Except as provided by this rule, appeals involving personal protection order matters must comply with subchapter 7.200. Appeals involving minor personal protection actions under the Juvenile Code must additionally comply with MCR 3.993.

(B) **From Entry of Personal Protection Order**.

(1) Either party has an appeal of right from

(a) an order granting or denying a personal protection order after a hearing under subrule 3.705(B)(6), or

(b) the ruling on respondent's first motion to rescind or modify the order if an ex parte order was entered.

(2) Appeals of all other orders are by leave to appeal.

(C) **From Finding after Violation Hearing**.

(1) The respondent has an appeal of right from a sentence for criminal contempt entered after a contested hearing.

(2) All other appeals concerning violation proceedings are by application for leave.

Subchapter 3.800 Adoption

Rule 3.800 Applicable Rules; Interested Parties; Indian Child

(A) **Generally**. Except as modified by MCR 3.801-3.807, adoption proceedings, are governed by Michigan Court Rules.

(B) **Interested Parties**.

(1) The persons interested in various adoption proceedings, including proceedings involving and Indian child, are as provided by MCL 710.24a except as otherwise provided in subrules (2) and (3).

(2) If the court knows or has reason to know the adoptee is an Indian child, in addition to subrule (B)(1), the persons interested are the Indian child's tribe and the Indian custodian, if any, and, if the Indian child's parent or Indian custodian, or tribe, is unknown, the Secretary of the Interior.

(3) The interested persons in a petition to terminate the rights of the noncustodial parent pursuant to MCL 710.51(6) are:

(a) the petitioner;

(b) the adoptee, if over 14 years of age;

(c) the noncustodial parent; and

(d) if the court knows or has reason to know the adoptee is an Indian child, the Indian child's tribe and the Indian custodian, if any, and, if the Indian child's parent or Indian custodian, or tribe, is unknown, the Secretary of the Interior.

Rule 3.801 Papers, Execution

(A) A waiver, affirmation, or disclaimer to be executed by the father of a child born out of wedlock may be executed any time after the conception of the child. If a putative father acknowledges paternity, he must receive notice of the hearing if the child is an Indian child.

(B) A release or consent is valid if executed in accordance with the law at the time of execution.

Rule 3.802 Manner and Method of Service

(A) **Service of Papers**.

(1) A notice of intent to release or consent pursuant to MCL 710.34(1) may only be served by personal service by a peace officer or a person authorized by the court.

(2) Notice of a petition to identify a putative father and to determine or terminate his rights, or a petition to terminate the rights of a noncustodial parent, must be served on the individual or the individual's attorney in the manner provided in MCR 5.105(B)(1)(a) or (b).

(3) Notice of Proceeding Concerning Indian Child. If the court knows or has reason to know an Indian child is the subject of an adoption proceeding and an Indian tribe does not have exclusive jurisdiction as defined in MCR 3.002(6),

(a) in addition to any other service requirements, the petitioner shall notify the parent or Indian custodian and the Indian child's tribe, by personal service or by registered mail with return receipt requested and delivery restricted to the addressee, of the pending proceedings on a petition for adoption of the Indian child and of their right of intervention on a form approved by the State Court Administrative Office. If the identity or location of the parent or Indian custodian, or of the Indian child's tribe, cannot be determined, notice shall be given to the Secretary of the Interior by registered mail with return receipt requested.

(b) the court shall notify the parent or Indian custodian and the Indian child's tribe of all other hearings pertaining to the adoption proceeding as provided in this rule. If the identity or location of the parent or Indian custodian, or of the Indian child's tribe, cannot be determined, notice of the hearings shall be given to the Secretary of the Interior. Such notice may be made by first-class mail.

(4) Except as provided in subrules (B) and (C), all other papers may be served by mail under MCR 2.107(C)(3).

(B) **Service When Identity or Whereabouts of Father is Unascertainable**.

(1) If service cannot be made under subrule (A)(2) because the identity of the father of a child born out of wedlock or the whereabouts of the identified father has not been ascertained after diligent inquiry, the petitioner must file proof, by affidavit or by declaration under MCR 2.114(B)(2), of the attempt to identify or locate the father. No further service is necessary before the hearing to identify the father and to determine or terminate his rights.

(2) At the hearing, the court shall take evidence concerning the attempt to identify or locate the father. If the court finds that a reasonable attempt was made, the court shall proceed under MCL 710.37(2). If the court finds that a reasonable attempt was not made, the court shall adjourn the hearing under MCL 710.36(7) and shall

(a) order a further attempt to identify or locate the father so that service can be made under subrule (A)(2)(a), or

(b) direct any manner of substituted service of the notice of hearing except service by publication.

(C) **Service When Whereabouts of Noncustodial Parent Is Unascertainable**. If service of a petition to terminate the parental rights of a noncustodial parent pursuant to MCL 710.51(6) cannot be made under subrule (A)(2) because the whereabouts of the noncustodial parent has not been ascertained after diligent inquiry, the petitioner must file proof, by affidavit or by declaration under MCR 2.114(B)(2), of the attempt to locate the noncustodial parent. If the court finds, on reviewing the affidavit or declaration, that service cannot be made because the whereabouts of the person has not been determined after reasonable efforts, the court may direct any manner of substituted service of the notice of hearing, including service by publication.

Rule 3.803 Financial Reports, Subsequent Orders

(A) **Updated Accounting and Statements**.

(1) The update of the accounting filed pursuant to MCL 710.54(8) may include by reference the total expenses itemized in the accounting required by MCL 710.54(7).

(2) Any verified statement filed pursuant to MCL 710.54(7) need not be filed again unless, at the time of the update required by MCL 710.54(8), any such statement does not reflect the facts at that time.

(B) **Subsequent Orders**.

(1) Only one order approving fees disclosed in the financial reports by MCL 710.54(7) need be entered, and it must be entered after the filing required by MCL 710.54(8).

(2) The order placing the child may be entered before the elapse of the 7-day period required by MCL 710.54(7).

(3) The final order of adoption may be entered before the elapse of the 21-day period required by MCL 710.54(8).

Rule 3.804 Consent and Release

(A) **Contents and Execution of Consent or Release**. In addition to the requirements of MCL 710.29 or MCL 710.44, if a parent of an Indian child intends to voluntarily consent to adoptive placement or the termination of his or her parental rights for the express purpose of adoption pursuant to MCL 712B.13, the following requirements must be met:

(1) except in stepparent adoptions under MCL 710.23a(4), both parents must consent.
(2) to be valid, consent must be executed on a form approved by the State Court Administrative Office, in writing, recorded before a judge of a court of competent jurisdiction, and accompanied by the presiding judge's certificate that the terms and consequences of the consent were fully explained in detail and were fully understood by the parent. The court shall also certify that either the parent fully understood the explanation in English or that it was interpreted into a language that the parent understood. Any consent given before, or within 10 days after, the birth of the Indian child is not valid.
(3) the consent must contain the information prescribed by MCL 712B.13(2).
(4) in a direct placement, as defined in MCL 710.22(o), a consent by a parent shall be accompanied by a verified statement that complies with MCL 712B.13(6).

(B) **Hearing**.
(1) The consent hearing required by MCL.710.44(1) must be promptly scheduled by the court after the court examines and approves the report of the investigation or foster family study filed pursuant to MCL 710.46. If an interested party has requested a consent hearing, the hearing shall be held within 7 days of the filing of the report or foster family study.
(2) A consent hearing involving an Indian child pursuant to MCL 712B.13 must be held in conjunction with either a consent to adopt, as required by MCL 710.44, or a release, as required by MCL 710.29. Notice of the hearing must be sent to the parties prescribed in MCR 3.800(B) in compliance with MCR 3.802(A)(3).

(C) **Withdrawal of Consent to Adopt Indian Child**. A parent who executes a consent under MCL 712B.13 may withdraw that consent at any time before entry of a final order of adoption by filing a written demand requesting the return of the child. Once a demand is filed with the court, the court shall order the return of the child. Withdrawal of consent under MCL 712B.13 constitutes a withdrawal of a release executed under MCL 710.29 or a consent to adopt executed under MCL 710.44.

Rule 3.805 Temporary Placements, Time for Service of Notice of Hearing to Determine Disposition of Child

(A) **Time for Personal Service**. Personal service of notice of hearing on a petition for disposition of a child pursuant to MCL 710.23e(1) must be served at least 3 days before the date set for hearing.

(B) **Time for Service by Mail**. Service by mail must be made at least 7 days before the date set for hearing.

(C) **Interested Party, Whereabouts Unknown**. If the whereabouts of an interested party, other than the putative father who did not join in the temporary placement, is unknown, service on that interested party will be sufficient if personal service or service by mail is attempted at the last known address of the interested party.

(D) **Putative Father, Identity or Whereabouts Unknown**. If the identity of the putative father is unknown or the whereabouts of a putative father who did not join in the temporary placement is unknown, he need not be served notice of the hearing.

Rule 3.806 Rehearings

(A) **Filing, Notice and Response**. A party may seek rehearing under MCL 710.64(1) by timely filing a petition stating the basis for rehearing. Immediately upon filing the petition, the petitioner must give all interested parties notice of its filing in accordance with MCR 5.105. Any interested party may file a response within 7 days of the date of service of notice on the interested party.

(B) **Procedure for Determining Whether to Grant a Rehearing**. The court must base a decision on whether to grant a rehearing on the record, the pleading filed, or a hearing on the petition. The court may grant a rehearing only for good cause. The reasons for its decision must be in writing or stated on the record.

(C) **Procedure if Rehearing Granted**. If the court grants a rehearing, the court may, after notice, take new evidence on the record. It may affirm, modify, or vacate its prior decision in whole or in part. The court must state the reasons for its action in writing or on the record.

(D) **Stay**. Pending a ruling on the petition for rehearing, the court may stay any order, or enter another order in the best interest of the minor.

Rule 3.807 Indian Child

(A) **Definitions.** If an Indian child, as defined by the Michigan Indian Family Preservation Act, MCL 712B.3, is the subject of an adoption proceeding, the definitions in MCR 3.002 shall control.

(B) **Jurisdiction, Notice, Transfer, Intervention**.
(1) If an Indian child is the subject of an adoption proceeding and an Indian tribe has exclusive jurisdiction as defined in MCR 3.002(6), the matter shall be dismissed.
(2) If an Indian child is the subject of an adoption proceeding and an Indian tribe does not have exclusive jurisdiction as defined in MCR 3.002(6), the court shall ensure that the petitioner has given notice of the proceedings to the persons prescribed

in MCR 3.800(B) in accordance with MCR 3.802(A)(3).

(a) If either parent or the Indian custodian or the Indian child's tribe petitions the court to transfer the proceeding to the tribal court, the court shall transfer the case to the tribal court unless either parent objects to the transfer of the case to tribal court jurisdiction or the court finds good cause not to transfer. When the court makes a good-cause determination under MCL 712B.7, adequacy of the tribe, tribal court, or tribal social services shall not be considered. A court may determine that good cause not to transfer a case to tribal court exists only if the person opposing the transfer shows by clear and convincing evidence that either of the following applies:

(i) The Indian tribe does not have a tribal court.

(ii) The requirement of the parties or witnesses to present evidence in tribal court would cause undue hardship to those parties or witnesses that the Indian tribe is unable to mitigate.

(b) The court shall not dismiss the matter until the transfer has been accepted by the tribal court.

(c) If the tribal court declines transfer, the Michigan Indian Family Preservation Act applies, as do the provisions of these rules that pertain to an Indian child (see MCL 712B.3 and MCL 712B.5.

(d) A petition to transfer may be made at any time in accordance with MCL 712B.7(3).

(3) The Indian custodian of the child, the Indian child's tribe, and the Indian child have a right to intervene at any point in the proceeding pursuant to MCL 712B.7(6).

(C) **Record of Tribal Affiliation**. Upon application by an Indian individual who has reached the age of 18 and who was the subject of an adoption placement, the court that entered the final decree shall inform such individual of the tribal affiliation, if any, of the individual's biological parents and provide such other information as may be necessary to protect any rights flowing from the individual's tribal relationship. (25 USC 1917.)

Subchapter 3.900 Proceedings Involving Juveniles

Rule 3.901 Applicability of Rules

(A) **Scope**.

(1) The rules in this subchapter, in subchapter 1.100, in MCR 5.113, and in subchapter 8.100 govern practice and procedure in the family division of the circuit court in all cases filed under the Juvenile Code.

(2) Other Michigan Court Rules apply to juvenile cases in the family division of the circuit court only when this subchapter specifically provides.

(3) The Michigan Rules of Evidence, except with regard to privileges, do not apply to proceedings under this subchapter, except where a rule in this subchapter specifically so provides. MCL 722.631 governs privileges in child protective proceedings.

(B) **Application**. Unless the context otherwise indicates:

(1) MCR 3.901-3.930, and 3.991-3.993 apply to delinquency proceedings and child protective proceedings;

(2) MCR 3.931-3.950 apply only to delinquency proceedings;

(3) MCR 3.951-3.956 apply only to designated proceedings;

(4) MCR 3.961-3.979 apply only to child protective proceedings;

(5) MCR 3.981-3.989 apply only to minor personal protection order proceedings.

Rule 3.902 Construction

(A) **In General**. The rules are to be construed to secure fairness, flexibility, and simplicity. The court shall proceed in a manner that safeguards the rights and proper interests of the parties. Limitations on corrections of error are governed by MCR 2.613.

(B) **Philosophy**. The rules must be interpreted and applied in keeping with the philosophy expressed in the Juvenile Code. The court shall ensure that each minor coming within the jurisdiction of the court shall:

(1) receive the care, guidance, and control, preferably in the minor's own home, that is conducive to the minor's welfare and the best interests of the public; and

(2) when removed from parental control, be placed in care as nearly as possible equivalent to the care that the minor's parents should have given the minor.

Rule 3.903 Definitions

(A) **General Definitions**. When used in this subchapter, unless the context otherwise indicates:

(1) "Case" means an action initiated in the family division of the circuit court by:

(a) submission of an original complaint, petition, or citation;

(b) acceptance of transfer of an action from another court or tribunal; or

(c) filing or registration of a foreign judgment or order.

(2) "Child protective proceeding" means a proceeding concerning an offense against a child.

(3) "Confidential file" means

(a) that part of a file made confidential by statute or court rule, including, but not limited to,

(i) the diversion record of a minor pursuant to the Juvenile Diversion Act, MCL 722.821 et seq.;
(ii) the separate statement about known victims of juvenile offenses, as required by the Crime Victim's Rights Act, MCL 780.751 et seq.;
(iii) the testimony taken during a closed proceeding pursuant to MCR 3.925(A)(2) and MCL 712A.17(7);
(iv) the dispositional reports pursuant to MCR 3.943(C)(3) and 3.973(E)(4);
(v) fingerprinting material required to be maintained pursuant to MCL 28.243;
(vi) reports of sexually motivated crimes, MCL 28.247;
(vii) test results of those charged with certain sexual offenses or substance abuse offenses, MCL 333.5129;

(b) the contents of a social file maintained by the court, including materials such as
(i) youth and family record fact sheet;
(ii) social study;
(iii) reports (such as dispositional, investigative, laboratory, medical, observation, psychological, psychiatric, progress, treatment, school, and police reports);
(iv) Department of Human Services records;
(v) correspondence;
(vi) victim statements;
(vii) information regarding the identity or location of a foster parent, preadoptive parent, relative caregiver, or juvenile guardian.

(4) "Court" means the family division of the circuit court.

(5) "Delinquency proceeding" means a proceeding concerning an offense by a juvenile, as defined in MCR 3.903(B)(3).

(6) "Designated proceeding" means a proceeding in which the prosecuting attorney has designated, or has requested the court to designate, the case for trial in the family division of the circuit court in the same manner as an adult.

(7) "Father" means:
(a) A man married to the mother at any time from a minor's conception to the minor's birth, unless a court has determined, after notice and a hearing, that the minor was conceived or born during the marriage, but is not the issue of the marriage;
(b) A man who legally adopts the minor;
(c) A man who by order of filiation or by judgment of paternity is judicially determined to be the father of the minor;
(d) A man judicially determined to have parental rights; or
(e) A man whose paternity is established by the completion and filing of an acknowledgment of parentage in accordance with the provisions of the Acknowledgment of Parentage Act, MCL 722.1001 et seq., or a previously applicable procedure. For an acknowledgment under the Acknowledgment of Parentage Act, the man and mother must each sign the acknowledgment of parentage before a notary public appointed in this state. The acknowledgment shall be filed at either the time of birth or another time during the child's lifetime with the state registrar.

(8) "File" means a repository for collection of the pleadings and other documents and materials related to a case.

(9) An authorized petition is deemed "filed" when it is delivered to, and accepted by, the clerk of the court.

(10) "Formal calendar" means judicial proceedings other than a delinquency proceeding on the consent calendar, a preliminary inquiry, or a preliminary hearing of a delinquency or child protective proceeding.

(11) "Guardian" means a person appointed as guardian of a child by a Michigan court pursuant to MCL 700.5204 or 700.5205, by a court of another state under a comparable statutory provision, or by parental or testamentary appointment as provided in MCL 700.5202, or a juvenile guardian appointed pursuant to MCL 712A.19a or MCL 712A.19c.

(12) "Juvenile Code" means 1944 (1st Ex Sess) PA 54, MCL 712A.1 et seq., as amended.

(13) "Juvenile Guardian" means a person appointed guardian of a child by a Michigan court pursuant to MCL 712A.19a or MCL 712A.19c. A juvenile guardianship is distinct from a guardianship authorized under the Estates and Protected Individuals Code.

(14) "Legal Custodian" means an adult who has been given legal custody of a minor by order of a circuit court in Michigan or a comparable court of another state or who possesses a valid power of attorney given pursuant to MCL 700.5103 or a comparable statute of another state. It also includes the term "Indian custodian" as defined in MCR 3.002(15).

(15) "Legally admissible evidence" means evidence admissible under the Michigan Rules of Evidence.

(16) "Minor" means a person under the age of 18, and may include a person of age 18 or older over whom the court has continuing jurisdiction pursuant to MCL 712A.2a.

(17) "Officer" means a government official with the power to arrest or any other person designated and

directed by the court to apprehend, detain, or place a minor.

(18) "Parent" means the mother, the father as defined in MCR 3.903(A)(7), or both, of the minor. It also includes the term "parent" as defined in MCR 3.002(20).

(19) "Party" includes the

(a) petitioner and juvenile in a delinquency proceeding;

(b) petitioner, child, respondent, and parent, guardian, or legal custodian in a protective proceeding.

(20) "Petition" means a complaint or other written allegation, verified in the manner provided in MCR 2.114(B), that a parent, guardian, nonparent adult, or legal custodian has harmed or failed to properly care for a child, or that a juvenile has committed an offense.

(21) "Petition authorized to be filed" refers to written permission given by the court to file the petition containing the formal allegations against the juvenile or respondent with the clerk of the court.

(22) "Petitioner" means the person or agency who requests the court to take action.

(23) "Preliminary inquiry" means informal review by the court to determine appropriate action on a petition.

(24) "Putative father" means a man who is alleged to be the biological father of a child who has no father as defined in MCR 3.903(A)(7).

(25) "Records" are as defined in MCR 1.109 and include pleadings, motions, authorized petition, notices, memoranda, briefs, exhibits, available transcripts, findings of the court, registers of actions, and court orders.

(26) "Register of actions" means the permanent case history maintained in accord with the Michigan Supreme Court Case File Management Standards. See MCR 8.119(D)(1)(c).

(27) "Trial" means the fact-finding adjudication of an authorized petition to determine if the minor comes within the jurisdiction of the court.

(B) **Delinquency Proceedings**. When used in delinquency proceedings, unless the context otherwise indicates:

(1) "Detention" means court-ordered removal of a juvenile from the custody of a parent, guardian, or legal custodian, pending trial, disposition, commitment, or further order.

(2) "Juvenile" means a minor alleged or found to be within the jurisdiction of the court for having committed an offense.

(3) "Offense by a juvenile" means an act that violates a criminal statute, a criminal ordinance, a traffic law, or a provision of MCL 712A.2(a) or (d).

(4) "Prosecuting attorney" means the prosecuting attorney for a county, an assistant prosecuting attorney for a county, the attorney general, the deputy attorney general, an assistant attorney general, a special prosecuting attorney, and, in connection with the prosecution of an ordinance violation, an attorney for the political subdivision or governmental entity that enacted the ordinance, charter, rule, or regulation upon which the ordinance violation is based.

(C) **Child Protective Proceedings**. When used in child protective proceedings, unless the context otherwise indicates:

(1) "Agency" means a public or private organization, institution, or facility responsible pursuant to court order or contractual arrangement for the care and supervision of a child.

(2) "Child" means a minor alleged or found to be within the jurisdiction of the court pursuant to MCL 712A.2(b).

(3) "Contrary to the welfare of the child" includes, but is not limited to, situations in which the child's life, physical health, or mental well-being is unreasonably placed at risk.

(4) "Foster care" means 24-hour a day substitute care for children placed away from their parents, guardians, or legal custodians, and for whom the court has given the Department of Human Services placement and care responsibility, including, but not limited to,

(a) care provided to a child in a foster family home, foster family group home, or child caring institution licensed or approved under MCL 722.111 et seq., or

(b) care provided to a child in a relative's home pursuant to an order of the court.

(5) "Lawyer-guardian ad litem" means that term as defined in MCL 712A.13a(1)(g).

(6) "Nonparent adult" means a person who is 18 years of age or older and who, regardless of the person's domicile, meets all the following criteria in relation to a child over whom the court takes jurisdiction under this chapter:

(a) has substantial and regular contact with the child,

(b) has a close personal relationship with the child's parent or with a person responsible for the child's health or welfare, and

(c) is not the child's parent or a person otherwise related to the child by blood or affinity to the third degree.

(7) "Offense against a child" means an act or omission by a parent, guardian, nonparent adult, or legal custodian asserted as grounds for bringing the child within the jurisdiction of the court pursuant to the Juvenile Code.

(8) "Placement" means court-approved transfer of physical custody of a child to foster care, a shelter home, a hospital, or a private treatment agency.
(9) "Prosecutor" or "prosecuting attorney" means the prosecuting attorney of the county in which the court has its principal office or an assistant to the prosecuting attorney.
(10) Except as provided in MCR 3.977(B), "respondent" means the parent, guardian, legal custodian, or nonparent adult who is alleged to have committed an offense against a child.

(D) **Designated Proceedings**.
(1) "Arraignment" means the first hearing in a designated case at which
(a) the juvenile is informed of the allegations, the juvenile's rights, and the potential consequences of the proceeding;
(b) the matter is set for a probable cause or designation hearing; and,
(c) if the juvenile is in custody or custody is requested pending trial, a decision is made regarding custody pursuant to MCR 3.935(C).
(2) "Court-designated case" means a case in which the court, pursuant to a request by the prosecuting attorney, has decided according to the factors set forth in MCR 3.952(C)(3) that the juvenile is to be tried in the family division of circuit court in the same manner as an adult for an offense other than a specified juvenile violation.
(3) "Designated case" means either a prosecutor-designated case or a court-designated case.
(4) "Designation hearing" means a hearing on the prosecuting attorney's request that the court designate the case for trial in the same manner as an adult in the family division of circuit court.
(5) "Preliminary examination" means a hearing at which the court determines whether there is probable cause to believe that the specified juvenile violation or alleged offense occurred and whether there is probable cause to believe that the juvenile committed the specified juvenile violation or alleged offense.
(6) "Prosecutor-designated case" means a case in which the prosecuting attorney has endorsed a petition charging a juvenile with a specified juvenile violation with the designation that the juvenile is to be tried in the same manner as an adult in the family division of the circuit court.
(7) "Sentencing" means the imposition of any sanction on a juvenile that could be imposed on an adult convicted of the offense for which the juvenile was convicted or the decision to delay the imposition of such a sanction.
(8) "Specified juvenile violation" means any offense, attempted offense, conspiracy to commit an offense, or solicitation to commit an offense, as enumerated in MCL 712A.2d, that would constitute:
(a) burning of a dwelling house, MCL 750.72;
(b) assault with intent to commit murder, MCL 750.83;
(c) assault with intent to maim, MCL 750.86;
(d) assault with intent to rob while armed, MCL 750.89;
(e) attempted murder, MCL 750.91;
(f) first-degree murder, MCL 750.316;
(g) second-degree murder, MCL 750.317;
(h) kidnaping, MCL 750.349;
(i) first-degree criminal sexual conduct, MCL 750.520b;
(j) armed robbery, MCL 750.529;
(k) carjacking, MCL 750.529a;
(l) robbery of a bank, safe, or vault, MCL 750.531;
(m) possession, manufacture, or delivery of, or possession with intent to manufacture or deliver, 650 grams(1,000 grams beginning March 1, 2003) or more of any schedule 1 or 2 controlled substance, MCL 333.7401, 333.7403;
(n) assault with intent to do great bodily harm less than murder, MCL 750.84, if armed with a dangerous weapon as defined by MCL 712A.2d(9)(b);
(o) first-degree home invasion, MCL 750.110a(2), if armed with a dangerous weapon as defined by MCL 712A.2d(9)(b);
(p) escape or attempted escape from a medium security or high security facility operated by the Department of Human Services or a high-security facility operated by a private agency under contract with the Department of Human Services, MCL 750.186a;
(q) any lesser-included offense of an offense described in subrules (a)-(p), if the petition alleged that the juvenile committed an offense described in subrules (a)-(p); or
(r) any offense arising out of the same transaction as an offense described in subrules (a)-(p), if the petition alleged that the juvenile committed an offense described in subrules (a)-(p).
(9) "Tried in the same manner as an adult" means a trial in which the juvenile is afforded all the legal and procedural protections that an adult would be given if charged with the same offense in a court of general criminal jurisdiction.

(E) **Minor Personal Protection Order Proceedings**. When used in minor personal protection order proceedings, unless the context otherwise indicates:
(1) "Minor personal protection order" means a personal protection order issued by a court against a minor under jurisdiction granted by MCL 712A.2(h).

(2) "Original petitioner" means the person who originally petitioned for the minor personal protection order.
(3) "Prosecutor" or "prosecuting attorney" means the prosecuting attorney of the county in which the court has its principal office or an assistant to the prosecuting attorney.

(F) **Michigan Indian Family Preservation Act**. If an Indian child, as defined by the Michigan Indian Family Preservation Act, MCL 712B.1 et seq., is the subject of a protective proceeding or is charged with a status offense in violation of MCL 712A.2(a)(2)-(4) or (d), the definitions in MCR 3.002 shall control.

Rule 3.904. Use of Interactive Video Technology.

(A) **Facilities**. Courts may use two-way interactive video technology to conduct the proceedings outlined in subrule (B).

(B) **Hearings**.
(1) *Delinquency Proceedings*. Two-way interactive video technology may be used to conduct preliminary hearings under MCR 3.935(A)(1), postdispositional progress reviews, and dispositional hearings where the court does not order a more restrictive placement or more restrictive treatment
(2) *Child Protective Proceedings*. Two-way interactive video technology may be used to conduct preliminary hearings or review hearings.

(C) **Mechanics of Use**. The use of two-way interactive video technology must be conducted in accordance with any requirements and guidelines established by the State Court Administrative Office. All proceedings at which such technology is used must be recorded verbatim by the court.

Rule 3.905 Indian Children; Jurisdiction, Notice, Transfer, Intervention

(A) If an Indian child is the subject of a protective proceeding or is charged with a status offense in violation of MCL 712A.2(a)(2)-(4) or (d), and if an Indian tribe has exclusive jurisdiction as defined in MCR 3.002(6), and the matter is not before the state court as a result of emergency removal pursuant to MCL 712B.7(2), the matter shall be dismissed.

(B) If an Indian child is the subject of a protective proceeding or is charged with a status offense in violation of MCL 712A.2(a)(2)-(4) or (d), and if an Indian tribe has exclusive jurisdiction as defined in MCR 3.002(6), and the matter is before the state court as a result of emergency removal pursuant to MCL 712B.7(2), and either the tribe notifies the state court that it is exercising its jurisdiction, or the emergency no longer exists, then the state court shall dismiss the matter.

(C) If an Indian child is the subject of a protective proceeding or is charged with a status offense in violation of MCL 712A.2(a)(2)-(4) or (d) and an Indian tribe does not have exclusive jurisdiction as defined in MCR 3.002(6), the court shall ensure that the petitioner has given notice of the proceedings to the persons described in MCR 3.921 in accordance with MCR 3.920(C).
(1) If either parent or the Indian custodian or the Indian child's tribe petitions the court to transfer the proceeding to the tribal court, the court shall transfer the case to the tribal court unless either parent objects to the transfer of the case to tribal court jurisdiction or the court finds good cause not to transfer. When the court makes a good-cause determination under this section, adequacy of the tribe, tribal court, or tribal social services shall not be considered. A court may determine that good cause not to transfer a case to tribal court exists only if the person opposing the transfer shows by clear and convincing evidence that either of the following applies:
(a) The Indian tribe does not have a tribal court.
(b) The requirement of the parties or witnesses to present evidence in tribal court would cause undue hardship to those parties or witnesses that the Indian tribe is unable to mitigate.
(2) The court shall not dismiss the matter until the transfer has been accepted by the tribal court.
(3) If the tribal court declines transfer, the Michigan Indian Family Preservation Act applies to the continued proceeding in state court, as do the provisions of these rules that pertain to an Indian child. See MCL 712B.3 and MCL 712B.5.
(4) A petition to transfer may be made at any time in accordance with MCL 712B.7(3).

(D) The Indian custodian of the child, the Indian child's tribe and the Indian child have a right to intervene at any point in the proceeding pursuant to MCL 712B.7(6).

Rule 3.911 Jury

(A) **Right**. The right to a jury in a juvenile proceeding exists only at the trial.

(B) **Jury Demand**. A party who is entitled to a trial by jury may demand a jury by filing a written demand with the court within:
(1) 14 days after the court gives notice of the right to jury trial, or
(2) 14 days after an appearance by an attorney or lawyer-guardian ad litem, whichever is later, but no later than 21 days before trial.

The court may excuse a late filing in the interest of justice.

(C) **Jury Procedure**. Jury procedure in juvenile cases is governed by MCR 2.508-2.516, except as provided in this subrule.
(1) In a delinquency proceeding,

(a) each party is entitled to 5 peremptory challenges, and
(b) the verdict must be unanimous.

(2) In a child protective proceeding,
(a) each party is entitled to 5 peremptory challenges, with the child considered a separate party, and
(b) a verdict in a case tried by 6 jurors will be received when 5 jurors agree.

(3) Two or more parties on the same side, other than a child in a child protective proceeding, are considered a single party for the purpose of peremptory challenges.
(a) When two or more parties are aligned on the same side and have adverse interests, the court shall allow each such party represented by a different attorney 3 peremptory challenges.
(b) When multiple parties are allowed more than 5 peremptory challenges under this subrule, the court may allow the opposite side a total number of peremptory challenges not to exceed the number allowed to the multiple parties.

(4) In a designated case, jury procedure is governed by MCR 6.401-6.420.

Rule 3.912 Judge

(A) **Judge Required**. A judge must preside at:
(1) a jury trial;
(2) a waiver proceeding under MCR 3.950;
(3) the preliminary examination, trial, and sentencing in a designated case;
(4) a proceeding on the issuance, modification, or termination of a minor personal protection order.

(B) **Right; Demand**. The parties have the right to a judge at a hearing on the formal calendar. A party may demand that a judge rather than a referee preside at a nonjury trial by filing a written demand with the court within:
(1) 14 days after the court gives notice of the right to a judge, or
(2) 14 days after an appearance by an attorney or lawyer-guardian ad litem, whichever is later, but no later than 21 days before trial.
The court may excuse a late filing in the interest of justice.

(C) **Designated Cases**.
(1) The judge who presides at the preliminary examination may not preside at the trial of the same designated case unless a determination of probable cause is waived. The judge who presides at a preliminary examination may accept a plea in the designated case.
(2) The juvenile has the right to demand that the same judge who accepted the plea or presided at the trial of a designated case preside at sentencing or delayed imposition of sentence, but not at a juvenile disposition of the designated case.

(D) **Disqualification of Judge**. The disqualification of a judge is governed by MCR 2.003.

Rule 3.913 Referees

(A) **Assignment of Matters to Referees**.
(1) *General*. Subject to the limitations in subrule (A)(2), the court may assign a referee to conduct a preliminary inquiry or to preside at a hearing other than those specified in MCR 3.912(A) and to make recommended findings and conclusions.
(2) *Attorney and Nonattorney Referees*.
(a) Delinquency Proceedings. Except as otherwise provided by MCL 712A.10, only a person licensed to practice law in Michigan may serve as a referee at a delinquency proceeding other than a preliminary inquiry or preliminary hearing, if the juvenile is before the court under MCL 712A.2(a)(1).
(b) Child Protective Proceedings. Only a person licensed to practice law in Michigan may serve as a referee at a child protective proceeding other than a preliminary inquiry, preliminary hearing, a progress review under MCR 3.974(A), or an emergency removal hearing under MCR 3.974(B). In addition, either an attorney or a nonattorney referee may issue an ex parte placement order under MCR 3.963(B).
(c) Designated Cases. Only a referee licensed to practice law in Michigan may preside at a hearing to designate a case or to amend a petition to designate a case and to make recommended findings and conclusions.
(d) Minor Personal Protection Actions. A nonattorney referee may preside at a preliminary hearing for enforcement of a minor personal protection order. Only a referee licensed to practice law in Michigan may preside at any other hearing for the enforcement of a minor personal protection order and make recommended findings and conclusions.

(B) **Duration of Assignment**. Unless a party has demanded trial by jury or by a judge pursuant to MCR 3.911 or 3.912, a referee may conduct the trial and further proceedings through disposition.

(C) **Advice of Right to Review of Referee's Recommendations**. During a hearing held by a referee, the referee must inform the parties of the right to file a request for review of the referee's recommended findings and conclusions as provided in MCR 3.991(B).

Rule 3.914 Prosecuting Attorney

(A) **General**. On request of the court, the prosecuting attorney shall review the petition for legal sufficiency and shall appear at any child protective proceeding or any delinquency proceeding.

(B) **Delinquency Proceedings.**

(1) Petition Approval. Only the prosecuting attorney may request the court to take jurisdiction of a juvenile under MCL 712A.2(a)(1).

(2) Appearance. The prosecuting attorney shall participate in every delinquency proceeding under MCL 712A.2(a)(1) that requires a hearing and the taking of testimony.

(C) **Child Protective Proceedings.**

(1) Legal Consultant to Agency. On request of the Michigan Family Independence Agency or of an agent under contract with the agency, the prosecuting attorney shall serve as a legal consultant to the agency or agent at all stages of a child protective proceeding.

(2) Retention of Counsel. In a child protective proceeding, the agency may retain legal representation of its choice when the prosecuting attorney does not appear on behalf of the agency or an agent under contract with the agency.

(D) **Designated Proceedings.**

(1) *Specified Juvenile Violation.* In a case in which the petition alleges a specified juvenile violation, only the prosecuting attorney may designate the case, or request leave to amend a petition to designate the case, for trial of the juvenile in the same manner as an adult.

(2) *Other Offenses.* In a case in which the petition alleges an offense other than the specified juvenile violation, only the prosecuting attorney may request the court to designate the case for trial of the juvenile in the same manner as an adult.

(E) **Minor Personal Protection Orders.** The prosecuting attorney shall prosecute criminal contempt proceedings as provided in MCR 3.987(B).

Rule 3.915 Assistance of Attorney

(A) **Delinquency Proceedings.**

(1) *Advice.* If the juvenile is not represented by an attorney, the court shall advise the juvenile of the right to the assistance of an attorney at each stage of the proceedings on the formal calendar, including trial, plea of admission, and disposition.

(2) *Appointment of an Attorney.* The court shall appoint an attorney to represent the juvenile in a delinquency proceeding if:

(a) the parent, guardian, or legal custodian refuses or fails to appear and participate in the proceedings;

(b) the parent, guardian, or legal custodian is the complainant or victim;

(c) the juvenile and those responsible for the support of the juvenile are found financially unable to retain an attorney, and the juvenile does not waive an attorney;

(d) those responsible for the support of the juvenile refuse or neglect to retain an attorney for the juvenile, and the juvenile does not waive an attorney; or

(e) the court determines that the best interests of the juvenile or the public require appointment.

(3) *Waiver of Attorney.* The juvenile may waive the right to the assistance of an attorney except where a parent, guardian, legal custodian, or guardian ad litem objects or when the appointment is based on subrule (A)(2)(e). The waiver by a juvenile must be made in open court to the judge or referee, who must find and place on the record that the waiver was voluntarily and understandingly made.

(B) **Child Protective Proceedings.**

(1) *Respondent.*

(a) Advice and Right to Counsel. At respondent's first court appearance, the court shall advise the respondent of the right to retain an attorney to represent the respondent at any hearing conducted pursuant to these rules and that

(i) the respondent has the right to a court appointed attorney at any hearing conducted pursuant to these rules, including the preliminary hearing, if the respondent is financially unable to retain an attorney, and,

(ii) if the respondent is not represented by an attorney, the respondent may request a court-appointed attorney at any later hearing.

(b) Appointment of an Attorney. The court shall appoint an attorney to represent the respondent at any hearing, including the preliminary hearing, conducted pursuant to these rules if

(i) the respondent requests appointment of an attorney, and

(ii) it appears to the court, following an examination of the record, through written financial statements, or otherwise, that the respondent is financially unable to retain an attorney.

(c) The respondent may waive the right to the assistance of an attorney, except that the court shall not accept the waiver by a respondent who is a minor when a parent, guardian, legal custodian, or guardian ad litem objects to the waiver.

(2) *Child.*

(a) The court must appoint a lawyer-guardian ad litem to represent the child at every hearing, including the preliminary hearing. The child may not waive the assistance of a lawyer-guardian ad litem. The duties of the lawyer-guardian ad litem are as provided by MCL 712A.17d. At each hearing, the court shall inquire whether the lawyer-guardian ad litem has met or had contact with the child, as required by the court or MCL 712A.17d(1)(d) and if the lawyer-guardian ad litem has not met or had contact with the child, the court shall require the lawyer-guardian ad litem to state, on the record, the reasons for failing to do so.

(b) If a conflict arises between the lawyer-guardian ad litem and the child regarding the child's best interests, the court may appoint an attorney to represent the child's stated interests.

(C) **Appearance**. The appearance of an attorney is governed by MCR 2.117(B).

(D) **Duration**.

(1) An attorney retained by a party may withdraw only on order of the court.

(2) An attorney or lawyer-guardian ad litem appointed by the court to represent a party shall serve until discharged by the court. The court may permit another attorney to temporarily substitute for the child's lawyer-guardian ad litem at a hearing, if that would prevent the hearing from being adjourned, or for other good cause. Such a substitute attorney must be familiar with the case and, for hearings other than a preliminary hearing or emergency removal hearing, must review the agency case file and consult with the foster parents and caseworker before the hearing unless the child's lawyer-guardian ad litem has done so and communicated that information to the substitute attorney. The court shall inquire on the record whether the attorneys have complied with the requirements of this subrule.

(E) **Costs**. When an attorney is appointed for a party under this rule, the court may enter an order assessing costs of the representation against the party or against a person responsible for the support of that party, which order may be enforced as provided by law.

Rule 3.916 Guardian Ad Litem

(A) **General**. The court may appoint a guardian ad litem for a party if the court finds that the welfare of the party requires it.

(B) **Appearance**. The appearance of a guardian ad litem must be in writing and in a manner and form designated by the court. The appearance shall contain a statement regarding the existence of any interest that the guardian ad litem holds in relation to the minor, the minor's family, or any other person in the proceeding before the court or in other matters.

(C) **Access to Information**. The appearance entitles the guardian ad litem to be furnished copies of all petitions, motions, and orders filed or entered, and to consult with the attorney of the party for whom the guardian ad litem has been appointed.

(D) **Costs**. The court may assess the cost of providing a guardian ad litem against the party or a person responsible for the support of the party, and may enforce the order of reimbursement as provided by law.

Rule 3.917 Court Appointed Special Advocate

(A) **General**. The court may, upon entry of an appropriate order, appoint a volunteer special advocate to assess and make recommendations to the court concerning the best interests of the child in any matter pending in the family division.

(B) **Qualifications**. All court appointed special advocates shall receive appropriate screening.

(C) **Duties**. Each court appointed special advocate shall maintain regular contact with the child, investigate the background of the case, gather information regarding the child's status, provide written reports to the court and all parties before each hearing, and appear at all hearings when required by the court.

(D) **Term of Appointment**. A court appointed special advocate shall serve until discharged by the court.

(E) **Access to Information**. Upon appointment by the court, the special advocate may be given access to all information, confidential or otherwise, contained in the court file if the court so orders. The special advocate shall consult with the child's lawyer-guardian ad litem.

Rule 3.920 Service of Process

(A) **General**.

(1) Unless a party must be summoned as provided in subrule (B), a party shall be given notice of a juvenile proceeding in any manner authorized by the rules in this subchapter.

(2) MCR 2.004 applies in juvenile proceedings involving incarcerated parties.

(B) **Summons**.

(1) *In General*. A summons may be issued and served on a party before any juvenile proceeding.

(2) *When Required*. Except as otherwise provided in these rules, the court shall direct the service of a summons in the following circumstances:

(a) In a delinquency proceeding, a summons must be served on the parent or parents, guardian, or legal custodian having physical custody of the juvenile, directing them to appear with the juvenile for trial. The juvenile must also be served with a summons to appear for trial. A parent without physical custody must be notified by service as provided in subrule (D), unless the whereabouts of the parent remain unknown after a diligent inquiry.

(b) In a child protective proceeding, a summons must be served on the respondent. A summons may be served on a person having physical custody of the child directing such person to appear with the child for hearing. A parent, guardian, or legal custodian who is not a respondent must be served with notice of hearing in the manner provided by subrule (D).

(c) In a personal protection order enforcement proceeding involving a minor respondent, a summons must be served on the minor. A summons must also be served on the parent or parents, guardian, or legal custodian, unless their whereabouts remain unknown after a diligent inquiry.

(3) *Content*. The summons must direct the person to whom it is addressed to appear at a time and place specified by the court and must:

(a) identify the nature of hearing;

(b) explain the right to an attorney and the right to trial by judge or jury, including, where appropriate, that there is no right to a jury at a termination hearing;

(c) if the summons is for a child protective proceeding, include a prominent notice that the hearings could result in termination of parental rights; and

(d) have a copy of the petition attached.

(4) *Manner of Serving Summons*.

(a) Except as provided in subrule (B)(4)(b), a summons required under subrule (B)(2) must be served by delivering the summons to the party personally.

(b) If the court finds, on the basis of testimony or a motion and affidavit, that personal service of the summons is impracticable or cannot be achieved, the court may by ex parte order direct that it be served in any manner reasonably calculated to give notice of the proceedings and an opportunity to be heard, including publication.

(c) If personal service of a summons is not required, the court may direct that it be served in a manner reasonably calculated to provide notice.

(5) *Time of Service*.

(a) A summons shall be personally served at least:

(i) 14 days before hearing on a petition that seeks to terminate parental rights or a permanency planning hearing,

(ii) 7 days before trial or a child protective dispositional review hearing, or

(iii) 3 days before any other hearing.

(b) If the summons is served by registered mail, it must be sent at least 7 days earlier than subrule (a) requires for personal service of a summons if the party to be served resides in Michigan, or 14 days earlier than required by subrule (a) if the party to be served resides outside Michigan.

(c) If service is by publication, the published notice must appear in a newspaper in the county where the party resides, if known, and, if not, in the county where the action is pending. The published notice need not include the petition itself. The notice must be published at least once 21 days before a hearing specified in subrule (a)(i), 14 days before trial or a hearing specified in subrule (a)(ii), or 7 days before any other hearing.

(C) **Notice of Proceeding Concerning Indian Child**. If the court knows or has reason to know an Indian child is the subject of a protective proceeding or is charged with a status offense in violation of MCL 712A.2(a)(2)-(4) or (d) and an Indian tribe does not have exclusive jurisdiction as defined in MCR 3.002(6):

(1) in addition to any other service requirements, the petitioner shall notify the parent or Indian custodian and the Indian child's tribe by registered mail with return receipt requested of the pending proceedings on a petition filed under MCR 3.931 or MCR 3.961 and of their right of intervention on a form approved by the State Court Administrative Office. If the identity or location of the parent or Indian custodian, or of the tribe, cannot be determined, notice shall be given to the Secretary of the Interior by registered mail with return receipt requested. Subsequent notices shall be served in accordance with this subrule for proceedings under MCR 3.967 and MCR 3.977.

(2) the court shall notify the parent or Indian custodian and the Indian child's tribe of all hearings other than those specified in subrule (1) as provided in subrule (D). If the identity or location of the parent or Indian custodian or the tribe cannot be determined, notice of the hearings shall be given to the Secretary of the Interior. Such notice may be by first-class mail.

(D) **Notice of Hearing**.

(1) *General*. Notice of a hearing must be given in writing or on the record at least 7 days before the hearing except as provided in subrules (D)(2) and (D)(3), or as otherwise provided in the rules.

(2) *Preliminary Hearing; Emergency Removal Hearing*.

(a) When a juvenile is detained, notice of the preliminary hearing must be given to the juvenile and to the parent of the juvenile as soon as the hearing is scheduled. The notice may be in person, in writing, on the record, or by telephone.

(b) When a child is placed outside the home, notice of the preliminary hearing or an emergency removal hearing under MCR

3.974(B)(3) must be given to the parent of the child as soon as the hearing is scheduled. The notice may be in person, in writing, on the record, or by telephone.

(3) *Permanency Planning Hearing; Termination Proceedings*.
   (a) Notice of a permanency planning hearing must be given in writing at least 14 days before the hearing.
   (b) Notice of a hearing on a petition requesting termination of parental rights in a child protective proceeding must be given in writing at least 14 days before the hearing.

(4) *Failure to Appear*. When a party fails to appear in response to a notice of hearing, the court may order the party's appearance by summons or subpoena.

(E) **Subpoenas**.
   (1) The attorney for a party or the court on its own motion may cause a subpoena to be served upon a person whose testimony or appearance is desired.
   (2) It is not necessary to tender advance fees to the person served a subpoena in order to compel attendance.
   (3) Except as otherwise stated in this subrule, service of a subpoena is governed by MCR 2.506.

(F) **Waiver of Notice and Service**. A person may waive notice of hearing or service of process. The waiver shall be in writing. When a party waives service of a summons required by subrule (B), the party must be provided the advice required by subrule (B)(3).

(G) **Subsequent Notices**. After a party's first appearance before the court, subsequent notice of proceedings and pleadings shall be served on that party or, if the party has an attorney, on the attorney for the party as provided in subrule (D), except that a summons must be served for trial or termination hearing as provided in subrule (B).

(H) **Notice Defects**. The appearance and participation of a party at a hearing is a waiver by that party of defects in service with respect to that hearing unless objections regarding the specific defect are placed on the record. If a party appears or participates without an attorney, the court shall advise the party that the appearance and participation waives notice defects and of the party's right to seek an attorney.

(I) **Proof of Service**.
   (1) *Summons*. Proof of service of a summons must be made in the manner provided in MCR 2.104(A).
   (2) *Other Papers*. Proof of service of other papers permitted or required to be served under these rules must be made in the manner provided in MCR 2.107(D).
   (3) *Publication*. If the manner of service used involves publication, proof of service must be made in the manner provided in MCR 2.106(G)(1), and (G)(3) if the publication is accompanied by a mailing.
   (4) *Content*. The proof of service must identify the papers served. A proof of service for papers served on a foster parent, preadoptive parent, or relative caregiver shall be maintained in the confidential social file as identified in MCR 3.903(A)(3)(b)(vii).
   (5) *Failure to File*. Failure to file proof of service does not affect the validity of the service.

Rule 3.921 Persons Entitled to Notice

(A) **Delinquency Proceedings**.
   (1) *General*. In a delinquency proceeding, the court shall direct that the following persons be notified of each hearing except as provided in subrule (A)(3):
      (a) the juvenile,
      (b) the custodial parents, guardian, or legal custodian of the juvenile,
      (c) the noncustodial parent who has requested notice at a hearing or in writing,
      (d) the guardian ad litem or lawyer-guardian ad litem of a juvenile appointed pursuant to these rules,
      (e) the attorney retained or appointed to represent the juvenile, and
      (f) the prosecuting attorney.
      (g) in accordance with the notice provisions of MCR 3.905, if the juvenile is charged with a status offense in violation of MCL 712A.2(a)(2)-(4) or (d) and if the court knows or has reason to know the juvenile is an Indian child:
         (i) the juvenile's tribe and, if the tribe is unknown, the Secretary of the Interior, and
         (ii) the juvenile's parents or Indian custodian, and if unknown, the Secretary of the Interior.
   (2) *Notice to the Petitioner*. The petitioner must be notified of the first hearing on the petition.
   (3) *Parent Without Physical Custody*. A parent of the minor whose parental rights over the minor have not been terminated at the time the minor comes to court, must be notified of the first hearing on the formal calendar, unless the whereabouts of the parent are unknown.

(B) **Protective Proceedings**.
   (1) *General*. In a child protective proceeding, except as provided in subrules (B)(2) and (3), the court shall ensure that the following persons are notified of each hearing:
      (a) the respondent,
      (b) the attorney for the respondent,
      (c) the lawyer-guardian ad litem for the child,
      (d) subject to subrule (D), the parents, guardian, or legal custodian, if any, other than the respondent,
      (e) the petitioner,

(f) a party's guardian ad litem appointed pursuant to these rules, and
(g) the foster parents, preadoptive parents, and relative caregivers of a child in foster care under the responsibility of the state, and
(h) in accordance with the notice provisions of MCR 3.905, if the court knows or has reason to know the child is an Indian child:
(i) the child's tribe and, if the tribe is unknown, the Secretary of the Interior, and
(ii) the child's parents or Indian custodian, and if unknown, the Secretary of the Interior, and
(i) any other person the court may direct to be notified.

(2) *Dispositional Review Hearings and Permanency Planning Hearings*. Before a dispositional review hearing or a permanency planning hearing, the court shall ensure that the following persons are notified in writing of each hearing:
(a) the agency responsible for the care and supervision of the child,
(b) the person or institution having court-ordered custody of the child,
(c) the parents of the child, subject to subrule (D), and the attorney for the respondent parent, unless parental rights have been terminated,
(d) the guardian or legal custodian of the child, if any,
(e) the guardian ad litem for the child,
(f) the lawyer-guardian ad litem for the child,
(g) the attorneys for each party,
(h) the prosecuting attorney if the prosecuting attorney has appeared in the case,
(i) the child, if 11 years old or older,
(j) if the court knows or has reason to know the child is an Indian child, the child's tribe,
(k) the foster parents, preadoptive parents, and relative caregivers of a child in foster care under the responsibility of the state, and
(l) if the court knows or has reason to know the child is an Indian child and the parents, guardian, legal custodian, or tribe are unknown, to the Secretary of Interior, and
(m) any other person the court may direct to be notified.

(3) *Termination of Parental Rights*. Written notice of a hearing to determine if the parental rights to a child shall be terminated must be given to those appropriate persons or entities listed in subrule (B)(2), except that if the court knows or has reason to know the child is an Indian child, notice shall be given in accordance with MCR 3.920(C)(1).

(C) **Juvenile Guardianships**. In a juvenile guardianship, the following persons shall be entitled to notice:
(1) the child, if 11 years old or older;
(2) the Department of Human Services;
(3) the parents of the child, unless parental rights over the child have been terminated;
(4) the juvenile guardian or proposed juvenile guardian;
(5) any court that previously had jurisdiction over the child in a child protective proceeding, if different than the court that entered an order authorizing a juvenile guardianship;
(6) the attorneys for any party;
(7) the prosecuting attorney, if the prosecuting attorney has appeared in the case;
(8) if the court knows or has reason to know the child is an Indian child, the child's tribe, Indian custodian, or if the tribe is unknown, the Secretary of the Interior;
(9) the Michigan Children's Institute superintendent;
(10) any other person the court may direct to be notified.

(D) **Putative Fathers**. If, at any time during the pendency of a proceeding, the court determines that the minor has no father as defined in MCR 3.903(A)(7), the court may, in its discretion, take appropriate action as described in this subrule.
(1) The court may take initial testimony on the tentative identity and address of the natural father. If the court finds probable cause to believe that an identifiable person is the natural father of the minor, the court shall direct that notice be served on that person in any manner reasonably calculated to provide notice to the putative father, including publication if his whereabouts remain unknown after diligent inquiry. Any notice by publication must not include the name of the putative father. If the court finds that the identity of the natural father is unknown, the court must direct that the unknown father be given notice by publication. The notice must include the following information:
(a) if known, the name of the child, the name of the child's mother, and the date and place of birth of the child;
(b) that a petition has been filed with the court;
(c) the time and place of hearing at which the natural father is to appear to express his interest, if any, in the minor; and
(d) a statement that failure to attend the hearing will constitute a denial of interest in the minor, a waiver of notice for all subsequent hearings, a waiver of a right to appointment of an attorney, and could result in termination of any parental rights.
(2) After notice to the putative father as provided in subrule (D)(1), the court may conduct a hearing and determine, as appropriate, that:
(a) the putative father has been served in a manner that the court finds to be reasonably calculated to provide notice to the putative father.

(b) a preponderance of the evidence establishes that the putative father is the natural father of the minor and justice requires that he be allowed 14 days to establish his relationship according to MCR 3.903(A)(7). The court may extend the time for good cause shown.

(c) there is probable cause to believe that another identifiable person is the natural father of the minor. If so, the court shall proceed with respect to the other person in accord with subrule (D).

(d) after diligent inquiry, the identity of the natural father cannot be determined. If so, the court may proceed without further notice and without appointing an attorney for the unidentified person.

(3) The court may find that the natural father waives all rights to further notice, including the right to notice of termination of parental rights, and the right to an attorney if

(a) he fails to appear after proper notice, or

(b) he appears, but fails to establish paternity within the time set by the court.

(E) **Failure to Appear; Notice by Publication**. When persons whose whereabouts are unknown fail to appear in response to notice by publication or otherwise, the court need not give further notice by publication of subsequent hearings, except a hearing on the termination of parental rights.

Rule 3.922 Pretrial Procedures in Delinquency and Child Protection Proceedings

(A) **Discovery**.

(1) The following materials are discoverable as of right in all proceedings provided they are requested no later than 21 days before trial unless the interests of justice otherwise dictate:

(a) all written or recorded statements and notes of statements made by the juvenile or respondent that are in possession or control of petitioner or a law enforcement agency, including oral statements if they have been reduced to writing;

(b) all written or recorded nonconfidential statements made by any person with knowledge of the events in possession or control of petitioner or a law enforcement agency, including police reports;

(c) the names of prospective witnesses;

(d) a list of all prospective exhibits;

(e) a list of all physical or tangible objects that are prospective evidence that are in the possession or control of petitioner or a law enforcement agency;

(f) the results of all scientific, medical, or other expert tests or experiments, including the reports or findings of all experts, that are relevant to the subject matter of the petition;

(g) the results of any lineups or showups, including written reports or lineup sheets; and

(h) all search warrants issued in connection with the matter, including applications for such warrants, affidavits, and returns or inventories.

(2) On motion of a party, the court may permit discovery of any other materials and evidence, including untimely requested materials and evidence that would have been discoverable of right under subrule (A)(1) if timely requested. Absent manifest injustice, no motion for discovery will be granted unless the moving party has requested and has not been provided the materials or evidence sought through an order of discovery.

(3) Depositions may only be taken as authorized by the court.

(4) Failure to comply with subrules (1) and (2) may result in such sanctions, as applicable, as set forth in MCR 2.313.

(B) **Notice of Defenses; Rebuttal**.

(1) Within 21 days after the juvenile has been given notice of the date of trial, but no later than 7 days before the trial date, the juvenile or the juvenile's attorney must file a written notice with the court and prosecuting attorney of the intent to rely on a defense of alibi or insanity. The notice shall include a list of the names and addresses of defense witnesses.

(2) Within 7 days after receipt of notice, but no later than 2 days before the trial date, the prosecutor shall provide written notice to the court and defense of an intent to offer rebuttal to the above-listed defenses. The notice shall include names and addresses of rebuttal witnesses.

(3) Failure to comply with subrules (1) and (2) may result in the sanctions set forth in MCL 768.21.

(C) **Motion Practice**. Motion practice in juvenile proceedings is governed by MCR 2.119.

(D) **Pretrial Conference**. The court may direct the parties to appear at a pretrial conference. The scope and effect of a pretrial conference are governed by MCR 2.401, except as otherwise provided in or inconsistent with the rules of this subchapter.

(E) **Notice of Intent**.

(1) Within 21 days after the parties have been given notice of the date of trial, but no later than 7 days before the trial date, the proponent must file with the court, and serve all parties, written notice of the intent to:

(a) use a support person, including the identity of the support person, the relationship to the witness, and the anticipated location of the support person during the hearing.

(b) request special arrangements for a closed courtroom or for restricting the view of the respondent/defendant from the witness or other special arrangements allowed under law and ordered by the court.
(c) use a videotaped deposition as permitted by law.
(d) admit out-of-court hearsay statements under MCR 3.972(C)(2), including the identity of the persons to whom a statement was made, the circumstances leading to the statement, and the statement to be admitted.

(2) Within 7 days after receipt or notice, but no later than 2 days before the trial date, the nonproponent parties must provide written notice to the court of an intent to offer rebuttal testimony or evidence in opposition to the request and must include the identity of the witnesses to be called.
(3) The court may shorten the time periods provided in subrule if good cause is shown.

Rule 3.923 Miscellaneous Procedures

(A) **Additional Evidence**. If at any time the court believes that the evidence has not been fully developed, it may:
(1) examine a witness,
(2) call a witness, or
(3) adjourn the matter before the court, and
(a) cause service of process on additional witnesses, or
(b) order production of other evidence.

(B) **Examination or Evaluation**. The court may order that a minor or a parent, guardian, or legal custodian be examined or evaluated by a physician, dentist, psychologist, or psychiatrist.

(C) **Fingerprinting and Photographing**. A juvenile must be fingerprinted when required by law. The court may permit fingerprinting or photographing, or both, of a minor concerning whom a petition has been filed. Fingerprints and photographs must be placed in the confidential files, capable of being located and destroyed on court order.

(D) **Lineup**. If a complaint or petition is filed against a juvenile alleging violation of a criminal law or ordinance, the court may, at the request of the prosecuting attorney, order the juvenile to appear at a place and time designated by the court for identification by another person, including a corporeal lineup pursuant to MCL 712A.32. If the court orders the juvenile to appear for such an identification procedure, the court must notify the juvenile and the juvenile's parent, guardian or legal custodian that the juvenile has the right to consult with an attorney and have an attorney present during the identification procedure and that if the juvenile and the juvenile's parent, guardian or legal custodian cannot afford an attorney, the court will appoint an attorney for the juvenile if requested on the record or in writing by the juvenile or the juvenile's parent, guardian or legal custodian.

(E) **Electronic Equipment; Support Person**. The court may allow the use of closed-circuit television, speaker telephone, or other similar electronic equipment to facilitate hearings or to protect the parties. The court may allow the use of videotaped statements and depositions, anatomical dolls, or support persons, and may take other measures to protect the child witness as authorized by MCL 712A.17b.

(F) **Impartial Questioner**. The court may appoint an impartial person to address questions to a child witness at a hearing as the court directs.

(G) **Adjournments**. Adjournments of trials or hearings in child protective proceedings should be granted only
(1) for good cause,
(2) after taking into consideration the best interests of the child, and
(3) for as short a period of time as necessary.

Rule 3.924 Information Furnished on Request by Court

Persons or agencies providing testimony, reports, or other information at the request of the court, including otherwise confidential information, records, or reports that are relevant and material to the proceedings following authorization of a petition, are immune from any subsequent legal action with respect to furnishing the information to the court.

Rule 3.925 Open Proceedings; Judgments and Orders; Records Confidentiality; Destruction of Court Files; Setting Aside Adjudications

(A) **Open Proceedings**.
(1) *General*. Except as provided in subrule (A)(2), juvenile proceedings on the formal calendar and preliminary hearings shall be open to the public.
(2) *Closed Proceedings; Criteria*. The court, on motion of a party or a victim, may close the proceedings to the public during the testimony of a child or during the testimony of the victim to protect the welfare of either. In making such a determination, the court shall consider the nature of the proceedings; the age, maturity, and preference of the witness; and, if the witness is a child, the preference of a parent, guardian, or legal custodian that the proceedings be open or closed. The court may not close the proceedings to the public during the testimony of the juvenile if jurisdiction is requested under MCL 712A.2(a)(1).

(B) **Record of Proceedings**. A record of all hearings must be made. All proceedings on the formal calendar must be recorded by stenographic recording or by mechanical or electronic recording as provided by statute or MCR 8.108. A plea of admission or no contest, including any agreement with or objection to the plea, must be recorded.

(C) **Judgments and Orders**. The form and signing of judgments are governed by MCR 2.602(A)(1) and (2). Judgments and orders may be served on a person by first-class mail to the person's last known address.

(D) **Public Access to Records; Confidential File**.

(1) *General*. Records of the juvenile cases, other than confidential files, must be open to the general public.

(2) *Confidential Files*. Only persons who are found by the court to have a legitimate interest may be allowed access to the confidential files. In determining whether a person has a legitimate interest, the court shall consider the nature of the proceedings, the welfare and safety of the public, the interest of the minor, and any restriction imposed by state or federal law.

(E) **Retention and Destruction of Court Case Files and Other Court Records**. This subrule governs the retention and destruction of court case files and other court records, as defined by MCR 8.119(D).

(1) *Destruction Generally; Effect*. The court may destroy its case files and other court records only as prescribed by this rule and the approved General Records Retention and Disposal Schedule #16 – Michigan Trial Courts. Destruction of a file does not negate, rescind, or set aside an adjudication.

(2) *Register of Actions, Indexes, and Orders*. The register of actions and numerical and alphabetical indexes must be maintained permanently. In addition, the court must permanently maintain the order of adjudication, the order terminating parental rights, and the order terminating jurisdiction for each child protective case; the order of adjudication and the order terminating jurisdiction for each delinquency case; the latest dispositive order for each designated case; and the order appointing a guardian for each juvenile guardianship case.

(3) *Delinquency and Motor Vehicle Code Case Files*.

(a) Except as provided in subrule (2), the court may destroy the diversion case file of a juvenile after the juvenile becomes 17 years of age.

(b) Except as provided in subrule (2), the court may destroy all case files of matters heard on the consent calendar after the juvenile becomes 17 years of age or after dismissal from court supervision, whichever is later, unless the juvenile subsequently comes within the jurisdiction of the court on the formal calendar. If the case is transferred to the consent calendar and a register of actions exists, the register of actions must be maintained permanently as a nonpublic record.

(c) Except as provided by subrules (2), (3)(a), and (3)(b), the court may destroy the legal records in the case files pertaining to a person's juvenile offenses when the person becomes 30 years of age. The social records in the case files pertaining to a person's juvenile offenses may be destroyed three years after entry of the order terminating jurisdiction of that person or when the person becomes 18 years old, whichever is later. The social records are the confidential files defined in MCR 3.903(A)(3). The court must destroy the records in traffic and local ordinance case files opened by issuance of a citation pursuant to the motor vehicle code or a local corresponding ordinance when the person becomes 30 years of age.

(d) If the court destroys its case files regarding a juvenile proceeding on the formal calendar, it shall retain the register of actions, and, if the information is not included in the register of actions, whether the juvenile was represented by an attorney or waived representation.

(4) *Child Protective Case Files*. Except as provided in subrule (2), the court may destroy the legal records in the child protective proceeding case files pertaining to a child, 25 years after the jurisdiction over the child ends, except that where records on more than one child in a family are retained in the same file, destruction is not allowed until 25 years after jurisdiction over the last child ends. The social records in the child protective proceeding case files pertaining to a child may be destroyed three years after entry of the order terminating jurisdiction of that child or when the child becomes 18 years of age, whichever is later. The social records are the confidential files defined in MCR 3.903(A)(3).

(5) *Personal Protection Proceeding Case Files*. The court may destroy the legal and social records in personal protection proceeding case files pertaining to a juvenile respondent three years after the expiration date of the personal protection order or the latest dispositive order on a violation of the personal protection order, or when the juvenile respondent becomes 18 years of age, whichever is later.

(6) *Juvenile Guardianship Case Files*. Except as provided in subrule (2), the court may destroy the records in juvenile guardianship case files 25 years after the order appointing a juvenile guardian.

(7) *Probation Case Files*. The court may destroy the records in probation case files pertaining to a juvenile three years after an order terminating jurisdiction or when the juvenile becomes 18 years of age, whichever is later.

(F) **Setting Aside Adjudications and Convictions.**
 (1) *Adjudications*. The setting aside of juvenile adjudications is governed by MCL 712A.18e.
 (2) *Convictions*. The court may only set aside a conviction as provided by MCL 780.621 et seq.

(G) **Access to Juvenile Offense Record of Convicted Adults.** When the juvenile offense record of an adult convicted of a crime is made available to the appropriate agency, as provided in MCL 791.228(1), the record must state whether, with regard to each adjudication, the juvenile had an attorney or voluntarily waived an attorney.

Rule 3.926 Transfer of Jurisdiction; Change of Venue

(A) **Definition.** As used in MCL 712A.2, a child is "found within the county" in which the offense against the child occurred, in which the offense committed by the juvenile occurred, or in which the minor is physically present.

(B) **Transfer to County of Residence.** When a minor is brought before the family division of the circuit court in a county other than that in which the minor resides, the court may transfer the case to the court in the county of residence before trial.
 (1) If both parents reside in the same county, or if the child resides in the county with a parent who has been awarded legal custody, a guardian, a legal custodian, or the child's sole legal parent, that county will be presumed to be the county of residence.
 (2) In circumstances other than those enumerated in subsection (1) of this section, the court shall consider the following factors in determining the child's county of residence:
  (a) The county of residence of the parent or parents, guardian, or legal custodian.
  (b) Whether the child has ever lived in the county, and, if so, for how long.
  (c) Whether either parent has moved to another county since the inception of the case.
  (d) Whether the child is subject to the prior continuing jurisdiction of another court.
  (e) Whether a court has entered an order placing the child in the county for the purpose of adoption.
  (f) Whether the child has expressed an intention to reside in the county.
  (g) Any other factor the court considers relevant.
 (3) If the child has been placed in a county by court order or by placement by a public or private agency, the child shall not be considered a resident of the county in which he or she has been placed, unless the child has been placed for the purpose of adoption.

(C) **Costs.** When a court other than the court in a county in which the minor resides orders disposition, it will be responsible for any costs incurred in connection with such order unless
 (1) the court in the county in which the minor resides agrees to pay the costs of such disposition, or
 (2) the minor is made a state ward pursuant to the Youth Rehabilitation Services Act, MCL 803.301 et seq., and the county of residence withholds consent to a transfer of the case.

(D) **Change of Venue; Grounds.** The court, on motion by a party, may order a case to be heard before a court in another county:
 (1) for the convenience of the parties and witnesses, provided that a judge of the other court agrees to hear the case; or
 (2) when an impartial trial cannot be had where the case is pending.
 All costs of the proceeding in another county are to be borne by the court ordering the change of venue.

(E) **Bifurcated Proceeding.** If the judge of the transferring court and the judge of the receiving court agree, the case may be bifurcated to permit adjudication in the transferring court and disposition in the receiving court. The case may be returned to the receiving court immediately after the transferring court enters its order of adjudication.

(F) **Transfer of Records.** The court entering an order of transfer or change of venue shall send the original pleadings and documents, or certified copies of the pleadings and documents, to the receiving court without charge. Where the courts have agreed to bifurcate the proceedings, the court adjudicating the case shall send any supplemented pleadings and records or certified copies of the supplemented pleadings and records to the court entering the disposition in the case.

(G) **Designated Cases.** Designated cases are to be filed in the county in which the offense is alleged to have occurred. Other than a change of venue for the purpose of trial, a designated case may not be transferred to any other county, except, after conviction, a designated case may be transferred to the juvenile's county of residence for entry of a juvenile disposition only. Sentencing of a juvenile, including delayed imposition of sentence, may only be done in the county in which the offense occurred.

Rule 3.927 Prior Court Orders

In a juvenile proceeding involving a minor who is subject to a prior order of another Michigan court, the manner of notice to the other court and the authority of the family division of the circuit court to proceed are governed by MCR 3.205.

Rule 3.928 Contempt of Court

(A) **Power**. The court has the authority to hold persons in contempt of court as provided by MCL 600.1701 and 712A.26. A parent, guardian, or legal custodian of a juvenile who is within the court's jurisdiction and who fails to attend a hearing as required is subject to the contempt power as provided in MCL 712A.6a.

(B) **Procedure**. Contempt of court proceedings are governed by MCL 600.1711, 600.1715, and MCR 3.606. MCR 3.982-3.989 govern proceedings against a minor for contempt of a minor personal protection order.

(C) **Contempt by Juvenile**. A juvenile under court jurisdiction who is convicted of criminal contempt of court, and who was at least 17 years of age when the contempt was committed, may be sentenced to up to 93 days in the county jail as a disposition for the contempt. Juveniles sentenced under this subrule need not be lodged separately and apart from adult prisoners. Younger juveniles found in contempt of court are subject to a juvenile disposition under these rules.

Rule 3.929 Use of Facsimile Communication Equipment

The parties may file records, as defined in MCR 3.903(A)(25), by the use of facsimile communication equipment. Filing of records by the use of facsimile communication equipment in juvenile proceedings is governed by MCR 2.406.

Rule 3.930 Receipt and Return or Disposal of Exhibits in Juvenile Proceedings

(A) **Receipt of Exhibits**. Except as otherwise required by statute or court rule, materials that are intended to be used as evidence at or during a trial shall not be filed with the clerk of the court, but shall be submitted to the judge for introduction into evidence as exhibits. Exhibits introduced into evidence at or during court proceedings shall be received and maintained as provided by the Michigan Supreme Court trial court case file management standards. As defined in MCR 1.109, exhibits received and accepted into evidence under this rule are not court records.

(B) **Return or Disposal of Exhibits.** At the conclusion of a trial or hearing, the court shall direct the parties to retrieve the exhibits submitted by them except that any weapons and drugs shall be returned to the confiscating agency for proper disposition. If the exhibits are not retrieved by the parties as directed within 56 days after conclusion of the trial or hearing, the court may properly dispose of the exhibits without notice to the parties.

(C) **Confidentiality**. If the court retains discovery materials filed pursuant to MCR 1.109(C) or an exhibit submitted pursuant to this rule after a hearing or trial and the material is confidential as provided by MCR 3.903(A)(3) or order of the court pursuant to MCR 8.119(I), the court must continue to maintain the material in a confidential manner.

Rule 3.931 Initiating Delinquency Proceedings

(A) **Commencement of Proceeding**. Any request for court action against a juvenile must be by written petition.

(B) **Content of Petition**. A petition must contain the following information:

- (1) the juvenile's name, address, and date of birth, if known;
- (2) the names and addresses, if known, of
  - (a) the juvenile's mother and father,
  - (b) the guardian, legal custodian, or person having custody of the juvenile, if other than a mother or father,
  - (c) the nearest known relative of the juvenile, if no parent, guardian, or legal custodian can be found, and
  - (d) the juvenile's membership or eligibility for membership in an Indian tribe, if any, and the identity of the tribe, and
  - (e) any court with prior continuing jurisdiction;
- (3) sufficient allegations that, if true, would constitute an offense by the juvenile;
- (4) a citation to the section of the Juvenile Code relied upon for jurisdiction;
- (5) a citation to the federal, state, or local law or ordinance allegedly violated by the juvenile;
- (6) the court action requested;
- (7) if applicable, the notice required by MCL 257.732(8), and the juvenile's Michigan driver's license number; and
- (8) information required by MCR 3.206(A)(4), identifying whether a family division matter involving members of the same family is or was pending.

(C) **Citation or Appearance Ticket**.

- (1) A citation or appearance ticket may be used to initiate a delinquency proceeding if the charges against the juvenile are limited to:
  - (a) violations of the Michigan Vehicle Code, or of a provision of an ordinance substantially corresponding to any provision of that law, as provided by MCL 712A.2b.
  - (b) offenses that, if committed by an adult, would be appropriate for use of an appearance ticket under MCL 764.9c.
- (2) The citation or appearance ticket shall be treated by the court as if it were a petition, except that it may not serve as a basis for pretrial detention.

(D) **Motor Vehicle Violations; Failure to Appear**. If the juvenile is a Michigan resident and fails to appear or otherwise to respond to any matter pending relative to a motor vehicle violation, the court

(1) must initiate the procedure required by MCL 257.321a for the failure to answer a citation, and

(2) may issue an order to apprehend the juvenile after a petition is filed with the court.

Rule 3.932 Summary Initial Proceedings

(A) **Preliminary Inquiry**. When a petition is not accompanied by a request for detention of the juvenile, the court may conduct a preliminary inquiry. Except in cases involving offenses enumerated in the Crime Victim's Rights Act, MCL 780.781(1)(g), the preliminary inquiry need not be conducted on the record. The court may, in the interest of the juvenile and the public:

(1) deny authorization of the petition;

(2) refer the matter to a public or private agency providing available services pursuant to the Juvenile Diversion Act, MCL 722.821 et seq.;

(3) direct that the juvenile and the parent, guardian, or legal custodian be notified to appear for further informal inquiry on the petition;

(4) proceed on the consent calendar as provided in subrule (C); or

(5) place the matter on the formal calendar as provided in subrule (D).

(B) **Offenses Listed in the Crime Victim's Rights Act**. A case involving the alleged commission of an offense listed in the Crime Victim's Rights Act, MCL 780.781(1)(f), may only be removed from the adjudicative process upon compliance with the procedures set forth in that act. See MCL 780.786b.

(C) **Consent Calendar**. If the court receives a petition, citation, or appearance ticket, and it appears that protective and supportive action by the court will serve the best interests of the juvenile and the public, the court may proceed on the consent calendar without authorizing a petition to be filed. No case may be placed on the consent calendar unless the juvenile and the parent, guardian, or legal custodian and the prosecutor, agree to have the case placed on the consent calendar. A court may not consider a case on the consent calendar that includes an offense listed as an assaultive crime by the Juvenile Diversion Act, MCL 722.822(a). The court may transfer a case from the formal calendar to the consent calendar at any time before disposition.

(1) *Notice*. Formal notice is not required for cases placed on the consent calendar except as required by article 2 of the Crime Victim's Rights Act, MCL 780.781 et seq.

(2) *Plea; Adjudication*. No formal plea may be entered in a consent calendar case unless the case is based on an alleged violation of the Michigan Vehicle Code, MCL 257.1 et seq. in which case the court shall enter a plea. The court must not enter an adjudication.

(3) *Conference*. The court shall conduct a consent calendar conference with the juvenile and the parent, guardian, or legal custodian to discuss the allegations. The victim may, but need not, be present.

(4) *Case Plan*. If it appears to the court that the juvenile has engaged in conduct that would subject the juvenile to the jurisdiction of the court, the court may issue a written consent calendar case plan.

(5) *Custody*. A consent calendar case plan must not contain a provision removing the juvenile from the custody of the parent, guardian, or legal custodian.

(6) *Disposition*. No order of disposition may be entered by the court in a case placed on the consent calendar.

(7) *Closure*. Upon successful completion by the juvenile of the consent calendar case plan, the court shall close the case and may destroy all records of the proceeding.

(8) *Transfer to Formal Calendar*. If it appears to the court at any time that the proceeding on the consent calendar is not in the best interest of either the juvenile or the public, the court may, without hearing, transfer the case from the consent calendar to the formal calendar on the charges contained in the original petition, citation, or appearance ticket. Statements made by the juvenile during the proceeding on the consent calendar may not be used against the juvenile at a trial on the formal calendar on the same charge.

(9) *Abstracting*. If the court finds that the juvenile has violated the Michigan Vehicle Code, the court must fulfill the reporting requirements imposed by MCL 712A.2b(d).

(D) **Formal Calendar**. The court may authorize a petition to be filed and docketed on the formal calendar if it appears to the court that formal court action is in the best interest of the juvenile and the public. The court shall not authorize an original petition under MCL 712A.2(a)(1), unless the prosecuting attorney has approved submitting the petition to the court. At any time before disposition, the court may transfer the matter to the consent calendar.

Rule 3.933 Acquiring Physical Control of Juvenile

(A) **Custody Without Court Order**. When an officer apprehends a juvenile for an offense without a court order and does not warn and release the juvenile, does not refer the juvenile to a diversion program, and does not have authorization from the prosecuting attorney to file a complaint and warrant charging the juvenile with an offense as though an adult pursuant to MCL 764.1f, the officer may:

(1) issue a citation or ticket to appear at a date and time to be set by the court and release the juvenile;
(2) accept a written promise of the parent, guardian, or legal custodian to bring the juvenile to court, if requested, at a date and time to be set by the court, and release the juvenile to the parent, guardian, or legal custodian; or
(3) take the juvenile into custody and submit a petition, if:
(a) the officer has reason to believe that because of the nature of the offense, the interest of the juvenile or the interest of the public would not be protected by release of the juvenile, or
(b) a parent, guardian, or legal custodian cannot be located or has refused to take custody of the juvenile.

(B) **Custody With Court Order**. When a petition is presented to the court, and probable cause exists to believe that a juvenile has committed an offense, the court may issue an order to apprehend the juvenile. The order may include authorization to
(1) enter specified premises as required to bring the juvenile before the court, and
(2) detain the juvenile pending preliminary hearing.

(C) **Notification of Court**. The officer who apprehends a juvenile must immediately contact the court when:
(1) the officer detains the juvenile,
(2) the officer is unable to reach a parent, guardian, or legal custodian who will appear promptly to accept custody of the juvenile, or
(3) the parent, guardian, or legal custodian will not agree to bring the juvenile to court as provided in subrule (A)(2).

(D) **Separate Custody of Juvenile**. While awaiting arrival of the parent, guardian, or legal custodian, appearance before the court, or otherwise, the juvenile must be maintained separately from adult prisoners to prevent any verbal, visual, or physical contact with an adult prisoner.

Rule 3.934 Arranging Court Appearance; Detained Juvenile

(A) **General**. Unless the prosecuting attorney has authorized a complaint and warrant charging the juvenile with an offense as though an adult pursuant to MCL 764.1f, when a juvenile is apprehended and not released, the officer shall:
(1) forthwith take the juvenile
(a) before the court for a preliminary hearing, or
(b) to a place designated by the court pending the scheduling of a preliminary hearing;
(2) ensure that the petition is prepared and presented to the court;
(3) notify the parent, guardian, or legal custodian of the detaining of the juvenile and of the need for the presence of the parent, guardian, or legal custodian at the preliminary hearing;
(4) prepare a custody statement for submission to the court including:
(a) the grounds for and the time and location of detention, and
(b) the names of persons notified and the times of notification, or the reason for failure to notify.

(B) **Temporary Detention; Court Not Open**.
(1) Grounds. A juvenile apprehended without court order when the court is not open may be detained pending preliminary hearing if the offense or the juvenile meets a circumstance set forth in MCR 3.935(D)(1), or if no parent, guardian, or legal custodian can be located.
(2) Designated Court Person. The court must designate a judge, referee, or other person who may be contacted by the officer taking a juvenile into custody when the court is not open. In each county there must be a designated facility open at all times at which an officer may obtain the name of the person to be contacted for permission to detain the juvenile pending preliminary hearing.

Rule 3.935 Preliminary Hearing

(A) **Time**.
(1) *Commencement*. The preliminary hearing must commence no later than 24 hours after the juvenile has been taken into court custody, excluding Sundays and holidays, as defined by MCR 8.110(D)(2), or the juvenile must be released.
(2) *General Adjournment*. The court may adjourn the hearing for up to 14 days:
(a) to secure the attendance of the juvenile's parent, guardian, or legal custodian or of a witness, or
(b) for other good cause shown.
(3) *Special Adjournment; Specified Juvenile Violation*. This subrule applies to a juvenile accused of an offense that allegedly was committed between the juvenile's 14th and 17th birthdays and that would constitute a specified juvenile violation listed in MCL 712A.2(a)(1).
(a) On a request of a prosecuting attorney who has approved the submission of a petition with the court, conditioned on the opportunity to withdraw it within 5 days if the prosecuting attorney authorizes the filing of a complaint and warrant with a magistrate, the court shall comply with subrules (i)-(iii).
(i) The court shall adjourn the preliminary hearing for up to 5 days to give the prosecuting attorney the opportunity to determine whether to authorize the filing of a criminal complaint and warrant charging the juvenile with an offense as

though an adult pursuant to MCL 764.1f, instead of unconditionally approving the filing of a petition with the court.
(ii) The court, during the special adjournment under subrule 3(a), must defer a decision regarding whether to authorize the filing of the petition.
(iii) The court, during the special adjournment under subrule (3)(a), must release the juvenile pursuant to MCR 3.935(E) or detain the juvenile pursuant to MCR 3.935(D).
(b) If, at the resumption of the preliminary hearing following special adjournment, the prosecuting attorney has not authorized the filing with a magistrate of a criminal complaint and warrant on the charge concerning the juvenile, approval of the petition by the prosecuting attorney shall no longer be deemed conditional and the court shall proceed with the preliminary hearing and decide whether to authorize the petition to be filed.
(c) This rule does not preclude the prosecuting attorney from moving for a waiver of jurisdiction over the juvenile under MCR 3.950.

(B) **Procedure**.
(1) The court shall determine whether the parent, guardian, or legal custodian has been notified and is present. The preliminary hearing may be conducted without a parent, guardian, or legal custodian present, provided a guardian ad litem or attorney appears with the juvenile.
(2) The court shall read the allegations in the petition.
(3) The court shall determine whether the petition should be dismissed, whether the matter should be referred to alternate services pursuant to the Juvenile Diversion Act, MCL 722.821 et seq., whether the matter should be heard on the consent calendar as provided by MCR 3.932(C), or whether to continue the preliminary hearing.
(4) If the hearing is to continue, the court shall advise the juvenile on the record in plain language of:
(a) the right to an attorney pursuant to MCR 3.915(A)(1);
(b) the right to trial by judge or jury on the allegations in the petition and that a referee may be assigned to hear the case unless demand for a jury or judge is filed pursuant to MCR 3.911 or 3.912; and
(c) the privilege against self-incrimination and that any statement by the juvenile may be used against the juvenile.
(5) If the charge is a status offense in violation of MCL 712A.2(a)(2)-(4) or (d), the court must inquire if the juvenile or a parent is a member of an Indian tribe. If the court knows or has reason to know the child is an Indian child, the court must determine the identity of the tribe and comply with MCR 3.905 before proceeding with the hearing.
(6) The juvenile must be allowed an opportunity to deny or otherwise plead to the allegations.
(7) Unless the preliminary hearing is adjourned, the court must decide whether to authorize the petition to be filed pursuant to MCR 3.932(D). If it authorizes the filing of the petition, the court must:
(a) determine if fingerprints must be taken as provided by MCL 712A.11(5) and MCR 3.936; and
(b) determine if the juvenile should be released, with or without conditions, or detained, as provided in subrules (C)-(F).
(8) The juvenile may be detained pending the completion of the preliminary hearing if the conditions for detention under subrule (D) are established.

(C) **Determination Whether to Release or Detain**.
(1) Factors. In determining whether the juvenile is to be released, with or without conditions, or detained, the court shall consider the following factors:
(a) the juvenile's family ties and relationships,
(b) the juvenile's prior delinquency record,
(c) the juvenile's record of appearance or nonappearance at court proceedings,
(d) the violent nature of the alleged offense,
(e) the juvenile's prior history of committing acts that resulted in bodily injury to others,
(f) the juvenile's character and mental condition,
(g) the court's ability to supervise the juvenile if placed with a parent or relative, and
(h) any other factor indicating the juvenile's ties to the community, the risk of nonappearance, and the danger to the juvenile or the public if the juvenile is released.
(2) Findings. The court must state the reasons for its decision to grant or deny release on the record or in a written memorandum. The court's statement need not include a finding on each of the enumerated factors.

(D) **Detention**.
(1) *Conditions for Detention*. A juvenile may be ordered detained or continued in detention if the court finds probable cause to believe the juvenile committed the offense, and that one or more of the following circumstances are present:
(a) the offense alleged is so serious that release would endanger the public safety;
(b) the juvenile is charged with an offense that would be a felony if committed by an adult and will likely commit another offense pending trial, if released, and

(i) another petition is pending against the juvenile,
(ii) the juvenile is on probation, or
(iii) the juvenile has a prior adjudication, but is not under the court's jurisdiction at the time of apprehension;

(c) there is a substantial likelihood that if the juvenile is released to the parent, guardian, or legal custodian, with or without conditions, the juvenile will fail to appear at the next court proceeding;

(d) the home conditions of the juvenile make detention necessary;

(e) the juvenile has run away from home;

(f) the juvenile has failed to remain in a detention facility or nonsecure facility or placement in violation of a valid court order; or

(g) pretrial detention is otherwise specifically authorized by law.

(2) *Waiver*. A juvenile may waive the probable cause determination required by subrule (1) only if the juvenile is represented by an attorney.

(3) *Evidence; Findings*. The juvenile may contest the sufficiency of evidence by cross-examination of witnesses, presentation of defense witnesses, or by other evidence. The court shall permit the use of subpoena power to secure attendance of defense witnesses. The Michigan Rules of Evidence do not apply, other than those with respect to privileges.

(4) *Type of Detention*. The detained juvenile must be placed in the least restrictive environment that will meet the needs of the juvenile and the public, and that will conform to the requirements of MCL 712A.15 and 712A.16.

(E) **Release; Conditions.**

(1) The court may release a juvenile to a parent pending the resumption of the preliminary hearing, pending trial, or until further order without conditions, or, if the court determines that release with conditions is necessary to reasonably ensure the appearance of the juvenile as required or to reasonably ensure the safety of the public, the court may, in its discretion, order that the release of the juvenile be on the condition or combination of conditions that the court determines to be appropriate, including, but not limited to:

(a) that the juvenile will not commit any offense while released,

(b) that the juvenile will not use alcohol or any controlled substance or tobacco product,

(c) that the juvenile will participate in a substance abuse assessment, testing, or treatment program,

(d) that the juvenile will participate in a treatment program for a physical or mental condition,

(e) that the juvenile will comply with restrictions on personal associations or place of residence,

(f) that the juvenile will comply with a specified curfew,

(g) that the juvenile will maintain appropriate behavior and attendance at an educational program, and

(h) that the juvenile's driver's license or passport will be surrendered.

(2) Violation of Conditions of Release. If a juvenile is alleged to have violated the conditions set by the court, the court may order the juvenile apprehended and detained immediately. The court may then modify the conditions or revoke the juvenile's release status after providing the juvenile an opportunity to be heard on the issue of the violation of conditions of release.

(F) **Bail**. In addition to any other conditions of release, the court may require a parent, guardian, or legal custodian to post bail.

(1) *Cash or Surety Bond*. The court may require a parent, guardian, or legal custodian to post a surety bond or cash in the full amount of the bail, at the option of the parent, guardian, or legal custodian. A surety bond must be written by a person or company licensed to write surety bonds in Michigan. Except as otherwise provided by this rule, MCR 3.604 applies to bonds posted under this rule.

(2) *Option to Deposit Cash or 10 Percent of Bail*. Unless the court requires a surety bond or cash in the full amount of the bail as provided in subrule (F)(1), the court shall advise the parent, guardian, or legal custodian of the option to satisfy the monetary requirement of bail by:

(a) posting either cash or a surety bond in the full amount of bail set by the court or a surety bond written by a person or company licensed to write surety bonds in Michigan, or

(b) depositing with the register, clerk, or cashier of the court currency equal to 10 percent of the bail, but at least $10.

(3) *Revocation or Modification*. The court may modify or revoke the bail for good cause after providing the parties notice and an opportunity to be heard.

(4) *Return of Bail*. If the conditions of bail are met, the court shall discharge any surety.

(a) If disposition imposes reimbursement or costs, the bail money posted by the parent must first be applied to the amount of reimbursement and costs, and the balance, if any, returned.

(b) If the juvenile is discharged from all obligations in the case, the court shall return the cash posted, or return 90 percent and retain 10 percent if the amount posted represented 10 percent of the bail.

(5) *Forfeiture*. If the conditions of bail are not met, the court may issue a writ for the apprehension of the juvenile and enter an order declaring the bail money, if any, forfeited.
   (a) The court must immediately mail notice of the forfeiture order to the parent at the last known address and to any surety.
   (b) If the juvenile does not appear and surrender to the court within 28 days from the forfeiture date, or does not within the period satisfy the court that the juvenile is not at fault, the court may enter judgment against the parent and surety, if any, for the entire amount of the bail and, when allowed, costs of the court proceedings.

Rule 3.936 Fingerprinting

(A) **General**. The court must permit fingerprinting of a juvenile pursuant to MCL 712A.11(5) and 712A.18(10), and as provided in this rule. Notice of fingerprinting retained by the court is confidential.
(B) **Order for Fingerprints**. At the time that the court authorizes the filing of a petition alleging a juvenile offense and before the court enters an order of disposition on a juvenile offense, the court shall examine the confidential files and verify that the juvenile has been fingerprinted. If it appears to the court that the juvenile has not been fingerprinted, the court must:
   (1) direct the juvenile to go to the law enforcement agency involved in the apprehension of the juvenile, or to the sheriff's department, so fingerprints may be taken; or
   (2) issue an order to the sheriff's department to apprehend the juvenile and to take the fingerprints of the juvenile.
(C) **Notice of Disposition**. The court shall notify the Department of State Police in writing:
   (1) of any juvenile who had been fingerprinted for a juvenile offense and who was found not to be within the jurisdiction of the court under MCL 712A.2(a)(1); or
   (2) that the court took jurisdiction of a juvenile under MCL 712A.2(a)(1), who was fingerprinted for a juvenile offense, specifying the offense, the method of adjudication, and the disposition ordered.
(D) **Order for Destruction of Fingerprints**. When a juvenile has been fingerprinted for a juvenile offense, but no petition on the offense is submitted to the court, the court does not authorize the petition, or the court does not take jurisdiction of the juvenile under MCL 712A.2(a)(1), if the records have not been destroyed as provided by MCL 28.243(7)-(8), the court, on motion filed pursuant to MCL 28.243(8), shall issue an order directing the Department of State Police, or other official holding the information, to destroy the fingerprints and arrest card of the juvenile pertaining to the offense, other than an offense as listed in MCL 28.243(12).

Rule 3.939 Case Transferred From District Court Pursuant to Subchapter 6.900

(A) **General Procedure**. Except as provided in subrule (B), the court shall hear and dispose of a case transferred pursuant to MCL 766.14 in the same manner as if the case had been commenced in the family division of circuit court. A petition that has been approved by the prosecuting attorney must be submitted to the court.
(B) **Probable Cause Finding of Magistrate**. The court may use the probable cause finding of the magistrate made at the preliminary examination to satisfy the probable cause requirement of MCR 3.935(D)(1).

Rule 3.941 Pleas of Admission or No Contest

(A) **Capacity**. A juvenile may offer a plea of admission or of no contest to an offense with the consent of the court. The court shall not accept a plea to an offense unless the court is satisfied that the plea is accurate, voluntary, and understanding.
(B) **Conditional Pleas**. The court may accept a plea of admission or of no contest conditioned on preservation of an issue for appellate review.
(C) **Plea Procedure**. Before accepting a plea of admission or of no contest, the court must personally address the juvenile and must comply with subrules (1)-(4).
   (1) *An Understanding Plea*. The court shall tell the juvenile:
      (a) the name of the offense charged,
      (b) the possible dispositions,
      (c) that if the plea is accepted, the juvenile will not have a trial of any kind, so the juvenile gives up the rights that would be present at trial, including the right:
         (i) to trial by jury,
         (ii) to trial by the judge if the juvenile does not want trial by jury,
         (iii) to be presumed innocent until proven guilty,
         (iv) to have the petitioner or prosecutor prove guilt beyond a reasonable doubt,
         (v) to have witnesses against the juvenile appear at the trial,
         (vi) to question the witnesses against the juvenile,
         (vii) to have the court order any witnesses for the juvenile's defense to appear at the trial,
         (viii) to remain silent and not have that silence used against the juvenile, and
         (ix) to testify at trial, if the juvenile wants to testify.

(2) *A Voluntary Plea.*
(a) The court shall confirm any plea agreement on the record.
(b) The court shall ask the juvenile if any promises have been made beyond those in a plea agreement or whether anyone has threatened the juvenile.
(3) *An Accurate Plea.* The court may not accept a plea of admission or of no contest without establishing support for a finding that the juvenile committed the offense:
(a) either by questioning the juvenile or by other means when the plea is a plea of admission, or
(b) by means other than questioning the juvenile when the juvenile pleads no contest. The court shall also state why a plea of no contest is appropriate.
(4) *Support for Plea.* The court shall inquire of the parent, guardian, legal custodian, or guardian ad litem, if present, whether there is any reason why the court should not accept the plea tendered by the juvenile.
(D) **Plea Withdrawal**. The court may take a plea of admission or of no contest under advisement. Before the court accepts the plea, the juvenile may withdraw the plea offer by right. After the court accepts the plea, the court has discretion to allow the juvenile to withdraw a plea.

Rule 3.942 Trial

(A) **Time**. In all cases the trial must be held within 6 months after the filing of the petition, unless adjourned for good cause. If the juvenile is detained, the trial has not started within 63 days after the juvenile is taken into custody, and the delay in starting the trial is not attributable to the defense, the court shall forthwith order the juvenile released pending trial without requiring that bail be posted, unless the juvenile is being detained on another matter.
(B) **Preliminary Matters**.
(1) The court shall determine whether all parties are present.
(a) The juvenile has the right to be present at the trial with an attorney, parent, guardian, legal custodian, or guardian ad litem, if any.
(b) The court may proceed in the absence of a parent, guardian, or legal custodian who was properly notified to appear.
(c) The victim has the right to be present at trial as provided by MCL 780.789.
(2) The court shall read the allegations contained in the petition, unless waived.
(3) The court shall inform the juvenile of the right to the assistance of an attorney pursuant to MCR 3.915 unless an attorney appears representing the juvenile. If the juvenile requests to proceed without the assistance of an attorney, the court must advise the juvenile of the dangers and disadvantages of self-representation and make sure the juvenile is literate and competent to conduct the defense.
(C) **Evidence; Standard of Proof**. The Michigan Rules of Evidence and the standard of proof beyond a reasonable doubt apply at trial.
(D) **Verdict**. In a delinquency proceeding, the verdict must be guilty or not guilty of either the offense charged or a lesser included offense.

Rule 3.943 Dispositional Hearing

(A) **General**. A dispositional hearing is conducted to determine what measures the court will take with respect to a juvenile and, when applicable, any other person, once the court has determined following trial or plea that the juvenile has committed an offense.
(B) **Time**. The interval between the plea of admission or trial and disposition, if any, is within the court's discretion. When the juvenile is detained, the interval may not be more than 35 days, except for good cause.
(C) **Evidence**.
(1) The Michigan Rules of Evidence, other than those with respect to privileges, do not apply at dispositional hearings. All relevant and material evidence, including oral and written reports, may be received by the court and may be relied upon to the extent of its probative value, even though such evidence may not be admissible at trial.
(2) The juvenile, or the juvenile's attorney, and the petitioner shall be afforded an opportunity to examine and controvert written reports so received and, in the court's discretion, may be allowed to cross-examine individuals making reports when those individuals are reasonably available.
(3) No assertion of an evidentiary privilege, other than the privilege between attorney and client, shall prevent the receipt and use, at a dispositional hearing, of materials prepared pursuant to a court-ordered examination, interview, or course of treatment.
(D) **Presence of Juvenile and Victim**.
(1) The juvenile may be excused from part of the dispositional hearing for good cause shown, but must be present when the disposition is announced.
(2) The victim has the right to be present at the dispositional hearing and to make an impact statement as provided by the Crime Victim's Rights Act, MCL 780.751 et seq.
(E) **Dispositions**.
(1) If the juvenile has been found to have committed an offense, the court may enter an order of disposition as provided by MCL 712A.18.
(2) In making second and subsequent dispositions in delinquency cases, the court must consider imposing increasingly severe sanctions, which may

include imposing additional conditions of probation; extending the term of probation; imposing additional costs; ordering a juvenile who has been residing at home into an out-of-home placement; ordering a more restrictive placement; ordering state wardship for a child who has not previously been a state ward; or any other conditions deemed appropriate by the court. Waiver of jurisdiction to adult criminal court, either by authorization of a warrant or by judicial waiver, is not considered a sanction for the purpose of this rule.

(3) Before a juvenile is placed in an institution outside the state of Michigan as a disposition, the court must find that:
   (a) institutional care is in the best interests of the juvenile,
   (b) equivalent facilities to meet the juvenile's needs are not available within Michigan, and
   (c) the placement will not cause undue hardship.

(4) The court shall not enter an order of disposition for a juvenile offense until the court verifies that the juvenile has been fingerprinted. If the juvenile has not been fingerprinted, the court shall proceed as provided by MCR 3.936.

(5) If the court enters an order pursuant to the Crime Victim's Rights Act, MCL 780.751 et seq., the court shall only order the payment of one assessment at any dispositional hearing, regardless of the number of offenses.

(6) The court shall prepare and forward to the Secretary of State an abstract of its findings at such times and for such offenses as are required by law.

(7) Mandatory Detention for Use of a Firearm.
   (a) In addition to any other disposition, a juvenile, other than a juvenile sentenced in the same manner as an adult under MCL 712A.18(1)(n), shall be committed under MCL 712A.18(1)(e) to a detention facility for a specified period of time if all the following circumstances exist:
      (i) the juvenile is under the jurisdiction of the court under MCL 712A.2(a)(1),
      (ii) the juvenile was found to have violated a law of this state or of the United States or a criminal municipal ordinance, and
      (iii) the juvenile was found to have used a firearm during the offense.
   (b) The length of the commitment to a detention facility shall not exceed the length of the sentence that could have been imposed if the juvenile had been sentenced as an adult.
   (c) "Firearm" means any weapon from which a dangerous projectile may be propelled by using explosives, gas, or air as a means of propulsion, except any smoothbore rifle or hand gun designed and manufactured exclusively for propelling BB's not exceeding .177 caliber by means of spring, gas, or air.

Rule 3.944 Probation Violation

(A) **Petition; Temporary Custody**.
   (1) Upon receipt of a sworn supplemental petition alleging that the juvenile has violated any condition of probation, the court may:
      (a) direct that the juvenile be notified pursuant to MCR 3.920 to appear for a hearing on the alleged violation, which notice must include a copy of the probation violation petition and a notice of the juvenile's rights as provided in subrule (C)(1); or
      (b) order that the juvenile be apprehended and brought to the court for a detention hearing, which must be commenced within 24 hours after the juvenile has been taken into court custody, excluding Sundays and holidays as defined in MCR 8.110 (D)(2).
   (2) When a juvenile is apprehended pursuant to court order as provided in subrule (A)(1)(b), the officer must:
      (a) forthwith take the juvenile
         (i) to the court for a detention hearing, or
         (ii) to the place designated by the court pending the scheduling of a detention hearing; and
      (b) notify the custodial parent, guardian, or legal custodian that the juvenile has been taken into custody, of the time and place of the detention hearing, if known, and of the need for the presence of the parent, guardian, or legal custodian at the detention hearing.

(B) **Detention Hearing; Procedure**. At the detention hearing:
   (1) The court must determine whether a parent, guardian, or legal custodian has been notified and is present. If a parent, guardian, or legal custodian has been notified, but fails to appear, the detention hearing may be conducted without a parent, guardian, or legal custodian if a guardian ad litem or attorney appears with the juvenile.
   (2) The court must provide the juvenile with a copy of the petition alleging probation violation.
   (3) The court must read the petition to the juvenile, unless the attorney or juvenile waives the reading.
   (4) The court must advise the juvenile of the juvenile's rights as provided in subrule (C)(1) and of the possible dispositions.
   (5) The juvenile must be allowed an opportunity to deny or otherwise plead to the probation violation. If the juvenile wishes to admit the probation violation or plead no contest, the court must comply with subrule (D) before accepting the plea.

(a) If the juvenile admits the probation violation or pleads no contest, and the court accepts the plea, the court may modify the existing order of probation or may order any disposition available under MCL 712A.18 or MCL 712A.18a.

(b) If the juvenile denies the probation violation or remains silent, the court must schedule a probation violation hearing, which must commence within 42 days. The court may order the juvenile detained without bond pending the probation violation hearing if there is probable cause to believe the juvenile violated probation. If the hearing is not commenced within 42 days, and the delay in commencing the hearing is not attributable to the juvenile, the juvenile must be released pending hearing without requiring that bail be posted.

(C) **Probation Violation Hearing**.

(1) At the probation violation hearing, the juvenile has the following rights:

(a) the right to be present at the hearing,

(b) the right to an attorney pursuant to MCR 3.915(A)(1),

(c) the right to have the petitioner prove the probation violation by a preponderance of the evidence,

(d) the right to have the court order any witnesses to appear at the hearing,

(e) the right to question witnesses against the juvenile,

(f) the right to remain silent and not have that silence used against the juvenile, and

(g) the right to testify at the hearing, if the juvenile wants to testify.

(2) At the probation violation hearing, the Michigan Rules of Evidence do not apply, other than those with respect to privileges. There is no right to a jury.

(3) If it is alleged that the juvenile violated probation by having been found, pursuant to MCR 3.941 or MCR 3.942, to have committed an offense, the juvenile may then be found to have violated probation pursuant to this rule.

(D) **Pleas of Admission or No Contest**. If the juvenile wishes to admit the probation violation or plead no contest, before accepting the plea, the court must:

(1) tell the juvenile the nature of the alleged probation violation;

(2) tell the juvenile the possible dispositions;

(3) tell the juvenile that if the plea is accepted, the juvenile will not have a contested hearing of any kind, so the juvenile would give up the rights that the juvenile would have at a contested hearing, including the rights as provided in subrule (C)(1);

(4) confirm any plea agreement on the record;

(5) ask the juvenile if any promises have been made beyond those in the plea agreement and whether anyone has threatened the juvenile;

(6) establish support for a finding that the juvenile violated probation,

(a) by questioning the juvenile or by other means when the plea is a plea of admission, or

(b) by means other than questioning the juvenile when the juvenile pleads no contest. The court must also state why a plea of no contest is appropriate;

(7) inquire of the parent, guardian, legal custodian, or guardian ad litem whether there is any reason why the court should not accept the juvenile's plea. Agreement or objection by the parent, guardian, legal custodian, or guardian ad litem to a plea of admission or of no contest by a juvenile shall be placed on the record if the parent, guardian, legal custodian, or guardian ad litem is present; and

(8) determine that the plea is accurately, voluntarily and understandingly made.

(E) **Disposition of Probation Violation; Reporting**.

(1) If, after hearing, the court finds that a violation of probation has occurred, the court may modify the existing order of probation or order any disposition available under MCL 712A.18 or MCL 712A.18a.

(2) If, after hearing, the court finds that a violation of probation occurred on the basis of the juvenile having committed an offense, that finding must be recorded as a violation of probation only and not a finding that the juvenile committed the underlying offense. That finding must not be reported to the State Police or the Secretary of State as an adjudication or a disposition.

Rule 3.945 Dispositional Review

(A) **Dispositional Review Hearings**.

(1) *Generally*. The court must conduct periodic hearings to review the dispositional orders in delinquency cases in which the juvenile has been placed outside the home. Such review hearings must be conducted at intervals designated by the court, or may be requested at any time by a party or by a probation officer or caseworker. The victim has a right to make a statement at the hearing or submit a written statement for use at the hearing, or both. At a dispositional review hearing, the court may modify or amend the dispositional order or treatment plan to include any disposition permitted by MCL 712A.18 and MCL 712A.18a or as otherwise permitted by law. The Michigan Rules of Evidence, other than those with respect to privileges, do not apply.

(2) *Required Review Hearings.*
   (a) If the juvenile is placed in out-of-home care, the court must hold dispositional review hearings no later than every 182 days after the initial disposition, as provided in MCL 712A.19(2).
   (b) A review hearing is required before a juvenile is moved to a more physically restrictive type of placement, unless the court in its dispositional order has provided for a more physically restrictive type of placement. A review hearing is not required if the juvenile and a parent consent to the new placement in a writing filed with the court. A juvenile, who has been ordered placed in a juvenile facility, may be released only with the approval of the court.

(B) **Hearing to Extend Jurisdiction.**
   (1) *When Required.* When a juvenile committed under MCL 712A.18(1)(e) for an offense specified in MCL 712A.18d remains under court jurisdiction after the juvenile's 18th birthday, the court must conduct a hearing to determine whether to extend the court's jurisdiction to age 21, pursuant to MCL 712A.18d.
      (a) Time of Hearing. Unless adjourned for good cause, a commitment review hearing must be held as nearly as possible to, but before, the juvenile's 19th birthday.
      (b) Notice of Hearing. Notice of the hearing must be given to the prosecuting attorney, the agency or the superintendent of the institution or facility to which the juvenile has been committed, the juvenile, and, if the address or whereabouts are known, the parent, guardian or legal custodian of the juvenile, at least 14 days before the hearing. The notice must clearly indicate that the court may extend jurisdiction over the juvenile until the juvenile reaches 21 years of age and must include advice to the juvenile and the parent, guardian, or legal custodian that the juvenile has the right to an attorney.
   (2) *Appointment of Attorney.* The court must appoint an attorney to represent the juvenile at the hearing unless an attorney has been retained.
   (3) *Evidence; Commitment Report.* The Michigan Rules of Evidence do not apply, other than those with respect to privileges. The institution, agency, or facility must prepare a report for use at the hearing to extend jurisdiction. The report must contain information required by MCL 803.225. The court must consider this information in determining whether to extend jurisdiction beyond the age of 19.
   (4) *Burden of Proof; Findings.* The court must extend jurisdiction over the juvenile until the age of 21, unless the juvenile proves by a preponderance of the evidence that the juvenile has been rehabilitated and does not present a serious risk to public safety. In making the determination, the court must consider the following factors:
      (a) the extent and nature of the juvenile's participation in education, counseling, or work programs;
      (b) the juvenile's willingness to accept responsibility for prior behavior;
      (c) the juvenile's behavior in the current placement;
      (d) the juvenile's prior record, character, and physical and mental maturity;
      (e) the juvenile's potential for violent conduct, as demonstrated by prior behavior;
      (f) the recommendations of the institution, agency, or facility charged with the juvenile's care regarding the appropriateness of the juvenile's release or continued custody; and
      (g) any other information the prosecuting attorney or the juvenile submits.

(C) **Review of Extended Jurisdiction Cases.**
   (1) *Out-of-Home Care.* If the juvenile is placed outside the home, the court must hold a dispositional review hearing no later than every 182 days after the hearing to extend jurisdiction.
   (2) *Periodic Review.* If the institution, agency, or facility to which the juvenile was committed believes that the juvenile has been rehabilitated and does not present a serious risk to public safety, the institution, agency, or facility may petition the court to conduct a review hearing at any time before the juvenile becomes 21 years of age.

(D) **Juvenile on Conditional Release.** The procedures set forth in MCR 3.944 apply to juveniles committed under MCL 712A.18 who have allegedly violated a condition of release after being returned to the community on release from a public institution. The court need not conduct such a hearing when there will be an administrative hearing by the agency to which the juvenile is committed, provided the court has not retained jurisdiction.

Rule 3.946 Post-Dispositional Secure Detention Pending Return to Placement

(A) If a juvenile who has been found to have committed an offense that would be a misdemeanor or a felony if committed by an adult has been placed out of the home by court order or by the Family Independence Agency, and the juvenile leaves such placement without authority, upon being apprehended the juvenile may be detained without the right to bail. Any detention must be authorized by the court.

(B) If a juvenile is placed in secure detention pursuant to this rule and no new petition is filed that would require a preliminary hearing pursuant to MCR 3.935, and no probation violation petition is filed, the court must conduct a detention hearing within 48 hours after the juvenile has been taken into custody, excluding Sundays and holidays as defined by MCR 8.110(D)(2).

(C) At the detention hearing the court must:
  (1) assure that the custodial parent, guardian, or legal custodian has been notified, if that person's whereabouts are known,
  (2) advise the juvenile of the right to be represented by an attorney,
  (3) determine whether the juvenile should be released or should continue to be detained.

Rule 3.950 Waiver of Jurisdiction

(A) **Authority**. Only a judge assigned to hear cases in the family division of the circuit court of the county where the offense is alleged to have been committed may waive jurisdiction pursuant to MCL 712A.4.

(B) **Definition**. As used in this rule, “felony” means an offense punishable by imprisonment for more than one year or an offense designated by law as a felony.

(C) **Motion by Prosecuting Attorney**. A motion by the prosecuting attorney requesting that the family division waive its jurisdiction to a court of general criminal jurisdiction must be in writing and must clearly indicate the charges and that if the motion is granted the juvenile will be prosecuted as though an adult.
  (1) A motion to waive jurisdiction of the juvenile must be filed within 14 days after the petition has been authorized to be filed. Absent a timely motion and good cause shown, the juvenile shall no longer be subject to waiver of jurisdiction on the charges.
  (2) A copy of the motion seeking waiver must be personally served on the juvenile and the parent, guardian, or legal custodian of the juvenile, if their addresses or whereabouts are known or can be determined by the exercise of due diligence.

(D) **Hearing Procedure**. The waiver hearing consists of two phases. Notice of the date, time, and place of the hearings may be given either on the record directly to the juvenile or to the attorney for the juvenile, the prosecuting attorney, and all other parties, or in writing, served on each individual.
  (1) *First Phase*. The first-phase hearing is to determine whether there is probable cause to believe that an offense has been committed that if committed by an adult would be a felony, and that there is probable cause to believe that the juvenile who is 14 years of age or older committed the offense.
    (a) The probable cause hearing shall be commenced within 28 days after the filing of the petition unless adjourned for good cause.
    (b) At the hearing, the prosecuting attorney has the burden to present legally admissible evidence to establish each element of the offense and to establish probable cause that the juvenile committed the offense.
    (c) The court need not conduct the first phase of the waiver hearing, if:
      (i) the court has found the requisite probable cause at a hearing under MCR 3.935(D)(1), provided that at the earlier hearing only legally admissible evidence was used to establish probable cause that the offense was committed and probable cause that the juvenile committed the offense; or
      (ii) the juvenile, after being informed by the court on the record that the probable cause hearing is equivalent to and held in place of preliminary examination in district court, waives the hearing. The court must determine that the waiver of hearing is freely, voluntarily, and understandingly given and that the juvenile knows there will be no preliminary examination in district court if the court waives jurisdiction.
  (2) *Second Phase*. If the court finds the requisite probable cause at the first-phase hearing, or if there is no hearing pursuant to subrule (D)(1)(c), the second-phase hearing shall be held to determine whether the interests of the juvenile and the public would best be served by granting the motion. However, if the juvenile has been previously subject to the general criminal jurisdiction of the circuit court under MCL 712A.4 or 600.606, the court shall waive jurisdiction of the juvenile to the court of general criminal jurisdiction without holding the second-phase hearing.
    (a) The second-phase hearing shall be commenced within 28 days after the conclusion of the first phase, or within 35 days after the filing of the petition if there was no hearing pursuant to subrule (D)(1)(c), unless adjourned for good cause.
    (b) The Michigan Rules of Evidence, other than those with respect to privileges, do not apply to the second phase of the waiver hearing.
    (c) The prosecuting attorney has the burden of establishing by a preponderance of the evidence that the best interests of the juvenile and the public would be served by waiver.
    (d) The court, in determining whether to waive the juvenile to the court having general criminal jurisdiction, shall consider and make findings on the following criteria, giving greater weight to the seriousness of the alleged offense and the juvenile's prior record of delinquency than to the other criteria:

(i) the seriousness of the alleged offense in terms of community protection, including, but not limited to, the existence of any aggravating factors recognized by the sentencing guidelines, the use of a firearm or other dangerous weapon, and the effect on any victim;

(ii) the culpability of the juvenile in committing the alleged offense, including, but not limited to, the level of the juvenile's participation in planning and carrying out the offense and the existence of any aggravating or mitigating factors recognized by the sentencing guidelines;

(iii) the juvenile's prior record of delinquency including, but not limited to, any record of detention, any police record, any school record, or any other evidence indicating prior delinquent behavior;

(iv) the juvenile's programming history, including, but not limited to, the juvenile's past willingness to participate meaningfully in available programming;

(v) the adequacy of the punishment or programming available in the juvenile justice system;

(vi) the dispositional options available for the juvenile.

(e) In determining whether to waive the juvenile to the court having general criminal jurisdiction, the court may also consider any stipulation by the defense to a finding that the best interests of the juvenile and the public support a waiver.

(E) **Grant of Waiver Motion.**

(1) If the court determines that it is in the best interests of the juvenile and public to waive jurisdiction over the juvenile, the court must:

(a) Enter a written order granting the motion to waive jurisdiction and transferring the matter to the appropriate court having general criminal jurisdiction for arraignment of the juvenile on an information.

(b) Make findings of fact and conclusions of law forming the basis for entry of the waiver order. The findings and conclusions may be incorporated in a written opinion or stated on the record.

(c) Advise the juvenile, orally or in writing, that

(i) the juvenile is entitled to appellate review of the decision to waive jurisdiction,

(ii) the juvenile must seek review of the decision in the Court of Appeals within 21 days of the order to preserve the appeal of right, and

(iii) if the juvenile is financially unable to retain an attorney, the court will appoint one to represent the juvenile on appeal.

(d) The court shall send, without cost, a copy of the order and a copy of the written opinion or transcript of the court's findings and conclusions, to the court having general criminal jurisdiction.

(2) Upon the grant of a waiver motion, a juvenile must be transferred to the adult criminal justice system and is subject to the same procedures used for adult criminal defendants. Juveniles waived pursuant to this rule are not required to be kept separate and apart from adult prisoners.

(F) **Denial of Waiver Motion**. If the waiver motion is denied, the court shall make written findings or place them on the record. A transcript of the court's findings or, if a written opinion is prepared, a copy of the written opinion must be sent to the prosecuting attorney and the juvenile, or juvenile's attorney, upon request. If the juvenile is detained and the trial of the matter in the family division has not started within 28 days after entry of the order denying the waiver motion, and the delay is not attributable to the defense, the court shall forthwith order the juvenile released pending trial without requiring that bail be posted, unless the juvenile is being detained on another matter.

(G) **Psychiatric Testimony**.

(1) A psychiatrist, psychologist, or certified social worker who conducts a court-ordered examination for the purpose of a waiver hearing may not testify at a subsequent criminal proceeding involving the juvenile without the juvenile's written consent.

(2) The juvenile's consent may only be given:

(a) in the presence of an attorney representing the juvenile or, if no attorney represents the juvenile, in the presence of a parent, guardian, or legal custodian;

(b) after the juvenile has had an opportunity to read the report of the psychiatrist, psychologist, or certified social worker; and

(c) after the waiver decision is rendered.

(3) Consent to testimony by the psychiatrist, psychologist, or certified social worker does not waive the juvenile's privilege against self-incrimination.

Rule 3.951 Initiating Designated Proceedings

(A) **Prosecutor-Designated Cases**. The procedures in this subrule apply if the prosecuting attorney submits a petition designating the case for trial in the same manner as an adult.

(1) *Time for Arraignment.*

(a) If the juvenile is in custody or custody is requested, the arraignment must commence no later than 24 hours after the juvenile has been taken into court custody, excluding Sundays and holidays as defined by MCR 8.110(D)(2), or the juvenile must be released. The court may adjourn the arraignment for up to 7 days to secure the attendance of the juvenile's parent, guardian, or legal custodian or of a witness, or for other good cause shown.

(b) If the juvenile is not in custody and custody is not requested, the juvenile must be brought before the court for an arraignment as soon as the juvenile's attendance can be secured.

(2) *Procedure.*

(a) The court shall determine whether the juvenile's parent, guardian, or legal custodian has been notified and is present. The arraignment may be conducted without a parent, guardian, or legal custodian, provided a guardian ad litem or attorney appears with the juvenile.

(b) The court shall read the allegations in the petition and advise the juvenile on the record in plain language:

(i) of the right to an attorney pursuant to MCR 3.915(A)(1);

(ii) of the right to trial by judge or jury on the allegations in the petition;

(iii) of the right to remain silent and that any statement made by the juvenile may be used against the juvenile;

(iv) of the right to have a preliminary examination within 14 days;

(v) that the case has been designated for trial in the same manner as an adult and, if the prosecuting attorney proves that there is probable cause to believe an offense was committed and there is probable cause to believe that the juvenile committed the offense, the juvenile will be afforded all the rights of an adult charged with the same crime and that upon conviction the juvenile may be sentenced as an adult; and

(vi) of the maximum possible prison sentence and any mandatory minimum sentence required by law.

(c) Unless the arraignment is adjourned, the court must decide whether to authorize the petition to be filed. If it authorizes the filing of the petition, the court must:

(i) determine if fingerprints must be taken as provided by MCR 3.936;

(ii) schedule a preliminary examination within 14 days before a judge other than the judge who would conduct the trial;

(iii) if the juvenile is in custody or custody is requested, determine whether to detain or release the juvenile as provided in MCR 3.935(C).

(d) If the juvenile is in custody or custody is requested, the juvenile may be detained pending the completion of the arraignment if it appears to the court that one of the circumstances in MCR 3.935(D)(1) is present.

(3) *Amendment of Petition.* If a petition submitted by the prosecuting attorney alleging a specified juvenile violation did not include a designation of the case for trial as an adult:

(a) The prosecuting attorney may, by right, amend the petition to designate the case during the preliminary hearing.

(b) The prosecuting attorney may request leave of the court to amend the petition to designate the case no later than the pretrial hearing or, if there is no pretrial hearing, at least 21 days before trial, absent good cause for further delay. The court may permit the prosecuting attorney to amend the petition to designate the case as the interests of justice require.

(B) **Court-Designated Cases**. The procedures in this subrule apply if the prosecuting attorney submits a petition charging an offense other than a specified juvenile violation and requests the court to designate the case for trial in the same manner as an adult.

(1) *Time for Arraignment.*

(a) If the juvenile is in custody or custody is requested, the arraignment must commence no later than 24 hours after the juvenile has been taken into court custody, excluding Sundays and holidays as defined by MCR 8.110(D)(2), or the juvenile must be released. The court may adjourn the arraignment for up to 7 days to secure the attendance of the juvenile's parent, guardian, or legal custodian or of a witness, or for other good cause shown.

(b) If the juvenile is not in custody and custody is not requested, the juvenile must be brought before the court for an arraignment as soon as the juvenile's attendance can be secured.

(2) *Procedure.*

(a) The court shall determine whether the juvenile's parent, guardian, or legal custodian has been notified and is present. The arraignment may be conducted without a parent, guardian, or legal custodian, provided a guardian ad litem or attorney appears with the juvenile.

(b) The court shall read the allegations in the petition, and advise the juvenile on the record in plain language:

(i) of the right to an attorney pursuant to MCR 3.915(A)(1);

(ii) of the right to trial by judge or jury on the allegations in the petition;

(iii) of the right to remain silent and that any statement made by the juvenile may be used against the juvenile;

(iv) of the right to have a designation hearing within 14 days;

(v) of the right to have a preliminary examination within 14 days after the case is designated if the juvenile is charged with a felony or offense for which an adult could be imprisoned for more than one year;

(vi) that if the case is designated by the court for trial in the same manner as an adult and, if a preliminary examination is required by law, the prosecuting attorney proves that there is probable cause to believe that an offense was committed and there is probable cause to believe that the juvenile committed the offense, the juvenile will be afforded all the rights of an adult charged with the same crime and that upon conviction the juvenile may be sentenced as an adult;

(vii) of the maximum possible prison sentence and any mandatory minimum sentence required by law.

(c) Unless the arraignment is adjourned, the court must decide whether to authorize the petition to be filed. If it authorizes the filing of the petition, the court must:

(i) determine if fingerprints must be taken as provided by MCR 3.936;

(ii) schedule a designation hearing within 14 days;

(iii) if the juvenile is in custody or custody is requested, determine whether to detain or release the juvenile as provided in MCR 3.935(C).

(d) If the juvenile is in custody or custody is requested, the juvenile may be detained pending the completion of the arraignment if it appears to the court that one of the circumstances in MCR 3.935(D)(1) is present.

(3) *Amendment of Petition*. If a petition submitted by the prosecuting attorney alleging an offense other than a specified juvenile violation did not include a request that the court designate the case for trial as an adult:

(a) The prosecuting attorney may, by right, amend the petition to request the court to designate the case during the preliminary hearing.

(b) The prosecuting attorney may request leave of the court to amend the petition to request the court to designate the case no later than the pretrial hearing or, if there is no pretrial hearing, at least 21 days before trial, absent good cause for further delay. The court may permit the prosecuting attorney to amend the petition to request the court to designate the case as the interests of justice require.

Rule 3.952 Designation Hearing

(A) **Time**. The designation hearing shall be commenced within 14 days after the arraignment, unless adjourned for good cause.

(B) **Notice**.

(1) A copy of the petition or a copy of the petition and separate written request for court designation must be personally served on the juvenile and the juvenile's parent, guardian, or legal custodian, if the address or whereabouts of the juvenile's parent, guardian, or custodian is known or can be determined by the exercise of due diligence.

(2) Notice of the date, time, and place of the designation hearing must be given to the juvenile, the juvenile's parent, guardian, or legal custodian, the attorney for the juvenile, if any, and the prosecuting attorney. The notice may be given either orally on the record or in writing, served on each individual by mail, or given in another manner reasonably calculated to provide notice.

(C) **Hearing Procedure**.

(1) *Evidence*. The Michigan Rules of Evidence, other than those with respect to privileges, do not apply.

(2) *Burden of Proof*. The prosecuting attorney has the burden of proving by a preponderance of the evidence that the best interests of the juvenile and the public would be served by designation.

(3) *Factors to be Considered*. In determining whether to designate the case for trial in the same manner as an adult, the court must consider all the following factors, giving greater weight to the seriousness of the alleged offense and the juvenile's prior delinquency record than to the other factors:

(a) the seriousness of the alleged offense in terms of community protection, including, but not limited to, the existence of any aggravating factors recognized by the sentencing guidelines, the use of a firearm or other dangerous weapon, and the effect on any victim;

(b) the culpability of the juvenile in committing the alleged offense, including, but not limited to, the level of the juvenile's participation in planning and carrying out the offense and the existence of any aggravating or mitigating factors recognized by the sentencing guidelines;

(c) the juvenile's prior record of delinquency, including, but not limited to, any record of

detention, any police record, any school record, or any other evidence indicating prior delinquent behavior;
(d) the juvenile's programming history, including, but not limited to, the juvenile's past willingness to participate meaningfully in available programming;
(e) the adequacy of the punishment or programming available in the juvenile justice system; and
(f) the dispositional options available for the juvenile.

(D) **Grant of Request for Court Designation**.
(1) If the court determines that it is in the best interests of the juvenile and the public that the juvenile be tried in the same manner as an adult in the family division of the circuit court, the court must:
(a) Enter a written order granting the request for court designation and
(i) schedule a preliminary examination within 14 days if the juvenile is charged with a felony or an offense for which an adult could be imprisoned for more than one year, or
(ii) schedule the matter for trial or pretrial hearing if the juvenile is charged with a misdemeanor.
(b) Make findings of fact and conclusions of law forming the basis for entry of the order designating the petition. The findings and conclusions may be incorporated in a written opinion or stated on the record.

(E) **Denial of Request for Designation**. If the request for court designation is denied, the court shall make written findings or place them on the record. Further proceedings shall be conducted pursuant to MCR 3.941-3.944.

Rule 3.953 Preliminary Examination in Designated Cases

(A) **Requirement**. A preliminary examination must be held only in designated cases in which the juvenile is alleged to have committed a felony or an offense for which an adult could be imprisoned for more than one year.

(B) **Waiver**. The juvenile may waive the preliminary examination if the juvenile is represented by an attorney and the waiver is made and signed by the juvenile in open court. The judge shall find and place on the record that the waiver was freely, understandingly, and voluntarily given.

(C) **Combined Hearing**. The preliminary examination may be combined with a designation hearing provided that the Michigan Rules of Evidence, except as otherwise provided by law, apply only to the preliminary examination phase of the combined hearing.

(D) **Time**. The preliminary examination must commence within 14 days of the arraignment in a prosecutor-designated case or within 14 days after court-ordered designation of a petition, unless the preliminary examination was combined with the designation hearing.

(E) **Procedure**. The preliminary examination must be conducted in accordance with MCR 6.110.

(F) **Findings**.
(1) If the court finds there is probable cause to believe that the alleged offense was committed and probable cause to believe the juvenile committed the offense, the court may schedule the matter for trial or a pretrial hearing.
(2) If the court does not find there is probable cause to believe that the alleged offense was committed or does not find there is probable cause to believe the juvenile committed the offense, the court shall dismiss the petition, unless the court finds there is probable cause to believe that a lesser included offense was committed and probable cause to believe the juvenile committed that offense.
(3) If the court finds there is probable cause to believe that a lesser included offense was committed and probable cause to believe the juvenile committed that offense, the court may, as provided in MCR 3.952, further determine whether the case should be designated as a case in which the juvenile should be tried in the same manner as an adult. If the court designates the case following the determination of probable cause under this subrule, the court may schedule the matter for trial or a pretrial hearing.

(G) **Confinement**. If the court has designated the case and finds probable cause to believe that a felony or an offense for which an adult could be imprisoned for more than one year has been committed and probable cause to believe that the juvenile committed the offense, the judge may confine the juvenile in the county jail pending trial. If the juvenile is under 17 years of age, the juvenile may be confined in jail only if the juvenile can be separated by sight and sound from adult prisoners and if the sheriff has approved the confinement.

Rule 3.954 Trial of Designated Cases

Trials of designated cases are governed by subchapter 6.400, except for MCR 6.402(A). The court may not accept a waiver of trial by jury until after the juvenile has been offered an opportunity to consult with a lawyer. Pleas in designated cases are governed by subchapter 6.300.

Rule 3.955 Sentencing or Disposition in Designated Cases

(A) **Determining Whether to Sentence or Impose Disposition**. If a juvenile is convicted under MCL

712A.2d, sentencing or disposition shall be made as provided in MCL 712A.18(1)(n) and the Crime Victim's Rights Act, MCL 780.751 et seq., if applicable. In deciding whether to enter an order of disposition, or impose or delay imposition of sentence, the court shall consider all the following factors, giving greater weight to the seriousness of the offense and the juvenile's prior record:

(1) the seriousness of the alleged offense in terms of community protection, including but not limited to, the existence of any aggravating factors recognized by the sentencing guidelines, the use of a firearm or other dangerous weapon, and the effect on any victim;

(2) the culpability of the juvenile in committing the alleged offense, including, but not limited to, the level of the juvenile's participation in planning and carrying out the offense and the existence of any aggravating or mitigating factors recognized by the sentencing guidelines;

(3) the juvenile's prior record of delinquency including, but not limited to, any record of detention, any police record, any school record, or any other evidence indicating prior delinquent behavior;

(4) the juvenile's programming history, including, but not limited to, the juvenile's past willingness to participate meaningfully in available programming;

(5) the adequacy of the punishment or programming available in the juvenile justice system; and

(6) the dispositional options available for the juvenile. The court also shall give the juvenile, the juvenile`s lawyer, the prosecutor, and the victim an opportunity to advise the court of any circumstances they believe the court should consider in deciding whether to enter an order of disposition or to impose or delay imposition of sentence.

(B) **Burden of Proof**. The court shall enter an order of disposition unless the court determines that the best interests of the public would be served by sentencing the juvenile as an adult. The prosecuting attorney has the burden of proving by a preponderance of the evidence that, on the basis of the criteria in subrule (A), it would be in the best interests of the public to sentence the juvenile as an adult.

(C) **Sentencing**. If the court determines that the juvenile should be sentenced as an adult, either initially or following a delayed imposition of sentence, the sentencing hearing shall be held in accordance with the procedures set forth in MCR 6.425.

(D) **Delayed Imposition of Sentence**. If the court determines that the juvenile should be sentenced as an adult, the court may, in its discretion, enter an order of disposition delaying imposition of sentence and placing the juvenile on probation on such terms and conditions as it considers appropriate, including ordering any disposition under MCL 712A.18. A delayed sentence may be imposed in accordance with MCR 3.956.

(E) **Disposition Hearing**. If the court does not determine that the juvenile should be sentenced as an adult, the court shall hold a dispositional hearing and comply with the procedures set forth in MCR 3.943.

Rule 3.956 Review Hearings; Probation Violation

(A) **Review Hearings in Delayed Imposition of Sentence Cases**.

(1) *When Required*. If the court entered an order of disposition delaying imposition of sentence, the court shall conduct a review hearing to determine whether the juvenile has been rehabilitated and whether the juvenile presents a serious risk to public safety.

(a) Time of Hearing.

(i) Annual Review. The court shall conduct an annual review of the probation, including, but not limited to, the services being provided to the juvenile, the juvenile's placement, and the juvenile's progress in placement. In conducting the review, the court must examine any report prepared under MCL 803.223, and any report prepared by the officer or agency supervising probation. The court may order changes in the juvenile's probation on the basis of the review including, but not limited to, imposition of sentence.

(ii) Review on Request of Institution or Agency. If an institution or agency to which the juvenile was committed believes that the juvenile has been rehabilitated and does not present a serious risk to public safety, the institution or agency may petition the court to conduct a review hearing at any time before the juvenile becomes 19 years of age or, if the court has extended jurisdiction, any time before the juvenile becomes 21 years of age.

(iii) Mandatory Review. The court shall schedule a review hearing to be held within 42 days before the juvenile attains the age of 19, unless adjourned for good cause.

(iv) Final Review. The court shall conduct a final review of the juvenile's probation not less than 91 days before the end of the probation period.

(b) Notice of Hearing. Notice of the hearing must be given at least 14 days before the hearing to

(i) the prosecuting attorney;

(ii) the agency or the superintendent of the institution or facility to which the juvenile has been committed;

(iii) the juvenile; and
(iv) if the address or whereabouts are known, the parent, guardian, or legal custodian of the juvenile.

The notice must clearly indicate that the court may extend jurisdiction over the juvenile or impose sentence and must advise the juvenile and the parent, guardian, or legal custodian of the juvenile that the juvenile has a right to an attorney.

(2) *Appointment of Attorney.* The court must appoint an attorney to represent the juvenile unless an attorney has been retained. The court may assess the cost of providing an attorney as costs against the juvenile or those responsible for the juvenile's support, or both, if the persons to be assessed are financially able to comply.

(3) *Evidence; Commitment Report.* The court may consider the commitment report prepared as provided in MCL 803.225 and any report prepared upon the court's order by the officer or agency supervising probation.

(4) *Burden of Proof; Findings.*

(a) Before the court may continue jurisdiction over the juvenile or impose sentence, the prosecuting attorney must demonstrate by a preponderance of the evidence that the juvenile has not been rehabilitated or that the juvenile presents a serious risk to public safety. The Michigan Rules of Evidence, other than those with respect to privileges, do not apply. In making the determination, the court must consider the following factors:

(i) the extent and nature of the juvenile's participation in education, counseling, or work programs;
(ii) the juvenile's willingness to accept responsibility for prior behavior;
(iii) the juvenile's behavior in the current placement;
(iv) the juvenile's prior record, character, and physical and mental maturity;
(v) the juvenile's potential for violent conduct as demonstrated by prior behavior;
(vi) the recommendation of the institution, agency, or facility charged with the juvenile's care for the juvenile's release or continued custody;
(vii) any other information the prosecuting attorney or the juvenile submit.

(b) Before the court may impose a sentence at the final review hearing, the court must determine that the best interests of the public would be served by the imposition of a sentence provided by law for an adult offender. In making the determination, the court must consider the following factors, in addition to the criteria specified in subrule (4)(a):

(i) the effect of treatment on the juvenile's rehabilitation;
(ii) whether the juvenile is likely to be dangerous to the public if released;
(iii) the best interests of the public welfare and the protection of public security.

(5) *Sentencing credit.* If a sentence of imprisonment is imposed, the juvenile shall receive credit for the time served on probation.

(B) **Violation of Probation in Delayed Imposition of Sentence Cases.**

(1) *Subsequent Conviction.* If a juvenile placed on probation under an order of disposition delaying imposition of sentence is found by the court to have violated probation by being convicted of a felony or a misdemeanor punishable by imprisonment for more than 1 year, or adjudicated as responsible for an offense that if committed by an adult would be a felony or a misdemeanor punishable by imprisonment for more than 1 year, the court shall revoke probation and sentence the juvenile to imprisonment for a term that does not exceed the penalty that could have been imposed for the offense for which the juvenile was originally convicted and placed on probation.

(2) *Other Violations of Probation.* If a juvenile placed on probation under an order of disposition delaying imposition of sentence is found by the court to have violated probation other than as provided in subrule (B)(1), the court may impose sentence or may order any of the following for the juvenile:

(a) A change in placement.
(b) Community service.
(c) Substance abuse counseling.
(d) Mental health counseling.
(e) Participation in a vocational-technical program.
(f) Incarceration in the county jail for not more than 30 days if the present county jail facility would meet all requirements under federal law and regulations for housing juveniles, and if the court has consulted with the sheriff to determine when the sentence will begin to ensure that space will be available for the juvenile. If the juvenile is under 17 years of age, the juvenile must be placed in a room or ward out of sight and sound from adult prisoners.
(g) Other participation or performance as the court considers necessary.

(3) *Hearing.* The probation violation hearing must be conducted pursuant to MCR 3.944(C).

(4) *Sentencing Credit.* If a sentence of imprisonment is imposed, the juvenile must receive credit for the time served on probation.

Rule 3.961 Initiating Child Protective Proceedings

(A) **Form**. Absent exigent circumstances, a request for court action to protect a child must be in the form of a petition.

(B) **Content of Petition**. A petition must contain the following information, if known:

(1) The child's name, address, and date of birth.

(2) The names and addresses of:

(a) the child's mother and father,

(b) the parent, guardian, legal custodian, or person who has custody of the child, if other than a mother or father,

(c) the nearest known relative of the child, if no parent, guardian, or legal custodian can be found, and

(d) any court with prior continuing jurisdiction.

(3) The essential facts that constitute an offense against the child under the Juvenile Code.

(4) A citation to the section of the Juvenile Code relied on for jurisdiction.

(5) The child's membership or eligibility for membership in an Indian tribe, if any, and the identity of the tribe.

(6) The type of relief requested. A request for removal of the child or a parent or for termination of parental rights at the initial disposition must be specifically stated. If the petition requests removal of an Indian child or if an Indian child was taken into protective custody pursuant to MCR 3.963 as a result of an emergency, the petition must specifically describe:

(a) the active efforts as defined in MCR 3.002, that have been made to provide remedial services and rehabilitative programs designed to prevent the breakup of the Indian family; and

(b) documentation, including attempts, to identify the child's tribe.

(7) The information required by MCR 3.206(A)(4), identifying whether a family division matter involving members of the same family is or was pending.

Rule 3.962 Preliminary Inquiry

(A) **Purpose**. When a petition is not accompanied by a request for placement of the child and the child is not in temporary custody, the court may conduct a preliminary inquiry to determine the appropriate action to be taken on a petition.

(B) **Action by Court**. A preliminary inquiry need not be conducted on the record or in the presence of the parties. At the preliminary inquiry, the court may:

(1) Deny authorization of the petition.

(2) Refer the matter to alternative services.

(3) Authorize the filing of the petition if it contains the information required by MCR 3.961(B), and there is probable cause to believe that one or more of the allegations is true. For the purpose of this subrule, probable cause may be established with such information and in such a manner as the court deems sufficient.

Rule 3.963 Acquiring Physical Custody of Child

(A) **Taking Custody Without Court Order**.

(1) An officer may without court order remove a child from the child's surroundings and take the child into protective custody if, after investigation, the officer has reasonable grounds to believe that a child is at substantial risk of harm or is in surroundings that present an imminent risk of harm and the child's immediate removal from those surroundings is necessary to protect the child's health and safety. If the child is an Indian child who resides or is domiciled on a reservation, but is temporarily located off the reservation, the officer may take the child into protective custody only when necessary to prevent imminent physical damage or harm to the child.

(2) An officer who takes a child into protective custody under this rule shall immediately notify the Department of Human Services. While awaiting the arrival of the Department of Human Services, the child shall not be held in a detention facility.

(3) If a child taken into protective custody under this subrule is not released, the Department of Human Services shall immediately contact the designated judge or referee as provided in subrule (D) to seek an ex parte court order for placement of the child pursuant to subrule (B)(4).

(B) **Court-Ordered Custody**.

(1) *Order to Take Child into Protective Custody*. The court may issue a written order, electronically or otherwise, authorizing a child protective services worker, an officer, or other person deemed suitable by the court to immediately take a child into protective custody when, after presentment of a petition or affidavit of facts to the court, the court has reasonable cause to believe that all the following conditions exist, together with specific findings of fact:

(a) The child is at substantial risk of harm or is in surroundings that present an imminent risk of harm and the child's immediate removal from those surroundings is necessary to protect the child's health and safety. If the child is an Indian child who resides or is domiciled on a reservation, but is temporarily located off the reservation, the child is subject to the exclusive jurisdiction of the tribal court. However, the state court may enter an order for protective custody of that child when it is necessary to

prevent imminent physical damage or harm to the child.
(b) The circumstances warrant issuing an order pending the hearing.
(c) Consistent with the circumstances, reasonable efforts were made to prevent or eliminate the need for removal of the child.
(d) No remedy other than protective custody is reasonably available to protect the child.
(e) Continuing to reside in the home is contrary to the child's welfare.

(2) The court may include in such an order authorization to enter specified premises to remove the child.

(3) The court shall inquire whether a member of the child's immediate or extended family is available to take custody of the child pending preliminary hearing, whether there has been a central registry clearance, and whether a criminal history check has been initiated.

(4) *Ex parte Placement Order*. If an officer has taken a child into protective custody without court order under subsection (A), or if the Department of Human Services is requesting the court grant it protective custody and placement authority, the Department of Human Services shall present to the court a petition or affidavit of facts and request a written ex parte placement order. If a judge finds all the factors in subrule (B)(1)(a)-(e) are present, the judge may issue a placement order; if a referee finds all the factors in subrule (B)(1)(a)-(e) are present, the referee may issue an interim placement order pending a preliminary hearing. The written order shall contain specific findings of fact. It shall be communicated, electronically or otherwise, to the Department of Human Services.

(C) **Arranging for Court Appearance**. An officer or other person who takes a child into protective custody must:

(1) immediately attempt to notify the child's parent, guardian, or legal custodian of the protective custody;
(2) inform the parent, guardian, or legal custodian of the date, time, and place of the preliminary or emergency removal hearing scheduled by the court;
(3) immediately bring the child to the court for preliminary hearing, or immediately contact the court for instructions regarding placement pending preliminary hearing;
(4) if the court is not open, DHS must contact the person designated under subrule (D) for permission to place the child pending the hearing;
(5) ensure that the petition is prepared and submitted to the court;
(6) file a custody statement with the court that includes:
(a) a specific and detailed account of the circumstances that led to the emergency removal, and
(b) the names of persons notified and the times of notification or the reason for failure to notify.

(D) **Designated Court Contact**

(1) When the Department of Human Services seeks a placement order for a child in protective custody under subrule (A) or (B), DHS shall contact a judge or referee designated by the court for that purpose.
(2) If the court is closed, the designated judge or referee may issue an ex parte order for placement upon receipt, electronically or otherwise, of a petition or affidavit of facts. The order must be communicated in writing, electronically or otherwise, to the appropriate county DHS office and filed with the court the next business day.

Rule 3.965 Preliminary Hearing

(A) **Time for Preliminary Hearing**.

(1) *Child in Protective Custody*. The preliminary hearing must commence no later than 24 hours after the child has been taken into protective custody, excluding Sundays and holidays, as defined by MCR 8.110(D)(2), unless adjourned for good cause shown, or the child must be released.
(2) *Severely Physically Injured or Sexually Abused Child*. When the Department of Human Services submits a petition in cases in which the child has been severely physically injured, as that term is defined in MCL 722.628(3)(c), or sexually abused, and subrule (A)(1) does not apply, the preliminary hearing must commence no later than 24 hours after the agency submits a petition or on the next business day following the submission of the petition.

(B) **Procedure**.

(1) The court must determine if the parent, guardian, or legal custodian has been notified, and if the lawyer-guardian ad litem for the child is present. The preliminary hearing may be adjourned for the purpose of securing the appearance of an attorney, parent, guardian, or legal custodian or may be conducted in the absence of the parent, guardian, or legal custodian if notice has been given or if the court finds that a reasonable attempt to give notice was made.
(2) The court must inquire if the child or either parent is a member of an Indian tribe. If the court knows or has reason to know the child is an Indian child, the court must determine the identity of the child's tribe and, if the child was taken into protective custody pursuant to MCR 3.963(A) or the petition requests removal of the child, follow the procedures set forth in MCR 3.967. If necessary, the court may adjourn the preliminary hearing pending the

conclusion of the removal hearing. A removal hearing may be held in conjunction with the preliminary hearing if all necessary parties have been notified as required by MCR 3.905, there are no objections by the parties to do so, and at least one qualified expert witness is present to provide testimony.

(3) The child's lawyer-guardian ad litem must be present to represent the child at the preliminary hearing. The court may make temporary orders for the protection of the child pending the appearance of an attorney or pending the completion of the preliminary hearing. The court must direct that the lawyer-guardian ad litem for the child receive a copy of the petition.

(4) If the respondent is present, the court must assure that the respondent has a copy of the petition. The court must read the allegations in the petition in open court, unless waived.

(5) The court shall determine if the petition should be dismissed or the matter referred to alternate services. If the court so determines the court must release the child. Otherwise, the court must continue the hearing.

(6) The court must advise the respondent of the right to the assistance of an attorney at the preliminary hearing and any subsequent hearing pursuant to MCR 3.915(B)(1)(a).

(7) The court must advise the respondent of the right to trial on the allegations in the petition and that the trial may be before a referee unless a demand for a jury or judge is filed pursuant to MCR 3.911 or 3.912.

(8) The court shall allow the respondent an opportunity to deny or admit the allegations and make a statement of explanation.

(9) The court must inquire whether the child is subject to the continuing jurisdiction of another court and, if so, which court.

(10) The court may adjourn the hearing for up to 14 days to secure the attendance of witnesses or for other good cause shown. If the court knows or has reason to know the child is an Indian, the court may adjourn the hearing for up to 21 days to ensure proper notice to the tribe or Secretary of the Interior as required by MCR 3.920(C)(1). If the preliminary hearing is adjourned, the court may make temporary orders for the placement of the child when necessary to assure the immediate safety of the child, pending the completion of the preliminary hearing and subject to subrule (C), and as applicable, MCR 3.967.

(11) Unless the preliminary hearing is adjourned, the court must decide whether to authorize the filing of the petition and, if authorized, whether the child should remain in the home, be returned home, or be placed in foster care pending trial. The court may authorize the filing of the petition upon a showing of probable cause, unless waived, that one or more of the allegations in the petition are true and fall within MCL 712A.2(b). The Michigan Rules of Evidence do not apply, other than those with respect to privileges, except to the extent that such privileges are abrogated by MCL 722.631.

(12) If the court authorizes the filing of the petition, the court:

(a) may release the child to a parent, guardian, or legal custodian and may order such reasonable terms and conditions believed necessary to protect the physical health or mental well-being of the child; or

(b) may order placement of the child after making the determinations specified in subrules (C), if those determinations have not previously been made. If the child is an Indian child, the child must be placed in descending order of preference with:

(i) a member of the child's extended family,

(ii) a foster home licensed, approved, or specified by the child's tribe,

(iii) an Indian foster family licensed or approved by the department,

(iv) an institution for children approved by an Indian tribe or operated by an Indian organization that has a program suitable to meet the child's needs.

The court may order another placement for good cause shown in accordance with MCL 712B.23(3)-(5). If the Indian child's tribe has established a different order of preference than the order prescribed above, placement shall follow that tribe's order of preference as long as the placement is the least restrictive setting appropriate to the particular needs of the child, as provided in MCL 712B.23(6). The standards to be applied in meeting the preference requirements above shall be the prevailing social and cultural standards of the Indian community in which the parent or extended family resides or with which the parent or extended family members maintain social and cultural ties.

(13) The court must inquire of the parent, guardian, or legal custodian regarding the identity of relatives of the child who might be available to provide care. If the father of the child has not been identified, the court must inquire of the mother regarding the identity and whereabouts of the father.

(C) **Pretrial Placement.**

(1) *Placement; Proofs.* If the child was not released under subrule (B), the court shall receive evidence, unless waived, to establish that the criteria for placement set forth in subrule 3.965(C)(2) are present. The respondent shall be given an

opportunity to cross-examine witnesses, to subpoena witnesses, and to offer proofs to counter the admitted evidence.

(2) *Criteria*. The court may order placement of the child into foster case if the court finds all of the following:

(a) Custody of the child with the parent presents a substantial risk of harm to the child's life, physical health, or mental well-being.

(b) No provision of service or other arrangement except removal of the child is reasonably available to adequately safeguard the child from the risk as described in subrule (A).

(c) Continuing the child's residence in the home is contrary to the child's welfare.

(d) Consistent with the circumstances, reasonable efforts were made to prevent or eliminate the need for removal of the child.

(e) Conditions of child custody away from the parent are adequate to safeguard the child's health and welfare.

(3) *Contrary to the Welfare Findings*. Contrary to the welfare findings must be made. If placement is ordered, the court must make a statement of findings, in writing or on the record, explicitly including the finding that it is contrary to the welfare of the child to remain at home and the reasons supporting that finding. If the "contrary to the welfare of the child" finding is placed on the record and not in a written statement of findings, it must be capable of being transcribed. The findings may be made on the basis of hearsay evidence that possesses adequate indicia of trustworthiness. If continuing the child's residence in the home is contrary to the welfare of the child, the court shall not return the child to the home, but shall order the child place in the most family-like setting available consistent with the child's needs.

(4) *Reasonable Efforts Findings*. Reasonable efforts findings must be made. In making the reasonable efforts determination under this subrule, the child's health and safety must be of paramount concern to the court. When the court has placed a child with someone other than the custodial parent, guardian, or legal custodian, the court must determine whether reasonable efforts to prevent the removal of the child have been made or that reasonable efforts to prevent removal are not required. The court must make this determination at the earliest possible time, but no later than 60 days from the date of removal, and must state the factual basis for the determination in the court order. Nunc pro tunc orders or affidavits are not acceptable. Reasonable efforts to prevent a child's removal from the home are not required if a court of competent jurisdiction has determined that

(a) the parent has subjected the child to aggravated circumstances as listed in sections 18(1) and (2) of the Child Protection Law, MCL 722.638(1) and (2); or

(b) the parent has been convicted of 1 or more of the following:

(i) murder of another child of the parent,

(ii) voluntary manslaughter of another child of the parent,

(iii) aiding or abetting, attempting, conspiring, or soliciting to commit such a murder or such a voluntary manslaughter, or

(iv) a felony assault that results in serious bodily injury to the child or another child of the parent; or

(c) parental rights of the parent with respect to a sibling have been terminated involuntarily; or

(d) the parent is required to register under the Sex Offender Registration Act.

(5) *Record Checks; Home Study*. If the child has been placed in a relative's home,

(a) the court may order the Family Independence Agency to report the results of a criminal record check and central registry clearance of the residents of the home to the court before, or within 7 days after, the placement, and

(b) the court must order the Family Independence Agency to perform a home study with a copy to be submitted to the court not more than 30 days after the placement.

(6) *No Right to Bail*. No one has the right to post bail in a protective proceeding for the release of a child in the custody of the court.

(7) *Parenting Time or Visitation*.

(a) Unless the court suspends parenting time pursuant to MCL 712A.19b(4), or unless the child has a guardian or legal custodian, the court must permit each parent frequent parenting time with a child in placement unless parenting time, even if supervised, may be harmful to the child.

(b) If the child was living with a guardian or legal custodian, the court must determine what, if any, visitation will be permitted with the guardian or legal custodian.

(8) *Medical Information*. Unless the court has previously ordered the release of medical information, the order placing the child in foster care must include:

(a) an order that the child's parent, guardian, or legal custodian provide the supervising agency with the name and address of each of the child's medical providers, and

(b) an order that each of the child's medical providers release the child's medical records.

(D) **Advice; Initial Service Plan**. If placement is ordered, the court must, orally or in writing, inform the parties:
(1) that the agency designated to care and supervise the child will prepare an initial service plan no later than 30 days after the placement;
(2) that participation in the initial service plan is voluntary unless otherwise ordered by the court;
(3) that the general elements of an initial service plan include:
(a) the background of the child and the family,
(b) an evaluation of the experiences and problems of the child,
(c) a projection of the expected length of stay in foster care, and
(d) an identification of specific goals and projected time frames for meeting the goals;
(4) that, on motion of a party, the court will review the initial service plan and may modify the plan if it is in the best interests of the child; and
(5) that the case may be reviewed for concurrent planning.
The court shall direct the agency to identify, locate, and consult with relatives to determine if placement with a relative would be in the child`s best interests, as required by MCL 722.954a(2). In a case to which MCL 712A.18f(6) applies, the court shall require the agency to provide the name and address of the child`s attending physician of record or primary care physician.

Rule 3.966 Other Placement Review Proceedings

(A) **Review of Placement Order and Initial Service Plan**.
(1) On motion of a party, the court must review the placement order or the initial service plan, and may modify the order and plan if it is in the best interest of the child and, if removal from the parent, guardian, or legal custodian is requested, determine whether the conditions in MCR 3.965(C)(2) exist.
(2) If the child is removed from the home and disposition is not completed, the progress of the child must be reviewed no later than 182 days from the date the child was removed from the home.
(B) **Petitions to Review Placement Decisions by Supervising Agency**.
(1) *General*. The court may review placement decisions when all of the following apply:
(a) a child has been removed from the home;
(b) the supervising agency has made a placement decision after identifying, locating, and consulting with relatives to determine placement with a fit and appropriate relative who would meet the child's developmental, emotional, and physical needs as an alternative to nonrelative foster care;
(c) the supervising agency has provided written notice of the placement decision;
(d) a person receiving notice has disagreed with the placement decision and has given the child's lawyer-guardian ad litem written notice of the disagreement within 5 days of the date on which the person receives notice; and
(e) the child's lawyer-guardian ad litem determines the decision is not in the child's best interest.
(2) *Petition for Review*. If the criteria in subrule (1) are met, within 14 days after the date of the agency's written placement decision, the child's lawyer-guardian ad litem must file a petition for review.
(3) *Hearing on Petition*. The court must commence a review hearing on the record within 7 days of the filing of the petition.
(C) **Disputes Between Agency and Foster Care Review Board Regarding Change In Placement**.
(1) *General*. The court must conduct a hearing upon notice from the Foster Care Review Board that, after an investigation, it disagrees with a proposed change in placement by the agency of a child who is not a permanent ward of the Michigan Children's Institute.
(2) *Procedure*.
(a) Time. The court must set the hearing no sooner than 7 days and no later than 14 days after receipt of the notice from the Foster Care Review Board that there is a disagreement regarding a placement change.
(b) Notice. The court must provide notice of the hearing date to the foster parents, each interested party, and the prosecuting attorney if the prosecuting attorney has appeared in the case.
(c) Evidence. The court may hear testimony from the agency and any other interested party. The court may consider any other evidence bearing upon the proposed change in placement. The Rules of Evidence do not apply to a hearing under this rule.
(d) Findings. The court must order the continuation or restoration of placement unless the court finds that the proposed change in placement is in the child's best interests.

Rule 3.967 Removal Hearing for Indian Child

(A) **Child in Protective Custody**. If an Indian child is taken into protective custody pursuant to MCR 3.963(A) or (B) or MCR 3.974, a removal hearing must be completed within 14 days after removal from a parent or Indian custodian unless that parent or Indian custodian has requested an additional 20 days for the hearing pursuant to MCL 712B.9(2) or the court adjourns the hearing pursuant to MCR 3.923(G). Absent extraordinary circumstances that make additional delay unavoidable, temporary emergency custody shall not be continued for more than 45 days.

(B) **Child Not in Protective Custody**. If an Indian child has not been taken into protective custody and the petition requests removal of that child, a removal hearing must be conducted before the court may enter an order removing the Indian child from the parent or Indian custodian.

(C) Notice of the removal hearing must be sent to the parties prescribed in MCR 3.921 in compliance with MCR 3.920(C)(1).

(D) **Evidence**. An Indian child may be removed from a parent or Indian custodian, or, for an Indian child already taken into protective custody pursuant to MCR 3.963 or MCR 3.974(B), remain removed from a parent or Indian custodian pending further proceedings, only upon clear and convincing evidence, including the testimony of at least one qualified expert witness, as described in MCL 712B.17, who has knowledge about the child-rearing practices of the Indian child's tribe, that active efforts as defined in MCR 3.002 have been made to provide remedial services and rehabilitative programs designed to prevent the breakup of the Indian family, that these efforts have proved unsuccessful, and that continued custody of the child by the parent or Indian custodian is likely to result in serious emotional or physical damage to the child. The active efforts must take into account the prevailing social and cultural conditions and way of life of the Indian child's tribe.

(E) A removal hearing may be combined with any other hearing.

(F) The Indian child, if removed from home, must be placed in descending order of preference with:
   (1) a member of the child's extended family,
   (2) a foster home licensed, approved, or specified by the child's tribe,
   (3) an Indian foster family licensed or approved by department,
   (4) an institution for children approved by an Indian tribe or operated by an Indian organization that has a program suitable to meet the child's needs.

   The court may order another placement for good cause shown in accordance with MCL 712B.23(3)-(5). If the Indian child's tribe has established a different order of preference than the order prescribed in subrule (F), placement shall follow that tribe's order of preference as long as the placement is the least restrictive setting appropriate to the particular needs of the child, as provided in MCL 712B.23(6).

   The standards to be applied in meeting the preference requirements above shall be the prevailing social and cultural standards of the Indian community in which the parent or extended family resides or with which the parent or extended family members maintain social and cultural ties.

Rule 3.971 Pleas of Admission or No Contest

(A) **General**. A respondent may make a plea of admission or of no contest to the original allegations in the petition. The court has discretion to allow a respondent to enter a plea of admission or a plea of no contest to an amended petition. The plea may be taken at any time after the filing of the petition, provided that the petitioner and the attorney for the child have been notified of a plea offer to an amended petition and have been given the opportunity to object before the plea is accepted.

(B) **Advice of Rights and Possible Disposition**. Before accepting a plea of admission or plea of no contest, the court must advise the respondent on the record or in a writing that is made a part of the file:
   (1) of the allegations in the petition;
   (2) of the right to an attorney, if respondent is without an attorney;
   (3) that, if the court accepts the plea, the respondent will give up the rights to
      (a) trial by a judge or trial by a jury,
      (b) have the petitioner prove the allegations in the petition by a preponderance of the evidence,
      (c) have witnesses against the respondent appear and testify under oath at the trial,
      (d) cross-examine witnesses, and
      (e) have the court subpoena any witnesses the respondent believes could give testimony in the respondent's favor;
   (4) of the consequences of the plea, including that the plea can later be used as evidence in a proceeding to terminate parental rights if the respondent is a parent.

(C) **Voluntary, Accurate Plea**.
   (1) *Voluntary Plea*. The court shall not accept a plea of admission or of no contest without satisfying itself that the plea is knowingly, understandingly, and voluntarily made.
   (2) *Accurate Plea*. The court shall not accept a plea of admission or of no contest without establishing support for a finding that one or more of the statutory grounds alleged in the petition are true, preferably by questioning the respondent unless the offer is to plead no contest. If the plea is no contest, the court shall not question the respondent, but, by some other means, shall obtain support for a finding that one or more of the statutory grounds alleged in the petition are true. The court shall state why a plea of no contest is appropriate.

Rule 3.972 Trial

(A) **Time**. If the child is not in placement, the trial must be held within 6 months after the filing of the petition unless adjourned for good cause under MCR 3.923(G). If the child is in placement, the trial must commence as soon as possible, but not later than 63 days after the child is removed from the home unless the trial is postponed:

(1) on stipulation of the parties for good cause;

(2) because process cannot be completed; or

(3) because the court finds that the testimony of a presently unavailable witness is needed.

When trial is postponed pursuant to subrule (2) or (3), the court shall release the child to the parent, guardian, or legal custodian unless the court finds that releasing the child to the custody of the parent, guardian, or legal custodian will likely result in physical harm or serious emotional damage to the child.

(B) If the child has been removed from the home, a review hearing must be held within 182 days of the date of the child's removal from the home, even if the trial has not been completed before the expiration of that 182-day period.

(C) **Preliminary Proceedings**.

(1) The court shall determine that the proper parties are present. The respondent has the right to be present, but the court may proceed in the absence of the respondent provided notice has been served on the respondent. The child may be excused as the court determines the child's interests require.

(2) The court shall read the allegations in the petition, unless waived.

(D) **Evidentiary Matters**.

(1) *Evidence; Standard of Proof*. Except as otherwise provided in these rules, the rules of evidence for a civil proceeding and the standard of proof by a preponderance of evidence apply at the trial, notwithstanding that the petition contains a request to terminate parental rights.

(2) *Child's Statement*. Any statement made by a child under 10 years of age or an incapacitated individual under 18 years of age with a developmental disability as defined in MCL 330.1100a(21) regarding an act of child abuse, child neglect, sexual abuse, or sexual exploitation, as defined in MCL 722.622 (f), (j), (w), or (x), performed with or on the child by another person may be admitted into evidence through the testimony of a person who heard the child make the statement as provided in this subrule.

(a) A statement describing such conduct may be admitted regardless of whether the child is available to testify or not, and is substantive evidence of the act or omission if the court has found, in a hearing held before trial, that the circumstances surrounding the giving of the statement provide adequate indicia of trustworthiness. This statement may be received by the court in lieu of or in addition to the child's testimony.

(b) If the child has testified, a statement denying such conduct may be used for impeachment purposes as permitted by the rules of evidence.

(c) If the child has not testified, a statement denying such conduct may be admitted to impeach a statement admitted under subrule (2)(a) if the court has found, in a hearing held before trial, that the circumstances surrounding the giving of the statement denying the conduct provide adequate indicia of trustworthiness.

(E) **Recommendation by Lawyer-Guardian ad Litem**. At the conclusion of the proofs, the lawyer-guardian ad litem for the child may make a recommendation to the finder of fact regarding whether one or more of the statutory grounds alleged in the petition have been proven.

(F) **Verdict**. In a child protective proceeding, the verdict must be whether one or more of the statutory grounds alleged in the petition have been proven.

Rule 3.973 Dispositional Hearing

(A) **Purpose**. A dispositional hearing is conducted to determine what measures the court will take with respect to a child properly within its jurisdiction and, when applicable, against any adult, once the court has determined following trial, plea of admission, or plea of no contest that one or more of the statutory grounds alleged in the petition are true.

(B) **Notice**. Unless the dispositional hearing is held immediately after the trial, notice of hearing may be given by scheduling it on the record in the presence of the parties or in accordance with MCR 3.920.

(C) **Time**. The interval, if any, between the trial and the dispositional hearing is within the discretion of the court. When the child is in placement, the interval may not be more than 28 days, except for good cause.

(D) **Presence of Parties**.

(1) The child may be excused from the dispositional hearing as the interests of the child require.

(2) The respondent has the right to be present or may appear through an attorney.

(3) The court may proceed in the absence of parties provided that proper notice has been given.

(E) **Evidence; Reports**.

(1) The Michigan Rules of Evidence do not apply at the initial dispositional hearing, other than those with respect to privileges. However, as provided by MCL 722.631, no assertion of an evidentiary privilege, other than the privilege between attorney and client, shall prevent the receipt and use, at the dispositional phase, of materials prepared pursuant to a court-ordered examination, interview, or course of treatment.

(2) All relevant and material evidence, including oral and written reports, may be received and may be relied on to the extent of its probative value. The

court shall consider the case service plan and any written or oral information concerning the child from the child's parent, guardian, legal custodian, foster parent, child caring institution, or relative with whom the child is placed. If the agency responsible for the care and supervision of the child recommends not placing the child with the parent, guardian, or legal custodian, the agency shall report in writing what efforts were made to prevent removal, or to rectify conditions that caused removal, of the child from the home.

(3) The parties shall be given an opportunity to examine and controvert written reports so received and may be allowed to cross-examine individuals making the reports when those individuals are reasonably available.

(4) Written reports, other than those portions made confidential by law, case service plans, and court orders, including all updates and revisions, shall be available to the foster parent, child caring institution, or relative with whom the child is placed. The foster parents, child caring institution, or relative with whom the child is placed shall not have the right to cross-examine individuals making such reports or the right to controvert such reports beyond the making of a written or oral statement concerning the child as provided in subrule (E)(2).

(5) The court, upon receipt of a local foster care review board's report, shall include the report in the court's confidential social file. The court shall ensure that all parties have had the opportunity to review the report and file objections before a dispositional order, dispositional review order, or permanency planning order is entered. The court may at its discretion include recommendations from the report in its orders.

(F) **Dispositional Orders.**

(1) The court shall enter an order of disposition as provided in the Juvenile Code and these rules.

(2) The court shall not enter an order of disposition until it has examined the case service plan as provided in MCL 712A.18f. The court may order compliance with all or part of the case service plan and may enter such orders as it considers necessary in the interest of the child.

(3) The court, on consideration of the written report prepared by the agency responsible for the care and supervision of the child pursuant to MCL 712A.18f(1), shall, when appropriate, include a statement in the order of disposition as to whether reasonable efforts were made:

(a) to prevent the child's removal from home, or

(b) to rectify the conditions that caused the child to be removed from the child's home.

(4) *Medical Information*. Unless the court has previously ordered the release of medical information, the order placing the child in foster care must include the following:

(a) an order that the child's parent, guardian, or legal custodian provide the supervising agency with the name and address of each of the child's medical providers, and

(b) an order that each of the child's medical providers release the child's medical records.

(5) *Child Support*. The court may include an order requiring one or both of the child's parents to pay child support. All child support orders entered under this subrule must comply with MCL 552.605 and MCR 3.211(D).

(G) **Subsequent Review**. When the court does not terminate jurisdiction upon entering its dispositional order, it must:

(1) follow the review procedures in MCR 3.975 for a child in placement, or

(2) review the progress of a child at home pursuant to the procedures of MCR 3.974(A).

(H) **Allegations of Additional Abuse or Neglect**.

(1) Proceedings on a supplemental petition seeking termination of parental rights on the basis of allegations of additional abuse or neglect, as defined in MCL 722.622(f) and (j), of a child who is under the jurisdiction of the court are governed by MCR 3.977.

(2) Where there is no request for termination of parental rights, proceedings regarding allegations of additional abuse or neglect, as defined in MCL 722.622(f) and (j), of a child who is under the jurisdiction of the court, including those made under MCL 712A.19(1), are governed by MCR 3.974 for a child who is at home or MCR 3.975 for a child who is in foster care.

Rule 3.974 Post-Dispositional Procedures: Child at Home

(A) **Review of Child's Progress.**

(1) *General*. The court shall periodically review the progress of a child not in foster care over whom it has retained jurisdiction.

(2) *Time*. If the child was never removed from the home, the progress of the child must be reviewed no later than 182 days from the date the petition was filed and no later than 91 days after that for the first year that the child is subject to the jurisdiction of the court. After that first year, a review hearing shall be held no later than 182 days from the immediately preceding review hearing before the end of the first year and no later than every 182 days from each preceding hearing until the court terminates its jurisdiction. The review shall occur no later than 182 days after the child returns home when the child is no longer in foster care. If the child was removed from the home and subsequently

returned home, review hearings shall be held in accordance with MCR 3.975.

(3) *Change of Placement*. Except as provided in subrule (B), the court may not order a change in the placement of a child solely on the basis of a progress review. If the child over whom the court has retained jurisdiction remains at home following the initial dispositional hearing or has otherwise returned home from foster care, the court must conduct a hearing before it may order the placement of the child. Such a hearing must be conducted in the manner provided in MCR 3.975(E), except as otherwise provided in this subrule for Indian children. If the child is an Indian child, in addition to the hearing prescribed by this subrule, the court must also conduct a removal hearing in accordance with MCR 3.967 before it may order the placement of the Indian child.

(B) **Emergency Removal; Protective Custody**.

(1) *General*. If the child, over whom the court has retained jurisdiction, remains at home following the initial dispositional hearing or has otherwise returned home from foster care, the court may order the child to be taken into protective custody pending an emergency removal hearing pursuant to the conditions listed in MCR 3.963(B)(1) and upon receipt, electronically or otherwise, of a petition or affidavit of fact. If the child is an Indian child and the child resides or is domiciled within a reservation, but is temporarily located off the reservation, the court may order the child to be taken into protective custody only when necessary to prevent imminent physical damage or harm to the child.

(2) *Notice*. The court shall ensure that the parties are given notice of the hearing as provided in MCR 3.920 and MCR 3.921.

(3) *Emergency Removal Hearing*. If the court orders the child to be taken into protective custody pursuant to MCR 3.963, the court must conduct an emergency removal hearing no later than 24 hours after the child has been taken into custody, excluding Sundays and holidays as defined in MCR 8.110(D)(2). If the child is an Indian child, the court must also conduct a removal hearing in accordance with MCR 3.967 in order for the child to remain removed from a parent or Indian custodian. Unless the child is returned to the parent pending the dispositional review, the court must make a written determination that the criteria for placement listed in MCR 3.965(C)(2) are satisfied.

(a) At the emergency removal hearing, the respondent parent, guardian, or legal custodian from whom the child is removed must receive a written statement of the reasons for removal and be advised of the following rights:

(i) to be represented by an attorney at the dispositional review hearing;

(ii) to contest the continuing placement at the dispositional review hearing within 14 days; and

(iii) to use compulsory process to obtain witnesses for the dispositional review hearing.

(b) At an emergency removal hearing, the parent, guardian, or legal custodian from whom the child was removed must be given an opportunity to state why the child should not be removed from, or should be returned to, the custody of the parent, guardian, or legal custodian.

(C) **Dispositional Review Hearing; Procedure**. If the child is in placement pursuant to subrule (B), the dispositional review hearing must commence no later than 14 days after the child is placed by the court, except for good cause shown. The dispositional review hearing may be combined with the removal hearing for an Indian child prescribed by MCR 3.967. The dispositional review hearing must be conducted in accordance with the procedures and rules of evidence applicable to a dispositional hearing.

Rule 3.975 Post-dispositional Procedures: Child in Foster Care

(A) **Dispositional Review Hearings**. A dispositional review hearing is conducted to permit court review of the progress made to comply with any order of disposition and with the case service plan prepared pursuant to MCL 712A.18f and court evaluation of the continued need and appropriateness for the child to be in foster care.

(B) **Notice**. The court shall ensure that written notice of a dispositional review hearing is given to the appropriate persons in accordance with MCR. 3.920 and MCR 3.921(B)(2). The notice must inform the parties of their opportunity to participate in the hearing and that any information they wish to provide should be submitted in advance to the court, the agency, the lawyer-guardian ad litem for the child, or an attorney for one of the parties.

(C) **Time**. The court must conduct dispositional review hearings at intervals as follows, as long as the child remains in foster care:

(1) not more than 182 days after the child's removal from his or her home and no later than every 91 days after that for the first year that the child is subject to the jurisdiction of the court. After the first year that the child has been removed from his or her home and is subject to the jurisdiction of the court, a review hearing shall be held not more than 182 days from the immediately preceding review hearing before the end of that first year and no later

than every 182 days from each preceding review hearing thereafter until the case is dismissed; or

(2) if a child is under the care and supervision of the agency and is either placed with a relative and the placement is intended to be permanent or is in a permanent foster family agreement, not more than 182 days after the child has been removed from his or her home and no later than 182 days after that so long as the child is subject to the jurisdiction of the court, the Michigan Children's Institute, or other agency as provided in MCR 3.976(E)(3).

A review hearing under this subrule shall not be canceled or delayed beyond the number of days required in this subrule, regardless of whether a petition to terminate parental rights or another matter is pending.

(D) **Early Review Option**. At the initial dispositional hearing and at every regularly scheduled dispositional review hearing, the court must decide whether it will conduct the next dispositional review hearing before what would otherwise be the next regularly scheduled dispositional review hearing as provided in subrule (C). In deciding whether to shorten the interval between review hearings, the court shall, among other factors, consider:

(1) the ability and motivation of the parent, guardian, or legal custodian to make changes needed to provide the child a suitable home environment;

(2) the reasonable likelihood that the child will be ready to return home earlier than the next scheduled dispositional review hearing.

(E) **Procedure**. Dispositional review hearings must be conducted in accordance with the procedures and rules of evidence applicable to the initial dispositional hearing. The report of the agency that is filed with the court must be accessible to the parties and offered into evidence. The court shall consider any written or oral information concerning the child from the child's parent, guardian, legal custodian, foster parent, child caring institution, or relative with whom a child is placed, in addition to any other relevant and material evidence at the hearing. The court, on request of a party or on its own motion, may accelerate the hearing to consider any element of a case service plan. The court, upon receipt of a local foster care review board's report, shall include the report in the court's confidential social file. The court shall ensure that all parties have had the opportunity to review the report and file objections before a dispositional order, dispositional review order, or permanency planning order is entered. The court may at its discretion include recommendations from the report in its orders.

(F) **Criteria**.

(1) *Review of Case Service Plan*. The court, in reviewing the progress toward compliance with the case service plan, must consider:

(a) the services provided or offered to the child and parent, guardian, or legal custodian of the child;

(b) whether the parent, guardian, or legal custodian has benefited from the services provided or offered;

(c) the extent of parenting time or visitation, including a determination regarding the reasons either was not frequent or never occurred;

(d) the extent to which the parent, guardian, or legal custodian complied with each provision of the case service plan, prior court orders, and any agreement between the parent, guardian, or legal custodian and the agency;

(e) any likely harm to the child if the child continues to be separated from his or her parent, guardian, or custodian;

(f) any likely harm to the child if the child is returned to the parent, guardian, or legal custodian; and

(g) if the child is an Indian child, whether the child's placement remains appropriate and complies with MCR 3.967(F).

(2) *Progress Toward Returning Child Home*. The court must decide the extent of the progress made toward alleviating or mitigating conditions that caused the child to be, and to remain, in foster care. The court shall also review the concurrent plan, if applicable.

(G) **Dispositional Review Orders**. The court, following a dispositional review hearing, may:

(1) order the return of the child home,

(2) change the placement of the child,

(3) modify the dispositional order,

(4) modify any part of the case service plan,

(5) enter a new dispositional order, or

(6) continue the prior dispositional order.

(H) **Returning Child Home Without Dispositional Review Hearing**. Unless notice is waived, if not less than 7 days written notice is given to all parties before the return of a child to the home, and if no party requests a hearing within the 7 days, the court may issue an order without a hearing permitting the agency to return the child home.

Rule 3.976 Permanency Planning Hearings

(A) **Permanency Plan**. At or before each permanency planning hearing, the court must determine whether the agency has made reasonable efforts to finalize the permanency plan. At the hearing, the court must review the permanency plan for a child in foster care. The court must determine whether and, if applicable, when:

(1) the child may be returned to the parent, guardian, or legal custodian;

(2) a petition to terminate parental rights should be filed;

(3) the child may be placed in a legal guardianship;

(4) the child may be permanently placed with a fit and willing relative; or
(5) the child may be placed in another planned permanent living arrangement, but only in those cases where the agency has documented to the court a compelling reason for determining that it would not be in the best interests of the child to follow one of the options listed in subrules (1)-(4).

(B) **Time**.
(1) An initial permanency planning hearing must be held within 28 days after a judicial determination that reasonable efforts to reunite the family or to prevent removal are not required given one of the following circumstances:
(a) There has been a judicial determination that the child's parent has subjected the child to aggravated circumstances as listed in sections 18(1) and (2) of the Child Protection Law, 1975 PA 238, MCL 722.638.
(b) The parent has been convicted of one of the following:
(i) murder of another child of the parent;
(ii) voluntary manslaughter of another child of the parent;
(iii) aiding or abetting, attempting, conspiring, or soliciting to commit such a murder or such a voluntary manslaughter; or
(iv) a felony assault that results in serious bodily injury to the child or another child of the parent.
(c) The parent has had rights to one of the child's siblings involuntarily terminated.
(2) If subrule (1) does not apply, the court must conduct an initial permanency planning hearing no later than 12 months after the child's removal from the home, regardless of whether any supplemental petitions are pending in the case.
(3) Requirement of Annual Permanency Planning Hearings. During the continuation of foster care, the court must hold permanency planning hearings beginning no later than 12 months after the initial permanency planning hearing. The interval between permanency planning hearings is within the discretion of the court as appropriate to the circumstances of the case, but must not exceed 12 months. The court may combine the permanency planning hearing with a review hearing.
(4) The judicial determination to finalize the court-approved permanency plan must be made within the time limits prescribed in subsections (1)-(3).

(C) **Notice**. The parties entitled to participate in a permanency planning hearing include the:
(1) parents of the child, if the parent's parental rights have not been terminated,
(2) child, if the child is of an appropriate age to participate,
(3) guardian,
(4) legal custodian,
(5) foster parents,
(6) pre-adoptive parents,
(7) relative caregivers, and
(8) if the child is an Indian child, the child's tribe.
Written notice of a permanency planning hearing must be given as provided in MCR 3.920 and MCR 3.921(B)(2). The notice must include a brief statement of the purpose of the hearing, and must include a notice that the hearing may result in further proceedings to terminate parental rights. The notice must inform the parties of their opportunity to participate in the hearing and that any information they wish to provide should be submitted in advance to the court, the agency, the lawyer-guardian ad litem for the child, or an attorney for one of the parties.

(D) **Hearing Procedure; Evidence**.
(1) *Procedure*. Each permanency planning hearing must be conducted by a judge or a referee. Paper reviews, ex parte hearings, stipulated orders, or other actions that are not open to the participation of (a) the parents of the child, unless parental rights have been terminated; (b) the child, if of appropriate age; and (c) foster parents or preadoptive parents, if any, are not permanency planning hearings.
(2) *Evidence*. The Michigan Rules of Evidence do not apply, other than those with respect to privileges, except to the extent such privileges are abrogated by MCL 722.631. At the permanency planning hearing all relevant and material evidence, including oral and written reports, may be received by the court and may be relied upon to the extent of its probative value. The court must consider any written or oral information concerning the child from the child's parent, guardian, custodian, foster parent, child caring institution, or relative with whom the child is placed, in addition to any other evidence offered at the hearing. The court shall obtain the child's views regarding the permanency plan in a manner appropriate to the child's age. The parties must be afforded an opportunity to examine and controvert written reports received and may be allowed to cross-examine individuals who made the reports when those individuals are reasonably available.
(3) The court, upon receipt of a local foster care review board's report, shall include the report in the court's confidential social file. The court shall ensure that all parties have had the opportunity to review the report and file objections before a dispositional order, dispositional review order, or permanency planning order is entered. The court may at its

discretion include recommendations from the report in its orders.

(E) **Determinations; Permanency Options.**

(1) In the case of a child who will not be returned home, the court shall consider in-state and out-of-state placement options. In the case of a child placed out of state, the court shall determine whether the out-of-state placement continues to be appropriate and in the child's best interests. The court shall ensure that the agency is providing appropriate services to assist a child who will transition from foster care to independent living.

(2) *Determining Whether to Return Child Home.* At the conclusion of a permanency planning hearing, the court must order the child returned home unless it determines that the return would cause a substantial risk of harm to the life, the physical health, or the mental well-being of the child. Failure to substantially comply with the case service plan is evidence that the return of the child to the parent may cause a substantial risk of harm to the child's life, physical health, or mental well-being. In addition, the court shall consider any condition or circumstance of the child that may be evidence that a return to the parent would cause a substantial risk of harm to the child's life, physical health, or mental well-being.

(3) *Continuing Foster Care Pending Determination on Termination of Parental Rights.* If the court determines at a permanency planning hearing that the child should not be returned home, it may order the agency to initiate proceedings to terminate parental rights. Except as otherwise provided in this subsection, if the child has been in foster care under the responsibility of the state for 15 of the most recent 22 months, the court shall order the agency to initiate proceedings to terminate parental rights. If the court orders the agency to initiate proceedings to terminate parental rights, the order must specify the date, or the time within which the petition must be filed. In either case, the petition must be filed no later than 28 days after the date the permanency planning hearing is concluded. The court is not required to order the agency to initiate proceedings to terminate parental rights if one or more of the following apply:

(a) The child is being cared for by relatives.

(b) The case service plan documents a compelling reason for determining that filing a petition to terminate parental rights would not be in the best interests of the child. A compelling reason not to file a petition to terminate parental rights includes, but is not limited to, any of the following:

(i) Adoption is not the appropriate permanency goal for the child.

(ii) No grounds to file a petition to terminate parental rights exist.

(iii) The child is an unaccompanied refugee minor as defined in 45 CFR 400.111.

(iv) There are international legal obligations or compelling foreign policy reasons that preclude terminating parental rights.

(c) The state has not provided the child's family, during the period set in the case service plan, with the services the state considers necessary for the child's safe return to his or her home, if reasonable efforts to reunify the family are required.

If the court does not require the agency to initiate proceedings to terminate parental rights under this provision, the court shall state on the record the reason or reasons for its decision.

(4) *Other Permanency Plans.* If the court does not return the child to the parent, guardian, or legal custodian and if the agency demonstrates that termination of parental rights is not in the best interests of the child, the court may

(a) continue the placement of the child in foster care for a limited period to be set by the court if the court while the agency continues to make reasonable efforts to finalize the court-approved permanency plan for the child,

(b) place the child with a fit and willing relative,

(c) upon a showing of compelling reasons, place the child in an alternative planned permanent living arrangement, or

(d) appoint a juvenile guardian for the child pursuant to MCL 712A.19a and MCR 3.979.

The court must articulate the factual basis for its determination in the court order adopting the permanency plan.

Rule 3.977 Termination of Parental Rights

(A) **General.**

(1) This rule applies to all proceedings in which termination of parental rights is sought . Proceedings for termination of parental rights involving an Indian child, are governed by 25 USC 1912 in addition to this rule.

(2) Parental rights of the respondent over the child may not be terminated unless termination was requested in an original, amended, or supplemental petition by:

(a) the agency,

(b) the child,

(c) the guardian, legal custodian, or representative of the child,

(d) a concerned person as defined in MCL 712A.19b(6),

(e) the state children's ombudsman, or

(f) the prosecuting attorney, without regard to whether the prosecuting attorney is representing or acting as a legal consultant to the agency or any other party.

(3) The burden of proof is on the party seeking by court order to terminate the rights of the respondent over the child. There is no right to a jury determination.

(B) **Definition**. When used in this rule, unless the context otherwise indicates, "respondent" includes

(1) the natural or adoptive mother of the child;

(2) the father of the child as defined by MCR 3.903(A)(7).

"Respondent" does not include other persons to whom legal custody has been given by court order, persons who are acting in the place of the mother or father, or other persons responsible for the control, care, and welfare of the child.

(C) **Notice; Priority**.

(1) Notice must be given as provided in MCR 3.920 and MCR 3.921(B)(3).

(2) Hearings on petitions seeking termination of parental rights shall be given the highest possible priority consistent with the orderly conduct of the court`s caseload.

(D) **Suspension of Parenting Time**. If a petition to terminate parental rights to a child is filed, the court may suspend parenting time for a parent who is a subject of the petition.

(E) **Termination of Parental Rights at the Initial Disposition**. The court shall order termination of the parental rights of a respondent at the initial dispositional hearing held pursuant to MCR 3.973, and shall order that additional efforts for reunification of the child with the respondent shall not be made, if

(1) the original, or amended, petition contains a request for termination;

(2) at the trial or plea proceedings, the trier of fact finds by a preponderance of the evidence that one or more of the grounds for assumption of jurisdiction over the child under MCL 712A.2(b) have been established;

(3) at the initial disposition hearing, the court finds on the basis of clear and convincing legally admissible evidence that had been introduced at the trial or plea proceedings, or that is introduced at the dispositional hearing, that one or more facts alleged in the petition:

(a) are true, and

(b) establish grounds for termination of parental rights under MCL 712A.19b(3)(a), (b), (d), (e), (f), (g), (h), (i), (j), (k), (l), (m), or (n);

(4) termination of parental rights is in the child's best interests.

(F) **Termination of Parental Rights on the Basis of Different Circumstances**. The court may take action on a supplemental petition that seeks to terminate the parental rights of a respondent over a child already within the jurisdiction of the court on the basis of one or more circumstances new or different from the offense that led the court to take jurisdiction.

(1) The court must order termination of the parental rights of a respondent, and must order that additional efforts for reunification of the child with the respondent must not be made, if

(a) the supplemental petition for termination of parental rights contains a request for termination;

(b) at the hearing on the supplemental petition, the court finds on the basis of clear and convincing legally admissible evidence that one or more of the facts alleged in the supplemental petition:

(i) are true; and

(ii) come within MCL 712A.19b(3)(a), (b), (c)(ii), (d), (e), (f), (g), (i), (j), (k), (l), (m), or (n);and

(c) termination of parental rights is in the child's best interests.

(2) Time for Hearing on Petition. The hearing on a supplemental petition for termination of parental rights under this subrule shall be held within 42 days after the filing of the supplemental petition. The court may, for good cause shown, extend the period for an additional 21 days.

(G) **Termination of Parental Rights; Indian Child**. In addition to the required findings in this rule, the parental rights of a parent of an Indian child must not be terminated unless:

(1) the court is satisfied that active efforts as defined in MCR 3.002 have been made to provide remedial service and rehabilitative programs designed to prevent the breakup of the Indian family and that these efforts have proved unsuccessful, and

(2) the court finds evidence beyond a reasonable doubt, including testimony of at least one qualified expert witness as described in MCL 712B.17, that parental rights should be terminated because continued custody of the child by the parent or Indian custodian will likely result in serious emotional or physical damage to the child.

(H) **Termination of Parental Rights; Other**. If the parental rights of a respondent over the child were not terminated pursuant to subrule (E) at the initial dispositional hearing or pursuant to subrule (F) at a hearing on a supplemental petition on the basis of different circumstances, and the child is within the jurisdiction of the court, the court must, if the child is in foster care, or may, if the child is not in foster care, following a dispositional review hearing under MCR 3.975, a progress review under MCR 3.974, or a permanency planning hearing under MCR 3.976, take action on a supplemental petition that seeks to terminate the parental rights of a respondent over the child on the basis of one or more grounds listed in MCL 712A.19b(3).

(1) *Time.*

(a) Filing Petition. The supplemental petition for termination of parental rights may be filed at any time after the initial dispositional review hearing, progress review, or permanency planning hearing, whichever occurs first.

(b) Hearing on Petition. The hearing on a supplemental petition for termination of parental rights under this subrule must be held within 42 days after the filing of the supplemental petition. The court may, for good cause shown, extend the period for an additional 21 days.

(2) *Evidence.* The Michigan Rules of Evidence do not apply, other than those with respect to privileges, except to the extent such privileges are abrogated by MCL 722.631. At the hearing all relevant and material evidence, including oral and written reports, may be received by the court and may be relied upon to the extent of its probative value. The parties must be afforded an opportunity to examine and controvert written reports received by the court and shall be allowed to cross-examine individuals who made the reports when those individuals are reasonably available.

(3) *Order.* The court must order termination of the parental rights of a respondent and must order that additional efforts for reunification of the child with the respondent must not be made, if the court finds

(a) on the basis of clear and convincing evidence admitted pursuant to subrule (H)(2) that one or more facts alleged in the petition:

(i) are true; and

(ii) come within MCL 712A.19b(3).

(b) that termination of parental rights is in the child's best interests.

(I) **Findings**.

(1) *General.* The court shall state on the record or in writing its findings of fact and conclusions of law. Brief, definite, and pertinent findings and conclusions on contested matters are sufficient. If the court does not issue a decision on the record following hearing, it shall file its decision within 28 days after the taking of final proofs, but no later than 70 days after the commencement of the hearing to terminate parental rights.

(2) *Denial of Termination.* If the court finds that the parental rights of respondent should not be terminated, the court must make findings of fact and conclusions of law.

(3) *Order of Termination.* An order terminating parental rights under the Juvenile Code may not be entered unless the court makes findings of fact, states its conclusions of law, and includes the statutory basis for the order.

(J) **Respondent's Rights Following Termination**.

(1) *Advice.* Immediately after entry of an order terminating parental rights, the court shall advise the respondent parent orally or in writing that:

(a) The respondent is entitled to appellate review of the order.

(b) If the respondent is financially unable to provide an attorney to perfect an appeal, the court will appoint an attorney and furnish the attorney with the portions of the transcript and record the attorney requires to appeal.

(c) A request for the assistance of an attorney must be made within 14 days after notice of the order is given or an order is entered denying a timely filed postjudgment motion. The court must then give a form to the respondent with the instructions (to be repeated on the form) that if the respondent desires the appointment of an attorney, the form must be returned to the court within the required period (to be stated on the form).

(d) The respondent has the right to file a denial of release of identifying information, a revocation of a denial of release, and to keep current the respondent's name and address as provided in MCL 710.27.

(2) *Appointment of Attorney.*

(a) If a request is timely filed and the court finds that the respondent is financially unable to provide an attorney, the court shall appoint an attorney within 14 days after the respondent's request is filed. The chief judge of the court shall bear primary responsibility for ensuring that the appointment is made within the deadline stated in this rule.

(b) In a case involving the termination of parental rights, the order described in (J)(2) and (3) must be entered on a form approved by the State Court Administrator's Office, entitled "Claim of Appeal and Order Appointing Counsel," and the court must immediately send to the Court of Appeals a copy of the Claim of Appeal and Order Appointing Counsel, a copy of the judgment or order being appealed, and a copy of the complete register of actions in the case. The court must also file in the Court of Appeals proof of having made service of the Claim of Appeal and Order Appointing Counsel on the respondent(s), appointed counsel for the respondent(s), the court reporter(s)/recorder(s), petitioner, the prosecuting attorney, the lawyer-guardian ad litem for the child(ren) under MCL 712A.13a(1)(f), and the guardian ad litem or attorney (if any) for the child(ren). Entry of the order by the trial court pursuant to this subrule constitutes a timely filed claim of appeal for the purposes of MCR 7.204.

(3) *Transcripts*. If the court finds that the respondent is financially unable to pay for the preparation of transcripts for appeal, the court must order transcripts prepared at public expense.

(K) **Review Standard**. The clearly erroneous standard shall be used in reviewing the court's findings on appeal from an order terminating parental rights.

Rule 3.978 Post-Termination Review Hearings

(A) **Review Hearing Requirement**. If a child remains in foster care following the termination of parental rights to the child, the court must conduct a hearing not more than 91 days after the termination of parental rights and not later than every 91 days after that hearing for the first year following the termination of parental rights to the child. At the post-termination review hearing, the court shall review the child's placement in foster care and the progress toward the child's adoption or other permanent placement, as long as the child is subject to the jurisdiction, control, or supervision of the court, or of the Michigan Children's Institute or other agency. If the child is residing in another permanent planned living arrangement or is placed with a fit and willing relative and the child's placement is intended to be permanent, the court must conduct a hearing not more than 182 days from the preceding review hearing.

(B) **Notice; Right to be Heard**. The foster parents (if any) of a child and any preadoptive parents or relative providing care to the child must be provided with notice of and an opportunity to be heard at each hearing.

(C) **Findings**. The court must make findings on whether reasonable efforts have been made to establish permanent placement for the child, and may enter such orders as it considers necessary in the best interests of the child, including appointment of a juvenile guardian pursuant to MCL 712A.19c and MCR 3.979.

(D) **Termination of Jurisdiction**. The jurisdiction of the court in the child protective proceeding may terminate when a court of competent jurisdiction enters an order:

(1) terminating the rights of the entity with legal custody and enters an order placing the child for adoption, or

(2) appointing a juvenile guardian under MCR 3.979 after conducting a review hearing under subsection (A) of this rule.

Rule 3.979 Juvenile Guardianships

(A) **Appointment of Juvenile Guardian; Process**. If the court determines at a posttermination review hearing or a permanency planning hearing that it is in the child's best interests, the court may appoint a juvenile guardian for the child pursuant to MCL 712A.19a or MCL 712A.19c.

(1) Under MCR 3.979(A), the court shall order the Department of Human Services to:

(a) conduct a criminal record check and central registry clearance of the residents of the home and submit the results to the court within 7 days; and

(b) perform a home study with a copy to be submitted to the court within 28 days, unless a home study has been performed within the immediately preceding 365 days, in which case a copy of that home study shall be submitted to the court.

(2) If a child for whom a juvenile guardianship is proposed is in foster care, the court shall continue the child's placement and order the information required above about the proposed juvenile guardian. If the information required above has already been provided to the court, the court may issue an order appointing the proposed juvenile guardian pursuant to subrule (B).

(3) If the parental rights over a child who is the subject of a proposed juvenile guardianship have been terminated, the court shall not appoint a guardian without the written consent of the Michigan Children's Institute (MCI) superintendent. The court may order the Department of Human Services to seek the consent of the MCI superintendent. The consent must be filed with the court no later than 28 days after the permanency planning hearing or the posttermination review hearing, or such longer time as the court may allow for good cause shown.

(a) If a person denied consent believes that the decision to withhold consent by the MCI superintendent is arbitrary or capricious, the person may file a motion with the court within 56 days of receipt of the decision to deny consent. A motion under this subsection shall contain information regarding both of the following:

(i) the specific steps taken by the person or agency to obtain the consent required and the results, if any, and

(ii) the specific reasons why the person or agency believes that the decision to withhold consent was arbitrary or capricious.

(b) If a motion is filed alleging that the MCI superintendent's failure to consent was arbitrary or capricious, the court shall set a hearing date and ensure that notice is provided to the MCI superintendent and all parties entitled to notice under MCR 3.921.

(c) If a hearing is held and the court finds by clear and convincing evidence that the decision to withhold consent was arbitrary or capricious, the court may approve the guardianship without the consent of the MCI superintendent.

The court shall determine the continuing necessity and appropriateness of the child's placement.

(B) **Order Appointing Juvenile Guardian**. After receiving the information ordered by the court under subsection (A)(1), and after finding that appointment of a juvenile guardian is in the child's best interests, the court may enter an order appointing a juvenile guardian. The order appointing a juvenile guardian shall be on a form approved by the state court administrator. Within 7 days of receiving the information, the court shall enter an order appointing a juvenile guardian or schedule the matter for a hearing. A separate order shall be entered for each child.

(1) Acceptance of Appointment. A juvenile guardian appointed by the court shall file an acceptance of appointment with the court on a form approved by the state court administrator. The acceptance shall state, at a minimum, that the juvenile guardian accepts the appointment, submits to personal jurisdiction of the court, will not delegate the juvenile guardian's authority, and will perform required duties.

(2) Letters of Authority. On the filing of the acceptance of appointment, the court shall issue letters of authority on a form approved by the state court administrator. Any restriction or limitation of the powers of the juvenile guardian must be set forth in the letters of authority, including but not limited to, not moving the domicile of the child from the state of Michigan without court approval.

(3) Certification. Certification of the letters of authority and a statement that on a given date the letters are in full force and effect may appear on the face of copies furnished to the juvenile guardian or interested persons.

(4) Notice. Notice of a proceeding relating to the juvenile guardianship shall be delivered or mailed to the juvenile guardian by first-class mail at the juvenile guardian's address as listed in the court records and to his or her address as then known to the petitioner. Any notice mailed first class by the court to the juvenile guardian's last address on file shall be considered notice to the juvenile guardian.

(C) **Court Jurisdiction; Review Hearings; Lawyer-Guardian ad Litem**.

(1) *Jurisdiction*. The court's jurisdiction over a juvenile guardianship shall continue until terminated by court order. The court's jurisdiction over a juvenile under section 2(b) of the Juvenile Code, MCL 712A.2(b), and the jurisdiction of the MCI under section 3 of 1935 PA 220, MCL 400.203, shall be terminated after the court appoints a juvenile guardian under this section and conducts a review hearing pursuant to MCR 3.975 when parental rights to the child have not been terminated, or a review hearing pursuant to MCR 3.978 when parental rights to the child have been terminated. Upon notice by the Department of Human Services that extended guardianship assistance beyond age 18 will be provided to a youth pursuant to MCL 400.665, the court shall retain jurisdiction over the guardianship until that youth no longer receives extended guardian assistance.

(2) *Review Hearings*. The review hearing following appointment of the juvenile guardian must be conducted within 91 days of the most recent review hearing if it has been one year or less from the date the child was last removed from the home, or within 182 days of the most recent review hearing if it has been more than one year from the date the child was last removed from the home.

(3) *Lawyer-Guardian ad Litem*. The appointment of the lawyer-guardian ad litem in the child protective proceeding terminates upon entry of the order terminating the court's jurisdiction pursuant to MCL 712A.2(b). At any time after a juvenile guardian is appointed, the court may reappoint the lawyer-guardian ad litem or may appoint a new lawyer-guardian ad litem if the court is satisfied that such action is warranted. A lawyer-guardian ad litem appointed under this subrule is subject to the provisions of MCL 712A.17d.

(D) **Court Responsibilities**.

(1) *Annual Review*.

(a) The court shall conduct a review of a juvenile guardianship annually. The review shall be commenced within 63 days after the anniversary date of the appointment of the guardian. The court may conduct a review of a juvenile guardianship at any time it deems necessary. If the report of the juvenile guardian has not been filed as required by subrule (E)(1), the court shall take appropriate action.

(b) If extended guardianship assistance has been provided to a youth pursuant to MCL 400.665, the court shall conduct an annual review hearing at least once every 12 months after the youth's eighteenth birthday to determine that the guardianship meets the criteria under MCL 400.667. Notice of the hearing shall be sent to the guardian and the youth as provided in MCR 3.920(D)(1). The court shall issue an order to support its determination and serve the order on the Department of Human Services, the guardian, and the youth.

(2) *Investigation*. The court shall appoint the Department of Human Services or another person to conduct an investigation of the juvenile guardianship of a child when deemed appropriate

by the court or upon petition by the Department of Human Services or an interested person. The investigator shall file a written report with the court within 28 days of such appointment and shall serve it on the other interested parties listed in MCR 3.921(C). The report shall include a recommendation regarding whether the juvenile guardianship should continue or be modified and whether a hearing should be scheduled. If the report recommends modification, the report shall state the nature of the modification.

(3) *Judicial Action.* After informal review of the report provided in subrule (D)(2), the court shall enter an order denying the modification or set a date for a hearing to be held within 28 days.

(4) Upon notice of a child's death the court shall enter an order of discharge. The court may schedule a hearing on the matter before entering an order of discharge.

(E) **Duties and Authority of Guardian Appointed to Juvenile Guardianship**. A juvenile guardianship approved under these rules is authorized by the Juvenile Code and is distinct from a guardianship authorized under the Estates and Protected Individuals Code. A juvenile guardian has all the powers and duties of a guardian set forth under section 5215 of the Estates and Protected Individuals Code.

(1) *Report of Juvenile Guardian.* A juvenile guardian shall file a written report annually within 56 days after the anniversary of appointment and at other times as the court may order. Reports must be on a form approved by the state court administrator. The juvenile guardian must serve the report on the persons listed in MCR 3.921.

(2) *Petition for Conservator.* At the time of appointing a juvenile guardian or during the period of the juvenile guardianship, the court shall determine whether there would be sufficient assets under the control of the juvenile guardian to require a conservatorship. If so, the court shall order the juvenile guardian to petition the probate court for a conservator pursuant to MCL 700.5401 et seq.

(3) *Address of Juvenile Guardian.* The juvenile guardian must keep the court informed in writing within 7 days of any change in the juvenile guardian's address.

(4) The juvenile guardian shall provide the court and interested persons with written notice within 14 days of the child's death.

(F) **Revocation or Termination of Guardianship**.

(1) *Motion or Petition.*

(a) Revocation of Juvenile Guardianship. The court shall, on its own motion or upon petition from the Department of Human Services or the child's lawyer-guardian ad litem, hold a hearing to determine whether a juvenile guardianship established under this section shall be revoked.

(b) Termination of Juvenile Guardian and Appointment of Successor. A juvenile guardian or other interested person may petition the court for permission to terminate the guardianship. A petition may include a request for appointment of a successor juvenile guardian.

(2) *Hearing.* If a petition for revocation or termination is filed with the court, the court shall hold a hearing within 28 days to determine whether to grant the petition to revoke or terminate the juvenile guardianship. The court may order temporary removal of the child under MCR 3.963 to protect the health, safety, or welfare of the child, pending the revocation or termination hearing. If the court orders removal of the child from the juvenile guardian to protect the child's health, safety, or welfare, the court must proceed under MCR 3.974(B).

(3) *Investigation and Report.* In preparation for the revocation or termination hearing, the court shall order the Department of Human Services to perform an investigation and file a written report of the investigation. The report shall be filed with the court no later than 7 days before the hearing. The report shall include the reasons for terminating a juvenile guardianship or revoking a juvenile guardianship, and a recommendation regarding temporary placement, if necessary.

(4) *Notice.* The court shall ensure that interested persons are given notice of the hearing as provided in MCR 3.920 and MCR 3.921. The court may proceed in the absence of interested persons provided that proper notice has been given. The notice must inform the interested persons of their opportunity to participate in the hearing and that any information they wish to provide should be submitted in advance to the court, the agency, the lawyer-guardian ad litem for the child, and an attorney for one of the parties.

(5) *Action Following Motion or Petition to Revoke Juvenile Guardianship.* After notice and a hearing on a petition to revoke the juvenile guardianship, if the court finds by a preponderance of evidence that continuation of the juvenile guardianship is not in the child's best interests, and upon finding that it is contrary to the welfare of the child to be placed in or remain in the juvenile guardian's home and that reasonable efforts were made to prevent removal, the court shall revoke the juvenile guardianship. The court shall enter an order revoking the juvenile guardianship and placing the child under the care and supervision of the Department of Human Services on a form approved by the state court

administrator. Jurisdiction over the child under MCL 712A.2(b) is reinstated under the previous child protective proceeding upon entry of the order revoking the juvenile guardianship.

(6) *Action Following Petition to Terminate Appointment of Juvenile Guardian.* After notice and a hearing on a petition to terminate the appointment of a juvenile guardian, if the court finds it is in the child's best interests to terminate the appointment and if there is:

(a) no successor, the court shall proceed according to subrule (F)(5); or

(b) a successor, the court shall terminate the appointment of the juvenile guardian and proceed with an investigation and appointment of a successor juvenile guardian in accordance with the requirements of this rule, and the court's jurisdiction over the juvenile guardianship shall continue. An order terminating a juvenile guardianship and appointing a successor juvenile guardian shall be entered on a form approved by the state court administrator.

(7) *Dispositional Review Hearing.* The court shall hold a dispositional review hearing pursuant to MCR 3.973 or MCR 3.978 within 42 days of revocation of a juvenile guardianship. The Department of Human Services shall prepare a case service plan and file it with the court no later than 7 days before the hearing. Subsequent postdispositional review hearings shall be scheduled in conformity with MCR 3.974 and MCR 3.975.

Rule 3.981 Minor Personal Protection Orders; Issuance; Modification; Recision; Appeal

Procedure for the issuance, dismissal, modification, or recision of minor personal protection orders is governed by subchapter 3.700. Procedure in appeals related to minor personal protection orders is governed by MCR 3.709 and MCR 3.993.

Rule 3.982 Enforcement of Minor Personal Protection Orders

(A) **In General**. A minor personal protection order is enforceable under MCL 600.2950(22), (25), 600.2950a(19), (22), 764.15b, and 600.1701 et seq. For the purpose of MCR 3.981-3.989, "minor personal protection order" includes a foreign protection order against a minor respondent enforceable in Michigan under MCL 600.2950l.

(B) **Procedure**. Unless indicated otherwise in these rules, contempt proceedings for the enforcement of minor personal protection orders where the respondent is under 18 years of age are governed by MCR 3.982-3.989.

(C) **Form of Proceeding**. A contempt proceeding brought in a court other than the one that issued the minor personal protection order shall be entitled "In the Matter of Contempt of [Respondent], a minor". The clerk shall provide a copy of the contempt proceeding to the court that issued the minor personal protection order.

Rule 3.983 Initiation of Contempt Proceedings by Supplemental Petition

(A) **Filing**. If a respondent allegedly violates a minor personal protection order, the original petitioner, a law enforcement officer, a prosecuting attorney, a probation officer, or a caseworker may submit a supplemental petition in writing to have the respondent found in contempt. The supplemental petition must contain a specific description of the facts constituting a violation of the personal protection order. There is no fee for such a petition.

(B) **Scheduling**. Upon receiving the supplemental petition, the court must either:

(1) set a date for a preliminary hearing on the supplemental petition, to be held as soon as practicable, and issue a summons to appear; or

(2) issue an order authorizing a peace officer or other person designated by the court to apprehend the respondent.

(C) **Service**. If the court sets a date for a preliminary hearing, the petitioner shall serve the supplemental petition and summons on the respondent and, if the relevant addresses are known or are ascertainable upon diligent inquiry, on the respondent's parent or parents, guardian, or custodian. Service must be in the manner provided by MCR 3.920 at least 7 days before the preliminary hearing.

(D) **Order to Apprehend**.

(1) A court order to apprehend the respondent may include authorization to:

(a) enter specified premises as required to bring the minor before the court, and

(b) detain the minor pending preliminary hearing if it appears there is a substantial likelihood of retaliation or continued violation.

(2) Upon apprehending a minor respondent under a court order, the officer shall comply with MCR 3.984(B) and (C).

Rule 3.984 Apprehension of Alleged Violator

(A) **Apprehension; Release to Parent, Guardian, or Custodian**. When an officer apprehends a minor for violation of a minor personal protection order without a court order for apprehension and does not warn and release the minor, the officer may accept a written promise of the minor's parent, guardian, or custodian to bring the minor to court, and release the minor to the parent, guardian, or custodian.

(B) **Custody; Detention**. When an officer apprehends a minor in relation to a minor personal protection order pursuant to a court order that specifies that the minor is to be brought directly to court; or when an officer apprehends a minor for an alleged violation of a minor personal protection order without a court order, and either the officer has failed to obtain a written promise from the minor's parent, guardian, or custodian to bring the minor to court, or it appears to the officer that there is a substantial likelihood of retaliation or violation by the minor, the officer shall immediately do the following:
  (1) If the whereabouts of the minor's parent or parents, guardian, or custodian is known, inform the minor's parent or parents, guardian, or custodian of the minor's apprehension and of the minor's whereabouts and of the need for the parent or parents, guardian, or custodian to be present at the preliminary hearing;
  (2) Take the minor
    (a) before the court for a preliminary hearing, or
    (b) to a place designated by the court pending the scheduling of a preliminary hearing;
  (3) Prepare a custody statement for submission to the court including:
    (a) the grounds for and the time and location of detention, and
    (b) the names of persons notified and the times of notification, or the reason for failure to notify; and
  (4) Ensure that a supplemental petition is prepared and filed with the court.

(C) **Separate Custody**. While awaiting arrival of the parent, guardian, or custodian, appearance before the court, or otherwise, a minor under 17 years of age must be maintained separately from adult prisoners to prevent any verbal, visual, or physical contact with an adult prisoner.

(D) **Designated Court Person**. The court must designate a judge, referee or other person who may be contacted by the officer taking a minor under 17 into custody when the court is not open. In each county there must be a designated facility open at all times at which an officer may obtain the name of the person to be contacted for permission to detain the minor pending preliminary hearing.

(E) **Out-of-County Violation**. Subject to MCR 3.985(H), if a minor is apprehended for violation of a minor personal protection order in a jurisdiction other than the jurisdiction where the minor personal protection order was issued, the apprehending jurisdiction may notify the issuing jurisdiction that it may request that the respondent be returned to the issuing jurisdiction for enforcement proceedings.

Rule 3.985 Preliminary Hearing

(A) **Time**.
  (1) *Commencement*. If the respondent was apprehended or arrested for violation of a minor personal protection order or was apprehended or arrested under a court order, and the respondent is taken into court custody or is jailed, the preliminary hearing must commence no later than 24 hours after the minor was apprehended or arrested, excluding Sundays and holidays, as defined in MCR 8.110(D)(2), or the minor must be released. Otherwise, the preliminary hearing must commence as soon as practicable after the apprehension or arrest, or the submission of a supplemental petition.
  (2) *General Adjournment*. The court may adjourn the hearing for up to 14 days:
    (a) to secure the attendance of witnesses or the minor's parent, guardian, or custodian, or
    (b) for other good cause shown.

(B) **Procedure**.
  (1) The court shall determine whether the parent, guardian, or custodian has been notified and is present. The preliminary hearing may be conducted without a parent, guardian, or custodian provided a guardian ad litem or attorney appears with the minor.
  (2) Unless waived by the respondent, the court shall read the allegations in the supplemental petition, and ensure that the respondent has received written notice of the alleged violation.
  (3) Immediately after the reading of the allegations, the court shall advise the respondent on the record in plain language of the rights to:
    (a) contest the allegations at a violation hearing;
    (b) an attorney at every stage in the proceedings, and, if the court determines it might sentence the respondent to jail or place the respondent in secure detention, the fact that the court will appoint an attorney at public expense if the respondent wants one and is financially unable to retain one;
    (c) a nonjury trial and that a referee may be assigned to hear the case unless demand for a judge is filed pursuant to MCR 3.912;
    (d) have witnesses against the respondent appear at a violation hearing and to question the witnesses;
    (e) have the court order any witnesses for the respondent's defense to appear at the hearing; and
    (f) remain silent and to not have that silence used against the respondent, and that any statement by the respondent may be used against the respondent.

(4) The court must decide whether to authorize the filing of the supplemental petition and proceed formally, or to dismiss the supplemental petition.

(5) The respondent must be allowed an opportunity to deny or otherwise plead to the allegations. If the respondent wishes to enter a plea of admission or of nolo contendere, the court shall follow MCR 3.986.

(6) If the court authorizes the filing of the supplemental petition, the court must:

(a) set a date and time for the violation hearing, or, if the court accepts a plea of admission or no contest, either enter a dispositional order or set the matter for dispositional hearing; and

(b) either release the respondent pursuant to subrule (E) or order detention of the respondent as provided in subrule (F).

(C) **Notification**. Following the preliminary hearing, if the respondent denies the allegations in the supplemental petition, the court must:

(1) notify the prosecuting attorney of the scheduled violation hearing;

(2) notify the respondent, respondent's attorney, if any, and respondent's parents, guardian, or custodian of the scheduled violation hearing and direct the parties to appear at the hearing and give evidence on the charge of contempt.

Notice of hearing must be given by personal service or ordinary mail at least 7 days before the violation hearing, unless the respondent is detained, in which case notice of hearing must be served at least 24 hours before the hearing.

(D) **Failure to Appear**. If the respondent was notified of the preliminary hearing and fails to appear for the preliminary hearing, the court may issue an order in accordance with MCR 3.983(D) authorizing a peace officer or other person designated by the court to apprehend the respondent.

(1) If the respondent is under 17 years of age, the court may order the respondent detained pending a hearing on the apprehension order; if the court releases the respondent it may set bond for the respondent's appearance at the violation hearing.

(2) If the respondent is 17 years of age, the court may order the respondent confined to jail pending a hearing on the apprehension order. If the court releases the respondent it must set bond for the respondent's appearance at the violation hearing.

(E) **Release of Respondent.**

(1) Subject to the conditions set forth in subrule (F), the respondent may be released, with conditions, to a parent, guardian, or custodian pending the resumption of the preliminary hearing or pending the violation hearing after the court considers available information on

(a) family ties and relationships,

(b) the minor's prior juvenile delinquency or minor personal protection order record, if any,

(c) the minor's record of appearance or nonappearance at court proceedings,

(d) the violent nature of the alleged violation,

(e) the minor's prior history of committing acts that resulted in bodily injury to others,

(f) the minor's character and mental condition,

(g) the court's ability to supervise the minor if placed with a parent or relative,

(h) the likelihood of retaliation or violation of the order by the respondent, and

(i) any other factors indicating the minor's ties to the community, the risk of nonappearance, and the danger to the respondent or the original petitioner if the respondent is released.

(2) Bail procedure is governed by MCR 3.935(F).

(F) **Detention Pending Violation Hearing**.

(1) *Conditions*. A minor shall not be removed from the parent, guardian, or custodian pending violation hearing or further court order unless:

(a) probable cause exists to believe the minor violated the minor personal protection order; and

(b) at the preliminary hearing the court finds one or more of the following circumstances to be present:

(i) there is a substantial likelihood of retaliation or continued violation by the minor who allegedly violated the minor personal protection order;

(ii) there is a substantial likelihood that if the minor is released to the parent, with or without conditions, the minor will fail to appear at the next court proceeding; or

(iii) detention pending violation hearing is otherwise specifically authorized by law.

(2) *Waiver*. A minor respondent in custody may waive the probable cause phase of a detention determination only if the minor is represented by an attorney.

(3) *Evidence; Findings*. At the preliminary hearing the minor respondent may contest the sufficiency of evidence to support detention by cross-examination of witnesses, presentation of defense witnesses, or by other evidence. The court shall permit the use of subpoena power to secure attendance of defense witnesses. A finding of probable cause under subrule (F)(1)(a) may be based on hearsay evidence which possesses adequate guarantees of trustworthiness.

(4) *Type of Detention*. The detained minor must be placed in the least restrictive environment that will meet the needs of the minor and the public, and conforms to the requirements of MCL 712A.15 and 712A.16.

(G) **Findings**. At the preliminary hearing the court must state the reasons for its decision to release or detain the minor on the record or in a written memorandum.

(H) **Out-of-County Violation**. When a minor is apprehended for violation of a minor personal protection order in a jurisdiction other than the one that issued the personal protection order, and the apprehending jurisdiction conducts the preliminary hearing, if it has not already done so, the apprehending jurisdiction must immediately notify the issuing jurisdiction that the latter may request that the respondent be returned to the issuing jurisdiction for enforcement proceedings.

Rule 3.986 Pleas of Admission or No Contest

(A) **Capacity**. A minor may offer a plea of admission or of no contest to the violation of a minor personal protection order with the consent of the court. The court shall not accept a plea to a violation unless the court is satisfied that the plea is accurate, voluntary, and understanding.

(B) **Qualified Pleas**. The court may accept a plea of admission or of no contest conditioned on preservation of an issue for appellate review.

(C) **Support of Plea by Parent, Guardian, Custodian**. The court shall inquire of the parents, guardian, custodian, or guardian ad litem whether there is any reason the court should not accept the plea tendered by the minor. Agreement or objection by the parent, guardian, custodian, or guardian ad litem to a plea of admission or of no contest by a minor must be placed on the record if that person is present.

(D) **Plea Withdrawal**. The court may take a plea of admission or of no contest under advisement. Before the court accepts the plea, the minor may withdraw the plea offer by right. After the court accepts a plea, the court has discretion to allow the minor to withdraw the plea.

Rule 3.987 Violation Hearing

(A) **Time**. Upon completion of the preliminary hearing the court shall set a date and time for the violation hearing if the respondent denies the allegations in the supplemental petition. The violation hearing must be held within 72 hours of apprehension, excluding Sundays and holidays, as defined in MCR 8.110(D)(2), if the respondent is detained. If the respondent is not detained the hearing must be held within 21 days.

(B) **Prosecution After Apprehension**. If a criminal contempt proceeding is commenced under MCL 764.15b, the prosecuting attorney shall prosecute the proceeding unless the petitioner retains an attorney to prosecute the criminal contempt proceeding. If the prosecuting attorney determines that the personal protection order was not violated or that it would not be in the interest of justice to prosecute the criminal contempt violation, the prosecuting attorney need not prosecute the proceeding.

(C) **Preliminary Matters**.

(1) The court must determine whether the appropriate parties have been notified and are present.

(a) The respondent has the right to be present at the violation hearing along with parents, guardian, or custodian, and guardian ad litem and attorney.

(b) The court may proceed in the absence of a parent properly noticed to appear, provided the respondent is represented by an attorney.

(c) The original petitioner has the right to be present at the violation hearing.

(2) The court must read the allegations contained in the supplemental petition, unless waived.

(3) Unless an attorney appears with the minor, the court must inform the minor of the right to the assistance of an attorney and that, if the court determines that it might sentence the respondent to jail or place the respondent in secure detention, the court will appoint an attorney at public expense if the respondent wants one and is financially unable to retain one. If the juvenile requests to proceed without the assistance of an attorney, the court must advise the minor of the dangers and disadvantages of self-representation and determine whether the minor is literate and competent to conduct the defense.

(D) **Jury**. There is no right to a jury trial.

(E) **Conduct of the Hearing**. The respondent has the right to be present at the hearing, to present evidence, and to examine and cross-examine witnesses.

(F) **Evidence; Burden of Proof**. The rules of evidence apply to both criminal and civil contempt proceedings. The petitioner or the prosecuting attorney has the burden of proving the respondent's guilt of criminal contempt beyond a reasonable doubt and the respondent's guilt of civil contempt by a preponderance of the evidence.

(G) **Judicial Findings**. At the conclusion of the hearing, the court must make specific findings of fact, state separately its conclusions of law, and direct entry of the appropriate judgment. The court must state its findings and conclusions on the record or in a written opinion made a part of the record.

Rule 3.988 Dispositional Hearing

(A) **Time**. The time interval between the entry of judgment finding a violation of a minor personal protection order and disposition, if any, is within the court's discretion, but may not be more than 35 days. When the minor is detained, the interval may not be more than 14 days, except for good cause.

(B) **Presence of Respondent and Petitioner**.
(1) The respondent may be excused from part of the dispositional hearing for good cause, but the respondent must be present when the disposition is announced.
(2) The petitioner has the right to be present at the dispositional hearing.

(C) **Evidence**.
(1) At the dispositional hearing all relevant and material evidence, including oral and written reports, may be received by the court and may be relied on to the extent of its probative value, even though such evidence may not be admissible at the violation hearing.
(2) The respondent, or the respondent's attorney, and the petitioner shall be afforded an opportunity to examine and controvert written reports so received and, in the court's discretion, may be allowed to cross-examine individuals making reports when such individuals are reasonably available.
(3) No assertion of an evidentiary privilege, other than the privilege between attorney and client, shall prevent the receipt and use, at the dispositional phase, of materials prepared pursuant to a court-ordered examination, interview, or course of treatment.

(D) **Dispositions**.
(1) If a minor respondent at least 17 years of age pleads or is found guilty of criminal contempt, the court may impose a sentence of incarceration of up to 93 days and may impose a fine of not more than $500.
(2) If a minor respondent pleads or is found guilty of civil contempt, the court shall
(a) impose a fine or imprisonment as specified in MCL 600.1715 and 600.1721, if the respondent is at least 17 years of age.
(b) subject the respondent to the dispositional alternatives listed in MCL 712A.18, if the respondent is under 17 years of age.
(3) In addition to the sentence, the court may impose other conditions to the minor personal protection order.

Rule 3.989 Supplemental Dispositions

When it is alleged that a minor placed on probation for the violation of a minor personal protection order has violated a condition of probation, the court shall follow the procedures for supplemental disposition as provided in MCR 3.944.

Rule 3.991 Review of Referee Recommendations

(A) **General**.
(1) Before signing an order based on a referee's recommended findings and conclusions, a judge of the court shall review the recommendations if requested by a party in the manner provided by subrule (B).
(2) If no such request is filed within the time provided by subrule (B)(3), the court may enter an order in accordance with the referee's recommendations.
(3) Nothing in this rule prohibits a judge from reviewing a referee's recommendation before the expiration of the time for requesting review and entering an appropriate order.
(4) After the entry of an order under subrule (A)(3), a request for review may not be filed. Reconsideration of the order is by motion for rehearing under MCR 3.992.

(B) **Form of Request; Time**. A party's request for review of a referee's recommendation must:
(1) be in writing,
(2) state the grounds for review,
(3) be filed with the court within 7 days after the conclusion of the inquiry or hearing or within 7 days after the issuance of the referee's written recommendations, whichever is later, and
(4) be served on the interested parties by the person requesting review at the time of filing the request for review with the court. A proof of service must be filed.

(C) **Response**. A party may file a written response within 7 days after the filing of the request for review.

(D) **Prompt Review; No Party Appearance Required**. Absent good cause for delay, the judge shall consider the request within 21 days after it is filed if the minor is in placement or detention. The judge need not schedule a hearing to rule on a request for review of a referee's recommendations.

(E) **Review Standard**. The judge must enter an order adopting the referee's recommendation unless:
(1) the judge would have reached a different result had he or she heard the case; or
(2) the referee committed a clear error of law, which
(a) likely would have affected the outcome, or
(b) cannot otherwise be considered harmless.

(F) **Remedy**. The judge may adopt, modify, or deny the recommendation of the referee, in whole or in part, on the basis of the record and the memorandums prepared, or may conduct a hearing, whichever the court in its discretion finds appropriate for the case.

(G) **Stay**. The court may stay any order or grant bail to a detained juvenile, pending its decision on review of the referee's recommendation.

Rule 3.992 Rehearings; New Trial

(A) **Time and Grounds**. Except for the case of a juvenile tried as an adult in the family division of the circuit court for a criminal offense, and except for a case in which parental rights are terminated, a party may seek a rehearing or new trial by filing a written motion stating the basis for the relief sought within 21 days after the date of the order resulting from the hearing or trial. In a case that involves termination of parental rights, a motion for new trial, rehearing, reconsideration, or other postjudgment relief shall be filed within 14 days after the date of the order terminating parental rights. The court may entertain an untimely motion for good cause shown. A motion will not be considered unless it presents a matter not previously presented to the court, or presented, but not previously considered by the court, which, if true, would cause the court to reconsider the case.

(B) **Notice**. All parties must be given notice of the motion in accordance with Rule 3.920.

(C) **Response by Parties**. Any response by parties must be in writing and filed with the court and served on the opposing parties within 7 days after notice of the motion.

(D) **Procedure**. The judge may affirm, modify, or vacate the decision previously made in whole or in part, on the basis of the record, the memoranda prepared, or a hearing on the motion, whichever the court in its discretion finds appropriate for the case.

(E) **Hearings**. The court need not hold a hearing before ruling on a motion. Any hearing conducted shall be in accordance with the rules for dispositional hearings and, at the discretion of the court, may be assigned to the person who conducted the hearing. The court shall state the reasons for its decision on the motion on the record or in writing.

(F) **Stay**. The court may stay any order, or grant bail to a detained juvenile, pending a ruling on the motion.

Rule 3.993 Appeals

(A) The following orders are appealable to the Court of Appeals by right:

- (1) an order of disposition placing a minor under the supervision of the court or removing the minor from the home,
- (2) an order terminating parental rights,
- (3) any order required by law to be appealed to the Court of Appeals, and
- (4) any final order.

(B) All orders not listed in subrule (A) are appealable to the Court of Appeals by leave.

(C) **Procedure; Delayed Appeals**.

- (1) *Applicable Rules*. Except as modified by this rule, chapter 7 of the Michigan Court Rules governs appeals from the family division of the circuit court.
- (2) *Delayed Appeals; Termination of Parental Rights*. The Court of Appeals may not grant an application for leave to appeal an order of the family division of the circuit court terminating parental rights if filed more than 63 days after entry of an order of judgment on the merits, or if filed more than 63 days after entry of an order denying reconsideration or rehearing.

CHAPTER 4. DISTRICT COURT

Subchapter 4.000 General Provisions

Rule 4.001 Applicability

The rules in this chapter apply to the specific types of proceedings within the jurisdiction of the district and municipal courts. Except as otherwise provided in this chapter, proceedings under this chapter are governed by Michigan Court Rules.

Rule 4.002 Transfer of Actions From District Court to Circuit Court

(A) **Counterclaim or Cross-Claim in Excess of Jurisdiction.**

(1) If a defendant asserts a counterclaim or cross-claim seeking relief of an amount or nature beyond the jurisdiction or power of the district court in which the action is pending, and accompanies the notice of the claim with an affidavit stating that the defendant is justly entitled to the relief demanded, the clerk shall record the pleading and affidavit and present them to the judge to whom the action is assigned. The judge shall either order the action transferred to the circuit court to which appeal of the action would ordinarily lie or inform the defendant that transfer will not be ordered without a motion and notice to the other parties.

(2) MCR 4.201(G)(2) and 4.202(I)(4) govern transfer of summary proceedings to recover possession of premises.

(B) **Change in Conditions**.

(1) A party may, at any time, file a motion with the district court in which an action is pending, requesting that the action be transferred to circuit court. The motion must be supported by an affidavit stating that

(a) due to a change in condition or circumstance, or

(b) due to facts not known by the party at the time the action was commenced, the party wishes to seek relief of an amount or nature that is beyond the jurisdiction or power of the court to grant.

(2) If the district court finds that the party filing the motion may be entitled to the relief the party now seeks to claim and that the delay in making the claim is excusable, the court shall order the action transferred to the circuit court to which an appeal of the action would ordinarily lie.

(C) **Conditions Precedent to Transfer**. The action may not be transferred under this rule until the party seeking transfer pays to the opposing parties the costs they have reasonably incurred up to that time that would not have been incurred if the action had originally been brought in circuit court, and pays the statutory circuit court filing fee to the clerk of the court from which the action is to be transferred. If a case is entirely transferred from district court to circuit court and the jury fee was paid in the district court, the district court clerk shall forward the fee to the circuit court with the papers and filing fee under subrule (D). If the amount paid to the district court for the jury fee is less than the circuit court jury fee, then the party requesting the jury shall pay the difference to the circuit court.

(D) **Filing in Circuit Court**. After the court has ordered transfer and the costs and fees required by subrule (C) have been paid, the clerk of the court from which the action is transferred shall forward to the clerk of the circuit court the original papers in the action and the circuit court filing fee.

(E) **Procedure After Transfer**. After transfer no further proceedings may be conducted in the district court, and the action shall proceed in the circuit court. The circuit court may order further pleadings and set the time when they must be filed.

Subchapter 4.100 Civil Infraction Actions

Rule 4.101 Civil Infraction Actions

(A) **Citation; Complaint; Summons; Warrant**.

(1) Except as otherwise provided by court rule or statute, a civil infraction action may be initiated by a law enforcement officer serving a written citation on the alleged violator, and filing the citation in the district court.

(a) If the infraction is a parking violation, the action may be initiated by an authorized person placing a citation securely on the vehicle or mailing a citation to the registered owner of the vehicle. In either event, the citation must be filed in the district court.

(b) If the infraction is a municipal civil infraction, the action may be initiated by an authorized local official serving a written citation on the alleged violator. If the infraction involves the use or occupancy of land or a building or other structure, service may be accomplished by posting the citation at the site and sending a copy to the owner by first-class mail.

The citation serves as the complaint in a civil infraction action, and may be filed either on paper or electronically.

(2) A violation alleged on a citation may not be amended except by the prosecuting official or a police officer for the plaintiff.

(3) The citation serves as a summons to command

(a) the initial appearance of the defendant; and

(b) a response from the defendant as to his or her responsibility for the alleged violation.

(4) A warrant may not be issued for a civil infraction unless permitted by statute.

(B) **Appearances; Failure to Appear; Default Judgment**.

(1) Depending on the nature of the violation and on the procedure appropriate to the violation, a defendant may appear in person, by representation, or by mail.

(2) A defendant may not appear by making a telephone call to the court, but a defendant may telephone the court to obtain a date to appear.

(3) A clerk of the court may enter a default after certifying, on a form to be furnished by the court, that the defendant has not made a scheduled appearance, or has not answered a citation within the time allowed by statute.

(4) If a defendant fails to appear or otherwise to respond to any matter pending relative to a civil infraction action, the court:

(a) must enter a default against the defendant;

(b) must make a determination of responsibility, if the complaint is sufficient;

(c) must impose a sanction by entering a default judgment;

(d) must send the defendant a notice of the entry of the default judgment and the sanctions imposed; and

(e) may retain the driver's license of a nonresident as permitted by statute, if the court has received that license pursuant to statute. The court need not retain the license past its expiration date.

(5) If a defendant fails to appear or otherwise to respond to any matter pending relative to a traffic civil infraction, the court

(a) must notify the secretary of state of the entry of the default judgment, as required by MCL 257.732, and

(b) must initiate the procedures required by MCL 257.321a.

(6) If a defendant fails to appear or otherwise to respond to any matter pending relative to a state civil infraction, the court must initiate the procedures required by MCL 257.321a.

(C) **Appearance by Police Officer at Informal Hearing**.

(1) If a defendant requests an informal hearing, the court shall schedule an informal hearing and notify the police officer who issued the citation to appear at the informal hearing.

(2) The attendance of the officer at the hearing may not be waived.

Except when the court is notified before the commencement of a hearing of an emergency preventing an on-duty officer from appearing, failure of the police officer to appear as required by this rule shall result in a dismissal of the case without prejudice.

(D) **Motion to Set Aside Default Judgment**.

(1) A defendant may move to set aside a default judgment within 14 days after the court sends notice of the judgment to the defendant. The motion

(a) may be informal,

(b) may be either written or presented to the court in person,

(c) must explain the reason for the nonappearance of the defendant,

(d) must state that the defendant wants to offer a defense to or an explanation of the complaint, and

(e) must be accompanied by a cash bond equal to the fine and costs due at the time the motion is filed.

(2) For good cause, the court may

(a) set aside the default and direct that a hearing on the complaint take place, or

(b) schedule a hearing on the motion to set aside the default judgment.

(3) A defendant who does not file this motion on time may use the procedure set forth in MCR 2.603(D).

(E) **Response**.

(1) Except as provided in subrule (4), an admission without explanation may be offered to and accepted by

(a) a district judge;

(b) a district court magistrate as authorized by the chief judge, the presiding judge, or the only judge of the district; or

(c) other district court personnel, as authorized by a judge of the district.

(2) Except as provided in subrule (4), an admission with explanation may be written or offered orally to a judge or district court magistrate, as authorized by the district judge.

(3) Except as provided in subrule (4), a denial of responsibility must be made by the defendant appearing at a time set either by the citation or as the result of a communication with the court.

(4) If the violation is a trailway municipal civil infraction, and there has been damage to property or a vehicle has been impounded, the defendant's response must be made at a formal hearing.

(F) **Contested Actions; Notice; Defaults**.

(1) A contested action may not be heard until a citation is filed with the court. If the citation is filed electronically, the court may decline to hear the matter until the citation is signed by the officer or official who issued it, and is filed on paper. A citation that is not signed and filed on paper, when required by the court, may be dismissed with prejudice.

(2) An informal hearing will be held unless

(a) a party expressly requests a formal hearing, or

(b) the violation is a trailway municipal civil infraction which requires a formal hearing pursuant to MCL 600.8717(4).

(3) The provisions of MCR 2.501(C) regarding the length of notice of trial assignment do not apply in civil infraction actions.

(4) A defendant who obtains a hearing date other than the date specified in the citation, but who does not appear to explain or contest responsibility, is in default, and the procedures established by subrules (B)(4)-(6) apply.

(G) **Postdetermination Orders; Sanctions, Fines, and Costs; Schedules**.

(1) A court may not increase a scheduled civil fine because the defendant has requested a hearing.

(2) Upon a finding of responsibility in a traffic civil infraction action, the court:

(a) must inform the secretary of state of the finding, as required by MCL 257.732; and

(b) must initiate the procedures required by MCL 257.321a, if the defendant fails to pay a fine or to comply with an order or judgment of the court.

(3) Upon a finding of responsibility in a state civil infraction action, the court must initiate the procedures required by MCL 257.321a(1), if the defendant fails to pay a fine or to comply with an order or judgment of the court.

(4) The court may waive fines, costs and fees, pursuant to statute or court rule, or to correct clerical error.

(H) **Appeal; Bond**.

(1) An appeal following a formal hearing is a matter of right. Except as otherwise provided in this rule, the appeal is governed by subchapter 7.100.

(a) A defendant who appeals must post with the district court, at the time the appeal is taken, a bond equal to the fine and costs imposed. A defendant who has paid the fine and costs is not required to post a bond.

(b) If a defendant who has posted a bond fails to comply with the requirements of MCR 7.104(D), the appeal may be considered abandoned, and the district court may dismiss the appeal on 14 days' notice to the parties pursuant to MCR 7.113. The court clerk must promptly notify the circuit court of a dismissal and the circuit court shall dismiss the claim of appeal. If the appeal is dismissed or the judgment is affirmed, the district court may apply the bond to the fine and costs.

(c) A plaintiff's appeal must be asserted by the prosecuting authority of the political unit that provided the plaintiff's attorney for the formal hearing. A bond is not required.

(2) An appeal following an informal hearing is a matter of right, and must be asserted in writing, within 7 days after the decision, on a form to be provided by the court. The appeal will result in a de novo formal hearing.

(a) A defendant who appeals must post a bond as provided in subrule (1)(a). If a defendant who has posted a bond defaults by failing to appear at the formal hearing, or if the appeal is dismissed or the judgment is affirmed, the bond may be applied to the fine and costs.

(b) A plaintiff's appeal must be asserted by the prosecuting authority of the political unit that is responsible for providing the plaintiff's attorney for the formal hearing. A bond is not required.

(3) There is no appeal of right from an admission of responsibility. However, within 14 days after the admission, a defendant may file with the district court a written request to withdraw the admission, and must post a bond as provided in subrule (1)(a). If the court grants the request, the case will be scheduled for either a formal hearing or an informal hearing, as ordered by the court. If the court denies the request, the bond may be applied to the fine and costs.

Subchapter 4.200 Landlord-Tenant Proceedings; Land Contract Forfeiture

Rule 4.201 Summary Proceedings to Recover Possession of Premises

(A) **Applicable Rules; Forms**. Except as provided by this rule and MCL 600.5701 et seq., a summary proceeding to recover possession of premises from a person in possession as described in MCL 600.5714 is governed by the Michigan Court Rules. Forms available for public distribution at the court clerk's office may be used in the proceeding.

(B) **Complaint**.

(1) *In General*. The complaint must

(a) comply with the general pleading requirements;

(b) have attached to it a copy of any written instrument on which occupancy was or is based;

(c) have attached to it copies of any notice to quit and any demand for possession (the copies must show when and how they were served);

(d) describe the premises or the defendant's holding if it is less than the entire premises;

(e) show the plaintiff's right to possession and indicate why the defendant's possession is improper or unauthorized; and

(f) demand a jury trial, if the plaintiff wishes one. The jury trial fee must be paid when the demand is made.

(2) *Specific Requirements.*
   (a) If rent or other money is due and unpaid, the complaint must show
      (i) the rental period and rate;
      (ii) the amount due and unpaid when the complaint was filed; and
      (iii) the date or dates the payments became due.
   (b) If the tenancy involves housing operated by or under the rules of a governmental unit, the complaint must contain specific reference to the rules or law establishing the basis for ending the tenancy.
   (c) If the tenancy is of residential premises, the complaint must allege that the lessor or licensor has performed his or her covenants to keep the premises fit for the use intended and in reasonable repair during the term of the lease or license, unless the parties to the lease or license have modified those obligations.
   (d) If possession is claimed for a serious and continuing health hazard or for extensive and continuing physical injury to the premises pursuant to MCL 600.5714(1)(d), the complaint must
      (i) describe the nature and the seriousness or extent of the condition on which the complaint is based, and
      (ii) state the period of time for which the property owner has been aware of the condition.
   (e) If possession is sought for trespass pursuant to MCL 600.5714(1)(f), the complaint must describe, when known by the plaintiff, the conditions under which possession was unlawfully taken or is unlawfully held and allege that no lawful tenancy of the premises has existed between the parties since defendant took possession.

(C) **Summons.**
   (1) The summons must comply with MCR 2.102, except that it must command the defendant to appear for trial in accord with MCL 600.5735(2), unless by local court rule the provisions of MCL 600.5735(4) have been made applicable.
   (2) The summons must also include the following advice to the defendant:
      [A] The defendant has the right to employ an attorney to assist in answering the complaint and in preparing defenses.
      [B] If the defendant does not have an attorney but does have money to retain one, he or she might locate an attorney through the State Bar of Michigan or a local lawyer referral service.
      [C] If the defendant does not have an attorney and cannot pay for legal help, he or she might qualify for assistance through a local legal aid office.
      [D] The defendant has a right to a jury trial which will be lost unless it is demanded in the first defense response, written or oral. The jury trial fee must be paid when the demand is made, unless payment of fees is waived or suspended under MCR 2.002.

(D) **Service of Process**. A copy of the summons and complaint and all attachments must be served on the defendant by mail. Unless the court does the mailing and keeps a record, the plaintiff must perfect the mail service by attaching a postal receipt to the proof of service. In addition to mailing, the defendant must be served in one of the following ways:
   (1) By a method provided in MCR 2.105;
   (2) By delivering the papers at the premises to a member of the defendant's household who is
      (a) of suitable age,
      (b) informed of the contents, and
      (c) asked to deliver the papers to the defendant; or
   (3) After diligent attempts at personal service have been made, by securely attaching the papers to the main entrance of the tenant's dwelling unit. A return of service made under subrule (D)(3) must list the attempts at personal service. Service under subrule (D)(3) is effective only if a return of service is filed showing that, after diligent attempts, personal service could not be made.

   An officer who files proof that service was made under subrule (D)(3) is entitled to the regular personal service fee.

(E) **Recording**. All landlord-tenant summary proceedings conducted in open court must be recorded by stenographic or mechanical means, and only a reporter or recorder certified under MCR 8.108(G) may file a transcript of the record in a Michigan court.

(F) **Appearance and Answer; Default.**
   (1) *Appearance and Answer*. The defendant or the defendant's attorney must appear and answer the complaint by the date on the summons. Appearance and answer may be made as follows:
      (a) By filing a written answer or a motion under MCR 2.115 or 2.116 and serving a copy on the plaintiff or the plaintiff's attorney. If proof of the service is not filed before the hearing, the defendant or the defendant's attorney may attest to service on the record.
      (b) By orally answering each allegation in the complaint at the hearing. The answers must be recorded or noted on the complaint.

(2) *Right to an Attorney*. If either party appears in person without an attorney, the court must inform that party of the right to retain an attorney. The court must also inform the party about legal aid assistance when it is available.

(3) *Jury Demand*. If the defendant wants a jury trial, he or she must demand it in the first response, written or oral. The jury trial fee must be paid when the demand is made.

(4) *Default*.

(a) If the defendant fails to appear, the court, on the plaintiff's motion, may enter a default and may hear the plaintiff's proofs in support of judgment. If satisfied that the complaint is accurate, the court must enter a default judgment under MCL 600.5741, and in accord with subrule (K). The default judgment must be mailed to the defendant by the court clerk and must inform the defendant that (if applicable)

(i) he or she may be evicted from the premises;

(ii) he or she may be liable for a money judgment.

(b) If the plaintiff fails to appear, a default judgment as to costs under MCL 600.5747 may be entered.

(c) If a party fails to appear, the court may adjourn the hearing for up to 7 days. If the hearing is adjourned, the court must mail notice of the new date to the party who failed to appear.

(G) **Claims and Counterclaims**.

(1) *Joinder*.

(a) A party may join:

(i) A money claim or counterclaim described by MCL 600.5739. A money claim must be separately stated in the complaint. A money counterclaim must be labeled and separately stated in a written answer.

(ii) A claim or counterclaim for equitable relief.

(b) Unless service of process under MCR 2.105 was made on the defendant, a money claim must be

(i) dismissed without prejudice, or

(ii) adjourned until service of process is complete

if the defendant does not appear or file an answer to the complaint.

(c) A court with a territorial jurisdiction which has a population of more than 1,000,000 may provide, by local rule, that a money claim or counterclaim must be tried separately from a claim for possession unless joinder is allowed by leave of the court pursuant to subrule (G)(1)(e).

(d) If trial of a money claim or counterclaim

(i) might substantially delay trial of the possession claim, or

(ii) requires that the premises be returned before damages can be determined,

the court must adjourn the trial of the money claim or counterclaim to a date no later than 28 days after the time expires for issuing an order of eviction. A party may file and serve supplemental pleadings no later than 7 days before trial, except by leave of the court.

(e) If adjudication of a money counterclaim will affect the amount the defendant must pay to prevent issuance of an order of eviction, that counterclaim must be tried at the same time as the claim for possession, subrules (G)(1)(c) and (d) notwithstanding, unless it appears to the court that the counterclaim is without merit.

(2) *Removal*.

(a) A summary proceedings action need not be removed from the court in which it is filed because an equitable defense or counterclaim is interposed.

(b) If a money claim or counterclaim exceeding the court's jurisdiction is introduced, the court, on motion of either party or on its own initiative, shall order removal of that portion of the action to the circuit court, if the money claim or counterclaim is sufficiently shown to exceed the court's jurisdictional limit.

(H) **Interim Orders**. On motion of either party, or by stipulation, for good cause, a court may issue such interim orders as are necessary, including, but not limited to the following:

(1) *Injunctions*. The interim order may award injunctive relief

(a) to prevent the person in possession from damaging the property; or

(b) to prevent the person seeking possession from rendering the premises untenantable or from suffering the premises to remain untenantable.

(2) *Escrow Orders*.

(a) If trial is adjourned more than 7 days and the plaintiff shows a clear need for protection, the court may order the defendant to pay a reasonable rent for the premises from the date the escrow order is entered, including a pro rata amount per day between the date of the order and the next date rent ordinarily would be due. In determining a reasonable rent, the court should consider evidence offered concerning the condition of the premises or other relevant factors. The order must provide that:

(i) payments be made to the court clerk within 7 days of the date of entry of the order, and thereafter within 7 days of the

date or dates each month when rent would ordinarily be due, until the right to possession is determined;
   - (ii) the plaintiff must not interfere with the obligation of the defendant to comply with the escrow order; and
   - (iii) if the defendant does not comply with the order, the defendant waives the right to a jury trial only as to the possession issue, and the plaintiff is entitled to an immediate trial within 14 days which may be by jury if a party requests it and if, in the court's discretion, the court's schedule permits it. The 14-day limit need not be rigidly adhered to if the plaintiff is responsible for a delay.

- (b) Only the court may order the disbursement of money collected under an escrow order. The court must consider the defendant's defenses. If trial was postponed to permit the premises to be repaired, the court may condition disbursement by requiring that the repairs be completed by a certain time. Otherwise, the court may condition disbursement as justice requires.

(I) **Consent Judgment When Party Is Not Represented**. The following procedures apply to consent judgments and orders entered when either party is not represented by an attorney.

- (1) The judgment or order may not be enforced until 3 regular court business days have elapsed after the judgment or order was entered. The judge shall review, in court, a proposed consent judgment or order with the parties, and shall notify them of the delay required by this subrule at the time the terms of the consent judgment or order are placed on the record.
- (2) A party who was not represented by an attorney at the time of the consent proceedings may move to set aside the consent judgment or order within the 3-day period. Such a motion stays the judgment or order until the court decides the motion or dismisses it after notice to the moving party.
- (3) The court shall set aside a consent judgment or order on a satisfactory showing that the moving party misunderstood the basis for, or the rights which were being relinquished in, the judgment or order.

(J) **Trial**.

- (1) *Time*. When the defendant appears, the court may try the action, or, if good cause is shown, may adjourn trial up to 56 days. If the court adjourns trial for more than 7 days, an escrow order may be entered pursuant to subrule (H)(2). The parties may adjourn trial by stipulation in writing or on the record, subject to the approval of the court.
- (2) *Pretrial Action*. At trial, the court must first decide pretrial motions and determine if there is a triable issue. If there is no triable issue, the court must enter judgment.
- (3) *Government Reports*. If the defendant claims that the plaintiff failed to comply with an ordinance or statute, the court may admit an authenticated copy of any relevant government employee's report filed with a government agency. Objections to the report affect the weight given it, not its admissibility.
- (4) *Payment or Acceptance of Money*. The payment or the acceptance of money by a party before trial does not necessarily prevent or delay the proceedings.

(K) **Judgment**.

- (1) *Requirements*. A judgment for the plaintiff must
   - (a) comply with MCL 600.5741;
   - (b) state when and under what conditions, if any, an order of eviction will issue;
   - (c) separately state possession and money awards; and
   - (d) advise the defendant of the right to appeal or file a postjudgment motion within 10 days.

  If the judgment is in favor of the defendant, it must comply with MCL 600.5747.
- (2) *Injunctions*. The judgment may award injunctive relief
   - (a) to prevent the person in possession from damaging the property; or
   - (b) to prevent the person seeking possession from rendering the premises untenantable, or from suffering the premises to remain untenantable.
- (3) *Partial Payment*. The judgment may provide that acceptance of partial payment of an amount due under the judgment will not prevent issuance of an order of eviction.
- (4) *Costs*. Only those costs permitted by MCL 600.5759 may be awarded.
- (5) *Notice*. The court must mail or deliver a copy of the judgment to the parties. The time period for applying for the order of eviction does not begin to run until the judgment is mailed or delivered.

(L) **Order of Eviction**.

- (1) *Request*. When the time stated in the judgment expires, a party awarded possession may apply for an order of eviction. The application must:
   - (a) be written;
   - (b) be verified by a person having knowledge of the facts stated;
   - (c) if any money has been paid after entry of the judgment, show the conditions under which it was accepted; and
   - (d) state whether the party awarded judgment has complied with its terms.
- (2) *Issuance of Order of Eviction and Delivery of Order*. Subject to the provisions of subrule (L)(4),

the order of eviction shall be delivered to the person serving the order for service within 7 days after the order is filed.

(3) *Issuance Immediately on Judgment.* The court may issue an order immediately on entering judgment if
  (a) the court is convinced the statutory requirements are satisfied, and
  (b) the defendant was given notice, before the judgment of a request for immediate issuance of the order.

  The court may condition the order to protect the defendant's interest.

(4) *Limitations on Time for Issuance and Execution.* Unless a hearing is held after the defendant has been given notice and an opportunity to appear, an order of eviction may not
  (a) be issued later than 56 days after judgment is entered,
  (b) be executed later than 56 days after it is issued.

(5) *Acceptance of Partial Payment.* An order of eviction may not be issued if any part of the amount due under the judgment has been paid, unless
  (a) a hearing is held after the defendant has been given notice and an opportunity to appear, or
  (b) the judgment provides that acceptance of partial payment of the amount due under the judgment will not prevent issuance of an order of eviction.

(M) **Postjudgment Motions.**

(1) Except as provided in MCR 2.612, or for a motion to set aside a default money judgment, any postjudgment motion must be filed no later than 10 days after judgment enters.

(2) If the motion challenges a judgment for possession, the court may not grant a stay unless
  (a) the motion is accompanied by an escrow deposit of 1 month's rent, or
  (b) the court is satisfied that there are grounds for relief under MCR 2.612(C), and issues an order that waives payment of the escrow; such an order may be ex parte.

  If a stay is granted, a hearing shall be held within 14 days after it is issued.

  A motion to set aside a default money judgment shall comply with MCR 2.603(D).

(3) If the judgment does not include an award of possession, the filing of the motion stays proceedings, but the plaintiff may move for an order requiring a bond to secure the stay. If the initial escrow deposit is believed inadequate, the plaintiff may apply for continuing adequate escrow payments in accord with subrule (H)(2). The filing of a postjudgment motion together with a bond, bond order, or escrow deposit stays all proceedings, including an order of eviction issued but not executed.

(N) **Appeals From Possessory Judgments.**

(1) *Rules Applicable.* Except as provided by this rule, appeals must comply with MCR 7.101 through 7.115.

(2) *Time.* An appeal of right must be filed within 10 days after the entry of judgment.

(3) *Stay of Order of Eviction.*
  (a) Unless a stay is ordered by the trial court, an order of eviction must issue as provided in subrule (L).
  (b) The filing of a claim of appeal together with a bond or escrow order of the court stays all proceedings, including an order of eviction issued but not executed.

(4) *Appeal Bond; Escrow.*
  (a) A plaintiff who appeals must file a bond providing that if the plaintiff loses he or she will pay the appeal costs.
  (b) A defendant who appeals must file a bond providing that if the defendant loses, he or she will pay
    (i) the appeal costs,
    (ii) the amount due stated in the judgment, and
    (iii) damages from the time of forcible entry, the detainer, the notice to quit, or the demand for possession.

    The court may waive the bond requirement of subrule (N)(4)(b)(i) on the grounds stated in MCR 2.002(C) or (D).
  (c) If the plaintiff won a possession judgment, the court shall enter an escrow order under subrule (H)(2) and require the defendant to make payments while the appeal is pending. This escrow order may not be retroactive as to arrearages preceding the date of the posttrial escrow order unless there was a pretrial escrow order entered under subrule (H)(2), in which case the total escrow amount may include the amount accrued between the time of the original escrow order and the filing of the appeal.
  (d) If it is established that an appellant cannot obtain sureties or make a sufficient cash deposit, the court must permit the appellant to comply with an escrow order.

(O) **Objections to Fees Covered by Statute for Orders of Eviction.** Objections shall be by motion. The fee to be paid shall be reasonable in light of all the circumstances. In determining the reasonableness of a fee, the court shall consider all issues bearing on reasonableness, including but not limited to

(1) the time of travel to the premises,
(2) the time necessary to execute the order,
(3) the amount and weight of the personal property removed from the premises,

(4) who removed the personal property from the premises,
(5) the distance that the personal property was moved from the premises, and
(6) the actual expenses incurred in executing the order of eviction.

Rule 4.202 Summary Proceedings; Land Contract Forfeiture

(A) **Applicable Rules**. Except as provided by this rule and MCL 600.5701 et seq., a summary proceeding to recover possession of premises after forfeiture of an executory contract for the purchase of premises as described in MCL 600.5726 is governed by the Michigan Court Rules.

(B) **Jurisdiction**.
  (1) *Status of Premises*. The proceeding may be brought when the premises are vacant or are in the possession of
    (a) the vendee,
    (b) a party to the contract,
    (c) an assignee of the contract, or
    (d) a third party.
  (2) *Powers of Court*. The court may do all things necessary to hear and resolve the proceeding, including but not limited to
    (a) hearing and deciding all issues,
    (b) ordering joinder of additional parties,
    (c) ordering or permitting amendments or additional pleadings, and
    (d) making and enforcing writs and orders.

(C) **Necessary Parties**. The plaintiff must join as defendants
  (1) the vendee named in the contract,
  (2) any person known to the plaintiff to be claiming an interest in the premises under the contract, and
  (3) any person in possession of the premises, unless that party has been released from liability.

(D) **Complaint**. The complaint must:
  (1) comply with the general pleading requirements;
  (2) allege
    (a) the original selling price,
    (b) the principal balance due, and
    (c) the amount in arrears under the contract;
  (3) state with particularity any other material breach claimed as a basis for forfeiture; and
  (4) have attached to it a copy of the notice of forfeiture, showing when and how it was served on each named defendant.

(E) **Summons**. The summons must comply with MCR 2.102 and MCL 600.5735, and command the defendant to appear and answer or take other action permitted by law within the time permitted by statute after service of the summons on the defendant.

(F) **Service of Process**. The defendant must be served with a copy of the complaint and summons under MCR 2.105.

(G) **Recording**. All executory contract summary proceedings conducted in open court must be recorded by stenographic or mechanical means, and only a reporter or recorder certified under MCR 8.108(G) may file a transcript of the record in a Michigan court.

(H) **Answer; Default**.
  (1) *Answer*. The answer must comply with general pleading requirements and allege those matters on which the defendant intends to rely to defeat the claim or any part of it.
  (2) *Default*.
    (a) If the defendant fails to appear, the court, on the plaintiff's motion, may enter a default and may hear the plaintiff's proofs in support of judgment. If satisfied that the complaint is accurate, the court must enter a default judgment under MCL 600.5741, and in accord with subrule (J). The default judgment must be mailed to the defendant by the court clerk and must inform the defendant that (if applicable)
      (i) he or she may be evicted from the premises;
      (ii) he or she may be liable for a money judgment.
    (b) If the plaintiff fails to appear, a default and judgment as to costs under MCL 600.5747 may be entered.
    (c) If a party fails to appear, the court may adjourn the hearing for up to 7 days. If the hearing is adjourned, the court must mail notice of the new date to the party who failed to appear.

(I) **Joinder; Removal**.
  (1) A party may join a claim or counterclaim for equitable relief or a money claim or counterclaim described by MCL 600.5739. A money claim must be separately stated in the complaint. A money counterclaim must be labeled and separately stated in a written answer. If such a joinder is made, the court may order separate summary disposition of the claim for possession, as described by MCL 600.5739.
  (2) A court with a territorial jurisdiction which has a population of more than 1,000,000 may provide, by local rule, that a money claim or counterclaim must be tried separately from a claim for possession unless joinder is allowed by leave of the court pursuant to subrule (I)(3).
  (3) If adjudication of a money counterclaim will affect the amount the defendant must pay to prevent the issuance of a writ of restitution, the counterclaim must be tried at the same time as the claim for possession, subrules (I)(1) and (2) notwithstanding,

unless it appears to the court that the counterclaim is without merit.

(4) If a money claim or counterclaim exceeding the court's jurisdiction is introduced, the court, on motion of either party or on its own initiative, shall order removal of that portion of the action, if the money claim or counterclaim is sufficiently shown to exceed the court's jurisdictional limit.

(J) **Judgment**. The judgment

(1) must comply with MCL 600.5741;

(2) must state when, and under what conditions, if any, a writ of restitution will issue;

(3) must state that an appeal or postjudgment motion to challenge the judgment may be filed within 10 days;

(4) may contain such other terms and conditions as the nature of the action and the rights of the parties require; and

(5) must be mailed or delivered by the court to the parties. The time period for applying for the writ of restitution does not begin to run until the judgment is mailed or delivered.

(K) **Order of Eviction**.

(1) *Request*. When the time stated in the judgment expires, a party awarded possession may apply for an order of eviction. The application must:

(a) be written;

(b) be verified by a person having knowledge of the facts stated;

(c) if any money due under the judgment has been paid, show the conditions under which it was accepted; and

(d) state whether the party awarded judgment has compiled with its terms.

(2) *Hearing Required if Part of Judgment Has Been Paid*. An order of eviction may not be issued if any part of the amount due under the judgment has been paid unless a hearing has been held after the defendant has been given notice and an opportunity to appear.

(L) **Appeal**. Except as provided by this rule or by law, the rules applicable to other appeals to circuit court (see MCR 7.101-7.115) apply to appeals from judgments in land contract forfeiture cases. However, in such cases the time limit for filing a claim of appeal under MCR 7.104(A) is 10 days.

Subchapter 4.300 Small Claims Actions

Rule 4.301 Applicability of Rules

Actions in a small claims division are governed by the procedural provisions of Chapter 84 of the Revised Judicature Act, MCL 600.8401 et seq., and by this subchapter of the rules. After judgment, other applicable Michigan Court Rules govern actions that were brought in a small claims division.

Rule 4.302 Statement of Claim

(A) **Contents**. The statement of the claim must be in an affidavit in substantially the form approved by the state court administrator. Affidavit forms shall be available at the clerk's office. The nature and amount of the claim must be stated in concise, nontechnical language, and the affidavit must state the date or dates when the claim arose.

(B) **Affidavit; Signature**.

(1) If the plaintiff is an individual, the affidavit must be signed by the plaintiff, or the plaintiff's guardian, conservator, or next friend.

(2) If the plaintiff is a sole proprietorship, a partnership, or a corporation, the affidavit must be signed by a person authorized to file the claim by MCL 600.8407(3).

(C) **Names**.

(1) The affidavit must state the full and correct name of the plaintiff and whether the plaintiff is a corporation or a partnership. If the plaintiff was acting under an assumed name when the claim arose, the assumed name must be given.

(2) The defendant may be identified as permitted by MCL 600.8426, or as is proper in other civil actions.

(D) **Claims in Excess of Statutory Limitation**. If the amount of the plaintiff's claim exceeds the statutory limitation, the actual amount of the claim must be stated. The claim must state that by commencing the action the plaintiff waives any claim to the excess over the statutory limitation, and that the amount equal to the statutory limitation, exclusive of costs, is claimed by the action. A judgment on the claim is a bar to a later action in any court to recover the excess.

Rule 4.303 Notice

(A) **Contents**. The notice to the defendant must meet the requirements of MCL 600.8404. The court clerk shall notify the plaintiff to appear at the time and place specified with the books, papers, and witnesses necessary to prove the claim, and that if the plaintiff fails to appear, the claim will be dismissed.

(B) **Certified Mail**. If the defendant is a corporation or a partnership, the certified mail described in MCL 600.8405 need not be deliverable to the addressee only, but may be deliverable to and signed for by an agent of the addressee.

(C) **Notice Not Served**. If it appears that notice was not received by the defendant at least 7 days before the appearance date and the defendant does not appear, the clerk must, at the plaintiff's request, issue further notice without additional cost to the plaintiff, setting the hearing for a future date. The notice may be served as provided in MCR 2.105.

Rule 4.304 Conduct of Trial

(A) **Appearance**. If the parties appear, the court shall hear the claim as provided in MCL 600.8411. The trial may be adjourned to a later date for good cause.

(B) **Nonappearance**.

(1) If a defendant fails to appear, judgment may be entered by default if the claim is liquidated, or on the ex parte proofs the court requires if the claim is unliquidated.

(2) If the plaintiff fails to appear, the claim may be dismissed for want of prosecution, the defendant may proceed to trial on the merits, or the action may be adjourned, as the court directs.

(3) If all parties fail to appear, the claim may be dismissed for want of prosecution or the court may order another disposition, as justice requires.

Rule 4.305 Judgments

(A) **Entry of Judgments**. A judgment must be entered at the time of the entry of the court's findings, and must contain the payment and stay provisions required by MCL 600.8410(2).

(B) **Modification; Vacation**. A judgment of the small claims division may be modified or vacated in the same manner as judgments in other civil actions, except that an appeal may not be taken.

(C) **Garnishment**. A writ of garnishment may not be issued to enforce the judgment until the expiration of 21 days after it was entered. If a judgment had been ordered to be paid by installments, an affidavit for a writ of garnishment must so state and must state that the order has been set aside or vacated.

Rule 4.306 Removal to Trial Court

(A) **Demand**. A party may demand that the action be removed from the small claims division to the trial court for further proceedings by

(1) signing a written demand for removal and filing it with the clerk at or before the time set for hearing; or

(2) appearing before the court at the time and place set for hearing and demanding removal.

(B) **Order; Fee**. On receiving a demand for removal, the court shall, by a written order filed in the action, direct removal to the trial court for further proceedings.

(1) The order must direct a defendant to file a written answer and serve it as provided in MCR 2.107 within 14 days after the date of the order.

(2) A copy of the order must be mailed to each party by the clerk.

(3) There is no fee for the removal, order, or mailing.

(C) **Motion for More Definite Statement**. After removal, the affidavit is deemed to be a sufficient statement of the plaintiff's claim unless a defendant, within the time permitted for answer, files a motion for a more definite statement.

(1) The motion must state the information sought and must be supported by an affidavit that the defendant

(a) does not have the information and cannot secure it with the exercise of reasonable diligence, and

(b) is unable to answer the plaintiff's claim without it.

(2) The court may decide the motion without a hearing on just and reasonable terms or may direct that a hearing be held after notice to both parties at a time set by the court.

(3) If the plaintiff fails to file a more definite statement after having been ordered to do so, the clerk shall dismiss the claim for want of prosecution.

(D) **Default**. On removal, if the defendant fails to file an answer or motion within the time permitted, the clerk shall enter the default of the defendant. MCR 2.603 governs further proceedings.

(E) **Procedure After Removal**. Except as provided in this rule, further proceedings in actions removed to the trial court are governed by the rules applicable to other civil actions.

Subchapter 4.400 Magistrates

Rule 4.401 Magistrates

(A) **Procedure**. Proceedings involving magistrates must be in accordance with relevant statutes and rules.

(B) **Duties**. Notwithstanding statutory provisions to the contrary, magistrates exercise only those duties expressly authorized by the chief judge of the district or division.

(C) **Control of Magisterial Action**. An action taken by a magistrate may be superseded, without formal appeal, by order of a district judge in the district in which the magistrate serves.

(D) **Appeals**. Appeals of right may be taken from a decision of the magistrate to the district court in the district in which the magistrate serves by filing a written claim of appeal in substantially the form provided by MCR 7.104 within 7 days of the entry of the decision of the magistrate. No fee is required on the filing of the appeal, except as otherwise provided by statute or court rule. The action is heard de novo by the district court.

CHAPTER 5. PROBATE COURT

Subchapter 5.000 General Provisions

Rule 5.001 Applicability

(A) **Applicability of Rules**. Procedure in probate court is governed by the rules applicable to other civil proceedings, except as modified by the rules in this chapter.

(B) **Terminology**.

(1) References to the "clerk" in the Michigan Court Rules also apply to the register in probate court proceedings.

(2) References to "pleadings" in the Michigan Court Rules also apply to petitions, objections, and claims in probate court proceedings.

Subchapter 5.100 General Rules of Pleading and Practice

Rule 5.101 Form and Commencement of Action; Confidential Records

(A) **Form of Action**. There are two forms of action, a "proceeding" and a "civil action."

(B) **Commencement of Proceeding**. A proceeding is commenced by filing an application or a petition with the court.

(C) **Civil Actions, Commencement, Governing Rules**. The following actions must be titled civil actions and commenced by filing a complaint and are governed by the rules applicable to civil actions in circuit court:

(1) Any action against another filed by a fiduciary or trustee.

(2) Any action filed by a claimant after notice that the claim has been disallowed.

(D) Records are public except as otherwise indicated in court rule and statute.

Rule 5.102 Notice of Hearing

A petitioner, fiduciary, or other moving party must cause to be prepared, served, and filed, a notice of hearing for all matters requiring notification of interested persons. It must state the time and date, the place, and the nature of the hearing. Hearings must be noticed for and held at times previously approved by the court.

Rule 5.103 Who May Serve

(A) **Qualifications**. Service may be made by any adult or emancipated minor, including an interested person.

(B) **Service in a Governmental Institution**. Personal service on a person in a governmental institution, hospital, or home must be made by the person in charge of the institution or a person designated by that person.

Rule 5.104 Proof of Service; Waiver and Consent; Unopposed Petition

(A) **Proof of Service**.

(1) Whenever service is required by statute or court rule, a proof of service must be filed promptly and at the latest before a hearing to which the paper relates or at the time the paper is required to be filed with the court if the paper does not relate to a hearing. The proof of service must include a description of the papers served, the date of service, the manner and method of service, and the person or persons served.

(2) Except as otherwise provided by rule, proof of service of a paper required or permitted to be served may be by

(a) a copy of the notice of hearing, if any;

(b) copies of other papers served with the notice of hearing, with a description of the papers in the proof of service;

(c) authentication under MCR 5.114(B) of the person making service.

(3) Subrule (A)(1) notwithstanding, in decedent estates, no proof of service need be filed in connection with informal proceedings or unsupervised administration unless required by court rule.

(4) In unsupervised administration of a trust, subrule (A)(1) notwithstanding, no proof of service need be filed unless required by court rule.

(B) **Waiver and Consent**.

(1) *Waiver*. The right to notice of hearing may be waived. The waiver must

(a) be stated on the record at the hearing, or

(b) be in a writing, which is dated and signed by the interested person or someone authorized to consent on the interested person's behalf and specifies the hearing to which it applies.

(2) *Consent*. The relief requested in an application, petition, or motion may be granted by consent. An interested person who consents to an application, petition, or motion does not have to be served with or waive notice of hearing on the application, petition, or motion. The consent must

(a) be stated on the record at the hearing, or

(b) be in a writing which is dated and signed by the interested person or someone authorized to consent on the interested person's behalf and must contain a declaration that the person signing has received a copy of the application, petition, or motion.

(3) *Who May Waive and Consent*. A waiver and a consent may be made

(a) by a legally competent interested person;

(b) by a person designated in these rules as eligible to be served on behalf of an interested person who is a legally disabled person; or

(c) on behalf of an interested person whether competent or legally disabled, by an attorney who has previously filed a written appearance.

However, a guardian, conservator, or trustee cannot waive or consent with regard to petitions, motions, accounts, or reports made by that person as guardian, conservator, or trustee.

(4) Order. If all interested persons have consented, the order may be entered immediately.

(C) **Unopposed Petition**. If a petition is unopposed at the time set for the hearing, the court may either grant the petition on the basis of the recitations in the petition or conduct a hearing. However, an order determining heirs based on an uncontested petition to determine heirs may only be entered on the basis of sworn testimony or a sworn testimony form. An order granting a petition to appoint a guardian may only be entered on the basis of testimony at a hearing.

Rule 5.105 Manner and Method of Service

(A) **Manner of Service**.

(1) Service on an interested person may be by personal service within or without the State of Michigan.

(2) Unless another method of service is required by statute, court rule, or special order of a probate court, service may be made to the current address of an interested person by registered, certified, or ordinary first-class mail. Foreign consul and the Attorney General may be served by mail.

(3) An interested person whose address or whereabouts is not known may be served by publication, if an affidavit or declaration under MCR 5.114(B) is filed with the court, showing that the address or whereabouts of the interested person could not be ascertained on diligent inquiry. Except in proceedings seeking a determination of a presumption of death based on absence pursuant to MCL 700.1208(2), after an interested person has once been served by publication, notice is only required on an interested person whose address is known or becomes known during the proceedings.

(4) The court, for good cause on ex parte petition, may direct the manner of service if

(a) no statute or court rule provides for the manner of service on an interested person, or

(b) service cannot otherwise reasonably be made.

(B) **Method of Service**.

(1) *Personal Service*.

(a) On an Attorney. Personal service of a paper on an attorney must be made by

(i) handing it to the attorney personally;

(ii) leaving it at the attorney's office with a clerk or with some person in charge or, if no one is in charge or present, by leaving it in some conspicuous place there, or by electronically delivering a facsimile to the attorney's office;

(iii) if the office is closed or the attorney has no office, by leaving it at the attorney's usual residence with some person of suitable age and discretion residing there; or

(iv) sending the paper by registered mail or certified mail, return receipt requested, and delivery restricted to the addressee; but service is not made for purpose of this subrule until the attorney receives the paper.

(b) On Other Individuals. Personal service of a paper on an individual other than an attorney must be made by

(i) handing it to the individual personally;

(ii) leaving it at the person's usual residence with some person of suitable age and discretion residing there; or

(iii) sending the paper by registered mail or certified mail, return receipt requested, and delivery restricted to the addressee; but service is not made for purpose of this subrule until the individual receives the paper.

(c) On Persons Other Than Individuals. Service on an interested person other than an individual must be made in the manner provided in MCR 2.105(C)-(G).

(2) *Mailing*. Mailing of a copy under this rule means enclosing it in a sealed envelope with first-class postage fully prepaid, addressed to the person to be served, and depositing the envelope and its contents in the United States mail. Service by mail is complete at the time of mailing.

(3) *Publication*. Service by publication must be made in the manner provided in MCR 5.106.

(4) *E-mail*. Unless otherwise limited or provided by this court rule, parties to a civil action or interested persons to a proceeding may agree to service by e-mail in the manner provided in and governed by MCR 2.107(C)(4).

(C) **Petitioner, Service Not Required**. For service of notice of hearing on a petition, the petitioner, although otherwise an interested person, is presumed to have waived notice and consented to the petition, unless the petition expressly indicates that the petitioner does not waive notice and does not consent to the granting of the requested prayers without a hearing. Although a petitioner or a fiduciary may in fact be an interested person, the petitioner need not indicate, either by written waiver or proof of service, that the petitioner has received a copy of any paper required by these rules to be served on interested persons.

(D) **Service on Persons Under Legal Disability or Otherwise Legally Represented**. In a guardianship or conservatorship proceeding, a petition or notice of hearing asking for an order that affects the ward or protected individual must be served on that ward or protected individual if he or she is 14 years of age or older. In all other circumstances, service on an interested person under legal disability or otherwise legally represented must be made on the following:
(1) The guardian of an adult, conservator, or guardian ad litem of a minor or other legally incapacitated individual, except with respect to:
(a) a petition for commitment or
(b) a petition, account, inventory, or report made as the guardian, conservator, or guardian ad litem.
(2) The trustee of a trust with respect to a beneficiary of the trust, except that the trustee may not be served on behalf of the beneficiary on petitions, accounts, or reports made by the trustee as trustee or as personal representative of the settlor's estate.
(3) The guardian ad litem of any person, including an unascertained or unborn person, except as otherwise provided in subrule (D)(1).
(4) A parent of a minor with whom the minor resides, provided the interest of the parent in the outcome of the hearing is not in conflict with the interest of the minor and provided the parent has filed an appearance on behalf of the minor.
(5) The attorney for an interested person who has filed a written appearance in the proceeding. If the appearance is in the name of the office of the United States attorney, the counsel for the Veterans' Administration, the Attorney General, the prosecuting attorney, or the county or municipal corporation counsel, by a specifically designated attorney, service must be directed to the attention of the designated attorney at the address stated in the written appearance.
(6) The agent of an interested person under an unrevoked power of attorney filed with the court. A power of attorney is deemed unrevoked until written revocation is filed or it is revoked by operation of law.

For purposes of service, an emancipated minor without a guardian or conservator is not deemed to be under legal disability.

(E) **Service on Beneficiaries of Future Interests**. A notice that must be served on unborn or unascertained interested persons not represented by a fiduciary or guardian ad litem is considered served on the unborn or unascertained interested persons if it is served as provided in this subrule.
(1) If an interest is limited to persons in being and the same interest is further limited to the happening of a future event to unascertained or unborn persons, notice and papers must be served on the persons to whom the interest is first limited.
(2) If an interest is limited to persons whose existence as a class is conditioned on some future event, notice and papers must be served on the persons in being who would comprise the class if the required event had taken place immediately before the time when the papers are served.
(3) If a case is not covered by subrule (E)(1) or (2), notice and papers must be served on all known persons whose interests are substantially identical to those of the unascertained or unborn interested persons.

Rule 5.106 Publication of Notice of Hearing

(A) **Requirements**. A notice of hearing or other notice required to be made by publication must be published in a newspaper as defined by MCR 2.106(F) one time at least 14 days before the date of the hearing, except that publication of a notice seeking a determination of a presumption of death based on absence pursuant to MCL 700.1208(2) must be made once a month for 4 consecutive months before the hearing.

(B) **Contents of Published Notice**. If notice is given to a person by publication because the person's address or whereabouts is not known and cannot be ascertained after diligent inquiry, the published notice must include the name of the person to whom the notice is given and a statement that the result of the hearing may be to bar or affect the person's interest in the matter.

(C) **Affidavit of Publication**. The person who orders the publication must cause to be filed with the court a copy of the publication notice and the publisher's affidavit stating
(1) the facts that establish the qualifications of the newspaper, and
(2) the date or dates the notice was published.

(D) **Service of Notice**. A copy of the notice:
(1) must be mailed to an interested person at his or her last known address if the person's present address is not known and cannot be ascertained by diligent inquiry;
(2) need not be mailed to an interested person if an address cannot be ascertained by diligent inquiry.

(E) **Location of Publication**. Publication must be in the county where the court is located unless a different county is specified by statute, court rule, or order of the court.

Rule 5.107 Other Papers Required to be Served

(A) **Other Papers to be Served**. The person filing a petition, an application, a sworn testimony form, supplemental sworn testimony form, a motion, a response or objection, an instrument offered or admitted to probate, an accounting, or a sworn closing statement with the court must serve a copy of that document on interested persons. The person who obtains an order from the court must serve a copy of the order on interested persons.

(B) **Exceptions.**

(1) Service of the papers listed in subrule (A) is not required to be made on an interested person whose address or whereabouts, on diligent inquiry, is unknown, or on an unascertained or unborn person. The court may excuse service on an interested person for good cause.

(2) Service is not required for a small estate filed under MCL 700.3982.

Rule 5.108 Time of Service

(A) **Personal**. Personal service of a petition or motion must be made at least 7 days before the date set for hearing, or an adjourned date, unless a different period is provided or permitted by court rule. This subrule applies regardless of conflicting statutory provisions.

(B) **Mail**.

(1) *Petition or Motion*. Service by mail of a petition or motion must be made at least 14 days before the date set for hearing, or an adjourned date.

(2) *Application by a Guardian or Conservator Appointed in Another State*.

(a) A court may appoint a temporary guardian or conservator without a hearing pursuant to MCL 700.5202a, MCL 700.5301a, or MCL 700.5433.

(b) If a court appoints a temporary guardian or conservator pursuant to MCL 700.5202a, MCL 700.5301a or MCL 700.5433, the temporary guardian or conservator must, not later than 14 days after the appointment, serve notice of the appointment by mail to all interested persons.

(C) **Exception: Foreign Consul**. This rule does not affect the manner and time for service on foreign consul provided by law.

(D) **Computation of Time**. MCR 1.108 governs computation of time in probate proceedings.

(E) **Responses**. A written response or objection may be served at any time before the hearing or at a time set by the court.

Rule 5.109 Notice of Guardianship Proceedings Concerning Indian Child

If an Indian child is the subject of a guardianship proceeding and an Indian tribe does not have exclusive jurisdiction as defined in MCR 3.002(2):

(1) in addition to any other service requirements, the petitioner shall notify the parent or Indian custodian and the Indian child's tribe, by personal service or by registered mail with return receipt requested and delivery restricted to the addressee, of the pending proceedings on a petition to establish guardianship over the Indian child and of their right of intervention on a form approved by the State Court Administrative Office. If the identity or location of the parent or Indian custodian, or of the Indian child's tribe, cannot be determined, notice shall be given to the Secretary of the Interior by registered mail with return receipt requested. If a petition is filed with the court that subsequently identifies the minor as an Indian child after a guardianship has been established, notice of that petition must be served in accordance with this subrule.

(2) the court shall notify the parent or Indian custodian and the Indian child's tribe of all other hearings pertaining to the guardianship proceeding as provided in MCR 5.105. If the identity or location of the parent or Indian custodian, or of the Indian child's tribe, cannot be determined, notice of the hearings shall be given to the Secretary of the Interior. Such notice may be made by first-class mail.

Rule 5.112 Prior Proceedings Affecting the Person of a Minor

Proceedings affecting the person of a minor subject to the prior continuing jurisdiction of another court of record are governed by MCR 3.205, including the requirement that petitions in such proceedings must contain allegations with respect to the prior proceedings.

Rule 5.113 Papers; Form and Filing

(A) **Forms of Papers Generally**.

(1) An application, petition, motion, inventory, report, account, or other paper in a proceeding must

(a) comply with MCR 1.109 and be legibly typewritten or printed in ink in the English language, and

(b) include the

(i) name of the court and title of the proceeding in which it is filed;

(ii) case number, if any, including a prefix of the year filed and a two-letter suffix for the case-type code (see MCR 8.117) according to the principal subject matter of the proceeding, and if the case is filed under the juvenile code, the petition number which also includes a prefix of the year filed and a two-letter suffix for the case-type code.

(iii) character of the paper; and

(iv) name, address, and telephone number of the attorney, if any, appearing for the person filing the paper, and

(c) be substantially in the form approved by the State Court Administrator, if a form has been approved for the use.

(2) A judge or register may reject nonconforming documents in accordance with MCR 8.119.

(B) **Contents of Petitions**.

(1) A petition must include allegations and representations sufficient to justify the relief sought and must:

(a) identify the petitioner, and the petitioner's interest in proceedings, and qualification to petition;

(b) include allegations as to residence, domicile, or property situs essential to establishing court jurisdiction;

(c) identify and incorporate, directly or by reference, any documents to be admitted, construed, or interpreted;

(d) include any additional allegations required by law or court rule;

(e) except when ex parte relief is sought, include a current list of interested persons, indicate the existence and form of incapacity of any of them, the mailing addresses of the persons or their representatives, the nature of representation and the need, if any, for special representation.

(2) The petition may incorporate by reference papers and lists of interested persons previously filed with the court if changes in the papers or lists are set forth in the incorporating petition.

(C) **Filing by Registered Mail**. Any document required by law to be filed in or delivered to the court by registered mail, may be filed or delivered by certified mail, return receipt requested.

(D) **Filing Additional Papers**. The court in its discretion may receive for filing a paper not required to be filed.

Rule 5.114 Signing and Authentication of Papers

(A) **Signing of Papers**.

(1) The provisions of MCR 2.114 regarding the signing of papers apply in probate proceedings except as provided in this subrule.

(2) When a person is represented by an attorney, the signature of the attorney is required on any paper filed in a form approved by the State Court Administrator only if the form includes a place for a signature.

(3) An application, petition, or other paper may be signed by the attorney for the petitioner, except that an inventory, account, acceptance of appointment, and sworn closing statement must be signed by the fiduciary or trustee. A receipt for assets must be signed by the person entitled to the assets.

(B) **Authentication by Verification or Declaration**.

(1) An application, petition, inventory, accounting, proof of claim, or proof of service must be either authenticated by verification under oath by the person making it, or, in the alternative, contain a statement immediately above the date and signature of the maker: "I declare under the penalties of perjury that this __________ has been examined by me and that its contents are true to the best of my information, knowledge, and belief." Any requirement of law that a document filed with the court must be sworn may be met by this declaration.

(2) In addition to the sanctions provided by MCR 2.114(E), a person who knowingly makes a false declaration under subrule (B)(1) is in contempt of court.

Rule 5.117 Appearance by Attorneys

(A) **Representation of Fiduciary**. An attorney filing an appearance on behalf of a fiduciary shall represent the fiduciary.

(B) **Appearance**.

(1) *In General*. An attorney may appear by an act indicating that the attorney represents an interested person in the proceeding. An appearance by an attorney for an interested person is deemed an appearance by the interested person. Unless a particular rule indicates otherwise, any act required to be performed by an interested person may be performed by the attorney representing the interested person.

(2) *Notice of Appearance*. If an appearance is made in a manner not involving the filing of a paper served with the court or if the appearance is made by filing a paper which is not served on the interested persons, the attorney must promptly file a written appearance and serve it on the interested persons whose addresses are known and on the fiduciary. The attorney's address and telephone number must be included in the appearance.

(3) *Appearance by Law Firm*.

(a) A pleading, appearance, motion, or other paper filed by a law firm on behalf of a client is deemed the appearance of the individual attorney first filing a paper in the action. All notices required by these rules may be served on that individual. That attorney's appearance continues until an order of substitution or withdrawal is entered. This subrule is not intended to prohibit other attorneys in the law firm from appearing in the action on behalf of the client.

(b) The appearance of an attorney is deemed to be the appearance of every member of the law firm. Any attorney in the firm may be required by the court to conduct a court-ordered conference or trial.

(C) **Duration of Appearance by Attorney**.

(1) *In General*. Unless otherwise stated in the appearance or ordered by the court, an attorney's appearance applies only in the court in which it is made or to which the action is transferred and only for the proceeding in which it is filed.

(2) *Appearance on Behalf of Fiduciary*. An appearance on behalf of a fiduciary applies until the proceedings are completed, the client is discharged, or an order terminating the appearance is entered.

(3) *Termination of Appearance on Behalf of a Personal Representative*. In unsupervised administration, the probate register may enter an order terminating an appearance on behalf of a personal representative if the personal representative consents in writing to the termination.

(4) *Other Appearance*. An appearance on behalf of a client other than a fiduciary applies until a final order is entered disposing of all claims by or against the client, or an order terminating the appearance is entered.

(5) *Substitution of Attorneys*. In the case of a substitution of attorneys, the court in a supervised administration or the probate register in an unsupervised administration may enter an order permitting the substitution without prior notice to the interested persons or fiduciary. If the order is entered, the substituted attorney must give notice of the substitution to all interested persons and the fiduciary.

(D) **Right to Determination of Compensation**. An attorney whose services are terminated retains the right to have compensation determined before the proceeding is closed.

Rule 5.118 Amending or Supplementing Papers

(A) **Papers Subject to Hearing**. A person who has filed a paper that is subject to a hearing may amend or supplement the paper

(1) before a hearing if notice is given pursuant to these rules, or

(2) at the hearing without new notice of hearing if the court determines that material prejudice would not result to the substantial rights of the person to whom the notice should have been directed.

(B) **Papers Not Subject to Hearing**. A person who has filed a paper that is not subject to a hearing may amend or supplement the paper if service is made pursuant to these rules.

Rule 5.119 Additional Petitions; Objections; Hearing Practices

(A) **Right to Hearing, New Matter**. An interested person may, within the period allowed by law or these rules, file a petition and obtain a hearing with respect to the petition. The petitioner must serve copies of the petition and notice of hearing on the fiduciary and other interested persons whose addresses are known.

(B) **Objection to Pending Matter**. An interested person may object to a pending petition orally at the hearing or by filing and serving a paper which conforms with MCR 5.113. The court may adjourn a hearing based on an oral objection and require that a proper written objection be filed and served.

(C) **Adjournment**. A petition that is not heard on the day for which it is noticed, in the absence of a special order, stands adjourned from day to day or until a day certain.

(D) **Briefs; Argument**. The court may require that briefs of law and fact and proposed orders be filed as a condition precedent to oral argument. The court may limit oral argument.

Rule 5.120 Action by Fiduciary in Contested Matter; Notice to Interested Persons; Failure to Intervene

The fiduciary represents the interested persons in a contested matter. The fiduciary must give notice to all interested persons whose addresses are known that a contested matter has been commenced and must keep such interested persons reasonably informed of the fiduciary's actions concerning the matter. The fiduciary must inform the interested persons that they may file a petition to intervene in the matter and that failure to intervene shall result in their being bound by the actions of the fiduciary. The interested person shall be bound by the actions of the fiduciary after such notice and until the interested person notifies the fiduciary that the interested person has filed with the court a petition to intervene.

Rule 5.121 Guardian Ad Litem; Visitor

(A) **Appointment**.

(1) *Guardian Ad Litem*. The court shall appoint a guardian ad litem when required by law. If it deems necessary, the court may appoint a guardian ad litem to appear for and represent the interests of any person in any proceeding. The court shall state the purpose of the appointment in the order of appointment. The order may be entered with or without notice.

(2) *Visitor*. The court may appoint a visitor when authorized by law.

(B) **Revocation**. If it deems necessary, the court may revoke the appointment and appoint another guardian ad litem or visitor.

(C) **Duties**. Before the date set for hearing, the guardian ad litem or visitor shall conduct an investigation and shall make a report in open court or file a written report of the investigation and recommendations. The guardian ad litem or visitor need not appear personally at the hearing unless required by law or directed by the court. Any written report must be filed with the court at least 24 hours before the hearing or such other time specified by the court.

(D) **Evidence**.

(1) *Reports, Admission Into Evidence*. Oral and written reports of a guardian ad litem or visitor may be received by the court and may be relied on to the extent of their probative value, even though such evidence may not be admissible under the Michigan Rules of Evidence.

(2) *Reports, Review and Cross-Examination*.

(a) Any interested person shall be afforded an opportunity to examine and controvert reports received into evidence.

(b) The person who is the subject of a report received under subrule (D)(1) shall be permitted to cross-examine the individual making the report if the person requests such an opportunity.

(c) Other interested persons may cross-examine the individual making a report on the contents of the report, if the individual is reasonably available. The court may limit cross-examination for good cause.

(E) **Attorney-Client Privilege**.

(1) *During Appointment of Guardian Ad Litem*. When the guardian ad litem appointed to represent the interest of a person is an attorney, that appointment does not create an attorney-client relationship. Communications between that person and the guardian ad litem are not subject to the attorney-client privilege. The guardian ad litem must inform the person whose interests are represented of this lack of privilege as soon as practicable after appointment. The guardian ad litem may report or testify about any communication with the person whose interests are represented.

(2) *Later Appointment as Attorney*. If the appointment of the guardian ad litem is terminated and the same individual is appointed attorney, the appointment as attorney creates an attorney-client relationship. The attorney-client privilege relates back to the date of the appointment of the guardian ad litem.

Rule 5.125 Interested Persons Defined

(A) **Special Persons**. In addition to persons named in subrule (C) with respect to specific proceedings, the following persons must be served:

(1) The Attorney General must be served if required by law or court rule. The Attorney General must be served in the specific proceedings enumerated in subrule (C) when the decedent is not survived by any known heirs, or the protected person has no known presumptive heirs.

(2) A foreign consul must be served if required by MCL 700.1401(4) or court rule. An attorney who has filed an appearance for a foreign consul must be served when required by subrule (A)(5).

(3) On a petition for the appointment of a guardian or conservator of a person on whose account benefits are payable by the Veterans' Administration, the Administrator of Veterans' Affairs must be served through the administrator's Michigan district counsel.

(4) A guardian, conservator, or guardian ad litem of a person must be served with notice of proceedings as to which the represented person is an interested person, except as provided by MCR 5.105(D)(1).

(5) An attorney who has filed an appearance must be served notice of proceedings concerning which the attorney's client is an interested person.

(6) A special fiduciary appointed under MCL 700.1309.

(7) A person who filed a demand for notice under MCL 700.3205 or a request for notice under MCL 700.5104 if the demand or request has not been withdrawn, expired, or terminated by court order.

(8) In a guardianship proceeding for a minor, if the minor is an Indian child as defined by the Michigan Indian Family Preservation Act, MCL 712B.1 *et seq.*, the minor's tribe and the Indian custodian, if any, and, if the Indian child's parent or Indian custodian or tribe is unknown, the Secretary of the Interior.

(B) **Special Conditions for Interested Persons**.

(1) *Claimant*. Only a claimant who has properly presented a claim and whose claim has not been disallowed and remains unpaid need be notified of specific proceedings under subrule (C).

(2) *Devisee*. Only a devisee whose devise remains unsatisfied, or a trust beneficiary whose beneficial interest remains unsatisfied, need be notified of specific proceedings under subrule (C).

(3) *Trust as Devisee*. If either a trust or a trustee is a devisee, the trustee is the interested person. If no trustee has qualified, the interested persons are the qualified trust beneficiaries described in MCL 700.7103(g)(i) and the nominated trustee, if any.

(4) *Father of a Child Born out of Wedlock*. Except as otherwise provided by law, the natural father of a child born out of wedlock need not be served notice of proceedings in which the child's parents are interested persons unless his paternity has been determined in a manner provided by law.

(5) *Decedent as Interested Person*. If a decedent is an interested person, the personal representative of the

decedent's estate is the interested person. If there is no personal representative, the interested persons are the known heirs of the estate of the decedent, and the known devisees. If there are no known heirs, the Attorney General must receive notice.

(C) **Specific Proceedings**. Subject to subrules (A) and (B) and MCR 5.105(E), the following provisions apply. When a single petition requests multiple forms of relief, the petitioner must give notice to all persons interested in each type of relief:

(1) The persons interested in an application or a petition to probate a will are the
   (a) devisees,
   (b) nominated trustee and qualified trust beneficiaries described in MCL 700.7103(g)(i) of a trust created under the will,
   (c) heirs,
   (d) nominated personal representative, and
   (e) trustee of a revocable trust described in MCL 700.7605(1).

(2) The persons interested in an application or a petition to appoint a personal representative, other than a special personal representative, of an intestate estate are the
   (a) heirs,
   (b) nominated personal representative, and
   (c) trustee of a revocable trust described in MCL 700.7605(1).

(3) The persons interested in a petition to determine the heirs of a decedent are the presumptive heirs.

(4) The persons interested in a petition of surety for discharge from further liability are the
   (a) principal on the bond,
   (b) co-surety,
   (c) devisees of a testate estate,
   (d) heirs of an intestate estate,
   (e) qualified trust beneficiaries, as referred to in MCL 700.7103(g)(i),
   (f) protected person and presumptive heirs of the protected person in a conservatorship, and
   (g) claimants.

(5) The persons interested in a proceeding for spouse's allowance are the
   (a) devisees of a testate estate,
   (b) heirs of an intestate estate,
   (c) claimants,
   (d) spouse, and
   (e) the personal representative, if the spouse is not the personal representative.

(6) The persons interested in a proceeding for examination of an account of a fiduciary are the
   (a) for a testate estate, the devisees under the will (and if one of the devisees is a trustee or a trust, the persons referred to in MCR 5.125[B][3]),
   (b) for an intestate estate, the heirs,
   (c) for a conservatorship, the protected individual (if he or she is 14 years of age or older), the presumptive heirs of the protected individual, and the guardian ad litem, if any,
   (d) for a final conservatorship or guardianship account following the death of the protected person, the personal representative, if one has been appointed,
   (e) for a guardianship, the ward (if he or she is 14 years of age or older), the presumptive heirs of the ward, and the guardian ad litem, if any,
   (f) for a revocable trust, the settlor (and if the petitioner has a reasonable basis to believe the settlor is an incapacitated individual, those persons who are entitled to be reasonably informed, as referred to in MCL 700.7603[2]), the current trustee, and any other person named in the terms of the trust to receive either an account or a notice of such a proceeding, including a trust protector,
   (g) for an irrevocable trust, the current trustee, the qualified trust beneficiaries, as defined in MCL 700.7103(g), and any other person named in the terms of the trust to receive either an account or a notice of such a proceeding, including a trust protector,
   (h) in all matters described in this subsection (6), any person whose interests would be adversely affected by the relief requested, including a claimant or an insurer or surety who might be subject to financial obligations as the result of the approval of the account.

(7) The persons interested in a proceeding for partial distribution of the estate of a decedent are the
   (a) devisees of a testate estate entitled to share in the residue,
   (b) heirs of an intestate estate,
   (c) claimants, and
   (d) any other person whose unsatisfied interests in the estate may be affected by such assignment.

(8) The persons interested in a petition for an order of complete estate settlement under MCL 700.3952 or a petition for discharge under MCR 5.311(B)(3) are the
   (a) devisees of a testate estate,
   (b) heirs unless there has been an adjudication that decedent died testate,
   (c) claimants, and
   (d) such other persons whose interests are affected by the relief requested.

(9) The persons interested in a proceeding for an estate settlement order pursuant to MCL 700.3953 are the
   (a) personal representative,
   (b) devisees,
   (c) claimants, and

(d) such other persons whose interests are affected by the relief requested.

(10) The persons interested in a proceeding for assignment and distribution of the share of an absent apparent heir or devisee in the estate of a decedent are the
(a) devisees of the will of the decedent,
(b) heirs of the decedent if the decedent did not leave a will,
(c) devisees of the will of the absent person, and
(d) presumptive heirs of the absent person.

(11) The persons interested in a petition for supervised administration after an estate has been commenced are the
(a) devisees, unless the court has previously found decedent died intestate,
(b) heirs, unless the court has previously found decedent died testate,
(c) personal representative, and
(d) claimants.

(12) The persons interested in an independent request for adjudication under MCL 700.3415 and a petition for an interim order under MCL 700.3505 are the
(a) personal representative, and
(b) other persons who will be affected by the adjudication.

(13) The persons interested in a petition for settlement of a wrongful-death action or distribution of wrongful-death proceeds are the
(a) heirs of the decedent,
(b) other persons who may be entitled to distribution of wrongful-death proceeds, and
(c) claimants whose interests are affected.

(14) The persons interested in a will contest settlement proceeding are the
(a) heirs of the decedent and
(b) devisees affected by settlement.

(15) The persons interested in a partition proceeding where the property has not been assigned to a trust under the will are the
(a) heirs in an intestate estate or
(b) devisees affected by partition.

(16) The persons interested in a partition proceeding where the property has been assigned to a trust under the will are the
(a) trustee and
(b) beneficiaries affected by the partition.

(17) The persons interested in a petition to establish the cause and date of death in an accident or disaster case under MCL 700.1208 are the heirs of the presumed decedent.

(18) The persons interested in a proceeding under the Mental Health Code that may result in an individual receiving involuntary mental health treatment or judicial admission of an individual with a developmental disability to a center are the
(a) individual,
(b) individual's attorney,
(c) petitioner,
(d) prosecuting attorney or petitioner's attorney,
(e) director of any hospital or center to which the individual has been admitted,
(f) the individual's spouse, if the spouse's whereabouts are known,
(g) the individual's guardian, if any,
(h) in a proceeding for judicial admission to a center, the community mental health program, and
(i) such other relatives or persons as the court may determine.

(19) The persons interested in an application for appointment of a guardian of a minor by a guardian appointed in another state and in a petition for appointment of a guardian of a minor are
(a) the minor, if 14 years of age or older;
(b) if known by the petitioner or applicant, each person who had the principal care and custody of the minor during the 63 days preceding the filing of the petition or application;
(c) the parents of the minor or, if neither of them is living, any grandparents and the adult presumptive heirs of the minor;
(d) the nominated guardian; and
(e) if known by the petitioner or applicant, a guardian or conservator appointed by a court in another state to make decisions regarding the person of a minor.

(20) The persons interested in the acceptance of parental appointment of the guardian of a minor under MCL 700.5202 are
(a) the minor, if 14 years of age or older,
(b) the person having the minor's care, and
(c) each grandparent and the adult presumptive heirs of the minor.

(21) The persons interested in a 7-day notice of acceptance of appointment as guardian of an incapacitated individual under MCL 700.5301 are the
(a) incapacitated individual,
(b) person having the care of the incapacitated individual, and
(c) presumptive heirs of the incapacitated individual.

(22) The persons interested in an application for appointment of a guardian of an incapacitated individual by a guardian appointed in another state or in a petition for appointment of a guardian of an alleged incapacitated individual are
(a) the alleged incapacitated individual or the incapacitated individual,

(b) if known, a person named as attorney in fact under a durable power of attorney,
(c) the alleged incapacitated individual's spouse or the incapacitated individual's spouse,
(d) the alleged incapacitated individual's adult children and the individual's parents or the incapacitated individual's adult children and parents,
(e) if no spouse, child, or parent is living, the presumptive heirs of the individual,
(f) the person who has the care and custody of the alleged incapacitated individual or the incapacitated individual,
(g) the nominated guardian, and
(h) if known by the petitioner or applicant, a guardian or conservator appointed by a court in another state to have care and control of the incapacitated individual.

(23) The persons interested in receiving a copy of the report of a guardian of a legally incapacitated individual on the condition of a ward are:
(a) the ward,
(b) the person who has principal care and custody of the ward, and
(c) the spouse and adult children or, if no adult children are living, the presumptive heirs of the individual.

(24) The persons interested in an application for appointment of a conservator for a protected individual by a conservator appointed in another state or for the petition for the appointment of a conservator or for a protective order are:
(a) the individual to be protected if 14 years of age or older,
(b) the presumptive heirs of the individual to be protected,
(c) if known, a person named as attorney in fact under a durable power of attorney,
(d) the nominated conservator,
(e) a governmental agency paying benefits to the individual to be protected or before which an application for benefits is pending, and
(f) if known by the petitioner or applicant, a guardian or conservator appointed by a court in another state to manage the protected individual's finances.

(25) The persons interested in a petition for the modification or termination of a guardianship or conservatorship or for the removal of a guardian or a conservator are
(a) those interested in a petition for appointment under subrule (C)(19), (21), (22), or (24) as the case may be, and
(b) the guardian or conservator.

(26) The persons interested in a petition by a conservator for instructions or approval of sale of real estate or other assets are
(a) the protected individual and
(b) those persons listed in subrule (C)(24) who will be affected by the instructions or order.

(27) The persons interested in receiving a copy of an inventory or account of a conservator or of a guardian are:
(a) the protected individual or ward, if he or she is 14 years of age or older,
(b) the presumptive heirs of the protected individual or ward,
(c) the claimants,
(d) the guardian ad litem, and
(e) the personal representative, if any.

(28) The persons interested in a petition for approval of a trust under MCR 2.420 are
(a) the protected individual if 14 years of age or older,
(b) the presumptive heirs of the protected individual,
(c) if there is no conservator, a person named as attorney in fact under a durable power of attorney,
(d) the nominated trustee, and
(e) a governmental agency paying benefits to the individual to be protected or before which an application for benefits is pending.

(29) The persons interested in a petition for emancipation of a minor are
(a) the minor,
(b) parents of the minor,
(c) the affiant on an affidavit supporting emancipation, and
(d) any guardian or conservator.

(30) Interested persons for any proceeding concerning a durable power of attorney for health care are
(a) the patient,
(b) the patient's advocate,
(c) the patient's spouse,
(d) the patient's adult children,
(e) the patient's parents if the patient has no adult children,
(f) if the patient has no spouse, adult children, or parents, the patient's minor children, or, if there are none, the presumptive heirs whose addresses are known,
(g) the patient's guardian and conservator, if any, and
(h) the patient's guardian ad litem.

(31) Persons interested in a proceeding to require, hear, or settle an accounting of an agent under a power of attorney are
(a) the principal,
(b) the attorney in fact or agent,

(c) any fiduciary of the principal,
(d) the principal's guardian ad litem or attorney, if any, and
(e) the principal's presumptive heirs.

(32) Subject to the provisions of Part 3 of Article VII of the Estates and Protected Individuals Code, the persons interested in the modification or termination of a noncharitable irrevocable trust are:
(a) the qualified trust beneficiaries affected by the relief requested,
(b) the settlor,
(c) if the petitioner has a reasonable basis to believe the settlor is an incapacitated individual, the settlor's representative, as referred to in MCL 700.7411(6);
(d) the trust protector, if any, as referred to in MCL 700.7103(n),
(e) the current trustee, and
(f) any other person named in the terms of the trust to receive notice of such a proceeding.

(33) Subject to the provisions of Part 3 of Article VII of the Estates and Protected Individuals Code, the persons interested in a proceeding affecting a trust other than those already covered by subrules (C)(6), (C)(28), and (C)(32) are:
(a) the qualified trust beneficiaries affected by the relief requested,
(b) the holder of a power of appointment affected by the relief requested,
(c) the current trustee,
(d) in a proceeding to appoint a trustee, the proposed trustee,
(e) the trust protector, if any, as referred to in MCL 700.7103(n),
(f) the settlor of a revocable trust, and
(g) if the petitioner has a reasonable basis to believe the settlor is an incapacitated individual, those persons who are entitled to be reasonably informed, as referred to in MCL 700.7603(2).

(D) The court shall make a specific determination of the interested persons if they are not defined by statute or court rule.

(E) In the interest of justice, the court may require additional persons be served.

Rule 5.126 Demand or Request for Notice

(A) **Applicability**. For purposes of this rule "demand" means a demand or request. This rule governs the procedures to be followed regarding a person who files a demand for notice pursuant to MCL 700.3205 or MCL 700.5104. This person under both sections is referred to as a "demandant."

(B) **Procedure**.

(1) *Obligation to Provide Notice or Copies of Documents*. Except in small estates under MCL 700.3982 and MCL 700.3983, the person responsible for serving a paper in a decedent estate, guardianship, or conservatorship in which a demand for notice is filed is responsible for providing copies of any orders and filings pertaining to the proceeding in which the demandant has requested notification. If no proceeding is pending at the time the demand is filed, the court must notify the petitioner or applicant at the time of filing that a demand for notice has been filed and of the responsibility to provide notice to the demandant.

(2) *Rights and Obligations of Demandant*.
(a) The demandant must serve on interested persons a copy of a demand for notice filed after a proceeding has been commenced.
(b) Unless the demand for notice is limited to a specified class of papers, the demandant is entitled to receive copies of all orders and filings subsequent to the filing of the demand. The copies must be mailed to the address specified in the demand. If the address becomes invalid and the demandant does not provide a new address, no further copies of papers need be provided to the demandant.

(C) **Termination, Withdrawal**.

(1) *Termination on Disqualification of Demandant*. The fiduciary or an interested person may petition the court to determine that a person who filed a demand for notice does not meet the requirements of statute or court rule to receive notification. The court on its own motion may require the demandant to show cause why the demand should not be stricken.

(2) *Expiration of Demand When no Proceeding is Opened*. If a proceeding is not opened, the demand expires three years from the date the demand is filed.

(3) *Withdrawal*. The demandant may withdraw the demand at any time by communicating the withdrawal in writing to the fiduciary.

Rule 5.127 Venue of Certain Actions

(A) **Defendant Found Incompetent to Stand Trial**. When a criminal defendant is found mentally incompetent to stand trial and is referred to the probate court for admission to a treating facility,
(1) if the defendant is a Michigan resident, venue is proper in the county where the defendant resides;
(2) if the defendant is not a Michigan resident, venue is proper in the county of the referring criminal court.

(B) **Guardian of Property of Nonresident With a Developmental Disability**. If an individual with a developmental disability is a nonresident of Michigan and needs a guardian for Michigan property under the

Mental Health Code, venue is proper in the probate court of the county where any of the property is located.

(C) **Guardian of Individual With a Developmental Disability Who is in a Facility**. If venue for a proceeding to appoint a guardian for an individual with a developmental disability who is in a facility is questioned, and it appears that the convenience of the individual with a developmental disability or guardian would not be served by proceeding in the county where the individual with a developmental disability was found, venue is proper in the county where the individual with a developmental disability most likely would reside if not disabled. In making its decision, the court shall consider the situs of the property of the individual with a developmental disability and the residence of relatives or others who have provided care.

Rule 5.128 Change of Venue

(A) **Reasons for Change**. On petition by an interested person or on the court's own initiative, the venue of a proceeding may be changed to another county by court order for the convenience of the parties and witnesses, for convenience of the attorneys, or if an impartial trial cannot be had in the county where the action is pending.

(B) **Procedure**. If venue is changed

(1) the court must send to the transferee court, without charge, copies of necessary documents on file as requested by the parties or the transferee court and the original of an unadmitted will or a certified copy of an admitted will; and

(2) except as provided in MCR 5.208(A) or unless the court directs otherwise, notices required to be published must be published in the county to which venue was changed.

Rule 5.131 Discovery Generally

(A) The general discovery rules apply in probate proceedings.

(B) Scope of Discovery in Probate Proceedings. Discovery in a probate proceeding is limited to matters raised in any petitions or objections pending before the court. Discovery for civil actions in probate court is governed by subchapter 2.300.

Rule 5.132 Proof of Wills

(A) **Deposition of Witness to Will**. If no written objection has been filed to the admission to probate of a document purporting to be the will of a decedent, the deposition of a witness to the will or of other witnesses competent to testify at a proceeding for the probate of the will may be taken and filed without notice. However, the deposition is not admissible in evidence if at the hearing on the petition for probate of the will an interested person who was not given notice of the taking of the deposition as provided by MCR 2.306(B) objects to its use.

(B) **Use of Copy of Will**. When proof of a will is required and a deposition is to be taken, a copy of the original will or other document made by photographic or similar process may be used at the deposition.

Rule 5.141 Pretrial Procedures; Conferences; Scheduling Orders

The procedures of MCR 2.401 shall apply in a contested proceeding.

Rule 5.142 Pretrial Motions in Contested Proceedings

In a contested proceeding, pretrial motions are governed by the rules that are applicable in civil actions in circuit court.

Rule 5.143 Alternative Dispute Resolution

(A) The court may submit to mediation, case evaluation, or other alternative dispute resolution process one or more requests for relief in any contested proceeding. MCR 2.410 applies to the extent possible.

(B) If a dispute is submitted to case evaluation, MCR 2.403 and 2.404 shall apply to the extent feasible, except that sanctions must not be awarded unless the subject matter of the case evaluation involves money damages or division of property.

Rule 5.144 Administratively Closed File

(A) **Administrative Closing**. The court may administratively close a file

(1) for failure to file a notice of continuing administration as provided by MCL 700.3951(3) or

(2) for other reasons as provided by MCR 5.203(D) or, after notice and hearing, upon a finding of good cause.

In a conservatorship, the court may administratively close a file only when there are insufficient assets in the estate to employ a successor or special fiduciary, or after notice and hearing upon a finding of good cause. If the court administratively closes the conservatorship, the court shall provide notice to the state court administrative office of the closure.

(B) **Reopening** Administratively Closed Estate. Upon petition by an interested person, with or without notice as the court directs, the court may order an administratively closed estate reopened. The court may appoint the previously appointed fiduciary, a successor fiduciary, a special fiduciary, or a special personal representative, or the court may order completion of the administration without appointing a fiduciary. In a decedent estate, the court may order supervised administration if it finds that supervised administration is necessary under the circumstances.

Rule 5.151 Jury Trial, Applicable Rules

Jury trials in probate proceedings shall be governed by MCR 2.508 through 2.516 except as modified by this subchapter or MCR 5.740 for mental health proceedings.

Rule 5.158 Jury Trial of Right in Contested Proceedings

(A) **Demand**. A party may demand a trial by jury of an issue for which there is a right to trial by jury by filing in a manner provided by these rules a written demand for a jury trial within 28 days after an issue is contested. However, if trial is conducted within 28 days of the issue being joined, the jury demand must be filed at least 4 days before trial. A party who was not served with notice of the hearing at least 7 days before the hearing or trial may demand a jury trial at any time before the time set for the hearing. The court may adjourn the hearing in order to impanel the jury. A party may include the demand in a pleading if notice of the demand is included in the caption of the pleading. The jury fee provided by law must be paid at the time the demand is filed.

(B) **Waiver**. A party who fails to file a demand or pay the jury fee as required by this rule waives trial by jury. A jury is waived if trial or hearing is commenced without a demand being filed.

Rule 5.162 Form and Signing of Judgments and Orders

(A) **Form of Judgments and Orders**. A proposed judgment or order must include the name, address, and telephone number of the attorney or party who prepared it. All judgments and orders of the court must be typewritten or legibly printed in ink and signed by the judge to whom the proceeding is assigned.

(B) **Procedure for Entry of Judgments and Orders**. In a contested matter, the procedure for entry of judgments and orders is as provided in MCR 2.602(B).

Subchapter 5.200 Provisions Common to Multiple Types of Fiduciaries

Rule 5.201 Applicability

Except for MCR 5.204 and MCR 5.208, which apply in part to trustees and trusts, rules in this subchapter contain requirements applicable to all fiduciaries except trustees and apply to all estates except trusts.

Rule 5.202 Letters of Authority

(A) **Issuance**. Letters of authority shall be issued after the appointment and qualification of the fiduciary. Unless ordered by the court, letters of authority will not have an expiration date.

(B) **Restrictions and Limitations**. The court may restrict or limit the powers of a fiduciary. The restrictions and limitations imposed must appear on the letters of authority. The court may modify or remove the restrictions and limitations with or without a hearing.

(C) **Certification**. A certification of the letters of authority and a statement that on a given date the letters are in full force and effect may appear on the face of copies furnished to the fiduciary or interested persons.

Rule 5.203 Follow-Up Procedures

Except in the instance of a personal representative who fails to timely comply with the requirements of MCL 700.3951(1), if it appears to the court that the fiduciary is not properly administering the estate, the court shall proceed as follows:

(A) **Notice of Deficiency**. The court must notify the fiduciary, the attorney for the fiduciary, if any, and each of the sureties for the fiduciary of the nature of the deficiency, together with a notice to correct the deficiency within 28 days, or, in the alternative, to appear before the court or an officer designated by it at a time specified within 28 days for a conference concerning the deficiency. Service is complete on mailing to the last known address of the fiduciary.

(B) **Conference, Memorandum**. If a conference is held, the court must prepare a written memorandum setting forth the date of the conference, the persons present, and any steps required to be taken to correct the deficiency. The steps must be taken within the time set by the court but not to exceed 28 days from the date of the conference. A copy of the memorandum must be given to those present at the conference and, if the fiduciary is not present at the conference, mailed to the fiduciary at the last known address.

(C) **Extension of Time**. For good cause, the court may extend the time for performance of required duties for a further reasonable period or periods, but any extended period may not exceed 28 days and shall only be extended to a day certain. The total period as extended may not exceed 56 days.

(D) **Suspension of Fiduciary, Appointment of Special Fiduciary**. If the fiduciary fails to perform the duties required within the time allowed, the court may do any of the following: suspend the powers of the dilatory fiduciary, appoint a special fiduciary, and close the estate administration. If the court suspends the powers of the dilatory fiduciary or closes the estate administration, the court must notify the dilatory fiduciary, the attorney of record for the dilatory fiduciary, the sureties on any bond of the dilatory fiduciary that has been filed, any financial institution listed on the most recent inventory or account where the fiduciary has deposited funds, any currently serving guardian ad litem, and the interested persons at their addresses shown in the court file. This rule does not preclude contempt proceedings as provided by law.

(E) **Reports on the Status of Estates**. The chief judge of each probate court must file with the state court administrator, on forms provided by the state court administrative office, any reports on the status of estates required by the state court administrator.

Rule 5.204 Appointment of Special Fiduciary

(A) **Appointment**. The court may appoint a special fiduciary or enjoin a person subject to the court's jurisdiction under MCL 700.1309 on its own initiative, on the notice it directs, or without notice in its discretion.

(B) **Duties and Powers**. The special fiduciary has all the duties and powers specified in the order of the court appointing the special fiduciary. Appointment of a special fiduciary suspends the powers of the general fiduciary unless the order of appointment provides otherwise. The appointment may be for a specified time and the special fiduciary is an interested person for all purposes in the proceeding until the appointment terminates.

Rule 5.205 Address of Fiduciary

A fiduciary must keep the court and the interested persons informed in writing within 7 days of any change in the fiduciary's address. Any notice sent to the fiduciary by the court by ordinary mail to the last address on file shall be notice to the fiduciary.

Rule 5.206 Duty to Complete Administration

A fiduciary and an attorney for a fiduciary must take all actions reasonably necessary to regularly administer and estate and close administration of an estate. If the fiduciary or the attorney fails to take such actions, the court may act to regularly close the estate and assess costs against the fiduciary or attorney personally.

Rule 5.207 Sale of Real Estate

(A) **Petition**. Any petition to approve the sale of real estate must contain the following:
   (1) the terms and purpose of the sale,
   (2) the legal description of the property,
   (3) the financial condition of the estate before the sale, and
   (4) an appended copy of the most recent assessor statement or tax statement showing the state equalized value of the property. If the court is not satisfied that the evidence provides the fair market value, a written appraisal may be ordered.

(B) **Bond**. The court may require a bond before approving a sale of real estate in an amount sufficient to protect the estate.

Rule 5.208 Notice to Creditors, Presentment of Claims

(A) **Publication of Notice to Creditors; Contents**. Unless the notice has already been given, the personal representative must publish, and a special personal representative may publish, in a newspaper, as defined by MCR 2.106(F), in a county in which a resident decedent was domiciled or in which the proceeding as to a nonresident was initiated, a notice to creditors as provided in MCL 700.3801. The notice must include:
   (1) The name, and, if known, the date of death, and date of birth of the decedent;
   (2) The name and address of the personal representative;
   (3) The name and address of the court where proceedings are filed; and
   (4) A statement that claims will be forever barred unless presented to the personal representative, or to both the court and the personal representative within 4 months after the publication of the notice.

(B) **Notice to Known Creditors and Trustee**. A personal representative who has published notice must cause a copy of the published notice or a similar notice to be served personally or by mail on each known creditor of the estate and to the trustee of a trust of which the decedent is settlor, as defined in MCL 700.7605(1). Notice need not be served on the trustee if the personal representative is the trustee.
   (1) Within the time limits prescribed by law, the personal representative must cause a copy of the published notice or a similar notice to be served personally or by mail on each creditor of the estate whose identity at the time of publication or during the 4 months following publication is known to, or can be reasonably ascertained by, the personal representative.
   (2) If, at the time of the publication, the address of a creditor is unknown and cannot be ascertained after diligent inquiry, the name of the creditor must be included in the published notice.

(C) **Publication of Notice to Creditors and Known Creditors by Trustee**. A notice that must be published under MCL 700.7608 must include:
   (1) The name, and, if known, date of death, and date of birth of the trust's deceased settlor;
   (2) The trust's name or other designation;
   (3) The date the trust was established;
   (4) The name and address of each trustee serving at the time of or as a result of the settlor's death;

(5) The name and address of the trustee's attorney, if any

and must be served on known creditors as provided in subrule (B) above.

(D) **No Notice to Creditors**. No notice need be given to creditors in the following situations:

(1) The decedent or settlor has been dead for more than 3 years;

(2) Notice need not be given to a creditor whose claim has been presented or paid;

(3) For a personal representative:

(a) The estate has no assets;

(b) The estate qualifies and is administered under MCL 700.3982, MCL 700.3983, or MCL 700.3987;

(c) Notice has previously been given under MCL 700.7608 in the county where the decedent was domiciled in Michigan.

(4) For a trustee, the costs of administration equal or exceed the value of the trust estate.

(E) **Presentment of Claims**. A claim shall be presented to the personal representative or trustee by mailing or delivering the claim to the personal representative or trustee, or the attorney for the personal representative or trustee, or, in the case of an estate, by filing the claim with the court and mailing or delivering a copy of the claim to the personal representative.

(F) A claim is considered presented

(1) on mailing, if addressed to the personal representative or trustee, or the attorney for the personal representative or trustee, or

(2) in all other cases, when received by the personal representative, or trustee or the attorney for the personal representative or trustee or in the case of an estate when filed with the court.

Subchapter 5.300 Proceedings In Decedent Estates

Rule 5.301 Applicability

The rules in this subchapter apply to decedent estate proceedings other than proceedings provided by law for small estates under MCL 700.3982.

Rule 5.302 Commencement of Decedent Estates

(A) **Methods of Commencement**. A decedent estate may be commenced by filing an application for an informal proceeding or a petition for a formal testacy proceeding. A request for supervised administration may be made in a petition for a formal testacy proceeding. When filing either an application or petition to commence a decedent estate, a copy of the death certificate must be attached. If the death certificate is not available, the petitioner may provide alternative documentation of the decedent's death. Requiring additional documentation, such as information about the proposed or appointed personal representative, is prohibited.

(B) **Sworn Testimony Form**. At least one sworn testimony form sufficient to establish the identity of heirs and devisees must be submitted with the application or petition that commences proceedings. A sworn testimony form must be executed before a person authorized to administer oaths.

(C) **Preservation of Testimony**. If a hearing is held, proofs included as part of the record are deemed preserved for further administration purposes.

(D) **Petition by Parent of Minor**. In the interest of justice, the court may allow a custodial parent who has filed an appearance to file a petition to commence proceedings in a decedent estate on behalf of a minor child where the child is an interested person in the estate.

Rule 5.304 Notice of Appointment

(A) **Notice of Appointment**. The personal representative must, not later than 14 days after appointment, serve notice of appointment as provided in MCL 700.3705 and the agreement and notice relating to attorney fees required by MCR 5.313(D). No notice of appointment need be served if the person serving as personal representative is the only person to whom notice must be given.

(B) **Publication of Notice**. If the address or identity of a person who is to receive notice of appointment is not known and cannot be ascertained with reasonable diligence, the notice of appointment must be published one time in a newspaper, as defined in MCR 2.106(F), in the county in which a resident decedent was domiciled or in the county in which the proceedings with respect to a nonresident were initiated. The published notice of appointment is sufficient if it includes:

(1) statements that estate proceedings have been commenced, giving the name and address of the court, and, if applicable, that a will has been admitted to probate,

(2) the name of any interested person whose name is known but whose address cannot be ascertained after diligent inquiry, and a statement that the result of the administration may be to bar or affect that person's interest in the estate, and

(3) the name and address of the person appointed personal representative, and the name and address of the court.

(C) **Prior Publication**. After an interested person has once been served by publication, notice of appointment is only required if that person's address is known or becomes known during the proceedings.

Rule 5.305 Notice to Spouse; Election

(A) **Notice to Spouse**. In the estate of a decedent who was domiciled in the state of Michigan at the time of death, the personal representative, except a special personal representative, must serve notice of the rights of election under part 2 of article II of the Estates and Protected Individuals Code, including the time for making the election and the rights to exempt property and allowances under part 4 of article II of the code, on the surviving spouse of the decedent within 28 days after the personal representative's appointment. An election as provided in subrule (C) may be filed in lieu of the notice. No notice need be given if the surviving spouse is the personal representative or one of several personal representatives or if there is a waiver under MCL 700.2205.

(B) **Proof of Service**. The personal representative is not required to file a proof of service of the notice of the rights of election.

(C) **Spouse's Election**. If the surviving spouse exercises the right of election, the spouse must serve a copy of the election on the personal representative personally or by mail. The election must be made within 63 days after the date for presentment of claims or within 63 days after the service of the inventory upon the surviving spouse, whichever is later. The election may be filed with the court.

(D) **Assignment of Dower**. A petition for the assignment of dower under MCL 558.1-558.29 must include:

(1) a full and accurate description of the land in Michigan owned by a deceased husband and of which he died seized, from which the petitioner asks to have the dower assigned;

(2) the name, age, and address of the widow and the names and addresses of the other heirs;

(3) the date on which the husband died and his domicile on the date of his death; and

(4) the fact that the widow's right to dower has not been barred and that she or some other person interested in the land wishes it set apart.

If there is a minor or other person other than the widow under legal disability having no legal guardian or conservator, there may not be a hearing on the petition until after the appointment of a guardian ad litem for such person.

Rule 5.307 Requirements Applicable to All Decedent Estates

(A) **Inventory Fee**. Within 91 days of the date of the letters of authority, the personal representative must submit to the court the information necessary for computation of the probate inventory fee. The inventory fee must be paid no later than the filing of the petition for an order of complete estate settlement under MCL 700.3952, the petition for settlement order under MCL 700.3953, or the sworn statement under MCL 700.3954, or one year after appointment, whichever is earlier.

(B) **Notice of Continued Administration.** If unable to complete estate administration within one year of the original personal representative's appointment, the personal representative must file with the court and serve on all interested persons a notice that the estate remains under administration, specifying the reason for the continuation of administration. The notice must be given within 28 days of the first anniversary of appointment and all subsequent anniversaries during which the administration remains uncompleted.

(C) **Notice to Personal Representative**. At the time of appointment, the court must provide the personal representative with written notice of information to be provided to the court. The notice should be substantially in the following form or in the form specified by MCR 5.310(E), if applicable:

"Inventory Information: Within 91 days of the date of the letters of authority, you must submit to the court the information necessary for computation of the probate inventory fee. You must also provide the name and address of each financial institution listed on your inventory at the time the inventory is presented to the court. The address for a financial institution shall be either that of the institution's main headquarters or the branch used most frequently by the personal representative.

"Change of Address: You must keep the court and all interested persons informed in writing within 7 days of any change in your address."

"Notice of Continued Administration: If you are unable to complete the administration of the estate within one year of the original personal representative's appointment, you must file with the court and all interested persons a notice that the estate remains under administration, specifying the reason for the continuation of the administration. You must give this notice within 28 days of the first anniversary of the original appointment and all subsequent anniversaries during which the administration remains uncompleted."

"Duty to Complete Administration of Estate: You must complete the administration of the estate and file appropriate closing papers with the court. Failure to do so may result in personal assessment of costs."

(D) **Claim by Personal Representative**. A claim by a personal representative against the estate for an obligation that arose before the death of the decedent shall only be allowed in a formal proceeding by order of the court.

(E) **Requiring or Filing of Additional Papers**. Except in formal proceedings and supervised administration, the court may not require the filing of any papers other than those required to be filed by statute or court rule. However, additional papers may be filed under MCR 5.113(D).

Rule 5.308 Formal Proceedings

(A) **Accounts**. Any account filed with the court must be in the form required by MCR 5.310(C)(2)(c).

(B) **Determination of Heirs**.

(1) *Determination During Estate Administration*. Every petition for formal probate of a will or for adjudication of intestacy shall include a request for a determination of heirs unless heirs were previously determined. Determination of heirs is also required whenever supervised administration is requested. No other petition for a formal proceeding, including a petition to appoint a personal representative which does not request formal probate of a will or adjudication of intestacy, need contain a request for determination of heirs. The personal representative or an interested person may at any time file a petition for determination of heirs. Heirs may only be determined in a formal hearing.

(2) *Determination Without Estate Administration*.

(a) Petition and Testimony Form. Any person may initiate a formal proceeding to determine intestacy and heirs without appointment of a personal representative by filing a petition and a sworn testimony form, executed before a person authorized to administer oaths, sufficient to establish the domicile of the decedent at the time of death and the identity of the interested persons.

(b) Notice, Publication. The petitioner must serve notice of hearing on all interested persons. If an interested person's address or whereabouts is not known, the petitioner shall serve notice on that person by publication as provided in MCR 5.105(A)(3). The court may require other publication if it deems necessary.

(c) Order. If notice and proofs are sufficient, the court must enter an order determining the date of death, the domicile of the decedent at the time of death, whether the decedent died intestate, and the names of the heirs.

(d) Closing File. If there are no further requests for relief and no appeal, the court may close its file.

Rule 5.309 Informal Proceedings

(A) **Denial of Application**. If the probate register denies the application for informal probate or informal appointment, the applicant may file a petition for a formal proceeding, which may include a request for supervised administration.

(B) **Effect of Form of Administration in Another State or Country**. The fact that any particular form of administration has been initiated in the estate of a decedent in another state or country does not preclude any other form of proceedings with respect to that decedent in Michigan without regard to the form of the proceeding in the other state or country.

(C) **Notice of Intent to Seek Informal Appointment as Personal Representative**.

(1) A person who desires to be appointed personal representative in informal proceedings must give notice of intent to seek appointment and a copy of the application to each person having a prior or equal right to appointment who does not renounce this right in writing before the appointment is made.

(2) Service of notice of intent to seek appointment and a copy of the application must be made at least 14 days by mail or 7 days by personal service before appointment as personal representative. If the address of one or more of the persons having a prior or equal right to appointment is unknown and cannot be ascertained after diligent inquiry, notice of the intent to file the application must be published pursuant to MCR 5.106 at least 14 days prior to the appointment, but a copy of the application need not be published.

(3) Proof of service must be filed with the court along with the application for informal appointment as personal representative.

(D) **Publication**. If the address of an heir, devisee, or other interested person entitled to the information on the informal probate under MCL 700.3306 is unknown and cannot be ascertained after diligent inquiry, the information in MCL 700.3306(2) must be provided by publication pursuant to MCR 5.106. Publication of notice under this rule is not required if a personal representative has been appointed and provided notice under MCR 5.304.

Rule 5.310 Supervised Administration

(A) **Applicability**. The other rules applicable to decedent estates apply to supervised administration unless they conflict with this rule.

(B) **Commencement of Supervised Administration**. A request for supervised administration in a decedent estate may be made in the petition for formal testacy and appointment proceedings. A petition for formal testacy and appointment proceedings including a request for supervised administration may be filed at any time during the estate proceedings if testacy has not previously been adjudicated. If testacy and appointment have been previously adjudicated, a separate petition for supervised administration may be filed at any time during administration of the estate. Whenever supervised administration is requested, the court must determine heirs unless heirs were previously determined, even if supervised administration is denied.

(C) **Filing Papers With the Court**. The personal representative must file the following additional papers with the court and serve copies on the interested persons:

(1) *Inventory.*

(a) Administration Commenced Supervised. If supervised administration is ordered at the commencement of the estate administration, the personal representative must file the inventory within 91 days of the date of the letters of authority.

(b) Administration Commenced Without Supervision. If supervised administration is ordered after a personal representative has been appointed, the court must specify in the order a time for that personal representative to file the inventory.

(2) *Accountings.*

(a) Time for Filing. Unless the court designates a shorter period, the personal representative must file accountings within 56 days after the end of the accounting period. A final account must be filed when the estate is ready for closing or on removal of a personal representative. The court may order an interim accounting at any time the court deems necessary.

(b) Accounting Period. The accounting period ends on the anniversary date of the issuance of the letters of authority or, if applicable, on the anniversary date of the close of the last period covered by an accounting. The personal representative may elect to change the accounting period so that it ends on a different date. If the personal representative elects to make such a change, the first accounting period thereafter shall not be more than a year. A notice of the change must be filed with the court.

(c) Contents. All accountings must be itemized, showing in detail receipts and disbursements during the accounting period, unless itemization is waived by all interested persons. A written description of services performed must be included or appended regarding compensation sought by a personal representative. This description need not be duplicated in the order. The accounting must include notice that (i) objections concerning the accounting must be brought to the court's attention by an interested person because the court does not normally review the accounting without an objection; (ii) interested persons have a right to review proofs of income and disbursements at a time reasonably convenient to the personal representative and the interested person; (iii) interested persons may object to all or part of an accounting by filing an objection with the court before allowance of the accounting; and (iv) if an objection is filed and not otherwise resolved, the court will hear and determine the objection.

(d) Proof of Income and Disbursements. After filing and before the allowance of an accounting, the personal representative must make proofs of income and disbursements reasonably available for examination by any interested person who requests to see them or as required by the court. An interested person, with or without examination of the proofs of income and disbursements, may file an objection to an accounting with the court. If an interested person files an objection without examining the proofs and the court concludes that such an examination would help resolve the objection, the court may order the interested person to examine the proofs before the court hears the objection.

(e) Deferral of Hearings on Accountings. Hearing on each accounting may be deferred in the discretion of the court. The court in any case at any time may require a hearing on an accounting with or without a request by an interested person.

(3) Notice of appointment.

(4) Fees notice pursuant to MCR 5.313.

(5) Notice to spouse.

(6) Affidavit of any required publication.

(7) Such other papers as are ordered by the court.

(D) **Tax Information**. The personal representative must file with the court

(1) in the case of a decedent dying before October 1, 1993, proof that all Michigan inheritance taxes have been paid or

(2) in the case of an estate of a decedent dying after September 30, 1993, either

(a) if a federal estate tax return was required to be filed for the decedent, proof from the Michigan Department of Treasury that all Michigan estate taxes have been paid, or

(b) if no federal estate tax return was required to be filed for the decedent, a statement that no Michigan estate tax is due.

(E) **Notice to Personal Representative**. When supervised administration is ordered, the court must serve a written notice of duties on the personal representative. The notice must be substantially as follows:

> "Inventories: You are required to file an inventory of the assets of the estate within 91 days of the date of your letters of authority or as ordered by the court. The inventory must list in reasonable detail all the property owned

by the decedent at the time of death, indicating, for each listed item, the fair market value at the time of decedent's death and the type and amount of any encumbrance. If the value of any item has been obtained through an appraiser, the inventory should include the appraiser's name and address with the item or items appraised by that appraiser.

"Accountings: You are required to file annually, or more often if the court directs, a complete itemized accounting of your administration of the estate, showing in detail all the receipts and disbursements and the property remaining in your hands together with the form of the property. When the estate is ready for closing, you are required to file a final accounting and an itemized and complete list of all properties remaining. Subsequent annual and final accountings must be filed within 56 days after the close of the accounting period.

"Change of Address: You are required to keep the court and interested persons informed in writing within 7 days of any change in your address.

"Notice of Continued Administration: If you are unable to complete the administration of the estate within one year of the original personal representative's appointment, you must file with the court and all interested persons a notice that the estate remains under administration, specifying the reason for the continuation of the administration. You must give this notice within 28 days of the first anniversary of the original appointment and all subsequent anniversaries during which the administration remains uncompleted.

"Duty to Complete Administration of Estate: You must complete the administration of the estate and file appropriate closing papers with the court. Failure to do so may result in personal assessment of costs."

(F) **Changing from Supervised to Unsupervised Administration**. At any time during supervised administration, any interested person or the personal representative may petition the court to terminate supervision of administration. The court may terminate supervision unless the court finds that proceeding with supervision is necessary under the circumstances. Termination of supervision does not discharge the personal representative.

(G) Approval of compensation of an attorney must be sought pursuant to MCR 5.313.

(H) **Order of Complete Estate Settlement**. An estate being administered in supervised administration must be closed under MCL 700.3952, using the procedures specified in MCR 5.311(B)(1).

Rule 5.311 Closing Estate

(A) **Closing by Sworn Statement**. In unsupervised administration, a personal representative may close an estate by filing a sworn closing statement under MCL 700.3954 or 700.3988.

(B) **Formal Proceedings**.

(1) *Requirements for Order of Complete Estate Settlement under MCL 700.3952*. An estate being administered in supervised administration must be closed by an order for complete estate settlement under MCL 700.3952. All other estates may be closed under that provision. A petition for complete estate settlement must state the relief requested. If the petitioner requests a determination of testacy, the petitioner must comply with the requirements of the statute and court rules dealing with a determination of testacy in a formal proceeding.

(2) *Requirements for Settlement Order under MCL 700.3953*. A personal representative or a devisee may file a petition for a settlement order under MCL 700.3953; only in an estate being administered under a will admitted to probate in an informal proceeding. The petition may not contain a request for a determination of the decedent testacy status in a formal proceeding.

(3) *Discharge*. A personal representative may petition for discharge from liability with notice to the interested persons. A personal representative who files such a petition with the court must also file the papers described in MCR 5.310(C) and (D), as applicable, proofs of service of those papers that are required to be served on interested persons, and such other papers as the court may require. The court may order the personal representative discharged if the court is satisfied that the personal representative has properly administered the estate.

(4) *Other Requests for Relief*. With respect to other requests for relief, the petitioner must file appropriate papers to support the request for relief.

(5) *Order*. If the estate administration is completed, the order entered under MCL 700.3952 or MCL 700.3953 shall, in addition to any other relief, terminate the personal representative's authority and close the estate.

(C) **Closing of Reopened Estate**. After completion of the reopened estate administration, the personal representative shall proceed to close the estate by filing a petition under MCL 700.3952 or MCL 700.3953 or a supplemental closing statement under MCL 700.3954. If a supplemental closing statement is filed, the personal representative must serve a copy on each interested person. If an objection is not filed within 28 days, the personal representative is entitled to receive a supplemental certificate of completion.

Rule 5.312 Reopening Decedent Estate

(A) **Reopening by Application**. If there is good cause to reopen a previously administered estate, other than an estate that was terminated in supervised administration, any interested person may apply to the register to reopen the estate and appoint the former personal representative or another person who has priority. For good cause and without notice, the register may reopen the estate, appoint the former personal representative or a person who has priority, and issue letters of authority with a specified termination date.

(B) **Reopening by Petition**. The previously appointed personal representative or an interested person may file a petition with the court to reopen the estate and appoint a personal representative under MCL 700.3959.

(C) **Calculation of Due Dates**. For purposes of determining when the inventory fee calculation, the inventory filing, the inventory fee payment, and the notice of continued administration are due, a reopened decedent estate is to be treated as a new case.

Rule 5.313 Compensation of Attorneys

(A) **Reasonable Fees and Costs**. An attorney is entitled to receive reasonable compensation for legal services rendered on behalf of a personal representative, and to reimbursement for costs incurred in rendering those services. In determining the reasonableness of fees, the court must consider the factors listed in MRPC 1.5(a). The court may also take into account the failure to comply with this rule.

(B) **Written Fee Agreement**. At the commencement of the representation, the attorney and the personal representative or the proposed personal representative must enter into a written fee agreement signed by them. A copy of the agreement must be provided to the personal representative.

(C) **Records**. Regardless of the fee agreement, every attorney who represents a personal representative must maintain time records for services that must reflect the following information: the identity of the person performing the services, the date the services are performed, the amount of time expended in performing the services, and a brief description of the services.

(D) **Notice to Interested Persons**. Within 14 days after the appointment of a personal representative or the retention of an attorney by a personal representative, whichever is later, the personal representative must mail to the interested persons whose interests will be affected by the payment of attorney fees, a notice in the form substantially approved by the State Court Administrator and a copy of the written fee agreement. The notice must state:

(1) the anticipated frequency of payment,

(2) that the person is entitled to a copy of each statement for services or costs upon request,

(3) that the person may object to the fees at any time prior to the allowance of fees by the court,

(4) that an objection may be made in writing or at a hearing and that a written objection must be filed with the court and a copy served on the personal representative or attorney.

(E) **Payment of Fees**. A personal representative may make, and an attorney may accept, payments for services and costs, on a periodic basis without prior court approval if prior to the time of payment

(1) the attorney and personal representative have entered a written fee agreement;

(2) copies of the fee agreement and the notice required by subrule (D) have been sent to all interested persons who are affected;

(3) a statement for services and costs (containing the information required by subrule [C]) has been sent to the personal representative and each interested person who has requested a copy of such statement; and

(4) no written, unresolved objection to the fees, current or past, has been served on the attorney and personal representative.

In all other instances, attorney fees must be approved by the court prior to payment. Costs may be paid without prior court approval. Attorney fees and costs paid without prior court approval remain subject to review by the court.

(F) **Claims for compensation, Required Information**. Except when the compensation is consented to by all the parties affected, the personal representative must append to an accounting, petition, or motion in which compensation is claimed a statement containing the information required by subrule (C).

(G) **Contingent Fee Agreements under MCR 8.121**. Subrules (C), (E), and (F) of this rule do not apply to a contingent fee agreement between a personal representative and an attorney under MCR 8.121.

Subchapter 5.400 Guardianship, Conservatorship, and Protective Order Proceedings

Rule 5.401 General Provisions

This subchapter governs guardianships, conservatorships, and protective order proceedings. The other rules in chapter 5 also apply to these proceedings unless they conflict with rules in this subchapter. Except as modified in this subchapter, proceedings for guardianships of adults and minors, conservatorships, and protective orders shall be in accordance with the Estates and Protected Individuals Code, 1998 PA 386 and, where applicable, the Michigan Indian Family Preservation Act, MCL 712B.1 *et seq.*, the Indian Child Welfare Act, 25 USC 1901 *et seq.*, or the Mental Health Code, 1974 PA 258, as amended.

Rule 5.402 Common Provisions

(A) **Petition; Multiple Prayers**. A petition for the appointment of a guardian or a conservator or for a protective order may contain multiple prayers for relief.

(B) **Petition by Minor**. A petition and a nomination for the appointment of a guardian or conservator of a minor may be executed and made by a minor 14 years of age or older.

(C) **Responsibility for Giving Notice; Manner of Service**. The petitioner is responsible for giving notice of hearing. Regardless of statutory provisions, an interested person may be served by mail, by personal service, or by publication when necessary; however, if the person who is the subject of the petition is 14 years of age or older, notice of the initial hearing must be served on the person personally unless another method of service is specifically permitted in the circumstances.

(D) **Letters of Authority**. On the filing of the acceptance of appointment or bond required by the order appointing a fiduciary, the court shall issue letters of authority on a form approved by the state court administrator. Any restriction or limitation of the powers of a guardian or conservator must be set forth in the letters of authority.

(E) **Indian Child; Definitions, Jurisdiction, Notice, Transfer, Intervention.**

(1) If an Indian child, as defined by the Michigan Indian Family Preservation Act, is the subject of a guardianship proceeding, the definitions in MCR 3.002 shall control.

(2) If an Indian child is the subject of a petition to establish guardianship of a minor and an Indian tribe has exclusive jurisdiction as defined in MCR 3.002(6), the matter shall be dismissed.

(3) If an Indian child is the subject of a petition to establish guardianship of a minor and an Indian tribe does not have exclusive jurisdiction as defined in MCR 3.002(6), the court shall ensure that the petitioner has given notice of the proceedings to the persons prescribed in MCR 5.125(A)(8) and (C)(19) in accordance with MCR 5.109(1).

(a) If either parent or the Indian custodian or the Indian child's tribe petitions the court to transfer the proceeding to the tribal court, the court shall transfer the case to the tribal court unless either parent objects to the transfer of the case to tribal court jurisdiction or the court finds good cause not to transfer. When the court makes a good-cause determination under MCL 712B.7, adequacy of the tribe, tribal court, or tribal social services shall not be considered. A court may determine that good cause not to transfer a case to tribal court exists only if the person opposing the transfer shows by clear and convincing evidence that either of the following applies:

(i) The Indian tribe does not have a tribal court.

(ii) The requirement of the parties or witnesses to present evidence in tribal court would cause undue hardship to those parties or witnesses that the Indian tribe is unable to mitigate.

(b) The court shall not dismiss the matter until the transfer has been accepted by the tribal court.

(c) If the tribal court declines transfer, the Michigan Indian Family Preservation Act applies, as do the provisions of these rules that pertain to an Indian child (see MCL 712B.3 and MCL 712B.5).

(d) A petition to transfer may be made at any time in accordance with MCL 712B.7(3).

(4) The Indian custodian of the child, the Indian child's tribe, and the Indian child have a right to intervene at any point in the proceeding pursuant to MCL 712B.7(6).

(5) If the court discovers a child may be an Indian child after a guardianship is ordered, the court shall provide notice of the guardianship and the potential applicability of the Indian Child Welfare Act and the Michigan Indian Family Preservation Act on a form approved by the State Court Administrative Office to the persons prescribed in MCR 5.125(A)(8), (C)(19), and (C)(25) in accordance with MCR 5.109(1). A copy of the notice shall be mailed to the guardian by first-class mail.

Rule 5.403 Proceedings on Temporary Guardianship

(A) **Limitation**. The court may appoint a temporary guardian only in the course of a proceeding for permanent guardianship or pursuant to an application to appoint a guardian serving in another state to serve as a guardian in this state.

(B) **Notice of Hearing, Minor**. For good cause stated on the record and included in the order, the court may shorten the period for notice of hearing or may dispense with notice of a hearing for the appointment of a temporary guardian of a minor, except that the minor shall always receive notice if the minor is 14 years of age or older. If a temporary guardian is appointed following an ex parte hearing in a case in which the notice period was shortened or eliminated, the court shall send notice of the appointment to all interested persons. The notice shall inform the interested persons about their right to object to the appointment, the process for objecting, and the date of the next hearing, if any. If an interested person objects to the appointment of a temporary guardian following an ex parte hearing in a case in which the notice period was shortened or eliminated, the court shall hold a hearing on the objection within 14 days from the date the objection is filed.

(C) **Temporary Guardian for Incapacitated Individual Where no Current Appointment; Guardian Ad Litem**. A petition for a temporary guardian for an alleged incapacitated individual shall specify in detail the emergency situation requiring the temporary guardianship. For the purpose of an emergency hearing, the court shall appoint a guardian ad litem unless such appointment would cause delay and the alleged incapacitated individual would likely suffer serious harm if immediate action is not taken. The duties of the guardian ad litem are to visit the alleged incapacitated individual, report to the court and take such other action as directed by the court. The requirement of MCL 700.5312(1) that the court hold the fully noticed hearing within 28 days applies only when the court grants temporary relief.

(D) **Temporary Guardian for Minor**.

(1) *Before Appointment of Guardian*. If necessary during proceedings for the appointment of a guardian for a minor, the court may appoint a temporary guardian after a hearing at which testimony is taken. The petition for a temporary guardian shall specify in detail the conditions requiring a temporary guardianship. Where a petition for appointment of a limited guardian has been filed, the court, before the appointment of a temporary guardian, shall take into consideration the limited guardianship placement plan in determining the powers and duties of the parties during the temporary guardianship.

(2) *When Guardian Previously Appointed*. If it comes to the attention of the court that a guardian of a minor is not properly performing the duties of a guardian, the court, after a hearing at which testimony is taken, may appoint a temporary guardian for a period not to exceed 6 months. The temporary guardian shall have the authority of the previously appointed guardian whose powers are suspended during the term of the temporary guardianship. The temporary guardian shall determine whether a petition to remove the guardian should be filed. If such a petition is not filed, the temporary guardian shall report to court with recommendations for action that the court should take in order to protect the minor upon expiration of the term of the temporary guardian. The report shall be filed within 1 month of the date of the expiration of the temporary guardianship.

Rule 5.404 Guardianship of Minor

(A) **Petition for Guardianship of Minor**.

(1) *Petition*. A petition for guardianship of a minor shall be filed on a form approved by the State Court Administrative Office. The petitioner shall state in the petition whether or not the minor is an Indian child or whether that fact is unknown. The petitioner shall document all efforts made to determine a child's membership or eligibility for membership in an Indian tribe and shall provide them, upon request, to the court, Indian tribe, Indian child, Indian child's lawyer-guardian ad litem, parent, or Indian custodian.

(2) *Investigation*. Upon the filing of a petition, the court may appoint a guardian ad litem to represent the interests of a minor and may order the Department of Human Services or a court employee or agent to conduct an investigation of the proposed guardianship and file a written report of the investigation in accordance with MCL 700.5204(1). If the petition involves an Indian child, the report shall contain the information required in MCL 712B.25(1). The report shall be filed with the court and served no later than 7 days before the hearing on the petition. If the petition for guardianship states that it is unknown whether the minor is an Indian child, the investigation shall include an inquiry into Indian tribal membership.

(3) *Guardianship of an Indian Child*. If the petition involves an Indian child and both parents intend to execute a consent pursuant to MCL 712B.13 and these rules, the court shall proceed under subrule (B). If the petition involves an Indian child and a consent will not be executed pursuant to MCL 712B.13 and these rules, the petitioner shall state in the petition what active efforts were made to provide remedial services and rehabilitative programs designed to prevent the breakup of the Indian family as defined in MCR 3.002(1). The court shall proceed under subrule (C).

(4) *Social History*. If the court requires the petitioner to file a social history before hearing a petition for guardianship of a minor, it shall do so on a form approved by the State Court Administrative Office. The social history for minor guardianship is confidential, and it is not to be released, except on order of the court, to the parties or the attorneys for the parties.

(5) *Limited Guardianship of the Child of a Minor*. On the filing of a petition for appointment of a limited guardian for a child whose parent is an unemancipated minor, the court shall appoint a guardian ad litem to represent the minor parent. A limited guardianship placement plan is not binding on the minor parent until consented to by the guardian ad litem.

(B) **Voluntary Consent to Guardianship of an Indian Child**. A voluntary consent to guardianship of an Indian child must be executed by both parents or the Indian custodian.

(1) *Form of Consent.* To be valid, the consent must contain the information prescribed by MCL 712B.13(2) and be executed on a form approved by the State Court Administrative Office, in writing, recorded before a judge of a court of competent jurisdiction, and accompanied by the presiding judge's certificate that the terms and consequences of the consent were fully explained in detail and were fully understood by the parent or Indian custodian. The court shall also certify that either the parent or Indian custodian fully understood the explanation in English or that it was interpreted into a language that the parent or Indian custodian understood. Any consent given before, or within 10 days after, the birth of the Indian child is not valid.

(2) Hearing. The court must conduct a hearing on a petition for voluntary guardianship of an Indian child in accordance with this rule before the court may enter an order appointing a guardian. Notice of the hearing on the petition must be sent to the persons prescribed in MCR 5.125(A)(8) and (C)(19) in compliance with MCR 5.109(1). At the hearing on the petition, the court shall determine:

(a) if the tribe has exclusive jurisdiction as defined in MCR 3.002(6). The court shall comply with MCR 5.402(E)(2).

(b) that a valid consent has been executed by both parents or the Indian custodian as required by MCL 712B.13 and this subrule.

(c) if it is in the Indian child's best interest to appoint a guardian.

(d) if a lawyer-guardian ad litem should be appointed to represent the Indian child.

(3) *Withdrawal of Consent.* A consent may be withdrawn at any time by sending written notice to the court substantially in compliance with a form approved by the State Court Administrative Office. Upon receipt of the notice, the court shall immediately enter an ex parte order terminating the guardianship and returning the Indian child to the parent or Indian custodian except, if both parents executed a consent, both parents must withdraw their consent or the court must conduct a hearing within 21 days to determine whether to terminate the guardianship.

(C) **Involuntary Guardianship of an Indian Child**.

(1) *Hearing.* The court must conduct a hearing on a petition for involuntary guardianship of an Indian child in accordance with this rule before the court may enter an order appointing a guardian. Notice of the hearing must be sent to the persons prescribed in MCR 5.125(A)(8) and (C)(19) in compliance with MCR 5.109(1). At the hearing on the petition, the court shall determine:

(a) if the tribe has exclusive jurisdiction as defined in MCR 3.002(6).The court shall comply with MCR 5.402(E)(2).

(b) if the placement with the guardian meets the placement requirements in subrule (C)(2) and (3).

(c) if it is in the Indian child's best interest to appoint a guardian.

(d) if a lawyer-guardian ad litem should be appointed to represent the Indian child.

(e) whether or not each parent wants to consent to the guardianship if consents were not filed with the petition. If each parent wants to consent to the guardianship, the court shall proceed in accordance with subrule (B).

(2) *Placement.* An Indian child shall be placed in the least restrictive setting that most approximates a family and in which his or her special needs, if any, may be met. The child shall be placed within reasonable proximity to his or her home, taking into account any special needs of the child. Absent good cause to the contrary, the placement of an Indian child must be in descending order of preference with:

(a) a member of the child's extended family,

(b) a foster home licensed, approved, or specified by the child's tribe,

(c) an Indian foster family licensed or approved by the Department of Human Services,

(d) an institution for children approved by an Indian tribe or operated by an Indian organization that has a program suitable to meet the child's needs.

(e) The standards to be applied in meeting the preference requirements above shall be the prevailing social and cultural standards of the Indian community in which the parent or extended family resides or with which the parent or extended family members maintain social and cultural ties.

(3) *Deviating from Placement.* The court may order another placement for good cause shown in accordance with MCL 712B.23(3)-(5) and 25 USC 1915(c). If the Indian child's tribe has established a different order of preference than the order prescribed in subrule (C)(2), placement shall follow that tribe's order of preference as long as the placement is the least restrictive setting appropriate to the particular needs of the child, as provided in MCL 712B.23(6). Where appropriate, the preference of the Indian child or parent shall be considered.

(D) **Hearing**. If the petition for guardianship of a minor does not indicate that the minor is an Indian child as defined in MCR 3.002(12), the court must inquire if the child or either parent is a member of an Indian tribe. If the child is a member or if a parent is a member and the child is eligible for membership in the tribe, the court shall either dismiss the petition or allow the petitioner to comply with MCR 5.404(A)(1).

(E) **Limited Guardianship Placement Plans and Court-Structured Plans.**

(1) All limited guardianship placement plans and court-structured plans shall at least include provisions concerning all of the following:

(a) visitation and contact with the minor by the parent or parents sufficient to maintain a parent and child relationship;

(b) the duration of the guardianship;

(c) financial support for the minor; and

(d) in a limited guardianship, the reason why the parent or parents are requesting the court to appoint a limited guardian for the minor.

(2) All limited guardianship placement plans and court-structured plans may include the following:

(a) a schedule of services to be followed by the parent or parents, child, and guardian and

(b) any other provisions that the court deems necessary for the welfare of the child.

(3) *Modification of Placement Plan.*

(a) The parties to a limited guardianship placement plan may file a proposed modification of the plan without filing a petition. The proposed modification shall be substantially in the form approved by the state court administrator.

(b) The court shall examine the proposed modified plan and take further action under subrules (c) and (d) within 14 days after the filing of the proposed modified plan.

(c) If the court approves the proposed modified plan, the court shall endorse the modified plan and notify the interested persons of its approval.

(d) If the court does not approve the modification, the court either shall set the proposed modification plan for a hearing or notify the parties of the objections of the court and that they may schedule a hearing or submit another proposed modified plan.

(F) **Evidence.**

(1) *Involuntary Guardianship of an Indian Child.* If a petition for guardianship involves an Indian child and the petition was not accompanied by a consent executed pursuant to MCL 712B.13 and these rules, the court may remove the Indian child from a parent or Indian custodian and place that child with a guardian only upon clear and convincing evidence that:

(a) active efforts have been made to provide remedial services and rehabilitative programs designed to prevent the breakup of the Indian family,

(b) these efforts have proved unsuccessful, and

(c) continued custody of the child by the parent or Indian custodian is likely to result in serious emotional or physical damage to the child.

The evidence shall include the testimony of at least one qualified expert witness, as described in MCL 712B.17, who has knowledge about the child-rearing practices of the Indian child's tribe. The active efforts must take into account the prevailing social and cultural conditions and way of life of the Indian child's tribe. If the petitioner cannot show active efforts have been made, the court shall dismiss the petition and may refer the petitioner to the Department of Human Services for child protective services or to the tribe for services.

(2) *Reports, Admission Into Evidence.* At any hearing concerning a guardianship of a minor, all relevant and material evidence, including written reports, may be received by the court and may be relied on to the extent of their probative value, even though such evidence may not be admissible under the Michigan Rules of Evidence.

(3) *Written Reports, Review and Cross-Examination.* Interested persons shall be afforded an opportunity to examine and controvert written reports so received and, in the court's discretion, may be allowed to cross-examine individuals making reports when such individuals are reasonably available.

(4) *Privilege, Abrogation.* No assertion of an evidentiary privilege, other than the privilege between attorney and client, shall prevent the receipt and use of materials prepared pursuant to a court-ordered examination, interview, or course of treatment.

(G) **Review of Guardianship for Minor.**

(1) *Periodic Review.* The court shall conduct a review of a guardianship of a minor annually in each case where the minor is under age 6 as of the anniversary of the qualification of the guardian. The review shall be commenced within 63 days after the anniversary date of the qualification of the guardian. The court may at any time conduct a review of a guardianship as it deems necessary.

(2) *Investigation.* The court shall appoint the Department of Human Services or any other person to conduct an investigation of the guardianship of a minor. The investigator shall file a written report with the court within 28 days after such appointment. The report shall include a recommendation regarding whether the guardianship should be continued or modified and whether a hearing should be scheduled. If the report recommends modification, the report shall state the nature of the modification.

(3) *Judicial Action.* After informal review of the report, the court shall enter an order continuing the guardianship or set a date for a hearing to be held within 28 days. If a hearing is set, an attorney may be appointed to represent the minor.

(H) **Termination of Guardianship**.

(1) *Necessity of Order.* A guardianship may terminate without order of the court on the minor's death, adoption, marriage, or attainment of majority or in accordance with subrule (H)(6). No full, testamentary, or limited guardianship shall otherwise terminate without an order of the court.

(2) *Continuation of Guardianship.* When a court has continued a guardianship for a period not exceeding one year, the court shall hold the final hearing not less than 28 days before the expiration of the period of continuance.

(3) *Petition for Family Division of Circuit Court to Take Jurisdiction.* If the court appoints an attorney or the Department of Human Services to investigate whether to file a petition with the family division of circuit court to take jurisdiction of the minor, the attorney or Department of Human Services shall, within 21 days, report to the court that a petition has been filed or why a petition has not been filed.

(a) If a petition is not filed with the family division, the court shall take such further action as is warranted, except the guardianship may not be continued for more than one year after the hearing on the petition to terminate.

(b) If a petition is filed with the family division, the guardianship shall terminate when the family division authorizes the petition under MCL 712A.11, unless the family division determines that continuation of such guardianship pending disposition is necessary for the well-being of the child.

(4) *Resignation of Limited Guardian.* A petition by a limited guardian to resign shall be treated as a petition for termination of the limited guardianship. The parents or the sole parent with the right to custody may file a petition for a new limited guardianship. If the court does not approve the new limited guardianship or if no petition is filed, the court may proceed in the manner for termination of a guardianship under section 5209 or 5219 of the Estates and Protected Individuals Code, MCL 700.5209 or MCL 700.5219.

(5) *Petition for Termination by a Party Other Than a Parent.* If a petition for termination is filed by other than a parent or Indian custodian, the court may proceed in the manner for termination of a guardianship under section 5209 of the Estates and Protected Individuals Code, MCL 700.5209.

(6) *Voluntary Consent Guardianship.* The guardianship of an Indian child established pursuant to subrule (C) shall be terminated in accordance with subrule (B)(3).

Rule 5.405 Proceedings on Guardianship of Incapacitated Individual

(A) **Examination by Physician or Mental Health Professional**.

(1) *Admission of Report.* The court may receive into evidence without testimony a written report of a physician or mental health professional who examined an individual alleged to be incapacitated, provided that a copy of the report is filed with the court five days before the hearing and that the report is substantially in the form required by the state court administrator. A party offering a report must promptly inform the parties that the report is filed and available. The court may issue on its own initiative, or any party may secure, a subpoena to compel the preparer of the report to testify.

(2) *Abrogation of Privilege.* A report ordered by the court may be used in guardianship proceedings without regard to any privilege. Any privilege regarding a report made as part of an independent evaluation at the request of a respondent is waived if the respondent seeks to have the report considered in the proceedings.

(3) *Determination of Fee.* As a condition of receiving payment, the physician or mental health professional shall submit an itemized statement of services and expenses for approval. In reviewing a statement, the court shall consider the time required for examination, evaluation, preparation of reports and court appearances; the examiner's experience and training; and the local fee for similar services.

(B) **Hearings at Site Other Than Courtroom**. When hearings are not held in the courtroom where the court ordinarily sits, the court shall ensure a quiet and dignified setting that permits an undisturbed proceeding and inspires the participants' confidence in the integrity of the judicial process.

(C) **Guardian of Incapacitated Individual Appointed by Will or Other Writing**.

(1) *Appointment.* A guardian appointed by will or other writing under MCL 700.5301 may qualify after the death or adjudicated incapacity of a parent or spouse who had been the guardian of an incapacitated individual by filing an acceptance of appointment with the court that has jurisdiction over the guardianship. Unless the court finds the person unsuitable or incompetent for the trust, the court shall issue to the nominated guardian letters of guardianship equivalent to those that had been issued to the deceased guardian.

(2) *Notice, Revocation.* The testamentary guardian shall notify the court in which the testamentary instrument has been or will be filed of the

appointment as guardian. The probating court shall notify the court having jurisdiction over the guardianship if the will is denied probate, and the court having the guardianship jurisdiction shall immediately revoke the letters of guardianship.

Rule 5.406 Testamentary Guardian of Individual With Developmental Disabilities

(A) **Appointment**. If the court has not appointed a standby guardian, a testamentary guardian may qualify after the death of a parent who had been the guardian of an individual with developmental disabilities by filing an acceptance of appointment with the court that appointed the deceased parent as guardian. If the nominated person is to act as guardian of the estate of the ward, the guardian should also file a bond in the amount last required of the deceased guardian. Unless the court finds the person unsuitable or incompetent for the appointment, the court shall issue to the testamentary guardian letters of authority equivalent to those that had been issued to the deceased guardian.

(B) **Notice, Revocation**. The testamentary guardian must notify the court in which the testamentary instrument has been or will be filed of the appointment as guardian. The probating court shall notify the court having jurisdiction over the guardianship if the will is denied probate, and the court having the guardianship jurisdiction shall immediately revoke the letters of authority.

Rule 5.407 Conservatorship; Settlements

A conservator may not enter into a settlement in any court on behalf of the protected person if the conservator will share in the settlement unless a guardian ad litem has been appointed to represent the protected person's interest and has consented to such settlement in writing or on the record or the court approves the settlement over any objection.

Rule 5.408 Review and Modification of Guardianships of Legally Incapacitated Individuals

(A) **Periodic Review of Guardianship**.

(1) *Periodic Review*. The court shall commence a review of a guardianship of a legally incapacitated individual not later than 1 year after the appointment of the guardian and not later than every 3 years thereafter.

(2) *Investigation*. The court shall appoint a person to investigate the guardianship and report to the court by a date set by the court. The person appointed must visit the legally incapacitated individual or include in the report to the court an explanation why a visit was not practical. The report shall include a recommendation on whether the guardianship should be modified.

(3) *Judicial Action*. After informal review of the report, the court shall enter an order continuing the guardianship, or enter an order appointing an attorney to represent the legally incapacitated individual for the purpose of filing a petition for modification of guardianship. In either case, the court shall send a copy of the report and the order to the legally incapacitated individual and the guardian.

(4) *Petition for Modification*. If an attorney is appointed under subrule (A)(3), the attorney shall file proper pleadings with the court within 14 days of the date of appointment.

(B) **Petition for Modification; Appointment of Attorney or Guardian Ad Litem**.

(1) *Petition by Legally Incapacitated Individual*. If a petition for modification or written request for modification comes from the legally incapacitated individual and that individual does not have an attorney, the court shall immediately appoint an attorney.

(2) *Petition by Person Other Than Legally Incapacitated Individual*. If a petition for modification or written request for modification comes from some other party, the court shall appoint a guardian ad litem. If the guardian ad litem ascertains that the legally incapacitated individual contests the relief requested, the court shall appoint an attorney for the legally incapacitated individual and terminate the appointment of the guardian ad litem.

Rule 5.409 Report of Guardian; Inventories and Accounts of Conservators

(A) **Reports**. A guardian shall file a written report annually within 56 days after the anniversary of appointment and at other times as the court may order. Reports must be substantially in the form approved by the state court administrator. The guardian must serve the report on the persons listed in MCR 5.125(C)(23).

(B) **Inventories**.

(1) *Guardian*. At the time of appointing a guardian, the court shall determine whether there would be sufficient assets under the control of the guardian to require the guardian to file an inventory. If the court determines that there are sufficient assets, the court shall order the guardian to file an inventory.

(2) *Filing and Service*. Within 56 days after appointment, a conservator or, if ordered to do so, a guardian shall file with the court a verified inventory of the estate of the protected person, serve copies on the persons required by law or court rule to be served, and file proof of service with the court.

(3) *Contents*. The guardian or conservator must provide the name and address of each financial institution

listed on the inventory. The address for a financial institution shall be either that of the institution's main headquarters or the branch used most frequently by the guardian or conservator. Property that the protected individual owns jointly or in common with others must be listed on the inventory along with the type of ownership and value.

(C) **Accounts**.

(1) *Filing, Service*. A conservator must file an annual account unless ordered not to by the court. A guardian must file an annual account if ordered by the court. The provisions of the court rules apply to any account that is filed with the court, even if the account was not required by court order. The account must be served on interested persons, and proof of service must be filed with the court. The copy of the account served on interested persons must include a notice that any objections to the account should be filed with the court and noticed for hearing. When required, an accounting must be filed within 56 days after the end of the accounting period.

(2) *Accounting Period*. The accounting period ends on the anniversary date of the issuance of the letters of authority, unless the conservator selects another accounting period or unless the court orders otherwise. If the conservator selects another accounting period, notice of that selection shall be filed with the court. The accounting period may be a calendar year or a fiscal year ending on the last day of a month. The conservator may use the same accounting period as that used for income tax reporting, and the first accounting period may be less than a year but not longer than a year.

(3) *Hearing*. On filing, the account may be set for hearing or the hearing may be deferred to a later time.

(4) *Exception, Conservatorship of Minor*. Unless otherwise ordered by the court, no accounting is required in a minor conservatorship where the assets are restricted or in a conservatorship where no assets have been received by the conservator. If the assets are ordered to be placed in a restricted account, proof of the restricted account must be filed with the court within 28 days of the conservator's qualification or as otherwise ordered by the court. The conservator must file with the court an annual verification of funds on deposit with a copy of the corresponding financial institution statement attached.

(5) *Contents*. The accounting is subject to the provisions of MCR 5.310(C)(2)(c) and (d), except that references to a personal representative shall be to a conservator. A copy of the corresponding financial institution statement must be presented to the court or a verification of funds on deposit must be filed with the court, either of which must reflect the value of all liquid assets held by a financial institution dated within 30 days after the end of the accounting period, unless waived by the court for good cause.

(6) *Periodic Review*. The court shall either review or allow accounts annually, unless no account is required under MCR 5.409(C)(1) or (C)(4). Accounts shall be set for hearing to determine whether they will be allowed at least once every three years.

(D) **Service and Notice**. A copy of the account must be sent to the interested persons as provided by these rules. Notice of hearing to approve the account must be given to interested persons as provided in subchapter 5.100 of these rules.

(E) **Procedures**. The procedures prescribed in MCR 5.203, 5.204 and 5.310(E) apply to guardianship and conservatorship proceedings, except that references to a personal representative shall be to a guardian or conservator, as the situation dictates.

(F) **Death of Ward**. If an individual who is subject to a guardianship or conservatorship dies, the guardian or conservator must give written notification to the court within 14 days of the individual's date of death. If accounts are required to be filed with the court, a final account must be filed within 56 days of the date of death.

5.411 Bond of Conservator

In all conservatorships in which there are unrestricted assets, the court may require a bond in the amount the court finds necessary to protect the estate or as required by statute. No bond shall be required of trust companies organized under the laws of Michigan or of banks with trust powers unless the court orders that a bond be required.

Subchapter 5.500 Trust Proceedings

Rule 5.501 Trust Proceedings in General

(A) **Applicability**. This subchapter applies to all trusts as defined in MCL 700.1107(n), including a trust established under a will and a trust created by court order or a separate document.

(B) **Unsupervised Administration of Trusts**. Unless an interested person invokes court jurisdiction, the administration of a trust shall proceed expeditiously, consistent with the terms of the trust, free of judicial intervention and without court order, approval, or other court action. Neither registration nor a proceeding concerning a trust results in continued supervisory proceedings.

(C) **Commencement of Trust Proceedings**. A proceeding concerning a trust is commenced by filing a petition in the court. Registration of the trust is not required for filing a petition.

(D) **Appointment of Trustee not Named in Creating Document**. An interested person may petition the court for appointment of a trustee when there is a vacancy in a trusteeship. The court may issue an order appointing as trustee the person nominated in the petition or another person. The order must state whether the trustee must file a bond or execute an acceptance.

(E) **Qualification of Trustee**. A trustee appointed by an order of the court, nominated as a trustee in a will that has been admitted to probate shall qualify by executing an acceptance indicating the nominee's willingness to serve. The trustee must serve the acceptance and order, if any, on the then known qualified trust beneficiaries described in MCL 700.7103(g)(i) and, in the case of a testamentary trustee, on the personal representative of the decedent estate, if one has been appointed. No letters of trusteeship shall be issued by the court. The trustee or the attorney for the trustee may establish the trustee's incumbency by executing an affidavit to that effect, identifying the trustee and the trust and indicating that any required bond has been filed with the court and is in force.

(F) **Transitional Rule**. A trustee of a trust under the jurisdiction of the court before April 1, 2000, may request an order of the court closing court supervision and the file. On request by the trustee or on its own initiative, the court may order the closing of supervision of the trust and close the file. The trustee must give notice of the order to all current trust beneficiaries. Closing supervision does not preclude any interested trust beneficiary from later petitioning the court for supervision. Without regard to whether the court file is closed, all letters of authority for existing trusts are canceled as of April 1, 2000, and the trustee's incumbency may be established in the manner provided in subrule (E).

Rule 5.502 Supervision of Trusts

If, during a trust proceeding, the court orders supervision of the trust, the court shall specify the terms of the supervision.

Subchapter 5.730 Mental Health Rules

Rule 5.730 Mental Health Code; Application

Except as modified by this subchapter, civil admission and discharge proceedings under the Mental Health Code are governed by the rules generally applicable to probate court.

Rule 5.731 Confidential Records

Records are public except as otherwise indicated in court rule or statute.

Rule 5.732 Attorneys

(A) **Continuing Appointment of Attorney**. The attorney of record must represent the individual in all probate court proceedings under the Mental Health Code until the attorney is discharged by court order or another attorney has filed an appearance on the individual's behalf.

(B) **Duties**. The attorney must serve as an advocate for the individual's preferred position. If the individual does not express a preference, the attorney must advocate for the position that the attorney believes is in the individual's best interest.

(C) **Waiver; Appointment of Guardian Ad Litem**. The individual may waive an attorney only in open court and after consultation with an attorney. The court may not accept the waiver if it appears that the waiver is not voluntarily and understandingly made. If an attorney is waived, the court may appoint a guardian ad litem for the individual.

Rule 5.733 Appointment of Independent Examiner; Determination of Fees and Expenses

(A) **Appointment**. When an indigent individual requests an independent clinical evaluation, the court must appoint the physician, psychiatrist, or licensed psychologist chosen by the individual, unless the person chosen refuses to examine the individual or the requested appointment would require unreasonable expense.

(B) **Determination of Fee**. In its order of appointment, a court must direct the independent examiner to submit an itemized statement of services and expenses for approval. In reviewing a fee, the court must consider:
   (1) the time required for examination, evaluation, preparation of reports, and court appearances;
   (2) the examiner's experience and training; and
   (3) the local fee for similar services.

Rule 5.734 Service of Papers; Notice of Subsequent Petitions; Time for Service

(A) **Service of Papers**. When required by the Mental Health Code, the court must have the necessary papers served. The individual must be served personally. The individual's attorney also must be served.

(B) **Notice of Subsequent Petitions**. The court must serve a copy of a petition for the second or continuing order of involuntary mental health treatment or petition for discharge and the notice of hearing on all persons required to be served with notice of hearing on the initial petition or application for hospitalization.

(C) **Time for Service**.
   (1) A notice of hearing must be served on the individual and the individual's attorney

(a) at least 2 days before the time of a hearing that is scheduled by the court to be held within 7 days or less; or
(b) at least 5 days before the time scheduled for other hearings.

(2) A notice of hearing must be served on other interested parties
(a) by personal service, at least 2 days before the time of a hearing that is scheduled by the court to be held within 7 days or less; or
(b) by personal service or by mail, at least 5 days before the time scheduled for other hearings.

The court may permit service of a notice of hearing on the individual, the individual's attorney, or other interested parties within a shorter period of time with the consent of the individual and the individual's attorney.

Rule 5.735 Adjournment

A hearing may be adjourned only for good cause. The reason for an adjournment must be submitted in writing to the court and to the opposing attorney or stated on the record.

Rule 5.737 Waiver of Rights

Unless a statute or court rule requires that a waiver be made by the individual personally and on the record, a waiver may be in writing signed by the individual, witnessed by the individual's attorney, and filed with the court.

Rule 5.738 Conditions at Hearings

(A) **Hearings at Hospitals**. When hearings are not held in the courtroom where the court ordinarily sits, the court shall ensure a quiet and dignified setting that permits an undisturbed proceeding and inspires the participants' confidence in the integrity of the judicial process.

(B) **Clothing**. The individual may attend a hearing in personal clothing.

(C) **Restraints at Hearing**. At a court hearing, the individual may not be handcuffed or otherwise restrained, except
(1) on the prior approval of the court, based on the individual's immediate past conduct indicating the individual is reasonably likely to try to escape or to inflict physical harm on himself or herself or others; or
(2) after an incident occurring during transportation in which the individual has attempted to escape or inflict physical harm on himself or herself or others.

Rule 5.738a Use of Interactive Video Technology

(A) Probate courts may use two-way interactive video technology to conduct the proceedings outlined in subrule (B).

(B) **Hearings**. Probate courts may use two-way interactive video technology to conduct hearings concerning initial involuntary treatment, continuing mental health treatment, and petitions for guardianship involving persons receiving treatment in mental health facilities.

(C) **Mechanics of Use**. The use of two-way interactive video technology must be conducted in accordance with any requirements and guidelines established by the State Court Administrative Office. All proceedings at which such technology is used must be recorded verbatim by the court.

Rule 5.740 Jury Trial

(A) **Persons Permitted to Demand Jury Trial**. Notwithstanding MCR 5.158(A), only an individual alleged to be in need of involuntary mental health treatment or an individual with mental retardation alleged to meet the criteria for judicial admission may demand a jury trial in a civil admission proceeding.

(B) **Time for Demand**. An individual may demand a jury trial any time before testimony is received at the hearing for which the jury is sought.

(C) **Verdict in Commitment Proceedings**. In proceedings involving possible commitment to a hospital or facility under the Mental Health Code, or to a correctional or training facility under the juvenile code, the jury's verdict must be unanimous.

(D) **Fee**. A jury fee is not required from a party demanding a jury trial under the Mental Health Code.

Rule 5.741 Inquiry Into Adequacy of Treatment

(A) **Written Report or Testimony Required**. Before ordering a course of involuntary mental health treatment or of care and treatment at a center, the court must receive a written report or oral testimony describing the type and extent of treatment that will be provided to the individual and the appropriateness and adequacy of this treatment.

(B) **Use of Written Report; Notice**. The court may receive a written report in evidence without accompanying testimony if a copy is filed with the court before the hearing. At the time of filing the report with the court, the preparer of the report must promptly provide the individual's attorney with a copy of the report. The attorney may subpoena the preparer of the report to testify.

Rule 5.743 Appeal by Individual Receiving Involuntary Mental Health Treatment Who is Returned to Hospital After Authorized Leave

(A) **Applicability**. This rule applies to an individual receiving involuntary mental health treatment who has been returned to a hospital following an authorized leave.

(B) **Notifications**. When an individual receiving involuntary mental health treatment has been returned to a hospital from an authorized leave in excess of 10 days, the director of the hospital must, within 24 hours, notify the court of the return and notify the individual of the right to appeal the return and have a hearing to determine the appeal. The court must notify the individual's attorney or appoint a new attorney to consult with the individual and determine whether the individual desires a hearing.

(C) **Request and Time for Hearing**. An individual who wishes to appeal must request a hearing in writing within 7 days of the notice to the individual under subrule (B). The court must schedule a requested hearing to be held within 7 days of the court's receipt of the request.

(D) **Reports Filed With Court**. At least 3 days before the hearing, the director of the hospital must deliver to the court, the individual, and the individual's attorney, copies of a clinical certificate and a current alternative treatment report.

(E) **Conduct of Hearing**. At the hearing, the director of the hospital must show that the individual requires treatment in a hospital. The clinical certificate may be admitted in evidence without accompanying testimony by the preparer. However, the individual's attorney may subpoena the preparer of the clinical certificate to testify.

(F) **Order After Hearing**. If the court finds that the individual requires treatment at a hospital, it must dismiss the appeal and order the individual returned to the hospital. If the court finds that the director lacked an adequate basis for concluding that the individual requires further treatment in the hospital, it must do one of the following:

- (1) order the individual returned to authorized leave status; or
- (2) order treatment through an alternative to hospitalization
  - (a) (if the individual was under an order of hospitalization of up to 60 days), for a period not to exceed the difference between 90 days and the combined time the individual has been hospitalized and on authorized leave status, or
  - (b) (if the individual was under an order of hospitalization of up to 90 days or under a continuing order), for a period not to exceed the difference between 1 year and the combined time the individual has been hospitalized and on authorized leave status.

Rule 5.743a Appeal by Administratively Admitted Individual Returned to Center After Authorized Leave

(A) **Applicability**. This rule applies to an individual with a developmental disability who was admitted to a center by an administrative admission and who has been returned to a center following an authorized leave.

(B) **Notifications**. When an administratively admitted individual has been returned to a center from an authorized leave in excess of 10 days, the director of the center must, within 24 hours, notify the court of the return and notify the individual of the right to appeal the return. The court must notify the individual's guardian, if any, and the parents of an individual who is a minor of the return and the right to appeal the return and have a hearing to determine the appeal.

(C) **Request for Hearing**. An individual who wishes to appeal that individual's return must request a hearing in writing within 7 days of the notice to the individual under subrule (B). If the individual is less than 13 years of age, the request may be made by the individual's parent or guardian. The court must schedule a requested hearing to be held within 7 days of the court's receipt of the request.

(D) **Statement Filed With Court**. At least 3 days before the hearing, the director of the center must deliver to the court, the individual, the individual's parents or guardian, if applicable, and the individual's attorney a statement setting forth:

- (1) the reason for the individual's return to the center;
- (2) the reason the individual is believed to need care and treatment at the center; and
- (3) the plan for further care and treatment.

(E) **Conduct of Hearing**. The hearing shall proceed as provided in § 511(4) of the Mental Health Code, MCL 330.1511. At the hearing, the director of the center must show that the individual needs care and treatment at the center and that no alternative to the care and treatment provided at the center is available and adequate to meet the individual's needs.

(F) **Order After Hearing**. If the court finds the individual requires care and treatment at the center, it must dismiss the appeal and order the individual to remain at the center. If the court finds the director did not sustain the burden of proof, it must order the individual returned to authorized leave status.

Rule 5.743b Appeal by Judicially Admitted Individual Returned to Center After Authorized Leave

(A) **Applicability**. This rule applies to an individual with mental retardation who has been admitted to a center by judicial order, and who has been on authorized leave for a continuous period of less than 1 year.

(B) **Notifications**. When a judicially admitted individual has been returned to a center from an authorized leave in excess of 10 days, the director of the center must, within 24 hours, notify the court of the return and notify the individual of the right to appeal the return and have a hearing to determine the appeal. The court must notify the individual's attorney or appoint a new attorney to consult with the individual and to determine whether the individual desires a hearing.

(C) **Request for Hearing**. An individual who wishes to appeal the return must request a hearing in writing within 7 days of the notice to the individual under subrule (B). The court must schedule a requested hearing to be held within 7 days of the court's receipt of the request.

(D) **Statement Filed With Court**. At least 3 days before the hearing, the director of the center must deliver to the court, the individual, and the individual's attorney a statement setting forth:
  (1) the reason for the individual's return to the center;
  (2) the reason the individual is believed to need care and treatment at the center; and
  (3) the plan for further care and treatment.

(E) **Report**. The court may order an examination of the individual and the preparation and filing with the court of a report that contains such information as the court deems necessary.

(F) **Conduct of Hearing**. The court shall proceed as provided in § 511(4) of the Mental Health Code, MCL 330.1511(4). At the hearing, the director of the center must show that the individual needs care and treatment at the center, and that no alternative to the care and treatment provided at the center is available and adequate to meet the individual's needs.

(G) **Order After Hearing**. If the court finds the individual requires care and treatment at the center, it must dismiss the appeal and order the individual to remain at the center. If the court finds the director did not sustain the burden of proof, it must do one of the following:
  (1) order the individual returned to authorized leave status; or
  (2) order the individual to undergo a program of care and treatment for up to one year as an alternative to remaining at the center.

Rule 5.744 Proceedings Regarding Hospitalization Without a Hearing

(A) **Scope of Rule**. This rule applies to any proceeding involving an individual hospitalized without a hearing as ordered by a court or a psychiatrist and the rights of that individual.

(B) **Notification**. A notification requesting an order of hospitalization or a notification requesting a change in an alternative treatment program, a notice of noncompliance, or a notice of hospitalization as ordered by a psychiatrist, must be in writing.

(C) **Service of Papers**. If the court enters a new or modified order without a hearing, the court must serve the individual with a copy of that order. If the order includes hospitalization, the court must also serve the individual with notice of the right to object and demand a hearing.

(D) **Objection; Scheduling Hearing**. An individual hospitalized without a hearing, either by order of the court or by a psychiatrist's order, may file an objection to the order not later than 7 days after receipt of notice of the right to object. The court must schedule a hearing to be held within 10 days after receiving the objection.

(E) **Conduct of Hearing**. A hearing convened under this rule is without a jury. At the hearing the party seeking hospitalization of the individual must present evidence that hospitalization is necessary.

Rule 5.744a Proceedings Regarding an Individual Subject to Judicial Admission who is Transferred to a Center from Alternative Setting

(A) **Applicability**. This rule applies to an individual with mental retardation under court order to undergo a program of care and treatment as an alternative to admission to a center.

(B) **Immediate Transfer**. After the court receives written notification concerning the need to transfer a judicially admitted individual receiving alternative care and treatment, the court may direct the filing of additional information and may do one of the following:
  (1) modify its original order and direct the individual's transfer to another program of alternative care and treatment for the remainder of the 1-year period;
  (2) enter a new order directing the individual's admission to either
    (a) a center recommended by the community mental health services program; or
    (b) a licensed hospital requested by the individual or the individual's family if private funds are to be used; or
  (3) set a date for a hearing.

(C) **Investigation Report**. On receipt of notification, the court must promptly obtain from the community mental health services program or other appropriate agency a report stating
  (1) the reason for concern about the adequacy of the care and treatment being received at the time of the notification;
  (2) the continued suitability of that care and treatment; and
  (3) the adequacy of care and treatment available at another alternative or at a center or licensed hospital.

(D) **Service of Papers**. If the court enters a new order without a hearing, it must serve the interested parties with a copy of that order and a copy of the investigation report when it becomes available. If the order includes transfer of the individual to a center, the court must also serve the interested parties with written notification of the individual's right to object and demand a hearing.

(E) **Hearing**. If within 7 days of service under subrule (D) the court receives a written objection from the individual or the individual's attorney, guardian, or presumptive heir, the court must schedule a hearing to be held within 10 days of the court's receipt of the objection.

(F) **Conduct of Hearing**. A hearing convened under this rule is without a jury. At the hearing, the person seeking transfer of the individual to a center must present evidence that the individual had not complied with the applicable order or that the order is not sufficient to prevent the individual from inflicting harm or injuries on himself, herself or others. The evidence must support a finding that transfer to another alternative, a center or a licensed hospital is necessary.

(G) **Order After Hearing**. The court may affirm or rescind the order issued under subrule (B), order a new program of care and treatment, or order discharge. The court may not place the individual in a center without inquiring into the adequacy of care and treatment for that individual at that center.

Rule 5.745 Multiple Proceedings

(A) **New Proceedings Not Prohibited**. The admission of an individual under the Mental Health Code may not be invalidated because the individual is already subject to a court order as a result of a prior admission proceeding.

(B) **Procedure**. On being informed that an individual is subject to a previous court order, the court must:

(1) if it was the court issuing the previous order, dismiss the new proceeding and determine the proper disposition of the individual under its previous order or vacate the previous order and proceed under the new petition; or

(2) if the previous order was issued by another court, continue the new proceeding and issue an appropriate order. After entry of the order, the court with the new proceeding must consult with the court with the prior proceeding to determine if the best interests of the individual will be served by changing venue of the prior proceeding to the county where the new proceeding has been initiated. If not, the court with the new proceeding must transfer the matter to the other court.

(C) **Disposition**. The court may treat a petition or certificate filed in connection with the more recent proceeding as "notification" under MCR 5.743 or 5.744 and proceed with disposition under those rules.

Rule 5.746 Placement of Individual with a Developmental Disability in a Facility

(A) **Petition for Authorization**. If placement in a facility of an individual with a developmental disability has not been authorized or if permission is sought for authorization to place the individual in a more restrictive setting than previously ordered, a guardian of the individual must petition the court for authorization to place the individual in a facility or in a more restricted setting.

(B) **Order**. If the court grants the petition for authorization, it may order that:

(1) the guardian may execute an application for the individual's administrative admission to a specific center;

(2) the guardian may request the individual's temporary admission to a center for a period not to exceed 30 days for each admission; or

(3) the guardian may place the individual in a specific facility or class of facility as defined in MCL 330.1600.

(C) **Notice of Hearing**. Notice of hearing on a petition for authorization to place an individual must be given to those persons required to be served with notice of hearing for the appointment of a guardian.

Rule 5.747 Petition for Discharge of Individual

At a hearing on a petition for discharge of an individual, the burden is on the person who seeks to prevent discharge to show that the individual is a person requiring treatment.

Rule 5.748 Transitional Provision on Termination of Indefinite Orders of Hospitalization

If on March 27, 1996, any individual is subject to any order that may result in the individual's hospitalization for a period beyond March 27, 1997, a petition for a determination that the individual continues to require involuntary mental health treatment must be filed on or before the time set for the second periodic review after March 27, 1996. The petition may be for involuntary health treatment for a period of not more than one year. This rule expires on March 28, 1997.

Subchapter 5.780 Miscellaneous Proceedings

Rule 5.784 Proceedings on a Durable Power of Attorney for Health Care or Mental Health Treatment

(A) **Petition, Who Shall File**. The petition concerning a durable power of attorney for health care or mental health treatment must be filed by any interested party or the patient's attending physician.

(B) **Venue**. Venue for any proceeding concerning a durable power of attorney for health care or mental health treatment is proper in the county in which the patient resides or the county where the patient is found.

(C) **Notice of Hearing, Service, Manner and Time**.

(1) *Manner of Service*. If the address of an interested party is known or can be learned by diligent inquiry, notice must be by mail or personal service, but service by mail must be supplemented by facsimile or telephone contact within the period for timely service when the hearing is an expedited

hearing or a hearing on the initial determination regarding whether the patient is unable to participate in medical or mental health treatment decisions.

(2) *Waiving Service.* At an expedited hearing or a hearing on an initial determination regarding whether the patient is unable to participate in medical or mental health treatment decisions, the court may dispense with notice of the hearing on those interested parties who could not be contacted after diligent effort by the petitioner.

(3) *Time of Service.* Notice of hearing must be served at least 2 days before the time of a hearing on an initial determination regarding whether the patient is unable to participate in medical or mental health treatment decisions. Notice of an expedited hearing must be served at such time as directed by the court. Notice of other hearings must be served at such time as directed by MCR 5.108.

(D) **Hearings**.

(1) *Time.* Hearings on a petition for an initial determination regarding whether a patient is unable to participate in a medical or mental health treatment decision must be held within 7 days of the filing of the petition. The court may order an expedited hearing on any petition concerning a durable power of attorney for health care or mental health treatment decisions on a showing of good cause to expedite the proceedings. A showing of good cause to expedite proceedings may be made ex parte.

(2) *Trial.* Disputes concerning durable powers of attorney for health care or mental health treatment decisions are tried by the court without a jury.

(3) *Proof.* The petitioner has the burden of proof by a preponderance of evidence on all contested issues except that the standard is by clear and convincing evidence on an issue whether a patient has authorized the patient advocate under a durable power of attorney for health care to decide to withhold or withdraw treatment, which decision could or would result in the patient's death, or authorized the patient advocate under a durable power of attorney for mental health treatment to seek the forced administration of medication or hospitalization.

(4) *Privilege, Waiver.* The physician-patient privilege must not be asserted.

(E) **Temporary Relief**. On a sufficient showing of need, the court may issue a temporary restraining order pursuant to MCR 3.310 pending a hearing on any petition concerning a durable power of attorney for health care or mental health treatment.

Subchapter 5.800 Appeals

Rule 5.801 Appeals to Other Courts

(A) **Right to Appeal**. An interested person aggrieved by an order of the probate court may appeal as provided by this rule.

(B) **Orders Appealable to Court of Appeals**. Orders appealable of right to the Court of Appeals are defined and limited to the following:

(1) a final order affecting the rights or interests of a party to a civil action commenced in the probate court under MCR 5.101(C).

(2) a final order affecting the rights or interests of an interested person in a proceeding involving a decedent estate, the estate of a person who has disappeared or is missing, a conservatorship or other protective proceeding, the estate of an individual with developmental disabilities, or an inter vivos trust or a trust created under a will. These are defined as and limited to orders resolving the following matters:

(a) appointing or removing a personal representative, conservator, trustee, or trust protector as referred to in MCL 700.7103(n), or denying such an appointment or removal;

(b) admitting or denying to probate of a will, codicil, or other testamentary instrument;

(c) determining the validity of a governing instrument;

(d) interpreting or construing a governing instrument;

(e) approving or denying a settlement relating to a governing instrument;

(f) reforming, terminating, or modifying or denying the reformation , termination or modification of a trust;

(g) granting or denying a petition to consolidate or divide trusts;

(h) discharging or denying the discharge of a surety on a bond from further liability;

(i) allowing, disallowing, or denying a claim;

(j) assigning, selling, leasing, or encumbering any of the assets of an estate or trust;

(k) authorizing or denying the continuation of a business;

(l) determining special allowances in a decedent's estate such as a homestead allowance, an exempt property allowance, or a family allowance;

(m) authorizing or denying rights of election;

(n) determining heirs, devisees, or beneficiaries;

(o) determining title to or rights or interests in property;

(p) authorizing or denying partition of property;

(q) authorizing or denying specific performance;

(r) ascertaining survivorship of parties;

(s) granting or denying a petition to bar a mentally incompetent or minor wife from dower in the property of her living husband;
(t) granting or denying a petition to determine cy pres;
(u) directing or denying the making or repayment of distributions;
(v) determining or denying a constructive trust;
(w) determining or denying an oral contract relating to a will;
(x) allowing or disallowing an account, fees, or administration expenses;
(y) surcharging or refusing to surcharge a fiduciary or trust protector as referred to in MCL 700.7103(n);
(z) determining or directing payment or apportionment of taxes;
(aa) distributing proceeds recovered for wrongful death under MCL 600.2922;
(bb) assigning residue;
(cc) granting or denying a petition for instructions;
(dd) authorizing disclaimers.
(ee) allowing or disallowing a trustee to change the principal place of a trust's administration;

(3) other appeals as may be hereafter provided by statute.

(C) **Final Orders Appealable to Circuit Court**. All final orders not enumerated in subrule (B) are appealable of right to the circuit court. These include, but are not limited to:

(1) a final order affecting the rights and interests of an adult or a minor in a guardianship proceeding;
(2) a final order affecting the rights or interests of a person under the Mental Health Code, except for a final order affecting the rights or interests of a person in the estate of an individual with developmental disabilities.

(D) **Interlocutory Orders**. An interlocutory order, such as an order regarding discovery; ruling on evidence; appointing a guardian ad litem; or suspending a fiduciary for failure to give a new bond, to file an inventory, or to render an account, may be appealed only to the circuit court and only by leave of that court. The circuit court shall pay particular attention to an application for leave to appeal an interlocutory order if the probate court has certified that the order involves a controlling question of law as to which there is substantial ground for difference of opinion and that an immediate appeal may materially advance the termination of the litigation.

(E) **Transfer of Appeals From Court of Appeals to Circuit Court**. If an appeal of right within the jurisdiction of the circuit court is filed in the Court of Appeals, the Court of Appeals may transfer the appeal to the circuit court, which shall hear the appeal as if it had been filed in the circuit court.

(F) **Appeals to Court of Appeals on Certification by Probate Court**. Instead of appealing to the circuit court, a party may appeal directly to the Court of Appeals if the probate court certifies that the order involves a controlling question of law as to which there is substantial ground for difference of opinion and that an appeal directly to the Court of Appeals may materially advance the ultimate termination of the litigation. An appeal to the Court of Appeals under this subrule is by leave only under the provisions of MCR 7.205. In lieu of granting leave to appeal, the Court of Appeals may remand the appeal to the circuit court for consideration as on leave granted.

Rule 5.802 Appellate Procedure; Stays Pending Appeal

(A) **Procedure**. Except as modified by this subchapter, chapter 7 of these rules governs appeals from the probate court.

(B) **Record**.

(1) An appeal from the probate court is on the papers filed and a written transcript of the proceedings in the probate court or on a record settled and agreed to by the parties and approved by the court.
(2) The probate register may transmit certified copies of the necessary documents and papers in the file if the original papers are needed for further proceedings in the probate court. The parties shall not be required to pay for the copies as costs or otherwise.

(C) **Stays Pending Appeals**. An order removing a fiduciary; appointing a special personal representative or a special fiduciary; granting a new trial or rehearing; granting an allowance to the spouse or children of a decedent; granting permission to sue on a fiduciary's bond; or suspending a fiduciary and appointing a special fiduciary, is not stayed pending appeal unless ordered by the court on motion for good cause.

CHAPTER 6: CRIMINAL PROCEDURE

Subchapter 6.000 General Provisions

Rule 6.001 Scope; Applicability of Civil Rules; Superseded Rules and Statutes

(A) **Felony Cases**. The rules in subchapters 6.000-6.500 govern matters of procedure in criminal cases cognizable in the circuit courts and in courts of equivalent criminal jurisdiction.

(B) **Misdemeanor Cases**. MCR 6.001-6.004, 6.005(B) and (C), 6.006, 6.102(D) and (F), 6.103, 6.104(A) and (D), 6.106, 6.125, 6.202, 6.427, 6.435, 6.440, 6.445(A)-(G), and the rules in subchapter 6.600 govern matters of procedure in criminal cases cognizable in the district courts.

(C) **Juvenile Cases**. The rules in subchapter 6.900 govern matters of procedure in the district courts and in circuit courts and courts of equivalent criminal jurisdiction in cases involving juveniles against whom the prosecutor has authorized the filing of a criminal complaint as provided in MCL 764.1f.

(D) **Civil Rules Applicable**. The provisions of the rules of civil procedure apply to cases governed by this chapter, except

(1) as otherwise provided by rule or statute,

(2) when it clearly appears that they apply to civil actions only, or

(3) when a statute or court rule provides a like or different procedure.

Depositions and other discovery proceedings under subchapter 2.300 may not be taken for the purposes of discovery in cases governed by this chapter. The provisions of MCR 2.501(C) regarding the length of notice of trial assignment do not apply in cases governed by this chapter.

(E) **Rules and Statutes Superseded**. The rules in this chapter supersede all prior court rules in this chapter and any statutory procedure pertaining to and inconsistent with a procedure provided by a rule in this chapter.

Rule 6.002 Purpose and Construction

These rules are intended to promote a just determination of every criminal proceeding. They are to be construed to secure simplicity in procedure, fairness in administration, and the elimination of unjustifiable expense and delay.

Rule 6.003 Definitions

For purposes of subchapters 6.000-6.800:

(1) "Party" includes the lawyer representing the party.

(2) "Defendant's lawyer" includes a self-represented defendant proceeding without a lawyer.

(3) "Prosecutor" includes any lawyer prosecuting the case.

(4) "Court" or "judicial officer" includes a judge, a magistrate, or a district court magistrate authorized in accordance with the law to perform the functions of a magistrate.

(5) "Court clerk" includes a deputy clerk.

(6) "Court reporter" includes a court recorder.

Rule 6.004 Speedy Trial

(A) **Right to Speedy Trial**. The defendant and the people are entitled to a speedy trial and to a speedy resolution of all matters before the court. Whenever the defendant's constitutional right to a speedy trial is violated, the defendant is entitled to dismissal of the charge with prejudice.

(B) **Priorities in Scheduling Criminal Cases**. The trial court has the responsibility to establish and control a trial calendar. In assigning cases to the calendar, and insofar as it is practicable,

(1) the trial of criminal cases must be given preference over the trial of civil cases, and

(2) the trial of defendants in custody and of defendants whose pretrial liberty presents unusual risks must be given preference over other criminal cases.

(C) **Delay in Felony and Misdemeanor Cases; Recognizance Release**. In a felony case in which the defendant has been incarcerated for a period of 180 days or more to answer for the same crime or a crime based on the same conduct or arising from the same criminal episode, or in a misdemeanor case in which the defendant has been incarcerated for a period of 28 days or more to answer for the same crime or a crime based on the same conduct or arising from the same criminal episode, the defendant must be released on personal recognizance, unless the court finds by clear and convincing evidence that the defendant is likely either to fail to appear for future proceedings or to present a danger to any other person or the community. In computing the 28-day and 180-day periods, the court is to exclude

(1) periods of delay resulting from other proceedings concerning the defendant, including but not limited to competency and criminal responsibility proceedings, pretrial motions, interlocutory appeals, and the trial of other charges,

(2) the period of delay during which the defendant is not competent to stand trial,

(3) the period of delay resulting from an adjournment requested or consented to by the defendant's lawyer,

(4) the period of delay resulting from an adjournment requested by the prosecutor, but only if the prosecutor demonstrates on the record either

(a) the unavailability, despite the exercise of due diligence, of material evidence that the

prosecutor has reasonable cause to believe will be available at a later date; or
   - (b) exceptional circumstances justifying the need for more time to prepare the state's case,
- (5) a reasonable period of delay when the defendant is joined for trial with a codefendant as to whom the time for trial has not run, but only if good cause exists for not granting the defendant a severance so as to enable trial within the time limits applicable, and
- (6) any other periods of delay that in the court's judgment are justified by good cause, but not including delay caused by docket congestion.

(D) **Untried Charges Against State Prisoner**.
- (1) The 180-Day Rule. Except for crimes exempted by MCL 780.131(2), the inmate shall be brought to trial within 180 days after the department of corrections causes to be delivered to the prosecuting attorney of the county in which the warrant, indictment, information, or complaint is pending written notice of the place of imprisonment of the inmate and a request for final disposition of the warrant, indictment, information, or complaint. The request shall be accompanied by a statement setting forth the term of commitment under which the prisoner is being held, the time already served, the time remaining to be served on the sentence, the amount of good time or disciplinary credits earned, the time of parole eligibility of the prisoner, and any decisions of the parole board relating to the prisoner. The written notice and statement shall be delivered by certified mail.
- (2) Remedy. In the event that action is not commenced on the matter for which request for disposition was made as required in subsection (1), no court of this state shall any longer have jurisdiction thereof, nor shall the untried warrant, indictment, information, or complaint be of any further force or effect, and the court shall enter an order dismissing the same with prejudice.

Rule 6.005 Right to Assistance of Lawyer; Advice; Appointment for Indigents; Waiver; Joint Representation; Grand Jury Proceedings

(A) **Advice of Right**. At the arraignment on the warrant or complaint, the court must advise the defendant
- (1) of entitlement to a lawyer's assistance at all subsequent court proceedings, and
- (2) that the court will appoint a lawyer at public expense if the defendant wants one and is financially unable to retain one.

The court must question the defendant to determine whether the defendant wants a lawyer and, if so, whether the defendant is financially unable to retain one.

(B) **Questioning Defendant About Indigency**. If the defendant requests a lawyer and claims financial inability to retain one, the court must determine whether the defendant is indigent. The determination of indigency must be guided by the following factors:
- (1) present employment, earning capacity and living expenses;
- (2) outstanding debts and liabilities, secured and unsecured;
- (3) whether the defendant has qualified for and is receiving any form of public assistance;
- (4) availability and convertibility, without undue financial hardship to the defendant and the defendant's dependents, of any personal or real property owned; and
- (5) any other circumstances that would impair the ability to pay a lawyer's fee as would ordinarily be required to retain competent counsel.

The ability to post bond for pretrial release does not make the defendant ineligible for appointment of a lawyer.

(C) **Partial Indigency**. If a defendant is able to pay part of the cost of a lawyer, the court may require contribution to the cost of providing a lawyer and may establish a plan for collecting the contribution.

(D) **Appointment or Waiver of a Lawyer**. If the court determines that the defendant is financially unable to retain a lawyer, it must promptly appoint a lawyer and promptly notify the lawyer of the appointment. The court may not permit the defendant to make an initial waiver of the right to be represented by a lawyer without first
- (1) advising the defendant of the charge, the maximum possible prison sentence for the offense, any mandatory minimum sentence required by law, and the risk involved in self-representation, and
- (2) offering the defendant the opportunity to consult with a retained lawyer or, if the defendant is indigent, the opportunity to consult with an appointed lawyer.

(E) **Advice at Subsequent Proceedings**. If a defendant has waived the assistance of a lawyer, the record of each subsequent proceeding (e.g., preliminary examination, arraignment, proceedings leading to possible revocation of youthful trainee status, hearings, trial or sentencing) need show only that the court advised the defendant of the continuing right to a lawyer's assistance (at public expense if the defendant is indigent) and that the defendant waived that right. Before the court begins such proceedings,
- (1) the defendant must reaffirm that a lawyer's assistance is not wanted; or
- (2) if the defendant requests a lawyer and is financially unable to retain one, the court must appoint one; or

(3) if the defendant wants to retain a lawyer and has the financial ability to do so, the court must allow the defendant a reasonable opportunity to retain one.

The court may refuse to adjourn a proceeding to appoint counsel or allow a defendant to retain counsel if an adjournment would significantly prejudice the prosecution, and the defendant has not been reasonably diligent in seeking counsel.

(F) **Multiple Representation**. When two or more indigent defendants are jointly charged with an offense or offenses or their cases are otherwise joined, the court must appoint separate lawyers unassociated in the practice of law for each defendant. Whenever two or more defendants who have been jointly charged or whose cases have been joined are represented by the same retained lawyer or lawyers associated in the practice of law, the court must inquire into the potential for a conflict of interest that might jeopardize the right of each defendant to the undivided loyalty of the lawyer. The court may not permit the joint representation unless:

(1) the lawyer or lawyers state on the record the reasons for believing that joint representation in all probability will not cause a conflict of interests;

(2) the defendants state on the record after the court's inquiry and the lawyer's statement, that they desire to proceed with the same lawyer; and

(3) the court finds on the record that joint representation in all probability will not cause a conflict of interest and states its reasons for the finding.

(G) **Unanticipated Conflict of Interest**. If, in a case of joint representation, a conflict of interest arises at any time, including trial, the lawyer must immediately inform the court. If the court agrees that a conflict has arisen, it must afford one or more of the defendants the opportunity to retain separate lawyers. The court should on its own initiative inquire into any potential conflict that becomes apparent, and take such action as the interests of justice require.

(H) **Scope of Trial Lawyer's Responsibilities**. The responsibilities of the trial lawyer who represents the defendant include

(1) representing the defendant in all trial court proceedings through initial sentencing,

(2) filing of interlocutory appeals the lawyer deems appropriate, and

(3) responding to any preconviction appeals by the prosecutor. The defendant's lawyer must either:

(i) file a substantive brief in response to the prosecutor's interlocutory application for leave to appeal, or

(ii) notify the Court of Appeals that the lawyer will not be filing a brief in response to the application.

(4) unless an appellate lawyer has been appointed or retained, or if retained trial counsel withdraws, the trial lawyer who represents the defendant is responsible for filing postconviction motions the lawyer deems appropriate, including motions for new trial, for a directed verdict of acquittal, to withdraw plea, or for resentencing.

(5) when an appellate lawyer has been appointed or retained, promptly making the defendant's file, including all discovery material obtained, available for copying upon request of that lawyer. The trial lawyer must retain the materials in the defendant's file for at least five years after the case is disposed in the trial court.

(I) **Assistance of Lawyer at Grand Jury Proceedings**.

(1) A witness called before a grand jury or a grand juror is entitled to have a lawyer present in the hearing room while the witness gives testimony. A witness may not refuse to appear for reasons of unavailability of the lawyer for that witness. Except as otherwise provided by law, the lawyer may not participate in the proceedings other than to advise the witness.

(2) The prosecutor assisting the grand jury is responsible for ensuring that a witness is informed of the right to a lawyer's assistance during examination by written notice accompanying the subpoena to the witness and by personal advice immediately before the examination. The notice must include language informing the witness that if the witness is financially unable to retain a lawyer, the chief judge in the circuit court in which the grand jury is convened will on request appoint one for the witness at public expense.

Rule 6.006 Video and Audio Proceedings

(A) **Defendant in the Courtroom or at a Separate Location**. District and circuit courts may use two-way interactive video technology to conduct the following proceedings between a courtroom and a prison, jail, or other location: initial arraignments on the warrant or complaint, arraignments on the information, pretrials conferences, pleas, sentencings for misdemeanor offenses, show cause hearings, waivers and adjournments of extradition, referrals for forensic determination of competency, and waivers and adjournments of preliminary examinations.

(B) **Defendant in the Courtroom - Preliminary Examinations**. As long as the defendant is either present in the courtroom or has waived the right to be present, on motion of either party, district courts may use telephonic, voice, or video conferencing, including two-way interactive video technology, to take testimony from an expert witness or, upon a showing of good cause, any person at another location in a preliminary examination.

(C) **Defendant in the Courtroom - Other Proceedings**. As long as the defendant is either present in the courtroom or has waived the right to be present, upon a showing of good cause, district and circuit courts may use two-way interactive video technology to take testimony from a person at another location in the following proceedings:
   (1) evidentiary hearings, competency hearings, sentencings, probation revocation proceedings, and proceedings to revoke a sentence that does not entail an adjudication of guilt, such as youthful trainee status;
   (2) with the consent of the parties, trials. A party who does not consent to the use of two-way interactive video technology to take testimony from a person at trial shall not be required to articulate any reason for not consenting.

(D) **Mechanics of Use**. The use of telephonic, voice, video conferencing, or two-way interactive video technology, must be in accordance with any requirements and guidelines established by the State Court Administrative Office, and all proceedings at which such technology is used must be recorded verbatim by the court.

Rule 6.007 Confidential Records

Records are public except as otherwise indicated in court rule or statute.

Subchapter 6.100 Preliminary Proceedings

Rule 6.101 The Complaint

(A) **Definition and Form**. A complaint is a written accusation that a named or described person has committed a specified criminal offense. The complaint must include the substance of the accusation against the accused and the name and statutory citation of the offense.

(B) **Signature and Oath**. The complaint must be signed and sworn to before a judicial officer or court clerk.

(C) **Prosecutor's Approval or Posting of Security**. A complaint may not be filed without a prosecutor's written approval endorsed on the complaint or attached to it, or unless security for costs is filed with the court.

Rule 6.102 Arrest on a Warrant

(A) **Issuance of Warrant**. A court must issue an arrest warrant, or a summons in accordance with MCR 6.103, if presented with a proper complaint and if the court finds probable cause to believe that the accused committed the alleged offense.

(B) **Probable Cause Determination**. A finding of probable cause may be based on hearsay evidence and rely on factual allegations in the complaint, affidavits from the complainant or others, the testimony of a sworn witness adequately preserved to permit review, or any combination of these sources.

(C) **Contents of Warrant; Court's Subscription**. A warrant must
   (1) contain the accused's name, if known, or an identifying name or description;
   (2) describe the offense charged in the complaint;
   (3) command a peace officer or other person authorized by law to arrest and bring the accused before a judicial officer of the judicial district in which the offense allegedly was committed or some other designated court; and
   (4) be signed by the court.

(D) **Warrant Specification of Interim Bail**. Where permitted by law, the court may specify on the warrant the bail that an accused may post to obtain release before arraignment on the warrant and, if the court deems it appropriate, include as a bail condition that the arrest of the accused occur on or before a specified date or within a specified period of time after issuance of the warrant.

(E) **Execution and Return of Warrant**. Only a peace officer or other person authorized by law may execute an arrest warrant. On execution or attempted execution of the warrant, the officer must make a return on the warrant and deliver it to the court before which the arrested person is to be taken.

(F) **Release on Interim Bail**. If an accused has been arrested pursuant to a warrant that includes an interim bail provision, the accused must either be arraigned promptly or released pursuant to the interim bail provision. The accused may obtain release by posting the bail on the warrant and by submitting a recognizance to appear before a specified court at a specified date and time, provided that
   (1) the accused is arrested prior to the expiration date, if any, of the bail provision;
   (2) the accused is arrested in the county in which the warrant was issued, or in which the accused resides or is employed, and the accused is not wanted on another charge;
   (3) the accused is not under the influence of liquor or controlled substance; and
   (4) the condition of the accused or the circumstances at the time of arrest do not otherwise suggest a need for judicial review of the original specification of bail.

Rule 6.103 Summons Instead of Arrest

(A) **Issuance of Summons**. If the prosecutor so requests, the court may issue a summons instead of an arrest warrant. If an accused fails to appear in response to a summons, the court, on request, must issue an arrest warrant.

(B) **Form**. A summons must contain the same information as an arrest warrant, except that it should summon the accused to appear before a designated court at a stated time and place.

(C) **Service and Return of Summons**. A summons may be served by
  (1) delivering a copy to the named individual; or
  (2) leaving a copy with a person of suitable age and discretion at the individual's home or usual place of abode; or
  (3) mailing a copy to the individual's last known address.

Service should be made promptly to give the accused adequate notice of the appearance date. The person serving the summons must make a return to the court before which the person is summoned to appear.

Rule 6.104 Arraignment on the Warrant or Complaint

(A) **Arraignment Without Unnecessary Delay**. Unless released beforehand, an arrested person must be taken without unnecessary delay before a court for arraignment in accordance with the provisions of this rule, or must be arraigned without unnecessary delay by use of two-way interactive video technology in accordance with MCR 6.006(A).

(B) **Place of Arraignment**. An accused arrested pursuant to a warrant must be taken to a court specified in the warrant. An accused arrested without a warrant must be taken to a court in the judicial district in which the offense allegedly occurred. If the arrest occurs outside the county in which these courts are located, the arresting agency must make arrangements with the authorities in the demanding county to have the accused promptly transported to the latter county for arraignment in accordance with the provisions of this rule. If prompt transportation cannot be arranged, the accused must be taken without unnecessary delay before the nearest available court for preliminary appearance in accordance with subrule (C). In the alternative, the provisions of this subrule may be satisfied by use of two-way interactive video technology in accordance with MCR 6.006(A).

(C) **Preliminary Appearance Outside County of Offense**. When, under subrule (B), an accused is taken before a court outside the county of the alleged offense either in person or by way of two-way interactive video technology, the court must advise the accused of the rights specified in subrule (E)(2) and determine what form of pretrial release, if any, is appropriate. To be released, the accused must submit a recognizance for appearance within the next 14 days before a court specified in the arrest warrant or, in a case involving an arrest without a warrant, before either a court in the judicial district in which the offense allegedly occurred or some other court designated by that court. The court must certify the recognizance and have it delivered or sent without delay to the appropriate court. If the accused is not released, the arresting agency must arrange prompt transportation to the judicial district of the offense. In all cases, the arraignment is then to continue under subrule (D), if applicable, and subrule (E) either in the judicial district of the alleged offense or in such court as otherwise is designated.

(D) **Arrest Without Warrant**. If an accused is arrested without a warrant, a complaint complying with MCR 6.101 must be filed at or before the time of arraignment. On receiving the complaint and on finding probable cause, the court must either issue a warrant or endorse the complaint as provided in MCL 764.1c. Arraignment of the accused may then proceed in accordance with subrule (E).

(E) **Arraignment Procedure; Judicial Responsibilities**. The court at the arraignment must
  (1) inform the accused of the nature of the offense charged, and its maximum possible prison sentence and any mandatory minimum sentence required by law;
  (2) if the accused is not represented by a lawyer at the arraignment, advise the accused that
    (a) the accused has a right to remain silent,
    (b) anything the accused says orally or in writing can be used against the accused in court,
    (c) the accused has a right to have a lawyer present during any questioning consented to, and
    (d) if the accused does not have the money to hire a lawyer, the court will appoint a lawyer for the accused;
  (3) advise the accused of the right to a lawyer at all subsequent court proceedings and, if appropriate, appoint a lawyer;
  (4) set a date within the next 14 days for the accused's preliminary examination and inform the accused of the date;
  (5) determine what form of pretrial release, if any, is appropriate; and
  (6) ensure that the accused has been fingerprinted as required by law.

The court may not question the accused about the alleged offense or request that the accused enter a plea.

(F) **Arraignment Procedure; Recording**. A verbatim record must be made of the arraignment.

(G) **Plan for Judicial Availability**. In each county, the court with trial jurisdiction over felony cases must adopt and file with the state court administrator a plan for judicial availability. The plan shall
  (1) make a judicial officer available for arraignments each day of the year, or
  (2) make a judicial officer available for setting bail for every person arrested for commission of a felony each day of the year conditioned upon
    (a) the judicial officer being presented a proper complaint and finding probable cause pursuant to MCR 6.102(A), and

(b) the judicial officer having available information to set bail.

This portion of the plan must provide that the judicial officer shall order the arresting officials to arrange prompt transportation of any accused unable to post bond to the judicial district of the offense for arraignment not later than the next regular business day.

Rule 6.106 Pretrial Release

(A) **In General**. At the defendant's first appearance before a court, unless an order in accordance with this rule was issued beforehand, the court must order that, pending trial, the defendant be
  (1) held in custody as provided in subrule (B);
  (2) released on personal recognizance or an unsecured appearance bond; or
  (3) released conditionally, with or without money bail (ten percent, cash or surety).

(B) **Pretrial Release/Custody Order Under Const 1963, art 1, § 15**.
  (1) The court may deny pretrial release to
    (a) a defendant charged with
      (i) murder or treason, or
      (ii) committing a violent felony and
        [A] at the time of the commission of the violent felony, the defendant was on probation, parole, or released pending trial for another violent felony, or
        [B] during the 15 years preceding the commission of the violent felony, the defendant had been convicted of 2 or more violent felonies under the laws of this state or substantially similar laws of the United States or another state arising out of separate incidents,

      if the court finds that proof of the defendant's guilt is evident or the presumption great;
    (b) a defendant charged with criminal sexual conduct in the first degree, armed robbery, or kidnapping with the intent to extort money or other valuable thing thereby, if the court finds that proof of the defendant's guilt is evident or the presumption great, unless the court finds by clear and convincing evidence that the defendant is not likely to flee or present a danger to any other person.
  (2) A "violent felony" within the meaning of subrule (B)(1) is a felony, an element of which involves a violent act or threat of a violent act against any other person.
  (3) If the court determines as provided in subrule (B)(1) that the defendant may not be released, the court must order the defendant held in custody for a period not to exceed 90 days after the date of the order, excluding delays attributable to the defense, within which trial must begin or the court must immediately schedule a hearing and set the amount of bail.
  (4) The court must state the reasons for an order of custody on the record and on a form approved by the State Court Administrator's Office entitled "Custody Order." The completed form must be placed in the court file.

(C) **Release on Personal Recognizance**. If the defendant is not ordered held in custody pursuant to subrule (B), the court must order the pretrial release of the defendant on personal recognizance, or on an unsecured appearance bond, subject to the conditions that the defendant will appear as required, will not leave the state without permission of the court, and will not commit any crime while released, unless the court determines that such release will not reasonably ensure the appearance of the defendant as required, or that such release will present a danger to the public.

(D) **Conditional Release**. If the court determines that the release described in subrule (C) will not reasonably ensure the appearance of the defendant as required, or will not reasonably ensure the safety of the public, the court may order the pretrial release of the defendant on the condition or combination of conditions that the court determines are appropriate including
  (1) that the defendant will appear as required, will not leave the state without permission of the court, and will not commit any crime while released, and
  (2) subject to any condition or conditions the court determines are reasonably necessary to ensure the appearance of the defendant as required and the safety of the public, which may include requiring the defendant to
    (a) make reports to a court agency as are specified by the court or the agency;
    (b) not use alcohol or illicitly use any controlled substance;
    (c) participate in a substance abuse testing or monitoring program;
    (d) participate in a specified treatment program for any physical or mental condition, including substance abuse;
    (e) comply with restrictions on personal associations, place of residence, place of employment, or travel;
    (f) surrender driver's license or passport;
    (g) comply with a specified curfew;
    (h) continue to seek employment;
    (i) continue or begin an educational program;
    (j) remain in the custody of a responsible member of the community who agrees to monitor the defendant and report any violation of any release condition to the court;
    (k) not possess a firearm or other dangerous weapon;

(l) not enter specified premises or areas and not assault, beat, molest or wound a named person or persons;

(m) comply with any condition limiting or prohibiting contact with any other named person or persons. If an order under this paragraph limiting or prohibiting contact with any other named person or persons is in conflict with another court order, the most restrictive provision of each order shall take precedence over the other court order until the conflict is resolved.

(n) satisfy any injunctive order made a condition of release; or

(o) comply with any other condition, including the requirement of money bail as described in subrule (E), reasonably necessary to ensure the defendant's appearance as required and the safety of the public.

(E) **Money Bail**. If the court determines for reasons it states on the record that the defendant's appearance or the protection of the public cannot otherwise be assured, money bail, with or without conditions described in subrule (D), may be required.

(1) The court may require the defendant to

(a) post, at the defendant's option,

(i) a surety bond that is executed by a surety approved by the court in an amount equal to 1/4 of the full bail amount, or

(ii) bail that is executed by the defendant, or by another who is not a surety approved by the court, and secured by

[A] a cash deposit, or its equivalent, for the full bail amount, or

[B] a cash deposit of 10 percent of the full bail amount, or, with the court's consent,

[C] designated real property; or

(b) post, at the defendant's option,

(i) a surety bond that is executed by a surety approved by the court in an amount equal to the full bail amount, or

(ii) bail that is executed by the defendant, or by another who is not a surety approved by the court, and secured by

[A] a cash deposit, or its equivalent, for the full bail amount, or, with the court's consent,

[B] designated real property.

(2) The court may require satisfactory proof of value and interest in property if the court consents to the posting of a bond secured by designated real property.

(F) **Decision; Statement of Reasons**.

(1) In deciding which release to use and what terms and conditions to impose, the court is to consider relevant information, including

(a) defendant's prior criminal record, including juvenile offenses;

(b) defendant's record of appearance or nonappearance at court proceedings or flight to avoid prosecution;

(c) defendant's history of substance abuse or addiction;

(d) defendant's mental condition, including character and reputation for dangerousness;

(e) the seriousness of the offense charged, the presence or absence of threats, and the probability of conviction and likely sentence;

(f) defendant's employment status and history and financial history insofar as these factors relate to the ability to post money bail;

(g) the availability of responsible members of the community who would vouch for or monitor the defendant;

(h) facts indicating the defendant's ties to the community, including family ties and relationships, and length of residence, and

(i) any other facts bearing on the risk of nonappearance or danger to the public.

(2) If the court orders the defendant held in custody pursuant to subrule (B) or released on conditions in subrule (D) that include money bail, the court must state the reasons for its decision on the record. The court need not make a finding on each of the enumerated factors.

(3) Nothing in subrules (C) through (F) may be construed to sanction pretrial detention nor to sanction the determination of pretrial release on the basis of race, religion, gender, economic status, or other impermissible criteria.

(G) **Custody Hearing**.

(1) *Entitlement to Hearing.* A court having jurisdiction of a defendant may conduct a custody hearing if the defendant is being held in custody pursuant to subrule (B) and a custody hearing is requested by either the defendant or the prosecutor. The purpose of the hearing is to permit the parties to litigate all of the issues relevant to challenging or supporting a custody decision pursuant to subrule (B).

(2) *Hearing Procedure.*

(a) At the custody hearing, the defendant is entitled to be present and to be represented by a lawyer, and the defendant and the prosecutor are entitled to present witnesses and evidence, to proffer information, and to cross-examine each other's witnesses.

(b) The rules of evidence, except those pertaining to privilege, are not applicable. Unless the court makes the findings required to enter an order under subrule (B)(1), the defendant must be ordered released under subrule (C) or (D). A verbatim record of the hearing must be made.

(H) **Appeals; Modification of Release Decision**.

(1) *Appeals*. A party seeking review of a release decision may file a motion in the court having appellate jurisdiction over the court that made the release decision. There is no fee for filing the motion. The reviewing court may not stay, vacate, modify, or reverse the release decision except on finding an abuse of discretion.

(2) *Modification of Release Decision*.

(a) Prior to Arraignment on the Information. Prior to the defendant's arraignment on the information, any court before which proceedings against the defendant are pending may, on the motion of a party or its own initiative and on finding that there is a substantial reason for doing so, modify a prior release decision or reopen a prior custody hearing.

(b) Arraignment on Information and Afterwards. At the defendant's arraignment on the information and afterwards, the court having jurisdiction of the defendant may, on the motion of a party or its own initiative, make a de novo determination and modify a prior release decision or reopen a prior custody hearing.

(c) Burden of Going Forward. The party seeking modification of a release decision has the burden of going forward.

(3) *Emergency Release*. If a defendant being held in pretrial custody under this rule is ordered released from custody as a result of a court order or law requiring the release of prisoners to relieve jail conditions, the court ordering the defendant's release may, if appropriate, impose conditions of release in accordance with this rule to ensure the appearance of the defendant as required and to protect the public. If such conditions of release are imposed, the court must inform the defendant of the conditions on the record or by furnishing to the defendant or the defendant's lawyer a copy of the release order setting forth the conditions.

(I) **Termination of Release Order**.

(1) If the conditions of the release order are met and the defendant is discharged from all obligations in the case, the court must vacate the release order, discharge anyone who has posted bail or bond, and return the cash (or its equivalent) posted in the full amount of the bail, or, if there has been a deposit of 10 percent of the full bail amount, return 90 percent of the deposited money and retain 10 percent.

(2) If the defendant has failed to comply with the conditions of release, the court may issue a warrant for the arrest of the defendant and enter an order revoking the release order and declaring the bail money deposited or the surety bond, if any, forfeited.

(a) The court must mail notice of any revocation order immediately to the defendant at the defendant's last known address and, if forfeiture of bail or bond has been ordered, to anyone who posted bail or bond.

(b) If the defendant does not appear and surrender to the court within 28 days after the revocation date, the court may continue the revocation order and enter judgment for the state or local unit of government against the defendant and anyone who posted bail or bond for an amount not to exceed the full amount of the bail, and costs of the court proceedings, or if a surety bond was posted, an amount not to exceed the full amount of the surety bond. If the amount of a forfeited surety bond is less than the full amount of the bail, the defendant shall continue to be liable to the court for the difference, unless otherwise ordered by the court. If the defendant does not within that period satisfy the court that there was compliance with the conditions of release other than appearance or that compliance was impossible through no fault of the defendant, the court may continue the revocation order and enter judgment for the state or local unit of government against the defendant alone for an amount not to exceed the full amount of the bond, and costs of the court proceedings.

(c) The 10 percent bail deposit made under subrule (E)(1)(a)(ii)[B] must be applied to the costs and, if any remains, to the balance of the judgment. The amount applied to the judgment must be transferred to the county treasury for a circuit court case, to the treasuries of the governments contributing to the district control unit for a district court case, or to the treasury of the appropriate municipal government for a municipal court case. The balance of the judgment may be enforced and collected as a judgment entered in a civil case.

(3) If money was deposited on a bail or bond executed by the defendant, the money must be first applied to the amount of any fine, costs, or statutory assessments imposed and any balance returned, subject to subrule (I)(1).

Rule 6.107 Grand Jury Proceedings

(A) **Right to Grand Jury Records**. Whenever an indictment is returned by a grand jury or a grand juror, the person accused in the indictment is entitled to the part of the record, including a transcript of the part of the testimony of all witnesses appearing before the grand jury or grand juror, that touches on the guilt or innocence of the accused of the charge contained in the indictment.

(B) **Procedure to Obtain Records**.

(1) To obtain the part of the record and transcripts specified in subrule (A), a motion must be addressed to the chief judge of the circuit court in the county in which the grand jury issuing the indictment was convened.

(2) The motion must be filed within 14 days after arraignment on the indictment or at a reasonable time thereafter as the court may permit on a showing of good cause and a finding that the interests of justice will be served.

(3) On receipt of the motion, the chief judge shall order the entire record and transcript of testimony taken before the grand jury to be delivered to the chief judge by the person having custody of it for an in-camera inspection by the chief judge.

(4) Following the in-camera inspection, the chief judge shall certify the parts of the record, including the testimony of all grand jury witnesses that touches on the guilt or innocence of the accused, as being all of the evidence bearing on that issue contained in the record, and have two copies of it prepared, one to be delivered to the attorney for the accused, or to the accused if not represented by an attorney, and one to the attorney charged with the responsibility for prosecuting the indictment.

(5) The chief judge shall then have the record and transcript of all testimony of grand jury witnesses returned to the person from whom it was received for disposition according to law.

Rule 6.110 The Preliminary Examination

(A) **Right to Preliminary Examination**. Where a preliminary examination is permitted by law, the people and the defendant are entitled to a prompt preliminary examination. If the court permits the defendant to waive the preliminary examination, it must bind the defendant over for trial on the charge set forth in the complaint or any amended complaint.

(B) **Time of Examination; Remedy**. Unless adjourned by the court, the preliminary examination must be held on the date specified by the court at the arraignment on the warrant or complaint. If the parties consent, for good cause shown, the court may adjourn the preliminary examination for a reasonable time. If a party objects, the court may not adjourn a preliminary examination unless it makes a finding on the record of good cause shown for the adjournment. A violation of this subrule is deemed to be harmless error unless the defendant demonstrates actual prejudice.

(C) **Conduct of Examination**. Each party may subpoena witnesses, offer proofs, and examine and cross-examine witnesses at the preliminary examination. Except as otherwise provided by law, the court must conduct the examination in accordance with the rules of evidence. A verbatim record must be made of the preliminary examination.

(D) **Exclusionary Rules**. If, during the preliminary examination, the court determines that evidence being offered is excludable, it must, on motion or objection, exclude the evidence. If, however, there has been a preliminary showing that the evidence is admissible, the court need not hold a separate evidentiary hearing on the question of whether the evidence should be excluded. The decision to admit or exclude evidence, with or without an evidentiary hearing, does not preclude a party from moving for and obtaining a determination of the question in the trial court on the basis of

(1) a prior evidentiary hearing, or

(2) a prior evidentiary hearing supplemented with a hearing before the trial court, or

(3) if there was no prior evidentiary hearing, a new evidentiary hearing.

(E) **Probable Cause Finding**. If, after considering the evidence, the court determines that probable cause exists to believe both that an offense not cognizable by the district court has been committed and that the defendant committed it, the court must bind the defendant over for trial. If the court finds probable cause to believe that the defendant has committed an offense cognizable by the district court, it must proceed thereafter as if the defendant initially had been charged with that offense.

(F) **Discharge of Defendant**. If, after considering the evidence, the court determines that probable cause does not exist to believe either that an offense has been committed or that the defendant committed it, the court must discharge the defendant without prejudice to the prosecutor initiating a subsequent prosecution for the same offense. Except as provided in MCR 8.111(C), the subsequent preliminary examination must be held before the same judicial officer and the prosecutor must present additional evidence to support the charge.

(G) **Return of Examination**. Immediately on concluding the examination, the court must certify and transmit to the court before which the defendant is bound to appear the prosecutor's authorization for a warrant application, the complaint, a copy of the register of actions, the examination return, and any recognizances received.

(H) **Motion to Dismiss**. If, on proper motion, the trial court finds a violation of subrule (C), (D), (E), or (F), it must either dismiss the information or remand the case to the district court for further proceedings.

(I) **Scheduling the Arraignment**. Unless the trial court does the scheduling of the arraignment on the information, the district court must do so in accordance with the administrative orders of the trial court.

Rule 6.111 Circuit Court Arraignment in District Court

(A) If the defendant, the defense attorney, and the prosecutor consent on the record, the circuit court arraignment may be conducted and a plea of not guilty, guilty, nolo contendere, guilty but mentally ill, or not guilty by reason of insanity may be taken by a district judge in criminal cases cognizable in the circuit court immediately after the bindover of the defendant. Following a plea, the case shall be transferred to the circuit court where the circuit judge shall preside over further proceedings, including sentencing.

(B) Arraignments conducted pursuant to this rule shall be conducted in conformity with MCR 6.113.

(C) Pleas taken pursuant to this rule shall be taken in conformity with MCR 6.301, 6.302, 6.303, and 6.304, as applicable, and, once taken, shall be governed by MCR 6.310.

(D) Each court intending to utilize this rule shall submit a local administrative order to the State Court Administrator pursuant to MCR 8.112(B) to implement the rule.

Rule 6.112 The Information or Indictment

(A) **Informations and Indictments; Similar Treatment**. Except as otherwise provided in these rules or elsewhere, the law and rules that apply to informations and prosecutions on informations apply to indictments and prosecutions on indictments.

(B) **Use of Information or Indictment**. A prosecution must be based on an information or an indictment. Unless the defendant is a fugitive from justice, the prosecutor may not file an information until the defendant has had or waives a preliminary examination. An indictment is returned and filed without a preliminary examination. When this occurs, the indictment shall commence judicial proceedings.

(C) **Time of Filing Information or Indictment**. The prosecutor must file the information or indictment on or before the date set for the arraignment.

(D) **Information; Nature and Contents; Attachments**. The information must set forth the substance of the accusation against the defendant and the name, statutory citation, and penalty of the offense allegedly committed. If applicable, the information must also set forth the notice required by MCL 767.45, and the defendant's Michigan driver's license number. To the extent possible, the information should specify the time and place of the alleged offense. Allegations relating to conduct, the method of committing the offense, mental state, and the consequences of conduct may be stated in the alternative. A list of all witnesses known to the prosecutor who may be called at trial and all res gestae witnesses known to the prosecutor or investigating law enforcement officers must be attached to the information. A prosecutor must sign the information.

(E) **Bill of Particulars**. The court, on motion, may order the prosecutor to provide the defendant a bill of particulars describing the essential facts of the alleged offense.

(F) **Notice of Intent to Seek Enhanced Sentence**. A notice of intent to seek an enhanced sentence pursuant to MCL 769.13 must list the prior convictions that may be relied upon for purposes of sentence enhancement. The notice must be filed within 21 days after the defendant's arraignment on the information charging the underlying offense or, if arraignment is waived or eliminated as allowed under MCR 6.113(E), within 21 days after the filing of the information charging the underlying offense.

(G) **Harmless Error**. Absent a timely objection and a showing of prejudice, a court may not dismiss an information or reverse a conviction because of an untimely filing or because of an incorrectly cited statute or a variance between the information and proof regarding time, place, the manner in which the offense was committed, or other factual detail relating to the alleged offense. This provision does not apply to the untimely filing of a notice of intent to seek an enhanced sentence.

(H) **Amendment of Information**. The court before, during, or after trial may permit the prosecutor to amend the information unless the proposed amendment would unfairly surprise or prejudice the defendant. On motion, the court must strike unnecessary allegations from the information.

Rule 6.113 The Arraignment on the Indictment or Information

(A) **Time of Conducting**. Unless the defendant waives arraignment or the court for good cause orders a delay, or as otherwise permitted by these rules, the court with trial jurisdiction must arraign the defendant on the scheduled date. The court may hold the arraignment before the preliminary examination transcript has been prepared and filed. Unless the defendant demonstrates actual prejudice, failure to hold the arraignment on the scheduled date is to be deemed harmless error.

(B) **Arraignment Procedure**. The prosecutor must give a copy of the information to the defendant before the defendant is asked to plead. Unless waived by the defendant, the court must either state to the defendant the substance of the charge contained in the information or require the information to be read to the defendant. If the defendant has waived legal representation, the court must advise the defendant of the pleading options. If the defendant offers a plea other than not guilty, the court must proceed in accordance with the rules in subchapter 6.300. Otherwise, the court must enter a plea of not guilty on the record. A verbatim record must be made of the arraignment.

(C) **Waiver**. A defendant represented by a lawyer may, as a matter of right, enter a plea of not guilty or stand mute without arraignment by filing, at or before the time set for the arraignment, a written statement signed by the defendant and the defendant's lawyer acknowledging that the defendant has received a copy of the information, has read or had it read or explained, understands the substance of the charge, waives arraignment in open court, and pleads not guilty to the charge or stands mute.

(D) **Preliminary Examination Transcript**. The court reporter shall transcribe and file the record of the preliminary examination if such is demanded or ordered pursuant to MCL 766.15.

(E) **Elimination of Arraignments**. A circuit court may submit to the State Court Administrator pursuant to MCR 8.112(B) a local administrative order that eliminates arraignment for a defendant represented by an attorney, provided other arrangements are made to give the defendant a copy of the information and any notice of intent to seek an enhanced sentence, as provided in MCR 6.112(F).

Rule 6.120 Joinder and Severance; Single Defendant

(A) **Charging Joinder**. The prosecuting attorney may file an information or indictment that charges a single defendant with any two or more offenses. Each offense must be stated in a separate count. Two or more informations or indictments against a single defendant may be consolidated for a single trial.

(B) **Postcharging Permissive Joinder or Severance**. On its own initiative, the motion of a party, or the stipulation of all parties, except as provided in subrule (C), the court may join offenses charged in two or more informations or indictments against a single defendant, or sever offenses charged in a single information or indictment against a single defendant, when appropriate to promote fairness to the parties and a fair determination of the defendant's guilt or innocence of each offense.

(1) Joinder is appropriate if the offenses are related. For purposes of this rule, offenses are related if they are based on

(a) the same conduct or transaction, or

(b) a series of connected acts, or

(c) a series of acts constituting parts of a single scheme or plan.

(2) Other relevant factors include the timeliness of the motion, the drain on the parties' resources, the potential for confusion or prejudice stemming from either the number of charges or the complexity or nature of the evidence, the potential for harassment, the convenience of witnesses, and the parties' readiness for trial.

(3) If the court acts on its own initiative, it must provide the parties an opportunity to be heard.

(C) **Right of Severance; Unrelated Offenses**. On the defendant's motion, the court must sever for separate trials offenses that are not related as defined in subrule (B)(1).

Rule 6.121 Joinder and Severance; Multiple Defendants

(A) **Permissive Joinder**. An information or indictment may charge two or more defendants with the same offense. It may charge two or more defendants with two or more offenses when

(1) each defendant is charged with accountability for each offense, or

(2) the offenses are related as defined in MCR 6.120(B).

When more than one offense is alleged, each offense must be stated in a separate count. Two or more informations or indictments against different defendants may be consolidated for a single trial whenever the defendants could be charged in the same information or indictment under this rule.

(B) **Right of Severance; Unrelated Offenses**. On a defendant's motion, the court must sever offenses that are not related as defined in MCR 6.120(B).

(C) **Right of Severance; Related Offenses**. On a defendant's motion, the court must sever the trial of defendants on related offenses on a showing that severance is necessary to avoid prejudice to substantial rights of the defendant.

(D) **Discretionary Severance**. On the motion of any party, the court may sever the trial of defendants on the ground that severance is appropriate to promote fairness to the parties and a fair determination of the guilt or innocence of one or more of the defendants. Relevant factors include the timeliness of the motion, the drain on the parties' resources, the potential for confusion or prejudice stemming from either the number of defendants or the complexity or nature of the evidence, the convenience of witnesses, and the parties' readiness for trial.

Rule 6.125 Mental Competency Hearing

(A) **Applicable Provisions**. Except as provided in these rules, a mental competency hearing in a criminal case is governed by MCL 330.2020 et seq.

(B) **Time and Form of Motion**. The issue of the defendant's competence to stand trial or to participate in other criminal proceedings may be raised at any time during the proceedings against the defendant. The issue may be raised by the court before which such proceedings are pending or being held, or by motion of a party. Unless the issue of defendant's competence arises during the course of proceedings, a motion raising the issue of defendant's competence must be in writing. If the competency issue arises during the course of proceedings, the court may adjourn the proceeding or, if the proceeding is defendant's trial, the court may, consonant with double jeopardy considerations, declare a mistrial.

(C) **Order for Examination**.

(1) On a showing that the defendant may be incompetent to stand trial, the court must order the defendant to undergo an examination by a certified or licensed examiner of the center for forensic psychiatry or other facility officially certified by the department of mental health to perform examinations relating to the issue of competence to stand trial.

(2) The defendant must appear for the examination as required by the court.

(3) If the defendant is held in detention pending trial, the examination may be performed in the place of detention or the defendant may be transported by the sheriff to the diagnostic facility for examination.

(4) The court may order commitment to a diagnostic facility for examination if the defendant fails to appear for the examination as required or if commitment is necessary for the performance of the examination.

(5) The defendant must be released from the facility on completion of the examination and, if (3) is applicable, returned to the place of detention.

(D) **Independent Examination**. On a showing of good cause by either party, the court may order an independent examination of the defendant relating to the issue of competence to stand trial.

(E) **Hearing**. A competency hearing must be held within 5 days of receipt of the report required by MCL 330.2028 or on conclusion of the proceedings then before the court, whichever is sooner, unless the court, on a showing of good cause, grants an adjournment.

(F) **Motions; Testimony**.

(1) A motion made while a defendant is incompetent to stand trial must be heard and decided if the presence of the defendant is not essential for a fair hearing and decision on the motion.

(2) Testimony may be presented on a pretrial defense motion if the defendant's presence could not assist the defense.

Subchapter 6.200 Discovery

Rule 6.201 Discovery

(A) **Mandatory Disclosure**. In addition to disclosures required by provisions of law other than MCL 767.94a, a party upon request must provide all other parties:

(1) the names and addresses of all lay and expert witnesses whom the party may call at trial; in the alternative, a party may provide the name of the witness and make the witness available to the other party for interview; the witness list may be amended without leave of the court no later than 28 days before trial;

(2) any written or recorded statement, including electronically recorded statements, pertaining to the case by a lay witness whom the party may call at trial, except that a defendant is not obliged to provide the defendant's own statement;

(3) the curriculum vitae of an expert the party may call at trial and either a report by the expert or a written description of the substance of the proposed testimony of the expert, the expert's opinion, and the underlying basis of that opinion;

(4) any criminal record that the party may use at trial to impeach a witness;

(5) a description or list of criminal convictions, known to the defense attorney or prosecuting attorney, of any witness whom the party may call at trial; and

(6) a description of and an opportunity to inspect any tangible physical evidence that the party may introduce at trial, including any document, photograph, or other paper, with copies to be provided on request. A party may request a hearing regarding any question of costs of reproduction, including the cost of providing copies of electronically recorded statements. On good cause shown, the court may order that a party be given the opportunity to test without destruction any tangible physical evidence.

(B) **Discovery of Information Known to the Prosecuting Attorney**. Upon request, the prosecuting attorney must provide each defendant:

(1) any exculpatory information or evidence known to the prosecuting attorney;

(2) any police report and interrogation records concerning the case, except so much of a report as concerns a continuing investigation;

(3) any written or recorded statements, including electronically recorded statements, by a defendant, codefendant, or accomplice pertaining to the case, even if that person is not a prospective witness at trial;

(4) any affidavit, warrant, and return pertaining to a search or seizure in connection with the case; and

(5) any plea agreement, grant of immunity, or other agreement for testimony in connection with the case.

(C) **Prohibited Discovery**.

(1) Notwithstanding any other provision of this rule, there is no right to discover information or evidence that is protected from disclosure by constitution, statute, or privilege, including information or

evidence protected by a defendant's right against self-incrimination, except as provided in subrule (2).

(2) If a defendant demonstrates a good-faith belief, grounded in articulable fact, that there is a reasonable probability that records protected by privilege are likely to contain material information necessary to the defense, the trial court shall conduct an in camera inspection of the records.

(a) If the privilege is absolute, and the privilege holder refuses to waive the privilege to permit an in camera inspection, the trial court shall suppress or strike the privilege holder's testimony.

(b) If the court is satisfied, following an in camera inspection, that the records reveal evidence necessary to the defense, the court shall direct that such evidence as is necessary to the defense be made available to defense counsel. If the privilege is absolute and the privilege holder refuses to waive the privilege to permit disclosure, the trial court shall suppress or strike the privilege holder's testimony.

(c) Regardless of whether the court determines that the records should be made available to the defense, the court shall make findings sufficient to facilitate meaningful appellate review.

(d) The court shall seal and preserve the records for review in the event of an appeal

(i) by the defendant, on an interlocutory basis or following conviction, if the court determines that the records should not be made available to the defense, or

(ii) by the prosecution, on an interlocutory basis, if the court determines that the records should be made available to the defense.

(e) Records disclosed under this rule shall remain in the exclusive custody of counsel for the parties, shall be used only for the limited purpose approved by the court, and shall be subject to such other terms and conditions as the court may provide.

(D) **Excision**. When some parts of material or information are discoverable and other parts are not discoverable, the party must disclose the discoverable parts and may excise the remainder. The party must inform the other party that nondiscoverable information has been excised and withheld. On motion, the court must conduct a hearing in camera to determine whether the reasons for excision are justifiable. If the court upholds the excision, it must seal and preserve the record of the hearing for review in the event of an appeal.

(E) **Protective Orders**. On motion and a showing of good cause, the court may enter an appropriate protective order. In considering whether good cause exists, the court shall consider the parties' interests in a fair trial; the risk to any person of harm, undue annoyance, intimidation, embarrassment, or threats; the risk that evidence will be fabricated; and the need for secrecy regarding the identity of informants or other law enforcement matters. On motion, with notice to the other party, the court may permit the showing of good cause for a protective order to be made in camera. If the court grants a protective order, it must seal and preserve the record of the hearing for review in the event of an appeal.

(F) **Timing of Discovery**. Unless otherwise ordered by the court, the prosecuting attorney must comply with the requirements of this rule within 21 days of a request under this rule and a defendant must comply with the requirements of this rule within 21 days of a request under this rule.

(G) **Copies**. Except as ordered by the court on good cause shown, a party's obligation to provide a photograph or paper of any kind is satisfied by providing a clear copy.

(H) **Continuing Duty to Disclose**. If at any time a party discovers additional information or material subject to disclosure under this rule, the party, without further request, must promptly notify the other party.

(I) **Modification**. On good cause shown, the court may order a modification of the requirements and prohibitions of this rule.

(J) **Violation**. If a party fails to comply with this rule, the court, in its discretion, may order the party to provide the discovery or permit the inspection of materials not previously disclosed, grant a continuance, prohibit the party from introducing in evidence the material not disclosed, or enter such other order as it deems just under the circumstances. Parties are encouraged to bring questions of noncompliance before the court at the earliest opportunity. Wilful violation by counsel of an applicable discovery rule or an order issued pursuant thereto may subject counsel to appropriate sanctions by the court. An order of the court under this section is reviewable only for abuse of discretion.

(K) Except as otherwise provided in MCR 2.302(B)(6), electronic materials are to be treated in the same manner as nonelectronic materials under this rule. Nothing in this rule shall be construed to conflict with MCL 600.2163a.

Rule 6.202. Disclosure of Forensic Laboratory Report and Certificate; Applicability; Admissibility of Report and Certificate; Extension of Time; Adjournment

(A) This rule shall apply to criminal trials in the district and circuit courts.

(B) **Disclosure**. Upon receipt of a forensic laboratory report and certificate, if applicable, by the examining expert, the prosecutor shall serve a copy of the laboratory report and certificate on the opposing party's attorney or party, if not represented by an attorney, within 14 days after receipt of the laboratory report and certificate. A proof of service of the report and certificate, if applicable, on the opposing party's attorney or party, if not represented by an attorney, shall be filed with the court.

(C) **Notice and Demand**.

(1) *Notice*. If a party intends to offer the report described in subsection (B) as evidence at trial, the party's attorney or party, if not represented by an attorney, shall provide the opposing party's attorney or party, if not represented by an attorney, with notice of that fact in writing. If the prosecuting attorney intends to offer the report as evidence at trial, notice to the defendant's attorney or the defendant, if not represented by an attorney, shall be included with the report. If the defendant intends to offer the report as evidence at trial, notice to the prosecuting attorney shall be provided within 14 days after receipt of the report. Except as provided in subrule (C)(2), the report and certification, if applicable, is admissible in evidence to the same effect as if the person who performed the analysis or examination had personally testified.

(2) *Demand*. Upon receipt of a copy of the laboratory report and certificate, if applicable, the opposing party's attorney or party, if not represented by an attorney, may file a written objection to the use of the laboratory report and certificate. The written objection shall be filed with the court in which the matter is pending, and shall be served on the opposing party's attorney or party, if not represented by an attorney, within 14 days of receipt of the notice. If a written objection is filed, the report and certificate are not admissible under subrule (C)(1). If no objection is made to the use of the laboratory report and certificate within the time allowed by this section, the report and certificate are admissible in evidence as provided in subrule (C)(1).

(3) For good cause the court shall extend the time period of filing a written objection.

(4) *Adjournment*. Compliance with this court rule shall be good cause for an adjournment of the trial.

(D) **Certification**. Except as otherwise provided, the analyst who conducts the analysis on the forensic sample and signs the report shall complete a certificate on which the analyst shall state (i) that he or she is qualified by education, training, and experience to perform the analysis, (ii) the name and location of the laboratory where the analysis was performed, (iii) that performing the analysis is part of his or her regular duties, and (iv) that the tests were performed under industry-approved procedures or standards and the report accurately reflects the analyst's findings and opinions regarding the results of those tests or analysis. A report submitted by an analyst who is employed by a laboratory that is accredited by a national or international accreditation entity that substantially meets the certification requirements described above may provide proof of the laboratory's accreditation certificate in lieu of a separate certificate.

Subchapter 6.300 Pleas

Rule 6.301 Available Pleas

(A) **Possible Pleas**. Subject to the rules in this subchapter, a defendant may plead not guilty, guilty, nolo contendere, guilty but mentally ill, or not guilty by reason of insanity. If the defendant refuses to plead or stands mute, or the court, pursuant to the rules, refuses to accept the defendant's plea, the court must enter a not guilty plea on the record. A plea of not guilty places in issue every material allegation in the information and permits the defendant to raise any defense not otherwise waived.

(B) **Pleas That Require the Court's Consent**. A defendant may enter a plea of nolo contendere only with the consent of the court.

(C) **Pleas That Require the Consent of the Court and the Prosecutor**. A defendant may enter the following pleas only with the consent of the court and the prosecutor:

(1) A defendant who has asserted an insanity defense may enter a plea of guilty but mentally ill or a plea of not guilty by reason of insanity. Before such a plea may be entered, the defendant must comply with the examination required by law.

(2) A defendant may enter a conditional plea of guilty, nolo contendere, guilty but mentally ill, or not guilty by reason of insanity. A conditional plea preserves for appeal a specified pretrial ruling or rulings notwithstanding the plea-based judgment and entitles the defendant to withdraw the plea if a specified pretrial ruling is overturned on appeal. The ruling or rulings as to which the defendant reserves the right to appeal must be specified orally on the record or in a writing made a part of the record. The appeal is by application for leave to appeal only.

(D) **Pleas to Lesser Charges**. The court may not accept a plea to an offense other than the one charged without the consent of the prosecutor.

Rule 6.302 Pleas of Guilty and Nolo Contendere

(A) **Plea Requirements**. The court may not accept a plea of guilty or nolo contendere unless it is convinced that the plea is understanding, voluntary, and accurate. Before accepting a plea of guilty or nolo contendere, the court must place the defendant or defendants under oath and personally carry out subrules (B)-(E).

(B) **An Understanding Plea**. Speaking directly to the defendant or defendants, the court must advise the defendant or defendants of the following and determine that each defendant understands:

(1) the name of the offense to which the defendant is pleading; the court is not obliged to explain the elements of the offense, or possible defenses;

(2) the maximum possible prison sentence for the offense and any mandatory minimum sentence required by law, including a requirement for mandatory lifetime electronic monitoring under MCL 750.520b or 750.520c;

(3) if the plea is accepted, the defendant will not have a trial of any kind, and so gives up the rights the defendant would have at a trial, including the right:

(a) to be tried by a jury;

(b) to be presumed innocent until proved guilty;

(c) to have the prosecutor prove beyond a reasonable doubt that the defendant is guilty;

(d) to have the witnesses against the defendant appear at the trial;

(e) to question the witnesses against the defendant;

(f) to have the court order any witnesses the defendant has for the defense to appear at the trial;

(g) to remain silent during the trial;

(h) to not have that silence used against the defendant; and

(i) to testify at the trial if the defendant wants to testify.

(4) if the plea is accepted, the defendant will be giving up any claim that the plea was the result of promises or threats that were not disclosed to the court at the plea proceeding, or that it was not the defendant's own choice to enter the plea;

(5) any appeal from the conviction and sentence pursuant to the plea will be by application for leave to appeal and not by right;

The requirements of subrules (B)(3) and (B)(5) may be satisfied by a writing on a form approved by the State Court Administrative Office. If a court uses a writing, the court shall address the defendant and obtain from the defendant orally on the record a statement that the rights were read and understood and a waiver of those rights. The waiver may be obtained without repeating the individual rights.

(C) **A Voluntary Plea**.

(1) The court must ask the prosecutor and the defendant's lawyer whether they have made a plea agreement. If they have made a plea agreement, which may include an agreement to a sentence to a specific term or within a specific range, the agreement must be stated on the record or reduced to writing and signed by the parties. The parties may memorialize their agreement on a form substantially approved by the SCAO. The written agreement shall be made part of the case file.

(2) If there is a plea agreement, the court must ask the prosecutor or the defendant's lawyer what the terms of the agreement are and confirm the terms of the agreement with the other lawyer and the defendant.

(3) If there is a plea agreement and its terms provide for the defendant's plea to be made in exchange for a sentence to a specified term or within a specified range or a prosecutorial sentence recommendation, the court may

(a) reject the agreement; or

(b) accept the agreement after having considered the presentence report, in which event it must sentence the defendant to a specified term or within a specified range as agreed to; or

(c) accept the agreement without having considered the presentence report; or

(d) take the plea agreement under advisement.

If the court accepts the agreement without having considered the presentence report or takes the plea agreement under advisement, it must explain to the defendant that the court is not bound to follow an agreement to a sentence for a specified term or within a specified range or a recommendation agreed to by the prosecutor, and that if the court chooses not to follow an agreement to a sentence for a specified term or within a specified range, the defendant will be allowed to withdraw from the plea agreement. A judge's decision not to follow the sentence recommendation does not entitle the defendant to withdraw the defendant's plea.

(4) The court must ask the defendant:

(a) (if there is no plea agreement) whether anyone has promised the defendant anything, or (if there is a plea agreement) whether anyone has promised anything beyond what is in the plea agreement;

(b) whether anyone has threatened the defendant; and

(c) whether it is the defendant's own choice to plead guilty.

(D) **An Accurate Plea**.

(1) If the defendant pleads guilty, the court, by questioning the defendant, must establish support for a finding that the defendant is guilty of the offense charged or the offense to which the defendant is pleading.

(2) If the defendant pleads nolo contendere, the court may not question the defendant about participation in the crime. The court must:

(a) state why a plea of nolo contendere is appropriate; and

(b) hold a hearing, unless there has been one, that establishes support for a finding that the defendant is guilty of the offense charged or the offense to which the defendant is pleading.

(E) **Additional Inquiries**. On completing the colloquy with the defendant, the court must ask the prosecutor and the defendant's lawyer whether either is aware of any promises, threats, or inducements other than those already disclosed on the record, and whether the court has complied with subrules (B)-(D). If it appears to the court that it has failed to comply with subrules (B)-(D), the court may not accept the defendant's plea until the deficiency is corrected.

(F) **Plea Under Advisement; Plea Record**. The court may take the plea under advisement. A verbatim record must be made of the plea proceeding.

Rule 6.303 Plea of Guilty but Mentally Ill

Before accepting a plea of guilty but mentally ill, the court must comply with the requirements of MCR 6.302. In addition to establishing a factual basis for the plea pursuant to MCR 6.302(D)(1) or (D)(2)(b), the court must examine the psychiatric reports prepared and hold a hearing that establishes support for a finding that the defendant was mentally ill, at the time of the offense to which the plea is entered. The reports must be made a part of the record.

Rule 6.304 Plea of Not Guilty by Reason of Insanity

(A) **Advice to Defendant**. Before accepting a plea of not guilty by reason of insanity, the court must comply with the requirements of MCR 6.302 except that subrule (C) of this rule, rather than MCR 6.302(D), governs the manner of determining the accuracy of the plea.

(B) **Additional Advice Required**. After complying with the applicable requirements of MCR 6.302, the court must advise the defendant, and determine whether the defendant understands, that the plea will result in the defendant's commitment for diagnostic examination at the center for forensic psychiatry for up to 60 days, and that after the examination, the probate court may order the defendant to be committed for an indefinite period of time.

(C) **Factual Basis**. Before accepting a plea of not guilty by reason of insanity, the court must examine the psychiatric reports prepared and hold a hearing that establishes support for findings that
  (1) the defendant committed the acts charged, and
  (2) that, by a preponderance of the evidence, the defendant was legally insane at the time of the offense.

(D) **Report of Plea**. After accepting the defendant's plea, the court must forward to the center for forensic psychiatry a full report, in the form of a settled record, of the facts concerning the crime to which the defendant pleaded and the defendant's mental state at the time of the crime.

Rule 6.310 Withdrawal or Vacation of Plea

(A) **Withdrawal Before Acceptance**. The defendant has a right to withdraw any plea until the court accepts it on the record.

(B) **Withdrawal After Acceptance but Before Sentence**. Except as provided in subsection (3), after acceptance but before sentence,
  (1) a plea may be withdrawn on the defendant's motion or with the defendant's consent, only in the interest of justice, and may not be withdrawn if withdrawal of the plea would substantially prejudice the prosecutor because of reliance on the plea. If the defendant's motion is based on an error in the plea proceeding, the court must permit the defendant to withdraw the plea if it would be required by subrule (C).
  (2) the defendant is entitled to withdraw the plea if
    (a) the plea involves an agreement for a sentence for a specified term or within a specified range, and the court states that it is unable to follow the agreement; the trial court shall then state the sentence it intends to impose, and provide the defendant the opportunity to affirm or withdraw the plea; or
    (b) the plea involves a statement by the court that it will sentence to a specified term or within a specified range, and the court states that it is unable to sentence as stated; the trial court shall provide the defendant the opportunity to affirm or withdraw the plea, but shall not state the sentence it intends to impose.
  (3) Except as allowed by the trial court for good cause, a defendant is not entitled to withdraw a plea under subsection (2)(a) or (2)(b) if the defendant commits misconduct after the plea is accepted but before sentencing. For purposes of this rule, misconduct is defined to include, but is not limited to: absconding or failing to appear for sentencing, violating terms of conditions on bond or the terms of any sentencing or plea agreement, or otherwise failing to comply with an order of the court pending sentencing.

(C) **Motion to Withdraw Plea After Sentence**. The defendant may file a motion to withdraw the plea within 6 months after sentence. Thereafter, the defendant may seek relief only in accordance with the procedure set forth in subchapter 6.500. If the trial court determines that there was an error in the plea proceeding that would entitle the defendant to have the plea set aside, the court must give the advice or make the inquiries necessary to rectify the error and then give the defendant the opportunity to elect to allow the plea and sentence to stand or to withdraw the plea. If the defendant elects to allow the plea and sentence to stand, the additional advice given and inquiries made become part of the plea proceeding for the purposes of further proceedings, including appeals.

(D) **Preservation of Issues**. A defendant convicted on the basis of a plea may not raise on appeal any claim of noncompliance with the requirements of the rules in this subchapter, or any other claim that the plea was not an understanding, voluntary, or accurate one, unless the defendant has moved to withdraw the plea in the trial court, raising as a basis for withdrawal the claim sought to be raised on appeal.

(E) **Vacation of Plea on Prosecutor's Motion**. On the prosecutor's motion, the court may vacate a plea if the defendant has failed to comply with the terms of a plea agreement.

Rule 6.312 Effect of Withdrawal or Vacation of Plea

If a plea is withdrawn by the defendant or vacated by the trial court or an appellate court, the case may proceed to trial on any charges that had been brought or that could have been brought against the defendant if the plea had not been entered.

Subchapter 6.400 Trials

Rule 6.401 Right to Trial by Jury or by the Court

The defendant has the right to be tried by a jury, or may, with the consent of the prosecutor and approval by the court, elect to waive that right and be tried before the court without a jury.

Rule 6.402 Waiver of Jury Trial by the Defendant

(A) **Time of Waiver**. The court may not accept a waiver of trial by jury until after the defendant has been arraigned or has waived an arraignment on the information, or, in a court where arraignment on the information has been eliminated under MCR 6.113(E), after the defendant has otherwise been provided with a copy of the information, and has been offered an opportunity to consult with a lawyer.

(B) **Waiver and Record Requirements**. Before accepting a waiver, the court must advise the defendant in open court of the constitutional right to trial by jury. The court must also ascertain, by addressing the defendant personally, that the defendant understands the right and that the defendant voluntarily chooses to give up that right and to be tried by the court. A verbatim record must be made of the waiver proceeding.

Rule 6.403 Trial by the Judge in Waiver Cases

When trial by jury has been waived, the court with jurisdiction must proceed with the trial. The court must find the facts specially, state separately its conclusions of law, and direct entry of the appropriate judgment. The court must state its findings and conclusions on the record or in a written opinion made a part of the record.

Rule 6.410 Jury Trial; Number of Jurors; Unanimous Verdict

(A) **Number of Jurors**. Except as provided in this rule, a jury that decides a case must consist of 12 jurors. At any time before a verdict is returned, the parties may stipulate with the court's consent to have the case decided by a jury consisting of a specified number of jurors less than 12. On being informed of the parties' willingness to stipulate, the court must personally advise the defendant of the right to have the case decided by a jury consisting of 12 jurors. By addressing the defendant personally, the court must ascertain that the defendant understands the right and that the defendant voluntarily chooses to give up that right as provided in the stipulation. If the court finds that the requirements for a valid waiver have been satisfied, the court may accept the stipulation. Even if the requirements for a valid waiver have been satisfied, the court may, in the interest of justice, refuse to accept a stipulation, but it must state its reasons for doing so on the record. The stipulation and procedure described in this subrule must take place in open court and a verbatim record must be made.

(B) **Unanimous Verdicts**. A jury verdict must be unanimous.

Rule 6.411 Additional Jurors

The court may impanel more than 12 jurors. If more than the number of jurors required to decide the case are left on the jury before deliberations are to begin, the names of the jurors must be placed in a container and names drawn from it to reduce the number of jurors to the number required to decide the case. The court may retain the alternate jurors during deliberations. If the court does so, it shall instruct the alternate jurors not to discuss the case with any other person until the jury completes its deliberations and is discharged. If an alternate juror replaces a juror after the jury retires to consider its verdict, the court shall instruct the jury to begin its deliberations anew.

Rule 6.412 Selection of the Jury

(A) **Selecting and Impaneling the Jury**. Except as otherwise provided by the rules in this subchapter, MCR 2.510 and 2.511 govern the procedure for selecting and impaneling the jury.

(B) **Instructions and Oath Before Selection**. Before beginning the jury selection process, the court should give the prospective jurors appropriate preliminary instructions and must have them sworn.

(C) **Voir Dire of Prospective Jurors**.

(1) *Scope and Purpose*. The scope of voir dire examination of prospective jurors is within the discretion of the court. It should be conducted for the purposes of discovering grounds for challenges for cause and of gaining knowledge to facilitate an intelligent exercise of peremptory challenges. The court should confine the examination to these purposes and prevent abuse of the examination process.

(2) *Conduct of the Examination*. The court may conduct the examination of prospective jurors or permit the lawyers to do so. If the court conducts the examination, it may permit the lawyers to supplement the examination by direct questioning or by submitting questions for the court to ask. On its own initiative or on the motion of a party, the court may provide for a prospective juror or jurors to be questioned out of the presence of the other jurors.

(D) **Challenges for Cause**.

(1) *Grounds*. A prospective juror is subject to challenge for cause on any ground set forth in MCR 2.511(D) or for any other reason recognized by law.

(2) *Procedure*. If, after the examination of any juror, the court finds that a ground for challenging a juror for cause is present, the court on its own initiative should, or on motion of either party must, excuse the juror from the panel.

(E) **Peremptory Challenges**.

(1) *Challenges by Right*. Each defendant is entitled to 5 peremptory challenges unless an offense charged is punishable by life imprisonment, in which case a defendant being tried alone is entitled to 12 peremptory challenges, 2 defendants being tried jointly are each entitled to 10 peremptory challenges, 3 defendants being tried jointly are each entitled to 9 peremptory challenges, 4 defendants being tried jointly are each entitled to 8 peremptory challenges, and 5 or more defendants being tried jointly are each entitled to 7 peremptory challenges. The prosecutor is entitled to the same number of peremptory challenges as a defendant being tried alone, or, in the case of jointly tried defendants, the total number of peremptory challenges to which all the defendants are entitled.

(2) *Additional Challenges*. On a showing of good cause, the court may grant one or more of the parties an increased number of peremptory challenges. The additional challenges granted by the court need not be equal for each party.

(F) **Oath After Selection**. After the jury is selected and before trial begins, the court must have the jurors sworn.

Rule 6.416 Presentation of Evidence

Subject to the rules in this chapter and to the Michigan rules of evidence, each party has discretion in deciding what witnesses and evidence to present.

Rule 6.419 Motion for Directed Verdict of Acquittal

(A) **Before Submission to Jury**. After the prosecutor has rested the prosecution's case-in-chief and before the defendant presents proofs, the court on its own initiative may, or on the defendant's motion must, direct a verdict of acquittal on any charged offense as to which the evidence is insufficient to support conviction. The court may not reserve decision on the defendant's motion. If the defendant's motion is made after the defendant presents proofs, the court may reserve decision on the motion, submit the case to the jury, and decide the motion before or after the jury has completed its deliberations.

(B) **After Jury Verdict**. After a jury verdict, the defendant may file an original or renewed motion for directed verdict of acquittal in the same manner as provided by MCR 6.431(A) for filing a motion for a new trial.

(C) **Bench Trial**. In an action tried without a jury, after the prosecutor has rested the prosecution's case-in-chief, the defendant, without waiving the right to offer evidence if the motion is not granted, may move for acquittal on the ground that a reasonable doubt exists. The court may then determine the facts and render a verdict of acquittal, or may decline to render judgment until the close of all the evidence. If the court renders a verdict of acquittal, the court shall make findings of fact.

(D) **Conditional New Trial Ruling**. If the court grants a directed verdict of acquittal after the jury has returned a guilty verdict, it must also conditionally rule on any motion for a new trial by determining whether it would grant the motion if the directed verdict of acquittal is vacated or reversed.

(E) **Explanation of Rulings on Record**. The court must state orally on the record or in a written ruling made a part of the record its reasons for granting or denying a motion for a directed verdict of acquittal and for conditionally granting or denying a motion for a new trial.

Rule 6.420 Verdict

(A) **Return**. The jury must return its verdict in open court.

(B) **Several Defendants**. If two or more defendants are jointly on trial, the jury at any time during its deliberations may return a verdict with respect to any defendant as to whom it has agreed. If the jury cannot reach a verdict with respect to any other defendant, the court may declare a mistrial as to that defendant.

(C) **Several Counts**. If a defendant is charged with two or more counts, and the court determines that the jury is deadlocked so that a mistrial must be declared, the court may inquire of the jury whether it has reached a unanimous verdict on any of the counts charged, and, if so, may accept the jury's verdict on that count or counts.

(D) **Poll of Jury**. Before the jury is discharged, the court on its own initiative may, or on the motion of a party must, have each juror polled in open court as to whether the verdict announced is that juror's verdict. If polling discloses the jurors are not in agreement, the court may (1) discontinue the poll and order the jury to retire for further deliberations, or (2) either (a) with the defendant's consent, or (b) after determining that the jury is deadlocked or that some other manifest necessity exists, declare a mistrial and discharge the jury.

Rule 6.425 Sentencing; Appointment of Appellate Counsel

(A) **Presentence Report; Contents.**

(1) Prior to sentencing, the probation officer must investigate the defendant's background and character, verify material information, and report in writing the results of the investigation to the court. The report must be succinct and, depending on the circumstances, include:

(a) a description of the defendant's prior criminal convictions and juvenile adjudications,

(b) a complete description of the offense and the circumstances surrounding it,

(c) a brief description of the defendant's vocational background and work history, including military record and present employment status,

(d) a brief social history of the defendant, including marital status, financial status, length of residence in the community, educational background, and other pertinent data,

(e) the defendant's medical history, substance abuse history, if any, and, if indicated, a current psychological or psychiatric report,

(f) information concerning the financial, social, psychological, or physical harm suffered by any victim of the offense, including the restitution needs of the victim,

(g) if provided and requested by the victim, a written victim's impact statement as provided by law,

(h) any statement the defendant wishes to make,

(i) a statement prepared by the prosecutor on the applicability of any consecutive sentencing provision,

(j) an evaluation of and prognosis for the defendant's adjustment in the community based on factual information in the report,

(k) a specific recommendation for disposition, and

(l) any other information that may aid the court in sentencing.

(2) A presentence investigation report shall not include any address or telephone number for the home, workplace, school, or place of worship of any victim or witness, or a family member of any victim or witness, unless an address is used to identify the place of the crime or to impose conditions of release from custody that are necessary for the protection of a named individual. Upon request, any other address or telephone number that would reveal the location of a victim or witness or a family member of a victim or witness shall be exempted from disclosure unless an address is used to identify the place of the crime or to impose conditions of release from custody that are necessary for the protection of a named individual.

(3) Regardless of the sentence imposed, the court must have a copy of the presentence report and of any psychiatric report sent to the Department of Corrections. If the defendant is sentenced to prison, the copies must be sent with the commitment papers.

(B) **Presentence Report; Disclosure Before Sentencing**. The court must provide copies of the presentence report to the prosecutor, and the defendant's lawyer, or the defendant if not represented by a lawyer, at a reasonable time, but not less than two business days, before the day of sentencing. The prosecutor and the defendant's lawyer, or the defendant if not represented by a lawyer, may retain a copy of the report or an amended report. If the presentence report is not made available to the prosecutor and the defendant's lawyer, or the defendant if not represented by a lawyer, at least two business days before the day of sentencing, the prosecutor and the defendant's lawyer, or the defendant if not represented by a lawyer, shall be entitled, on oral motion, to an adjournment of the day of sentencing to enable the moving party to review the presentence report and to prepare any necessary corrections, additions, or deletions to present to the court. The court may exempt from disclosure information or diagnostic opinion that might seriously disrupt a program of rehabilitation and sources of information that have been obtained on a promise of confidentiality. When part of the report is not disclosed, the court must inform the parties that information has not been disclosed and state on the record the reasons for nondisclosure. To the extent it can do so without defeating the purpose of nondisclosure, the court also must provide the parties with a written or oral summary of the nondisclosed information and give them an opportunity to comment on it. The court must have the information exempted from disclosure specifically noted in the report. The court's decision to exempt part of the report from disclosure is subject to appellate review.

(C) **Presentence Report; Disclosure After Sentencing**. After sentencing, the court, on written request, must provide the prosecutor, the defendant's lawyer, or the defendant not represented by a lawyer, with a copy of the presentence report and any attachments to it. The court must exempt from disclosure any information the sentencing court exempted from disclosure pursuant to subrule (B).

(D) **Sentencing Guidelines**. The court must use the sentencing guidelines, as provided by law. Proposed scoring of the guidelines shall accompany the presentence report.

(E) **Sentencing Procedure**.

(1) The court must sentence the defendant within a reasonably prompt time after the plea or verdict unless the court delays sentencing as provided by law. At sentencing, the court must, on the record:

(a) determine that the defendant, the defendant's lawyer, and the prosecutor have had an opportunity to read and discuss the presentence report,

(b) give each party an opportunity to explain, or challenge the accuracy or relevancy of, any information in the presentence report, and resolve any challenges in accordance with the procedure set forth in subrule (E)(2),

(c) give the defendant, the defendant's lawyer, the prosecutor, and the victim an opportunity to advise the court of any circumstances they believe the court should consider in imposing sentence,

(d) state the sentence being imposed, including the minimum and maximum sentence if applicable, together with any credit for time served to which the defendant is entitled,

(e) if the sentence imposed is not within the guidelines range, articulate the substantial and compelling reasons justifying that specific departure, and

(f) order that the defendant make full restitution as required by law to any victim of the defendant's course of conduct that gives rise to the conviction, or to that victim's estate.

(2) Resolution of Challenges. If any information in the presentence report is challenged, the court must allow the parties to be heard regarding the challenge, and make a finding with respect to the challenge or determine that a finding is unnecessary because it will not take the challenged information into account in sentencing. If the court finds merit in the challenge or determines that it will not take the challenged information into account in sentencing, it must direct the probation officer to

(a) correct or delete the challenged information in the report, whichever is appropriate, and

(b) provide defendant's lawyer with an opportunity to review the corrected report before it is sent to the Department of Corrections.

(F) **Advice Concerning the Right to Appeal; Appointment of Counsel**.

(1) In a case involving a conviction following a trial, immediately after imposing sentence, the court must advise the defendant, on the record, that

(a) the defendant is entitled to appellate review of the conviction and sentence,

(b) if the defendant is financially unable to retain a lawyer, the court will appoint a lawyer to represent the defendant on appeal, and

(c) the request for a lawyer must be made within 42 days after sentencing.

(2) In a case involving a conviction following a plea of guilty or nolo contendere, immediately after imposing sentence, the court must advise the defendant, on the record, that

(a) the defendant is entitled to file an application for leave to appeal,

(b) if the defendant is financially unable to retain a lawyer, the court will appoint a lawyer to represent the defendant on appeal, and

(c) the request for a lawyer must be made within 42 days after sentencing.

(3) The court also must give the defendant a request for counsel form containing an instruction informing the defendant that the form must be completed and returned to the court within 42 days after sentencing if the defendant wants the court to appoint a lawyer.

(4) When imposing sentence in a case in which sentencing guidelines enacted in 1998 PA 317, MCL 777.1 et seq., are applicable, if the court imposes a minimum sentence that is longer or more severe than the range provided by the sentencing guidelines, the court must advise the defendant on the record and in writing that the defendant may seek appellate review of the sentence, by right if the conviction followed trial or by application if the conviction entered by plea, on the ground that it is longer or more severe than the range provided by the sentencing guidelines.

(G) **Appointment of Lawyer; Trial Court Responsibilities in Connection with Appeal**.

(1) *Appointment of Lawyer*.

(a) Unless there is a postjudgment motion pending, the court must rule on a defendant's request for a lawyer within 14 days after receiving it. If there is a postjudgment motion pending, the court must rule on the request after the court's disposition of the pending motion and within 14 days after that disposition.

(b) In a case involving a conviction following a trial, if the defendant is indigent, the court must enter an order appointing a lawyer if the request is filed within 42 days after sentencing or within the time for filing an appeal of right. The court should liberally grant an untimely request as long as the defendant may file an application for leave to appeal.

(c) In a case involving a conviction following a plea of guilty or nolo contendere, if the defendant is indigent, the court must enter an order appointing a lawyer if the request is filed within 42 days after sentencing.

(d) Scope of Appellate Lawyer's Responsibilities. The responsibilities of the appellate lawyer appointed to represent the defendant include representing the defendant

(i) in available postconviction proceedings in the trial court the lawyer deems appropriate,

(ii) in postconviction proceedings in the Court of Appeals,

(iii) in available proceedings in the trial court the lawyer deems appropriate under MCR 7.208(B) or 7.211(C)(1), and

(iv) as appellee in relation to any postconviction appeal taken by the prosecutor.

(2) *Order to Prepare Transcript*. The appointment order also must

(a) direct the court reporter to prepare and file, within the time limits specified in MCR 7.210,

(i) the trial or plea proceeding transcript,

(ii) the sentencing transcript, and

(iii) such transcripts of other proceedings, not previously transcribed, that the court directs or the parties request, and

(b) provide for the payment of the reporter's fees.

The court must promptly serve a copy of the order on the prosecutor, the defendant, the appointed lawyer, the court reporter, and the Michigan Appellate Assigned Counsel System. If the appointed lawyer timely requests additional transcripts, the trial court shall order such transcripts within 14 days after receiving the request.

(3) *Order as Claim of Appeal; Trial Cases*. In a case involving a conviction following a trial, if the defendant's request for a lawyer, timely or not, was made within the time for filing a claim of appeal, the order described in subrules (G)(1) and (2) must be entered on a form approved by the State Court Administrative Office, entitled “Claim of Appeal and Appointment of Counsel,” and the court must immediately send to the Court of Appeals a copy of the order and a copy of the judgment being appealed. The court also must file in the Court of Appeals proof of having made service of the order as required in subrule (G)(2). Entry of the order by the trial court pursuant to this subrule constitutes a timely filed claim of appeal for the purposes of MCR 7.204.

Rule 6.427 Judgment

Within 7 days after sentencing, the court must date and sign a written judgment of sentence that includes:

(1) the title and file number of the case;

(2) the defendant's name;

(3) the crime for which the defendant was convicted;

(4) the defendant's plea;

(5) the name of the defendant's attorney if one appeared;

(6) the jury's verdict or the finding of guilt by the court;

(7) the term of the sentence;

(8) the place of detention;

(9) the conditions incident to the sentence; and

(10) whether the conviction is reportable to the Secretary of State pursuant to statute, and, if so, the defendant's Michigan driver's license number.

If the defendant was found not guilty or for any other reason is entitled to be discharged, the court must enter judgment accordingly. The date a judgment is signed is its entry date.

Rule 6.428 Reissuance of Judgment.

If the defendant did not appeal within the time allowed by MCR 7.204(A)(2) and demonstrates that the attorney or attorneys retained or appointed to represent the defendant on direct appeal from the judgment either disregarded the defendant's instruction to perfect a timely appeal of right, or otherwise failed to provide effective assistance, and, but for counsel's deficient performance, the defendant would have perfected a timely appeal of right, the trial court shall issue an order restarting the time in which to file an appeal of right.

Rule 6.429 Correction and Appeal of Sentence

(A) **Authority to Modify Sentence**. A motion to correct an invalid sentence may be filed by either party. The court may correct an invalid sentence, but the court may not modify a valid sentence after it has been imposed except as provided by law.

(B) **Time For Filing Motion**.

(1) A motion to correct an invalid sentence may be filed before the filing of a timely claim of appeal.

(2) If a claim of appeal has been filed, a motion to correct an invalid sentence may only be filed in accordance with the procedure set forth in MCR 7.208(B) or the remand procedure set forth in MCR 7.211(C)(1).

(3) If the defendant may only appeal by leave or fails to file a timely claim of appeal, a motion to correct an invalid sentence may be filed within 6 months of entry of the judgment of conviction and sentence.

(4) If the defendant is no longer entitled to appeal by right or by leave, the defendant may seek relief pursuant to the procedure set forth in subchapter 6.500.

(C) **Preservation of Issues Concerning Sentencing Guidelines Scoring and Information Considered in Sentencing**. A party shall not raise on appeal an issue challenging the scoring of the sentencing guidelines or challenging the accuracy of information relied upon in determining a sentence that is within the appropriate guidelines sentence range unless the party has raised the issue at sentencing, in a proper motion for resentencing, or in a proper motion to remand filed in the court of appeals.

Rule 6.431 New Trial

(A) **Time for Making Motion**.

(1) A motion for a new trial may be filed before the filing of a timely claim of appeal.

(2) If a claim of appeal has been filed, a motion for a new trial may only be filed in accordance with the procedure set forth in MCR 7.208(B) or the remand procedure set forth in MCR 7.211(C)(1).

(3) If the defendant may only appeal by leave or fails to file a timely claim of appeal, a motion for a new trial may be filed within 6 months of entry of the judgment of conviction and sentence.

(4) If the defendant is no longer entitled to appeal by right or by leave, the defendant may seek relief pursuant to the procedure set forth in subchapter 6.500.

(B) **Reasons for Granting**. On the defendant's motion, the court may order a new trial on any ground that would support appellate reversal of the conviction or because it believes that the verdict has resulted in a miscarriage of justice. The court must state its reasons for granting or denying a new trial orally on the record or in a written ruling made a part of the record.

(C) **Trial Without Jury**. If the court tried the case without a jury, it may, on granting a new trial and with the defendant's consent, vacate any judgment it has entered, take additional testimony, amend its findings of fact and conclusions of law, and order the entry of a new judgment.

(D) **Inclusion of Motion for Judgment of Acquittal**. The court must consider a motion for a new trial challenging the weight or sufficiency of the evidence as including a motion for a directed verdict of acquittal.

Rule 6.433 Documents for Postconviction Proceedings; Indigent Defendant

(A) **Appeals of Right**. An indigent defendant may file a written request with the sentencing court for specified court documents or transcripts, indicating that they are required to pursue an appeal of right. The court must order the clerk to provide the defendant with copies of documents without cost to the defendant, and, unless the transcript has already been ordered as provided in MCR 6.425(G)(2), must order the preparation of the transcript.

(B) **Appeals by Leave**. An indigent defendant who may file an application for leave to appeal may obtain copies of transcripts and other documents as provided in this subrule.

(1) The defendant must make a written request to the sentencing court for specified documents or transcripts indicating that they are required to prepare an application for leave to appeal.

(2) If the requested materials have been filed with the court and not provided previously to the defendant, the court clerk must provide a copy to the defendant. If the requested materials have been provided previously to the defendant, on defendant's showing of good cause to the court, the clerk must provide the defendant with another copy.

(3) If the request includes the transcript of a proceeding that has not been transcribed, the court must order the materials transcribed and filed with court. After the transcript has been prepared, court clerk must provide a copy to the defendant.

(C) **Other Postconviction Proceedings**. An indigent defendant who is not eligible to file an appeal of right or an application for leave to appeal may obtain records and documents as provided in this subrule.

(1) The defendant must make a written request to the sentencing court for specific court documents or transcripts indicating that the materials are required to pursue postconviction remedies in a state or federal court and are not otherwise available to the defendant.

(2) If the documents or transcripts have been filed with the court and not provided previously to the defendant, the clerk must provide the defendant with copies of such materials without cost to the defendant. If the requested materials have been provided previously to the defendant, on defendant's showing of good cause to the court, the clerk must provide the defendant with another copy.

(3) The court may order the transcription of additional proceedings if it finds that there is good cause for doing so. After such a transcript has been prepared, the clerk must provide a copy to the defendant.

(4) Nothing in this rule precludes the court from ordering materials to be supplied to the defendant in a proceeding under subchapter 6.500.

Rule 6.435 Correcting Mistakes

(A) **Clerical Mistakes**. Clerical mistakes in judgments, orders, or other parts of the record and errors arising from oversight or omission may be corrected by the court at any time on its own initiative or on motion of a party, and after notice if the court orders it.

(B) **Substantive Mistakes**. After giving the parties an opportunity to be heard, and provided it has not yet entered judgment in the case, the court may reconsider and modify, correct, or rescind any order it concludes was erroneous.

(C) **Correction of Record**. If a dispute arises as to whether the record accurately reflects what occurred in the trial court, the court, after giving the parties the opportunity to be heard, must resolve the dispute and, if necessary, order the record to be corrected.

(D) **Correction During Appeal**. If a claim of appeal has been filed or leave to appeal granted in the case, corrections under this rule are subject to MCR 7.208(A) and (B).

Rule 6.440 Disability of Judge

(A) **During Jury Trial**. If, by reason of death, sickness, or other disability, the judge before whom a jury trial has commenced is unable to continue with the trial, another judge regularly sitting in or assigned to the court, on certification of having become familiar with the record of the trial, may proceed with and complete the trial.

(B) **During Bench Trial**. If a judge becomes disabled during a trial without a jury, another judge may be substituted for the disabled judge, but only if

(1) both parties consent in writing to the substitution, and

(2) the judge certifies having become familiar with the record of the trial, including the testimony previously given.

(C) **After Verdict**. If, after a verdict is returned or findings of fact and conclusions of law are filed, the trial judge because of disability becomes unable to perform the remaining duties the court must perform, another judge regularly sitting in or assigned to the court may perform those duties; but if that judge is not satisfied of an ability to perform those duties because of not having presided at the trial or determines that it is appropriate for any other reason, the judge may grant the defendant a new trial.

Rule 6.445 Probation Revocation

(A) **Issuance of Summons; Warrant**. On finding probable cause to believe that a probationer has violated a condition of probation, the court may

(1) issue a summons in accordance with MCR 6.103(B) and (C) for the probationer to appear for arraignment on the alleged violation, or

(2) issue a warrant for the arrest of the probationer.

An arrested probationer must promptly be brought before the court for arraignment on the alleged violation.

(B) **Arraignment on the Charge**. At the arraignment on the alleged probation violation, the court must

(1) ensure that the probationer receives written notice of the alleged violation,

(2) advise the probationer that

(a) the probationer has a right to contest the charge at a hearing, and

(b) the probationer is entitled to a lawyer's assistance at the hearing and at all subsequent court proceedings, and that the court will appoint a lawyer at public expense if the probationer wants one and is financially unable to retain one,

(3) if requested and appropriate, appoint a lawyer,

(4) determine what form of release, if any, is appropriate, and

(5) subject to subrule (C), set a reasonably prompt hearing date or postpone the hearing.

(C) **Scheduling or Postponement of Hearing**. The hearing of a probationer being held in custody for an alleged probation violation must be held within 14 days after the arraignment or the court must order the probationer released from that custody pending the hearing. If the alleged violation is based on a criminal offense that is a basis for a separate criminal prosecution, the court may postpone the hearing for the outcome of that prosecution.

(D) **Continuing Duty to Advise of Right to Assistance of Lawyer**. Even though a probationer charged with probation violation has waived the assistance of a lawyer, at each subsequent proceeding the court must comply with the advice and waiver procedure in MCR 6.005(E).

(E) **The Violation Hearing**.

(1) *Conduct of the Hearing*. The evidence against the probationer must be disclosed to the probationer. The probationer has the right to be present at the hearing, to present evidence, and to examine and cross-examine witnesses. The court may consider only evidence that is relevant to the violation alleged, but it need not apply the rules of evidence except those pertaining to privileges. The state has the burden of proving a violation by a preponderance of the evidence.

(2) *Judicial Findings*. At the conclusion of the hearing, the court must make findings in accordance with MCR 6.403.

(F) **Pleas of Guilty**. The probationer may, at the arraignment or afterward, plead guilty to the violation. Before accepting a guilty plea, the court, speaking directly to the probationer and receiving the probationer's response, must

(1) advise the probationer that by pleading guilty the probationer is giving up the right to a contested hearing and, if the probationer is proceeding without legal representation, the right to a lawyer's assistance as set forth in subrule (B)(2)(b),

(2) advise the probationer of the maximum possible jail or prison sentence for the offense,

(3) ascertain that the plea is understandingly, voluntarily, and accurately made, and

(4) establish factual support for a finding that the probationer is guilty of the alleged violation.

(G) **Sentencing**. If the court finds that the probationer has violated a condition of probation, or if the probationer pleads guilty to a violation, the court may continue probation, modify the conditions of probation, extend the probation period, or revoke probation and impose a sentence of incarceration. The court may not sentence the probationer to prison without having considered a current presentence report and having complied with the provisions set forth in MCR 6.425(B) and (E).

(H) **Review**.

(1) In a case involving a sentence of incarceration under subrule (G), the court must advise the probationer on the record, immediately after imposing sentence, that

(a) the probationer has a right to appeal, if the underlying conviction occurred as a result of a trial, or

(b) the probationer is entitled to file an application for leave to appeal, if the underlying conviction was the result of a plea of guilty or nolo contendere.

(2) In a case that involves a sentence other than incarceration under subrule (G), the court must advise the probationer on the record, immediately after imposing sentence, that the probationer is entitled to file an application for leave to appeal.

Subchapter 6.500 Postappeal Relief

Rule 6.501 Scope of Subchapter

Unless otherwise specified by these rules, a judgment of conviction and sentence entered by the circuit court not subject to appellate review under subchapters 7.200 or 7.300 may be reviewed only in accordance with the provisions of this subchapter.

Rule 6.502 Motion for Relief From Judgment

(A) **Nature of Motion**. The request for relief under this subchapter must be in the form of a motion to set aside or modify the judgment. The motion must specify all of the grounds for relief which are available to the defendant and of which the defendant has, or by the exercise of due diligence, should have knowledge.

(B) **Limitations on Motion**. A motion may seek relief from one judgment only. If the defendant desires to challenge the validity of additional judgments, the defendant must do so by separate motions. For the purpose of this rule, multiple convictions resulting from a single trial or plea proceeding shall be treated as a single judgment.

(C) **Form of Motion**. The motion may not be noticed for hearing, and must be typed or legibly handwritten and include a verification by the defendant or defendant's lawyer in accordance with MCR 2.114. Except as otherwise ordered by the court, the combined length of the motion and any memorandum of law in support may not exceed 50 pages double-spaced, exclusive of attachments and exhibits. If the court enters an order increasing the page limit for the motion, the same order shall indicate that the page limit for the prosecutor's response provided for in MCR 6.506(A) is increased by the same amount. The motion must be substantially in the form approved by the State Court Administrative Office, and must include:

(1) The name of the defendant;

(2) The name of the court in which the defendant was convicted and the file number of the defendant's case;

(3) The place where the defendant is confined, or, if not confined, the defendant's current address;

(4) The offenses for which the defendant was convicted and sentenced;

(5) The date on which the defendant was sentenced;

(6) Whether the defendant was convicted by a jury, by a judge without jury, or on a plea of guilty, guilty but mentally ill, or nolo contendere;

(7) The sentence imposed (probation, fine, and/or imprisonment), the length of the sentence imposed, and whether the defendant is now serving that sentence;

(8) The name of the judge who presided at trial and imposed sentence;

(9) The court, title, and file number of any proceeding (including appeals and federal court proceedings) instituted by the defendant to obtain relief from conviction or sentence, specifying whether a proceeding is pending or has been completed;

(10) The name of each lawyer who represented the defendant at any time after arrest, and the stage of the case at which each represented the defendant;

(11) The relief requested;

(12) The grounds for the relief requested;

(13) The facts supporting each ground, stated in summary form;

(14) Whether any of the grounds for the relief requested were raised before; if so, at what stage of the case, and, if not, the reasons they were not raised;

(15) Whether the defendant requests the appointment of counsel, and, if so, information necessary for the court to determine whether the defendant is entitled to appointment of counsel at public expense.

Upon request, the clerk of each court with trial level jurisdiction over felony cases shall make available blank motion forms without charge to any person desiring to file such a motion.

(D) **Return of Insufficient Motion**. If a motion is not submitted on a form approved by the State Court Administrative Office, or does not substantially comply with the requirements of these rules, the court shall either direct that it be returned to the defendant with a statement of the reasons for its return, along with the appropriate form, or adjudicate the motion under the provisions of these rules. The clerk of the court shall retain a copy of the motion.

(E) **Attachments to Motion**. The defendant may attach to the motion any affidavit, document, or evidence to support the relief requested.

(F) **Amendment and Supplementation of Motion**. The court may permit the defendant to amend or supplement the motion at any time.

(G) **Successive Motions**.

(1) Except as provided in subrule (G)(2), regardless of whether a defendant has previously filed a motion for relief from judgment, after August 1, 1995, one and only one motion for relief from judgment may be filed with regard to a conviction. The court shall return without filing any successive motions for relief from judgment. A defendant may not appeal the denial or rejection of a successive motion.

(2) A defendant may file a second or subsequent motion based on a retroactive change in law that occurred after the first motion for relief from judgment or a claim of new evidence that was not discovered before the first such motion. The clerk shall refer a successive motion that asserts that one of these exceptions is applicable to the judge to whom the case is assigned for a determination whether the motion is within one of the exceptions.

Rule 6.503 Filing and Service of Motion

(A) **Filing; Copies**.

(1) A defendant seeking relief under this subchapter must file a motion, and a copy of the motion with the clerk of the court in which the defendant was convicted and sentenced.

(2) Upon receipt of a motion, the clerk shall file it under the same number as the original conviction.

(B) **Service**. The defendant shall serve a copy of the motion and notice of its filing on the prosecuting attorney. Unless so ordered by the court as provided in this subchapter, the filing and service of the motion does not require a response by the prosecutor.

Rule 6.504 Assignment; Preliminary Consideration by Judge; Summary Denial

(A) **Assignment to Judge**. The motion shall be presented to the judge to whom the case was assigned at the time of the defendant's conviction. If the appropriate judge is not available, the motion must be assigned to another judge in accordance with the court's procedure for the reassignment of cases. The chief judge may reassign cases in order to correct docket control problems arising from the requirements of this rule.

(B) **Initial Consideration by Court**.

(1) The court shall promptly examine the motion, together with all the files, records, transcripts, and correspondence relating to the judgment under attack. The court may request that the prosecutor provide copies of transcripts, briefs, or other records.

(2) If it plainly appears from the face of the materials described in subrule (B)(1) that the defendant is not entitled to relief, the court shall deny the motion without directing further proceedings. The order must include a concise statement of the reasons for the denial. The clerk shall serve a copy of the order on the defendant and the prosecutor. The court may dismiss some requests for relief or grounds for relief while directing a response or further proceedings with respect to other specified grounds.

(3) If the motion is summarily dismissed under subrule (B)(2), the defendant may move for reconsideration of the dismissal within 21 days after the clerk serves the order. The motion must concisely state why the court's decision was based on a clear error and that a different decision must result from correction of the error. A motion which merely presents the same matters that were considered by the court will not be granted.

(4) If the entire motion is not dismissed under subrule (B)(2), the court shall order the prosecuting attorney to file a response as provided in MCR 6.506, and shall conduct further proceedings as provided in MCR 6.505-6.508.

Rule 6.505 Right to Legal Assistance

(A) **Appointment of Counsel**. If the defendant has requested appointment of counsel, and the court has determined that the defendant is indigent, the court may appoint counsel for the defendant at any time during the proceedings under this subchapter. Counsel must be appointed if the court directs that oral argument or an evidentiary hearing be held.

(B) **Opportunity to Supplement the Motion**. If the court appoints counsel to represent the defendant, it shall afford counsel 56 days to amend or supplement the motion. The court may extend the time on a showing that a necessary transcript or record is not available to counsel.

Rule 6.506 Response by Prosecutor

(A) **Contents of Response**. On direction of the court pursuant to MCR 6.504(B)(4), the prosecutor shall respond in writing to the allegations in the motion. The trial court shall allow the prosecutor a minimum of 56 days to respond. If the response refers to transcripts or briefs that are not in the court's file, the prosecutor shall submit copies of those items with the response. Except as otherwise ordered by the court, the response shall not exceed 50 pages double-spaced, exclusive of attachments and exhibits.

(B) **Filing and Service**. The prosecutor shall file the response and one copy with the clerk of the court and serve one copy on the defendant.

Rule 6.507 Expansion of Record

(A) **Order to Expand Record**. If the court does not deny the motion pursuant to MCR 6.504(B)(2), it may direct the parties to expand the record by including any additional materials it deems relevant to the decision on the merits of the motion. The expanded record may include letters, affidavits, documents, exhibits, and answers under oath to interrogatories propounded by the court.

(B) **Submission to Opposing Party**. Whenever a party submits items to expand the record, the party shall serve copies of the items to the opposing party. The court shall afford the opposing party an opportunity to admit or deny the correctness of the items.

(C) **Authentication**. The court may require the authentication of any item submitted under this rule.

Rule 6.508 Procedure; Evidentiary Hearing; Determination

(A) **Procedure Generally**. If the rules in this subchapter do not prescribe the applicable procedure, the court may proceed in any lawful manner. The court may apply the rules applicable to civil or criminal proceedings, as it deems appropriate.

(B) **Decision Without Evidentiary Hearing**. After reviewing the motion and response, the record, and the expanded record, if any, the court shall determine whether an evidentiary hearing is required. If the court decides that an evidentiary hearing is not required, it may rule on the motion or, in its discretion, afford the parties an opportunity for oral argument.

(C) **Evidentiary Hearing**. If the court decides that an evidentiary hearing is required, it shall schedule and conduct the hearing as promptly as practicable. At the hearing, the rules of evidence other than those with respect to privilege do not apply. The court shall assure that a verbatim record is made of the hearing.

(D) **Entitlement to Relief**. The defendant has the burden of establishing entitlement to the relief requested. The court may not grant relief to the defendant if the motion

- (1) seeks relief from a judgment of conviction and sentence that still is subject to challenge on appeal pursuant to subchapter 7.200 or subchapter 7.300;
- (2) alleges grounds for relief which were decided against the defendant in a prior appeal or proceeding under this subchapter, unless the defendant establishes that a retroactive change in the law has undermined the prior decision;
- (3) alleges grounds for relief, other than jurisdictional defects, which could have been raised on appeal from the conviction and sentence or in a prior motion under this subchapter, unless the defendant demonstrates
  - (a) good cause for failure to raise such grounds on appeal or in the prior motion, and
  - (b) actual prejudice from the alleged irregularities that support the claim for relief. As used in this subrule, "actual prejudice" means that,
    - (i) in a conviction following a trial, but for the alleged error, the defendant would have had a reasonably likely chance of acquittal;
    - (ii) in a conviction entered on a plea of guilty, guilty but mentally ill, or nolo contendere, the defect in the proceedings was such that it renders the plea an involuntary one to a degree that it would be manifestly unjust to allow the conviction to stand;
    - (iii) in any case, the irregularity was so offensive to the maintenance of a sound judicial process that the conviction should not be allowed to stand regardless of its effect on the outcome of the case;
    - (iv) in the case of a challenge to the sentence, the sentence is invalid.

  The court may waive the "good cause" requirement of subrule (D)(3)(a) if it concludes that there is a significant possibility that the defendant is innocent of the crime.

(E) **Ruling**. The court, either orally or in writing, shall set forth in the record its findings of fact and its conclusions of law, and enter an appropriate order disposing of the motion.

Rule 6.509 Appeal

(A) **Availability of Appeal**. Appeals from decisions under this subchapter are by application for leave to appeal to the Court of Appeals pursuant to MCR 7.205. The 6-month time limit provided by MCR 7.205(G)(3), runs from the decision under this subchapter. Nothing in this subchapter shall be construed as extending the time to appeal from the original judgment.

(B) **Responsibility of Appointed Counsel**. If the trial court has appointed counsel for the defendant during the proceeding, that appointment authorizes the attorney to represent the defendant in connection with an application for leave to appeal to the Court of Appeals.

(C) **Responsibility of the Prosecutor**. If the prosecutor has not filed a response to the defendant's application for leave to appeal in the appellate court, the prosecutor must file an appellee's brief if the appellate court grants the defendant's application for leave to appeal. The prosecutor must file an appellee's brief within 56 days after an order directing a response pursuant to subrule (D).

(D) **Responsibility of the Appellate Court**. If the appellate court grants the defendant's application for leave to appeal and the prosecutor has not filed a response in the appellate court, the appellate court must direct the prosecutor to file an appellee's brief, and give the prosecutor the opportunity to file an appellee's brief pursuant to subrule (C), before granting further relief to the defendant.

Subchapter 6.600 Criminal Procedure in District Court

Rule 6.610 Criminal Procedure Generally

(A) **Precedence**. Criminal cases have precedence over civil actions.

(B) **Pretrial**. The court, on its own initiative or on motion of either party, may direct the prosecutor and the defendant, and, if represented, the defendant's attorney to appear for a pretrial conference. The court may require collateral matters and pretrial motions to be filed and argued no later than this conference.

(C) **Record**. Unless a writing is permitted, a verbatim record of the proceedings before a court under subrules (D)-(F) must be made.

(D) **Arraignment; District Court Offenses**.

(1) Whenever a defendant is arraigned on an offense over which the district court has jurisdiction, the defendant must be informed of

(a) the name of the offense;

(b) the maximum sentence permitted by law; and

(c) the defendant's right

(i) to the assistance of an attorney and to a trial;

(ii) (if subrule [D][2] applies) to an appointed attorney; and

(iii) to a trial by jury, when required by law.

The information may be given in a writing that is made a part of the file or by the court on the record.

(2) An indigent defendant has a right to an appointed attorney whenever the offense charged requires on conviction a minimum term in jail or the court determines it might sentence to a term of incarceration, even if suspended.

If an indigent defendant is without an attorney and has not waived the right to an appointed attorney, the court may not sentence the defendant to jail or to a suspended jail sentence.

(3) The right to the assistance of an attorney, to an appointed attorney, or to a trial by jury is not waived unless the defendant

(a) has been informed of the right; and

(b) has waived it in a writing that is made a part of the file or orally on the record.

(4) The court may allow a defendant to enter a plea of not guilty or to stand mute without formal arraignment by filing a written statement signed by the defendant and any defense attorney of record, reciting the general nature of the charge, the maximum possible sentence, the rights of the defendant at arraignment, and the plea to be entered. The court may require that an appropriate bond be executed and filed and appropriate and reasonable sureties posted or continued as a condition precedent to allowing the defendant to be arraigned without personally appearing before the court.

(E) **Pleas of Guilty and Nolo Contendere**. Before accepting a plea of guilty or nolo contendere, the court shall in all cases comply with this rule.

(1) The court shall determine that the plea is understanding, voluntary, and accurate. In determining the accuracy of the plea,

(a) if the defendant pleads guilty, the court, by questioning the defendant, shall establish support for a finding that defendant is guilty of the offense charged or the offense to which the defendant is pleading, or

(b) if the defendant pleads nolo contendere, the court shall not question the defendant about the defendant's participation in the crime, but shall make the determination on the basis of other available information.

(2) The court shall inform the defendant of the right to the assistance of an attorney. If the offense charged requires on conviction a minimum term in jail, the court shall inform the defendant that if the defendant is indigent the defendant has the right to an appointed attorney. The court shall also give

such advice if it determines that it might sentence to a term of incarceration, even if suspended.

(3) The court shall advise the defendant of the following:

(a) the mandatory minimum jail sentence, if any, and the maximum possible penalty for the offense,

(b) that if the plea is accepted the defendant will not have a trial of any kind and that the defendant gives up the following rights that the defendant would have at trial:

(i) the right to have witnesses called for the defendant's defense at trial,

(ii) the right to cross-examine all witnesses called against the defendant,

(iii) the right to testify or to remain silent without an inference being drawn from said silence,

(iv) the presumption of innocence and the requirement that the defendant's guilt be proven beyond a reasonable doubt.

(4) A defendant or defendants may be informed of the trial rights listed in subrule (3)(b) as follows:

(a) on the record,

(b) in a writing made part of the file, or

(c) in a writing referred to on the record.

If the court uses a writing pursuant to subrule (E)(4)(b) or (c), the court shall address the defendant and obtain from the defendant orally on the record a statement that the rights were read and understood and a waiver of those rights. The waiver may be obtained without repeating the individual rights.

(5) The court shall make the plea agreement a part of the record and determine that the parties agree on all the terms of that agreement. The court shall accept, reject or indicate on what basis it accepts the plea.

(6) The court must ask the defendant:

(a) (if there is no plea agreement) whether anyone has promised the defendant anything, or (if there is a plea agreement) whether anyone has promised anything beyond what is in the plea agreement;

(b) whether anyone has threatened the defendant; and

(c) whether it is the defendant's own choice to plead guilty.

(7) A plea of guilty or nolo contendere in writing is permissible without a personal appearance of the defendant and without support for a finding that defendant is guilty of the offense charged or the offense to which the defendant is pleading if

(a) the court decides that the combination of the circumstances and the range of possible sentences makes the situation proper for a plea of guilty or nolo contendere;

(b) the defendant acknowledges guilt or nolo contendere, in a writing to be placed in the district court file, and waives in writing the rights enumerated in subrule (3)(b); and

(c) the court is satisfied that the waiver is voluntary.

(8) The following provisions apply where a defendant seeks to challenge the plea.

(a) A defendant may not challenge a plea on appeal unless the defendant moved in the trial court to withdraw the plea for noncompliance with these rules. Such a motion may be made either before or after sentence has been imposed. After imposition of sentence, the defendant may file a motion to withdraw the plea within the time for filing an application for leave to appeal under MCR 7.105(F)(2).

(b) If the trial court determines that a deviation affecting substantial rights occurred, it shall correct the deviation and give the defendant the option of permitting the plea to stand or of withdrawing the plea. If the trial court determines either a deviation did not occur, or that the deviation did not affect substantial rights, it may permit the defendant to withdraw the plea only if it does not cause substantial prejudice to the people because of reliance on the plea.

(c) If a deviation is corrected, any appeal will be on the whole record including the subsequent advice and inquiries.

(9) The State Court Administrator shall develop and approve forms to be used under subrules (E)(4)(b) and (c) and (E)(7)(b).

(F) **Sentencing.**

(1) For sentencing, the court shall:

(a) require the presence of the defendant's attorney, unless the defendant does not have one or has waived the attorney's presence;

(b) provide copies of the presentence report (if a presentence report was prepared) to the prosecutor and the defendant's lawyer, or the defendant if not represented by a lawyer, at a reasonable time, but not less than two business days before the day of sentencing. The prosecutor and the defendant's lawyer, or the defendant if not represented by a lawyer, may retain a copy of the report or an amended report. If the presentence report is not made available to the prosecutor and the defendant's lawyer, or the defendant if not represented by a lawyer, at least two business days before the day of sentencing, the prosecutor and the defendant's lawyer, or the defendant if not represented by a lawyer, shall be entitled, on oral motion, to an adjournment to enable the moving party to review the presentence report and to prepare any necessary corrections, additions or deletions to present to the court, or otherwise advise the court of circumstances the prosecutor or defendant believes should be considered in imposing sentence. A presentence investigation report shall not include any address or telephone number for the home, workplace, school, or place of worship of any victim or witness, or a family member of any victim or witness, unless an address is used to identify the place of the crime or to impose conditions of release from custody that are necessary for the protection of a named individual. Upon request, any other address or telephone number that would reveal the location of a victim or witness or a family member of a victim or witness shall be exempted from disclosure unless an address is used to identify the place of the crime or to impose conditions of release from custody that are necessary for the protection of a named individual.

(c) inform the defendant of credit to be given for time served, if any.

(2) Unless a defendant who is entitled to appointed counsel is represented by an attorney or has waived the right to an attorney, a subsequent charge or sentence may not be enhanced because of this conviction and the defendant may not be incarcerated for violating probation or any other condition imposed in connection with this conviction.

(3) Immediately after imposing a sentence of incarceration, even if suspended, the court must advise the defendant, on the record or in writing, that:

(a) if the defendant wishes to file an appeal and is financially unable to retain a lawyer, the court will appoint a lawyer to represent the defendant on appeal, and

(b) the request for a lawyer must be made within 14 days after sentencing.

(G) **Motion for New Trial**. A motion for a new trial must be filed within 21 days after the entry of judgment. However, if an appeal has not been taken, a delayed motion may be filed within the time for filing an application for leave to appeal.

(H) **Arraignment; Offenses Not Cognizable by the District Court**. In a prosecution in which a defendant is charged with a felony or a misdemeanor not cognizable by the district court, the court shall

(1) inform the defendant of the nature of the charge;

(2) inform the defendant of

(a) the right to a preliminary examination;

(b) the right to an attorney, if the defendant is not represented by an attorney at the arraignment;

(c) the right to have an attorney appointed at public expense if the defendant is indigent; and

(d) the right to consideration of pretrial release.

If a defendant not represented by an attorney waives the preliminary examination, the court shall ascertain that the waiver is freely, understandingly, and voluntarily given before accepting it.

Rule 6.615 Misdemeanor Traffic Cases

(A) **Citation; Complaint; Summons; Warrant**.

(1) A misdemeanor traffic case may be begun by one of the following procedures:

(a) Service by a law enforcement officer on the defendant of a written citation, and the filing of the citation in the district court.

(b) The filing of a sworn complaint in the district court and the issuance of an arrest warrant. A citation may serve as the sworn complaint and as the basis for a misdemeanor warrant.

(c) Other special procedures authorized by statute.

(2) The citation serves as a summons to command

(a) the initial appearance of the defendant; and

(b) a response from the defendant as to his or her guilt of the violation alleged.

(B) **Appearances; Failure To Appear**. If a defendant fails to appear or otherwise to respond to any matter pending relative to a misdemeanor traffic citation, the court shall proceed as provided in this subrule.

(1) If the defendant is a Michigan resident, the court

(a) must initiate the procedures required by MCL 257.321a for the failure to answer a citation; and

(b) may issue a warrant for the defendant's arrest.

(2) If the defendant is not a Michigan resident,

(a) the court may mail a notice to appear to the defendant at the address in the citation;

(b) the court may issue a warrant for the defendant's arrest; and

(c) if the court has received the driver's license of a nonresident, pursuant to statute, it may retain the license as allowed by statute. The court need not retain the license past its expiration date.

(C) **Arraignment**. An arraignment in a misdemeanor traffic case may be conducted by

(1) a judge of the district, or

(2) a district court magistrate as authorized by statute and by the judges of the district.

(D) **Contested Cases**.

(1) A contested case may not be heard until a citation is filed with the court. If the citation is filed electronically, the court may decline to hear the matter until the citation is signed by the officer or

official who issued it, and is filed on paper. A citation that is not signed and filed on paper, when required by the court, may be dismissed with prejudice.

(2) A misdemeanor traffic case must be conducted in compliance with the constitutional and statutory procedures and safeguards applicable to misdemeanors cognizable by the district court.

Rule 6.620 Impaneling the Jury

(A) **Alternate Jurors**. The court may direct that 7 or more jurors be impaneled to sit in a criminal case. After the instructions to the jury have been given and the case submitted, the names of the jurors must be placed in a container and names drawn to reduce the number of jurors to 6, who shall constitute the jury. The court may retain the alternate jurors during deliberations. If the court does so, it shall instruct the alternate jurors not to discuss the case with any other person until the jury completes its deliberations and is discharged. If an alternate juror replaces a juror after the jury retires to consider its verdict, the court shall instruct the jury to begin its deliberations anew.

(B) **Peremptory Challenges**.

(1) Each defendant is entitled to three peremptory challenges. The prosecutor is entitled to the same number of peremptory challenges as a defendant being tried alone, or, in the case of jointly tried defendants, the total number of peremptory challenges to which all the defendants are entitled.

(2) Additional Challenges. On a showing of good cause, the court may grant one or more of the parties an increased number of peremptory challenges. The additional challenges granted by the court need not be equal for each party.

Rule 6.625 Appeal; Appointment of Appellate Counsel

(A) An appeal from a misdemeanor case is governed by subchapter 7.100.

(B) If the court imposed a sentence of incarceration, even if suspended, and the defendant is indigent, the court must enter an order appointing a lawyer if, within 14 days after sentencing, the defendant files a request for a lawyer or makes a request on the record. Unless there is a postjudgment motion pending, the court must rule on a defendant's request for a lawyer within 14 days after receiving it. If there is a postjudgment motion pending, the court must rule on the request after the court's disposition of the pending motion and within 14 days after that disposition. If a lawyer is appointed, the 21 days for taking an appeal pursuant to MCR 7.104(A)(3) and MCR 7.105(A)(3) shall commence on the day of the appointment.

Subchapter 6.900 Rules Applicable to Juveniles Charged With Specified Offenses Subject to the Jurisdiction of the Circuit or District Court

Rule 6.901 Applicability

(A) **Precedence**. The rules in this subchapter take precedence over, but are not exclusive of, the rules of procedure applicable to criminal actions against adult offenders.

(B) **Scope**. The rules apply to criminal proceedings in the district court and the circuit court concerning a juvenile against whom the prosecuting attorney has authorized the filing of a criminal complaint charging a specified juvenile violation instead of approving the filing of a petition in the family division of the circuit court. The rules do not apply to a person charged solely with an offense in which the family division has waived jurisdiction pursuant to MCL712A.4.

Rule 6.903 Definitions

When used in this subchapter, unless the context otherwise indicates:

(A) "Commitment review hearing" includes a hearing as required by MCL 769.1 to decide whether the jurisdiction of the court shall continue over a juvenile who was placed on juvenile probation and committed to state wardship.

(B) "Commitment review report" means a report on a juvenile committed to state wardship for use at a commitment review hearing prepared by the Family Independence Agency pursuant to MCL 803.225 (§ 5 of the Juvenile Facilities Act).

(C) "Court" means the circuit court as provided in MCL 600.606, but does not include the family division of the circuit court.

(D) "Family division" means the family division of the circuit court.

(E) "Juvenile" means a person 14 years of age or older, who is subject to the jurisdiction of the court for having allegedly committed a specified juvenile violation on or after the person's 14th birthday and before the person's 17th birthday.

(F) "Juvenile sentencing hearing" means a hearing conducted by the court following a criminal conviction to determine whether the best interests of the juvenile and of the public would be served:

(1) by retaining jurisdiction over the juvenile, placing the juvenile on juvenile probation, and committing the juvenile to a state institution or agency as a state ward, as provided in MCL 769.1; or

(2) by imposing sentence as provided by law for an adult offender.

(G) "Juvenile facility" means an institution or facility operated by the juvenile division of the circuit court, or a state institution or agency described in the Youth

Rehabilitation Services Act, MCL 803.301 et seq., or a county facility or institution operated as an agency of the county other than a facility designed or used to incarcerate adults.

(H) "Specified Juvenile Violation" means one or more of the following offenses allegedly committed by a juvenile in which the prosecuting attorney has authorized the filing of a criminal complaint and warrant instead of proceeding in the family division of the circuit court:

(1) burning a dwelling house, MCL 750.72;
(2) assault with intent to commit murder, MCL 750.83;
(3) assault with intent to maim, MCL 750.86;
(4) assault with intent to rob while armed, MCL 750.89;
(5) attempted murder, MCL 750.91;
(6) first-degree murder, MCL 750.316;
(7) second-degree murder, MCL 750.317;
(8) kidnaping, MCL 750.349;
(9) first-degree criminal sexual conduct, MCL 750.520b;
(10) armed robbery, MCL 750.529;
(11) carjacking, MCL 750.529a;
(12) bank, safe, or vault robbery, MCL 750.531;
(13) assault with intent to do great bodily harm, MCL 750.84, if armed with a dangerous weapon;
(14) first-degree home invasion, MCL 750.110a(2), if armed with a dangerous weapon;
(15) escape or attempted escape from a medium-security or high-security juvenile facility operated by the Family Independence Agency, or a high-security facility operated by a private agency under contract with the Family Independence Agency, MCL 750.186a;
(16) possession of [MCL 333.7403(2)(a)(i)] or manufacture, delivery, or possession with intent to manufacture or deliver of 650 grams(1,000 grams beginning March 1, 2003) or more of a schedule 1 or 2 controlled substance [MCL 333.7401(2)(a)(i)];
(17) any attempt, MCL 750.92; solicitation, MCL 750.157b; or conspiracy, MCL 750.157a; to commit any of the offenses listed in subrules (1)-(16);
(18) any lesser-included offense of an offense listed in subrules (1)-(17) if the juvenile is charged with a specified juvenile violation;
(19) any other violation arising out of the same transaction if the juvenile is charged with one of the offenses listed in subrules (1)-(17).

(I) "Dangerous Weapon" means one of the following:

(1) a loaded or unloaded firearm, whether operable or inoperable;
(2) a knife, stabbing instrument, brass knuckles, blackjack, club, or other object specifically designed or customarily carried or possessed for use as a weapon;
(3) an object that is likely to cause death or bodily injury when used as a weapon and that is used as a weapon, or carried or possessed for use as a weapon;
(4) an object or device that is used or fashioned in a manner leading a person to believe the object or device is an object or device described in subrules (1)-(3).

(J) "Magistrate" means a judge of the district court or a municipal court as defined in MCL 761.1(f).

(K) "Progress report" means the report on a juvenile in state wardship prepared by the Family Independence Agency for the court as required by MCL 803.223 (§ 3 of the Juvenile Facilities Act) and by these rules.

(L) "Social report" means the written report on a juvenile for use at the juvenile sentencing hearing prepared by the Family Independence Agency as required by MCL 803.224 (§ 4 of the Juvenile Facilities Act).

(M) "State wardship" means care and control of a juvenile until the juvenile's 21st birthday by an institution or agency within or under the supervision of the Family Independence Agency as provided in the Youth Rehabilitation Services Act, MCL 803.301 et seq., while the juvenile remains under the jurisdiction of the court on the basis of a court order of juvenile probation and commitment as provided in MCL 769.1.

Rule 6.905 Assistance of Attorney

(A) **Advice of Right**. If the juvenile is not represented by an attorney, the magistrate or court shall advise the juvenile at each stage of the criminal proceedings of the right to the assistance of an attorney. If the juvenile has waived the right to an attorney, the court at later proceedings must reaffirm that the juvenile continues to not want an attorney.

(B) **Court-Appointed Attorney**. Unless the juvenile has a retained attorney, or has waived the right to an attorney, the magistrate or the court must appoint an attorney to represent the juvenile.

(C) **Waiver of Attorney**. The magistrate or court may permit a juvenile to waive representation by an attorney if:

(1) an attorney is appointed to give the juvenile advice on the question of waiver;
(2) the magistrate or the court finds that the juvenile is literate and is competent to conduct a defense;
(3) the magistrate or the court advises the juvenile of the dangers and of the disadvantages of self-representation;
(4) the magistrate or the court finds on the record that the waiver is voluntarily and understandingly made; and
(5) the court appoints standby counsel to assist the juvenile at trial and at the juvenile sentencing hearing.

(D) **Cost**. The court may assess cost of legal representation, or part thereof, against the juvenile or against a person responsible for the support of the juvenile, or both. The order assessing cost shall not be binding on a person responsible for the support of the juvenile unless an opportunity for a hearing has been given and until a copy of the order is served on the person, personally or by first class mail to the person's last known address.

Rule 6.907 Arraignment on Complaint and Warrant

(A) **Time**. When the prosecuting attorney authorizes the filing of a complaint and warrant charging a juvenile with a specified juvenile violation instead of approving the filing of a petition in the family division of the circuit court, the juvenile in custody must be taken to the magistrate for arraignment on the charge. The prosecuting attorney must make a good-faith effort to notify the parent of the juvenile of the arraignment. The juvenile must be released if arraignment has not commenced:
- (1) within 24 hours of the arrest of the juvenile; or
- (2) within 24 hours after the prosecuting attorney authorized the complaint and warrant during special adjournment pursuant to MCR 3.935(A)(3), provided the juvenile is being detained in a juvenile facility.

(B) **Temporary Detention Pending Arraignment**. If the prosecuting attorney has authorized the filing of a complaint and warrant charging a specified juvenile violation instead of approving the filing of a petition in the family division of the circuit court, a juvenile may, following apprehension, be detained pending arraignment:
- (1) in a juvenile facility operated by the county;
- (2) in a regional juvenile detention facility operated by the state; or
- (3) in a facility operated by the family division of the circuit court with the consent of the family division or an order of a court as defined in MCR 6.903(C).

If no juvenile facility is reasonably available and if it is apparent that the juvenile may not otherwise be safely detained, the magistrate may, without a hearing, authorize that the juvenile be lodged pending arraignment in a facility used to incarcerate adults. The juvenile must be kept separate from adult prisoners as required by law.

(C) **Procedure**. At the arraignment on the complaint and warrant:
- (1) The magistrate shall determine whether a parent, guardian, or an adult relative of the juvenile is present. Arraignment may be conducted without the presence of a parent, guardian, or adult relative provided the magistrate appoints an attorney to appear at arraignment with the juvenile or provided an attorney has been retained and appears with the juvenile.
- (2) The magistrate shall set a date for the juvenile's preliminary examination within the next 14 days, less time given and used by the prosecuting attorney under special adjournment pursuant to MCR 3.935(A)(3), up to three days' credit. The magistrate shall inform the juvenile and the parent, guardian, or adult relative of the juvenile, if present, of the preliminary examination date. If a parent, guardian, or an adult relative is not present at the arraignment, the court shall direct the attorney for the juvenile to advise a parent or guardian of the juvenile of the scheduled preliminary examination.

Rule 6.909 Releasing or Detaining Juveniles Before Trial or Sentence

(A) **Bail; Detention**.
- (1) *Bail*. Except as provided in subrule (2) the magistrate or court must advise the juvenile of a right to bail as provided for an adult accused. The magistrate or the court may order a juvenile released to a parent or guardian on the basis of any lawful condition, including that bail be posted.
- (2) *Detention Without Bail*. If the proof is evident or if the presumption is great that the juvenile committed the offense, the magistrate or the court may deny bail:
  - (a) to a juvenile charged with first-degree murder, second-degree murder, or
  - (b) to a juvenile charged with first-degree criminal sexual conduct, or armed robbery,
    - (i) who is likely to flee, or
    - (ii) who clearly presents a danger to others.

(B) **Place of Confinement**.
- (1) *Juvenile Facility*. Except as provided in subrule (B)(2) and in MCR 6.907(B), a juvenile charged with a crime and not released must be placed in a juvenile facility while awaiting trial and, if necessary, sentencing, rather than being placed in a jail or similar facility designed and used to incarcerate adult prisoners.
- (2) *Jailing of Juveniles; Restricted*. On motion of a prosecuting attorney or a superintendent of a juvenile facility in which the juvenile is detained, the magistrate or court may order the juvenile confined in a jail or similar facility designed and used to incarcerate adult prisoners upon a showing that
  - (a) the juvenile's habits or conduct are considered a menace to other juveniles; or
  - (b) the juvenile may not otherwise be safely detained in a juvenile facility.
- (3) *Family Division Operated Facility*. The juvenile shall not be placed in an institution operated by the family division of the circuit court except with the

consent of the family division or on order of a court as defined in MCR 6.903(C).

(4) *Separate Custody of Juvenile*. The juvenile in custody or detention must be maintained separately from the adult prisoners or adult accused as required by MCL 764.27a.

(C) **Speedy Trial**. Within 7 days of the filing of a motion, the court shall release a juvenile who has remained in detention while awaiting trial for more than 91 days to answer for the specified juvenile violation unless the trial has commenced. In computing the 91-day period, the court is to exclude delays as provided in MCR 6.004(C)(1)-(6) and the time required to conduct the hearing on the motion.

Rule 6.911 Preliminary Examination

(A) **Waiver**. The juvenile may waive a preliminary examination if the juvenile is represented by an attorney and the waiver is made and signed by the juvenile in open court. The magistrate shall find and place on the record that the waiver was freely, understandingly, and voluntarily given.

(B) **Transfer to Family Division of Circuit Court**. If the magistrate, following preliminary examination, finds that there is no probable cause to believe that a specified juvenile violation occurred or that there is no probable cause to believe that the juvenile committed the specified juvenile violation, but that some other offense occurred that if committed by an adult would constitute a crime, and that there is probable cause to believe that the juvenile committed that offense, the magistrate shall transfer the matter to the family division of the circuit court in the county where the offense is alleged to have been committed for further proceedings. If the court transfers the matter to the family division, a transcript of the preliminary examination shall be sent to the family division without charge upon request.

Rule 6.931 Juvenile Sentencing Hearing

(A) **General**. If the juvenile has been convicted of an offense listed in MCL 769.1(1)(a)-(l), the court must sentence the juvenile in the same manner as an adult. Unless a juvenile is required to be sentenced in the same manner as an adult, a judge of a court having jurisdiction over a juvenile shall conduct a juvenile sentencing hearing unless the hearing is waived as provided in subrule (B). At the conclusion of the juvenile sentencing hearing, the court shall determine whether to impose a sentence against the juvenile as though an adult offender or whether to place the juvenile on juvenile probation and commit the juvenile to state wardship pursuant to MCL 769.1b.

(B) **No Juvenile Sentencing Hearing; Consent**. The court need not conduct a juvenile sentencing hearing if the prosecuting attorney, the juvenile, and the attorney for the juvenile, consent that it is not in the best interest of the public to sentence the juvenile as though an adult offender. If the juvenile sentence hearing is waived, the court shall not impose a sentence as provided by law for an adult offender. The court must place the juvenile on juvenile probation and commit the juvenile to state wardship.

(C) **Notice of Juvenile Sentencing Hearing Following Verdict**. If a juvenile sentencing hearing is required, the prosecuting attorney, the juvenile, and the attorney for the juvenile must be advised on the record immediately following conviction of the juvenile by a guilty plea or verdict of guilty that a hearing will be conducted at sentencing, unless waived, to determine whether to sentence the juvenile as an adult or to place the juvenile on juvenile probation and commit the juvenile to state wardship as though a delinquent. The court may announce the scheduled date of the hearing. On request, the court shall notify the victim of the juvenile sentencing hearing.

(D) **Review of Reports**. The court must give the prosecuting attorney, the juvenile, and the attorney for the juvenile, an opportunity to review the presentence report and the social report before the juvenile sentencing hearing. The court may exempt information from the reports as provided in MCL 771.14 and 771.14a.

(E) **Juvenile Sentencing Hearing Procedure**.

(1) *Evidence*. At the juvenile sentencing hearing all relevant and material evidence may be received by the court and relied upon to the extent of its probative value, even though such evidence may not be admissible at trial. The rules of evidence do not apply. The court shall receive and consider the presentence report prepared by the probation officer and the social report prepared by the Family Independence Agency.

(2) *Standard of Proof*. The court must sentence the juvenile in the same manner as an adult unless the court determines by a preponderance of the evidence, except as provided in subrule (3)(c), that the best interests of the public would be served by placing the juvenile on probation and committing the juvenile to state wardship.

(3) *Alternative Sentences For Juveniles Convicted of Certain Controlled Substance Offenses*. If a juvenile is convicted of a violation or conspiracy to commit a violation of MCL 333.7403(2)(a)(i), the court shall determine whether the best interests of the public would be served by:

(a) imposing the sentence provided by law for an adult offender;

(b) placing the individual on probation and committing the individual to a state institution or agency as provided in MCL 769.1(3); or

(c) imposing a sentence of imprisonment for any term of years, but not less than 25 years, if the court determines by clear and convincing evidence that such a sentence would serve the best interests of the public.

In making its determination, the court shall use the criteria set forth in subrule (4).

(4) *Criteria*. The court shall consider the following criteria in determining whether to sentence the juvenile as though an adult offender or whether to place the juvenile on juvenile probation and commit the juvenile to state wardship, giving more weight to the seriousness of the alleged offense and the juvenile's prior record of delinquency:

(a) the seriousness of the alleged offense in terms of community protection, including, but not limited to, the existence of any aggravating factors recognized by the sentencing guidelines, the use of a firearm or other dangerous weapon, and the impact on any victim;

(b) the culpability of the juvenile in committing the alleged offense, including, but not limited to, the level of the juvenile's participation in planning and carrying out the offense and the existence of any aggravating or mitigating factors recognized by the sentencing guidelines;

(c) the juvenile's prior record of delinquency, including, but not limited to, any record of detention, any police record, any school record, or any other evidence indicating prior delinquent behavior;

(d) the juvenile's programming history, including, but not limited to, the juvenile's past willingness to participate meaningfully in available programming;

(e) the adequacy of the punishment or programming available in the juvenile justice system; and

(f) the dispositional options available for the juvenile.

(5) *Findings*. The court must make findings of fact and conclusions of law forming the basis for the juvenile probation and commitment decision or the decision to sentence the juvenile as though an adult offender. The findings and conclusions may be incorporated in a written opinion or stated on the record.

(F) **Postjudgment Procedure; Juvenile Probation and Commitment to State Wardship**. If the court retains jurisdiction over the juvenile, places the juvenile on juvenile probation, and commits the juvenile to state wardship, the court shall comply with subrules (1)-(11):

(1) The court shall enter a judgment that includes a provision for reimbursement by the juvenile or those responsible for the juvenile's support, or both, for the cost of care and services pursuant to MCL 769.1(7). An order assessing such cost against a person responsible for the support of the juvenile shall not be binding on the person, unless an opportunity for a hearing has been given and until a copy of the order is served on the person, personally or by first class mail to the person's last known address.

(2) The court shall advise the juvenile at sentencing that if the juvenile, while on juvenile probation, is convicted of a felony or a misdemeanor punishable by more than one year's imprisonment, the court must revoke juvenile probation and sentence the juvenile to a term of years in prison not to exceed the penalty that might have been imposed for the offense for which the juvenile was originally convicted.

(3) The court shall assure that the juvenile receives a copy of the social report.

(4) The court shall send a copy of the order and a copy of the written opinion or transcript of the findings and conclusions of law to the Family Independence Agency.

(5) The court shall not place the juvenile on deferred sentencing, as provided in MCL 771.1(2).

(6) The court shall not place the juvenile on life probation for conviction of a controlled substance violation, as set forth in MCL 771.1(4).

(7) The five-year limit on the term of probation for an adult felony offender shall not apply.

(8) The court shall not require as a condition of juvenile probation that the juvenile report to a department of corrections probation officer.

(9) The court shall not, as a condition of juvenile probation, impose jail time against the juvenile except as provided in MCR 6.933(B)(2).

(10) The court shall not commit the juvenile to the Department of Corrections for failing to comply with a restitution order.

(11) The court shall not place the juvenile in a Department of Corrections camp for one year, as otherwise provided in MCL 771.3a(1).

Rule 6.933 Juvenile Probation Revocation

(A) **General Procedure**. When a juvenile, who was placed on juvenile probation and committed to an institution as a state ward, is alleged to have violated juvenile probation, the court shall proceed as provided in MCR 6.445(A)-(F).

(B) **Disposition in General**.

(1) *Certain Criminal Offense Violations*.

(a) If the court finds that the juvenile has violated juvenile probation by being convicted of a felony or a misdemeanor punishable by more than one year's imprisonment, the court must revoke the probation of the juvenile and order the juvenile committed to the Department of Corrections for a term of years not to exceed the penalty that could have been imposed for the offense that led to the probation. The court in imposing sentence shall grant credit against the sentence as required by law.

(b) The court may not revoke probation and impose sentence under subrule (B)(1) unless at the original sentencing the court gave the advice, as required by MCR 6.931(F)(2), that subsequent conviction of a felony or a misdemeanor punishable by more than one year's imprisonment would result in the revocation of juvenile probation and in the imposition of a sentence of imprisonment.

(2) *Other Violations*. If the court finds that the juvenile has violated juvenile probation, other than as provided in subrule (B)(1), the court may order the juvenile committed to the Department of Corrections as provided in subrule (B)(1), or may order the juvenile continued on juvenile probation and under state wardship, and may order any of the following:

(a) a change of placement,
(b) restitution,
(c) community service,
(d) substance abuse counseling,
(e) mental health counseling,
(f) participation in a vocational-technical education program,
(g) incarceration in a county jail for not more than 30 days, and
(h) any other participation or performance as the court considers necessary.

If the court determines to place the juvenile in jail for up to 30 days, and the juvenile is under 17 years of age, the juvenile must be placed separately from adult prisoners as required by law.

(3) If the court revokes juvenile probation pursuant to subrule (B)(1), the court must receive an updated presentence report and comply with MCR 6.445(G) before it imposes a prison sentence on the juvenile.

(C) **Disposition Regarding Specific Underlying Offenses**.

(1) *Controlled Substance Violation Punishable by Mandatory Nonparolable Life Sentence For Adults*. A juvenile who was placed on probation and committed to state wardship for manufacture, delivery, or possession with the intent to deliver 650 grams(1,000 grams beginning March 1, 2003) or more of a controlled substance, MCL 333.7401(2)(a)(i), may be resentenced only to a term of years following mandatory revocation of probation for commission of a subsequent felony or a misdemeanor punishable by more than one year of imprisonment.

(2) *First-Degree Murder*. A juvenile convicted of first-degree murder who violates juvenile probation by being convicted of a felony or a misdemeanor punishable by more than one year's imprisonment may only be sentenced to a term of years, not to nonparolable life.

(D) **Review**. The juvenile may appeal as of right from the imposition of a sentence of incarceration after a finding of juvenile probation violation.

Rule 6.935 Progress Review of Court-Committed Juveniles

(A) **General**. When a juvenile is placed on probation and committed to a state institution or agency, the court retains jurisdiction over the juvenile while the juvenile is on probation and committed to that state institution or agency. The court shall review the progress of a juvenile it has placed on juvenile probation and committed to state wardship.

(B) **Time**.

(1) *Semiannual Progress Reviews*. The court must conduct a progress review no later than 182 days after the entry of the order placing the juvenile on juvenile probation and committing the juvenile to state wardship. A review shall be made semiannually thereafter as long as the juvenile remains in state wardship.

(2) *Annual Review*. The court shall conduct an annual review of the services being provided to the juvenile, the juvenile's placement, and the juvenile's progress in that placement.

(C) **Progress Review Report**. In conducting these reviews, the court shall examine the progress review report prepared by the Family Independence Agency, covering placement and services being provided the juvenile and the progress of the juvenile, and the court shall also examine the juvenile's annual report prepared under MCL 803.223 (§ 3 of the Juvenile Facilities Act). The court may order changes in the juvenile's placement or treatment plan including, but not limited to, committing the juvenile to the jurisdiction of the Department of Corrections, on the basis of the review.

(D) **Hearings for Progress and Annual Reviews**. Unless the court orders a more restrictive placement or treatment plan, there shall be no requirement that the court hold a hearing when conducting a progress review for a court-committed juvenile pursuant to MCR 6.935(B). However, the court may not order a more physically restrictive change in the level of placement of the juvenile or order more restrictive treatment absent a hearing as provided in MCR 6.937.

Rule 6.937 Commitment Review Hearing

(A) **Required Hearing Before Age 19 for Court-Committed Juveniles**. The court shall schedule and hold, unless adjourned for good cause, a commitment review hearing as nearly as possible to, but before, the juvenile's 19th birthday.

(1) *Notice*. The Family Independence Agency or agency, facility, or institution to which the juvenile is committed, shall advise the court at least 91 days before the juvenile attains age 19 of the need to schedule a commitment review hearing. Notice of the hearing must be given to the prosecuting attorney, the agency or the superintendent of the facility to which the juvenile has been committed, the juvenile, and the parent of the juvenile if the parent's address or whereabouts are known, at least 14 days before the hearing. Notice must clearly indicate that the court may extend jurisdiction over the juvenile until the age of 21. The notice shall include advice to the juvenile and the parent of the juvenile that the juvenile has the right to an attorney.

(2) *Appointment of an Attorney*. The court must appoint an attorney to represent the juvenile at the hearing unless an attorney has been retained or is waived pursuant to MCR 6.905(C).

(3) *Reports*. The state institution or agency charged with the care of the juvenile must prepare a commitment report as required by MCL 769.1b(4) and 803.225(1). The commitment report must contain all of the following, as required by MCL 803.225(1)(a)-(d):

(a) the services and programs currently being utilized by, or offered to, the juvenile and the juvenile's participation in those services and programs;

(b) where the juvenile currently resides and the juvenile's behavior in the current placement;

(c) the juvenile's efforts toward rehabilitation; and

(d) recommendations for the juvenile's release or continued custody.

The report created pursuant to MCL 803.223 for the purpose of annual reviews may be combined with a commitment review report.

(4) *Findings; Criteria*. Before the court continues the jurisdiction over the juvenile until the age of 21, the prosecutor must demonstrate by a preponderance of the evidence that the juvenile has not been rehabilitated or that the juvenile presents a serious risk to public safety. The rules of evidence do not apply. In making the determination, the court must consider the following factors:

(a) the extent and nature of the juvenile's participation in education, counseling, or work programs;

(b) the juvenile's willingness to accept responsibility for prior behavior;

(c) the juvenile's behavior in the current placement;

(d) the prior record and character of the juvenile and physical and mental maturity;

(e) the juvenile's potential for violent conduct as demonstrated by prior behavior;

(f) the recommendations of the state institution or agency charged with the juvenile's care for the juvenile's release or continued custody; and

(g) other information the prosecuting attorney or the juvenile may submit.

(B) **Other Commitment Review Hearings**. The court, on motion of the institution, agency, or facility to which the juvenile is committed, may release a juvenile at any time upon a showing by a preponderance of evidence that the juvenile has been rehabilitated and is not a risk to public safety. The notice provision in subrule (A), other than the requirement that the court clearly indicate that it may extend jurisdiction over the juvenile until the age of 21, and the criteria in subrule (A) shall apply. The rules of evidence shall not apply. The court must appoint an attorney to represent the juvenile at the hearing unless an attorney has been retained or the right to counsel waived. The court, upon notice and opportunity to be heard as provided in this rule, may also move the juvenile to a more restrictive placement or treatment program.

Rule 6.938 Final Review Hearings

(A) **General**. The court must conduct a final review of the juvenile's probation and commitment not less than 3 months before the end of the period that the juvenile is on probation and committed to the state institution or agency. If the court determines at this review that the best interests of the public would be served by imposing any other sentence provided by law for an adult offender, the court may impose that sentence.

(B) **Notice Requirements**. Not less than 14 days before a final review hearing is to be conducted, the prosecuting attorney, juvenile, and, if addresses are known, the juvenile's parents or guardian must be notified. The notice must state that the court may impose a sentence upon the juvenile and must advise the juvenile and the juvenile's parent or guardian of the right to legal counsel.

(C) **Appointment of Counsel**. If an attorney has not been retained or appointed to represent the juvenile, the court must appoint an attorney and may assess the cost of providing an attorney as costs against the juvenile or those responsible for the juvenile's support, or both, if the persons to be assessed are financially able to comply.

(D) **Criteria**. In determining whether the best interests of the public would be served by imposing sentence, the court shall consider the following:

(1) the extent and nature of the juvenile's participation in education, counseling, or work programs;

(2) the juvenile's willingness to accept responsibility for prior behavior;

(3) the juvenile's behavior in the current placement;

(4) the prior record and character of the juvenile and the juvenile's physical and mental maturity;

(5) the juvenile's potential for violent conduct as demonstrated by prior behavior;

(6) the recommendations of the state institution or agency charged with the juvenile's care for the juvenile's release or continued custody;

(7) the effect of treatment on the juvenile's rehabilitation;

(8) whether the juvenile is likely to be dangerous to the public if released;

(9) the best interests of the public welfare and the protection of public security; and

(10) other information the prosecuting attorney or juvenile may submit.

(E) **Credit for Time Served on Probation**. If a sentence is imposed, the juvenile must receive credit for the period of time served on probation and committed to a state agency or institution.

CHAPTER 7. APPELLATE RULES

Subchapter 7.100 Appeals to Circuit Court

Rule 7.101 Scope of Rules

(A) **Scope of Rules**. The rules in this subchapter govern appeals to the circuit court.
(B) **Rules Do Not Affect Jurisdiction**. These rules do not restrict or enlarge the appellate jurisdiction of the circuit court.

Rule 7.102 Definitions

For purposes of this subchapter:
(1) "agency" means any governmental entity other than a "trial court," the decisions of which are subject to appellate review in the circuit court;
(2) "appeal" means judicial review by the circuit court of a judgment, order, or decision of a "trial court" or "agency," even if the statute or constitutional provision authorizing circuit court appellate review uses a term other than "appeal." "Appeal" does not include actions commenced under the Freedom of Information Act, MCL 15.231 et seq., proceedings described in MCR 3.302 through MCR 3.306, and motions filed under MCR 6.110(H);
(3) "appeal fee" means the fee required to be paid to the circuit court upon filing an appeal and any fee required to be paid to the "trial court" or "agency" in conjunction with the appeal;
(4) "clerk" means clerk of the court;
(5) "court" means the circuit court;
(6) "date of filing" means the date of receipt of a document by the "clerk";
(7) "entry" is as defined in MCR 7.204(A);
(8) "final judgment" or "final order" is as defined in MCR 7.202(6); and
(9) "trial court" means the district, probate, or municipal court from which the "appeal" is taken.

Rule 7.103 Appellate Jurisdiction of the Circuit Court

(A) **Appeal of Right**. The circuit court has jurisdiction of an appeal of right filed by an aggrieved party from the following:
(1) a final judgment or final order of a district or municipal court, except a judgment based on a plea of guilty or nolo contendere;
(2) a final order of a probate court under MCR 5.801(C);
(3) a final order or decision of an agency governed by the Administrative Procedures Act, MCL 24.201 et seq.; and
(4) a final order or decision of an agency from which an appeal of right to the circuit court is provided by law.
(B) **Appeal by Leave**. The circuit court may grant leave to appeal from:
(1) a judgment or order of a trial court when
(a) no appeal of right exists, or
(b) an appeal of right could have been taken but was not timely filed;
(2) a final order or decision of an agency from which an appeal by leave to the circuit court is provided by law;
(3) an interlocutory order or decision of an agency if an appeal of right would have been available for a final order or decision and if waiting to appeal of right would not be an adequate remedy;
(4) a final order or decision of an agency if an appeal of right was not timely filed and a statute authorizes a late appeal; and
(5) a decision of the Michigan Parole Board to grant parole.

Rule 7.104 Filing Appeal of Right

(A) **Time Requirements**. The time limit for an appeal of right is jurisdictional. See MCR 7.103(A). Time is computed as provided in MCR 1.108. An appeal of right to the circuit court must be taken within:
(1) 21 days or the time allowed by statute after entry of the judgment, order, or decision appealed, or
(2) 21 days after the entry of an order denying a motion for new trial, a motion for rehearing or reconsideration, or a motion for other relief from the judgment, order, or decision, if the motion was filed within:
(a) the initial 21-day period, or
(b) further time the trial court or agency may have allowed during that 21-day period.
(3) If a criminal defendant requests appointment of an attorney within 21 days after entry of the judgment of sentence, an appeal of right must be taken within 21 days after entry of an order:
(a) appointing or denying the appointment of an attorney, or
(b) denying a timely filed motion described in subrule (2).
(B) **Manner of Filing**. To vest the circuit court with jurisdiction in an appeal of right, an appellant must file with the clerk of the circuit court within the time for taking an appeal:
(1) the claim of appeal, and
(2) the circuit court's appeal fee, unless the appellant is indigent.
(C) **Claim of Appeal**.
(1) *Form*.
(a) The caption of a claim of appeal shall comply with MCR 2.113(C)(1).

(b) In an appeal from a trial court, the claim of appeal should name the parties in the same order as they appear in the trial court, with the added designation "appellant" or "appellee."

(2) *Content*. The claim should state:

"[name of appellant(s)] claim[s] an appeal from the [judgment or order] entered on [date] in the [name of trial court] by [name of judge]."

(3) *Signature*. The appellant or the appellant's attorney must date and sign the claim of appeal.

(D) **Other Documents**. The appellant shall file the following documents with the claim of appeal:

(1) a copy of the judgment, order, or decision appealed;

(2) a copy of the certificate of the court reporter or recorder or a statement that the transcript has been ordered, pursuant to MCR 7.109(B)(3)(a). If there is nothing to be transcribed, the appellant must file a statement so indicating;

(3) in an agency appeal, a copy of a written request or order for a certified copy of the record to be sent to the circuit court;

(4) if the appellant has filed a bond, a true copy of the bond;

(5) proof that money, property, or documents have been delivered or deposited as required by law;

(6) a copy of the register of actions, if any;

(7) proof that the appeal fee of the trial court or agency has been tendered;

(8) anything else required by law to be filed; and

(9) proof that a copy of the claim of appeal and other documents required by this subrule were served on all parties, the trial court or agency, and any other person or officer entitled by law to notice of the appeal.

(E) **Service Requirements in Trial Court or Agency**. Within the time for taking the appeal, the appellant shall serve on the trial court or agency from which the appeal is taken:

(1) a copy of the claim of appeal;

(2) any fee required by law;

(3) any bond required by law as a condition for taking the appeal;

(4) in an agency appeal, a copy of a written request for a certified copy of the record to be sent to the circuit court; and

(5) unless there is nothing to be transcribed, the certificate of the court reporter or recorder or a statement that the transcript has been ordered and payment for it made or secured. If a statement is filed, the certificate of the court reporter or recorder must be filed within 7 days after a transcript is ordered by a party or the court.

(F) **Appearance**. Within 14 days after being served with the claim of appeal, the appellee shall file an appearance in the circuit court identifying the individual appellate attorneys. An appellee who does not file an appearance is not entitled to notice of further proceedings.

Rule 7.105 Application for Leave to Appeal

(A) **Time Requirements**. An application for leave to appeal must be filed with the clerk of the circuit court within:

(1) 21 days or the time allowed by statute after entry of the judgment, order, or decision appealed, or

(2) 21 days after the entry of an order denying a motion for new trial, a motion for rehearing or reconsideration, or a motion for other relief from the judgment, order, or decision if the motion was filed within:

(a) the initial 21-day period, or

(b) such further time as the trial court or agency may have allowed during that 21-day period.

(3) If a criminal defendant, who has pled guilty or nolo contendere, requests appointment of an attorney within 21 days after entry of the judgment of sentence, an application must be filed within 21 days after entry of an order:

(a) appointing or denying the appointment of an attorney, or

(b) denying a timely filed motion described in subrule (2).

(B) **Manner of Filing**. To apply for leave to appeal, the appellant must file:

(1) a signed application for leave to appeal:

(a) stating the date and nature of the judgment, order, or decision appealed;

(b) concisely reciting the appellant's allegations of error and the relief sought;

(c) setting forth a concise argument in support of the appellant's position on each issue that conforms with MCR 7.212(C); and

(d) if the order appealed is interlocutory, setting forth facts showing how the appellant would suffer substantial harm by awaiting final judgment before taking an appeal;

(2) a copy of the judgment, order, or decision appealed and the opinion or findings of the trial court or agency;

(3) if the appeal is from a trial court, a copy of the register of actions;

(4) if the appeal is from an agency, a copy of the written request or order for a certified copy of the record to be sent to the circuit court;

(5) unless waived by stipulation of the parties or trial court order, a copy of certain transcripts as follows:

(a) in an appeal relating to an evidentiary hearing in a civil or criminal case, the transcript of the evidentiary hearing, including the opinion or findings of the court that conducted the hearing;

(b) in an appeal challenging jury instructions, the transcript of the entire charge to the jury;

(c) in an appeal from a judgment in a criminal case entered pursuant to a plea of guilty or nolo contendere, the transcripts of the plea and sentence;
(d) in an appeal from an order granting or denying a new trial, the portion of the transcript permitting the circuit court to determine whether the trial court's decision on the motion was for a legally recognized reason based on arguable support in the record;
(e) in an appeal raising a sentencing issue, the transcript of the sentencing proceeding and the transcript of any hearing on a motion related to sentencing;
(f) in an appeal raising any other issue, the portion of the transcript substantiating the existence of the issue, objections or lack thereof, arguments of counsel, and any comment or ruling of the trial judge; or
(g) if the transcript is not yet available, the appellant must file a copy of the certificate of the court reporter or recorder or a statement that a transcript has been ordered, in which case the certificate of the court reporter or recorder must be filed within 7 days after a transcript is ordered by a party or the court. If there is nothing to be transcribed, the appellant must file a statement so indicating within 7 days after the transcript is ordered;

(6) proof that a copy of the application was served on all other parties and that a notice of the filing of the application was filed with the trial court or agency. If service cannot be reasonably accomplished, the appellant may ask the circuit court to prescribe service under MCR 2.107(E); and
(7) the circuit court's appeal fee, unless the appellant is indigent.

(C) **Answer**. Any other party in the case may file, within 21 days of service of the application:
(1) a signed answer to the application conforming to MCR 7.212(D), and
(2) proof that a copy was served on all other parties.

(D) **Reply**. Within 7 days after service of the answer, the appellant may file a reply brief that conforms to MCR 7.212.

(E) **Decision**.
(1) There is no oral argument unless directed by the court.
(2) Absent good cause, the court shall decide the application within 35 days of the filing date.
(3) The court may grant or deny leave to appeal or grant other relief. The court shall promptly serve a copy of the order on the parties and the trial court or agency.
(4) If an application is granted, MCR 7.104 governs further proceedings, except that:
(a) the filing of a claim of appeal is not required,
(b) the appellant must complete the acts required by MCR 7.104(D) and (E) within 7 days after the entry of the order granting leave to appeal, and
(c) an appellee may file a claim of cross appeal within 14 days after service of the order granting leave to appeal.
(5) Unless otherwise ordered, the appeal is limited to the issues raised in the application.

(F) **Immediate Consideration**. When an appellant requires a decision on an application in fewer than 35 days, the appellant must file a motion for immediate consideration concisely stating why an immediate decision is required.

(G) **Late Appeal**.
(1) When an appeal of right or an application for leave was not timely filed, the appellant may file an application as prescribed under subrule (B) accompanied by a statement of facts explaining the delay. The answer may challenge the claimed reasons for the delay. The circuit court may consider the length of and the reasons for the delay in deciding whether to grant the application.
(2) A late application may not be filed more than 6 months after entry of:
(a) the order, judgment, or decision appealed;
(b) an order denying a motion for a new trial, a motion for rehearing or reconsideration, or a motion for other relief from the judgment, order, or decision, if the motion was timely filed; or
(c) an order denying a motion for new trial under MCR 6.610(G) or a motion to withdraw a plea under MCR 6.610(E)(8).

Rule 7.106 Cross Appeals

(A) **Right of Cross Appeal**.
(1) Any appellee may file a cross appeal when:
(a) an appeal of right is filed, or
(b) the circuit court grants leave to appeal.
(2) If there is more than one plaintiff or defendant in a civil action and one party appeals, any other party may file a cross appeal against all or any of the other parties as well as against the party who first appealed. If the cross appeal operates against a party not affected by the first appeal or in a manner different from the first appeal, that party may file a further cross appeal.

(B) **Time Requirements**. A cross appeal must be filed with the clerk of the circuit court within 14 days after the claim of appeal is served on the cross appellant or the order granting leave to appeal is entered.

(C) **Manner of Filing**. To file a cross appeal, the cross appellant must file:

(1) a claim of cross appeal in the form required by MCR 7.104(C);
(2) any required fee;
(3) a copy of the judgment, order, or decision from which the cross appeal is taken; and
(4) proof that a copy of the claim of cross appeal was served on all parties.

(D) **Additional Requirements**. The cross appellant must perform the steps required by MCR 7.104(D) and (E) unless compliance with this subrule would duplicate the appellant's filing of the same document. The cross appellant is not required to order a transcript or file a court reporter's certificate, unless the initial appeal is dismissed.

(E) **Dismissed Appeal**. If the initial appeal is dismissed, the cross appeal may continue. If there is a transcript to be produced and the certificate of the court reporter or recorder has not been filed, the cross appellant must file the certificate within 14 days after the order dismissing the appeal. If there is nothing to be transcribed, the cross appellant must file a statement so indicating within 14 days after the order dismissing the appeal.

(F) **Delayed Cross Appeal**. A party seeking leave to take a delayed cross appeal must proceed under MCR 7.105(F).

Rule 7.107 Authority of Trial Court or Agency

After a claim of appeal is filed or leave to appeal is granted, jurisdiction vests in the circuit court. The trial court or agency may not set aside or amend the judgment, order, or decision appealed except by circuit court order or as otherwise provided by law. In all other respects, the authority of the trial court or agency is governed by MCR 7.208(C) through (I).

Rule 7.108 Stay of Proceedings; Bond; Review

(A) **General Provisions**.

(1) A motion for bond or a stay pending appeal may not be filed in the circuit court unless such a motion was decided by the trial court. The motion must include a copy of the trial court's opinion and order and a copy of the transcript of the hearing, unless its production has been waived.

(2) Except as otherwise provided by rule or law, the circuit court may amend the amount of bond, order an additional or different bond and set the amount, or require different or additional sureties. The circuit court may also remand a bond matter to the trial court. The circuit court may grant a stay of proceedings in the trial court or stay the effect or enforcement of any judgment or order of a trial court on terms the circuit court deems just.

(B) **Civil Actions**.

(1) *Automatic Stay*. Unless otherwise provided by rule, statute, or court order, an execution may not issue and proceedings may not be taken to enforce an order or judgment until expiration of the time for taking an appeal of right.

(2) *Effect of Appeal*. An appeal does not stay execution unless:

(a) the appellant files a bond in an amount not less than 1-1/4 times the amount of the judgment or order being enforced, including any costs, interest, attorney fees, and sanctions assessed to date of filing the bond. When the bond is filed, the judgment or order shall automatically be stayed pending entry of a final order under MCR 7.108(B)(4)(c) to stay enforcement of the judgment even though objections to the bond or surety may be filed, or

(b) the trial court grants a stay with or without bond under MCR 3.604(L), MCR 7.209(E)(1), or MCL 600.2605. The stay order must conform to any condition expressly required by the statute authorizing review.

(3) *Bond Form and Content*. The bond must:

(a) recite the names and designations of the parties and the judge in the trial court; identify the parties for whom and against whom judgment was entered; and state the amount of the judgment, including any costs, interest, attorney fees, and sanctions assessed;

(b) contain the promises and conditions that the appellant will:

(i) diligently file and prosecute the appeal to decision taken from the judgment or order stayed, and will perform and satisfy the judgment or order stayed if it is not set aside or reversed;

(ii) perform or satisfy the judgment or order stayed if the appeal is dismissed;

(iii) pay and satisfy any judgment or order entered and any costs assessed against the principal on the bond in the circuit court, Court of Appeals, or Supreme Court; and

(iv) do any other act which is expressly required in the statute authorizing appeal or ordered by the court;

(c) be executed by the appellant along with one or more sufficient sureties as required by MCR 3.604; and

(d) include the conditions provided in MCR 4.201(N)(4) if the appeal is from a judgment for the possession of land.

(4) *Notice of Bond; Objections; Stay Orders*.

(a) A copy of a bond and any accompanying power of attorney or affidavit must be promptly served on all parties in the manner prescribed in MCR 2.107. At the same time, the party seeking the stay shall file a proposed stay order pursuant to MCR 2.602(B)(3). Proof of service must be filed promptly with the trial court in which the bond has been filed.

(b) Objections shall be filed and served within 7 days after service of the notice of bond. Objections to the amount of the bond are governed by MCR 2.602(B)(3). Objections to the surety are governed by MCR 3.604(E).

(c) If no timely objections to the bond, surety, or stay order are filed, the trial court shall promptly enter the order staying enforcement of the judgment or order pending all appeals. Unless otherwise ordered, the stay shall continue until jurisdiction is again vested in the trial court or until further order of an appellate court.

(d) Any stay order must be promptly served on all parties in the manner prescribed in MCR 2.107. Proof of service must be filed promptly with the trial court.

(e) All hearings under this rule may be held by telephone conference as provided in MCR 2.402.

(5) For good cause shown, the trial court may set the amount of the bond in a greater or lesser amount adequate to protect the interests of the parties.

(6) A bond may be secured under MCL 600.2631.

(7) If an execution has issued, it is suspended by giving notice of filing of the bond to the officer holding the execution.

(C) **Criminal Cases**.

(1) *Immediate Effect*. A criminal judgment may be executed immediately even though the time for taking an appeal has not elapsed. The granting of bond and its amount are within the discretion of the trial court, subject to the applicable laws and rules on bonds pending appeals in criminal cases.

(2) *Bond Form and Content*. If a bond is granted, the defendant must promise in writing:

(a) to prosecute the appeal to decision;

(b) if the sentence is one of incarceration, to surrender immediately to the county sheriff or as otherwise directed, if the judgment of sentence is affirmed on appeal or if the appeal is dismissed;

(c) if the sentence is other than one of incarceration, to perform and comply with the judgment of sentence if it is affirmed on appeal or if the appeal is dismissed;

(d) to appear in the trial court if the case is remanded for retrial or further proceedings or if a conviction is reversed and retrial is allowed;

(e) to remain in Michigan unless the court gives written approval to leave;

(f) to notify the trial court clerk in writing of a change of address; and

(g) to comply with any other conditions imposed by law or the court.

(3) *Notice of Bond; Objections*. A criminal defendant filing a bond after conviction shall give notice to the prosecuting attorney of the time and place the bond will be filed. The bond is subject to the objection procedure provided in MCR 3.604.

(D) **Civil Infractions**. An appeal bond and stay in a civil infraction proceeding is governed by MCR 4.101(H)(1).

(E) **Probate Actions**.

(1) The probate court has continuing jurisdiction to decide other matters pertaining to the proceeding from which an appeal was filed.

(2) A stay in an appeal from the probate court is governed by MCL 600.867 and MCR 5.802(C).

Rule 7.109 Record on Appeal

(A) **Content of Record**. Appeals to the circuit court are heard on the original record.

(1) *Appeal From Trial Court*. The record is as defined in MCR 7.210(A)(1).

(2) *Appeal From Agency*. The record is as defined in MCR 7.210(A)(2).

(3) *Excluded Evidence*. The record on appeal must include the substance of the excluded evidence or the transcript of proceedings in the trial court or agency excluding it. Excluded exhibits must be maintained by the party offering them.

(4) *Stipulations*. The parties may stipulate in writing regarding any matters relevant to the trial court or agency record if the stipulation is made a part of the record on appeal and sent to the circuit court.

(B) **Transcript**.

(1) *Appellant's Duties; Orders; Stipulations*.

(a) The appellant is responsible for securing the filing of the transcript as provided in this rule. Unless otherwise provided by circuit court order or this subrule, the appellant shall order the full transcript of testimony and other proceedings in the trial court or agency. Under MCR 7.104(D)(2), a party must serve a copy of any request for transcript preparation on the opposing party and file a copy with the circuit court.

(b) In an appeal from probate court, only that portion of the transcript concerning the order appealed need be filed. The appellee may file additional portions of the transcript.

(c) On the appellant's motion, with notice to the appellee, the trial court or agency may order that no transcript or some portion less than the full transcript be included in the record on appeal. The motion must be filed within the time required for filing an appeal, and, if the motion is granted, the appellee may file any portions of the transcript omitted by the appellant.

(d) The parties may stipulate that no transcript or some portion less than the full transcript be filed.

(e) The parties may agree on a statement of facts without procuring the transcript and the statement signed by the parties may be filed with the trial court or agency and sent as the record of testimony in the action.

(2) *Transcript Unavailable*. When a transcript of the proceedings in the trial court or agency cannot be obtained, the appellant shall file a settled statement of facts using the procedure in MCR 7.210(B)(2) unless a statute provides otherwise.

(3) *Duties of Court Reporter or Recorder*.

(a) Certificate. Within 7 days after a transcript is ordered by a party or the court, the court reporter or recorder shall furnish a certificate stating that the transcript has been ordered and payment for it made or secured and that it will be filed as soon as possible or has already been filed.

(b) Time for Filing.

(i) The court reporter or recorder shall file the transcript in the trial court or agency within:

[A] 14 days after a transcript is ordered by a party or the court for an application for leave to appeal from an order granting or denying a motion to suppress evidence in a criminal case;

[B] 28 days after a transcript is ordered by a party or the court in an appeal of a criminal conviction based on a plea of guilty, guilty but mentally ill, or nolo contendere or an appeal from the dismissal or reduction of a felony charge following a preliminary examination; or

[C] 56 days after a transcript is ordered by a party or the court in all other cases.

(ii) The circuit court may extend or shorten these time limits in an appeal pending in the court on motion filed by the court reporter or recorder or a party.

(c) Copies. Additional copies of the transcripts required by the appellant may be ordered from the court reporter or recorder. Photocopies of the transcript furnished by the court reporter or recorder may also be made.

(d) Form of Transcript. The transcript must be prepared in the form provided by MCR 7.210(B)(3)(d).

(e) Notice. Immediately after the transcript is filed, the court reporter or recorder shall notify the circuit court and all parties that it has been filed and file in the circuit court an affidavit of mailing of notice to the parties.

(f) Discipline. A court reporter or recorder failing to comply with the requirements of these rules is subject to disciplinary action, including punishment for contempt of court.

(g) Responsibility When More Than One Reporter or Recorder. In a case in which portions of the transcript must be prepared by more than one reporter or recorder, the person who recorded the beginning of the proceeding is responsible for ascertaining that the entire transcript has been prepared, filing it, and giving the notice required by subrule (B)(3)(e), unless the court has designated another person.

(C) **Exhibits**. Unless otherwise ordered by the circuit court, trial court, or agency, the offering parties shall maintain exhibits in their possession.

(D) **Reproduction of Records**. The trial court or agency shall procure copies of file contents as provided in MCR 7.210(D).

(E) **Record on Motion**. If, before the complete record on appeal is sent to the circuit court, a party files a motion that requires the circuit court to have the record, the trial court or agency shall, on request of a party or the circuit court, send the circuit court the documents needed.

(F) **Service of the Record**. Within 14 days after the transcript is filed with the trial court or agency, the appellant shall serve a copy of the entire record on appeal, including the transcripts and exhibits in his or her possession, on each appellee. However, copies of documents the appellee already possesses need not be served. On request, the appellant shall make available to the appellee exhibits incapable of being copied. Proof that the record was served must be promptly filed with the circuit court and the trial court or agency. If the filing of a transcript has been excused as provided in subrule (B), the record shall be served within 14 days after the filing of the transcript substitute.

(G) **Transmission of Record**.

(1) Within 14 days after the complete transcript has been filed or a certified copy of the record has been requested, the trial court or agency shall promptly send the record to the circuit court, except for those things omitted by written stipulation of the parties. The trial court may order removal of exhibits, if any, from the record. Weapons, drugs, or money are not to be sent unless requested by the circuit court. The trial court or agency shall append a certificate identifying the name of the case, listing the papers with reasonable definiteness, and indicating that the required fees have been paid and any required bond filed. The record transmitted shall include:

(a) a register of actions in the case;

(b) any exhibits on file;
(c) all documents and papers from the court file;
(d) all transcripts;
(e) all opinions, findings, and orders of the trial court or agency; and
(f) the order or judgment appealed.

(2) Transcripts and all other documents which are part of the record on appeal must be attached in one or more file folders or other suitable hard-surfaced binders showing the name of the trial court or agency, the title of the case, and the file number.

(3) The circuit court must immediately send written notice to the parties when the record is filed in the circuit court.

(H) **Return of Record**. After deciding the appeal, the circuit court shall promptly send the original record with a certified copy of its order and any written opinion

(1) to the clerk of the Court of Appeals if a timely application for leave to appeal is filed in the Court of Appeals, or

(2) to the clerk of the trial court or agency from which the record was received if no timely application for leave to appeal is filed in the Court of Appeals.

(I) **Notice of Return of Record**. The trial court or agency clerk shall promptly notify all parties of the return of the record.

Rule 7.110 Motions in Circuit Court Appeals

Motion practice in a circuit court appeal is governed by MCR 2.119. Motions may include special motions identified in MCR 7.211(C). Absent good cause, the court shall decide motions within 28 days after the hearing date.

Rule 7.111 Briefs

(A) **Time for Filing and Service.**

(1) *Appellant's Brief.*

(a) Within 28 days after the circuit court provides written notice under MCR 7.109(G)(3) that the record on appeal is filed with the circuit court, the appellant must file a brief conforming to MCR 7.212(C) and serve it on all other parties to the appeal. The time may be extended for 14 days by stipulation and order. The circuit court may extend the time on motion. The filing of a motion does not stay the time for filing a brief.

(b) If an appellant does not file a brief within the time provided by subrule (A)(1)(a), the appeal may be considered abandoned, and the circuit court may dismiss the appeal on 14 days' notice to the parties. Compliance with subrule (A)(1)(a) after notice is sent does not preclude a dismissal of the appeal unless the appellant shows a reasonable excuse for the late filing.

(2) *Appellee's Brief.* Within 21 days after the appellant's brief is served on the appellee, the appellee may file a brief. The brief must conform to MCR 7.212(D) and must be served on all other parties to the appeal. The time may be extended for 14 days by stipulation and order. The circuit court may extend the time on motion. The filing of the motion does not stay the time for filing a brief.

(3) Within 14 days after the appellee's brief is served on appellant, the appellant may file a reply brief. The brief must conform to MCR 7.212(G) and must be served on all other parties to the appeal

(4) *Briefs in Cross Appeals.* The filing and service of briefs by a cross appellant and a cross appellee are governed by subrules (A)(1)-(3).

(5) Earlier Filing and Service. For good cause shown, the circuit court may grant a motion to shorten the time for filing and serving briefs.

(6) Late Filing. Any party failing to timely file and serve a brief under these rules forfeits oral argument. For good cause shown, the court may grant a motion to reinstate oral argument.

(B) **Length and Form of Briefs**. The appellant's brief must comply with MCR 7.212(B) and (C), and the appellee's brief must comply with MCR 7.212(B) and (D).

(C) **Request for Oral Argument**. A party filing a timely brief is entitled to oral argument by writing "ORAL ARGUMENT REQUESTED" in capital letters or boldface type on the title page of the brief.

(D) **Nonconforming Briefs**. If, on its own initiative or on a party's motion, the circuit court concludes that a brief does not substantially comply with the requirements in this rule, it may order the party filing the brief to correct the deficiencies within a specified time or it may strike the nonconforming brief.

Rule 7.112 Miscellaneous Relief

In addition to its general appellate powers, the circuit court may grant relief as provided in MCR 7.216.

Rule 7.113 Dismissal

(A) **Involuntary Dismissal**.

(1) *Dismissal.* If the appellant fails to pursue the appeal in conformity with the court rules, the circuit court will notify the parties that the appeal shall be dismissed unless the deficiency is remedied within 14 days after service of the notice.

(2) *Reinstatement.* Within 14 days after the date of the dismissal order, the appellant may move for reinstatement by showing mistake, inadvertence, or excusable neglect.

(B) **Voluntary Dismissal**. In all cases where the parties file a signed stipulation agreeing to dismiss the appeal or the appellant files an unopposed motion to withdraw the appeal, the circuit court shall enter an order of dismissal.

(C) **Notice of Dismissal**. Immediately upon entry, a copy of an order dismissing an appeal must be sent to the parties and the trial court or agency.

Rule 7.114 Oral Argument; Decision and Effect of Judgment, Reconsideration

(A) **Oral Argument**. If requested in accord with MCR 7.111(C), the court shall schedule oral argument unless it concludes that the briefs and record adequately present the facts and legal arguments, and the court's deliberation would not be significantly aided by oral argument.

(B) **Decision**. The circuit court shall decide the appeal by oral or written opinion and issue an order. The court's order is its judgment.

(C) **Effect of Judgment**. Unless otherwise ordered by the circuit court or the Court of Appeals, a judgment is effective after expiration of the period for filing a timely application for leave to appeal or, if such an application is filed, after the Court of Appeals decides the case. Enforcement is to be obtained in the trial court or agency after the record is returned as provided in MCR 7.109(H).

(D) **Reconsideration**. A motion for reconsideration is governed by MCR 2.119(F).

Rule 7.115 Taxation of Costs, Fees.

(A) **Right to Costs**. Except as the circuit court otherwise directs, the prevailing party in a civil case is entitled to costs.

(B) **Time for Filing**. Within 28 days after the dispositive order, opinion, or order denying rehearing is mailed, the prevailing party may file a certified or verified bill of costs with the clerk and serve a copy on all other parties. Each item claimed in the bill must be specified. Failure to file a bill of costs within the time prescribed waives the right to costs.

(C) **Objections**. Any other party may file objections to the bill of costs with the clerk within 7 days after a copy of the bill is served. The objecting party must serve a copy of the objections on the prevailing party and file proof of that service.

(D) **Taxation**. The clerk will promptly verify the bill and tax those costs available.

(E) **Review**. The action by the clerk will be reviewed by the circuit court on motion of either party filed within 7 days from the date of taxation, but on review only those affidavits or objections that were previously filed with the clerk may be considered by the court.

(F) **Taxable Costs and Fees**. A prevailing party may tax only the reasonable costs and fees incurred in the appeal, including:

(1) printing of briefs, or if briefs were typewritten, a charge of $1 per original page;
(2) obtaining any stay bond;
(3) the transcript and necessary copies of it;
(4) documents required for the record on appeal;
(5) fees paid to the clerk or to the trial court clerk incident to the appeal;
(6) taxable costs and fees allowed by law in appeals under MCL 600.2441;
(7) the additional costs incurred when a party to an appeal under the Administrative Procedures Act unreasonably refused to stipulate to shortening the record as provided in MCL 24.304(2); and
(8) other expenses taxable under applicable court rules or statutes.

Rule 7.116 Appeals Under the Michigan Employment Security Act

(A) **Scope**. This rule governs appeals to the circuit court under the Michigan Employment Security Act, MCL 421.1 et seq. Unless this rule provides otherwise, MCR 7.101 through 7.115 apply.

(B) **Time Requirements**. An appeal of right from an order or decision of the Michigan Compensation Appellate Commission must be taken within 30 days after the mailing of the commission's decision.

(C) **Manner of Filing**. Except as provided in subrule (B), the claim of appeal shall conform with MCR 7.104 and must include statements of jurisdiction and venue. In addition, proof that the claim of appeal was served on the Michigan Compensation Appellate Commission and all interested parties must be filed in the circuit court. The unemployment agency is a party to any appeal under MCL 421.38(3), but the Michigan Compensation Appellate Commission is not a party to the appeal.

(D) **Venue**. Venue is determined under MCL 421.38(1).

(E) **Appearance of Appellee**. Within 14 days after service of the claim of appeal, the appellee must file an appearance in the circuit court.

(F) **Record on Appeal**. Within 42 days after the claim of appeal is served on the Michigan Compensation Appellate Commission, or within further time as the circuit court allows, the Michigan Compensation Appellate Commission must transmit to the clerk of the circuit court a certified copy of the record of proceedings before the administrative law judge and the Michigan Compensation Appellate Commission. The Michigan Compensation Appellate Commission must notify the parties that the record was transmitted.

(G) **Standard of Review and Decision on Appeal**. Under MCL 421.38, the circuit court may reverse an order or decision of the Michigan Compensation Appellate Commission only if it finds that the order or decision is contrary to law or is not supported by competent, material, and substantial evidence on the whole record. In all other respects, MCR 7.114 applies.

Rule 7.117 Appeals from the Michigan Civil Service Commission

(A) **Scope**. This rule governs appeals to the circuit court from the Michigan Civil Service Commission. Unless this rule provides otherwise, MCR 7.101 through 7.115 apply.

(B) **Procedure**. An appeal from a decision of the Michigan Civil Service Commission must comply with MCR 7.119.

(C) **Commission as Party**. An appeal challenging any decision, rule, or regulation of the Michigan Civil Service Commission must name the commission as a party and must serve the commission at the Office of the State Personnel Director in Lansing, Michigan.

Rule 7.118 Appeals from the Michigan Parole Board

(A) **Scope**. This rule governs appeals to the circuit court from the Michigan Parole Board. Unless this rule provides otherwise, MCR 7.101 through 7.115 apply.

(B) **No Appeal of Right**. There is no appeal of right from a decision of the parole board.

(C) **Access to Reports and Guidelines**. Upon request, the prosecutor, the victim, and the prisoner shall receive the parole eligibility report, any prior parole eligibility reports that are mentioned in the parole board's decision, and any parole guidelines that support the action taken.

(D) **Application for Leave to Appeal**.

(1) *Parties*.

(a) Only the prosecutor or a victim may file an application for leave to appeal.

(b) The prisoner shall be the appellee.

(c) The parole board may move to intervene as an appellee.

(2) *Time Requirements*. An application for leave to appeal must be filed within 28 days after the parole board mails a notice of action granting parole and a copy of any written opinion to the prosecutor and the victim, if the victim requested notification under MCL 780.771.

(3) *Manner of Filing*. An application for leave must comply with MCR 7.105, must include statements of jurisdiction and venue, and must be served on the parole board and the prisoner. If the victim seeks leave, the prosecutor must be served. If the prosecutor seeks leave, the victim must be served if the victim requested notification under MCL 780.771.

(a) Service on the parole board, the victim, or the prosecutor must be accomplished by certified mail, return receipt requested, in compliance with MCR 2.105(A)(2).

(b) Service on a prisoner incarcerated in a state correctional facility must be accomplished by serving the application for leave on the warden or administrator, along with the form approved by the State Court Administrative Office for personal service on a prisoner. Otherwise, service must be accomplished by certified mail, return receipt requested, as described in MCR 2.103(C) and MCR 2.104(A)(2) or in compliance with MCR 2.105(A)(2). In addition to the pleadings, service on the prisoner must also include a notice in a form approved by the State Court Administrative Office advising the prisoner that:

(i) the prisoner may respond to the application for leave to appeal through retained counsel or in propria persona, although no response is required, and

(ii) if an order of parole is issued under MCL 791.236 before the completion of appellate proceedings, a stay may be granted in the manner provided by MCR 7.108, except that no bond is required.

(c) Proof of service must be promptly filed with the clerk of the circuit court and must include a copy of the return receipt and, in the case of the prisoner, a copy of the certificate of service executed by the appropriate prison official.

(4) *Venue*. An application for leave to appeal a decision of the parole board may only be filed in the circuit court of the sentencing county under MCL 791.234(11).

(E) **Late Application**. A late application for leave to appeal may be filed under MCR 7.105(F).

(F) **Stay of Order of Parole**.

(1) An order of parole issued under MCL 791.236 shall not be executed until 28 days after the mailing of the notice of action.

(2) If an order is issued under MCL 791.235 before completion of appellate proceedings, a stay may be granted in the manner provided by MCR 7.108, except that no bond is required.

(G) **Decision to Grant Leave to Appeal**.

(1) The circuit court shall make its determination within 28 days after the application for leave to appeal is filed.

(2) If the court does not make its determination within 28 days, the court shall enter an order to produce the prisoner before the court for a show cause hearing to determine whether the prisoner shall be released on parole pending disposition of the appeal.

(H) **Procedure After Leave to Appeal Granted**. If leave to appeal is granted, MCR 7.105(D)(4) applies along with the following:

(1) *Record on Appeal*.

(a) The record on appeal shall consist of the prisoner's central office file at the Department of Corrections and any other documents considered by the parole board in reaching its decision.

(b) Within 14 days after being served with an order granting leave to appeal, the parole board shall send copies of the record to the circuit court and the other parties. In all other respects, the record on appeal shall be processed in compliance with MCR 7.109.

(c) The expense of preparing and serving the record on appeal may be taxed as costs to a nonprevailing appellant, except that expenses may not be taxed to an indigent party.

(2) *Briefs*. Briefs must comply with MCR 7.111, except:

(a) the appellant's brief is due 28 days after the record is served on the parties, and

(b) the appellee's brief, if filed, is due 21 days after the appellant's brief is served on the appellee.

(3) *Burden of Proof*. The appellant has the burden of establishing that the decision of the parole board was

(a) in violation of the Michigan Constitution, a statute, an administrative rule, or a written agency regulation that is exempted from promulgation pursuant to MCL 24.207, or

(b) a clear abuse of discretion.

(4) *Remand to the Parole Board*. On motion by a party or on the court's own motion, the court may remand the matter to the parole board for an explanation of its decision.

(a) The parole board shall hear and decide the matter within 28 days of the date of the order, unless the board determines that an adjournment is necessary to obtain evidence or there is other good cause for an adjournment.

(b) The time for filing briefs on appeal under subrule (H)(2) is tolled while the matter is pending on remand.

(I) **Subsequent Appeal to the Court of Appeals**. An appeal of a circuit court decision is by emergency application for leave to appeal to the Court of Appeals under MCR 7.205(E), and the Court of Appeals shall expedite the matter.

(J) **Parole Board Responsibility After Reversal or Remand**.

(1) If a decision of the parole board is reversed or remanded, the board shall review the matter and take action consistent with the circuit court's decision within 28 days.

(2) If the circuit court order requires the board to undertake further review of the file or to reevaluate its prior decision, the board shall provide the parties with an opportunity to be heard.

(3) An appeal to the Court of Appeals does not affect the board's jurisdiction to act under this subsection.

Rule 7.119 Appeals from Agencies Governed by the Administrative Procedures Act

(A) **Scope**. This rule governs an appeal to the circuit court from an agency decision where MCL 24.201 et seq. applies. Unless this rule provides otherwise, MCR 7.101 through MCR 7.115 apply.

(B) **Appeal of Right**.

(1) *Time Requirements*. Judicial review of a final decision or order shall be by filing a claim of appeal in the circuit court within 60 days after the date of mailing of the notice of the agency's final decision or order. If a rehearing before the agency is timely requested, then the claim of appeal must be filed within 60 days after delivery or mailing of the notice of the agency's decision or order on rehearing, as provided in the statute or constitutional provision authorizing appellate review.

(2) *Manner of Filing*.

(a) Claim of Appeal - Form. The claim of appeal shall conform with the requirements of MCR 7.104(C)(1), except that:

(i) the party aggrieved by the agency decision is the appellant and is listed first in the caption; and

(ii) the party seeking to sustain the agency's decision is the appellee; or

(iii) if there is no appellee, then the caption may read "In re [name of appellant or other identification of the subject of the appeal]," followed by the designation of the appellant. Except where otherwise provided by law, the agency or another party to the case may become an appellee by filing an appearance within 21 days after service of the claim of appeal.

(b) Claim of Appeal – Content. The claim of appeal must:

(i) state "[Name of appellant] claims an appeal from the decision entered on [date] by [name of the agency]," and

(ii) include concise statements of the following:

[A] the statute, rule, or other authority enabling the agency to conduct the proceedings;

[B] the statute or constitutional provision authorizing appellate review of the agency's decision or order in the circuit court; and

[C] the facts on which venue is based under MCL 24.303(1).

(c) Signature. The claim of appeal must be signed as stated in MCR 7.104(C)(3).
(d) Other Documents. In addition to the claim of appeal, the appellant shall also comply with MCR 7.104(D).
(e) Filing Requirements in the Agency. The appellant must comply with MCR 7.104(E).
(f) Service. In addition to the service requirements found in MCR 7.104(D)(9), the appellant must also serve the Attorney General.

(3) *Appearance*. The appellee shall file an appearance that complies with MCR 7.104(F) within 14 days after service of the claim of appeal.

(C) **Application for Interlocutory Appeal**. A preliminary procedural or intermediate agency action or ruling is not immediately reviewable, except that a court may grant interlocutory appeal of a preliminary, procedural, or intermediate decision by an agency only on a showing that review of the final decision would not be an adequate remedy.

(1) Time Requirements. An application for interlocutory appeal must be filed with the court within 14 days of the decision.

(2) Manner of Filing. In addition to the requirements of MCR 7.105(B), the application must:
(a) include a jurisdictional statement citing:
(i) the statute, rule, or other authority enabling the agency to conduct proceedings, and
(ii) the statute or constitutional provision authorizing appellate review of the agency's decision or order in the circuit court;
(b) include a statement of venue with supporting facts;
(c) set forth why review of the agency's final decision will not be an adequate remedy; and
(d) state the relief sought.

(3) Answer. An appellee may file an answer to an application for interlocutory appeal under MCR 7.105(C). The circuit court may require the filing of an answer.

(4) If Application is Granted. If the application is granted, the appeal proceeds in the same manner as an appeal of right.

(D) **Late Appeal**. The appellant may file an application for late appeal if permitted by statute.

(1) *Time Requirements*. Unless inconsistent with the statute authorizing the appeal, the application must be filed within six months after entry of the agency decision or order.

(2) *Manner of Filing*. In addition to the requirements of MCR 7.105(B), the application must include:
(a) a statement citing the statute authorizing a late appeal;
(b) a statement of facts explaining the delay; and
(c) statements of jurisdiction and venue complying with subrules (C)(2)(a) and (b).

(3) *Answer*. An appellee may file an answer to the application for late appeal under MCR 7.105(C). The circuit court may require the filing of an answer.

(4) *If Application is Granted*. If the application is granted, the appeal proceeds in the same manner as an appeal of right.

(E) **Stay of Enforcement**. The filing of an appeal does not stay enforcement of the agency's decision or order.

(1) A party may file a motion seeking a stay in the circuit court.

(2) For purposes of this subrule, the agency is entitled to notice even if it has not filed an appearance in the appeal.

(3) The court may order a stay on appropriate terms and conditions if it finds that:
(a) the moving party will suffer irreparable injury if a stay is not granted;
(b) the moving party made a strong showing that it is likely to prevail on the merits;
(c) the public interest will not be harmed if a stay is granted; and
(d) the harm to the moving party in the absence of a stay outweighs the harm to the other parties to the proceedings if a stay is granted.

(4) If the motion for stay is granted, the circuit court may set appropriate terms and conditions for the posting of a bond
(a) in the amount required by any applicable statute authorizing the appeal, or
(b) in an amount and with sureties that the circuit court deems adequate to protect the public and the parties when there are no statutory instructions.

(5) *Temporary Stay*.
(a) The circuit court may grant a temporary stay of enforcement without written notice only if
(i) it clearly appears from facts alleged in the motion that immediate and irreparable injury will result if a stay is not entered before a hearing, and
(ii) the moving party certifies to the court in writing that it made reasonable efforts to contact the other parties and agency, but was unsuccessful.
(b) A temporary stay may be granted by the court until a hearing can be held. A hearing on a motion to dissolve a temporary stay will be heard on 24 hours' notice, or less on order of the court for good cause shown, and takes precedence over all matters except previously filed matters of the same character.

(F) **Stipulations**. The parties may stipulate regarding any issue on appeal or any part of the record on appeal if the stipulation is embodied in an order entered by the court.

(G) **Additional Evidence**. A motion to present proofs of alleged irregularity in procedure before the agency, or to allow the taking of additional evidence before the agency, is timely only if it is filed with or included with the claim of appeal or application. The appellant shall promptly notice the motion for decision. If the court orders the taking of additional evidence, the time for filing briefs is stayed until the taking of the evidence is completed.

(H) **Decision**. The court may affirm, reverse, remand, or modify the decision of the agency and may grant further relief as appropriate based on the record, findings, and conclusions.

(1) If the agency's decision or order is not supported by competent, material, and substantial evidence on the whole record, the court shall specifically identify the finding or findings that lack support.

(2) If the agency's decision or order violates the Constitution or a statute, is affected by a material error of law, or is affected by an unlawful procedure resulting in material prejudice to a party, the court shall specifically identify the agency's conclusions of law that are being reversed.

Rule 7.120 Licensing Appeals Under the Michigan Vehicle Code

(A) **Scope**. This rule governs appeals to the circuit court under the Michigan Vehicle Code, MCL 257.1 et seq., from a final determination by the Secretary of State pertaining to an operator's license, a chauffeur's license, a vehicle group designation, or an indorsement. Unless this rule provides otherwise, MCR 7.101 through 7.115 apply.

(B) **Appeal of Right**.

(1) *Time Requirements*. The time for filing an appeal of right is governed by MCL 257.323(1).

(2) *Manner of Filing*.

(a) Claim of Appeal – Form. The claim of appeal shall conform to the requirements of MCR 7.104(C)(1), except that the party aggrieved by the Secretary of State's determination is the appellant.

(b) Claim of Appeal – Content. The claim of appeal must:

(i) state the appellant's full name, current address, birth date, and driver's license number;

(ii) state "[name of appellant] claims an appeal from the decision on [date] by the Secretary of State"; and

(iii) include concise statements of the following:

[A] the nature of any determination by the Secretary of State;

[B] the statute authorizing the Secretary of State's determination;

[C] the subsection of MCL 257.323 under which the appeal is taken; and

[D] the facts on which venue is based.

(c) Signature. The claim of appeal must be signed as stated in MCR 7.104(C)(3).

(d) Other Documents. The appellant must attach as exhibits accompanying the claim of appeal:

(i) a copy of the Secretary of State's determination, and

(ii) any affidavits supporting the claim of appeal.

(e) Service. The appellant shall serve the claim of appeal on all parties.

(3) *Appearance*. The appellee shall file an appearance within 14 days that complies with MCR 7.104(F).

(C) **Application for Late Appeal**.

(1) *Time Requirements*. An application for late appeal must be filed within the time set forth in MCL 257.323(1).

(2) *Manner of Filing*. In addition to the requirements of MCR 7.105(B), the application must comply with MCR 7.120(B)(2)(b) and must include a statement showing good cause for the delay.

(3) *Answer*. An appellee may file an answer to the application for late appeal under MCR 7.105(C). The circuit court may require the filing of an answer.

(4) *If Application is Granted*. If the application is granted, the appeal proceeds in the same manner as an appeal of right.

(D) **Stay of Enforcement**. The filing of a claim of appeal or an application for late appeal does not stay enforcement of the Secretary of State's decision or order. The appellant may file for a stay of enforcement under MCL 257.323a. The appellant shall serve a copy of the order granting or denying the stay on the Secretary of State. The Secretary of State may file a motion challenging the stay.

(E) **Stipulations**. The parties may stipulate regarding any issue on appeal or any part of the record on appeal if the stipulation is embodied in an order entered by the court.

(F) **Proceedings Under MCL 257.323(3)**.

(1) *Briefs*. The court may require briefs and may enter an order setting a briefing schedule. Unless otherwise ordered, briefs must comply with MCR 7.111.

(2) *Hearing*. The court shall schedule a hearing under MCL 257.323(2). During the hearing, the court may take testimony and examine all the facts and circumstances relating to the denial, suspension, or restriction of the person's license under MCL 257.303(1)(d), MCL 257.320, MCL 257.904(10),

MCL 257.904(11), MCL 257.310d, or for a first violation of MCL 257.625f.

(3) *Decision*. For denials, suspensions, or restrictions of the person's license under MCL 257.303(1)(d), MCL 257.320, MCL 257.904(10), MCL 257.904(11), MCL 257.310d, or for a first violation of MCL 257.625f, the circuit court may affirm, modify, or set aside the restriction, suspension, or denial. The circuit court, however, shall not order the Secretary of State to issue a restricted or unrestricted chauffeur's license that would permit the person to drive a commercial motor vehicle that hauls hazardous materials.

(4) *Appellant's Responsibility After Decision*. Pursuant to MCL 257.323(3), the appellant shall file a certified copy of the circuit court's order with the Secretary of State's office in Lansing within 7 days after entry of the order for denials, suspensions, or restrictions of the person's license arising under MCL 257.303(1)(d), MCL 257.320, MCL 257.904(10), MCL 257.904(11), MCL 257.310d, or for a first violation of MCL 257.625f.

(G) **Proceedings Under MCL 257.323(4)**.

(1) *Briefs*. Unless otherwise ordered, the parties must file briefs complying with MCR 7.111.

(2) *Oral Argument*. If requested in accord with MCR 7.111(C), the court shall schedule oral argument unless it concludes that the briefs and record adequately present the facts and legal arguments, and the court's deliberation would not be significantly aided by oral argument.

(3) *Decision*. The court shall confine its consideration to a review of the record prepared under MCL 257.322, MCL 257.625f, or MCL 257.204a for statutory legal issues and shall not grant restricted driving privileges. The court shall set aside the Secretary of State's determination only if the appellant's substantial rights have been prejudiced because the determination is:

(a) in violation of the Constitution of the United States, the Michigan Constitution, or a statute;

(b) in excess of the Secretary of State's statutory authority or jurisdiction;

(c) made upon unlawful procedure that results in material prejudice to the appellant;

(d) not supported by competent, material, and substantial evidence on the whole record;

(e) arbitrary, capricious, or clearly an abuse or unwarranted exercise of discretion; or

(f) affected by other substantial and material error of law.

Rule 7.121 Appeals From Concealed Weapon Licensing Boards

(A) **Scope**. This rule governs appeals to the circuit court from a final determination of a concealed weapon licensing board refusing to restore rights under MCL 28.424 or denying, failing to issue, revoking, or suspending a license to carry a concealed pistol. Unless this rule provides otherwise, MCR 7.101 through MCR 7.115 apply.

(B) **Appeal of Right**.

(1) *Time Requirements*. Time requirements are governed by MCR 7.104(A).

(2) *Manner of Filing*.

(a) Claim of Appeal – Form. The claim of appeal shall conform with the requirements of MCR 7.104(C)(1), except that:

(i) the license applicant is the appellant, and

(ii) the board is the appellee.

(b) Claim of Appeal – Content. The claim of appeal must:

(i) state:

[A] "[Name of appellant] claims an appeal from the decision on [date] by [name of the county] Concealed Weapon Licensing Board," or

[B] "[Name of appellant] claims an appeal from the failure of the [name of the county] Concealed Weapon Licensing Board to issue a decision on the application for a license by [date]," and

(ii) include concise statements of the following:

[A] the nature of the proceedings before the board, including citation to the statute authorizing the board's decision;

[B] citation to the statute or Const 1963, art 6 § 28 authorizing appellate review;

[C] the facts on which venue is based.

(c) Signature. The claim of appeal must be signed as stated in MCR 7.104(C)(3).

(d) Other Documents. In addition to the documents required under MCR 7.104(D), the claim of appeal shall include a copy of the board's decision and any materials accompanying the board's decision. If the appeal is from the board's failure to issue a timely decision, the claim of appeal shall state the date on which the application was filed and shall include a statement addressing whether the application complied with MCL 28.425b(1), (5), and (9).

(e) Service. The appellant shall serve the claim of appeal on all parties.

(f) Request for Certified Record. Within the time for filing a claim of appeal, the appellant shall send a written request to the board to send a certified copy of the record to the circuit court.

(3) *Appearance*. The appellee shall file an appearance that complies with MCR 7.104(F) within 14 days after service of the claim of appeal.

(C) **Hearing De Novo from Denial of License for Grounds Specified in MCL 28.425b(7)(n).**

(1) *Briefs*. The court may require briefs and may enter an order setting a briefing schedule. Unless otherwise ordered, briefs must comply with MCR 7.111.

(2) *Hearing*. The court shall hold a hearing de novo that comports with MCL 28.425d(1). Any determination that the appellant is unfit under MCL 28.425b(7)(n) shall be based on clear and convincing evidence.

(3) *Decision*. The circuit court shall enter an order either affirming the board's denial or finding the applicant qualified under MCL 28.425b(7)(n) and ordering the board to issue a license.

(D) **Procedure in All Other Appeals.**

(1) *Briefs*. Unless otherwise ordered, the parties must file briefs complying with MCR 7.111.

(2) *Oral Argument*. If requested in accord with MCR 7.111(C), the court shall hold oral argument within 14 days after the appellee's brief was filed or due. The court may dispense with oral argument under MCR 7.114(A).

(3) *Decision*. The court shall confine its consideration to a review of the record. If the court determines that the denial of a license was clearly erroneous, the court shall order the board to issue a license as required by the act. If the court determines that the board erroneously refused to restore rights pursuant to MCL 28.424(3), the court shall order the board to restore the applicant's rights. If the court determines that the board erroneously revoked or suspended a license, the court shall order the board to reinstate the license. If the court determines that the board failed to issue a license pursuant to MCL 28.425b(13), the court shall order the board to act on the application within 14 days. The court shall retain jurisdiction to review the board's decision.

(E) **Notice of Decision**. The circuit court shall serve the parties with a copy of its order resolving the appeal.

(F) **Costs and Attorney Fees.**

(1) *Arbitrary and Capricious Board Decision*. If the court determines that the decision of the board to deny issuance of a license to an applicant was arbitrary and capricious, the court shall order the state to pay 1/3 and the county in which the concealed weapon licensing board is located to pay 2/3 of the actual costs and actual attorney fees of the applicant in appealing the denial.

(2) *Frivolous Appeal*. If the court determines that an applicant's appeal was frivolous, the court shall order the applicant to pay the actual costs and actual attorney fees of the board in responding to the appeal.

Rule 7.122 Appeals From Zoning Ordinance Determinations

(A) **Scope.**

(1) This rule governs appeals to the circuit court from a determination under a zoning ordinance by any officer, agency, board, commission, or zoning board of appeals, and by any legislative body of a city, village, township, or county authorized to enact zoning ordinances. Unless this rule provides otherwise, MCR 7.101 through MCR 7.115 apply. This rule does not apply to legislative decisions of a city, village, township, or county, such as the adoption of or amendment to a zoning ordinance.

(2) This rule does not restrict the right of a party to bring a complaint for relief relating to a determination under a zoning ordinance. A party may seek a stay of enforcement under MCR 7.123(E).

(3) An appeal under this section is an appeal of right.

(B) **Time Requirements**. An appeal under this rule must be filed within the time prescribed by the statute applicable to the appeal. If no time is specified in the applicable statute, the appeal must be filed within 30 days after the certification of the minutes of the board or commission from which the appeal is taken or within 30 days after the board or commission issued its decision in writing, whichever deadline comes first.

(C) **Manner of Filing.**

(1) *Claim of Appeal – Form*. The claim of appeal shall conform to the requirements of MCR 7.104(C)(1), except that:

(a) the party aggrieved by the determination shall be designated the appellant; and

(b) the city, village, township, or county under whose ordinance the determination was made shall be designated the "appellee," except that when a city, village, township, county, or an officer or entity authorized to appeal on its behalf, appeals a determination as an aggrieved party, then the appellee(s) shall be designated as the board, commission, or other entity that made the determination and the party that prevailed before the board, commission, or other entity that made the determination.

(2) *Claim of Appeal – Content*. The claim of appeal must:

(a) state "[Name of appellant] claims an appeal from the decision on [date] by [name of the officer or entity]"; and

(b) include concise statements of the following:

(i) the nature of the determination by the officer or entity;

(ii) the statute authorizing the officer or entity's proceedings and determination;
(iii) the statute or constitutional provision under which the appeal is taken;
(iv) the facts on which venue is based;
(v) the grounds on which relief is sought, stated in as many separate paragraphs as there are separate grounds alleged; and
(vi) the relief sought.

(3) *Signature*. The claim of appeal must be signed as stated in MCR 7.104(C)(3).

(4) *Other Documents*. The appellant must attach to the claim of appeal a copy of the order and/or minutes of the officer or entity from which the appeal is taken or must indicate that there is no such document to attach.

(5) *Service*. Upon filing the claim of appeal, the appellant, shall serve a copy of the claim of appeal and all attachments upon the clerk of the city, village, township, or county as well as the board, commission, or other entity that made a determination that is the subject of the appeal. Service shall be in the manner provided in MCR 2.107, and appellant shall promptly file a proof of service with the court.

(D) **Bond**. An appellant shall not be required to post a bond unless so ordered by the court.

(E) **Record on Appeal; Transmittal of the Record**.

(1) The record includes the original or a copy certified by the city, village, township, or county clerk of the application, all documents and material submitted by any person or entity with respect to the application, the minutes of all proceedings, and any determination of the officer or entity.

(2) Within 28 days after service of the claim of appeal, the clerk of the city, village, township, or county from which the appeal is taken must file the record with the court.

(3) If the record is not available within 28 days after service of the claim of appeal, the clerk of the city, village, township, or county from which the appeal is taken shall notify the court of the estimated date of transmittal of the record.

(4) If the clerk of the city, village, township, or county postpones transmittal of the record or transmittal is otherwise delayed, the court may on motion or its own initiative exercise superintending control over the clerk to prevent delay.

(5) The clerk of the city, village, township, or county from which the appeal is taken must notify the appellant and appellee of the transmittal of the record to the court.

(6) Motions regarding the contents of the record or to prepare a transcript of proceedings before the officer or entity must be filed within 21 days after transmission of the record to the court.

(F) **Briefs**. Unless otherwise ordered, the parties must file briefs complying with MCR 7.111.

(G) **Decision**.

(1) *Appeals Under MCL 125.3606*.

(a) In an appeal from a city, village, township, or county board of zoning appeals, the court shall apply the standard of review under MCL 125.3606(1).

(b) If the court finds the record inadequate to review the decision or finds that additional material evidence exists that with good reason was not presented, the court shall order further zoning board of appeals proceedings on conditions that the court considers proper. The zoning board of appeals may modify the findings and decision as a result of the new proceedings or may affirm the original decision. The supplementary record and decision shall be filed with the court.

(c) The court may affirm, reverse, or modify the decision of the board of appeals.

(2) *Other Appeals*. In an appeal from a final determination under a zoning ordinance where no right of appeal to a zoning board of appeals exists, the court shall determine whether the decision was authorized by law and the findings were supported by competent, material, and substantial evidence on the whole record.

(H) **Notice of Decision**. The court shall serve the parties with a copy of its order resolving the appeal.

Rule 7.123 Appeals From Agencies not Governed by Another Rule

(A) **Scope**. This rule governs an appeal to the circuit court from an agency decision that is not governed by another rule in this subchapter. Unless this rule provides otherwise, MCR 7.101 through 7.115 apply.

(B) **Appeal of Right**.

(1) *Time Requirements*. Time requirements are governed by MCR 7.104(A).

(2) *Manner of Filing*.

(a) Claim of Appeal – Form. The claim of appeal shall conform to the requirements of MCR 7.119(B)(2)(a).

(b) Claim of Appeal – Content. The claim of appeal must:

(i) state "[Name of appellant] claims an appeal from the decision on [date] by [name of the agency]," and
(ii) include concise statements of the following:
[A] the nature of the proceedings before the agency;
[B] citation to the statute, rule, or other authority enabling the agency to conduct the proceedings;

[C] citation to the statute or constitutional provision authorizing appellate review of the agency's decision or order in the circuit court; and

[D] the facts on which venue is based.

(c) Signature. The claim of appeal must be signed as stated in MCR 7.104(C)(3).

(d) Other Documents. The appellant must also comply with MCR 7.104(D).

(e) Filing Requirements in the Agency. The appellant must comply with MCR 7.104(E).

(f) Service. The appellant must comply with MCR 7.104(D)(7).

(3) *Appearance*. The appellee shall file an appearance that complies with MCR 7.104(F) within 14 days after service of the claim of appeal.

(C) **Application for Leave to Appeal or for Interlocutory Appeal**.

(1) *Time Requirements*. An application must comply with MCR 7.105(A).

(2) *Manner of Filing*. An application must comply with MCR 7.105 and MCR 7.123(B)(2)(b)(ii). An application for interlocutory appeal shall also state why review of the agency's final decision will not be an adequate remedy.

(3) *Answer*. An appellee may file an answer to an application that complies with MCR 7.105(C). The circuit court may require the filing of an answer.

(4) *If Application is Granted*. If the application is granted, the appeal proceeds as an appeal of right.

(D) **Late Appeal**. The appellant may file an application for late appeal if permitted by statute.

(1) *Time Requirements*. Unless inconsistent with the statute authorizing late appeal, the application must be filed within six months after entry of the agency decision or order.

(2) *Manner of Filing*. In addition to the requirements of MCR 7.105(B), the application must include:

(a) a statement citing the statute authorizing a late appeal;

(b) a statement of facts explaining the delay; and

(c) statements of jurisdiction and venue complying with MCR 7.123(B)(2)(b)(ii).

(3) *Answer*. An appellee may file an answer to the application for late appeal under MCR 7.105(C). The circuit court may require the filing of an answer.

(4) *If Application is Granted*. If the application is granted, the appeal proceeds in the same manner as an appeal of right.

(E) **Stay of Enforcement**. The filing of an appeal or an application for leave to appeal does not stay enforcement of the agency's decision or order.

(1) A party may file a motion seeking a stay in the circuit court.

(2) For purposes of this subrule, the agency is entitled to notice even if it has not filed an appearance in the appeal.

(3) The court may order a stay on appropriate terms and conditions if it finds that:

(a) the moving party will suffer irreparable injury if a stay is not granted;

(b) the moving party made a strong showing that it is likely to prevail on the merits;

(c) the public interest will not be harmed if a stay is granted; and

(d) the harm to the moving party in the absence of a stay outweighs the harm to the other parties to the proceedings if a stay is granted.

(4) If the motion for stay is granted, the circuit court may set appropriate terms and conditions for the posting of a bond:

(a) in the amount required by any applicable statute authorizing the appeal, or

(b) in an amount and with sureties that the circuit court deems adequate to protect the public and the parties when there are no statutory instructions.

(5) *Temporary Stay*.

(a) The circuit court may grant a temporary stay of enforcement without written notice only if

(i) it clearly appears from facts alleged in the motion that immediate and irreparable injury will result if a stay is not entered before a hearing, and

(ii) the moving party certifies to the court in writing that it made reasonable efforts to contact the other parties and agency, but was unsuccessful.

(b) A temporary stay may be granted by the court until a hearing can be held. A hearing on a motion to dissolve a temporary stay will be heard on 24 hours' notice, or less on order of the court for good cause shown, and takes precedence over all matters except previously filed matters of the same character.

(F) **Stipulations**. The parties may stipulate regarding any issue on appeal or any part of the record on appeal if the stipulation is embodied in an order entered by the court.

(G) **Decision**. The court may affirm, reverse, remand, or modify the decision of the agency and may grant further relief as appropriate based on the record, findings, and conclusions.

(1) If the agency's decision or order is not supported by competent, material, and substantial evidence on the whole record, the court shall specifically identify the finding or findings that lack support.

(2) If the agency's decision or order violates the Constitution or a statute, is affected by a material error of law, or is affected by an unlawful procedure resulting in material prejudice to a party,

the court shall specifically identify the agency's conclusions of law that are being reversed.

Subchapter 7.200 Court of Appeals

Rule 7.201 Organization and Operation of Court of Appeals

(A) **Chief Judge and Chief Judge Pro Tempore**.

(1) The Supreme Court shall select a judge of the Court of Appeals to serve as chief judge. No later than October 1 of each odd-numbered year, the Court of Appeals may submit the names of no fewer than two judges whom the judges of that court recommend for selection as chief judge.

(2) The chief judge shall select a chief judge pro tempore, who shall fulfill such functions as the chief judge assigns.

(3) The chief judge and chief judge pro tempore shall serve a two-year term beginning on January 1 of each even-numbered year, provided that the chief judge serves at the pleasure of the Supreme Court and the chief judge pro tempore serves at the pleasure of the chief judge.

(B) **Court of Appeals Clerk; Place of Filing Papers; Fees**.

(1) The court shall appoint a chief clerk who is subject to the requirements imposed on the Supreme Court clerk in MCR 7.319. The clerk's office must be located in Lansing and be operated under the court's direction. With the court's approval, the clerk may appoint assistant and deputy clerks.

(2) Papers to be filed with the court or the clerk must be filed in the clerk's office in Lansing or with a deputy clerk in Detroit, Troy, or Grand Rapids. Fees paid to a deputy clerk must be forwarded to the clerk's office in Lansing. Claims of appeal, applications, motions, and complaints need not be accepted for filing until all required documents have been filed and the requisite fees have been paid.

(3) If a case is accepted for filing without all of the required documents, transcripts, or fees, the appellant, or the plaintiff in an original action under MCR 7.206, must supply the missing items within 21 days after the date of the clerk's notice of deficiency. The chief judge or another designated judge may dismiss the appeal and assess costs if the deficiency is not remedied within that time.

(C) **Sessions of Court**. There are 9 regular sessions of the court each year. Except as otherwise required for the efficient administration of the court, each session begins on the first Tuesday during the months of October through June. Each session continues for the number of days necessary to conclude the hearing of cases scheduled for argument. The chief judge may order a special session.

(D) **Panels**. The court shall sit to hear cases in panels of 3 judges. The decision of a majority of the judges of a panel in attendance at the hearing is the decision of the court. Except as modified by the Supreme Court, a decision of the court is final. The judges must be rotated so that each judge sits with every other judge with equal frequency, consistent with the efficient administration of the court's business. The Supreme Court may assign persons to act as temporary judges of the court, under the constitution and statutes. Only one temporary judge may sit on a 3-judge panel.

(E) **Assignments and Presiding Judge**. Before the calendar for each session is prepared, the chief judge shall assign the judges to each panel and the cases to be heard by them and designate one of them as presiding judge. A presiding judge presides at a hearing and performs other functions the court or the Supreme Court by rule or special order directs. The chief judge may assign a motion or any other matter to any panel.

(F) **Place of Hearing**. The court shall sit in Detroit, Lansing, Grand Rapids, and Marquette, or another place the chief judge designates. A calendar case will be assigned for hearing in the city nearest to the court or tribunal from which the appeal was taken or as the parties stipulate, except as otherwise required for the efficient administration of the court's business.

(G) **Judicial Conferences**. At least once a year and at other times the chief judge finds necessary, the judges shall meet to consider proposals to amend the rules of the court, improve the administration of justice, including the operations of the court, and transact any business which properly comes before them.

(H) **Approval of Expenses**. The state court administrator shall approve the expenses for operation of the court and the expense accounts of the judges, including attendance at a judicial conference. The state court administrator shall prepare a budget for the court.

Rule 7.202 Definitions

For purposes of this subchapter:

(1) "clerk" means the Court of Appeals clerk, unless otherwise stated;

(2) "date of filing" means the date of receipt of a document by a court clerk;

(3) "entry fee" means the fee required by law or, in lieu of that fee, a motion to waive fees or a copy of an order appointing an attorney;

(4) "filing" means the delivery of a document to a court clerk and the receipt and acceptance of the document by the clerk with the intent to enter it in the record of the court;

(5) "custody case" means a domestic relations case in which the custody of a minor child is an issue, an adoption case, or a case in which the family division of circuit court has entered an order

terminating parental rights or an order of disposition removing a child from the child's home;

(6) "final judgment" or "final order" means:
  (a) In a civil case,
    (i) the first judgment or order that disposes of all the claims and adjudicates the rights and liabilities of all the parties, including such an order entered after reversal of an earlier final judgment or order
    (ii) an order designated as final under MCR 2.604(B);
    (iii) in a domestic relations action, a postjudgment order affecting the custody of a minor,
    (iv) a postjudgment order awarding or denying attorney fees and costs under MCR 2.403, 2.405, 2.625 or other law or court rule,
    (v) an order denying governmental immunity to a governmental party, including a governmental agency, official, or employee underMCR 2.116(C)(7) or an order denying a motion for summary disposition under MCR 2.116(C)(10) based on a claim of governmental immunity;
  (b) In a criminal case,
    (i) an order dismissing the case;
    (ii) the original sentence imposed following conviction;
    (iii) a sentence imposed following the granting of a motion for resentencing;
    (iv) a sentence imposed, or order entered, by the trial court following a remand from an appellate court in a prior appeal of right; or
    (v) a sentence imposed following revocation of probation.

Rule 7.203 Jurisdiction of the Court of Appeals

(A) **Appeal of Right**. The court has jurisdiction of an appeal of right filed by an aggrieved party from the following:
  (1) A final judgment or final order of the circuit court, or court of claims, as defined in MCR 7.202(6), except a judgment or order of the circuit court
    (a) on appeal from any other court or tribunal;
    (b) in a criminal case in which the conviction is based on a plea of guilty or nolo contendere;
  An appeal from an order described in MCR 7.202(6)(a)(iii)-(v) is limited to the portion of the order with respect to which there is an appeal of right.
  (2) A judgment or order of a court or tribunal from which appeal of right to the Court of Appeals has been established by law or court rule;

(B) **Appeal by Leave**. The court may grant leave to appeal from:
  (1) a judgment or order of the circuit court and court of claims that is not a final judgment appealable of right;
  (2) a final judgment entered by the circuit court on appeal from any other court;
  (3) a final order of an administrative agency or tribunal which by law is appealable to or reviewable by the Court of Appeals or the Supreme Court;
  (4) any other judgment or order appealable to the Court of Appeals by law or rule;
  (5) any judgment or order when an appeal of right could have been taken but was not timely filed.

(C) **Extraordinary Writs, Original Actions, and Enforcement Actions**. The court may entertain an action for:
  (1) superintending control over a lower court or a tribunal immediately below it arising out of an action or proceeding which, when concluded, would result in an order appealable to the Court of Appeals;
  (2) mandamus against a state officer (see MCL 600.4401);
  (3) habeas corpus (see MCL 600.4304);
  (4) quo warranto involving a state office or officer;
  (5) any original action required by law to be filed in the Court of Appeals or Supreme Court;
  (6) any action to enforce a final order of an administrative tribunal or agency required by law to be filed in the Court of Appeals or Supreme Court.

(D) **Other Appeals and Proceedings**. The court has jurisdiction over any other appeal or action established by law. An order concerning the assignment of a case to the business court under MCL 600.8301 et seq. shall not be appealed to the Court of Appeals.

(E) **Appeals by Prosecution**. Appeals by the prosecution in criminal cases are governed by MCL 770.12, except as provided by MCL 770.3.

(F) **Dismissal**.
  (1) Except when a motion to dismiss has been filed, the chief judge or another designated judge may, acting alone, dismiss an appeal or original proceeding for lack of jurisdiction.
  (2) The appellant or plaintiff may file a motion for reconsideration within 21 days after the date of the order of dismissal. The motion shall be submitted to a panel of 3 judges. No entry fee is required for a motion filed under this subrule.
  (3) The clerk will not accept for filing a motion for reconsideration of an order issued by a 3-judge panel that denies a motion for reconsideration filed under subrule (2).

(G) **Appeals from Orders Granting or Denying Motions for Summary Disposition**. Appeals arising solely from orders granting or denying motions for summary disposition under MCR 2.116 are to be processed in accordance with Administrative Order 2004-5.

Rule 7.204 Filing Appeal of Right; Appearance

(A) **Time Requirements**. The time limit for an appeal of right is jurisdictional. See MCR 7.203(A). The provisions of MCR 1.108 regarding computation of time apply. For purposes of subrules (A)(1) and (A)(2), "entry" means the date a judgment or order is signed, or the date that data entry of the judgment or order is accomplished in the issuing tribunal's register of actions.

(1) An appeal of right in a civil action must be taken within

(a) 21 days after entry of the judgment or order appealed from;

(b) 21 days after the entry of an order deciding a motion for new trial, a motion for rehearing or reconsideration, or a motion for other relief from the order or judgment appealed, if the motion was filed within the initial 21-day appeal period or within further time the trial court has allowed for good cause during that 21-day period;

(c) 14 days after entry of an order of the family division of the circuit court terminating parental rights under the Juvenile Code, or entry of an order denying a motion for new trial, rehearing, reconsideration, or other postjudgment relief from an order terminating parental rights, if the motion was filed within the initial 14-day appeal period or within further time the trial court may have allowed during that period; or

(d) another time provided by law.

If a party in a civil action is entitled to the appointment of an attorney and requests the appointment within 14 days after the final judgment or order, the 14-day period for the taking of an appeal or the filing of a postjudgment motion begins to run from the entry of an order appointing or denying the appointment of an attorney. If a timely postjudgment motion is filed before a request for appellate counsel, the party may request counsel within 14 days after the decision on the motion.

(2) An appeal of right in a criminal case must be taken

(a) in accordance with MCR 6.425(G)(3);

(b) within 42 days after entry of an order denying a timely motion for the appointment of a lawyer pursuant to MCR 6.425(G)(1);

(c) within 42 days after entry of the judgment or order appealed from; or

(d) within 42 days after the entry of an order denying a motion for a new trial, for directed verdict of acquittal, or to correct an invalid sentence, if the motion was filed within the time provided in MCR 6.419(B), 6.429(B), or 6.431(A), as the case may be.

(e) If a claim of appeal is received by the court after the expiration of the periods set forth above, and if the appellant is an inmate in the custody of the Michigan Department of Corrections and has submitted the claim as a pro se party, the claim shall be deemed presented for filing on the date of deposit of the claim in the outgoing mail at the correctional institution in which the inmate is housed. Timely filing may be shown by a sworn statement, which must set forth the date of deposit and state that first-class postage has been prepaid. The exception applies to claims of appeal from decisions or orders rendered on or after March 1, 2010. This exception also applies to an inmate housed in a penal institution in another state or in a federal penal institution who seeks to appeal in a Michigan court.

A motion for rehearing or reconsideration of a motion mentioned in subrules (A)(1)(b) or (A)(2)(d) does not extend the time for filing a claim of appeal, unless the motion for rehearing or reconsideration was itself filed within the 21- or 42-day period.

(3) Where service of the judgment or order on appellant was delayed beyond the time stated in MCR 2.602, the claim of appeal must be accompanied by an affidavit setting forth facts showing that the service was beyond the time stated in MCR 2.602. Appellee may file an opposing affidavit within 14 days after being served with the claim of appeal and affidavit. If the Court of Appeals finds that service of the judgment or order was delayed beyond the time stated in MCR 2.602 and the claim of appeal was filed within 14 days after service of the judgment or order, the claim of appeal will be deemed timely.

(B) **Manner of Filing**. To vest the Court of Appeals with jurisdiction in an appeal of right, an appellant shall file with the clerk within the time for taking an appeal

(1) the claim of appeal, and

(2) the entry fee.

(C) **Other Documents**. With the claim of appeal, the appellant shall file the following documents with the clerk:

(1) a copy of the judgment or order appealed from;

(2) a copy of the certificate of the court reporter or recorder filed under subrule (E)(4), a statement by the attorney that the transcript has been ordered (in which case the certificate of the court reporter or recorder must be filed as soon as possible thereafter), or a statement by the attorney that there is no record to be transcribed;

(3) proof that a copy of the claim of appeal was served on all other parties in the case and on any other person or officer entitled by rule or law to notice of the appeal;
(4) if the appellant has filed a bond, a true copy of the bond;
(5) a copy of the register of actions of the lower court, tribunal, or agency; and
(6) a jurisdictional checklist on a form provided by the clerk's office.

(D) **Form of Claim of Appeal**.
(1) A claim of appeal is entitled "In the Court of Appeals." The parties are named in the same order as they appear in the trial court, with the added designation "appellant" or "appellee" as appropriate. The claim must be substantially in the following form:

[Name of appellant], [plaintiff or defendant], claims an appeal from the [judgment or order] entered [date of judgment or order or date sentence imposed] in the [name of court or tribunal from which the appeal is taken] by [name of judge or officer who entered the judgment, order, or sentence].

(2) The claim of appeal must be dated and signed, and must list the appropriate business address and telephone number under the signature.
(3) If the case involves
(a) a contest as to the custody of a minor child, or
(b) a ruling that a provision of the Michigan Constitution, a Michigan statute, a rule or regulation included in the Michigan Administrative Code, or any other action of the legislative or executive branch of state government is invalid, that the fact must be stated in capital letters on the claim of appeal. In an appeal specified in subrule (D)(3)(b), the Court of Appeals shall give expedited consideration to the appeal, and, if the state or an officer or agency of the state is not a party to the appeal, the Court of Appeals shall send copies of the claim of appeal and the judgment or order appealed from to the Attorney General.

(E) **Trial Court Filing Requirements**. Within the time for taking the appeal, the appellant shall file in the court or the tribunal from which the appeal is taken
(1) a copy of the claim of appeal;
(2) any fee required by law;
(3) any bond required by law as a condition for taking the appeal; and
(4) unless there is no record to be transcribed, the certificate of the court reporter or recorder stating that a transcript has been ordered and payment for it made or secured, and that it will be filed as soon as possible or has already been filed.

(F) **Other Requirements**. Within the time for taking the appeal, the appellant shall also
(1) make any delivery or deposit of money, property, or documents, and do any other act required by the statute authorizing the appeal, and file with the clerk an affidavit or other evidence of compliance;
(2) serve on all other parties in the case and on any other person or officer entitled by rule or law to notice of the appeal a copy of the claim of appeal and a copy of any bond filed under subrule (C)(4).

(G) **Appearance**. Within 14 days after being served with the claim of appeal, the appellee shall file an appearance (identifying the individual attorneys of record) in the Court of Appeals and in the court or tribunal from which the appeal is taken. An appellee who does not file a timely appearance is not entitled to notice of further proceedings until an appearance is filed.

(H) **Docketing Statement**. In all civil appeals, within 28 days after the claim of appeal is filed, the appellant must file two copies of a docketing statement with the clerk of the Court of Appeals and serve a copy on the opposing parties.
(1) *Contents*. The docketing statement must contain the information required from time to time by the Court of Appeals through the office of the Chief Clerk on forms provided by the Clerk's office and must set forth:
(a) the nature of the proceeding;
(b) the date of entry of the judgment or order sought to be reviewed as defined in MCR 7.204(A) or MCR 7.205(A), and whether the appeal was timely filed and is within the court's jurisdiction;
(c) a concise, accurate summary of all facts material to consideration of the issues presented, but transcripts are not required at this stage;
(d) the issues presented by the appeal, including a concise summary of how they arose and how they were preserved in the trial court. General conclusory statements such as, "the judgment of the trial court is not supported by the law or the facts," will not be accepted;
(e) a reference to all related or prior appeals, and the appropriate citation, if any.
(2) *Amendment*. The Court of Appeals may, upon motion and good cause shown, allow for the amendment of the docketing statement.
(3) *Cross Appeals*. A party who files a cross appeal shall file a docketing statement in accordance with this rule within 28 days after filing the cross appeal.
(4) *Dismissal*. If the appellant fails to file a timely docketing statement, the chief judge may dismiss the appeal pursuant to MCR 7.217.

Rule 7.205 Application for Leave to Appeal

(A) **Time Requirements**. An application for leave to appeal must be filed within

(1) 21 days after entry of the judgment or order to be appealed from or within other time as allowed by law or rule; or

(2) 21 days after entry of an order deciding a motion for new trial, a motion for rehearing or reconsideration, or a motion for other relief from the order or judgment appealed, if the motion was filed within the initial 21-day appeal period or within further time the trial court has allowed for good cause during that 21-day period.

For purposes of subrules (A)(1) and (A)(2),"entry" means the date a judgment or order is signed, or the date that data entry of the judgment or order is accomplished in the issuing tribunal's register of actions.

(3) If an application for leave to appeal in a criminal case is received by the court after the expiration of the periods set forth above or the period set forth in MCR 7.205(G), and if the appellant is an inmate in the custody of the Michigan Department of Corrections and has submitted the application as a pro se party, the application shall be deemed presented for filing on the date of deposit of the application in the outgoing mail at the correctional institution in which the inmate is housed. Timely filing may be shown by a sworn statement, which must set forth the date of deposit and state that first-class postage has been prepaid. The exception applies to applications for leave to appeal from decisions or orders rendered on or after March 1, 2010. This exception also applies to an inmate housed in a penal institution in another state or in a federal penal institution who seeks to appeal in a Michigan court.

(B) **Manner of Filing**. To apply for leave to appeal, the appellant shall file with the clerk:

(1) 5 copies of an application for leave to appeal (one signed), stating the date and nature of the judgment or order appealed from; concisely reciting the appellant's allegations of error and the relief sought; setting forth a concise argument, conforming to MCR 7.212(C), in support of the appellant's position on each issue; and, if the order appealed from is interlocutory, setting forth facts showing how the appellant would suffer substantial harm by awaiting final judgment before taking an appeal;

(2) 5 copies of the judgment or order appealed from, of the register of actions of the lower court, tribunal, or agency, of the opinion or findings of the lower court, tribunal, or agency, and of any opinion or findings reviewed by the lower court, tribunal, or agency.

(3) if the appeal is from an administrative tribunal or agency, or from a circuit court on review of an administrative tribunal or agency, evidence that the tribunal or agency has been requested to send its record to the Court of Appeals;

(4) 1 copy of certain transcripts, as follows:

(a) in an appeal relating to the evidence presented at an evidentiary hearing in a civil or criminal case, the transcript of the evidentiary hearing, including the opinion or findings of the court which conducted the hearing;

(b) in an appeal from the circuit court after an appeal from another court, the transcript of proceedings in the court reviewed by the circuit court;

(c) in an appeal challenging jury instructions, the transcript of the entire charge to the jury;

(d) in an appeal from a judgment in a criminal case entered pursuant to a plea of guilty or nolo contendere, the transcripts of the plea and sentence;

(e) in an appeal from an order granting or denying a new trial, such portion of the transcript of the trial as, in relation to the issues raised, permits the court to determine whether the trial court's decision on the motion was for a legally recognized reason and based on arguable support in the record;

(f) in an appeal raising a sentencing issue, the transcript of the sentencing proceeding and the transcript of any hearing on a motion relating to sentencing;

(g) in an appeal raising any other issue, such portion of the transcript as substantiates the existence of the issue, objections or lack thereof, arguments of counsel, and any comment or ruling of the trial judge.

If the transcript is not yet available, or if there is no record to be transcribed, the appellant shall file a copy of the certificate of the court reporter or recorder or a statement by the appellant's attorney as provided in MCR 7.204(C)(2). The appellant must file the transcript with the Court of Appeals as soon as it is available.

(5) if the appeal is from a probate court order, 5 copies of the probate court's certification of the issue, as required by law;

(6) proof that a copy of the filed documents was served on all other parties; and

(7) the entry fee.

(C) **Answer**. Any other party in the case may file with the clerk, within 21 days of service of the application,

(1) 5 copies of an answer to the application (one signed) conforming to MCR 7.212(D), except that transcript page references are not required unless a transcript has been filed; and

(2) proof that a copy was served on the appellant and any other appellee.

(D) **Reply**. A reply brief may be filed as provided by MCR 7.212(G).

(E) **Decision**.

(1) There is no oral argument. The application is decided on the documents filed and, in an appeal from an administrative tribunal or agency, the certified record.

(2) The court may grant or deny the application; enter a final decision; grant other relief; request additional material from the record; or require a certified concise statement of proceedings and facts from the court, tribunal, or agency whose order is being appealed. The clerk shall enter the court's order and mail copies to the parties.

(3) If an application is granted, the case proceeds as an appeal of right, except that the filing of a claim of appeal is not required and the time limits for the filing of a cross appeal and for the taking of the other steps in the appeal, including the filing of the docketing statement (28 days), and the filing of the court reporter's or recorder's certificate if the transcript has not been filed (14 days), run from the date the order granting leave is certified.

(4) Unless otherwise ordered, the appeal is limited to the issues raised in the application and supporting brief.

(F) **Emergency Appeal**.

(1) If the order appealed requires acts or will have consequences within 56 days of the date the application is filed, appellant shall alert the clerk of that fact by prominent notice on the cover sheet or first page of the application, including the date by which action is required.

(2) When an appellant requires a hearing on an application in less than 21 days, the appellant shall file and serve a motion for immediate consideration, concisely stating facts showing why an immediate hearing is required. A notice of hearing of the application and motion or a transcript is not required. An answer may be filed within the time the court directs. If a copy of the application and of the motion for immediate consideration are personally served under MCR 2.107(C)(1) or (2), the application may be submitted to the court immediately on filing. If mail service is used, it may not be submitted until the first Tuesday 7 days after the date of service, unless the party served acknowledges receipt. In all other respects, submission, decision, and further proceedings are as provided in subrule (D).

(3) Where the trial court makes a decision on the admissibility of evidence and the prosecutor or the defendant files an interlocutory application for leave to appeal seeking to reverse that decision, the trial court shall stay proceedings pending resolution of the application in the Court of Appeals, unless the trial court makes findings that the evidence is clearly cumulative or that an appeal is frivolous because legal precedent is clearly against the party's position. The appealing party must pursue the appeal as expeditiously as practicable, and the Court of Appeals shall consider the matter under the same priority as that granted to an interlocutory criminal appeal under MCR 7.213(C)(1). If the application for leave to appeal is filed by the prosecutor and the defendant is incarcerated, the defendant may request that the trial court reconsider whether pretrial release is appropriate.

(G) **Late Appeal**.

(1) When an appeal of right was not timely filed or was dismissed for lack of jurisdiction, or when an application for leave was not timely filed, the appellant may file an application as prescribed in subrule (B), file 5 copies of a statement of facts explaining the delay, and serve 1 copy on all other parties. The answer may challenge the claimed reasons for delay. The court may consider the length of and the reasons for delay in deciding whether to grant the application. In all other respects, submission, decision, and further proceedings are as provided in subrule (E).

(2) In a criminal case, the defendant may not file an application for leave to appeal from a judgment of conviction and sentence if the defendant has previously taken an appeal from that judgment by right or leave granted or has sought leave to appeal that was denied.

(3) Except as provided in subrules (G)(4)and (G)(5), leave to appeal may not be granted if an application for leave to appeal is filed more than 6 months after the later of:

(a) entry of a final judgment or other order that could have been the subject of an appeal of right under MCR 7.203(A), but if a motion described in MCR 7.204(A)(1)(b) was filed within the time prescribed in that rule, then the 6 months are counted from the time of entry of the order denying that motion; or

(b) entry of the order or judgment to be appealed from, but if a motion for new trial, a motion for rehearing or reconsideration, or a motion for other relief from the order or judgment appealed was filed within the initial 21-day appeal period or within further time the trial court has allowed for good cause during that 21-day period, then the 6 months are counted from the entry of the order deciding the motion.

(4) The limitation provided in subrule (G)(3) does not apply to an application for leave to appeal by a

criminal defendant if the defendant files an application for leave to appeal within 21 days after the trial court decides a motion for a new trial, for directed verdict of acquittal, to withdraw a plea, or to correct an invalid sentence, if the motion was filed within the time provided in MCR 6.310(C), MCR 6.419(B), MCR 6.429(B), and MCR 6.431(A), or if

(a) the defendant has filed a delayed request for the appointment of counsel pursuant to MCR 6.425(G)(1) within the 6-month period,

(b) the defendant or defendant's lawyer, if one is appointed, has ordered the appropriate transcripts within 28 days of service of the order granting or denying the delayed request for counsel, unless the transcript has already been filed or has been ordered by the court under MCR 6.425(G)(2), and

(c) the application for leave to appeal is filed in accordance with the provisions of this rule within 42 days after the filing of the transcript. If the transcript was filed before the order appointing or denying the appointment of counsel, the 42-day period runs from the date of that order.

A motion for rehearing or reconsideration of a motion mentioned in subrule (G)(4) does not extend the time for filing an application for leave to appeal, unless the motion for rehearing or reconsideration was itself filed within 21 days after the trial court decides the motion mentioned in subrule (G)(4), and the application for leave to appeal is filed within 21 days after the court decides the motion for rehearing or reconsideration.

A defendant who seeks to rely on one of the exceptions in subrule (G)(4) must file with the application for leave to appeal an affidavit stating the relevant docket entries, a copy of the register of actions of the lower court, tribunal, or agency, or other documentation showing that the application is filed within the time allowed.

(5) Notwithstanding the 6-month limitation period otherwise provided in subrule (G)(3), leave to appeal may be granted if a party's claim of appeal is dismissed for lack of jurisdiction within 21 days before the expiration of the 6-month limitation period, or at any time after the 6-month limitation period has expired, and the party files a late application for leave to appeal from the same lower court judgment or order within 21 days of the dismissal of the claim of appeal or within 21 days of denial of a timely filed motion for reconsideration. A party filing a late application in reliance on this provision must note the dismissal of the prior claim of appeal in the statement of facts explaining the delay.

(6) The time limit for late appeals from orders terminating parental rights is 63 days, as provided by MCR 3.993(C)(2).

(H) **Certified Concise Statement**.

(1) When the Court of Appeals requires a certified concise statement of proceedings and facts, the appellant shall, within 7 days after the order requiring the certified concise statement is certified, serve on all other parties a copy of a proposed concise statement of proceedings and facts, describing the course of proceedings and the facts pertinent to the issues raised in the application, and notice of hearing with the date, time, and place for settlement of the concise statement.

(2) Hearing on the proposed concise statement must be within 14 days after the proposed concise statement and notice is served on the other parties.

(3) Objections to the proposed concise statement must be filed in writing with the trial court and served on the appellant and any other appellee before the time set for settlement.

(4) The trial court shall promptly settle objections to the proposed concise statement and may correct it or add matters of record necessary to present the issues properly. When a court's discretionary act is being reviewed, the trial court may add to the statement its reasons for the act. Within 7 days after the settlement hearing, the trial court shall certify the proposed or a corrected concise statement of proceedings and facts as fairly presenting the factual basis for the questions to be reviewed as directed by the Court of Appeals. Immediately after certification, the trial court shall send the certified concise statement to the Court of Appeals clerk and serve a copy on each party.

Rule 7.206 Extraordinary Writs, Original Actions, and Enforcement Actions

(A) **General Rules of Pleading**. Except as otherwise provided in this rule, the general rules of pleading apply as nearly as practicable. See MCR 2.111-2.114.

(B) **Superintending Control, Mandamus, and Habeas Corpus**. To the extent that they do not conflict with this rule, the rules in subchapter 3.300 apply to actions for superintending control, mandamus, and habeas corpus.

(C) **Quo Warranto**. In a quo warranto action, the Attorney General also must be served with a copy of each pleading and document filed in the Court of Appeals. The Attorney General has the right to intervene as a party on either side.

(D) **Actions for Extraordinary Writs and Original Actions**.

(1) *Filing of Complaint*. To commence an original action, the plaintiff shall file with the clerk:

(a) 5 copies of a complaint (1 signed), which may have copies of supporting documents or affidavits attached to each copy;
(b) 5 copies of a supporting brief (1 signed) conforming to MCR 7.212(C) to the extent possible;
(c) proof that a copy of each of the filed documents was served on every named defendant and, in a superintending control action, on any other party involved in the case which gave rise to the complaint for superintending control; and
(d) the entry fee.

(2) *Answer*. The defendant or any other interested party must file with the clerk within 21 days of service of the complaint and any supporting documents or affidavits:
(a) 5 copies of an answer to the complaint (1 signed), which may have copies of supporting documents or affidavits attached to each copy;
(b) 5 copies of an opposing brief (1 signed) conforming to MCR 7.212(D) to the extent possible; and
(c) proof that a copy of each of the filed documents was served on the plaintiff and any other interested party.

(3) *Electronic Filing*. The parties may file all pleadings and other papers permitted by this rule electronically with the Court of Appeals. All electronically filed documents must be in PDF digital format, while appendices and other nonoriginal filings may be scanned. All electronic filings must be submitted in accordance with the instructions set forth on the website of the Michigan Court of Appeals. Pro se parties may file pleadings and other papers in paper form.

(4) *Preliminary Hearing*. There is no oral argument on preliminary hearing of a complaint. The court may deny relief, grant peremptory relief, or allow the parties to proceed to full hearing on the merits in the same manner as an appeal of right either with or without referral to a judicial circuit or tribunal or agency for the taking of proofs and report of factual findings. If the case is ordered to proceed to full hearing, the time for filing a brief by the plaintiff begins to run from the date the order allowing the case to proceed is certified or the date the transcript or report of factual findings on referral is filed, whichever is later. The plaintiff's brief must conform to MCR 7.212(C). An opposing brief must conform to MCR 7.212(D). In a habeas corpus proceeding, the prisoner need not be brought before the Court of Appeals.

(E) **Actions to Enforce the Headlee Amendment, Pursuant to Const 1963, art 9, § 32.**

(1) *Filing of Complaint*. To commence an action pursuant to Const 1963, art 9, § 32, the plaintiff shall file with the clerk:
(a) 5 copies of the complaint (1 signed), which conforms with the special pleading requirements of MCR 2.112(M) and indicates, inter alia, whether there are any factual questions that are anticipated to require resolution by the court and whether the plaintiff(s) anticipate(s) the need for discovery and the development of a factual record;
(b) 5 copies of a supporting brief (1 signed) conforming to MCR 7.212(C) to the extent possible;
(c) proof that a copy of each of the filed documents was served on every named defendant and the office of the attorney general; and
(d) the entry fee.

(2) *Answer*. The named defendant(s) shall file with the clerk within 21 days of service of the complaint:
(a) 5 copies of an answer to the complaint (1 signed), which conforms with the special pleading requirements of MCR 2.112(M) and indicates, inter alia, whether there are any factual questions that are anticipated to require resolution by the court and whether the named defendant(s) anticipate(s) the need for discovery and the development of a factual record;
(b) 5 copies of a supporting brief (1 signed) conforming to MCR 7.212(C) to the extent possible;
(c) proof that a copy of each of the filed documents was served on every named plaintiff.

(3) *Subsequent proceedings*. Following receipt of the answer:
(a) the chief clerk shall promptly select a panel of the court by random draw and assign that panel to commence proceedings in the suit; and
(b) the panel of the court may deny relief or grant peremptory relief without oral argument; or
(c) if the panel of the court determines that the issues framed in the parties' pleadings and supporting briefs solely present jurisprudentially significant questions of law, the panel shall direct that the suit proceed to a full hearing on the merits in the same manner as an appeal as of right and notify the parties of the date for the filing of supplemental briefs, if such briefs are determined to be necessary, and of the date for oral argument, which shall be on an expedited basis; or

(d) if the panel of the court determines that the issues framed in the parties' pleadings and supplemental briefs present factual questions for resolution, the panel shall refer the suit to a judicial circuit for the purposes of holding pretrial proceedings, conducting a hearing to receive evidence and arguments of law, and issuing a written report for the panel setting forth proposed findings of fact and conclusions of law. The proceedings before the circuit court shall proceed as expeditiously as due consideration of the circuit court's docket, facts and issues of law requires. Following the receipt of the report from the circuit court, the panel shall notify counsel for the parties of the schedule for filing briefs in response to the circuit court's report and of the date for oral argument, which shall be on an expedited basis.

(F) **Enforcement of Administrative Tribunal or Agency Orders**.

(1) *Complaint*. To obtain enforcement of a final order of an administrative tribunal or agency, the plaintiff shall file with the clerk within the time limit provided by law:

(a) 5 copies of a complaint (one signed) concisely stating the basis for relief and the relief sought;

(b) 5 copies of the order sought to be enforced;

(c) 5 copies of a supporting brief (one signed) which conforms to MCR 7.212(C) to the extent possible;

(d) a notice of preliminary hearing on the complaint on the first Tuesday at least 21 days after the complaint and supporting documents are served on the defendant, the agency (unless the agency is the plaintiff), and any other interested party;

(e) proof that a copy of each of the filed documents was served on the defendant, the agency (unless the agency is the plaintiff), and any other interested party;

(f) the certified tribunal or agency record or evidence the plaintiff has requested that the certified record be sent to the Court of Appeals; and

(g) the entry fee.

(2) *Answer*. The defendant must file, and any other interested party may file, with the clerk before the date of the preliminary hearing:

(a) 5 copies of an answer to the complaint (one signed);

(b) 5 copies of an opposing brief (one signed) conforming to MCR 7.212(D) to the extent possible; and

(c) proof that a copy of each of the filed documents was served on the plaintiff, the agency, and any other interested party.

(3) *Preliminary Hearing*. There is no oral argument on preliminary hearing of a complaint. The court may deny relief, grant peremptory relief, or allow the parties to proceed to full hearing on the merits in the same manner as an appeal of right. If the case is ordered to proceed to full hearing, the time for filing of a brief by the plaintiff begins to run from the date the clerk certifies the order allowing the case to proceed. The plaintiff's brief must conform to MCR 7.212(C). An opposing brief must conform to MCR 7.212(D). The case is heard on the certified record transmitted by the tribunal or agency. MCR 7.210(A)(2), regarding the content of the record, applies.

Rule 7.207 Cross Appeals

(A) **Right of Cross Appeal**.

(1) When an appeal of right is filed or the court grants leave to appeal any appellee may file a cross appeal.

(2) If there is more than 1 party plaintiff or defendant in a civil action and 1 party appeals, any other party, whether on the same or opposite side as the party first appealing, may file a cross appeal against all or any of the other parties to the case as well as against the party who first appealed. If the cross appeal operates against a party not affected by the first appeal or in a manner different from the first appeal, that party may file a further cross appeal as if the cross appeal affecting that party had been the first appeal.

(B) **Manner of Filing**. To file a cross appeal, the cross appellant shall file with the clerk a claim of cross appeal in the form required by MCR 7.204(D) and the entry fee

(1) within 21 days after the claim of appeal is filed with the Court of Appeals or served on the cross appellant, whichever is later, if the first appeal was of right; or

(2) within 21 days after the clerk certifies the order granting leave to appeal, if the appeal was initiated by application for leave to appeal.

The cross appellant shall file proof that a copy of the claim of cross appeal was served on the cross appellee and any other party in the case. A copy of the judgment or order from which the cross appeal is taken must be filed with the claim.

(C) **Additional Requirements**. The cross appellant shall perform the steps required by MCR 7.204(E) and (F), except that the cross appellant is not required to order a transcript or file a court reporter's or recorder's certificate unless the initial appeal is abandoned or dismissed. Otherwise the cross appeal proceeds in the same manner as an ordinary appeal.

(D) **Abandonment or Dismissal of Appeal**. If the appellant abandons the initial appeal or the court dismisses it, the cross appeal may nevertheless be prosecuted to its conclusion. Within 21 days after the clerk certifies the order dismissing the initial appeal, if there is a record to be transcribed, the cross appellant shall file a certificate of the court reporter or recorder that a transcript has been ordered and payment for it made or secured and will be filed as soon as possible or has already been filed.

(E) **Delayed Cross Appeal**. A party seeking leave to take a delayed cross appeal shall proceed under MCR 7.205.

Rule 7.208 Authority of Court or Tribunal Appealed From

(A) **Limitations**. After a claim of appeal is filed or leave to appeal is granted, the trial court or tribunal may not set aside or amend the judgment or order appealed from except

- (1) by order of the Court of Appeals,
- (2) by stipulation of the parties,
- (3) after a decision on the merits in an action in which a preliminary injunction was granted, or
- (4) as otherwise provided by law.

In a criminal case, the filing of the claim of appeal does not preclude the trial court from granting a timely motion under subrule (B).

(B) **Postjudgment Motions in Criminal Cases**.

- (1) No later than 56 days after the commencement of the time for filing the defendant-appellant's brief as provided by MCR 7.212(A)(1)(a)(iii), the defendant may file in the trial court a motion for a new trial, for judgment of acquittal, to withdraw a plea, or to correct an invalid sentence.
- (2) A copy of the motion must be filed with the Court of Appeals and served on the prosecuting attorney.
- (3) The trial court shall hear and decide the motion within 28 days of filing, unless the court determines that an adjournment is necessary to secure evidence needed for the decision on the motion or that there is other good cause for an adjournment.
- (4) Within 28 days of the trial court's decision, the court reporter or recorder must file with the trial court clerk the transcript of any hearing held.
- (5) If the motion is granted in whole or in part,
  - (a) the defendant must file the appellant's brief or a notice of withdrawal of the appeal within 42 days after the trial court's decision or after the filing of the transcript of any hearing held, whichever is later;
  - (b) the prosecuting attorney may file a cross appeal in the manner provided by MCR 7.207 within 21 days after the trial court's decision. If the defendant has withdrawn the appeal before the prosecuting attorney has filed a cross appeal, the prosecuting attorney may file a claim of appeal or an application for leave to appeal within the 21-day period.
- (6) If the motion is denied, defendant-appellant's brief must be filed within 42 days after the decision by the trial court, or the filing of the transcript of any trial court hearing, whichever is later.

(C) **Correction of Defects**. Except as otherwise provided by rule and until the record is filed in the Court of Appeals, the trial court or tribunal has jurisdiction

- (1) to grant further time to do, properly perform, or correct any act in the trial court or tribunal in connection with the appeal that was omitted or insufficiently done, other than to extend the time for filing a claim of appeal or for paying the entry fee or to allow delayed appeal;
- (2) to correct any part of the record to be transmitted to the Court of Appeals, but only after notice to the parties and an opportunity for a hearing on the proposed correction.

After the record is filed in the Court of Appeals, the trial court may correct the record only with leave of the Court of Appeals.

(D) **Supervision of Property**. When an appeal is filed while property is being held for conservation or management under the order or judgment of the trial court, that court retains jurisdiction over the property pending the outcome of the appeal, except as the Court of Appeals otherwise orders.

(E) **Temporary Orders**. A trial court order entered before final judgment concerning custody, control, and management of property; temporary alimony, support or custody of a minor child, or expenses in a domestic relations action; or a preliminary injunction, remains in effect and is enforceable in the trial court, pending interlocutory appeal, except as the trial court or the Court of Appeals may otherwise order.

(F) **Stays and Bonds**. The trial court retains authority over stay and bond matters, except as the Court of Appeals otherwise orders.

(G) **Matters Pertaining to Appointment of Attorney**. Throughout the pendency of an appeal involving an indigent person, the trial court retains authority to appoint, remove, or replace an attorney except as the Court of Appeals otherwise orders.

(H) **Acts by Other Judges**. Whenever the trial judge who has heard a case dies, resigns, or vacates office, or is unable to perform any act necessary to an appeal of a case within the time prescribed by law or these rules, another judge of the same court, or if another judge of that court is unavailable, another judge assigned by the state court administrator, may perform the acts necessary to the review process. Whenever a case is heard by a judge assigned from another court, the judicial acts necessary in the preparation of a record for appeal may be performed, with consent of the parties, by a judge of the court in which the case was heard.

(I) **Attorney Fees and Costs**. The trial court may rule on requests for costs or attorney fees under MCR 2.403, 2.405, 2.625 or other law or court rule, unless the Court of Appeals orders otherwise.

Rule 7.209 Bond; Stay of Proceedings

(A) **Effect of Appeal; Prerequisites.**

(1) Except for an automatic stay pursuant to MCR 2.614, an appeal does not stay the effect or enforceability of a judgment or order of a trial court unless the trial court or the Court of Appeals otherwise orders. An automatic stay under MCR 2.614(D) operates to stay any and all proceedings in a cause in which a party has appealed a trial court's denial of the party's claim of governmental immunity.

(2) A motion for bond or for a stay pending appeal may not be filed in the Court of Appeals unless such a motion was decided by the trial court.

(3) A motion for bond or a stay pending appeal filed in the Court of Appeals must include a copy of the trial court's opinion and order, and a copy of the transcript of the hearing on the motion in the trial court.

(B) **Responsibility for Setting Amount of Bond in Trial Court**.

(1) *Civil Actions*. Unless determined by law, the dollar amount of a stay or appeal bond in a civil action must be set by the trial court in an amount adequate to protect the opposite party.

(2) *Criminal Cases*. In a criminal case the granting of bond pending appeal and the amount of it are within the discretion of the trial court, subject to applicable law and rules. Bond must be sufficient to guarantee the appearance of the defendant. Unless bond pending appeal is allowed and a bond is filed with the trial court, a criminal judgment may be executed immediately, even though the time for taking an appeal has not elapsed.

(C) **Amendment of Bond**. On motion, the trial court may order an additional or different bond, set the amount, and approve or require different sureties.

(D) **Review by Court of Appeals**. Except as otherwise provided by rule or law, on motion filed in a case pending before it, the Court of Appeals may amend the amount of bond set by the trial court, order an additional or different bond and set the amount, or require different or additional sureties. The Court of Appeals may also refer a bond or bail matter to the court from which the appeal is taken. The Court of Appeals may grant a stay of proceedings in the trial court or stay of effect or enforcement of any judgment or order of a trial court on the terms it deems just.

(E) **Stay of Proceedings by Trial Court**.

(1) Except as otherwise provided by law or rule, the trial court may order a stay of proceedings, with or without a bond as justice requires.

(a) When the stay is sought before an appeal is filed and a bond is required, the party seeking the stay shall file a bond, with the party in whose favor the judgment or order was entered as the obligee, by which the party promises to

(i) perform and satisfy the judgment or order stayed if it is not set aside or reversed; and

(ii) prosecute to completion any appeal subsequently taken from the judgment or order stayed and perform and satisfy the judgment or order entered by the Court of Appeals or Supreme Court.

(b) If a stay is sought after an appeal is filed, any bond must meet the requirements set forth in subrule 7.209(F).

(2) If a stay bond filed under this subrule substantially meets the requirements of subrule (F), it will be a sufficient bond to stay proceedings pending disposition of an appeal subsequently filed.

(3) The stay order must conform to any condition expressly required by the statute authorizing review.

(4) If a government party files a claim of appeal from an order described in MCR 7.202(6)(a)(v), the proceedings shall be stayed during the pendency of the appeal, unless the court of Appeals directs otherwise.

(F) **Conditions of Appeal Bond**.

(1) *Civil Actions*. In a bond filed for stay pending appeal in a civil action, the appellant shall promise in writing:

(a) to prosecute the appeal to decision;

(b) to perform or satisfy a judgment or order of the Court of Appeals or the Supreme Court;

(c) to perform or satisfy the judgment or order appealed from, if the appeal is dismissed;

(d) in an action involving the possession of land or judgment for foreclosure of a mortgage or land contract, to pay the appellee the damages which may result from the stay of proceedings; and

(e) to do any other act which is expressly required in the statute authorizing appeal.

(2) *Criminal Cases*. A criminal defendant for whom bond pending appeal is allowed after conviction shall promise in writing:

(a) to prosecute the appeal to decision;

(b) if the sentence is one of incarceration, to surrender himself or herself to the sheriff of the county in which he or she was convicted or other custodial authority if the sentence is

affirmed on appeal or if the appeal is dismissed;
(c) if the judgment or order appealed is other than a sentence of incarceration, to perform and comply with the order of the trial court if it is affirmed on appeal or if the appeal is dismissed;
(d) to appear in the trial court if the case is remanded for retrial or further proceedings or if a conviction is reversed and retrial is allowed;
(e) to remain in Michigan unless the court gives written approval to leave; and
(f) to notify the trial court clerk of a change of address.

(G) **Sureties and Filing of Bond**. Except as otherwise specifically provided in this rule, MCR 3.604 applies. A bond must be filed with the clerk of the court which entered the order or judgment to be stayed.
(1) *Civil Actions*. A bond in a civil action need not be approved by a court or clerk before filing but is subject to the objection procedure provided in MCR 3.604.
(2) *Criminal Cases*. A criminal defendant filing a bond after conviction shall give notice to the county prosecuting attorney of the time and place the bond will be filed. The bond is subject to the objection procedure provided in MCR 3.604.

(H) **Stay of Execution**.
(1) If a bond is filed before execution issues, and notice is given to the officer having authority to issue execution, execution is stayed. If the bond is filed after the issuance but before execution, and notice is given to the officer holding it, execution is suspended.
(2) The Court of Appeals may stay or terminate a stay of any order or judgment of a lower court or tribunal on just terms.
(3) When the amount of the judgment is more than $1000 over the insurance policy coverage or surety obligation, then the policy or obligation does not qualify to stay execution under MCL 500.3036 on the portion of the judgment in excess of the policy or bond limits. Stay pending appeal may be achieved by complying with that statute and by filing a bond in an additional amount adequate to protect the opposite party or by obtaining a trial court or Court of Appeals order waiving the additional bond.
(4) A statute exempting a municipality or other governmental agency from filing a bond to stay execution supersedes the requirements of this rule.

(I) **Ex Parte Stay**. Whenever an ex parte stay of proceedings is necessary to allow a motion in either the trial court or the Court of Appeals, the court before which the motion will be heard may grant an ex parte stay for that purpose. Service of a copy of the order, with a copy of the motion, any affidavits on which the motion is based, and notice of hearing on the motion, shall operate as a stay of proceedings until the court rules on the motion unless the court supersedes or sets aside the order in the interim. Proceedings may not be stayed for longer than necessary to enable the party to make the motion according to the practice of the court, and if made, until the decision of the court.

Rule 7.210 Record on Appeal

(A) **Content of Record**. Appeals to the Court of Appeals are heard on the original record.
(1) *Appeal From Court*. In an appeal from a lower court, the record consists of the original papers filed in that court or a certified copy, the transcript of any testimony or other proceedings in the case appealed, and the exhibits introduced. In an appeal from probate court in an estate or trust proceeding, only the order appealed from and those petitions, opinions, and other documents pertaining to it need be included.
(2) *Appeal From Tribunal or Agency*. In an appeal from an administrative tribunal or agency, the record includes all documents, files, pleadings, testimony, and opinions and orders of the tribunal, agency, or officer (or a certified copy), except those summarized or omitted in whole or in part by stipulation of the parties. Testimony not transcribed when the certified record is sent for consideration of an application for leave to appeal, and not omitted by stipulation of the parties, must be filed and sent to the court as promptly as possible.
(3) *Excluded Evidence*. The substance or transcript of excluded evidence offered at a trial and the proceedings at the trial in relation to it must be included as part of the record on appeal.
(4) *Stipulations*. The parties in any appeal to the Court of Appeals may stipulate in writing regarding any matters relevant to the lower court or tribunal or agency record if the stipulation is made a part of the record on appeal and sent to the Court of Appeals.

(B) **Transcript**.
(1) *Appellant's Duties; Orders; Stipulations*.
(a) The appellant is responsible for securing the filing of the transcript as provided in this rule. Except in cases governed by MCR 3.977(J)(3) or MCR 6.425(G)(2), or as otherwise provided by Court of Appeals order or the remainder of this subrule, the appellant shall order from the court reporter or recorder the full transcript of testimony and other proceedings in the trial court or tribunal. Once an appeal is filed in the Court of Appeals, a party must serve a copy of any request for transcript preparation on opposing counsel and file a copy with the Court of Appeals.

(b) In an appeal from probate court in an estate or trust proceeding, only that portion of the transcript concerning the order appealed from need be filed. The appellee may file additional portions of the transcript.

(c) On the appellant's motion, with notice to the appellee, the trial court or tribunal may order that some portion less than the full transcript (or no transcript at all) be included in the record on appeal. The motion must be filed within the time required for filing an appeal, and, if the motion is granted, the appellee may file any portions of the transcript omitted by the appellant. The filing of the motion extends the time for filing the court reporter's or recorder's certificate until 7 days after entry of the trial court's or tribunal's order on the motion.

(d) The parties may stipulate that some portion less than the full transcript (or none) be filed.

(e) The parties may agree on a statement of facts without procuring the transcript and the statement signed by the parties may be filed with the trial court or tribunal clerk and sent as the record of testimony in the action.

(2) *Transcript Unavailable*. When a transcript of the proceedings in the trial court or tribunal cannot be obtained from the court reporter or recorder, the appellant shall take the following steps to settle the record and to cause the filing of a certified settled statement of facts to serve as a substitute for the transcript.

(a) No later than 56 days after the filing of the available transcripts, or 28 days after the filing of the available transcripts in a child custody case or interlocutory criminal appeal, or, if no transcripts are available, within 14 days after filing the claim of appeal, the appellant shall file with the trial court or tribunal clerk, and serve on each appellee, a motion to settle the record and, where reasonably possible, a proposed statement of facts. A proposed statement of facts must concisely set forth the substance of the testimony, or the oral proceedings before the trial court or tribunal if no testimony was taken, in sufficient detail to provide for appellate review.

(b) Except as otherwise provided, the appellant shall notice the motion to settle the record for hearing before the trial court or tribunal to held within 21 days of the filing of the motion. If it is not the typical practice of a tribunal to conduct hearings, the motion to settle the record must be filed with the tribunal for consideration by the tribunal within 21 days of the filing of the motion. The motion shall be filed and served at least 14 days before the date noticed for hearing or consideration to settle the record. If appellant filed a proposed statement of facts with the motion, appellee must file and serve on the appellant and other appellees an amendment or objection to the proposed statement of facts in the trial court or tribunal at least 7 days before the time set for the settlement hearing or consideration. The trial court may adopt and file the appellant's proposed statement of facts as the certified settled statement of facts.

(c) The trial court or tribunal shall settle any controversy and certify a settled statement of facts as an accurate, fair, and complete statement of the proceedings before it. The certified settled statement of facts must concisely set forth the substance of the testimony, or the oral proceedings before the trial court or tribunal if no testimony was taken, in sufficient detail to provide for appellate review.

(d) The appellant shall file the settled statement of facts and the certifying order with the trial court or tribunal clerk and Court of Appeals.

(3) *Duties of Court Reporter or Recorder*.

(a) Certificate. Within 7 days after a transcript is ordered by a party or the court, the court reporter or recorder shall furnish a certificate stating:

(i) that the transcript has been ordered, that payment for the transcript has been made or secured, that it will be filed as soon as possible or has already been filed, and the estimated number of pages for each of the proceedings requested;

(ii) as to each proceeding requested, whether the court reporter or recorder filing the certificate recorded the proceeding; and if not,

(iii) the name and certification number of the court reporter or recorder responsible for the transcript of that proceeding.

(b) Time for Filing. The court reporter or recorder shall give precedence to transcripts necessary for interlocutory criminal appeals and custody cases. The court reporter or recorder shall file the transcript with the trial court or tribunal clerk within

(i) 14 days after it is ordered for an application for leave to appeal from an order granting or denying a motion to suppress evidence in a criminal case;

(ii) 28 days after it is ordered in an appeal of a criminal conviction based on a plea of guilty, guilty but mentally ill, or nolo contendere;

(iii) 42 days after it is ordered in any other interlocutory criminal appeal or custody case;

(iv) 91 days after it is ordered in other cases.

The Court of Appeals may extend or shorten these time limits in an appeal pending in the court on motion filed by the court reporter or recorder or a party.

(c) Copies. Additional copies of the transcripts required by the appellant may be ordered from the court reporter or recorder or photocopies may be made of the transcript furnished by the court reporter or recorder.

(d) Form of Transcript. The transcript must be filed in one or more volumes under a hard-surfaced or other suitable cover, stating the title of the action, and prefaced by a table of contents showing the subject matter of the transcript with page references to the significant parts of the trial or proceedings, including the testimony of each witness by name, the arguments of the attorneys, and the jury instructions. The pages of the transcript must be consecutively numbered on the bottom of each page. Transcripts with more than one page, reduced in size, printed on a single page are permitted and encouraged, but a page in that format may not contain more than four reduced pages of transcript.

(e) Notice. Immediately after the transcript is filed, the court reporter or recorder shall notify the Court of Appeals and all parties that it has been filed and file in the Court of Appeals an affidavit of mailing of notice to the parties.

(f) Discipline. A court reporter or recorder failing to comply with the requirements of these rules is subject to disciplinary action by the courts, including punishment for contempt of court, on the court's own initiative or motion of a party.

(g) Responsibility When More Than One Reporter or Recorder. In a case in which portions of the transcript must be prepared by more than one reporter or recorder, unless the court has designated another person, the person who recorded the beginning of the proceeding is responsible for ascertaining that the entire transcript has been prepared, filing it, and giving the notice required by subrule (B)(3)(e).

(C) **Exhibits**. Within 21 days after the claim of appeal is filed, a party possessing any exhibits offered in evidence, whether admitted or not, shall file them with the trial court or tribunal clerk, unless by stipulation of the parties or order of the trial court or tribunal they are not to be sent, or copies, summaries, or excerpts are to be sent. Xerographic copies of exhibits may be filed in lieu of originals unless the trial court or tribunal orders otherwise. When the record is returned to the trial court or tribunal, the trial court or tribunal clerk shall return the exhibits to the parties who filed them.

(D) **Reproduction of Records**. Where facilities for the copying or reproduction of records are available to the clerk of the court or tribunal whose action is to be reviewed, the clerk, on a party's request and on deposit of the estimated cost or security for the cost, shall procure for the party as promptly as possible and at the cost to the clerk the requested number of copies of documents, transcripts, and exhibits on file.

(E) **Record on Motion**. If, before the time the complete record on appeal is sent to the Court of Appeals, a party files a motion that requires the Court of Appeals to have the record, the trial court or tribunal clerk shall, on request of a party or the Court of Appeals, send the Court of Appeals the documents needed.

(F) **Service of Record**. Within 21 days after the transcript is filed with the trial court clerk, the appellant shall serve a copy of the entire record on appeal, including the transcript and exhibits, on each appellee. However, copies of documents the appellee already possesses need not be served. Proof that the record was served must be promptly filed with the Court of Appeals and the trial court or tribunal clerk. If the filing of a transcript has been excused as provided in subrule (B), the record is to be served within 21 days after the filing of the transcript substitute.

(G) **Transmission of Record**. Within 21 days after the briefs have been filed or the time for filing the appellee's brief has expired, or when the court requests, the trial court or tribunal clerk shall send to the Court of Appeals the record on appeal in the case pending on appeal, except for those things omitted by written stipulation of the parties. Weapons, drugs, or money are not to be sent unless the Court of Appeals requests. The trial court or tribunal clerk shall append a certificate identifying the name of the case and the papers with reasonable definiteness and shall include as part of the record:

(1) a register of actions in the case;

(2) all opinions, findings, and orders of the court or tribunal; and

(3) the order or judgment appealed from.

Transcripts and all other documents which are part of the record on appeal must be attached in one or more file folders or other suitable hard-surfaced binders showing the name of the trial court or tribunal, the title of the case, and the file number.

(H) **Return of Record**. After the Court of Appeals disposes of an appeal, the Court of Appeals shall promptly send the original record, together with a certified copy of the opinion, judgment, or order entered by the Court of Appeals

(1) to the Clerk of the Supreme Court if an application for leave to appeal is filed in the Supreme Court, or
(2) to the clerk of the court or tribunal from which it was received when
  (a) the period for an application for leave to appeal to the Supreme Court has expired without the filing of an application, and
  (b) there is pending in the Court of Appeals no
    (i) timely motion for reconsideration,
    (ii) timely petition for a special panel under MCR 7.215 (I), or
    (iii) timely request by a judge of the Court of Appeals for a special panel under MCR 7.215 (I),
  and the period for such a timely motion, petition, or request has expired.

(I) **Notice by Trial Court or Tribunal Clerk**. The trial court or tribunal clerk shall promptly notify all parties of the return of the record in order that they may take the appropriate action in the trial court or tribunal under the Court of Appeals mandate.

Rule 7.211 Motions in Court of Appeals

(A) **Manner of Making Motion**. A motion is made in the Court of Appeals by filing:
(1) 5 copies of a motion (one signed) stating briefly but distinctly the facts and the grounds on which it is based and the relief requested;
(2) the entry fee;
(3) for a motion to dismiss, to affirm, or for peremptory reversal, 5 copies of a supporting brief. A supporting brief may be filed with any other motion. A brief must conform to MCR 7.212(C) as nearly as possible, except that page references to a transcript are not required unless the transcript is relevant to the issue raised in the motion. A brief in conformance with MCR 7.212(C) is not required in support of a motion to affirm when the appellant argues that:
  (a) the trial court's findings of fact are clearly erroneous;
  (b) the trial court erred in applying established law;
  (c) the trial court abused its discretion; or
  (d) a sentence which is within the sentencing guidelines is invalid.
  Instead of a brief in support of a motion to affirm in such a circumstance, the movant may append those portions of the transcript that are pertinent to the issues raised in the motion; in that case, the motion must include a summary of the movant's position;
(4) a motion for immediate consideration if the party desires a hearing on a date earlier than the applicable date set forth in subrules (B)(2)(a)-(e);
(5) proof that a copy of the motion, the motion for immediate consideration if one has been filed, and any other supporting papers were served on all other parties to the appeal.

(B) **Answer**.
(1) A party to an appeal may answer a motion by filing:
  (a) 5 copies of an answer (one signed); and
  (b) proof that a copy of the answer and any other opposing papers were served on all other parties to the appeal.
(2) Subject to subrule (3), the answer must be filed within
  (a) 21 days after the motion is served on the other parties, for a motion to dismiss, to remand, or to affirm;
  (b) 35 days after the motion is served on the appellee, if the motion is for peremptory reversal;
  (c) 56 days after the motion is served on the defendant, for a motion to withdraw as the appointed appellate attorney;
  (d) 14 days after the motion is served on the other parties, for a motion for reconsideration of an opinion or an order, to stay proceedings in the trial court, to strike a full or partial pleading on appeal, to file an amicus brief, to hold an appeal in abeyance, or to reinstate an appeal after dismissal under MCR 7.217(D);
  (e) 7 days after the motion is served on the other parties, for all other motions.
  If a motion for immediate consideration has been filed, all answers to all affected motions must be filed within 7 days if the motions for immediate consideration was served by mail, or within such time as the Court of Appeals directs. See subrule (C)(6).
(3) In its discretion, the Court of Appeals may dispose of the following motions before the answer period has expired: motion to extend time to order or file transcripts, to extend time to file a brief or other appellate pleading, to substitute one attorney for another, for oral argument when the right to oral argument was not otherwise preserved as described in MCR 7.212, or for an out-of-state attorney to appear and practice in Michigan.
(4) Five copies of an opposing brief may be filed. A brief must conform to MCR 7.212(D) as nearly as possible, except that page references to a transcript are not required unless the transcript is relevant to the issue raised in the motion.

(C) **Special Motions**. If the record on appeal has not been sent to the Court of Appeals, except as provided in subrule (C)(6), the party making a special motion shall request the clerk of the trial court or tribunal to send the record to the Court of Appeals. A copy of the request must be filed with the motion.

(1) *Motion to Remand.*
   (a) Within the time provided for filing the appellant's brief, the appellant may move to remand to the trial court. The motion must identify an issue sought to be reviewed on appeal and show
      (i) that the issue is one that is of record and that must be initially decided by the trial court; or
      (ii) that development of a factual record is required for appellate consideration of the issue.

      A motion under this subrule must be supported by affidavit or offer of proof regarding the facts to be established at a hearing.
   (b) A timely motion must be granted if it is accompanied by a certificate from the trial court that it will grant a motion for new trial.
   (c) In a case tried without a jury, the appellant need not file a motion for remand to challenge the great weight of the evidence in order to preserve the issue for appeal.
   (d) If a motion to remand is granted, further proceedings in the Court of Appeals are stayed until completion of the proceedings in the trial court pursuant to the remand, unless the Court of Appeals orders otherwise. Unless the Court of Appeals sets another time, the appellant's brief must be filed within 21 days after the trial court's decision or after the filing of the transcript of any hearing held, whichever is later.
(2) *Motion to Dismiss.* An appellee may file a motion to dismiss an appeal any time before it is placed on a session calendar on the ground that
   (a) the appeal is not within the Court of Appeals jurisdiction;
   (b) the appeal was not filed or pursued in conformity with the rules; or
   (c) the appeal is moot.
(3) *Motion to Affirm.* After the appellant's brief has been filed, an appellee may file a motion to affirm the order or judgment appealed from on the ground that
   (a) it is manifest that the questions sought to be reviewed are so unsubstantial as to need no argument or formal submission; or
   (b) the questions sought to be reviewed were not timely or properly raised.

   The decision to grant a motion to affirm must be unanimous. An order denying a motion to affirm may identify the judge or judges who would have granted it but for the unanimity requirement of this subrule.
(4) *Motion for Peremptory Reversal.* The appellant may file a motion for peremptory reversal on the ground that reversible error is so manifest that an immediate reversal of the judgment or order appealed from should be granted without formal argument or submission. The decision to grant a motion for peremptory reversal must be unanimous. An order denying a motion for peremptory reversal may identify the judge or judges who would have granted it but for the unanimity requirement of this subrule.
(5) *Motion to Withdraw.* A court-appointed appellate attorney for an indigent appellant may file a motion to withdraw if the attorney determines, after a conscientious and thorough review of the trial court record, that the appeal is wholly frivolous.
   (a) A motion to withdraw is made by filing:
      (i) 5 copies of a motion to withdraw (one signed) which identifies any points the appellant seeks to assert and any other matters that the attorney has considered as a basis for appeal;
      (ii) 5 copies of a brief conforming to MCR 7.212(C), which refers to anything in the record that might arguably support the appeal, contains relevant record references, and cites and deals with those authorities which appear to bear on the points in question;
      (iii) proof that copies of the motion, brief in support, and notice that the motion may result in the conviction or trial court judgment being affirmed were served on the appellant by certified mail; and
      (iv) proof that a copy of the motion only and not the brief was served the appellee.
   (b) The motion to withdraw and supporting papers will be submitted to the court for decision on the first Tuesday
      (i) 28 days after the appellant is served in appeals from orders of the family division of the circuit court terminating parental rights under the Juvenile Code, or
      (ii) 56 days after the appellant is served in all other appeals.

      The appellant may file with the court an answer and brief in which he or she may make any comments and raise any points that he or she chooses concerning the appeal and the attorney's motion. The appellant must file proof that a copy of the answer was served on his or her attorney.
   (c) If the court finds that the appeal is wholly frivolous, it may grant the motion and affirm

the conviction or trial court judgment. If the court grants the motion to withdraw, the appellant's attorney shall mail to the appellant a copy of the transcript within 14 days after the order affirming is certified and file proof of that service. If the court finds any legal point arguable on its merits, it will deny the motion and the court appointed attorney must file an appellant's brief in support of the appeal.

(6) *Motion for Immediate Consideration*. A party may file a motion for immediate consideration to expedite hearing on another motion. The motion must state facts showing why immediate consideration is required. If a copy of the motion for immediate consideration and a copy of the motion of which immediate consideration is sought are personally served under MCR 2.107(C)(1) or (2), the motions may be submitted to the court immediately on filing. If mail service is used, motions may not be submitted until the first Tuesday 7 days after the date of service, unless the party served acknowledges receipt. The trial court or tribunal record need not be requested unless it is required as to the motion of which immediate consideration is sought.

(7) *Confession of Error by Prosecutor*. In a criminal case, if the prosecutor concurs in the relief requested by the defendant, the prosecutor shall file a confession of error so indicating, which may state reasons why concurrence in the relief requested is appropriate. The confession of error shall be submitted to one judge pursuant to MCR 7.211(E). If the judge approves the confession of error, the judge shall enter an order or opinion granting the relief. If the judge rejects the confession of error, the case shall be submitted for decision through the ordinary processes of the court, and the confession of error shall be submitted to the panel assigned to decide the case.

(8) *Vexatious Proceedings*. A party's request for damages or other disciplinary action under MCR 7.216(C) must be contained in a motion filed under this rule. A request that is contained in any other pleading, including a brief filed under MCR 7.212, will not constitute a motion under this rule. A party may file a motion for damages or other disciplinary action under MCR 7.216(C) at any time within 21 days after the date of the order or opinion that disposes of the matter that is asserted to have been vexatious.

(9) *Motion to Seal Court of Appeals File in Whole or in Part*.

(a) Trial court files that have been sealed in whole or in part by a trial court order will remain sealed while in the possession of the Court of Appeals. Public requests to view such trial court files will be referred to the trial court.

(b) Materials that are subject to a protective order entered under MCR 2.302(C) may be submitted for inclusion in the Court of Appeals file in sealed form if they are accompanied by a copy of the protective order. A party objecting to such sealed submissions may file an appropriate motion in the Court of Appeals.

(c) Except as otherwise provided by statute or court rule, the procedure for sealing a Court of Appeals file is governed by MCR 8.119(I). Materials that are subject to a motion to seal a Court of Appeals file in whole or in part shall be held under seal pending the court's disposition of the motion.

(d) Any party or interested person may file an answer in response to a motion to seal a Court of Appeals file within 7 days after the motion is served on the other parties, or within 7 days after the motion is filed in the Court of Appeals, whichever is later.

(e) An order granting a motion shall include a finding of good cause, as defined by MCR 8.119(I)(2), and a finding that there is no less restrictive means to adequately and effectively protect the specific interest asserted.

(f) An order granting or denying a motion to seal a Court of Appeals file in whole or in part may be challenged by any person at any time during the pendency of an appeal.

(D) **Submission of Motions**. Motions in the Court of Appeals are submitted on Tuesday of each week. There is no oral argument on motions, unless ordered by the court.

(E) **Decision on Motions**.

(1) Except as provided in subrule (E)(2), orders may be entered only on the concurrence of the majority of the judges to whom the motion has been assigned.

(2) The chief judge or another designated judge may, acting alone, enter an order disposing of an administrative motion. Administrative motions include, but are not limited to:

(a) a motion to consolidate;

(b) a motion to extend the time to file a transcript or brief;

(c) a motion to strike a nonconforming brief;

(d) a motion for oral argument in a case that has not yet been placed on a session calendar;

(e) a motion to adjourn the hearing date of an application, complaint, or motion;

(f) a motion to dismiss a criminal appeal on the grounds that the defendant has absconded;

(g) a motion to file an amicus curiae brief;

(h) a motion to allow an out-of-state attorney to appear and practice.

Rule 7.212 Briefs

(A) **Time for Filing and Service.**

(1) *Appellant's Brief.*

(a) Filing. The appellant shall file 5 typewritten, xerographic, or printed copies of a brief with the Court of Appeals within

(i) 28 days after the claim of appeal is filed, the order granting leave is certified, the transcript is filed with the trial court, or a settled statement of facts and certifying order is filed with the trial court or tribunal, whichever is later, in a child custody case or an interlocutory criminal appeal. This time may be extended only by the Court of Appeals on motion; or

(ii) the time provided by MCR 7.208(B)(5)(a), 7.208(B)(6), or 7.211(C)(1), in a case in which one of those rules applies; or

(iii) 56 days after the claim of appeal is filed, the order granting leave is certified, the transcript is filed with the trial court or tribunal, or a settled statement of facts and certifying order is filed with the trial court or tribunal, whichever is later, in all other cases. In a criminal case in which substitute counsel is appointed for the defendant, the time runs from the date substitute counsel is appointed, the transcript is filed, or a settled statement of facts and certifying order is filed, whichever is later. The parties may extend the time within which the brief must be filed for 28 days by signed stipulation filed with the Court of Appeals. The Court of Appeals may extend the time on motion.

(b) Service. Within the time for filing the appellant's brief, 1 copy must be served on all other parties to the appeal and proof of that service filed with the Court of Appeals and served with the brief.

(2) *Appellee's Brief.*

(a) Filing. The appellee shall file 5 typewritten, xerographic, or printed copies of a brief with the Court of Appeals within

(i) 21 days after the appellant's brief is served on the appellee, in an interlocutory criminal appeal or a child custody case. This time may be extended only by the Court of Appeals on motion;

(ii) 35 days after the appellant's brief is served on the appellee, in all other cases. The parties may extend this time for 28 days by signed stipulation filed with the Court of Appeals. The Court of Appeals may extend the time on motion.

(b) Service. Within the time for filing the appellee's brief, 1 copy must be served on all other parties to the appeal and proof of that service must be filed with the Court of Appeals.

(3) Earlier Filing and Service. The time for filing and serving the appellant's or the appellee's brief may be shortened by order of the Court of Appeals on motion showing good cause.

(4) Late Filing. Any party failing to timely file and serve a brief required by this rule forfeits the right to oral argument.

(5) Motions. The filing of a motion does not stay the time for filing a brief.

(B) **Length and Form of Briefs**. Except as permitted by order of the Court of Appeals, and except as provided in subrule (G), briefs are limited to 50 pages double-spaced, exclusive of tables, indexes, and appendixes. Quotations and footnotes may be single-spaced. At least one-inch margins must be used, and printing shall not be smaller than 12-point type. A motion for leave to file a brief in excess of the page limitations of this subrule must be filed at least 21 days before the due date of the brief. Such motions are disfavored and will be granted only for extraordinary and compelling reasons.

(C) **Appellant's Brief; Contents**. The appellant's brief must contain, in the following order:

(1) A title page, stating the full title of the case and in capital letters or boldface type "ORAL ARGUMENT REQUESTED" or "ORAL ARGUMENT NOT REQUESTED." If the appeal involves a ruling that a provision of the Michigan Constitution, a Michigan Statute, a rule or regulation included in the Michigan Administrative Code, or any other action of the legislative or executive branch of state government is invalid, the title page must include the following in capital letters or boldface type: "THE APPEAL INVOLVES A RULING THAT A PROVISION OF THE CONSTITUTION, A STATUTE, RULE OR REGULATION, OR OTHER STATE GOVERNMENTAL ACTION IS INVALID";

(2) A table of contents, listing the subject headings of the brief, including the principal points of argument, in the order of presentation, with the numbers of the pages where they appear in the brief;

(3) An index of authorities, listing in alphabetical order all case authorities cited, with the complete citations including the years of decision, and all other authorities cited, with the numbers of the pages where they appear in the brief.

(4) A statement of the basis of jurisdiction of the Court of Appeals.

(a) The statement concerning appellate jurisdiction must identify the statute, court rule, or court decision believed to confer jurisdiction on the Court of Appeals and the following information:

(i) the date of signing the judgment or order, or the date of data entry of the judgment or order in the issuing tribunal's register of actions, as applicable to confer jurisdiction on the Court of Appeals under MCR 7.204 or MCR 7.205.

(ii) the filing date of any motion claimed to toll the time within which to appeal, the disposition of such a motion, and the date of entry of the order disposing of it;

(iii) in cases where appellate counsel is appointed, the date the request for appointment of appellate counsel was filed;

(iv) in cases where appellate counsel is retained or the party is proceeding in propria persona, the filing date of the claim of appeal or the date of the order granting leave to appeal or leave to proceed under MCR 7.206.

(b) If the order sought to be reviewed adjudicates fewer than all the claims, or the rights and liabilities of fewer than all the parties, the statement must provide enough information to enable the court to determine whether there is jurisdiction.

(5) A statement of questions involved, stating concisely and without repetition the questions involved in the appeal. Each question must be expressed and numbered separately and be followed by the trial court's answer to it or the statement that the trial court failed to answer it and the appellant's answer to it. When possible, each answer must be given as "Yes" or "No";

(6) A statement of facts that must be a clear, concise, and chronological narrative. All material facts, both favorable and unfavorable, must be fairly stated without argument or bias. The statement must contain, with specific page references to the transcript, the pleadings, or other document or paper filed with the trial court,

(a) the nature of the action;
(b) the character of pleadings and proceedings;
(c) the substance of proof in sufficient detail to make it intelligible, indicating the facts that are in controversy and those that are not;
(d) the dates of important instruments and events;
(e) the rulings and orders of the trial court;
(f) the verdict and judgment; and
(g) any other matters necessary to an understanding of the controversy and the questions involved;

(7) The arguments, each portion of which must be prefaced by the principal point stated in capital letters or boldface type. As to each issue, the argument must include a statement of the applicable standard or standards of review and supporting authorities. Facts stated must be supported by specific page references to the transcript, the pleadings, or other document or paper filed with the trial court. Page references to the transcript, the pleadings, or other document or paper filed with the trial court must also be given to show whether the issue was preserved for appeal by appropriate objection or by other means. If determination of the issues presented requires the study of a constitution, statute, ordinance, administrative rule, court rule, rule of evidence, judgment, order, written instrument, or document, or relevant part thereof, this material must be reproduced in the brief or in an addendum to the brief. If an argument is presented concerning the sentence imposed in a criminal case, the appellant's attorney must send a copy of the presentence report to the court at the time the brief is filed;

(8) The relief, stating in a distinct, concluding section the order or judgment requested; and

(9) A signature.

(D) **Appellee's Brief; Contents**.

(1) Except as otherwise provided in this subrule, the appellee's brief must conform to subrule (C).

(2) The appellee must state whether the jurisdictional summary and the standard or standards of review stated in the appellant's brief are complete and correct. If they are not, the appellee must provide a complete jurisdictional summary and a counterstatement of the standard or standards of review, and supporting authorities.

(3) Unless under the headings "Statement of Questions Involved" and "Statement of Facts" the appellee accepts the appellant's statements, the appellee shall include:

(a) a counter-statement of questions involved, stating the appellee's version of the questions involved; and

(b) a counter-statement of facts, pointing out the inaccuracies and deficiencies in the appellant's statement of facts without repeating that statement and with specific page references to the transcript, the pleadings, or other document or paper filed with the trial court, to support the appellee's assertions.

(E) **Briefs in Cross Appeals**. The filing and service of briefs by a cross appellant and a cross appellee are governed by subrules (A)-(D).

(F) **Supplemental Authority**. Without leave of court, a party may file an original and four copies of a one-page communication, titled "supplemental authority," to call the court's attention to new authority released after the party filed its brief. Such a communication,

(1) may not raise new issues;

(2) may only discuss how the new authority applies to the case, and may not repeat arguments or authorities contained in the party's brief;

(3) may not cite unpublished opinions.

(G) **Reply Briefs**. An appellant or a cross-appellant may reply to the brief of an appellee or cross-appellee within 21 days after service of the brief of the appellee or cross-appellee. Reply briefs must be confined to rebuttal of the arguments in the appellee's or cross-appellee's brief and must be limited to 10 pages, exclusive of tables, indexes, and appendices, and must include a table of contents and an index of authorities. No additional or supplemental briefs may be filed except as provided by subrule (F) or by leave of the Court.

(H) **Amicus Curiae**.

(1) An amicus curiae brief may be filed only on motion granted by the Court of Appeals. The motion must be filed within 21 days after the appellee's brief is filed. If the motion is granted, the order will state the date by which the brief must be filed.

(2) The brief is limited to the issues raised by the parties. An amicus curiae may not participate in oral argument except by court order.

(I) **Nonconforming Briefs**. If, on its own initiative or on a party's motion, the court concludes that a brief does not substantially comply with the requirements in this rule, it may order the party who filed the brief to file a supplemental brief within a specified time correcting the deficiencies, or it may strike the nonconforming brief.

Rule 7.213 Calendar Cases

(A) **Pre-Argument Conference in Calendar Cases**.

(1) At any time before submission of a case, the Court of Appeals may direct the attorneys for the parties and client representatives with information and authority adequate for responsible and effective participation in settlement discussions to appear in person or by telephone for a pre-argument conference. The conference will be conducted by the court, or by a judge, retired judge or attorney designated by the court, known as a mediator. The conference shall consider the possibility of settlement, the simplification of the issues, and any other matters which the mediator determines may aid in the handling of or the disposition of the appeal. The mediator shall make an order that recites the action taken at the conference and the agreements made by the parties as to any of the matters considered, and that limits the issues to those not disposed of by the admissions or agreements of counsel. Such order, when entered, controls the subsequent proceedings, unless modified to prevent manifest injustice.

(2) All civil cases will be examined to determine if a pre-argument conference would be of assistance to the court or the parties. An attorney or a party may request a pre-argument conference in any case. Such a request shall be confidential. The pre-argument conference shall be conducted by

(a) the court, or by a judge, retired judge or attorney designated by the court;

(b) if the parties unanimously agree, a special mediator designated by the court or selected by unanimous agreement of the parties. The special mediator shall be an attorney, licensed in Michigan, who possesses either mediation-type experience or expertise in the subject matter of the case. The special mediator may charge a reasonable fee, which shall be divided and borne equally by the parties unless agreed otherwise and paid by the parties directly to the mediator. If a party does not agree upon the fee requested by the mediator, upon motion of the party, the Court of Appeals shall set a reasonable fee.

When a case has been selected for participation in a pre-argument conference, participation in the conference is mandatory; however, the Court of Appeals may except the case from participation on motion for good cause shown if it finds that a pre-argument conference in that case would be inappropriate.

(3) Any judge who participates in a pre-argument conference or becomes involved in settlement discussions under this rule may not thereafter consider any aspect of the merits of the case, except that participation in a pre-argument conference shall not preclude the judge from considering the case pursuant to MCR 7.215(J).

(4) Statements and comments made during the pre-argument conference are confidential, except to the extent disclosed by the pre-argument conference order, and shall not be disclosed by the mediator or by the participants in briefs or in argument.

(5) To facilitate the pre-argument conference, unless one has already been filed, an appellant must file the docketing statement required by MCR 7.204(H).

(6) Upon failure by a party or attorney to comply with a provision of this rule or the pre-argument conference order, the Court of Appeals may assess reasonable expenses caused by the failure, including attorney's fees, may assess all or a portion of appellate costs, or may dismiss the appeal.

(B) **Notice of Calendar Cases**. After the briefs of both parties have been filed, or after the expiration of the time for filing the appellee's brief, the clerk shall notify the parties that the case will be submitted as a "calendar case" at the next available session of the court.

(C) **Priority on Calendar**. The priority of cases on the session calendar is in accordance with the initial filing dates of the cases, except that precedence shall be given to:
  (1) interlocutory criminal appeals;
  (2) child custody cases;
  (3) interlocutory appeals from the grant of a preliminary injunction
  (4) appeals from all cases involving election issues, including, but not limited to, recall elections and petition disputes;
  (5) appeals of decisions holding that a provision of the Michigan Constitution, a Michigan statute, a rule or regulation included in the Michigan Administrative Code, or any other action of the legislative or executive branch of state government is invalid; and
  (6) actions brought under Const 1963, art 9, § 29-34 (Headlee actions); and
  (7) cases that the court orders expedited.

(D) **Arrangement of Calendar**. Twenty-one days before the first day of the session, the clerk shall mail to all parties in each calendar case notice of the designated panel, location, day, and order in which the cases will be called.

(E) **Adjournment**. A change may not be made in the session calendar, except by order of the court on its own initiative or in response to timely motions filed by the parties. A calendar case will not be withdrawn after being placed on the session calendar, except on a showing of extreme emergency.

Rule 7.214 Argument of Calendar Cases

(A) **Request for Argument**. Oral argument of a calendar case is not permitted, except on order of the court, unless a party has stated on the title page of his or her brief in capital letters or boldface type "ORAL ARGUMENT REQUESTED." The failure of a party to properly request oral argument or to timely file and serve a brief waives the right to oral argument. If neither party is entitled to oral argument, the clerk will list the case as submitted on briefs.

(B) **Length of Argument**. In a calendar case the time allowed for argument is 30 minutes for each side. When only one side is represented, only 15 minutes is allowed to that side. The time for argument may be extended by the court on motion filed at least 21 days before the session begins, or by the presiding judge during argument.

(C) **Call for Argument**. The court, on each day of the session, will call the cases for argument in the order they appear on the session calendar as arranged.

(D) **Submission on Briefs**. A case may be submitted on briefs by stipulation at any time.

(E) **Decision Without Oral Argument**. Cases may be assigned to panels of judges for appropriate review and disposition without oral argument as provided in this subrule.
  (1) If, as a result of review under this rule, the panel unanimously concludes that
    (a) the dispositive issue or issues have been recently authoritatively decided;
    (b) the briefs and record adequately present the facts and legal arguments, and the court's deliberation would not be significantly aided by oral argument; or
    (c) the appeal is without merit;

  the panel may enter without oral argument an appropriate order or opinion dismissing the appeal, affirming, reversing, or vacating the judgment or order appealed from, or remanding the case for additional proceedings.
  (2) Any party's brief may include, at the conclusion of the brief, a statement setting forth the reasons why oral argument should be heard.

Rule 7.215 Opinions, Orders, Judgments, and Final Process for Court of Appeals

(A) **Opinions of Court**. An opinion must be written and bear the writer's name or the label "per curiam" or "memorandum" opinion. An opinion of the court that bears the writer's name shall be published by the Supreme Court reporter of decisions. A memorandum opinion shall not be published. A per curiam opinion shall not be published unless one of the judges deciding the case directs the reporter to do so at the time it is filed with the clerk. A copy of an opinion to be published must be delivered to the reporter no later than when it is filed with the clerk. The reporter is responsible for having those opinions published as are opinions of the Supreme Court, but in separate volumes containing opinions of the Court of Appeals only, in a form and under a contract approved by the Supreme Court.

(B) **Standards for Publication**. A court opinion must be published if it:
  (1) establishes a new rule of law;
  (2) construes a provision of a constitution, statute, ordinance, or court rule;
  (3) alters or modifies an existing rule of law or extends it to a new factual context;
  (4) reaffirms a principle of law not applied in a recently reported decision;
  (5) involves a legal issue of continuing public interest;
  (6) criticizes existing law; or
  (7) creates or resolves an apparent conflict of authority, whether or not the earlier opinion was reported; or
  (8) decides an appeal from a lower court order ruling that a provision of the Michigan Constitution, a Michigan Statute, a rule or regulation included in the Michigan Administrative Code, or any other

action of the legislative or executive branch of state government is invalid.

(C) **Precedent of Opinions.**

(1) An unpublished opinion is not precedentially binding under the rule of stare decisis. A party who cites an unpublished opinion must provide a copy of the opinion to the court and to opposing parties with the brief or other paper in which the citation appears.

(2) A published opinion of the Court of Appeals has precedential effect under the rule of stare decisis. The filing of an application for leave to appeal to the Supreme Court or a Supreme Court order granting leave to appeal does not diminish the precedential effect of a published opinion of the Court of Appeals.

(D) **Requesting Publication.**

(1) Any party may request publication of an authored or per curiam opinion not designated for publication by

(a) filing with the clerk 4 copies of a letter stating why the opinion should be published, and

(b) mailing a copy to each party to the appeal not joining in the request, and to the clerk of the Supreme Court.

Such a request must be filed within 21 days after release of the unpublished opinion or, if a timely motion for rehearing is filed, within 21 days after the denial of the motion.

(2) Any party served with a copy of the request may file a response within 14 days in the same manner as provided in subrule (D)(1).

(3) Promptly after the expiration of the time provided in subrule (D)(2), the clerk shall submit the request, and any response that has been received, to the panel that filed the opinion. Within 21 days after submission of the request, the panel shall decide whether to direct that the opinion be published. The opinion shall be published only if the panel unanimously so directs. Failure of the panel to act within 21 days shall be treated as a denial of the request.

(4) The Court of Appeals shall not direct publication if the Supreme Court has denied an application for leave to appeal under MCR 7.302.

(E) **Judgment.**

(1) When the Court of Appeals disposes of an original action or an appeal, whether taken as of right, by leave granted, or by order in lieu of leave being granted, its opinion or order is its judgment. An order denying leave to appeal is not deemed to dispose of an appeal.

(2) The clerk shall send a certified copy of the opinion or order, with the date of filing stamped on it, to each party and, in an appeal, to the court or tribunal from which the appeal was received. In criminal cases, the clerk shall provide an additional copy of any opinion or order disposing of an appeal or of any order denying leave to appeal to the defendant's lawyer, which the lawyer must promptly send to the defendant. An opinion or order is notice of the entry of judgment of the Court of Appeals.

(F) **Execution and Enforcement.**

(1) *Routine Issuance.* Unless otherwise ordered by the Court of Appeals or the Supreme Court or as otherwise provided by these rules,

(a) the Court of Appeals judgment is effective after the expiration of the time for filing an application for leave to appeal to the Supreme Court, or, if such an application is filed, after the disposition of the case by the Supreme Court;

(b) execution on the Court of Appeals judgment is to be obtained or enforcement proceedings had in the trial court or tribunal after the record has been returned (by the clerk under MCR 7.210[H] or by the Supreme Court clerk under MCR 7.311[B]) with a certified copy of the court's judgment or, if a record was not transmitted to the Court of Appeals, after the time specified for return of the record had it been transmitted.

(2) *Exceptional Issuance.* The court may order that a judgment described in subrule (E) has immediate effect. The order does not prevent the filing of a motion for rehearing, but the filing of the motion does not stay execution or enforcement.

(G) **Entry, Issuance, Execution on, and Enforcement of All Other Orders.** An order other than one described in subrule (E) is entered on the date of filing. The clerk must promptly send a certified copy to each party and to the trial court or tribunal. Unless otherwise stated, an order is effective on the date it is entered.

(H) **Certain Dispositive Orders and Opinions in Criminal Cases; Expedited Notice to Prosecutor.** In a criminal case, if the prosecuting attorney files a notice of a victim's request for information and proof that copies of the notice were served on the other parties to the appeal, then, coincident with issuing an order or opinion that reverses a conviction, vacates a sentence, remands a case to the trial court for a new trial, or denies the prosecuting attorney's appeal, the clerk of the court must electronically transmit a copy of the order or opinion to the prosecuting attorney at a facsimile number or electronic mail address provided by the prosecuting attorney in the notice.

(I) **Reconsideration.**

(1) A motion for reconsideration may be filed within 21 days after the date of the order or the date stamped on an opinion. The motion shall include all facts, arguments, and citations to authorities in a single document and shall not exceed 10 double-

spaced pages. A copy of the order or opinion of which reconsideration is sought must be included with the motion. Motions for reconsideration are subject to the restrictions contained in MCR 2.119(F)(3).

(2) A party may answer a motion for reconsideration within 14 days after the motion is served on the party. An answer to a motion for reconsideration shall be a single document and shall not exceed 7 double-spaced pages.

(3) The clerk will not accept for filing a motion for reconsideration of an order denying a motion for reconsideration.

(4) The clerk will not accept for filing a late motion for reconsideration.

(J) **Resolution of Conflicts in Court of Appeals Decisions.**

(1) *Precedential Effect of Published Decisions.* A panel of the Court of Appeals must follow the rule of law established by a prior published decision of the Court of Appeals issued on or after November 1, 1990, that has not been reversed or modified by the Supreme Court, or by a special panel of the Court of Appeals as provided in this rule.

(2) *Conflicting Opinion.* A panel that follows a prior published decision only because it is required to do so by subrule (1) must so indicate in the text of its opinion, citing this rule and explaining its disagreement with the prior decision. The panel's opinion must be published in the official reports of opinions of the Court of Appeals.

(3) *Convening of Special Panel.*

(a) Poll of Judges. Except as provided in subrule (3)(b), within 28 days after release of the opinion indicating disagreement with a prior decision as provided in subrule (2), the chief judge must poll the judges of the Court of Appeals to determine whether the particular question is both outcome determinative and warrants convening a special panel to rehear the case for the purpose of resolving the conflict that would have been created but for the provisions of subrule (1). Special panels may be convened to consider outcome-determinative questions only.

(b) Effect of Pending Supreme Court Appeal. No poll shall be conducted and a special panel shall not be convened if, at the time the judges are required to be polled, the Supreme Court has granted leave to appeal in the controlling case.

(c) Order. Immediately following the poll, an order reflecting the result must be entered. The chief clerk of the Court of Appeals must provide a copy of the order to the Clerk of the Supreme Court. The order must be published in the official reports of opinions of the Court of Appeals.

(4) *Composition of Panel.* A special panel convened pursuant to this rule consists of 7 judges of the Court of Appeals selected by lot, except that judges who participated in either the controlling decision or the opinion in the case at bar may not be selected.

(5) *Consideration of Case by Panel.* An order directing the convening of a special panel must vacate only that portion of the prior opinion in the case at bar addressing the particular question that would have been decided differently but for the provisions of subrule (1). The special panel shall limit its review to resolving the conflict that would have been created but for the provisions of subrule (1) and applying its decision to the case at bar. The parties are permitted to file supplemental briefs, and are entitled to oral argument before the special panel unless the panel unanimously agrees to dispense with oral argument. The special panel shall return to the original panel for further consideration any remaining, unresolved issues, as the case may require.

(6) *Decision.* The decision of the special panel must be by published opinion or order and is binding on all panels of the Court of Appeals unless reversed or modified by the Supreme Court.

(7) *Reconsideration; Appeal.* There is no appeal from the decision of the Court of Appeals as to whether to convene a special panel. As to the decision in the case at bar, the time limits for moving for rehearing or for filing an application for leave to appeal to the Supreme Court run from the date of the order declining to convene a special panel or, if a special panel is convened, from the date of the decision of the special panel, except that, if the case is returned to the original panel for further consideration in accordance with subrule (5), the time limits shall run from the date of the original panel's decision, after return from the special panel. If a motion for reconsideration is filed, it shall be submitted to the special panel, which, if appropriate, may refer some or all of the issues presented to the original panel.

Rule 7.216 Miscellaneous Relief

(A) **Relief Obtainable.** The Court of Appeals may, at any time, in addition to its general powers, in its discretion, and on the terms it deems just:

(1) exercise any or all of the powers of amendment of the trial court or tribunal;

(2) allow substitution, addition, or deletion of parties or allow parties to be rearranged as appellants or appellees, on reasonable notice;

(3) permit amendment or additions to the grounds for appeal;

(4) permit amendments, corrections, or additions to the transcript or record;
(5) remand the case to allow additional evidence to be taken;
(6) draw inferences of fact;
(7) enter any judgment or order or grant further or different relief as the case may require;
(8) if a judgment notwithstanding the verdict is set aside on appeal, grant a new trial or other relief as necessary;
(9) direct the parties as to how to proceed in any case pending before it;
(10) dismiss an appeal or an original proceeding for lack of jurisdiction or failure of the appellant or the plaintiff to pursue the case in conformity with the rules.

(B) **Allowing Act After Expiration of Time**. When any nonjurisdictional act is required to be done within a designated time, the Court of Appeals may permit it to be done after expiration of the period on motion showing that there was good cause for delay or that it was not due to the culpable negligence of the party or attorney.

(C) **Vexatious Proceedings**.

(1) The Court of Appeals may, on its own initiative or on the motion of any party filed under MCR 7.211(C)(8), assess actual and punitive damages or take other disciplinary action when it determines that an appeal or any of the proceedings in an appeal was vexatious because
(a) the appeal was taken for purposes of hindrance or delay or without any reasonable basis for belief that there was a meritorious issue to be determined on appeal; or
(b) a pleading, motion, argument, brief, document, record filed in the case or any testimony presented in the case was grossly lacking in the requirements of propriety, violated court rules, or grossly disregarded the requirements of a fair presentation of the issues to the court.

(2) Damages may not exceed actual damages and expenses incurred by the opposing party because of the vexatious appeal or proceeding, including reasonable attorney fees, and punitive damages in an added amount not exceeding the actual damages. The court may remand the case to the trial court or tribunal for a determination of actual damages.

Rule 7.217 Involuntary Dismissal of Cases

(A) **Dismissal**. If the appellant, or the plaintiff in an original action under MCR 7.206, fails to order a transcript, file a brief, or comply with court rules, the clerk will notify the parties that the appeal may be dismissed for want of prosecution unless the deficiency is remedied within 21 days after the date of the clerk's notice of deficiency. If the deficiency is not remedied within that time, the chief judge or another designated judge may dismiss the appeal for want of prosecution.

(B) **Notice**. A copy of an order dismissing an appeal for want of prosecution will be sent to the parties and the court or tribunal from which the appeal originated.

(C) **Other Action**. In all instances of failure to prosecute an appeal to hearing as required, the chief judge or another designated judge may take such other action as is deemed appropriate.

(D) **Reinstatement**.

(1) Within 21 days after the date of the clerk's notice of dismissal pursuant to this rule, the appellant or plaintiff may seek relief from dismissal by showing mistake, inadvertence, or excusable neglect.
(2) The chief judge of the Court of Appeals will decide all untimely motions for reinstatement of an appeal.

Rule 7.218 Voluntary Dismissal

(A) **Dismissal by Appellant**. In all cases where the appellant or plaintiff in an original action under MCR 7.206 files an unopposed motion to withdraw the appeal, the clerk will enter an order of dismissal.

(B) **Stipulation to Dismiss**. The parties to a case in the Court of Appeals may file with the clerk a signed stipulation agreeing to dismissal of an appeal or an action brought under MCR 7.206. On payment of all fees, the clerk will enter an order dismissing the appeal or the action under MCR 7.206, except that class actions or cases submitted on a session calendar may not be dismissed except by order of the Court of Appeals.

Rule 7.219 Taxation of Costs; Fees

(A) **Right to Costs**. Except as the Court of Appeals otherwise directs, the prevailing party in a civil case is entitled to costs.

(B) **Time for Filing**. Within 28 days after the dispositive order, opinion, or order denying reconsideration is mailed, the prevailing party may file a certified or verified bill of costs with the clerk and serve a copy on all other parties. Each item claimed in the bill must be specified. Failure to file a bill of costs within the time prescribed waives the right to costs.

(C) **Objections**. Any other party may file objections to the bill of costs with the clerk within 7 days after a copy of the bill is served. The objecting party must serve a copy of the objections on the prevailing party and file proof of that service.

(D) **Taxation**. The clerk will promptly verify the bill and tax those costs allowable.

(E) **Review**. The action by the clerk will be reviewed by the Court of Appeals on motion of either party filed within 7 days from the date of taxation, but on review only those affidavits or objections which were previously filed with the clerk may be considered by the court.

(F) **Costs Taxable**. A prevailing party may tax only the reasonable costs incurred in the Court of Appeals, including:
   (1) printing of briefs, or if briefs were typewritten, a charge of $1 per original page;
   (2) any appeal or stay bond;
   (3) the transcript and necessary copies of it;
   (4) documents required for the record on appeal;
   (5) fees paid to the clerk or to the trial court clerk incident to the appeal;
   (6) taxable costs allowed by law in appeals to the Supreme Court (MCL 600.2441); and
   (7) other expenses taxable under applicable court rules.

(G) **Fees Paid to Clerk**. The clerk shall collect the following fees, which may be taxed as costs:
   (1) the fee required by law for a claim of appeal, application for leave to appeal, application for delayed appeal, original complaint, or motion;
   (2) 50¢ per page for a certified copy of a paper from a public record;
   (3) $5 for certified docket entries;
   (4) $1 per document for certification of a copy presented to the clerk; and
   (5) 50¢ per page for a copy of an opinion; however, one copy must be given without charge to each party in a case.

   A person who is unable to pay a filing fee may ask the court to waive the fee by filing a motion and an affidavit disclosing the reason for the inability.

(H) **Rule Applicable**. Except as provided in this rule, MCR 2.625 applies generally to taxation of costs in the Court of Appeals.

(I) **Violation of Rules**. The Court of Appeals may impose costs on a party or an attorney when in its discretion they should be assessed for violation of these rules.

Subchapter 7.300 Supreme Court

Rule 7.301 Jurisdiction and Term

(A) **Jurisdiction**. The Supreme Court may:
   (1) review a Judicial Tenure Commission order recommending discipline, removal, retirement, or suspension (see MCR 9.223-9.226);
   (2) review by appeal a case pending in the Court of Appeals or after decision by the Court of Appeals (see MCR 7.302);
   (3) review by appeal a final order of the Attorney Discipline Board (see MCR 9.122);
   (4) give an advisory opinion (see Const 1963, art 3, § 8);
   (5) respond to a certified question (see MCR 7.305);
   (6) exercise superintending control over a lower court or tribunal (see, e.g., MCR 7.304);
   (7) exercise other jurisdiction as provided by the constitution or by law.

(B) **Term**. The Court will hold an annual term beginning on August 1 and ending on July 31. At every term, the Court will announce a date after which it will not call cases for argument except pursuant to order on a showing of special cause. Except as provided in MCR 7.312(E), the end of a term has no effect on pending cases.

Rule 7.302 Application for Leave to Appeal

(A) **What to File**. To apply for leave to appeal, a party must file:
   (1) 8 copies of an application for leave to appeal (one must be signed) prepared in conformity with MCR 7.212(B) and consisting of the following:
      (a) a statement identifying the judgment or order appealed from and indicating the relief sought;
      (b) the questions presented for review related in concise terms to the facts of the case;
      (c) a table of contents and index of authorities conforming to MCR 7.212(C)(2) and (3);
      (d) a concise statement of the material proceedings and facts conforming to MCR 7.212(C)(6);
      (e) a concise argument, conforming to MCR 7.212(C)(7), in support of the appellant's position on each of the stated questions;
      (f) any opinion, findings, or judgment of the trial court relevant to the question as to which leave to appeal is sought;
      (g) the opinion or order of the Court of Appeals, unless review of a pending case is being sought;
   (2) A notice for hearing stating that the application will be submitted to the Court on a date which is on a Tuesday at least 21 days after the filing of the application;
   (3) Proof that a copy of the application was served on all other parties, and that a notice of the filing of the application was served on the clerks of the Court of Appeals and the trial court; and
   (4) The fee provided by MCR 7.319(B)(7)(a).

(B) **Grounds**. The application must show that
   (1) the issue involves a substantial question as to the validity of a legislative act;
   (2) the issue has significant public interest and the case is one by or against the state or one of its agencies or subdivisions or by or against an officer of the state or one of its agencies or subdivisions in the officer's official capacity;
   (3) the issue involves legal principles of major significance to the state's jurisprudence;
   (4) in an appeal before decision by the Court of Appeals,
      (a) delay in final adjudication is likely to cause substantial harm, or
      (b) the appeal is from a ruling that a provision of the Michigan Constitution, a Michigan Statute,

a rule or regulation included in the Michigan Administrative Code, or any other action of the legislative or executive branch of state government is invalid;

(5) in an appeal from a decision of the Court of Appeals, the decision is clearly erroneous and will cause material injustice or the decision conflicts with a Supreme Court decision or another decision of the Court of Appeals; or

(6) in an appeal from the Attorney Discipline Board, the decision is erroneous and will cause material injustice.

(C) **When to File**.

(1) *Before Court of Appeals Decision*. In an appeal before the Court of Appeals decision, the application must be filed within 42 days

(a) after a claim of appeal is filed in the Court of Appeals;

(b) after an application for leave to appeal is filed in the Court of Appeals; or

(c) after entry of an order by the Court of Appeals granting an application for leave to appeal.

(2) *Other Appeals*. Except as provided in subrule (C)(4), in other appeals the application must be filed within 42 days in civil cases, or within 56 days in criminal cases,

(a) after the Court of Appeals clerk mails notice of an order entered by the Court of Appeals;

(b) after the filing of the opinion appealed from; or

(c) after the Court of Appeals clerk mails notice of an order denying a timely filed motion for rehearing.

However, the time limit is 28 days where the appeal is from an order terminating parental rights or an order of discipline or dismissal entered by the Attorney Discipline Board.

(3) *Late Application, Exception*. Late applications will not be accepted except as allowed under this subrule. If an application for leave to appeal in a criminal case is received by the clerk more than 56 days after the Court of Appeals decision, and the appellant is an inmate in the custody of the Michigan Department of Corrections and has submitted the application as a pro se party, the application shall be deemed presented for filing on the date of deposit of the application in the outgoing mail at the correctional institution in which the inmate is housed. Timely filing may be shown by a sworn statement, which must set forth the date of deposit and state that first-class postage has been prepaid. The exception applies to applications from decisions of the Court of Appeals rendered on or after March 1, 2010. This exception also applies to an inmate housed in a penal institution in another state or in a federal penal institution who seeks to appeal in a Michigan court.

(4) *Decisions Remanding for Further Proceedings*. If the decision of the Court of Appeals remands the case to a lower court for further proceedings, an application for leave may be filed within 28 days in appeals from orders terminating parental rights, 42 days in other civil cases, or 56 days in criminal cases, after

(a) the Court of Appeals decision ordering the remand,

(b) the Court of Appeals clerk mails notice of an order denying a timely filed motion for rehearing of a decision remanding the case to the lower court for further proceedings, or

(c) the Court of Appeals decision disposing of the case following the remand procedure, in which case an application may be made on all issues raised in the Court of Appeals, including those related to the remand question.

(5) *Effect of Appeal on Decision Remanding Case*. If a party appeals a decision which remands for further proceedings as provided in subrule (C)(4)(a), the following provisions apply:

(a) If the Court of Appeals decision is a judgment under MCR 7.215(E)(1), an application for leave to appeal stays proceedings on remand unless the Court of Appeals or the Supreme Court orders otherwise.

(b) If the Court of Appeals decision is an order other than a judgment under MCR 7.215(E)(1), the proceedings on remand are not stayed by an application for leave to appeal unless so ordered by the Court of Appeals or the Supreme Court.

(6) *Orders Denying Motions to Remand*. If the Court of Appeals has denied a motion to remand, the appellant may raise issues relating to that denial in an application for leave to appeal from the decision on the merits.

(D) **Opposing Brief; Cross Appeal**.

(1) Any party may file 8 copies of an opposing brief before the day the application is noticed for hearing. He or she must file proof that a copy of the brief was served on all other parties.

(2) An application for leave to appeal as cross appellant may be filed with the clerk within 28 days after the appellant's application is filed. Late applications will not be accepted. The application must comply with subrule (A).

(E) **Reply Briefs**. A reply brief may be filed as provided by MCR 7.212(G).

(F) If, on its own initiative or on a party's motion, the court concludes that a brief does not substantially comply with the requirements of this rule, it may order that party who filed the brief to file a supplemental brief within a specified time correcting the deficiencies, or it may strike the nonconforming brief.

(G) **Emergencies**. Any party may move for immediate consideration of a pending application by showing what injury would occur if usual procedures were followed. The motion or an accompanying affidavit must explain the manner of service of the motion on the other parties.

(H) **Decision**.

(1) *Possible Court Actions*. The Court may grant or deny the application, enter a final decision, or issue a peremptory order. There is no oral argument on applications unless ordered by the Court. The clerk shall issue the order entered and mail copies to the parties and to the Court of Appeals clerk.

(2) *Appeal Before Court of Appeals Decision*. If leave to appeal is granted, the appeal is thereafter pending in the Supreme Court only, and subchapter 7.300 applies.

(3) *Appeal After Court of Appeals Decision*. If leave to appeal is denied, the Court of Appeals decision becomes the final adjudication and may be enforced in accordance with its terms. If leave to appeal is granted, jurisdiction over the case is vested in the Supreme Court, and subchapter 7.300 applies.

(4) *Issues on Appeal*.

(a) Unless otherwise ordered by the Court, appeals shall be limited to the issues raised in the application for leave to appeal.

(b) On motion of any party, for good cause, the Court may grant a request to add additional issues not raised in the application for leave to appeal or in the order granting leave to appeal. Permission to brief and argue such additional issues does not extend the time for filing of briefs and appendixes.

(I) **Stay of Proceedings**. MCR 7.209 applies to appeals to the Supreme Court. When a stay bond has been filed on appeal to the Court of Appeals under MCR 7.209 or a stay has been entered or takes effect pursuant to MCR 7.209(E)(4), it operates to stay proceedings pending disposition of the appeal in the Supreme Court unless otherwise ordered by the Supreme Court or Court of Appeals.

Rule 7.304 Original Proceedings

(A) **When Available**. A complaint may be filed in the Supreme Court to implement the Court's superintending control power when an application for leave to appeal cannot be filed. A complaint may be filed to implement the Court's superintending control power over the Board of Law Examiners, the Attorney Discipline Board, or the Attorney Grievance Commission.

(B) **What to File**. To initiate an original proceeding, a plaintiff must file with the clerk:

(1) 8 copies of a complaint;

(2) 8 copies of a brief conforming as nearly as possible to MCR 7.212(B) and (C);

(3) a notice of hearing, which must state that the complaint will be submitted to the Court on a date which is a Tuesday at least 21 days after the complaint is filed;

(4) proof that a copy of the complaint and brief was served on the defendant; and

(5) the fee provided by MCR 7.319(B)(7)(b).

Copies of documents, record evidence, or supporting affidavits may be attached as exhibits to the complaint. The complaint must be entitled:

"[Plaintiff] v [Court of Appeals, Board of Law Examiners, Attorney Discipline Board, or Attorney Grievance Commission],"

and the clerk is directed to re-entitle any papers otherwise entitled.

(C) **Answer**.

(1) The defendant must file 8 copies of an answer and a brief conforming with MCR 7.212(B) and (D) before the date the complaint is noticed for hearing. The defendant must serve 1 copy on the plaintiff and file proof of that service with the clerk.

(2) The grievance administrator's answer to a complaint against the Attorney Grievance Commission must show the investigatory steps taken and other pertinent information.

(D) **Actions Against Attorney Grievance Commission; Confidentiality**. The clerk shall keep the file in an action against the Attorney Grievance Commission or the grievance administrator confidential and not open to the public if it appears that the complaint relates to matters that are confidential under MCR 9.126. In the answer to a complaint, the grievance administrator shall certify to the clerk whether the matters involved in the action are deemed confidential under MCR 9.126. The protection provided by MCR 9.126 continues, unless the Court otherwise orders.

(E) **Decision**. The Court may set the case for argument as on leave granted, grant or deny the relief requested, or enter another order it finds appropriate, including an order to show cause why the relief sought in the complaint should not be granted. There is no oral argument on complaints unless ordered by the Court.

Rule 7.305 Certified Questions

(A) **From Michigan Courts**.

(1) Whenever a court or tribunal from which an appeal may be taken to the Court of Appeals or to the Supreme Court has pending before it an action or proceeding involving a controlling question of public law, and the question is of such public moment as to require early determination according to executive message of the Governor addressed to the Supreme Court, the Supreme Court may authorize the court or tribunal to certify the question to the Supreme Court with a statement of

the facts sufficient to make clear the application of the question. Further proceedings relative to the case are stayed to the extent ordered by the court or tribunal, pending receipt of an answer from the Supreme Court.

(2) If any question is not properly stated, or if sufficient facts are not given, the Supreme Court may require a further and better statement of the question or of the facts.

(3) The answer to a certified question is given by the Supreme Court in the ordinary form of an opinion, to be published with other opinions of the Supreme Court.

(4) After the answer of the Supreme Court has been sent, the court or tribunal will proceed with or dispose of the case in accordance with the Supreme Court's answer.

(B) **From Other Courts**.

(1) When a federal court, state appellate court, or tribal court considers a question that Michigan law may resolve and that is not controlled by Michigan Supreme Court precedent, the court may on its own initiative or that of an interested party certify the question to the Michigan Supreme Court.

(2) A certificate may be prepared by stipulation or at the certifying court's direction, and must contain

(a) the case title;

(b) a factual statement; and

(c) the question to be answered.

The presiding judge must sign it, and the clerk must certify it under seal.

(3) With the certificate, the parties shall submit

(a) briefs conforming with MCR 7.306 and 7.309;

(b) a joint appendix conforming with MCR 7.307, 7.308, and 7.309; and

(c) a request for oral argument, if oral argument is desired.

(4) If the Supreme Court responds to the question certified, the clerk shall send a copy to the certifying court under seal.

(5) The Supreme Court shall divide costs equally among the parties, subject to redistribution by the certifying court.

Rule 7.306 Briefs in Calendar Cases

(A) **Form of Briefs**. Briefs in calendar cases must be prepared in the form provided in MCR 7.212(B),(C), and (D) and produced as provided in MCR 7.309. For the purposes of this rule, references in MCR 7.212(C) and (D) to the "record" should be read as referring to the appendix.

(B) **Length of Brief; Summary of Argument**. In a brief in which the argument of any one issue exceeds 20 pages, a summary of argument must be included. The summary must be a succinct, accurate, and clear condensation of the argument actually made in the body of the brief and may not be a mere repetition of the headings under which the argument is arranged. Unless the Court allows a longer brief, a brief prepared in the manner authorized under MCR 7.309 may not exceed 50 pages, excluding the table of contents, index of authorities, and appendix, but including the summary of argument.

(C) **Reply Briefs**. A reply brief may be filed as provided by MCR 7.212(G).

(D) **Amicus Curiae Briefs**.

(1) Except as provided in subsection (2), an amicus curiae brief may be filed only on motion granted by the Court and must conform to subrules (A) and (B) and MCR 7.309. The brief of an amicus curiae is to be filed within 21 days after the brief of the appellee, or at such other time as the Court directs. An amicus curiae may not participate in oral argument except by Court order.

(2) No motion for leave to file an amicus curiae brief is necessary if the brief is presented on behalf of the people of the state of Michigan or the state of Michigan, or any of its agencies or officials, by the Attorney General; on behalf of any political subdivision of the state when submitted by its authorized legal officer, its authorized agent, or an association representing a political subdivision; or on behalf of the Prosecuting Attorneys Association of Michigan or the Criminal Defense Attorneys of Michigan.

Rule 7.307 Appellant's Appendix

(A) **Contents of Appendix**. An appendix, entitled "Appellant's Appendix," must be separately bound. Each page number must be followed by the letter "a" (e.g., 1a). The appendix must contain

(1) a table of contents,

(2) the relevant docket entries both in the lower court and in the Court of Appeals arranged chronologically in a single column;

(3) the trial court judgment, order, or decision in question and the Court of Appeals opinion or order;

(4) any relevant finding or opinion of the trial court;

(5) any relevant portions of the pleadings or other parts of the record; and

(6) any relevant portions of the transcript, including the complete jury instructions if an issue is raised regarding a jury instruction.

The items listed in subrules (A)(3)-(6) shall be arranged in chronological order.

(B) **Joint Appendix**.

(1) The parties may stipulate to prepare a joint appendix, so designated, containing the matters that both want the justices to read to decide fairly the questions involved. A joint appendix shall meet the requirements of this rule and shall be separately bound and served with the appellant's brief.

(2) The stipulation to use a joint appendix may provide that either party may prepare, as a supplemental appendix, any additional portion of the record not covered by the joint appendix.

Rule 7.308 Appellee's Appendix

An appendix, entitled "Appellee's Appendix," may be filed, but must be separately bound. It may contain the part of the record the appellee wants the justices to read that has not been included in the appellant's appendix. The appellee's appendix must comply with the provisions of MCR 7.307. Each page number must be followed by the letter "b" (e.g., 1b). Material in the appellant's appendix may not be repeated in the appellee's appendix, except to clarify the subject matter included.

Rule 7.309 Preparation, Filing, and Serving Briefs and Appendixes

(A) **Form**.

(1) Briefs and appendixes shall be produced on good white unglazed paper by any printing, duplicating, or copying process that provides a clear image. Original typewritten pages may be used, but not carbon copies. Briefs and appendixes must be prepared in conformity with MCR 7.212(B), except that briefs must be printed on only one side of the page and appendixes must be printed on both sides of the page.

The necessary expense of preparation of briefs and appendixes to be taxed as costs pursuant to MCR 7.319 shall not exceed $2 per original page.

(2) The pages of the appendix must be numbered separately from the brief. In each appendix, brief running heads must be printed at the top of each page indicating the character of the matter contained on the page including, for testimony, the name of the witness, and, for documents, the nature of them. The clerk must refuse to receive a brief or appendix which has not been prepared in substantial conformity with this rule. The submission to the clerk of a nonconforming brief or appendix does not satisfy the time limitations for filing briefs and appendixes.

(3) A brief and appendix must have a suitable cover of heavy paper. The cover page must follow this form:

In the Supreme Court
Appeal from the [court or tribunal appealed from]
[judge or presiding officer]

____

Plaintiff-[Appellant or Appellee],
V
Docket No.

____

____

Defendant-[Appellee or Appellant].
Brief on Appeal – [Appellant or Appellee]
ORAL ARGUMENT [NOT] REQUESTED

____

Attorney for [Plaintiff or Defendant]-
[Appellant or Appellee]
[Business Address]

____

____

____

Appendixes shall be similarly endorsed, but shall be designated as appendixes instead of briefs. The cover of the brief of the appellant must be blue; that of the appellee, red; that of an intervenor or amicus curiae, green; that of any reply brief, gray; that of an appendix, yellow.

(B) **Filing and Service; Dismissal**.

(1) *Appellant's Brief and Appendix*. The appellant shall

(a) file 24 copies of a brief and appendix with the clerk within 56 days after leave to appeal is granted;

(b) serve 2 copies on each attorney who has appeared in the case for a separate party or group of parties and on each party who has appeared in person;

(c) serve 1 copy on the Attorney General in a criminal case or in a case in which the state is a party or interested; and

(d) file proof of service with the clerk.

(2) *Appellee's Brief and Appendix*. The appellee shall

(a) file 24 copies of a brief and appendix with the clerk within 35 days after the appellant's brief and appendix is served on the appellee;

(b) serve 2 copies on each attorney who has appeared in the case for a separate party or group of parties and on each party who has appeared in person;

(c) serve 1 copy on the Attorney General in a criminal case or in a case in which the state is a party or interested; and

(d) file proof of service with the clerk.

(3) *Failure to File*. If the appellant fails to file the brief and appendix within the time required, the Court may dismiss the case and award costs to the appellee, or affirm the judgment or order appealed from. A party filing a brief late forfeits the right to oral argument. The Court may extend the time on a party's motion.

(C) **Earlier Filing and Serving**. The time provided for filing and serving of the appellant's or the appellee's brief and appendix may be shortened on order of the Court on motion of either party or on the Court's own initiative.

Rule 7.310 Stipulations

The parties may stipulate in writing regarding any matter constituting the basis for an application for leave to appeal, or regarding any matter relevant to a part of the record on appeal. The parties may file with the clerk a stipulation agreeing to the dismissal of an application for leave to appeal or an appeal. The clerk shall present the stipulation to the Court, which shall enter the dismissal unless it concludes that the appeal should be decided notwithstanding the stipulation.

Rule 7.311 Filing Record on Appeal

(A) **Transmission of Record**. An appeal is heard on the original papers, which constitute the record on appeal. When requested by the Supreme Court clerk, the Court of Appeals clerk or the lower court clerk shall send to the Supreme Court clerk all papers on file in the Court of Appeals or the lower court, certified by the clerk. For an appeal originating from an administrative board, office, or tribunal, the record on appeal is the certified record filed with the Court of Appeals clerk and the papers filed with the Court of Appeals clerk.

(B) **Return of Record**. After final adjudication or other disposition of an appeal, the clerk shall return the original record to the Court of Appeals clerk, to the clerk of the lower court or tribunal in which the record was made, or to the clerk of the court to which the case has been remanded for further proceedings, and the clerk of the lower court to which the original record has been sent shall promptly notify the attorneys of the receipt of the record. The Supreme Court clerk shall forward a certified copy of the order or judgment entered by the Supreme Court to the Court of Appeals clerk and to the clerk of the trial court or tribunal from which the appeal was taken.

Rule 7.312 Supreme Court Calendar

(A) **Definition**. A case in which leave to appeal has been granted, or a case initiated in the Supreme Court which the Court determines will be heard and argued, is termed a "calendar case."

(B) **Notice of Hearing; Request for Oral Argument**.

(1) After the briefs of both parties have been filed or the time for filing the appellee's brief has expired, the clerk shall notify the parties that the case will be heard at a session of the Supreme Court not less than 35 days after the date of the notice. The Court may shorten the 35-day period.

(2) Except on order of the Court, a party is not entitled to oral argument unless that party advises the clerk, in writing, of the desire to argue orally at least 21 days before the first day of the session. If neither party is entitled to oral argument, the clerk will list the case as submitted on briefs. The Court may direct that a case be submitted on briefs without oral argument.

(C) **Arrangement of Calendar**. Twenty-one days before the first day of the session, the clerk will place cases on the session calendar and arrange the order in which they are to be heard. The cases will be called and heard in that order except as provided in subrule (D).

(D) **Adjournments; Rearrangement of Calendar**. By stipulation filed with the clerk at least 21 days before the first day of the session, a case may be specially placed on the session calendar, grouped to suit the convenience of the attorneys, or placed at the end of the call. After the rearrangement of cases by the clerk, further changes may not be made by the attorneys. A motion to adjourn to another session may be made only for good cause and on notice to the opposing attorney at least 48 hours before the time set for hearing, unless the opposing attorney consents to it in writing.

(E) **Reargument of Undecided Cases**. When a calendar case, other than one argued pursuant to special order under MCR 7.301(B), remains undecided at the end of the term in which it was argued, either party may file a supplemental brief. In addition, if either party requests within 14 days after the beginning of the new term, the clerk shall schedule the case for reargument.

Rule 7.313 Motions in Supreme Court

(A) **What to File**. To have a motion heard, a party must file with the clerk:

(1) a motion stating briefly but distinctly the grounds on which it is based and the relief required;

(2) an affidavit supporting any allegations of fact in the motion;

(3) a notice that the motion will be heard on a Tuesday at least 7 days after the motion is filed;

(4) the fee provided by MCR 7.319(B)(7)(c) or (d); and

(5) proof that the motion and supporting papers were served on the opposing party.

Eight copies of the motion must be filed, except only 2 copies need be filed of a motion to extend time, to place a case on or withdraw a case from the session calendar, or for oral argument. The attorney must sign the motion. By filing a motion for immediate consideration, a party may obtain an earlier hearing on the motion.

(B) **Motion Day**. Tuesday of each week is motion day. There is no oral argument on motions, unless ordered by the Court.

(C) **Answer**. An answer may be filed at any time before an order is entered on the motion.

(D) **Motion to Seal File**. Except as otherwise provided by statute or court rule, the procedure for sealing a Supreme Court file is governed by MCR 8.119(F). Materials that are subject to a motion to seal a file in whole or in part shall be held under seal pending the court's disposition of the motion.

(E) **Motion for Rehearing**.

(1) To move for rehearing, a party must file within 21 days after the opinion was filed (the date of an

opinion is stamped on the upper right corner of the first page):
    (a) 24 copies of a motion prepared as provided in MCR 7.309, if the opinion decided a case placed on a session calendar; or
    (b) 14 typewritten copies of a motion, if the opinion decided a noncalendar case; and
    (c) proof that a copy was served on the parties.

The motion for rehearing must include reasons why the Court should modify its opinion. Motions for rehearing are subject to the restrictions contained in MCR 2.119(F)(3).

(2) Unless otherwise ordered by the Court, timely filing of a motion postpones issuance of the Court's judgment order until the motion is denied by the Court or, if granted, until at least 21 days after the filing of the Court's opinion on rehearing.

(3) Any party may answer a motion within 14 days after it is served by filing
    (a) 24 or 14 copies of the motion, depending on whether the motion was filed under subrule (D)(1)(a) or (b); and
    (b) proof that a copy was served on the other parties.

(4) Unless ordered by the Court, there is no oral argument.

(F) **Motion for Reconsideration**. To move for reconsideration of a court order, a party must file the items required by subrule (A) within 21 days after the date of certification of the order. Motions for reconsideration are subject to the restrictions contained in MCR 2.119(F)(3). The clerk shall refuse to accept for filing any motion for reconsideration of an order denying a motion for reconsideration. The filing of a motion for reconsideration does not stay the effect of the order addressed in the motion.

Rule 7.314 Appeals in Which No Progress Has Been Made

(A) **Designation**. If a brief has not been filed under MCR 7.309(B)(1) within 182 days after the entry of the order granting leave to appeal or directing that the action be heard as a calendar case, the case shall be designated as one in which no progress has been made. In calculating the 182-day period, adjournments granted by the Court are excluded.

(B) **Notice; Dismissal**. When a case is so designated, the clerk shall mail to each party notice that unless cause is shown to the contrary, the case will be dismissed. The clerk shall file proof of that notice. The clerk shall place as the first item for each session calendar all cases in which notice of no progress has been mailed at least 21 days before the first day of that session. On the first day of each session, the Court shall dismiss each case appearing on the calendar as one in which no progress has been made, unless cause is shown to the contrary.

(C) The court may dismiss an appeal, application, or an original proceeding for lack of jurisdiction or failure of a party to pursue the case in substantial conformity with the rules.

Rule 7.315 Call and Argument of Cases in Supreme Court

(A) **Call; Notice of Argument; Withdrawal From Call**. The Court, on the first day of each session, will call the cases for argument in the order they stand on the calendar as arranged, and proceed from day to day during the session in the same order. A case may not be withdrawn after being placed on the call, except on a showing of extreme emergency. A case may be submitted on briefs by stipulation at any time.

(B) **Argument**. In a calendar case, the time allowed for argument is 30 minutes for each side unless the Court orders otherwise. When only one side is represented, only 15 minutes is allowed unless the Court orders otherwise. The time for argument may be extended by the Court on motion filed at least 14 days before the session begins or by the Chief Justice during the argument. Oral argument should emphasize and clarify the written argument appearing in the brief filed. The Court looks with disfavor on an argument that is read from a prepared text.

Rule 7.316 Miscellaneous Relief Obtainable in Supreme Court

(A) **Relief Obtainable**. The Supreme Court may, at any time, in addition to its general powers:
    (1) exercise any or all of the powers of amendment of the court or tribunal below;
    (2) on reasonable notice as it may require, allow substitution of parties by reason of marriage, death, bankruptcy, assignment, or any other cause; allow new parties to be added or parties to be dropped; or allow parties to be rearranged as appellants or appellees;
    (3) permit the reasons or grounds of appeal to be amended or new grounds to be added;
    (4) permit the transcript or record to be amended by correcting errors or adding matters which should have been included;
    (5) adjourn the case until further evidence is taken and brought before it, as the Court may deem necessary in order to do justice;
    (6) draw inferences of fact;
    (7) enter any judgment or order that ought to have been entered, and enter other and further orders and grant relief as the case may require; or
    (8) if a judgment notwithstanding the verdict is set aside on appeal, grant a new trial or other relief as it deems just.

(9) dismiss an appeal, application, or an original proceeding for lack of jurisdiction or failure of a party to pursue the case in substantial conformity with the rules.

(B) **Allowing Act After Expiration of Time**. When, under the practice relating to appeals or stay of proceedings, a nonjurisdictional act is required to be done within a designated time, the Supreme Court may at any time, on motion and notice, permit it to be done after the expiration of the period on a showing made to the court that there was good cause for the delay or that it was not due to the culpable negligence of the appellant. The Court will not entertain a motion to file a late application for leave to appeal under MCR 7.302(C)(3) or MCR 7.302(D)(2) or a late motion for reconsideration under MCR 7.313(F).

(C) **Decision by Supreme Court**. A motion may not be decided or an order entered by the Court unless all required documents have been filed with the Court and the requisite fees have been paid. Except for affirmance of action by a lower court or tribunal by even division of the justices, a decision of the Supreme Court must be made by concurrence of a majority of the justices voting.

(D) **Vexatious Proceedings**.

(1) The Court may, on its own initiative or the motion of any party filed before a case is placed on a session calendar, dismiss an appeal, assess actual and punitive damages, or take other disciplinary action when it determines that an appeal or any of the proceedings in an appeal was vexatious because

(a) the appeal was taken for purposes of hindrance or delay or without any reasonable basis for belief that there was a meritorious issue to be determined on appeal; or

(b) a pleading, motion, argument, brief, document, or record filed in the case or any testimony presented in the case was grossly lacking in the requirements of propriety, violated court rules, or grossly disregarded the requirements of a fair presentation of the issues to the Court.

(2) Damages may not exceed actual damages and expenses incurred by the opposing party because of the vexatious appeal or proceeding, including reasonable attorney fees, and punitive damages in an added amount not exceeding the actual damages. The Court may remand the case to the trial court or tribunal for a determination of actual damages.

Rule 7.317 Opinions, Orders, and Judgments of Supreme Court

(A) **Opinions of Court**. An opinion must be written and bear the writer's name or the label "per curiam." Each justice deciding a case must sign an opinion.

(B) **Filing and Publication**. The Court shall file a signed opinion with the clerk, who shall stamp the date of filing on it. The Supreme Court reporter of decisions is responsible for having the opinions printed, in a form and under a contract approved by the Court.

(C) **Orders or Judgments Pursuant to Opinions**.

(1) *Entry*. The clerk shall enter an order or judgment pursuant to an opinion as of the date the opinion is filed with the clerk.

(2) *Routine Issuance*.

(a) If a motion for rehearing is not timely filed under MCR 7.313(E)(1), the clerk shall send a certified copy of the order or judgment to the Court of Appeals with its file, and to the court or tribunal which tried the case with its record, not less than 21 days nor more than 28 days after entry of the order or judgment.

(b) If a motion for rehearing is timely filed, the clerk shall fulfill the responsibilities under subrule (C)(2)(a) promptly after the Court denies the motion or, if the motion is granted, enter a new order or judgment after the Court's opinion on rehearing.

(3) *Exceptional Issuance*. The Court may direct the clerk to dispense with the time requirement of subrule (C)(2)(a) and issue the order or judgment when its opinion is filed. An order or judgment issued under this subrule does not preclude the filing of a motion for rehearing, but the filing of a motion does not stay execution or enforcement.

(4) *Execution or Enforcement*. Unless otherwise ordered by the Court, an order or judgment is effective when it is issued under subrule (C)(2)(a) or (b) or (C)(3), and enforcement is to be obtained in the trial court.

(D) **Entry, Issuance, Execution, and Enforcement of Other Orders and Judgments of Court**. An order or judgment, other than those by opinion under subrule (C), is entered on the date of filing. Unless otherwise stated, an order or judgment is effective the date it is entered. The clerk must promptly send a certified copy to each party, to the Court of Appeals, and to the lower court or tribunal.

Rule 7.318 Taxation of Costs

(A) **Rules Applicable**. The procedure for taxation of costs in the Supreme Court is as provided by MCR 7.219.

(B) **Expenses Taxable**. Unless the Court otherwise orders, a prevailing party may tax only the reasonable costs incurred in the Supreme Court, including the necessary expense of printing the briefs and appendixes required by these rules.

Rule 7.319 Supreme Court Clerk

(A) **Appointment; General Provisions**. The Supreme Court will appoint a clerk who shall keep the clerk's office in Lansing under the direction of the Court.

Where the term "clerk" appears in this subchapter without modification, it means the Supreme Court clerk. The clerk may not practice law other than as clerk while serving as clerk.

(B) **Duties**. The clerk shall do the following:

(1) Furnish bond before taking office. The bond must be in favor of the people of the state and in the penal sum of $10,000, approved by the Chief Justice and filed with the Secretary of State, and conditioned on the faithful performance of the clerk's official duties. The fee for the bond is a state expense.

(2) Collect the fees provided for by statute or court rule.

(3) Deposit monthly with the State Treasurer the fees collected, securing and filing a receipt for them.

(4) Provide for the recording of Supreme Court proceedings as the Court directs.

(5) Care for and maintain custody of all records, seals, books, and papers pertaining to the clerk's office and filed or deposited there.

(6) After an appeal has been decided by the Court, return the original record as provided in MCR 7.311(B).

(7) Collect the following fees, which may be taxed as costs when costs are allowed by the Court:

(a) $375 for an application for leave to appeal;

(b) $375 for an original proceeding;

(c) $150 for a motion for immediate consideration or a motion to expedite appeal, except that a prosecuting attorney is exempt from paying a fee under this subdivision in an appeal arising out of a criminal proceeding, if the defendant is represented by a court-appointed lawyer;

(d) $75 for all other motions;

(e) 50 cents per page for a certified copy of a paper, from a public record;

(f) $5 for certified docket entries;

(g) $1 for certification of a copy presented to the clerk;

(h) 50 cents per page for a copy of an opinion; however, one copy must be given without charge to the attorney for each party in the case.

A person who is unable to pay a filing fee may ask the Court to waive the fee by filing a motion and an affidavit disclosing the reason for that inability.

Rule 7.320 Deputy Supreme Court Clerks

The Supreme Court may appoint deputy Supreme Court clerks. A deputy clerk shall carry out the duties assigned by the clerk and perform the duties of the clerk if the clerk is absent or unable to act.

Rule 7.321 Reporter of Decisions

The Supreme Court will appoint a reporter. The reporter shall:

(1) prepare the decisions, including dissenting opinions, of the Supreme Court for publication in volumes of not less than 700 nor more than 750 pages;

(2) write a brief statement of the facts of each case and headnotes containing the points made;

(3) publish each opinion in advance sheets as soon as practicable but not later than 2 months after it is issued; and

(4) publish bound volumes within 9 months after the last opinion included in it is issued.

(5) The reasons for denying leave to appeal, required by Const 1963, art 6, § 6 and filed in the clerk's office, are not to be published, and are not to be regarded as precedent.

Rule 7.322 Supreme Court Crier

The Supreme Court crier shall

(1) have charge of the Supreme Court room and the rooms assigned to the Supreme Court justices;

(2) have the power to serve an order, process, or writ issued by the Supreme Court; collect the fee for that service allowed by law to sheriffs; and deposit monthly with the State Treasurer all the fees collected, securing a receipt for them.

Rule 7.323 Selection of Chief Justice

At the first meeting of the Supreme Court in each odd-numbered year, the justices shall select by majority vote one among them to be Chief Justice.

CHAPTER 8. ADMINISTRATIVE RULES OF COURT

Subchapter 8.100 General Administrative Orders

Rule 8.101 Applicability of Administrative Rules

The administrative rules of subchapter 8.100 apply to all courts established by the constitution and laws of Michigan, unless a rule otherwise provides.

Rule 8.103 State Court Administrator

The state court administrator, under the Supreme Court's supervision and direction, shall:

(1) supervise and examine the administrative methods and systems employed in the offices of the courts, including the offices of the clerks and other officers, and make recommendations to the Supreme Court for the improvement of the administration of the courts;

(2) examine the status of court calendars, determine the need for assistance to a court, and report to the Supreme Court;

(3) on receipt of the quarterly reports as provided in MCR 8.110(C)(5), investigate each case in an effort to determine the reason for delays, recommend actions to eliminate delays, and recommend further actions to expedite process to insure speedy trials of criminal cases;

(4) recommend to the Supreme Court the assignment of judges where courts are in need of assistance and carry out the direction of the Supreme Court as to the assignment of judges;

(5) collect and compile statistical and other data, make reports of the business transacted by the courts, and transmit the reports to the Supreme Court so that the statistics and other data may be used in taking proper action in the administration of justice;

(6) prepare and submit budget estimates of state appropriations necessary for the maintenance and operation of the judicial system;

(7) obtain reports from courts, and the judges, clerks, and other officers of the courts, in accordance with rules adopted by the Supreme Court on cases and other judicial business conducted or pending in the courts, and report on them to the Supreme Court;

(8) recommend to the Supreme Court policies for the improvement of the judicial system;

(9) approve and publish forms as required by these rules, and such other recommended forms as the administrator deems advisable; and

(10) attend to other matters assigned by the Supreme Court.

Rule 8.104 Judicial Meetings

(A) **Meetings to be Called by State Court Administrator**. The state court administrator, under the Supreme Court's supervision and direction, may call

(1) an annual statewide meeting of the circuit, recorder's, and Court of Appeals judges;

(2) an annual statewide meeting of the probate judges;

(3) an annual statewide meeting of the district judges; and

(4) additional statewide or regional meetings of judges as may be desirable.

(B) **Presiding Officer**. The Chief Justice of the Supreme Court or another person designated by the Chief Justice shall preside at judicial meetings called by the state court administrator.

(C) **Secretary**. The state court administrator or deputy administrator acts as secretary at judicial meetings called by the state court administrator.

(D) **Purposes**. At the meetings, the judges are to

(1) study the organization, rules, methods of procedure, and practice of the judicial system in general;

(2) study the problems of administration confronting the courts and judicial system in general; and

(3) make recommendations for

(a) modifying or ameliorating existing conditions,

(b) harmonizing and improving laws, and

(c) amending the rules and statutes relating to practice and procedure.

Rule 8.105 General Duties of Clerks

(A) **Office Hours**. The office of the clerk of every court of record must be open, and the clerk or deputy clerk must be in attendance, during business hours on all days except Saturdays, Sundays, and legal holidays, and at other times that the court is in session.

(B) **Court Records and Reporting Duties**. The clerk of every circuit court shall maintain court records and make reports as prescribed by MCR 8.119.

(C) **Notice of Judgments, Orders, and Opinions**. Notice of a judgment, final order, written opinion or findings filed or entered in a civil action in a court of record must be given forthwith in writing by the court clerk to the attorneys of record in the case, in the manner provided in MCR 2.107.

(D) **Filing of Assurance of Discontinuance Under MCL 445.870**. The clerk of every judicial circuit shall, without charge, receive and file an assurance of discontinuance accepted by the Attorney General under MCL 445.870.

Rule 8.106 Money Paid Into Court

(A) **When Court Order Required**. Except as otherwise provided by law or when the money is in the form of cash bonds, the clerk may not perform services in handling money under MCL 600.2529(1)(f) without a signed order of the court.

(B) **Disposition of Interest Earned**. If the clerk deposits money in an interest-bearing account, the clerk retains as a fee one-tenth of the interest earned, but not more than $100 each year or part of the year. The fee must be deposited in the county general fund, as required by law. The balance of the interest earned and the principal must be disbursed to the persons entitled to the balance.

(C) **Accounts; Records**. The accounts of the clerk with the banks in which the money is directed to be deposited must be kept in a single trust fund, with the designation of the rights in the fund appearing on the court's records.

(D) **Orders to Pay out Funds**. Orders on the banks for the payment of money out of court are made payable to the order of the person entitled to the money or of that person's duly authorized attorney, and must specify in what action or on what account the money is to be paid out, and the time when the judgment or order authorizing the payment was made.

(E) NSF Checks. A court may assess costs for reasonable expenses incurred for checks returned to the court due to nonsufficient funds.

Rule 8.107 Statement by Trial Judge as to Matters Undecided

(A) **Time**. Matters under submission to a judge or judicial officer should be promptly determined. Short deadlines should be set for presentation of briefs and affidavits and for production of transcripts. Decisions, when possible, should be made from the bench or within a few days of submission; otherwise a decision should be rendered no later than 35 days after submission. For the purpose of this rule, the time of submission is the time the last argument or presentation in the matter was made, or the expiration of the time allowed for filing the last brief or production of transcripts, as the case may be.

(B) **Report as to Matters Undecided**. On the first business day of January, April, July, and October of each year, every trial judge shall file a certified statement with the chief judge in the form prescribed by the state court administrator. The statement shall provide information on all matters pending during the reporting period that were not decided within 56 days from submission. The judge shall state the reason that a decision was not made within 56 days. A report is required regardless of whether there is any case to report. The chief judge shall sign and file, or electronically submit, the statement with the state court administrator.

Rule 8.108 Court Reporters and Recorders

(A) **Scope of Rule**. This rule prescribes the duties of court reporters and recorders, the procedure for certifying them, the effect of noncertification, objections to certification, and display requirements.

(B) **Attendance at Court; Taking Testimony**.

(1) The court reporter or recorder shall attend the court sessions under the direction of the court and take a verbatim record of the following:

(a) the voir dire of prospective jurors;

(b) the testimony;

(c) the charge to the jury;

(d) in a jury trial, the opening statements and final arguments;

(e) the reasons given by the court for granting or refusing any motion made by a party during the course of a trial; and

(f) opinions and orders dictated by the court and other matters as may be prescribed by the court.

This subrule does not apply to actions tried in the small claims division of the district court or in the municipal courts. In the probate court proceedings, the reporter or recorder shall take a verbatim record of proceedings as required by law and chapter 5 of these rules.

(2) The court reporter or recorder who begins to record a case shall take the record of the entire case unless he or she shows good cause for failure to do so or is otherwise excused by the court.

(C) **Records Kept**. All records, as defined in MCR 8.119(F) and regardless of format, that are created and kept by the court reporter or recorder belong to the court, must remain in the physical possession of the court, and are subject to access in accordance with MCR 8.119(H). The court reporter or recorder who takes the testimony on the trial or the hearing of any case shall prefix the record of the testimony of each witness with the full name of the witness and the date and time the testimony was taken. At the conclusion of the trial of the case the reporter or recorder shall secure all of the records and properly entitle them on the outside, and shall safely keep them in the court according to the Michigan Trial Court Case File Management Standards. If the court reporter or recorder needs access to the records for purposes of transcribing off-site, the reporter or recorder may take only a reproduction of the original recording, which must be returned to the court upon filing of the transcript.

(D) **Transfer of Records; Inspection**. If the court reporter or recorder dies, resigns, is removed from office, or leaves the state, records he or she created and kept in each case pursuant to subrule (C) must be transferred to the clerk of the court in which the case was tried. The clerk shall safely keep the records in accordance with the Michigan Trial Court Case File Management Standards and MCR 8.119(F). On order of the court, a transcript shall be made from the records and filed as a part of the public record in the case.

(E) **Furnishing Transcript**. The court reporter or recorder shall furnish without delay, in legible English, a transcript of the records taken by him or her (or any part thereof) to any party on request. The reporter or recorder is entitled to receive the compensation prescribed in the statute on fees from the person who makes the request.

(F) **Filing Transcript.**

(1) On order of the trial court, the court reporter or recorder shall make and file in the clerk's office a transcript of his or her records, in legible English, of any civil or criminal case (or any part thereof) without expense to either party; the transcript is a part of the records in the case.

(2) Except when otherwise provided by contract, the court reporter or recorder shall receive from the appropriate governmental unit the compensation specified in the statute on fees for a transcript ordered by a court.

(G) **Certification.**

(1) *Certification Requirement.*

(a) Only reporters, recorders, or voice writers certified pursuant to this subrule may record or prepare transcripts of proceedings held in Michigan courts or of depositions taken in Michigan pursuant to these rules. This rule applies to the preparation of transcripts of videotaped courtroom proceedings or videotaped or audiotaped depositions, but not to the recording of such proceedings or depositions by means of videotaping. An operator holding a CEO certification under subrule (G)(7)(b) may record proceedings, but may not prepare transcripts.

(b) Proceedings held pursuant to MCR 6.102 or 6.104 need not be recorded by persons certified under this rule; however, transcripts of such proceedings must be prepared by court reporters, recorders, or voice writers certified pursuant to this rule.

(c) An indigent party who is represented by a nonprofit legal aid program providing free civil legal services to the indigent may use persons who are not certified pursuant to this rule to transcribe and file depositions taken by videotaping or audiotaping. Such depositions shall be otherwise prepared and certified in accordance with this rule.

(d) Any person who acts in the capacity of a court reporter or recorder shall not maintain an action in the courts of this state for the collection of compensation for the performance of an act for which certification is required by this rule without alleging and proving that the person was certified under this rule at the time of the performance of the act. "Person" refers to both individuals and the entity or entities for which a court reporter or recorder performs services.

(e) Any other court rule notwithstanding, an objection to the status of a court reporter's or recorder's certification or lack thereof must be placed on the record at the outset of the court proceeding or deposition or that objection is waived. If the objection is waived, the use of transcripts of the court proceeding or deposition for any purpose provided in these rules shall be allowed.

(f) Prior to the beginning of any deposition taken under these rules, the court reporter or recorder must display to all counsel initially present, and to each other person attending the deposition who is not represented by counsel, proof that the reporter or recorder has been certified as required by this rule. Proof of such certification, by certification number, shall also be displayed on the title page and certificate page of each court and deposition transcript and on the stationery and business cards, if any, of each court reporter or recorder required to be certified by this rule.

(2) *Court Reporting and Recording Board of Review.*

(a) The Supreme Court shall appoint a Court Reporting and Recording Board of Review, composed of

(i) a Court of Appeals judge, to be the chairperson;

(ii) a circuit judge;

(iii) a probate judge;

(iv) a district judge;

(v) a court reporter who is an employee of a Michigan court;

(vi) a court recorder who is an employee of a Michigan court;

(vii) a court reporter who is not an employee of a Michigan court;

(viii) a court recorder who is not an employee of a Michigan court; and,

(ix) an attorney.

(b) Appointments to the board shall be for terms of 4 years. A board member may be reappointed to a new term. Initial appointments may be of different lengths so that no more than 3 terms expire in the same year. The Supreme Court may remove a member at any time.

(c) If a position on the board becomes vacant because of death, resignation, or removal, or because a member is no longer employed in the capacity in which he or she was appointed, the board shall notify the Supreme Court Clerk and the Court shall appoint a successor to serve the remainder of the term.

(d) The state court administrator shall assign a staff person to serve as board secretary.

(3) *Certification by Testing.*

(a) At least twice each year the board shall administer an examination testing knowledge and speed, and, as to a recorder, operator, or voice writer, familiarity with basic logging techniques and minor repair and maintenance procedures. The board shall determine the passing score.

(b) In order to be eligible for registration for an examination, an applicant must

(i) be at least 18 years of age,

(ii) be a high school graduate, and

(iii) not have been under sentence for a felony for a period of two years.

(c) In addition, an applicant for the certified shorthand reporter examination must have satisfactorily completed a post-high school approved, accredited, or recognized course of study in court reporting and submit documentation of same prior to testing.

(d) An applicant for the CER/CSMR/CEO examination must have satisfactorily completed a post-high school board-approved workshop or course of study, or other board-approved curriculum and submit documentation of same prior to testing.

(e) All CERs/CSMRs/CEOs who are fully certified by December 31, 2005, are exempt from the requirements of subparagraph (d).

(f) The registration fee is $60.

(4) *Reciprocal Certification.* A reporter, recorder, operator, or voice writer certified in another state may apply to the board for certification based on the certification already obtained.

(5) *Temporary Certification.* A new reporter, recorder, operator, or voice writer may receive one temporary certification to enable him or her to work until the results of the next test are released. If the person does not take the test, the temporary certification may not be extended unless good cause is shown. If the person takes the test and fails, the board may extend the temporary certification.

(6) *Renewal, Review, and Revocation of Certification.*

(a) Certifications under this rule must be renewed annually. The fee for renewal is $30. Renewal applications must be filed by August 1. A renewal application filed after that date must be accompanied by an additional late fee of $100. The board may require certified reporters, recorders, operators, and voice writers to submit, as a condition of renewal, such information as the board reasonably deems necessary to determine that the reporter, recorder, operator, or voice writer has used his or her reporting or recording skills during the preceding year.

(b) The board must review the certification of a reporter, recorder, operator, or voice writer who has not used his or her skills in the preceding year, and shall determine whether the certification of such a reporter, recorder, operator, or voice writer may be renewed without the necessity of a certification test.

(c) The board may review the certification of a reporter, recorder, operator, or voice writer and may impose sanctions, including revoking the certification, for good cause after a hearing before the board.

(d) If, after a reporter's, recorder's, operator's, or voice writer's certification is revoked or voided by the board and the reporter, recorder, operator, or voice writer applies to take the certification examination and passes, the board may issue a conditional certification for a prescribed period imposing restrictions or conditions that must be met for continued certification. At the end of the conditional period, an unconditional certification may be issued.

(7) *Designations.* The board shall assign an identification number to each person certified. A court reporter, recorder, operator, or voice writer must place the identification number assigned on his or her communications with the courts, including certificates, motions, affidavits, and transcripts. The board will use the following certification designations:

(a) certified electronic recorder (CER);

(b) certified electronic operator (CEO);

(c) certified shorthand reporter (CSR);

(d) certified voice writer/stenomask reporter (CSMR).

The designations are to be used only by reporters, recorders, operators, or voice writers certified by the board. A reporter, recorder, operator, or voice writer may be given more than one designation by passing different tests.

Rule 8.109 Mechanical Recording of Court Proceedings

(A) **Official Record**. If a trial court uses audio or video recording devices for making the record of court proceedings, it shall use only recording devices that meet the standards as published by the State Court Administrative Office.

(B) **Other Recordings**. On motion of an attorney or of a party appearing on his or her own behalf, a court may permit audio recording of a part or all of a proceeding and may permit photographic recording of visual exhibits. The court may regulate the manner of audio or photographic recording so that it does not disrupt the proceeding. An audio or photographic recording made under this rule may be used solely to assist in the prosecution or defense during the proceeding recorded; it may not be used publicly.

Rule 8.110 Chief Judge Rule

(A) **Applicability**. This rule applies to all trial courts: i.e., the judicial circuits of the circuit court, the districts of the district court, the probate court in each county or a probate district established by law, and the municipal courts.

(B) **Chief Judge, Chief Judge Pro Tempore, and Presiding Judges of Divisions**.

(1) The Supreme Court shall select a judge to serve as chief judge of each trial court. When SCAO is considering recommending appointment of a chief judge of a specific group of courts, SCAO shall inform and seek input from those courts. Any judge of a court or group of courts may submit an application or recommendation to SCAO regarding the selection of a chief judge for that court or group of courts.

(2) Unless a chief judge pro tempore or presiding judge is named by the Supreme Court, the chief judge shall select a chief judge pro tempore and a presiding judge of any division of the trial court. The chief judge pro tempore and any presiding judges shall fulfill such functions as the chief judge assigns.

(3) The chief judge, chief judge pro tempore, and any presiding judges shall serve a two-year term beginning on January 1 of each even-numbered year, provided that the chief judge serves at the pleasure of the Supreme Court and the chief judge pro tempore and any presiding judges serve at the pleasure of the chief judge.

(4) The Supreme Court may appoint a judge of another court to serve as chief judge of a trial court.

(a) Apart from the duties of a chief judge described under this rule, the chief probate judge has various obligations imposed by statute. If the chief judge of a probate court is not a probate judge, the senior probate judge shall serve as the chief probate judge in meeting the statutory obligations of a chief probate judge.

(b) The senior probate judge is the judge with the longest service as a probate judge. If two judges have the same number of years of service, the judge who received the highest number of votes in the first election is the senior probate judge.

(C) **Duties and Powers of Chief Judge**.

(1) A chief judge shall act in conformity with the Michigan Court Rules, administrative orders of the Supreme Court, and local court rules, and should freely solicit the advice and suggestions of the other judges of his or her bench and geographic jurisdiction. If a local court management council has adopted the by-laws described in AO 1998-5 the chief judge shall exercise the authority and responsibilities under this rule in conformity with the provisions of AO 1998-5.

(2) As the presiding officer of the court, a chief judge shall:

(a) call and preside over meetings of the court;

(b) appoint committees of the court;

(c) initiate policies concerning the court's internal operations and its position on external matters affecting the court;

(d) meet regularly with all chief judges whose courts are wholly or partially within the same county;

(e) represent the court in its relations with the Supreme Court, other courts, other agencies of government, the bar, the general public, and the news media, and in ceremonial functions;

(f) counsel and assist other judges in the performance of their responsibilities; and

(g) cooperate with all investigations conducted by the Judicial Tenure Commission.

(3) As director of the administration of the court, a chief judge shall have administrative superintending power and control over the judges of the court and all court personnel with authority and responsibility to:

(a) supervise caseload management and monitor disposition of the judicial work of the court;

(b) direct the apportionment and assignment of the business of the court, subject to the provisions of MCR 8.111;

(c) determine the hours of the court and the judges; coordinate and determine the number of judges and court personnel required to be present at any one time to perform necessary judicial administrative work of the court, and require their presence to perform that work;

(d) supervise the performance of all court personnel, with authority to hire, discipline, or discharge such personnel, with the exception of a judge's secretary and law clerk, if any;

(e) coordinate judicial and personnel vacations and absences, subject to the provisions of subrule (D);

(f) supervise court finances, including financial planning, the preparation and presentation of budgets, and financial reporting;

(g) request assignments of visiting judges and direct the assignment of matters to the visiting judges;

(h) effect compliance by the court with all applicable court rules and provisions of the law; and

(i) perform any act or duty or enter any order necessarily incidental to carrying out the purposes of this rule.

(4) If a judge does not timely dispose of his or her assigned judicial work or fails or refuses to comply with an order or directive from the chief judge made under this rule, the chief judge shall report the facts to the state court administrator who will, under the Supreme Court's direction, initiate whatever corrective action is necessary.

(5) The chief judge of the court in which criminal proceedings are pending shall have filed with the state court administrator a quarterly report listing the following cases in a format prescribed by the state court administrator:

(a) felony cases in which there has been a delay of more than 301 days between the order binding the defendant over to circuit court and adjudication;

(b) misdemeanor cases and cases involving local ordinance violations that have criminal penalties in which there has been a delay of more than 126 days between the date of the defendant's first appearance on the warrant and complaint or citation and adjudication;

(c) In computing the 126-day and 301-day periods, the court shall exclude periods of delay

(i) between the time a preadjudication warrant is issued and a defendant is arraigned;

(ii) between the time a defendant is referred for evaluation to determine whether he or she is competent to stand trial and the receipt of the report; or

(iii) during the time a defendant is deemed incompetent to stand trial.

(iv) during the time an order is in effect that stays the disposition or proceedings of the case pending interlocutory appellate review.

(6) A chief judge may delegate administrative duties to a trial court administrator or others.

(7) Where a court rule or statute does not already require it, the chief judge may, by administrative order, direct the clerk of the court to provide litigants and attorneys with copies of forms approved by the state court administrator. In addition, except when a court rule or statute specifies that the court or clerk of the court must provide certain forms without charge, the administrative order may allow the clerk to provide the forms at the cost of reproduction to the clerk.

(D) **Court Hours; Court Holidays; Judicial Absences**.

(1) *Court Hours*. The chief judge shall enter an administrative order under MCR 8.112(B) establishing the court's hours.

(2) *Court Holidays; Local Modification*.

(a) The following holidays are to be observed by all state courts, except those courts which have adopted modifying administrative orders pursuant to MCR 8.112(B):

New Year's Day, January 1;
Martin Luther King, Jr., Day, the third Monday in January in conjunction with the federal holiday;
Presidents' Day, the third Monday in February;
Memorial Day, the last Monday in May;
Independence Day, July 4;
Labor Day, the first Monday in September;
Veterans' Day, November 11;
Thanksgiving Day, the fourth Thursday in November; Friday after Thanksgiving;
Christmas Eve, December 24;
Christmas Day, December 25;
New Year's Eve, December 31;

(b) When New Year's Day, Independence Day, Veterans' Day, or Christmas Day falls on Saturday, the preceding Friday shall be a holiday. When New Year's Day, Independence Day, Veterans' Day, or Christmas Day falls on Sunday, the following Monday shall be a holiday. When Christmas Eve or New Year's Eve falls on Friday, the preceding Thursday shall be a holiday. When Christmas Eve or New Year's Eve falls on Saturday or Sunday, the preceding Friday shall be a holiday.

(c) Courts are encouraged to promulgate a modifying administrative order if appropriate to accommodate or achieve uniformity with the holiday practices of local governmental units regarding local public employees.

(d) With the prior approval of the chief judge, a judge may continue a trial in progress or dispose of judicial matters on any of the listed holidays if he or she finds it to be necessary.

(e) Any action taken by a court on February 12, Lincoln's birthday, or on the second Monday in October, Columbus Day, shall be valid.

(3) *Judicial Vacation Standard*. A judge is expected to take an annual vacation leave of 20 days with the approval of the chief judge to ensure docket coordination and coverage. A judge may take an additional 10 days of annual vacation leave with the approval of the chief judge. A maximum of 30 days of annual vacation unused due to workload constraints may be carried from one calendar year

into the first quarter of the next calendar year and used during that quarter, if approved by the chief judge. Vacation days do not include:
(a) attendance at Michigan judicial conferences;
(b) attendance, with the chief judge's approval, at educational meetings or seminars;
(c) attendance, with the chief judge's approval, at meetings of judicial committees or committees substantially related to judicial administration of justice;
(d) absence due to illness; or
(e) administrative leave, with the chief judge's approval.

(4) *Judicial Education Leave Standard.* A judge is expected to take judicial education leave of 2 weeks every 3 years to participate in continuing legal education and training at Michigan judicial training programs and nationally recognized judicial education programs, including graduate and refresher courses. Judicial education leave does not include judicial conferences for which attendance is required. The use of judicial education leave approved by the chief judge does not affect a judge's annual leave.

(5) *Judicial Professional Leave Standard.* Judges are encouraged, as part of their regular judicial responsibilities, to participate in professional meetings and conferences that advance the administration of justice or the public's understanding of the judicial system; to serve on commissions and committees of state and national organizations that contribute to the improvement of the law or that advance the interests of the judicial system; and to serve on Supreme Court-appointed or in-house assignments or committees. The use of judicial professional leave approved by the chief judge does not affect a judge's annual leave or education leave.

(6) *Approval of Judicial Absences.* A judge may not be absent from the court without the chief judge's prior approval, except for personal illness. In making the decision on a request to approve a vacation or other absence, the chief judge shall consider, among other factors, the pending caseload of the judge involved. The chief judge shall withhold approval of vacation, judicial education, or judicial professional leave that conforms to these standards only if withholding approval is necessary to ensure the orderly conduct of judicial business. The chief judge shall maintain records of absences to be available at the request of the Supreme Court.

Rule 8.111 Assignment of Cases

(A) **Application**. The rule applies to all courts defined in subrule 8.110(A).

(B) **Assignment**. All cases must be assigned by lot, unless a different system has been adopted by local court administrative order under the provisions of subrule 8.112. Assignment will occur at the time the case is filed or before a contested hearing or uncontested dispositional hearing in the case, as the chief judge directs. Civil actions must be assigned within appropriate categories determined by the chief judge. The chief judge may receive fewer assignments in order to perform the duties of chief judge.

(C) **Reassignment**.
(1) If a judge is disqualified or for other good cause cannot undertake an assigned case, the chief judge may reassign it to another judge by a written order stating the reason. To the extent feasible, the alternate judge should be selected by lot. The chief judge shall file the order with the trial court clerk and have the clerk notify the attorneys of record. The chief judge may also designate a judge to act temporarily until a case is reassigned or during a temporary absence of a judge to whom a case has been assigned.
(2) If a judge is reassigned under a concurrent jurisdiction plan or a family court plan, the successor judge will be assigned all cases filed after the date of reassignment, any pending matters, and postjudgment matters that relate to disposed cases. The chief judge shall submit a local administrative order under MCR 8.112 identifying the revised caseload distribution.

(D) **Actions Arising out of Same Transaction or Occurrence**. Subject to subrule 8.110(C),
(1) if one of two or more actions arising out of the same transaction or occurrence has been assigned to a judge, the other action or actions must be assigned to that judge;
(2) if an action arises out of the same transaction or occurrence as a civil action previously dismissed or transferred, the action must be assigned to the judge to whom the earlier action was assigned;
(3) the attorney for the party bringing the other action under subrule (1) or the new action under subrule (2) shall notify the clerk of the fact in writing in the manner prescribed in MCR 2.113(C)(2). An attorney who knowingly fails to do so is subject to disciplinary action.
(4) The chief judge may reassign cases, other than those encompassed by subrule 8.111(D)(1), in order to correct docket control problems resulting from the requirements of this rule.

Rule 8.112 Local Court Rules; Administrative Orders

(A) **Local Court Rules**.
(1) A trial court may adopt rules regulating practice in that court if the rules are not in conflict with these

rules and regulate matters not covered by these rules.

(2) If a practice of a trial court is not specifically authorized by these rules, and
   (a) reasonably depends on attorneys or litigants being informed of the practice for its effectiveness, or
   (b) requires an attorney or litigant to do some act in relation to practice before that court, the practice, before enforcement, must be adopted by the court as a local court rule and approved by the Supreme Court.

(3) Unless a trial court finds that immediate action is required, it must give reasonable notice and an opportunity to comment on a proposed local court rule to the members of the bar in the affected judicial circuit, district, or county. The court shall send the rule and comments received to the Supreme Court clerk.

(4) If possible, the number of a local court rule supplementing an area covered by these rules must correspond with the numbering of these rules and bear the prefix LCR. For example, a local rule supplementing MCR 2.301 should be numbered LCR 2.301.

(B) **Administrative Orders**.
   (1) A trial court may issue an administrative order governing only internal court management.
   (2) Administrative orders must be sequentially numbered during the calendar year of their issuance. E.g., Recorder's Court Administrative Orders Nos. 1984-1, 1984-2.
   (3) Before its effective date, an administrative order must be sent to the state court administrator. If the state court administrator directs, a trial court shall stay the effective date of an administrative order or shall revoke it. A trial court may submit such an order to the Supreme Court as a local court rule.

Rule 8.113 Requests for Investigation of Courts

(A) **Submission of Request**. A request for investigation of a court may be submitted to the state court administrator.

(B) **Action by State Court Administrator**. The state court administrator may
   (1) attempt to informally resolve the dispute,
   (2) inform the complainant that an investigation pursuant to this rule is not appropriate under the circumstances,
   (3) direct the complainant to the Judicial Tenure Commission or the Attorney Grievance Commission,
   (4) request an investigation by the Judicial Tenure Commission or the Attorney Grievance Commission,
   (5) refer a matter to the Supreme Court for possible exercise of the Supreme Court's power of superintending control over the judiciary, or
   (6) take any other appropriate action.

(C) **Cooperation With Inquiry**. Judges, court employees, and members of the bar shall cooperate with the state court administrator on request for assistance in inquiries pursuant to this rule.

(D) **Review Prohibited; Action Without Prejudice to Other Proceedings**. There is no appeal from or review of any action taken by the state court administrator under this rule, but nothing in this rule limits the right of any person to request an investigation by the Judicial Tenure Commission or the Attorney Grievance Commission or to file an action for superintending control in an appropriate court.

Rule 8.115 Courtroom Decorum; Policy Regarding Use of Cell Phones or Other Portable Electronic Communication Devices

(A) **Display of Flags**. The flags of the United States and of the State of Michigan must be displayed in a conspicuous place adjacent to the bench at all times when court is in session.

(B) **Judicial Robe**. When acting in his or her official capacity in the courtroom, a judge shall wear a black robe.

(C) **Establishment of a Policy Regarding Portable Electronic Communication Devices**.
   (1) A facility that contains a courtroom may determine use of electronic equipment in nonjudicial areas of the facility.
   (2) The chief judge may establish a policy regarding the use of cell phones or other portable electronic communication devices within the court, except that no photographs may be taken of any jurors or witnesses, and no photographs may be taken inside any courtroom without permission of the court. The policy regarding the use of cell phones or other portable electronic communication devices shall be posted in a conspicuous location outside and inside each courtroom. Failure to comply with this section or with the policy established by the chief judge may result in a fine, including confiscation of the device, incarceration, or both for contempt of court.

Rule 8.116 Sessions of Court

(A) **Opening Court; Recesses**. A definite time must be set for all court sessions, and the judge shall promptly open a session. Recesses shall be taken regularly, but should be short, and court must resume on time.

(B) **Participants to be Punctual**. Persons having business with a court must be in court and ready to begin at the opening of the session, and must otherwise be punctual for all court business.

(C) **Staggered Scheduling**. A judge shall stagger the docket schedule so that an attorney or party may be heard within a time reasonably close to the scheduled time, and, except for good cause, the docket shall be called in order.

(D) **Access to Court Proceedings**.

(1) Except as otherwise provided by statute or court rule, a court may not limit access by the public to a court proceeding unless

(a) a party has filed a written motion that identifies the specific interest to be protected, or the court sua sponte has identified a specific interest to be protected, and the court determines that the interest outweighs the right of access;

(b) the denial of access is narrowly tailored to accommodate the interest to be protected, and there is no less restrictive means to adequately and effectively protect the interest; and

(c) the court states on the record the specific reasons for the decision to limit access to the proceeding.

(2) Any person may file a motion to set aside an order that limits access to a court proceeding under this rule, or an objection to entry of such an order. MCR 2.119 governs the proceedings on such a motion or objection. If the court denies the motion or objection, the moving or objecting person may file an application for leave to appeal in the same manner as a party to the action.

(3) Whenever the court enters an order limiting access to a proceeding that otherwise would be public, the court must forward a copy of the order to the State Court Administrative Office.

Rule 8.117 Case Classification Codes

Use of Case-Type Code. As required by MCR 2.113(C)(1)(c), the plaintiff must assign one case-type code from a list provided by the State Court Administrator according to the principal subject matter of the action (not the nature of the proceedings), and include this code in the caption of the complaint. The case code must be included in the caption of all papers thereafter filed in the case.
[The current case classification codes may be found at http://courts.mi.gov/Administration/SCAO/Resources/Documents/standards/cf_casetypecodes.pdf

Rule 8.119 Court Records and Reports; Duties of Clerks

(A) **Applicability**. This rule applies to all records in every trial court. For purposes of this rule, records are as defined in MCR 1.109, MCR 3.218, MCR 3.903, and MCR 8.119(D)-(G).

(B) **Records Standards**. The clerk of the court shall comply with the records standards in this rule, MCR 1.109, and as otherwise prescribed by the Michigan Supreme Court.

(C) **Filing of Documents and Other Materials**. The clerk of the court shall endorse on the first page of every document the date on which it is filed. Documents and other materials filed with the court as defined in MCR 2.107(G) must comply with Michigan Court Rules and Michigan Supreme Court records standards. The clerk of the court may only reject documents that do not meet the following minimum filing requirements:

(1) standards prescribed by MCR 1.109,

(2) legibility and language as prescribed by MCR 2.113(B) and MCR 5.113,

(3) captioning prescribed by MCR 2.113(C)(1) and MCR 5.113,

(4) signature prescribed by MCR 2.114(C) and MCR 5.114, and

(5) the filing fee is not paid at the time of filing, unless waived or suspended by court order.

(D) **Records Kept by the Clerk of the Court**. The clerk of the court shall keep the following case records in accordance with Michigan Supreme Court records standards and local court plans. Documents and other materials made confidential by court rule, statute, or order of the court pursuant to subrule (I) must be designated as confidential and maintained to allow only authorized access. In the event of transfer or appeal of a case, every rule, statute, or order of the court pursuant to subrule (I) that makes a document or other materials in that case confidential applies uniformly to every court in Michigan, irrespective of the court in which the document or other materials were originally filed.

(1) *Indexes and Case Files*. Except for civil infractions, the clerk shall keep and maintain records of each case consisting of a numerical index, an alphabetical index, a register of actions, and a case file in such form and style as may be prescribed by the Supreme Court. Each case shall be assigned a case number on receipt of a complaint, petition, or other initiating document. The case number shall comply with MCR 2.113(C)(1)(c) or MCR 5.113(A)(1)(b)(ii) as applicable. In addition to the case number, a separate petition number shall be assigned to each petition filed under the Juvenile Code as required under MCR 5.113(A)(1)(b)(ii). The case number (and petition number if applicable) shall be recorded on the register of actions, file, numerical index, and alphabetical index. The records shall include the following characteristics:

(a) Numerical Index. The clerk shall maintain a numerical index as a list of consecutive case numbers on which the date of filing and the names of the parties are recorded. The index may be maintained either as a central index for all cases filed in the court or as separate lists for particular types of cases or particular divisions of the court.

(b) Alphabetical Index. The clerk shall maintain a central alphabetical index or separate alphabetical indexes for particular types of cases or particular divisions of the court on which the date of filing, names of all parties, and the case number are recorded.

(c) Register of Actions. The clerk shall keep a case history of each case, known as a register of actions. The register of actions shall contain both pre- and post-judgment information. When a case is commenced, a register of actions form shall be created. The case identification information in the alphabetical index shall be entered on the register of actions. In addition, the following shall be noted chronologically on the register of actions as it pertains to the case:

(i) the offense (if one);
(ii) the judge assigned to the case;
(iii) the fees paid;
(iv) the date and title of each filed item;
(v) the date process was issued and returned, as well as the date of service;
(vi) the date of each event and type and result of action;
(vii) the date of scheduled trials, hearings, and all other appearances or reviews, including a notation indicating whether the proceedings were heard on the record and the name and certification number of the court reporter or recorder present;
(viii) the orders, judgments, and verdicts;
(ix) the judge at adjudication and disposition;
(x) the date of adjudication and disposition; and
(xi) the manner of adjudication and disposition.

Each notation shall be brief, but shall show the nature of each item filed, each order or judgment of the court, and the returns showing execution. Each notation shall be dated with not only the date of filing, but with the date of entry and shall indicate the person recording the action.

(d) Case File. The clerk of the court shall maintain a paper and/or electronic file for each action, bearing the case number assigned to it, in which the clerk shall keep all pleadings, process, written opinions and findings, orders, and judgments filed in the action. Additionally, the clerk shall keep in the file all other materials prescribed by court rule, statute, or as ordered by the court to be filed with the clerk of the court. If other records of a case file are maintained separately from the file, the clerk shall keep them as prescribed by trial court case file management standards.

(2) *Calendars*. The clerk may maintain calendars of actions. A calendar is a schedule of cases ready for court action that identifies times and places of activity.

(3) *Abolished Records*.

(a) Journals. Except for recording marriages, journals shall not be maintained.

(b) Dockets. A register of actions replaces a docket. Wherever these rules or applicable statutes require entries on a docket, those entries shall be entered on the register of actions.

(E) **Other Case Records**. The clerk or other persons designated by the chief judge of the court shall keep in the manner prescribed by these rules, other materials filed with or handled by the court for purposes of case processing, including but not limited to wills for safekeeping, case evaluations, exhibit logs, probation files, and friend of the court records.

(F) **Court Recordings, Log Notes, Jury Seating Charts, and Media**. Court recordings, log notes, jury seating charts, and all other records such as tapes, backup tapes, discs, and any other medium used or created in the making of a record of proceedings and kept pursuant to MCR 8.108 are court records and are subject to access in accordance with subrule (H)(2)(b).

(G) **Other Court Records**. All court records not included in subrules (D), (E), and (F) are considered administrative and fiscal records or nonrecord materials and are not subject to public access under subrule (H). These records are defined in the approved records retention and disposal schedule for trial courts.

(H) **Access to Records**. Except as otherwise provided in subrule (F), only case records as defined in subrule (D) are public records, subject to access in accordance with these rules. The clerk may not permit any case record to be taken from the court without the order of the court. A court may provide access to the public information in a register of actions through a publicly accessible website and business court opinions may be made available as part of an indexed list as required under MCL 600.8039; however, all other public information in its case records may be provided through electronic means only upon request. The court may provide access to any case record that is not a document, as defined by MCR 1.109(B), if it can reasonably accommodate the request. Any materials filed with the court pursuant to MCR 1.109(C)(2), in a medium in which the court does not have the means to readily access and reproduce those materials, may be made available for public inspection using court equipment only. The court is not required to provide the means to access or reproduce the contents of those materials if the means is not already available.

(1) Unless access to a case record or information contained in a record as defined in subrule (D) is restricted by statute, court rule, or an order entered pursuant to subrule (I), any person may inspect that record and may obtain copies as provided in subrule (J). In accordance with subrule (J), the court may collect a fee for the cost of this service, including the cost of providing the new record in a particular medium.

(2) Every court shall adopt an administrative order pursuant to MCR 8.112(B) to

(a) make reasonable regulations necessary to protect its public records and prevent excessive and unreasonable interference with the discharge of its functions;

(b) establish a policy for whether to provide access for records defined in subrule (F) and if access is to be provided, outline the procedure for accessing those records;

(c) specify the reasonable cost of reproduction of records provided under subrule (J); and

(d) specify the process for determining costs under subrule (J).

(I) **Sealed Records**.

(1) Except as otherwise provided by statute or court rule, a court may not enter an order that seals courts records, in whole or in part, in any action or proceeding, unless

(a) a party has filed a written motion that identifies the specific interest to be protected,

(b) the court has made a finding of good cause, in writing or on the record, which specifies the grounds for the order, and

(c) there is no less restrictive means to adequately and effectively protect the specific interest asserted.

(2) In determining whether good cause has been shown, the court must consider,

(a) the interests of the parties, including, where there is an allegation of domestic violence, the safety of the alleged or potential victim of the domestic violence, and

(b) the interest of the public.

(3) The court must provide any interested person the opportunity to be heard concerning the sealing of the records.

(4) For purposes of this rule, "court records" includes all documents and records of any nature that are filed with the clerk in connection with the action. Nothing in this rule is intended to limit the court's authority to issue protective orders pursuant to MCR 2.302(C). Materials that are subject to a motion to seal a record in whole or in part shall be held under seal pending the court's disposition of the motion.

(5) A court may not seal a court order or opinion, including an order or opinion that disposes of a motion to seal the record.

(6) Any person may file a motion to set aside an order that disposes of a motion to seal the record, or an objection to entry of a proposed order. MCR 2.119 governs the proceedings on such a motion or objection. If the court denies a motion to set aside the order or enters the order after objection is filed, the moving or objecting person may file an application for leave to appeal in the same manner as a party to the action. See MCR 8.116(D).

(7) Whenever the court grants a motion to seal a court record, in whole or in part, the court must forward a copy of the order to the Clerk of the Supreme Court and to the State Court Administrative Office.

(J) **Access and Reproduction Fees**.

(1) A court may not charge an access or reproduction fee for a case record that the court is required by law or court rule to provide without charge to a person or other entity, irrespective of the medium in which the case record is retained, the manner in which access to the case record is provided, and the technology used to create, store, retrieve, reproduce, and maintain the case record.

(2) The court may provide access to its public case records in any medium authorized by the records reproduction act, 1992 PA 116; MCL 24.401 to 24.403. If a court maintains its public records in electronic format only,

(a) the court may not charge a fee to access those case records when access is made on-site through a public terminal or when a verbal request for public information is made on-site to the clerk.

(b) the court or a contracted entity may charge a fee, in accordance with Supreme Court order, to access those case records when the access is made off-site through a document management, imaging, or other electronic records management system.

(3) Reproduction of a case record means the act of producing a copy of that record through any medium authorized by the records reproduction act, 1992 PA 116; MCL 24.401 to 24.403.

(a) A court may charge only for the actual cost of labor and supplies and the actual use of the system, including printing from a public terminal, to reproduce a case record and not the cost associated with the purchase and maintenance of any system or technology used to store, retrieve, and reproduce a case record.

(b) If a person wishes to obtain copies of documents in a file, the clerk shall provide copies upon receipt of the actual cost of reproduction.

(c) Except as otherwise directed by statute or court rule, a standard fee may be established, pursuant to (H)(2), for providing copies of documents on file.

(4) A court is not required to create a new record out of its existing records. A new record means the compilation of information into a format that does not currently exist or that cannot be generated electronically using predefined formats available through a court's case management system. Providing access to documents or furnishing copies of documents in an existing file does not constitute creation of a new record, even when the output appears in a format different than the format of the original record or document because the output is the result of predefined formats.

(a) A court may create a new record or compilation of records pertaining to case files or case-related information on request, provided that the record created or compiled does not disclose information that would otherwise be confidential or restricted by statute, court rule, or an order entered pursuant to subrule (I).

(b) A court may charge only for the actual cost of labor and supplies and the actual use of the system to develop, generate, and validate the accuracy of a new record and not the cost associated with the purchase and maintenance of any system or technology used to store, retrieve, and reproduce the information or documents for creating a new record.

(c) If a court creates a new record, the clerk shall provide access to the new record upon receipt of the actual cost of creating the record.

(K) **Retention Periods**. For purposes of retention, the records of the trial courts include: (1) administrative and fiscal records, (2) case records, (3) and nonrecord material. The records of the trial courts shall be retained in the medium prescribed by MCR 1.109. The records of a trial court may not be destroyed except upon order by the chief judge of that court. Before destroying records subject to the order, the court shall first transfer to the Archives of Michigan any records specified as such by State Archives in the Michigan trial courts approved records retention and disposal schedule. An order of destruction shall comply with the retention periods established by the State Court Administrative Office and approved by the state court administrator, Attorney General, State Administrative Board, and Archives and Records Management Services of the Department of Management and Budget, in accordance with MCL 399.5.

(L) **Reporting Duties**.

(1) The clerk of every court shall submit reports and records as required by statute and court rule.

(2) The clerk of every court shall submit reports or provide records as required by the State Court Administrative Office, without costs.

Rule 8.120 Law Students and Recent Graduates; Participation in Legal Aid Clinics, Defender Offices, and Legal Training Programs

(A) **Legal Aid Clinics; Defender Offices**. Effective legal service for each person in Michigan, regardless of that person's ability to pay, is important to the directly affected person, to our court system, and to the whole citizenry. Law students and recent law graduates, under supervision by a member of the state bar, may staff public and nonprofit defender offices, and legal aid clinics that are organized under a city or county bar association or an accredited law school or for the primary purpose of providing free legal services to indigent persons.

(B) **Legal Training Programs**. Law students and recent law graduates may participate in legal training programs organized in the offices of county prosecuting attorneys, county corporation counsel, city attorneys, the Attorney Grievance Commission, and the Attorney General.

(C) **Eligible Students**. A student in a law school approved by the American Bar Association who has received a passing grade in law school courses and has completed the first year is eligible to participate in a clinic or program listed in subrules (A) and (B) if the student meets the academic and moral standards established by the dean of that school. For the purpose of this rule, a "recent law graduate" is a person who has graduated from law school within the last year. The student or graduate must certify in writing that he or she has read and is familiar with the Michigan Rules of Professional Conduct and the Michigan Court Rules, and shall take an oath which is reasonably equivalent to the Michigan Lawyer's Oath in requiring at a minimum the promise to: (a) support the Constitution of the United States; (b) support the Constitution of the State of Michigan; (c) maintain the respect due to courts of justice and judicial officers; (d) never seek to mislead a judge or jury by any artifice or false statement of fact or law; (e) maintain the confidence and preserve inviolate the secrets of the client; (f) abstain from all offensive personality; (g) advance no fact prejudicial to the honor or reputation of a party or witness, unless required by the justice of the cause; and (h) in all other respects conduct himself or herself personally and professionally in conformity with the high standards of conduct imposed upon members of the state bar of Michigan.

(D) **Scope; Procedure**.

(1) A member of the legal aid clinic, in representing an indigent person, is authorized to advise the person and to negotiate and appear on the person's behalf in all Michigan courts except the Supreme Court. Except as otherwise provided in this rule, the indigent person that will be assisted by the student must consent in writing to the representation. In a situation in which a law student provides short-term, limited-scope legal advice by telephone in the context of a clinical program intended to assist indigent persons offered as part of a law school curriculum, the clinic patron shall be informed that:
   (a) the advice provided may be rendered by a law student, and
   (b) by proceeding to the consultation following notification that the advice may be provided by a law student, the clinic patron consents to such representation.

(2) Representation must be conducted under the supervision of a state bar member. Supervision by a state bar member includes the duty to examine and sign all pleadings filed. It does not require the state bar member to be present
   (a) while a law student or graduate is advising an indigent person or negotiating on the person's behalf, or
   (b) during a courtroom appearance of a law student or graduate, except
      (i) during an appellate argument or
      (ii) in a criminal or juvenile case exposing the client to a penalty of imprisonment.

   The supervising attorney shall assume all personal professional responsibility for the student's or graduate's work, and should consider purchasing professional liability insurance to cover the practice of such student or graduate.

(3) A law student or graduate may not appear in a case in a Michigan court without the approval of the judge or a majority of the panel of judges to which the case is assigned. If the judge or a majority of the panel grants approval, the judge or a majority of the panel may suspend the proceedings at any stage if the judge or a majority of the panel determines that the representation by the law student or graduate
   (a) is professionally inadequate, and
   (b) substantial justice requires suspension.

   In the Court of Appeals, a request for a law student or graduate to appear at oral argument must be submitted by motion to the panel that will hear the case. The panel may deny the request or establish restrictions or other parameters for the representation on a case-by-case basis.

(4) A law student or graduate serving in a prosecutor's, county corporation counsel's, city attorney's, Attorney Grievance Commission's, or Attorney General's program may be authorized to perform comparable functions and duties assigned by the prosecuting attorney, county attorney, city attorney, Attorney Grievance Commission attorney, or Attorney General, except that
   (a) the law student or graduate is subject to the conditions and restrictions of this rule; and
   (b) the law student or graduate may not be appointed as an assistant prosecutor, assistant corporation counsel, assistant city attorney, assistant Attorney Grievance Commission attorney, or assistant Attorney General.

Rule 8.121 Contingent Fees in Claims or Actions for Personal Injury, Wrongful Death, and No-Fault Benefits

(A) **Allowable Contingent Fee Agreements**. In any claim or action for personal injury or wrongful death based upon the alleged conduct of another or for no-fault benefits, in which an attorney enters into an agreement, expressed or implied, whereby the attorney's compensation is dependent or contingent in whole or in part upon successful prosecution or settlement or upon the amount of recovery, the receipt, retention, or sharing by such attorney, pursuant to agreement or otherwise, of compensation which is equal to or less than the fee stated in subrule (B) is deemed to be fair and reasonable. The receipt, retention, or sharing of compensation which is in excess of such a fee shall be deemed to be the charging of a "clearly excessive fee" in violation of MRPC 1.5(a), unless such fee is received as a result of an award of attorney fees payable pursuant to MCL 500.3148, or other award or sanction made pursuant to statute, court rule, or the common law.

(B) **Maximum Fee**. The maximum allowable fee for the claims and actions referred to in subrule (A) is one-third of the amount recovered.

(C) **Computation**.
   (1) The amount referred to in subrule (B) shall be computed on the net sum recovered after deducting from the amount recovered all disbursements properly chargeable to the enforcement of the claim or prosecution of the action. In computing the fee, the costs as taxed and any interest included in or upon the amount of a judgment shall be deemed part of the amount recovered.
   (2) In the case of a settlement payable in installments, the amount referred to in subrule (B) shall be computed using the present value of the future payments.
      (a) If an annuity contract will be used to fund the future payments, "present value" is the actual cost of purchasing the annuity contract. The attorney for the defendant must disclose to the court and the parties the amount paid for the

annuity contract, after any rebates or other discounts.

(b) If the defendant will make the future payments directly, "present value" is the amount that an entity of the same financial standing as the defendant would pay for an annuity contract. The court may appoint an independent expert to certify the "present value" as defined in this paragraph. The court may base its findings on the expert's testimony or affidavit.

(D) **Agreements for Lower Fees**. An attorney may enter into contingent fee arrangements calling for less compensation than that allowed by subrule (B).

(E) **Advice to Client**. An attorney must advise a client, before entering into a contingent fee arrangement, that attorneys may be employed under other fee arrangements in which the attorney is compensated for the reasonable value of the services performed, such as on an hourly or per diem basis. The method of compensation used by an individual attorney remains the attorney's option, and this rule does not require an attorney to accept compensation in a manner other than that chosen by the attorney.

(F) **Agreements to be in Writing**. Contingent fee arrangements made by an attorney with a client must be in writing and a copy provided to the client.

(G) **Applicability**. This rule does not apply to agreements reduced to writing before May 3, 1975. The one-third provision of subrule (B) applies to contingent fee agreements entered into after July 9, 1981. Earlier agreements are subject to the rule in effect at the time the agreement was made.

Rule 8.122 Claims by Clients Against Attorneys

Attorneys are officers of Michigan's one court of justice and are subject to the summary jurisdiction of the court. The circuit court of the county in which an attorney resides or maintains an office has jurisdiction, on verified written complaint of a client, and after reasonable notice and hearing, to enter an order for the payment of money or for the performance of an act by the attorney which law and justice may require. All courts have like jurisdiction over similar complaints regarding matters arising from actions or proceedings in those courts.

Rule 8.123 Counsel Appointments; Procedure and Records

(A) **Applicability**. This rule applies to all trial courts, which means all circuit courts, district courts, probate courts, and municipal courts.

(B) **Plan for Appointment**. Each trial court must adopt a local administrative order that describes the court's procedures for selecting, appointing, and compensating counsel who represent indigent parties in that court.

(C) **Approval by State Court Administrator**. The trial court must submit the local administrative order to the State Court Administrator for review pursuant to MCR 8.112(B)(3). The State Court Administrator shall approve a plan if its provisions will protect the integrity of the judiciary.

(D) **Required Records**. At the end of each calendar year, a trial court must compile an annual electronic report of the total public funds paid to each attorney for appointments by that court.

This subrule applies to appointments of attorneys in any capacity, regardless of the indigency status of the represented party. Trial courts that contract for services to be provided by an affiliated group of attorneys may treat the group as a single entity when compiling the required records.

The records required by this subrule must be retained for the period specified by the State Court Administrative Office`s General Schedule 16.

(E) **Public Access to Records**. The records must be available at the trial court for inspection by the public, without charge. The court may adopt reasonable access rules, and may charge a reasonable fee for providing copies of the records.

(F) **Reports to State Court Administrator**. A trial court must submit its annual electronic report to the state court administrator in the form specified by the state court administrator. When requested by the state court administrator, a trial court must cooperate in providing additional data on an individual attorney, judge, or attorney group for a period specified by the request, including the number of appointments by each judge, the number of appointments received by an individual attorney or attorney group, and the public funds paid for appointments by each judge.

Rule 8.125 Electronic Filing of Citation

(A) **Applicability**. This rule applies to all civil infraction and misdemeanor actions initiated by a Michigan Uniform Law Citation or a Michigan Uniform Municipal Civil Infraction Citation.

(B) **Citation; Complaint; Filing**. A citation may be filed with the court either on paper or electronically. The filing of a citation constitutes the filing of a complaint. An electronic citation must contain all the information that would be required if the citation were filed on paper. A citation that contains the full name of the police officer or authorized local official who issued it will be deemed to have been signed pursuant to MCL 257.727c(3), 600.8705(3), or 600.8805(3).

(C) **Contested Actions**. If an electronic citation is contested, the court may decline to hear the matter until the citation is signed and filed on paper. A citation that is not signed and filed on paper, when required by the court, will be dismissed with prejudice.

Rule 8.126 Temporary Admission to the Bar

(A) **Temporary Admission**. Any person who is licensed to practice law in another state or territory, or in the District of Columbia, of the United States of America, or in any foreign country, and who is not disbarred or suspended in any jurisdiction, and who is eligible to practice in at least one jurisdiction, may be permitted to appear and practice in a specific case in a court, before an administrative tribunal or agency, or in a specific arbitration proceeding in this state when associated with and on motion of an active member of the State Bar of Michigan who appears of record in the case. An out-of-state attorney may appear and practice under this rule in no more than five cases in a 365-day period. Permission to appear and practice is within the discretion of the court, administrative tribunal or agency, or arbitrator and may be revoked at any time for misconduct. For purposes of this rule, an out-of-state attorney is one who is licensed to practice law in another state or territory, or in the District of Columbia, of the United States of America, or in a foreign country and who is not a member of the State Bar of Michigan.

(1) *Procedure.*

(a) Motion. An attorney seeking temporary admission must be associated with a Michigan attorney. The Michigan attorney with whom the out-of-state attorney is associated shall file with the court or administrative tribunal or agency an appearance and a motion that seeks permission for the temporary admission of the out-of-state attorney. The motion shall be supported by a current certificate of good standing issued by a jurisdiction where the out-of-state attorney is licensed and eligible to practice and an affidavit of the out-of-state attorney seeking temporary admission, which affidavit shall verify

(i) the jurisdictions in which the attorney is or has been licensed or has sought licensure;

(ii) the jurisdiction where the attorney is presently eligible to practice;

(iii) that the attorney is not disbarred, or suspended in any jurisdiction, and is not the subject of any pending disciplinary action, and that the attorney is licensed and is in good standing in all jurisdictions where licensed; and

(iv) that he or she is familiar with the Michigan Rules of Professional Conduct, Michigan Court Rules, and the Michigan Rules of Evidence.

The out-of-state attorney must attach to the affidavit copies of any disciplinary dispositions, and a copy of the acknowledgment letter supplied by the State Bar of Michigan showing that the required fee has been paid. The motion shall include an attestation of the Michigan attorney that the attorney has read the out-of-state attorney's affidavit, has made a reasonable inquiry concerning the averments made therein, believes the out-of-state attorney's representations are true, and agrees to ensure that the procedures of this rule are followed. The motion shall also include the addresses of both attorneys.

(b) The Michigan attorney shall send a copy of the motion and supporting affidavit to the Attorney Grievance Commission. Within seven days after receipt of the copy of the motion, the Attorney Grievance Commission must notify the court, administrative tribunal or agency, or arbitrator and both attorneys whether the out-of-state attorney has been granted permission to appear temporarily in Michigan within the past 365 days, and, if so, the number of such appearances. No order or other writing granting permission to appear in a case shall be entered by a court, administrative tribunal or agency, or arbitrator until the notification is received from the Attorney Grievance Commission.

(c) Order. Following notification by the Attorney Grievance Commission, if the out-of-state attorney has been granted permission to appear temporarily in fewer than 5 cases within the past 365 days, the court, administrative tribunal or agency, or arbitrator may enter an order granting permission to the out-of-state attorney to appear temporarily in a case. If an order or other writing granting permission is entered, the court, administrative tribunal or agency, or arbitrator shall send a copy of the order or writing to the Michigan attorney, the out-of-state attorney, and the Attorney Grievance Commission.

(d) Fee. In each case in which an out-of-state attorney seeks temporary admission in Michigan, a fee equal to the discipline and client-protection portions of a bar member's annual dues must be paid. The discipline portion of the fee shall be paid to the State Bar of Michigan for allocation to the attorney discipline system, and the client-protection portion shall be paid to the State Bar of Michigan for allocation to the Client Protection Fund. Upon receipt of payment of the fee, the State Bar of Michigan shall within three business days send to the out-of-state attorney an acknowledgment letter that the fee has been paid.

(e) By seeking permission to appear under this rule, an out-of-state attorney consents to the jurisdiction of Michigan's attorney disciplinary system.

Rule 8.127 Foreign Language Board of Review and Regulation of Foreign Language Interpreters

(A) **Foreign Language Board of Review.**

(1) The Supreme Court shall appoint a Foreign Language Board of Review, which shall include:

(a) a circuit judge;

(b) a probate judge;

(c) a district judge;

(d) a court administrator;

(e) a fully-certified foreign language interpreter who practices regularly in Michigan courts;

(f) an advocate representing the interests of the limited English proficiency populations in Michigan;

(g) a prosecuting attorney in good standing and with experience using interpreters in the courtroom;

(h) a criminal defense attorney in good standing and with experience using interpreters in the courtroom;

(i) a family law attorney in good standing and with experience using interpreters in the courtroom

(2) Appointments to the board shall be for terms of three years. A board member may be appointed to no more than two full terms. Initial appointments may be of different lengths so that no more than three terms expire in the same year. The Supreme Court may remove a member at any time.

(3) If a position on the board becomes vacant because of death, resignation, or removal, or because a member is no longer employed in the capacity in which he or she was appointed, the board shall notify the state court administrator who will recommend a successor to the Supreme Court to serve the remainder of the term.

(4) The state court administrator shall assign a staff person to serve as executive secretary to the board.

(B) **Responsibilities of Foreign Language Board of Review.** The Foreign Language Board of Review has the following responsibilities:

(1) The board shall recommend to the state court administrator a Michigan Code of Professional Responsibility for Court Interpreters, which the state court administrator may adopt in full, in part, or in a modified form. The Code shall govern the conduct of Michigan court interpreters.

(2) The board must review a complaint that the State Court Administrative Office schedules before it pursuant to subrule (D). The board must review the complaint and any response and hear from the interpreter and any witnesses at a meeting of the board. The board shall determine what, if any, action it will take, which may include revoking certification, prohibiting the interpreter from obtaining certification, suspending the interpreter from participating in court proceedings, placing the interpreter on probation, imposing any fines authorized by law, and placing any remedial conditions on the interpreter.

(3) *Interpreter Certification Requirements*. The board shall recommend requirements for interpreters to the state court administrator that the state court administrator may adopt in full, in part, or in a modified form concerning the following:

(a) requirements for certifying interpreters as defined in MCR 1.111(A)(5). At a minimum, those requirements must include that the applicant is at least 18 years of age and not under sentence for a felony for at least two years and that the interpreter attends an orientation program for new interpreters.

(b) requirements for interpreters to be qualified as defined in MCR 1.111(A)(7).

(c) requirements under which an interpreter certified in another state or in the federal courts may apply for certification based on the certification already obtained. The certification must be a permanent or regular certification and not a temporary or restricted certification.

(d) requirements for interpreters as defined in MCR 1.111(A)(5) to maintain their certification.

(e) requirements for entities that provide interpretation services by telecommunications equipment to be qualified as defined in MCR 1.111(A)(7).

(C) **Interpreter Registration.**

(1) Interpreters who meet the requirements of MCR 1.111(A)(5) and MCR 1.111(A)(7)(a) and (b) must register with the State Court Administrative Office and renew their registration before October 1 of each year in order to maintain their status. The fee for registration is $60. The fee for renewal is $30. The renewal application shall include a statement showing that the applicant has used interpreting skills during the 12 months preceding registration. Renewal applications must be filed or postmarked on or before September 30. Any application filed or postmarked after that date must be accompanied by a late fee of $100. Any late registration made after December 31 or any application that does not demonstrate efforts to maintain proficiency shall require board approval.

(2) Entities that employ a certified foreign language interpreter as defined in MCR 1.111(A)(5), or a qualified foreign language interpreter as defined in MCR 1.111(A)(7) must also register with the State

Court Administrative Office and pay the registration fee and renewal fees.

(D) **Interpreter Misconduct or Incompetence**.

(1) An interpreter, trial court judge, or attorney who becomes aware of misconduct on the part of an interpreter committed in the course of a trial or other court proceeding that violates the Michigan Code of Professional Responsibility for Court Interpreters must report details of the misconduct to the State Court Administrative Office.

(2) Any person may file a complaint in writing on a form provided by the State Court Administrative Office. The complaint shall describe in detail the incident and the alleged incompetence, misconduct, or omission. The State Court Administrative Office may dismiss the complaint if it is plainly frivolous, insufficiently clear, or alleges conduct that does not violate this rule. If the complaint is not dismissed, the State Court Administrative Office shall send the complaint to the interpreter by regular mail or electronically at the address on file with the office.

(3) The interpreter shall answer the complaint within 28 days after the date the complaint is sent. The answer shall admit, deny, or further explain each allegation in the complaint. If the interpreter fails to answer, the allegations in the complaint are considered true and correct.

(4) The State Court Administrative Office may review records and interview the complainant, the interpreter, and witnesses, or set the matter for a hearing before the Foreign Language Board of Review. Before setting the matter for a hearing, the State Court Administrative Office may propose a resolution to which the interpreter may stipulate.

(5) If the complaint is not resolved by stipulation, the State Court Administrative Office shall notify the Foreign Language Board of Review, which shall hold a hearing. The State Court Administrative Office shall send notice of the date, time, and place of the hearing to the interpreter by regular mail or electronically. The hearing shall be closed to the public. A record of the proceedings shall be maintained but shall not be public.

(6) The interpreter may attend all of the hearings except the board's deliberations. The interpreter may be represented by counsel and shall be permitted to make a statement, obtain testimony from the complainant and witnesses, and comment on the claims and evidence.

(7) The State Court Administrative Office shall maintain a record of all interpreters who are sanctioned for incompetence or misconduct. If the interpreter is certified in Michigan under MCR 1.111(A)(5) because of certification pursuant to another state or federal test, the state court administrator shall report the findings and any sanctions to the certification authority in the other jurisdiction.

(8) This subrule shall not be construed to:

(a) restrict an aggrieved person from seeking to enforce this rule in the proceeding, including an appeal; or

(b) require exhaustion of administrative remedies.

(9) The State Court Administrative Office shall make complaint forms readily available and shall also provide complaint forms in such languages as determined by the State Court Administrative Office.

(10) Entities that employ interpreters are subject to the same requirements and procedures established by this subrule.

Subchapter 8.200 Administrative Rules Applicable in District Court

Rule 8.201 Allocation of Costs in Third-Class Districts

(A) **Duties of Clerks of Each Third-Class Control Unit Having a Clerk**.

(1) On the last day of March, June, September, and December of each year, the clerk of each third-class control unit having a clerk (see MCL 600.8281) shall determine the total number of civil and criminal cases filed during the preceding three months in the district and each political subdivision of the district under subrule (B). These figures are the total number of cases entered and commenced in that district and each political subdivision.

(2) The clerk shall determine the total cost of maintaining, financing, and operating the district court within the district.

(3) The clerk shall determine the proper share of the costs to be borne by each political subdivision by use of the following formula: (the number of cases entered and commenced in each political subdivision divided by the total number of cases entered and commenced in the district) multiplied by the total cost of maintaining, financing, and operating the district court.

(4) The clerk shall determine the proper share of the salary of the court reporter or recorder under MCL 600.8621(1) by use of the following formula: (the number of cases entered and commenced in each political subdivision divided by the total number of cases entered and commenced in the district) multiplied by the total salary of the court reporter or recorder.

(5) The clerk shall certify the figures determined under subrules (A)(3) and (4) to the treasurer of each political subdivision in the district. Payment by each political subdivision of any unpaid portion of

its certified share of the cost and salaries is then due.

(B) **Determination of Cases Entered and Commenced**.

(1) *In the District*. The total number of cases entered and commenced in the district is the total number of civil and criminal cases filed in the district for the time period in question, excepting those cases not attributable to a specific political subdivision under subrules (B)(2)(b) and (B)(3)(b).

(2) *In Each Political Subdivision Having a District Court Clerk*. The total number of cases entered and commenced in each political subdivision having a district court clerk is the total number of civil and criminal cases filed in the political subdivision for the time period in question, excepting those cases involving a filing plaintiff and one or more defendants whose residences are outside the political subdivision where filed.

(a) Cases in which a filing plaintiff and one or more defendants reside in the same political subdivision are deemed to have been entered and commenced in that political subdivision, even though filed elsewhere for purposes of MCL 600.8104.

(b) Cases in which the filing plaintiff and one or more defendants reside outside the political subdivision where the case was filed, but none of the defendants resides in the same political subdivision as the plaintiff, are to be disregarded for purposes of this rule and MCL 600.8104.

(3) *In Each Political Subdivision Having No District Court Clerk*.

(a) The total number of cases entered and commenced for the time period in question in each political subdivision having no district court clerk is the total number of civil and criminal cases in which the filing plaintiff and one or more defendants reside in the political subdivision, no matter where the case is filed.

(b) If more than one political subdivision qualifies under subrule (B)(3)(a), all are credited with one case for purposes of this rule and MCL 600.8104.

Rule 8.202 Payment of Assigned Attorneys and Transcript Costs

(A) **Misdemeanor Cases**. The political subdivision or subdivisions responsible for maintaining, financing, and operating the appointing court are responsible for paying assigned attorneys, regardless of whether the defendant is charged with violating a state law or an ordinance, and regardless of whether a fine or costs are actually assessed. If a county board of commissioners has taken or takes formal action to relieve cities or townships of part or all of the cost of paying assigned attorneys, that formal action shall control the payment of assigned attorneys in that county.

(B) **Appeals**. If an indigent defendant appealing to circuit court from a district or municipal court conviction is entitled to an assigned attorney or a transcript, the cost shall be paid by the same political subdivision or divisions that were responsible for or would have been responsible for paying an assigned attorney under subrule (A).

Rule 8.203 Records and Entries Kept by Clerk

The clerk of every district court shall maintain court records and make reports as prescribed by MCR 8.119.

Rule 8.204 Bonds for Clerks, Deputies, Magistrates, and Official Process Servers

All clerks, deputy clerks, magistrates, and official process servers of the district court must file with the chief judge a bond approved by the chief judge in a penal sum determined by the state court administrator, conditioned that the officer will

(1) perform the duties as clerk, deputy clerk, magistrate, or process server of that court; and

(2) account for and pay over all money which may be received by the officer to the person or persons lawfully entitled.

The bonds must be in favor of the court and the state.

Rule 8.205 Magistrates

The court shall provide the name, address, and telephone number of each magistrate to the clerk of the district court for the district in which the magistrate serves.

Subchapter 8.300 Administrative Rules Applicable in Probate Court

Rule 8.301 Powers of Register of Probate, Deputy Registers, and Clerks

(A) **Judicial Responsibility**. The judges of probate are responsible for the direction and supervision of the registers of probate, deputy registers of probate, probate clerks, and other personnel employed by the court to assist in the work of the court.

(B) **Entry of Order Specifying Authority**.

(1) To the extent authorized by the chief judge of a probate court by a general order, the probate register, the deputy probate register, the clerks of the probate court, and other court employees designated in the order, have the authority, until the further order of the court, to do all acts required of the probate judge except judicial acts in a contested matter and acts forbidden by law to be performed by the probate register.

(2) The order of the chief judge may refer to the power
(a) to set the time and place for hearings in all matters; take acknowledgements; administer oaths; sign notices to fiduciaries, attorneys, and sureties; sign citations and subpoenas; conduct conferences with fiduciaries required to ensure prompt administration of estates; and take testimony as provided by law or court rule; and
(b) to sign or by device indicate the name of a judge to all orders and letters of authority of the court, with the same force and effect as though the judge had signed them. In all such cases, the register or the designated deputy must place his or her initials under the name of the judge.

(C) **Statutory Authority**. In addition to the powers which may be granted by order of the chief judge, the probate registers and deputy registers have the authority granted by statute and may take acknowledgments to the same extent as a notary public.

Rule 8.302 Documents and Files

Original orders and letters of authority, after being recorded, must be placed in the files of the court. For security purposes, testamentary documents of deceased persons, bonds, orders, and such other documents as the court directs must be copied by microfilming or other means promptly after filing or issuance and preserved in the records of the court separately from the files. In addition, the clerk of every probate court shall maintain court records and make reports as prescribed by MCR 8.119.

CHAPTER 9. PROFESSIONAL DISCIPLINARY PROCEEDINGS

Subchapter 9.100 Attorney Grievance Commission; Attorney Discipline Board

Rule 9.101 Definitions

As used in subchapter 9.100:

(1) "board" means the Attorney Discipline Board;
(2) "commission" means the Attorney Grievance Commission;
(3) "administrator" means the grievance administrator;
(4) "investigator" means a person specially designated by the administrator to assist him or her in the investigation of alleged misconduct or requested reinstatement;
(5) "attorney" or "lawyer" means a person regularly licensed, specially admitted, permitted to practice law in Michigan on a temporary or other limited basis, or who is otherwise subject to the disciplinary authority of Michigan pursuant to order or rule of the Supreme Court;
(6) "respondent" means an attorney named in a request for investigation or complaint, or proceedings for reciprocal discipline, based on a judgment of conviction, or transfers to inactive status under MCR 9.121;
(7) "request for investigation" means the first step in bringing alleged misconduct to the administrator's attention;
(8) "complaint" means the formal charge prepared by the administrator and filed with the board;
(9) "review" means examination by the board of a hearing panel's order on petition by the administrator, complainant, or respondent;
(10) "appeal" means judicial re-examination by the Supreme Court of the board's final order on petition by the administrator, complainant, or respondent;
(11) "grievance" means alleged misconduct;
(12) "investigation" means fact finding on alleged misconduct under the administrator's direction.
(13) "disbarment" means revocation of the license to practice law.
(14) "complainant" means a person who signs a request for investigation.
(15) "disability inactive status" means inactive status to which a lawyer has been transferred pursuant to MCR 9.121 or a similar rule of another jurisdiction.
(16) "disciplinary proceeding" means a proceeding commenced under this subchapter seeking the imposition of discipline for misconduct.

Rule 9.102 Construction; Severability

(A) **Construction**. Subchapter 9.100 is to be liberally construed for the protection of the public, the courts, and the legal profession and applies to all pending matters of misconduct and reinstatement and to all future proceedings, even though the alleged misconduct occurred before the effective date of subchapter 9.100. Procedures must be as expeditious as possible.

(B) **Severability**. If a court finds a portion of subchapter 9.100 or its application to a person or circumstances invalid, the invalidity does not affect the remaining portions or other applications. To this end the rules are severable.

Rule 9.103 Standards of Conduct for Attorneys

(A) **General Principles**. The license to practice law in Michigan is, among other things, a continuing proclamation by the Supreme Court that the holder is fit to be entrusted with professional and judicial matters and to aid in the administration of justice as an attorney and counselor and as an officer of the court. It is the duty of every attorney to conduct himself or herself at all times in conformity with standards imposed on members of the bar as a condition of the privilege to practice law. These standards include, but are not limited to, the rules of professional responsibility and the rules of judicial conduct that are adopted by the Supreme Court.

(B) **Duty to Assist Public to Request Investigation**. An attorney shall assist a member of the public to communicate to the administrator, in appropriate form, a request for investigation of a member of the bar. An attorney shall not charge or collect a fee in connection with answering a request for investigation unless he or she is acting as counsel for a respondent in connection with a disciplinary investigation or proceeding.

(C) **Duty to Assist Administrator**. An attorney other than a respondent or respondent's attorney shall cooperate with the administrator in the investigation, prosecution, and disposition of a request for investigation or proceeding under this subchapter.

Rule 9.104 Grounds for Discipline in General

The following acts or omissions by an attorney, individually or in concert with another person, are misconduct and grounds for discipline, whether or not occurring in the course of an attorney-client relationship:

(1) conduct prejudicial to the proper administration of justice;
(2) conduct that exposes the legal profession or the courts to obloquy, contempt, censure, or reproach;
(3) conduct that is contrary to justice, ethics, honesty, or good morals;
(4) conduct that violates the standards or rules of professional conduct adopted by the Supreme Court;

(5) conduct that violates a criminal law of a state or of the United States, an ordinance, or tribal law pursuant to MCR 2.615;
(6) knowing misrepresentation of any facts or circumstances surrounding a request for investigation or complaint;
(7) failure to answer a request for investigation or complaint in conformity with MCR 9.113 and 9.115(D);
(8) contempt of the board or a hearing panel; or
(9) violation of an order of discipline.
(10) entering into and agreement or attempting to obtain an agreement, that:
  (a) the professional misconduct or the terms of a settlement of a claim for professional misconduct shall not be reported to the administrator;
  (b) the plaintiff shall withdraw a request for investigation or shall not cooperate with the investigation or prosecution of misconduct by the administrator; or
  (c) the record of any civil action for professional misconduct shall be sealed from review by the administrator.

Rule 9.105 Purpose and Funding of Disciplinary Proceedings

(A) **Purpose**. Discipline for misconduct is not intended as punishment for wrongdoing, but for the protection of the public, the courts, and the legal profession. The fact that certain misconduct has remained unchallenged when done by others or when done at other times or has not been earlier made the subject of disciplinary proceedings is not an excuse.

(B) **Funding**. The legal profession, through the State Bar of Michigan, is responsible for the reasonable and necessary expenses of the board, the commission, and the administrator, as determined by the Supreme Court.

Rule 9.106 Types of Discipline; Minimum Discipline

Misconduct is grounds for:

(1) disbarment of an attorney from the practice of law in Michigan;
(2) suspension of the license to practice law in Michigan for a specified term, not less than 30 days, with such additional conditions relevant to the established misconduct as a hearing panel, the board, or the Supreme Court may impose, and, if the term exceeds 179 days, until the further order of a hearing panel, the board, or the Supreme Court;
(3) reprimand with such conditions relevant to the established misconduct as a hearing panel, the board, or the Supreme Court may impose;
(4) probation ordered by a hearing panel, the board, or the Supreme Court under MCR 9.121(C); or
(5) requiring restitution, in an amount set by a hearing panel, the board, or the Supreme Court, as a condition of an order of discipline.

Rule 9.107 Rules Exclusive on Discipline

(A) **Proceedings for Discipline**. Subchapter 9.100 governs the procedure to discipline attorneys. A proceeding under subchapter 9.100 is subject to the superintending control of the Supreme Court. An investigation or proceeding may not be held invalid because of a nonprejudicial irregularity or an error not resulting in a miscarriage of justice.

(B) **Local Bar Associations**. A local bar association may not conduct a separate proceeding to discipline an attorney.

Rule 9.108 Attorney Grievance Commission

(A) **Authority of Commission**. The Attorney Grievance Commission is the prosecution arm of the Supreme Court for discharge of its constitutional responsibility to supervise and discipline Michigan attorneys and those temporarily admitted to practice under MCR 8.126 or otherwise subject to the disciplinary authority of the Supreme Court.

(B) **Composition**. The commission consists of 3 laypersons and 6 attorneys appointed by the Supreme Court. The members serve 3-year terms. A member may not serve more than 2 full terms.

(C) **Chairperson and Vice-Chairperson**. The Supreme Court shall designate from among the members of the commission a chairperson and a vice-chairperson who shall serve 1-year terms in those offices. The commencement and termination dates for the 1-year terms shall coincide appropriately with the 3-year membership terms of those officers and the other commission members. The Supreme Court may reappoint these officers for additional terms and may remove these officers prior to the expiration of a term. An officer appointed to fill a mid-term vacancy shall serve the remainder of that term and may be reappointed to serve up to 2 more full terms.

(D) **Internal Rules**.
  (1) The commission must elect annually from among its membership a secretary to keep the minutes of the commission's meetings and issue the required notices.
  (2) Five members constitute a quorum. The commission acts by majority vote of the members participating in the meeting.
  (3) The commission must meet monthly at a time and place the chairperson designates. Notice of a regular monthly meeting is not required.
  (4) A special meeting may be called by the chairperson or by petition of 3 commission members on 7 days' written notice. The notice may be waived in writing

or by attending the meeting. Special meetings may be conducted through electronic means.

(E) **Powers and Duties**. The commission has the power and duty to:
  (1) recommend attorneys to the Supreme Court for appointment as administrator and deputy administrator;
  (2) supervise the investigation of attorney misconduct, including requests for investigation of and complaints against attorneys;
  (3) supervise the administrator;
  (4) seek an injunction from the Supreme Court against an attorney's misconduct when prompt action is required, even if a disciplinary proceeding concerning that conduct is not pending before the board;
  (5) annually propose a budget for the commission and the administrator's office, including compensation, and submit it to the Supreme Court for approval;
  (6) submit to the Supreme Court proposed changes in these rules;
  (7) compile and maintain a list of out-of-state attorneys who have been admitted to practice temporarily and the dates those attorneys were admitted, and otherwise comply with the requirements of MCR 8.126, and
  (8) perform other duties provided in these rules.

Rule 9.109 Grievance Administrator

(A) **Appointment**. The administrator and the deputy administrator must be attorneys. The commission may recommend one or more candidates for appointment as administrator and deputy administrator. The Supreme Court shall appoint the administrator and the deputy administrator, may terminate their appointments at any time with or without cause, and shall determine their salaries and the other terms and conditions of their employment.

(B) **Powers and Duties**. The administrator has the power and duty to:
  (1) employ or retain attorneys, investigators, and staff with the approval of the commission;
  (2) supervise the attorneys, investigators, and staff;
  (3) assist the public in preparing requests for investigation;
  (4) maintain the commission records created as a result of these rules;
  (5) investigate alleged misconduct of attorneys, including initiating an investigation in his or her own name if necessary;
  (6) prosecute complaints the commission authorizes;
  (7) prosecute or defend reviews and appeals as the commission authorizes; and
  (8) report to the Supreme Court at least quarterly regarding the commission's activities, and to submit a joint annual report with the board that summarizes the activities of both agencies during the past year; and
  (9) perform other duties provided in these rules or assigned by the commission.

(C) **Legal Counsel for the Administrator**.
  (1) The administrator may appoint and retain volunteer legal counsel needed to prosecute proceedings under these rules.
  (2) Legal counsel may
    (a) commence proceedings under this subchapter;
    (b) present evidence relating to disciplinary and court proceedings;
    (c) prepare and file arguments and briefs;
    (d) inform the administrator about the progress of cases assigned; and
    (e) perform other duties assigned by the administrator.

Rule 9.110 Attorney Discipline Board

(A) **Authority of Board**. The Attorney Discipline Board is the adjudicative arm of the Supreme Court for discharge of its exclusive constitutional responsibility to supervise and discipline Michigan attorneys and those temporarily admitted to practice under MCR 8.126 or otherwise subject to the disciplinary authority of the Supreme Court.

(B) **Composition**. The board consists of 6 attorneys and 3 laypersons appointed by the Supreme Court. The members serve 3-year terms. A member may not serve more than 2 full terms.

(C) **Chairperson and Vice-Chairperson**. The Supreme Court shall designate from among the members of the board a chairperson and a vice-chairperson who shall serve 1-year terms in those offices. The commencement and termination dates of the 1-year terms shall coincide appropriately with the 3-year board terms of those officers and the other board members. The Supreme Court may reappoint these officers for additional terms and may remove an officer prior to the expiration of a term. An officer appointed to fill a midterm vacancy shall serve the remainder of that term and may be reappointed to serve two full terms.

(D) **Internal Rules**.
  (1) The board must elect annually from among its membership a secretary to supervise the keeping of the minutes of the board's meetings and the issuance of the required notices.
  (2) Five members constitute a quorum. The board acts by a majority vote of the members present.
  (3) The board shall meet monthly as often as necessary to maintain a current docket, but no less than every 2 months, at a time and place the chairperson designates.
  (4) A special meeting may be called by the chairperson or by petition of 3 board members on 7 days'

written notice. The notice may be waived in writing or by attending the meeting.

(E) **Powers and Duties**. The board has the power and duty to:

(1) appoint an attorney to serve as its general counsel and executive director;

(2) appoint hearing panels, masters, monitors and mentors;

(3) assign a proceeding under this subchapter to a hearing panel or to a master, except that a proceeding for reinstatement under MCR 9.124 may not be assigned to a master;

(4) on request of the respondent, the administrator, or the complainant, review a final order of discipline or dismissal by a hearing panel;

(5) on leave granted by the board, review a nonfinal order of a hearing panel;

(6) discipline and reinstate attorneys under these rules and exercise continuing jurisdiction over orders of discipline and reinstatement;

(7) file with the Supreme Court clerk its orders of suspension, disbarment, and reinstatement;

(8) annually propose a budget for the board and submit it to the Supreme Court for approval;

(9) report to the Supreme Court at least quarterly regarding its activities, and to submit a joint annual report with the Attorney Grievance Commission that summarizes the activities of both agencies during the past year; and

(10) submit to the Supreme Court proposed changes in these rules.

Rule 9.111 Hearing Panels

(A) **Composition; Quorum**. The board must establish hearing panels from a list of volunteer lawyers maintained by its executive director. The board must annually appoint 3 attorneys to each hearing panel and must fill a vacancy as it occurs. Following appointment, the board may designate the panel's chairperson, vice-chairperson and secretary. Thereafter, a hearing panel may elect a chairperson, vice-chairperson and secretary. A hearing panel must convene at the time and place designated by its chairperson or by the board. Two members constitute a quorum. A hearing panel acts by a majority vote. If a panel is unable to reach a majority decision, the matter shall be referred to the board for reassignment to a new panel.

(B) **Hearing Panelists or Masters; Discipline**.

(1) An attorney shall not be appointed as a hearing panelist or master if he or she:

(a) has ever been the subject of an order that imposes discipline, or

(b) has been admonished or placed on contractual probation within the preceding 5 years.

(2) A hearing panelist or master who becomes the subject of an order imposing discipline, an admonition, or placement on contractual probation shall be removed from the roster of hearing panelists. A hearing panelist or master who becomes the subject of a formal discipline proceeding shall be removed from consideration of any pending matter; shall be placed on the ADB's roster of inactive panelists; and shall not be assigned to a panel until the formal discipline proceeding has been resolved. A hearing panelist or master who becomes the subject of an otherwise confidential request for investigation must disclose that investigation to the parties in the matter before the panelist or master, or must disqualify himself or herself from participation in the matter.

(C) **Powers and Duties**. A hearing panel shall do the following:

(1) Schedule a public hearing on a proceeding under this subchapter assigned to it within 56 days after the proceeding is commenced or after the date that notice of the reinstatement is published, except that a proceeding for reciprocal discipline shall be governed by MCR 9.120. A hearing must be concluded within 91 days after it is begun, unless the board grants an extension for good cause.

(2) Receive evidence and make written findings of fact.

(3) Discipline and reinstate attorneys or dismiss a complaint by order under these rules and exercise continuing jurisdiction over its orders of discipline and reinstatement.

(4) Report its actions to the board within 35 days of the later of the filing of the transcript or the closing of the record, unless extended by the board chairperson.

(5) Perform other duties provided in these rules.

Rule 9.112 Requests for Investigation

(A) **Availability to Public**. The administrator shall furnish a form for a request for investigation to a person who alleges misconduct against an attorney. Use of the form is not required for filing a request for investigation.

(B) **Form of Request**. A request for investigation of alleged misconduct must

(1) be in writing;

(2) describe the alleged misconduct, including the approximate time and place of it;

(3) be signed by the complainant; and

(4) be filed with the administrator.

(C) **Handling by Administrator**.

(1) *Request for Investigation of Attorney*. After a preliminary review, the administrator shall either

(a) notify the complainant and the respondent that the allegations of the request for investigation are inadequate, incomplete, or insufficient to warrant the further attention of the commission; or

(b) serve a copy of the request for investigation on the respondent by ordinary mail at the respondent's address on file with the State Bar as required by Rule 2 of the Supreme Court Rules Concerning the State Bar of Michigan. Service is effective at the time of mailing, and nondelivery does not affect the validity of service. If a respondent has not filed an answer, no formal complaint shall be filed with the board unless the administrator has served the request for investigation by registered or certified mail return receipt requested.

(2) *Request for Investigation of Judge*. The administrator shall forward to the Judicial Tenure Commission a request for investigation of a judge, even if the request arises from the judge's conduct before he or she became a judge or from conduct unconnected with his or her judicial office. MCR 9.116 thereafter governs.

(3) *Request for Investigation of Member or Employee of Commission or Board*. Except as modified by MCR 9.131, MCR 9.104-9.130 apply to a request for investigation of an attorney who is a member of or is employed by the board or the commission.

(D) **Subpoenas**.

(1) After the request for investigation has been served on the respondent, the commission may issue subpoenas to require the appearance of a witness or the production of documents or other tangible things concerning matters then under investigation. Upon request filed with the board, the board chairperson may quash or modify the subpoena if compliance would be unreasonable or oppressive. Documents or other tangible things so produced may be retained by the grievance administrator, copied, or may be subjected to nondestructive testing. Subpoenas shall be returnable before the administrator or a person designated by the administrator.

(2) A person who without just cause, after being commanded by a subpoena, fails or refuses to appear or give evidence, to be sworn or affirmed, or to answer a proper question after being ordered to do so is in contempt. The administrator may initiate a contempt proceeding before the board chairperson or his or her designee, or under MCR 3.606 in the circuit court for the county where the act or refusal to act occurred. In the event of a finding of contempt by the respondent, the respondent's license to practice law may be suspended until he or she complies with the order of the board chairperson or his or her designee.

(3) A subpoena issued pursuant to this subrule and certified by the commission chairperson shall be sufficient authorization for taking a deposition or seeking the production of evidence outside the State of Michigan. If the deponent or the person possessing the subpoenaed evidence will not comply voluntarily, the proponent of the subpoena may utilize MCR 2.305(D) or any similar provision in a statute or court rule of Michigan or of the state, territory, or country where the deponent or possessor resides or is present.

(4) Upon receipt of a subpoena certified to be duly issued under the rules or laws of another lawyer disciplinary or admissions jurisdiction, the administrator may issue a subpoena directing a person domiciled or found within the state of Michigan to give testimony and/or produce documents or other things for use in the other lawyer disciplinary proceedings as directed in the subpoena of the other jurisdiction. The practice and procedure applicable to subpoenas issued under this subdivision shall be that of the other jurisdiction, except that:

(a) the testimony or production shall be only in the county where the person resides or is employed, or as otherwise fixed by the grievance administrator for good cause shown; and,

(b) compliance with any subpoena issued pursuant to this subdivision and contempt for failure in this respect shall be sought as elsewhere provided in this subchapter.

Rule 9.113 Answer by Respondent

(A) **Answer**. Within 21 days after being served with a request for investigation under MCR 9.112(C)(1)(b) or such further time as permitted by the administrator, the respondent shall file with the administrator a written answer signed by respondent in duplicate fully and fairly disclosing all the facts and circumstances pertaining to the alleged misconduct. Misrepresentation in the answer is grounds for discipline. Respondent's signature constitutes verification that he or she has read the document. The administrator shall provide a copy of the answer and any supporting documents, or documents related to a refusal to answer under MCR 9.113(B)(1), to the person who filed the request for investigation. If the administrator determines that there is cause for not disclosing some or all of the answer or documents supporting the answer, then the administrator need not provide those portions of the answer or the supporting documents to the person who filed the request for investigation.

(B) **Refusal or Failure to Answer**.

(1) A respondent may refuse to answer a request for investigation on expressed constitutional or professional grounds.

(2) The failure of a respondent to answer within the time period required under these rules other than as permitted in subrule (B)(1), or as further permitted

by the administrator is misconduct. See MCR 9.104(A)(7).

(3) If a respondent refuses to answer under subrule (B)(1), the refusal may be submitted under seal to a hearing panel for adjudication. If a panel finds that the refusal was not proper, it shall direct the attorney to answer the request for investigation within 21 days after its order.

(C) **Attorney-Client Privilege**. A person who files a request for investigation of an attorney irrevocably waives any attorney-client privilege that he or she may have as to matters relating to the request for the purposes of the commission's investigation.

(D) **Representation by Attorney**. The respondent may be represented by an attorney.

Rule 9.114 Action by Administrator or Commission After Answer

(A) **Action After Investigation**. After an answer is filed or the time for filing an answer has expired, the administrator may

(1) dismiss the request for investigation and notify the complainant and the respondent of the reasons for the dismissal,

(2) conduct further investigation. Upon completion of the investigation, the grievance administrator shall refer the matter to the commission for its review. The commission may direct that a complaint be filed, that the file be closed, that the respondent be admonished or placed on contractual probation with the respondent's consent, or

(3) close a file administratively where warranted under the circumstances.

(B) **Admonition**. With a respondent's consent, a respondent may be admonished by the commission without filing a complaint. An admonition does not constitute discipline and shall be confidential except as provided by this rule, MCR 9.115(J)(3) and by MCR 9.126(D)(4).

(1) The administrator shall notify the respondent of the provisions of this rule by ordinary mail at the respondent's address on file with the state bar as required by Rule 2 of the Supreme Court Rules Concerning the State Bar of Michigan, or as otherwise directed by respondent.

(2) The respondent may, within 21 days of service of the admonition or such additional time as permitted by the administrator, notify the commission in writing that respondent objects to the admonition. Upon timely receipt of the written objection, the commission shall vacate the admonition and either dismiss the request for investigation or authorize the filing of a complaint. Failure of a respondent to object constitutes an acceptance.

(C) **Contractual Probation**. For purposes of this subrule, "contractual probation" means the placement of a consenting respondent on probation by the commission, without the filing of formal charges. Contractual probation does not constitute discipline, and shall be confidential under MCR 9.126 except as provided by MCR 9.115(J)(3).

(1) If the commission finds that the alleged misconduct, if proven, would not result in disbarment or a substantial suspension of a respondent's license to practice law, the commission may defer disposition of the matter and place the respondent on contractual probation for a period not to exceed three years, provided the following criteria are met:

(a) the misconduct is significantly related to respondent's substance abuse problem, or mental or physical infirmity or disability,

(b) the terms and conditions of the contractual probation, which shall include an appropriate period of treatment, are agreed upon by the commission and the respondent, and

(c) the commission determines that contractual probation is appropriate and in the best interests of the public, the courts, the legal profession, and the respondent.

(2) A contractual probation may include one or more of these requirements:

(a) Periodic alcohol or drug testing.

(b) Attendance at support-group or comparable meetings.

(c) Professional counseling on a regular basis.

(d) An initial written diagnosis and prognosis by the provider followed by quarterly verification of treatment by the provider as agreed upon by the commission and the respondent. The provider shall notify the commission of any failure to adhere to the treatment plan.

(3) The respondent is responsible for any costs associated with the contractual probation and related treatment.

(4) Upon written notice to the respondent and an opportunity to file written objections, the commission may terminate the contractual probation and file disciplinary proceedings or take other appropriate action based on the misconduct, if

(a) the respondent fails to satisfactorily complete the terms and conditions of the contractual probation, or

(b) the commission concludes that the respondent has committed other misconduct that warrants the filing of a formal complaint.

(5) The placing of a respondent on contractual probation shall constitute a final disposition that entitles the complainant to notice in accordance with MCR 9.114(D), and to file an action in accordance with MCR 9.122(A)(2).

(D) **Assistance of Law Enforcement Agencies**. The administrator may request a law enforcement office to assist in an investigation by furnishing all available information about the respondent. Law enforcement officers are requested to comply promptly with each request.

(E) **Assistance of Courts**. If the grievance administrator determines that a nonpublic court file exists, including files on expunged convictions, and that it is relevant to a pending investigation concerning a respondent attorney, the administrator may request that a court release to the Attorney Grievance Commission the nonpublic court file. Courts are requested to comply promptly with each request.

(F) **Report by Administrator**. The administrator shall inform the complainant and, if the respondent answered, the respondent, of the final disposition of every request for investigation.

(G) **Retention of Records**. All files and records relating to allegations of misconduct by an attorney must be retained by the commission for the lifetime of the attorney, except as follows:

(1) Where 3 years have passed from the conclusion of formal disciplinary action or the issuance of an admonishment, nonessential documents may be discarded.

(2) The administrator may destroy the files or records relating to a closed or dismissed request for investigation after 3 years have elapsed from the date of dismissal or closing.

(3) If no request for investigation was pending when the files or records were created or acquired, and no related request for investigation was filed subsequently, the administrator may destroy the files or records after 1 year has elapsed from the date when they were created or acquired by the commission.

Rule 9.115 Hearing Panel Procedure

(A) **Rules Applicable**. Except as otherwise provided in these rules, the rules governing practice and procedure in a nonjury civil action apply to a proceeding before a hearing panel. Pleadings must conform as nearly as practicable to the requirements of subchapter 2.100. The original of the formal complaint and all other pleadings must be filed with the board. The formal complaint must be served on the respondent. All other pleadings must be served on the opposing party and each member of the hearing panel. Proof of service of the formal complaint may be filed at any time prior to the date of the hearing. Proof of service of all other pleadings must be filed with the original pleadings.

(B) **Complaint**. Except as provided by MCR 9.120, a complaint setting forth the facts of the alleged misconduct begins proceedings before a hearing panel. The administrator shall prepare the complaint, file it with the board, and serve it on the respondent and a respondent's employer. The unwillingness of a complainant to proceed, or a settlement between the complainant and the respondent, does not itself affect the right of the administrator to proceed.

(C) **Service**. Service of the complaint and a default must be made by personal service or by registered or certified mail addressed to the person at the person's last known address. An attorney's last known address is the address on file with the state bar as required by Rule 2 of the Supreme Court Rules Concerning the State Bar of Michigan. A respondent's attorney of record must also be served, but service may be made under MCR 2.107. Service is effective at the time of mailing, and nondelivery does not affect the validity of the service.

(D) **Answer**.

(1) A respondent must serve and file a signed answer or take other action permitted by law or these rules within 21 days after being served with the complaint in the manner provided in MCR 9.115(C). A signature constitutes verification that the respondent has read the answer or other response.

(2) A default, with the same effect as a default in a civil action, may enter against a respondent who fails within the time permitted to file an answer admitting, denying, or explaining the complaint, or asserting the grounds for failing to do so.

(E) **Representation by Attorney**. The respondent may be represented by an attorney, who must enter an appearance, which has the same effect as an appearance under MCR 2.117.

(F) **Prehearing Procedure**.

(1) *Extensions*. If good cause is shown, the hearing panel chairperson may grant one extension of time per party for filing pleadings and may grant one adjournment per party. Additional requests may be granted by the board chairperson if good cause is shown. Pending criminal or civil litigation of substantial similarity to the allegations of the complaint is not necessarily grounds for an adjournment.

(2) *Motion to Disqualify*.

(a) Within 14 days after an answer has been filed or the time for filing the answer has expired, each member of the hearing panel shall disclose in a writing filed with the board any information that the member believes could be grounds for disqualification under the guidelines of MCR 2.003(C), including pending requests for investigation filed against the member. The duty to disclose shall be a continuing one. The board shall serve a copy of the disclosure on each party and each panel member.

(b) A motion to disqualify must be filed within 14 days after the moving party discovers the ground for disqualification. If the discovery is made within 14 days of the hearing date, the motion must be made forthwith. If a motion is not timely filed, untimeliness is a factor in deciding whether the motion should be granted. All known grounds for disqualification must be included at the time the motion is filed. An affidavit must accompany the motion. The board chairperson shall decide the motion under the guidelines of MCR 2.003.

(c) The board must assign a substitute for a disqualified member of a hearing panel. If all are disqualified, the board must reassign the complaint to another panel.

(3) *Amendment of Pleadings*. The administrator and the respondent each may amend a pleading once as a matter of course within 14 days after being served with a responsive pleading by the opposing party, or within 15 days after serving the pleading if it does not require a responsive pleading. Otherwise, a party may amend a pleading only by leave granted by the hearing panel chairperson or with the written consent of the advserse party.

(4) *Discovery*. Pretrial or discovery proceedings are not permitted, except as follows:

(a) Within 21 days after the service of a formal complaint, a party may demand in writing that documentary evidence that is to be introduced at the hearing by the opposing party be made available for inspection or copying. Within 14 days after service of a written demand, the documents shall be made available, provided that the administrator need not comply prior to the filing of the respondent's answer; in such case, the administrator shall comply with the written demand within 14 days after the filing of the respondent's answer. The respondent shall comply with the written demand within 14 days, except that the respondent need not comply until the time for filing an answer to the formal complaint has expired. Any other documentary evidence to be introduced at the hearing by either party shall be supplied to the other party no later than 14 days prior to the hearing. Any documentary evidence not so supplied shall be excluded from the hearing except for good cause shown.

(i) Within 21 days after the service of a formal complaint, a party may demand in writing that the opposing party supply written notification of the name and address of any person to be called as a witness at the hearing. Within 14 days after the service of a written demand, the notification shall be supplied. However, the administrator need not comply prior to the filing of the respondent's answer to the formal complaint; in such cases, the administrator shall comply with the written demand within 14 days of the filing of the respondent's answer to the formal complaint. The respondent shall comply with the written demand within 14 days, except that the respondent need not comply until the time for filing an answer to the formal complaint has expired. Except for good cause shown, a party who is required to give said notification must give supplemental notice to the adverse party within 7 days after any additional witness has been identified, and must give the supplemental notice immediately if the additional witness is identified less than 14 days before a scheduled hearing.

(ii) Within 21 days following the filing of an answer, the administrator and respondent shall exchange the names and addresses of all persons having knowledge of relevant facts and comply with reasonable requests for (1) nonprivileged information and evidence relevant to the charges against the respondent, and (2) other material upon good cause shown to the chair of the hearing panel.

(b) A deposition may be taken of a witness who lives outside the state or is physically unable to attend the hearing. For good cause shown, the hearing panel may allow the parties to depose other witnesses.

(c) The hearing panel may order a prehearing conference held before a panel member to obtain admissions or otherwise narrow the issues presented by the pleadings.

If a party fails to comply with subrule (F)(4)(a), the hearing panel or the board may, on motion and showing of material prejudice as a result of the failure, impose one or more of the sanctions set forth in MCR 2.313(B)(2)(a)-(c).

(5) *Discipline by Consent*. A respondent may offer to plead no contest or to admit all essential facts contained in the complaint or any of its allegations in exchange for a stated form of discipline and on the condition that the plea or admission and discipline agreed on is accepted by the commission and the hearing panel. The respondent's offer shall first be submitted to the commission. If the offer is accepted by the commission, the administrator and the respondent shall prepare a stipulation for a consent order of discipline that includes all prior discipline, admonishments, and contractual probations, if any, and file the stipulation with the hearing panel. If the stipulation contains any

nonpublic information, it shall be filed in camera. At the time of the filing, the administrator shall serve a copy of the proposed stipulation upon the complainant. If the hearing panel approves the stipulation, it shall enter a final order of discipline. If not approved, the offer is deemed withdrawn and statements or stipulations made in connection with the offer are inadmissible in disciplinary proceedings against the respondent and not binding on the respondent or the administrator. If the stipulation is not approved, the matter must then be referred for hearing to a hearing panel other than the one that passed on the proposed discipline.

(G) **Hearing Time and Place; Notice**. The board or the chairperson of the hearing panel shall set the time and place for a hearing. Notice of a hearing must be served by the board or the chairperson of the hearing panel on the administrator, the respondent, the complainant, and any attorney of record at least 21 days before the initial hearing. Unless the board or the chairperson of the hearing panel otherwise directs, the hearing must be in the county in which the respondent has or last had an office or residence. If the hearing panel fails to convene or complete its hearing within a reasonable time, the board may reassign the complaint to another panel or to a master. A party may file a motion for a change of venue. The motion must be filed with the board and shall be decided by the board chairperson, in part, on the basis of the guidelines in MCR 2.221. Notwithstanding MRE 615, there shall be a presumption that a complainant is entitled to be present during a hearing, which may only be overcome upon a finding by the panel, supported by facts that are particular to the proceeding, that testimony by the complainant is likely to be materially affected by exposure to other testimony at the hearing.

(H) **Respondent's Appearance**. The respondent shall personally appear at the hearing, unless excused by the panel, and is subject to cross-examination as an opposite party under MCL 600.2161.

(1) Where satisfactory proofs are entered into the record that a respondent possessed actual notice of the proceedings, but who still failed to appear, a panel shall suspend him or her effective 7 days from the date of entry of the order and until further order of the panel or the board.

(2) If the respondent, or the respondent's attorney on his or her behalf, claims physical or mental incapacity as a reason for the respondent's failure to appear before a hearing panel or the board, the panel or the board on its own initiative may, effective immediately, suspend the respondent from the practice of law until further order of the panel or board. The order of suspension must be filed and served as other orders of discipline.

(I) **Hearing; Contempt**.

(1) A hearing panel may issue subpoenas (including subpoenas for production of documents and other tangible things), cause testimony to be taken under oath, and rule on the admissibility of evidence under the Michigan Rules of Evidence. The oath or affirmation may be administered by a panel member. A subpoena must be issued in the name and under the seal of the board. It must be signed by a panel or board member, by the administrator, or by the respondent or the respondent's attorney. A subpoenaed witness must be paid the same fee and mileage as a witness subpoenaed to testify in the circuit court. Parties must notify their own witnesses of the date, time, and place of the hearing.

(2) A person who without just cause fails or refuses to appear and give evidence as commanded by a subpoena, to be sworn or affirmed, or to answer a proper question after he or she has been ordered to do so, is in contempt. The administrator may initiate a contempt proceeding under MCR 3.606 in the circuit court for the county where the act or refusal to act occurred.

(3) Upon a showing of good cause by a party, a panel may permit a witness to testify by telephonic, voice, or video conferencing.

(J) **Decision**.

(1) The hearing panel must file a report on its decisions regarding the misconduct charges and, if applicable, the resulting discipline. The report must include a certified transcript, a summary of the evidence, pleadings, exhibits and briefs, and findings of fact. The discipline section of the report must also include a summary of all previous misconduct for which the respondent was disciplined, admonished, or placed on contractual probation.

(2) Upon a finding of misconduct, the hearing panel shall conduct a separate sanction hearing to determine the appropriate discipline. The sanction hearing shall be conducted as soon after the finding of misconduct as is practicable and may be held immediately following the panel's ruling that misconduct has been established.

(3) If the hearing panel finds that the charge of misconduct is established by a preponderance of the evidence, it must enter an order of discipline. The order shall take effect 21 days after it is served on the respondent unless the panel finds good cause for the order to take effect on a different date, in which event the panel's decision must explain the reasons for ordering a different effective date. The discipline ordered may be concurrent or consecutive to other discipline. In determining the discipline to be imposed, any and all relevant

evidence of aggravation or mitigation shall be admissible, including, but not limited to, records of the board, previous admonitions and orders of discipline, and the previous placement of the respondent on contractual probation.

(4) If the hearing panel finds that the charge of misconduct is not established by a preponderance of the evidence, it must enter an order dismissing the complaint.

(5) The report and order must be signed by the panel chairperson and filed with the board and the administrator. A copy must be served on the parties as required by these rules.

(K) **Stay of Discipline**. If a discipline order is a suspension of 179 days or less, a stay of the discipline order will automatically issue on the timely filing by the respondent of a petition for review and a petition for a stay of the discipline. If the discipline ordered is more severe than a suspension of 179 days, the respondent may petition the board for a stay pending review of the discipline order. Once granted, a stay remains effective until the further order of the board.

(L) **Enforcement**. The administrator shall take the necessary steps to enforce a discipline order after it is effective.

(M) **Resignation by Respondent; Admission of Charges**. An attorney's resignation may not be accepted while a request for investigation or a complaint is pending, except pursuant to an order of disbarment.

Rule 9.116 Judges; Former Judges

(A) **Judges**. The administrator or commission may not take action against an incumbent judge, except that this rule does not prohibit an action by the administrator or commission against:

(1) a magistrate or referee for misconduct unrelated to judicial functions, whether before or during the period when the person serves as a magistrate or referee; or

(2) a visiting judge as provided in MCR 9.203(E). If the Judicial Tenure Commission receives a request for investigation of a magistrate or referee or visiting judge arising from the practice of law, the Judicial Tenure Commission shall refer the matter to the administrator or commission for investigation in the first instance. If the administrator or the commission dismisses the request for investigation referred by the Judicial Tenure Commission, or a request for investigation of a magistrate, referee or visiting judge submitted directly to the commission by a complainant, the administrator or commission shall notify the Judicial Tenure Commission, which may take action as it deems appropriate.

(B) **Former Judges**. The administrator or commission may take action against a former judge for conduct resulting in removal as a judge, and for any conduct which was not the subject of a disposition by the Judicial Tenure Commission or by the Court. The administrator or commission may not take action against a former judge for conduct where the court imposed a sanction less than removal or the Judicial Tenure Commission has taken any action under MCR 9.207(B)(1)-(5).

(C) **Judicial Tenure Commission Record**. The record of the Judicial Tenure Commission proceeding is admissible at a hearing involving a former judge. The administrator or the respondent may introduce additional evidence.

Rule 9.117 Hearing Procedure Before Master

If the board assigns a complaint to a master, the master shall hold a public hearing on the complaint and receive evidence. To the extent that MCR 9.115 may be applied, it governs procedure before a master. After the hearing, the master shall prepare a report containing

(1) a brief statement of the proceedings,
(2) findings of fact, and
(3) conclusions of law.

The master shall file the report with a hearing panel designated by the board and serve a copy on the administrator and the respondent. Within 14 days after the report is filed, the administrator or the respondent may file objections to the report and a supporting brief. The panel must determine if the record supports the findings of fact and conclusions of law and impose discipline, if warranted. Further proceedings are governed by MCR 9.118.

Rule 9.118 Review of Order of Hearing Panel

(A) **Review of Order; Time**.

(1) The administrator, the complainant, or the respondent may petition the board in writing to review the order of a hearing panel filed under MCR 9.113(B), 9.116, 9.120, 9.121 or 9.124. The board may grant review of a nonfinal order and decide such interlocutory matters without a hearing. A petition for review must set forth the reasons and the grounds on which review is sought and must be filed with the board within 21 days after the order is served. The petitioner must serve copies of the petition and the accompanying documents on the other party and the complainant and file a proof of service with the board.

(2) A cross-petition for review may be filed within 21 days after the petition for review is served on the cross-petitioner. The cross-petition must be served on the other party and the complainant, and a proof of service must be filed with the board.

(3) A delayed petition for review may be considered by the board chairperson under the guidelines of MCR 7.205(F). If a petition for review is filed more than 12 months after the order of the hearing panel is entered, the petition may not be granted.

(B) **Order to Show Cause**. If a petition for review is timely filed or a delayed petition for review is accepted for filing, the board shall issue an order to show cause, at a date and time specified, why the order of the hearing panel should not be affirmed. The order shall establish a briefing schedule for all parties and may require that an answer to the petition or cross-petition be filed. An opposing party may file an answer even if the order does not require one. The board must serve the order to show cause on the administrator, respondent, and complainant at least 21 days before the hearing. Failure to comply with the order to show cause, including, but not limited to, a requirement for briefs, may be grounds for dismissal of a petition for review. Dismissal of a petition for review shall not affect the validity of a cross-petition for review.

(C) **Hearing**.

(1) A hearing on the order to show cause must be heard by a subboard of at least 3 board members assigned by the chairperson. The board must make a final decision on consideration of the whole record, including a transcript of the presentation made to the subboard and the subboard's recommendation. The respondent shall appear personally at the review hearing unless excused by the board. Failure to appear may result in denial of any relief sought by the respondent, or any other action allowable under MCR 9.118(D).

(2) If the board believes that additional testimony should be taken, it may refer the case to a hearing panel or a master. The panel or the master shall then take the additional testimony and shall make a supplemental report, including a transcript of the additional testimony, pleadings, exhibits, and briefs with the board. Notice of the filing of the supplemental report and a copy of the report must be served as an original report and order of a hearing panel.

(D) **Decision**. After the hearing on the order to show cause, the board may affirm, amend, reverse, or nullify the order of the hearing panel in whole or in part or order other discipline. A discipline order is not effective until 28 days after it is served on the respondent unless the board finds good cause for the order to take effect earlier.

(E) **Motion for Reconsideration; Stay**. A motion for reconsideration may be filed at any time before the board's order takes effect. An answer to a motion for reconsideration may be filed. If the discipline order is a suspension for 179 days or less, a stay of the discipline order will automatically issue on the timely filing by the respondent of a motion for reconsideration. If the discipline is greater than a 179-day suspension, the respondent may petition for a stay. If the board grants a stay, the stay remains effective for 28 days after the board enters its order granting or denying reconsideration.

(F) **Filing Orders**. The board must file a copy of its discipline order with the Supreme Court clerk and the clerk of the county where the respondent resides and where his or her office is located. The order must be served on all parties. If the respondent requests it in writing, a dismissal order must be similarly filed and served.

Rule 9.119 Conduct of Disbarred, Suspended, or Inactive Attorneys

(A) **Notification to Clients**. An attorney who has resigned under Rule 3 of the Rules Concerning the State Bar of Michigan, or been disbarred, or suspended, or who is transferred to inactive status pursuant to MCR 9.121, or who is suspended for nondisciplinary reasons pursuant to Rule 4 of the Supreme Court Rules Concerning the State Bar of Michigan, shall, within 7 days of the effective date of the order of discipline, resignation, the transfer to inactive status or the nondisciplinary suspension, notify all his or her active clients, in writing, by registered or certified mail, return receipt requested, of the following:

(1) the nature and duration of the discipline imposed, the transfer to inactive status, or the nondisciplinary suspension, or the resignation;

(2) the effective date of such discipline, transfer to inactive status, or nondisciplinary suspension, or resignation;

(3) the attorney's inability to act as an attorney after the effective date of such discipline, transfer to inactive status, nondisciplinary suspension, or resignation;

(4) the location and identity of the custodian of the clients' files and records, which will be made available to them or to substitute counsel;

(5) that the clients may wish to seek legal advice and counsel elsewhere; provided that, if the disbarred, suspended, inactive, or resigned attorney was a member of a law firm, the firm may continue to represent each client with the client's express written consent;

(6) the address to which all correspondence to the attorney may be addressed.

(B) **Conduct in Litigated Matters**. In addition to the requirements of subsection (A) of this rule, the affected attorney must, by the effective date of the order of disbarment, suspension, transfer to inactive status, or resignation, in every matter in which the attorney is representing a client in litigation, file with the tribunal and all parties a notice of the attorney's disqualification from the practice of law. The affected attorney shall either file a motion to withdraw from the representation, or, with the client’s knowledge and consent, a substitution of counsel.

(C) **Filing of Proof of Compliance**. Within 14 days after the effective date of the order of disbarment, suspension, or transfer to inactive status, pursuant to MCR 9.121, or resignation the disbarred, suspended, inactive, or resigned attorney shall file with the administrator and the board an affidavit showing full compliance with this rule. The affidavit must include as an appendix copies of the disclosure notices and mailing receipts required under subrules (A) and (B) of this rule. The affidavit must set forth any claim by the affected attorney that he or she does not have active clients at the time of the effective date of the change in status. A disbarred, suspended, inactive, or resigned attorney shall keep and maintain records of the various steps taken under this rule so that, in any subsequent proceeding instituted by or against him or her, proof of compliance with this rule and with the disbarment or suspension order will be available.

(D) **Conduct After Entry of Order Prior to Effective Date**. A disbarred or suspended attorney, after entry of the order of disbarment or suspension and prior to its effective date, shall not accept any new retainer or engagement as attorney for another in any new case or legal matter of any nature, unless specifically authorized by the board chairperson upon a showing of good cause and a finding that it is not contrary to the interests of the public and profession. However, during the period between the entry of the order and its effective date, the suspended or disbarred attorney may complete, on behalf of any existing client, all matters that were pending on the entry date.

(E) **Conduct After Effective Date of Order**. An attorney who is disbarred, suspended, transferred to inactive status pursuant to MCR 9.121, or who resigns is, during the period of disbarment, suspension, or inactivity, or from and after the date of resignation, forbidden from:

(1) practicing law in any form;

(2) having contact either in person, by telephone, or by electronic means, with clients or potential clients of a lawyer or law firm either as a paralegal, law clerk, legal assistant, or lawyer;

(3) appearing as an attorney before any court, judge, justice, board, commission, or other public authority; and

(4) holding himself or herself out as an attorney by any means.

(F) **Compensation of Disbarred, Suspended, Resigned, or Inactive Attorney**. An attorney who has been disbarred or suspended, has resigned, or who is transferred to inactive status pursuant to MCR 9.121 may not share in any legal fees for legal services performed by another attorney during the period of disqualification from the practice of law. A disbarred, suspended, resigned, or inactive attorney may be compensated on a quantum meruit basis for legal services rendered and expenses paid by him or her prior to the effective date of the disbarment, suspension, resignation, or transfer to inactive status.

(G) **Receivership**.

(1) *Attorney with a firm*. If an attorney who is a member of a firm is disbarred, suspended, is transferred to inactive status pursuant to MCR 9.121, or resigns his or her license to practice law, the firm may continue to represent each client with the client's express written consent. Copies of the signed consents shall be maintained with the client file.

(2) *Attorney practicing alone*. If an attorney is transferred to inactive status, resigns, or is disbarred or suspended and fails to give notice under the rule, or disappears, is imprisoned, or dies, and there is no partner, executor or other responsible person capable of conducting the attorney's affairs, the administrator may ask the chief judge in the judicial circuit in which the attorney maintained his or her practice to appoint a person to act as a receiver with necessary powers, including:

(a) to obtain and inventory the attorney's files;

(b) to take any action necessary to protect the interests of the attorney and the attorney's clients;

(c) to change the address at which the attorney's mail is delivered and to open the mail; or

(d) to secure (garner) the lawyer's bank accounts.

The person appointed is analogous to a receiver operating under the direction of the circuit court.

(3) *Confidentiality*. The person appointed may not disclose to any third parties any information protected by MRPC 1.6 without the client's written consent.

(4) *Publication of Notice*. Upon receipt of notification from the receiver, the state bar shall publish in the Michigan Bar Journal notice of the receivership, including the name and address of the subject attorney, and the name, address, and telephone number of the receiver.

Rule 9.120 Conviction of Criminal Offense; Reciprocal Discipline

(A) **Notification of the Grievance Administrator and the Attorney Discipline Board**.

(1) When a lawyer is convicted of a crime, the lawyer, the prosecutor or other authority who prosecuted the lawyer, and the defense attorney who represented the lawyer must notify the grievance administrator and the board of the conviction. This notice must be given in writing within 14 days after the conviction.

(2) A lawyer who has been the subject of an order of discipline or transferred to inactive status by any court of record or any body authorized by law or by rule of court to conduct disciplinary proceedings

against attorneys, of the United States, or of any state or territory of the United States or of the District of Columbia, or who has resigned from the bar or roster of attorneys in lieu of discipline by, or during the pendency of, discipline proceedings before such court or body shall inform the grievance administrator and board of entry of such order, transfer, or resignation within 14 days of the entry of the order, transfer, or resignation.

(B) **Criminal Conviction.**

(1) On conviction of a felony, an attorney is automatically suspended until the effective date of an order filed by a hearing panel under MCR 9.115(J). A conviction occurs upon the return of a verdict of guilty or upon the acceptance of a plea of guilty or nolo contendere. The board may, on the attorney's motion, set aside the automatic suspension when it appears consistent with the maintenance of the integrity and honor of the profession, the protection of the public, and the interests of justice. The board must set aside the automatic suspension if the felony conviction is vacated, reversed, or otherwise set aside for any reason by the trial court or an appellate court.

(2) In a disciplinary proceeding instituted against an attorney based on the attorney's conviction of a criminal offense, a certified copy of the judgment of conviction is conclusive proof of the commission of the criminal offense.

(3) The administrator may file with the board a judgment of conviction showing that an attorney has violated a criminal law of a state or of the United States, an ordinance, or tribal law pursuant to MCR 2.615. The board shall then order the attorney to show cause why a final order of discipline should not be entered, and the board shall refer the proceeding to a hearing panel for hearing. At the hearing, questions as to the validity of the conviction, alleged trial errors, and the availability of appellate remedies shall not be considered. After the hearing, the panel shall issue an order under MCR 9.115(J).

(4) On a pardon the board may, and on a reversal of the conviction the board must, by order filed and served under MCR 9.118(F), vacate the order of discipline. The attorney's name must be returned to the roster of Michigan attorneys and counselors at law, but the administrator may nevertheless proceed against the respondent for misconduct which had led to the criminal charge.

(C) **Reciprocal Discipline.**

(1) A certified copy of a final adjudication by any court of record or any body authorized by law or by rule of court to conduct disciplinary proceedings against attorneys by any state or territory of the United States or of the District of Columbia, a United States court, or a federal administrative agency, determining that an attorney, whether or not admitted in that jurisdiction, has committed misconduct or has been transferred to disability inactive status, shall establish conclusively the misconduct or the disability for purposes of a proceeding under subchapter 9.100 of these rules and comparable discipline or transfer shall be imposed in the Michigan proceeding unless the respondent was not afforded due process of law in the course of the original proceedings, the imposition of comparable discipline or transfer in Michigan would be clearly inappropriate, or the reason for the original transfer to disability inactive status no longer exists.

(2) Upon the filing by the grievance administrator of a certified copy of final adjudication described in paragraph (C)(1) with the board, the board shall issue an order directed to the lawyer and the administrator:

(a) attaching a copy of the order from the other jurisdiction; and

(b) directing, that, within 21 days from service of the order, the lawyer and administrator shall inform the board (i) of any objection to the imposition of comparable discipline or disability inactive status in Michigan based on the grounds set forth in paragraph (C)(1) of this rule, and (ii) whether a hearing is requested.

(3) Upon receipt of an objection to the imposition of comparable discipline or disability inactive status raising one or more of the issues identified in paragraph (C)(1) of this rule, the board shall assign the matter to a hearing panel for disposition. The opposing party shall have 21 days to reply to an objection. If a hearing is requested, and the hearing panel grants the request, the hearing shall be held in accordance with the procedures set forth in MCR 9.115 except as otherwise provided in this rule.

(4) Papers filed under this rule shall conform as nearly as practicable to the requirements of subchapter 2.100 and shall be filed with the board and served on the opposing party and each member of the hearing panel once assigned.

(5) The burden is on the party seeking to avoid the imposition of comparable discipline or transfer to disability inactive status to demonstrate that it is not appropriate for one or more of the grounds set forth in paragraph (C)(1). "Comparable" discipline does not mean that the dates of a period of disqualification from practice in this state must coincide with the dates of the period of disqualification, if any, in the original jurisdiction.

(6) If the 21-day period discussed in paragraph (C)(2)(b) has expired without objection by either party, the respondent is in default, with the same

effect as a default in a civil action, and the board shall impose comparable discipline or transfer to disability inactive status unless it appears that one of the grounds set forth in paragraph (C)(1) of this rule requires a different result, in which case the board shall schedule a hearing in accord with paragraph (3) of this rule. An order entered pursuant to this subparagraph may be set aside if the requirements of MCR 2.603(D) are established.

(7) In the event the discipline or transfer to disability inactive status imposed in the original jurisdiction is stayed, any reciprocal discipline imposed in Michigan shall be deferred until the stay expires.

Rule 9.121 Attorney Declared to be Incompetent or Alleged to be Incapacitated or Asserting Impaired Ability

(A) **Adjudication by Court**. If an attorney has been judicially declared incompetent or involuntarily committed on the grounds of incompetency or disability, the board, on proper proof of the fact, must enter an order effective immediately transferring the attorney to inactive status for an indefinite period and until further order of the board.

(B) **Allegations of Incompetency or Incapacity**.

(1) If it is alleged in a complaint by the administrator that an attorney is incapacitated to continue the practice of law because of mental or physical infirmity or disability or because of addiction to drugs or intoxicants, a hearing panel shall take action necessary to determine whether the attorney is incapacitated.

(a) Examination.

(i) Upon a showing of good cause that a mental or physical condition is the basis of respondent's incompetency or incapacity as alleged in a complaint by the administrator, a hearing panel may order respondent to submit to one or more medical examination(s) or psychological examination(s) that are relevant to a condition of respondent shown to be in controversy.

(ii) If testing is ordered, the administrator and respondent may stipulate to the expert(s) who will conduct the examination(s), prepare a report within 28 days of the conclusion of the examination(s), and provide a copy of said report to both parties. The content of a report prepared by an expert(s) pursuant to this paragraph is admissible into evidence in the proceedings, subject to relevancy objections.

(iii) If the administrator and/or respondent hire their own expert(s) to conduct the examination(s), the expert(s) will conduct the examination(s), prepare a report within 28 days of the conclusion of the examination(s), and provide a copy of said report to both parties. A report prepared pursuant to this paragraph is only admissible as substantive evidence upon stipulation by both parties. The respondent will be responsible for the expenses incurred by retaining his or her examiner.

(iv) On its own motion or on the motion of either party, the hearing panel may appoint an expert of its own selection to conduct the necessary examination(s). The expert so appointed will conduct the examination(s), prepare a report within 28 days of the conclusion of the examination(s), and provide a copy of said report to both parties. The content of a report prepared by an expert(s) pursuant to this paragraph is admissible into evidence in the proceedings unless, within 14 days of delivery of the report, a party objects, in which case either party may subpoena the expert(s) to testify at the hearing at that party's expense.

(b) Expert's Report. The expert's report as required by paragraph (a) shall include:

(i) the expert's resume or curriculum vitae;

(ii) a statement of facts, and a list of the tests that were administered and the test results;

(iii) a diagnosis, prognosis, a statement of limitations on the opinion because of the scope of the examination or testing, and recommendation for treatment, if any; and

(iv) no physician-patient privilege shall apply under this rule.

(2) The hearing panel shall provide notice to the attorney of the proceedings. Upon the request of a party, or on its own motion, and following a finding of good cause, a panel may recommend the appointment of counsel by the board to represent the respondent if he or she is without representation.

(3) If, after a hearing, the hearing panel concludes that the attorney is incapacitated from continuing to practice law, it shall enter an order transferring him or her to inactive status for an indefinite period and until further order of the board.

(4) Pending disciplinary proceedings against the attorney must be held in abeyance.

(5) Proceedings conducted under this subrule are subject to review by the board as provided in MCR 9.118.

(C) **Assertion of Impaired Ability; Probation**.

(1) If, in response to a formal complaint filed under subrule 9.115(B), the respondent asserts in mitigation and thereafter demonstrates by a preponderance of the evidence that

(a) during the period when the conduct that is the subject of the complaint occurred, his or her ability to practice law competently was materially impaired by physical or mental disability or by drug or alcohol addiction,

(b) the impairment was the cause of or substantially contributed to that conduct,

(c) the cause of the impairment is susceptible to treatment, and

(d) he or she in good faith intends to undergo treatment, and submits a detailed plan for such treatment, the hearing panel, the board, or the Supreme Court may enter an order placing the respondent on probation for a specific period not to exceed 3 years if it specifically finds that an order of probation is not contrary to the public interest.

(2) If the respondent alleges impairment by physical or mental disability or by drug or alcohol addiction pursuant to subrule (C)(1), the hearing panel may order the respondent to submit to a physical or mental examination in accord with the procedure set for the in MCR 9.121(B)(1)(a). The panel may direct that the expense of the examination be paid by the respondent. A respondent who fails or refuses to comply with an examination order, or refuses to undergo an examination requested by the administrator, shall not be eligible for probation.

(3) The probation order

(a) must specify the treatment the respondent is to undergo,

(b) may require the respondent to practice law only under the direct supervision of other attorneys, or

(c) may include any other terms the evidence shows are likely to eliminate the impairment without subjecting the respondent's clients or the public to a substantial risk of harm because the respondent is permitted to continue to practice law during the probation period.

(4) A respondent may be placed on probation for up to 3 years. The probation order expires on the date specified in it unless the administrator petitions for, and the hearing panel, board, or court grants, an extension. An extension may not exceed 3 years. A probation order may be dissolved if the respondent demonstrates that the impairment giving rise to the probation order has been removed and that the probation order has been fully complied with, but only one motion to accelerate dissolution of a probation order may be filed during the probation period.

(5) On proof that a respondent has violated a probation order, he or she may be suspended or disbarred.

(D) **Publication of Change in Status**. The board must publish in the Michigan Bar Journal a notice of transfer to inactive status. A copy of the notice and the order must be filed and served under MCR 9.118.

(E) **Reinstatement**. An attorney transferred to inactive status under this rule may not resume active status until reinstated by the board's order and, if inactive 3 years or more, recertified by the Board of Law Examiners. The attorney may petition for reinstatement to active status once a year or at shorter intervals as the board may direct. A petition for reinstatement must be granted by a panel on a showing by clear and convincing evidence that the attorney's disability has been removed and that he or she is fit to resume the practice of law. A panel may take the action necessary to determine whether the attorney's disability has been removed, including an examination of the attorney conducted in accord with the procedure set forth in MCR 9.121(B)(1)(a). The panel may direct that the expense of the examination be paid by the attorney. If an attorney was transferred to inactive status under subrule 9.121(A) and subsequently has been judicially declared to be competent, a panel may dispense with further evidence that the disability has been removed and may order reinstatement to active status on terms it finds proper and advisable, including recertification.

(F) **Waiver of Privilege**. By filing a petition for reinstatement to active status under this rule, the attorney waives the doctor-patient privilege with respect to treatment during the period of his or her disability. The attorney shall disclose the name of every psychiatrist, psychologist, physician, and hospital or other institution by whom or in which the attorney has been examined or treated since the transfer to inactive status. The attorney shall furnish to a panel written consent for each to divulge whatever information and records are requested by the panel's medical or psychological experts.

Rule 9.122 Review by Supreme Court

(A) **Kinds Available; Time for Filing**.

(1) A party aggrieved, including the complainant, by a final order entered by the board on review under MCR 9.118, may apply for leave to appeal to the Supreme Court under MCR 7.302 within 28 days after the order is entered. If a motion for reconsideration is filed before the board's order takes effect, the application for leave to appeal to the Supreme Court may be filed within 28 days after the board enters its order granting or denying reconsideration.

(2) If a request for investigation has been dismissed under MCR 9.112(C)(1)(a) or 9.114(A), a party aggrieved by the dismissal may file a complaint in the Supreme Court under MCR 7.304.

(B) **Rules Applicable**. Except as modified by this rule, subchapter 7.300 governs an appeal.

(C) **Stay of Order**. If the discipline order is a suspension of 179 days or less, a stay of the order will automatically issue on the timely filing of an appeal by the respondent. The stay remains effective for 21 days following the conclusion of the appeal or further order of the Supreme Court. The respondent may petition the Supreme Court for a stay pending appeal of other orders of the board.

(D) **Record on Appeal**. The original papers constitute the record on appeal. The board shall certify the original record and file it with the Supreme Court promptly after the briefs of the parties have been filed. The record must include a list of docket entries, a transcript of testimony taken, and all pleadings, exhibits, briefs, findings of fact, and orders in the proceeding. If the record contains material protected, the protection continues unless otherwise ordered by the Supreme Court.

(E) **Disposition**. The Supreme Court may make any order it deems appropriate, including dismissing the appeal. The parties may stipulate to dismiss the appeal with prejudice.

Rule 9.123 Eligibility for Reinstatement

(A) **Suspension, 179 Days or Less**. An attorney whose license has been suspended for 179 days or less is automatically reinstated by filing with the Supreme Court clerk, the board, and the administrator an affidavit showing that the attorney has fully complied with the terms and conditions of the suspension order. A materially false statement contained in the affidavit is ground for disbarment.

(B) **Disbarment or Suspension More Than 179 Days**. An attorney whose license to practice law has been revoked or suspended for more than 179 days is not eligible for reinstatement until the attorney has petitioned for reinstatement under MCR 9.124 and has established by clear and convincing evidence that:

(1) he or she desires in good faith to be restored to the privilege of practicing law in Michigan;

(2) the term of the suspension ordered has elapsed or 5 years have elapsed since his or her disbarment or resignation;

(3) he or she has not practiced or attempted to practice law contrary to the requirement of his or her suspension or disbarment;

(4) he or she has complied fully with the order of discipline;

(5) his or her conduct since the order of discipline has been exemplary and above reproach;

(6) he or she has a proper understanding of and attitude toward the standards that are imposed on members of the bar and will conduct himself or herself in conformity with those standards;

(7) taking into account all of the attorney's past conduct, including the nature of the misconduct which led to the revocation or suspension, he or she nevertheless can safely be recommended to the public, the courts, and the legal profession as a person fit to be consulted by others and to represent them and otherwise act in matters of trust and confidence, and in general to aid in the administration of justice as a member of the bar and as an officer of the court;

(8) he or she is in compliance with the requirements of subrule (C), if applicable; and

(9) he or she has reimbursed the client security fund of the State Bar of Michigan or has agreed to an arrangement satisfactory to the fund to reimburse the fund for any money paid from the fund as a result of his or her conduct. Failure to fully reimburse as agreed is ground for vacating an order of reinstatement.

(C) **Reinstatement After Three Years**. An attorney who, as a result of disciplinary proceedings, resigns, is disbarred, or is suspended for any period of time, and who does not practice law for 3 years or more, whether as the result of the period of discipline or voluntarily, must be recertified by the Board of Law Examiners before the attorney may be reinstated to the practice of law.

(D) **Petition for Reinstatement; Filing Limitations**.

(1) Except as provided in subrule (D)(3), an attorney whose license to practice law has been suspended may not file a petition for reinstatement earlier than 56 days before the term of suspension ordered has fully elapsed.

(2) An attorney whose license to practice law has been revoked or who has resigned may not file a petition for reinstatement until 5 years have elapsed since the attorney's resignation or disbarment.

(3) An attorney whose license to practice law has been suspended because of conviction of a felony for which a term of incarceration was imposed may not file a petition for reinstatement until six months after completion of the sentence, including any period of parole.

(4) An attorney who has been disbarred or suspended and who has been denied reinstatement may not file a new petition for reinstatement until at least 1 year from the effective date of the most recent hearing panel order granting or denying reinstatement.

Rule 9.124 Procedure for Reinstatement

(A) **Filing of Petition**. An attorney petitioning for reinstatement shall file the original petition for reinstatement with the Supreme Court clerk and a copy with the board and the commission.

(B) **Petitioner's Responsibilities.**

(1) Separately from the petition for reinstatement, the petitioner must serve only upon the administrator a personal history affidavit. The affidavit is to become part of the administrator's investigative file and may not be disclosed to the public except under the provisions of MCR 9.126. The affidavit must contain the following information:

(a) every residence address since the date of disqualification from the practice of law;

(b) employment history since the time of disqualification, including the nature of employment, the name and address of every employer, the duration of such employment, and the name of the petitioner's immediate supervisor at each place of employment; if requested by the grievance administrator, the petitioner must provide authorization to obtain a copy of the petitioner's personnel file from the employer;

(c) a copy of a current driver's license;

(d) any continuing legal education in which the petitioner participated during the period of disqualification from the practice of law;

(e) bank account statements, from the date of disqualification until the filing of the petition for reinstatement, for each and every bank account in which petitioner is named in any capacity;

(f) copies of the petitioner's personal and business federal, state, and local tax returns from the date of disqualification until the filing of the petition for reinstatement, and if the petitioner owes outstanding income taxes, interest, and penalties, the petitioner must provide a current statement from the taxation authority of the current amount due; if requested by the grievance administrator, the petitioner must provide a waiver granting the grievance administrator authority to obtain information from the tax authority;

(g) any and all professional or occupational licenses obtained or maintained during the period of disqualification and whether any were suspended or revoked;

(h) any and all names used by petitioner since the time of disqualification;

(i) petitioner's place and date of birth;

(j) petitioner's social security number;

(k) whether, since the time of disqualification, petitioner was a party or a witness in any civil case, and the title, docket number, and court in which the case occurred;

(l) whether the petitioner was a party to any civil case, including the title, docket number, and court in which such case was filed; the petitioner must provide copies of the complaints and any dispositional orders or judgments, including settlement agreements, in such cases;

(m) whether the petitioner was a defendant or a witness in any criminal case, and the title, docket number, and court in which such case was filed; the petitioner must provide copies of the indictments or complaints and any dispositional orders or judgments of conviction in cases in which the petitioner was a defendant;

(n) whether the petitioner was subject to treatment or counseling for mental or emotional impairments, or for substance abuse or gambling addictions since the time of disqualification; if so, the petitioner must provide a current statement from the petitioner's service provider setting forth an evaluative conclusion regarding the petitioner's impairment(s), the petitioner's treatment records, and prognosis for recovery.

(2) The petitioner must, contemporaneously with the filing of the petition for reinstatement and service on the administrator of the personal history affidavit, remit

(a) to the administrator the fee for publication of a reinstatement notice in the Michigan Bar Journal.

(b) to the board the basic administrative costs required under MCR 9.128(B)(1)

(i) an administrative cost of $750 where the discipline imposed was a suspension of less than 3 years;

(ii) an administrative cost of $1,500 where the discipline imposed was a suspension of 3 years or more or disbarment.

(3) If the petition is facially sufficient and the petitioner has provided proof of service of the personal history affidavit upon the administrator and paid the publication fee required by subrule (B)(2), the board shall assign the petition to a hearing panel. Otherwise, the board may dismiss the petition without prejudice, on its own motion or the motion of the administrator.

(4) A petitioner who files the petition before the term of suspension ordered has fully elapsed must file an updated petition and serve upon the administrator an updated personal history affidavit within 14 days after the term of suspension ordered has fully elapsed. All petitioners remain under a continuing

obligation to provide updated information bearing upon the petition or the personal history affidavit.

(5) The petitioner must cooperate fully in the investigation by the administrator into the petitioner's eligibility for reinstatement by promptly providing any information requested. If requested, the petitioner must participate in a recorded interview and answer fully and fairly under oath all questions about eligibility for reinstatement.

(C) **Administrator's Responsibilities**.

(1) Within 14 days after the commission receives its copy of the petition for reinstatement, the administrator shall submit to the Michigan Bar Journal for publication a notice briefly describing the nature and date of the discipline, the misconduct for which the petitioner was disciplined, and the matters required to be proved for reinstatement.

(2) The administrator shall investigate the petitioner's eligibility for reinstatement before a hearing on it, report the findings in writing to the board and the hearing panel within 56 days of the date the board assigns the petition to the hearing panel, and serve a copy on the petitioner.

(a) For good cause, the hearing panel may allow the administrator to file the report at a later date, but in no event later than 7 days before the hearing.

(b) The report must summarize the facts of all previous misconduct and the available evidence bearing on the petitioner's eligibility for reinstatement. The report is part of the record but does not restrict the parties in the presentation of additional relevant evidence at the hearing. Any evidence omitted from the report or received by the administrator after the filing of the report must be disclosed promptly to the hearing panel and to the opposing party.

(D) **Hearing on Petition**. A reinstatement hearing may not be held earlier than 28 days after the administrator files the investigative report with the hearing panel unless the hearing panel has extended the deadline for filing the report. The proceeding on a petition for reinstatement must conform as nearly as practicable to a hearing on a complaint. The petitioner shall appear personally before the hearing panel for cross-examination by the administrator and the hearing panel and answer fully and fairly under oath all questions regarding eligibility for reinstatement. The administrator and the petitioner may call witnesses or introduce evidence bearing upon the petitioner's eligibility for reinstatement. The hearing panel must enter an order granting or denying reinstatement and make a written report signed by the chairperson, including a transcript of the testimony taken, pleadings, exhibits and briefs, and its findings of fact. A reinstatement order may grant reinstatement subject to conditions that are relevant to the established misconduct or otherwise necessary to insure the integrity of the profession, to protect the public, and to serve the interests of justice. The report and order must be filed and served under MCR 9.118(F).

(E) **Review**. Review is available under the rules governing review of other hearing panel orders.

Rule 9.125 Immunity

A person is absolutely immune from suit for statements and communications transmitted solely to the administrator, the commission, or the commission staff, or given in an investigation or proceeding on alleged misconduct or reinstatement. The administrator, legal counsel, investigators, members of hearing panels, masters, receivers appointed under MCR 9.119(G), voluntary investigators, fee arbitrators, mentors, practice monitors, the commission, the board, and their staffs are absolutely immune from suit for conduct arising out of the performance of their duties.

A medical or psychological expert who administers testing or provides a report pursuant to MCR 9.114(C) or MCR 9.121 is absolutely immune from suit for statements and communications transmitted solely to the administrator, the commission, or the commission staff, or given in an investigation or formal disciplinary proceeding.

Rule 9.126 Open Hearings; Priviliged, Confidential Files and Records

(A) **Investigations**. Except as provided in these rules, investigations by the administrator or the staff are privileged from disclosure, confidential, and may not be made public. At the respondent's option, final disposition of a request for investigation not resulting in formal charges may be made public. In addition, any interested person may inspect the request for investigation and the respondent's answer thereto if a disciplinary proceeding has been filed.

(B) **Hearings**. Hearings before a hearing panel and the board must be open to the public, but not their deliberations.

(C) **Papers**. Formal pleadings, reports, findings, recommendations, discipline, reprimands, transcripts, and orders resulting from hearings must be open to the public. A personal history affidavit filed pursuant to MCR 9.124(B)(1) is a confidential document that is not open to the public. This subrule does not apply to a request for a disclosure authorization submitted to the board or the Supreme Court pursuant to subrules (D)(8) or (E)(8).

(D) **Other Records**. Other files and records of the board, the commission, the administrator, legal counsel, hearing panels and their members, and the staff of each may not be examined by or disclosed to anyone except

(1) the commission,

(2) the administrator,

(3) the respondent as provided under MCR 9.115(F)(4),
(4) members of hearing panels or the board,
(5) authorized employees,
(6) the Supreme Court, or
(7) other persons who are expressly authorized by the board or the Supreme Court.

(E) If a disclosure is made to the Supreme Court, the board, or a hearing panel, the information must also be disclosed to the respondent, except as it relates to an investigation, unless the court otherwise orders.

(F) **Other Information**. Notwithstanding any prohibition against disclosure set forth in this rule or elsewhere, the commission shall disclose the substance of information concerning attorney or judicial misconduct to the Judicial Tenure Commission, upon request. The commission also may make such disclosure to the Judicial Tenure Commission, absent a request, and to:
(1) the State Bar of Michigan Client Security Fund,
(2) the State Bar of Michigan:
(a) Committee on Judicial Qualifications;
(b) Lawyers and Judges Assistance Program;
(c) District and Standing Committees on Character and Fitness; or
(d) Unauthorized Practice of Law Committee,
(3) any court-authorized attorney disciplinary or admissions agency, including any federal district court or federal disciplinary agency considering the licensing of attorneys in its jurisdiction,
(4) the Michigan Appellate Assigned Counsel System,
(5) any Michigan court considering the appointment of a lawyer in a pending matter as house counsel, or a standing appointment,
(6) a lawyer representing the respondent in an unrelated disciplinary investigation or proceeding;
(7) law enforcement agencies; or
(8) other persons who are expressly authorized by the board or the Supreme Court.

Rule 9.127 Enforcement

(A) **Interim Suspension**. The Supreme Court, the board, or a hearing panel may order the interim suspension of a respondent who fails to comply with its lawful order. The suspension shall remain in effect until the respondent complies with the order or no longer has the power to comply. If the respondent is ultimately disciplined, the respondent shall not receive credit against the disciplinary suspension or disbarment for any time of suspension under this rule. All orders of hearing panels under this rule shall be reviewable immediately under MCR 9.118. All orders of the board under this rule shall be appealable immediately under MCR 9.122. The reviewing authority may issue a stay pending review or appeal.

(B) **Contempt**. The administrator may enforce a discipline order or an order granting or denying reinstatement by proceeding against a respondent for contempt of court. The proceeding must conform to MCR 3.606. The petition must be filed by the administrator in the circuit court in the county in which the alleged contempt took place, or in which the respondent resides, or has or had an office. Enforcement proceedings under this rule do not bar the imposition of additional discipline upon the basis of the same noncompliance with the discipline order.

Rule 9.128 Costs

(A) **Generally**. The hearing panel and the board, in an order of discipline or an order granting or denying reinstatement, must include a provision directing the payment of costs within a specified period of time. Under exceptional circumstances, the board may grant a motion to reduce administrative costs assessed under this rule, but may not reduce the assessment for actual expenses. Reimbursement must be a condition in a reinstatement order.

(B) **Amount and Nature of Costs Assessed**. The costs assessed under these rules shall include both basic administrative costs and disciplinary expenses actually incurred by the board, the commission, a master, or a panel for the expenses of that investigation, hearing, review and appeal, if any.
(1) Basic Administrative Costs:
(a) for discipline by consent pursuant to MCR 9.115(F)(5), $750;
(b) for all other orders imposing discipline, $1,500;
(c) with the filing of a petition for reinstatement as set forth in MCR 9.124(B)(2)(b)(i) and (ii);
(2) *Actual Expenses*. Within 14 days of the conclusion of a proceeding before a panel or a written request from the board, whichever is later, the grievance administrator shall file with the board an itemized statement of the commission's expenses allocable to the hearing, including expenses incurred during the grievance administrator's investigation. Copies shall be served upon the respondent and the panel. An itemized statement of the expenses of the board, the commission, and the panel, including the expenses of a master, shall be a part of the report in all matters of discipline and reinstatement.

(C) **Certification of Nonpayment**. If the respondent fails to pay the costs within the time prescribed, the board shall serve a certified notice of the nonpayment upon the respondent. Copies must be served on the administrator and the State Bar of Michigan. Commencing on the date a certified report of nonpayment is filed, interest on the unpaid fees and costs shall accrue thereafter at the rates applicable to civil judgments.

(D) **Automatic Suspension for Nonpayment**. The respondent will be suspended automatically, effective 7 days from the mailing of the certified notice of nonpayment, and until the respondent pays the costs assessed or the board approves a suitable plan for payment. The board shall file a notice of suspension with the clerk of the Supreme Court and the State Bar of Michigan. A copy must be served on the respondent and the administrator. A respondent who is suspended for nonpayment of costs under this rule is required to comply with the requirements imposed by MCR 9.119 on suspended attorneys.

(E) **Reinstatement**. A respondent who has been automatically suspended under this rule and later pays the costs or obtains approval of a payment plan, and is otherwise eligible, may seek automatic reinstatement pursuant to MCR 9.123(A) even if the suspension under this rule exceeded 179 days. However, a respondent who is suspended under this rule and, as a result, does not practice law in Michigan for 3 years or more, must be recertified by the Board of Law Examiners before the respondent may be reinstated.

Rule 9.129 Expenses; Reimbursement

The state bar must reimburse each investigator, legal counsel, hearing panel member, board member, master, and commission member for the actual and necessary expenses the board, commission, or administrator certifies as incurred as a result of these rules.

Rule 9.130 MCR 8.122 Cases; Arbitration; Discipline; Filing Complaint by Administrator

(A) **Arbitration**. On written agreement between an attorney and his or her client, the administrator or an attorney the administrator assigns may arbitrate a dispute and enter an award in accordance with the arbitration laws. Except as otherwise provided by this subrule, the arbitration is governed by MCR 3.602. The award and a motion for entry of an order or judgment must be filed in the court having jurisdiction under MCR 8.122. If the award recommends discipline of the attorney, it must also be treated as a request for investigation.

(B) **Complaint**. If the administrator finds that the filing of a complaint in the appropriate court under MCR 8.122 will be a hardship to the client and that the client may have a meritorious claim, the administrator may file the complaint on behalf of the client and prosecute it to completion without cost to the client.

Rule 9.131 Investigation of Member or Employee of Board or Commission; Investigation of Attorney Representing Respondent or Witness; Representation by Member or Employee of Board or Commission

(A) **Investigation of Commission Member or Employee**. If the request is for investigation of an attorney who is a member or employee of the commission, the following provisions apply:

(1) The administrator shall serve a copy of the request for investigation on the respondent by ordinary mail. Within 21 days after service, the respondent shall file with the administrator an answer to the request for investigation conforming to MCR 9.113. The administrator shall send a copy of the answer to the complainant.

(2) After the answer is filed or the time for answer has expired, the administrator shall send copies of the request for investigation and the answer to the Supreme Court clerk.

(3) The Supreme Court shall review the request for investigation and the answer and shall either dismiss the request for investigation or appoint volunteer legal counsel to investigate the matter.

(4) If, after conducting the investigation, appointed counsel determines that the request for investigation does not warrant the filing of a formal complaint, he or she shall file a report setting out the reasons for that conclusion with the administrator, who shall send a copy of the report to the Supreme Court clerk, the respondent, and the complainant. Review of a decision not to file a formal complaint is limited to a proceeding under MCR 9.122(A)(2). If appointed counsel determines not to file a complaint, the administrator shall close and maintain the file under MCR 9.114(E). MCR 9.126(A) governs the release of information regarding the investigation.

(5) If, after conducting the investigation, appointed counsel determines that the request for investigation warrants the filing of a formal complaint, he or she shall prepare and file a complaint with the board under MCR 9.115(B).

(6) Further proceedings are as in other cases except that the complaint will be prosecuted by appointed counsel rather than by the administrator.

If the request is for investigation of the administrator, the term “administrator” in this rule means a member of the commission or some other employee of the commission designated by the chairperson.

(B) **Investigation of Board Member or Employee**. Before the filing of a formal complaint, the procedures regarding a request for investigation of a member or employee of the board are the same as in other cases. Thereafter, the following provisions apply:

(1) The administrator shall file the formal complaint with the board and send a copy to the Supreme Court clerk.

(2) The chief justice shall appoint a hearing panel and may appoint a master to conduct the hearing. The hearing procedure is as provided in MCR 9.115, 9.117, or 9.120, as is appropriate, except that no matters shall be submitted to the board. Procedural

matters ordinarily within the authority of the board shall be decided by the hearing panel, except that a motion to disqualify a member of the panel shall be decided by the chief justice.

(3) The order of the hearing panel is effective 21 days after it is filed and served as required by MCR 9.115(J), and shall be treated as a final order of the board. The administrator shall send a copy of the order to the Supreme Court clerk.

(4) MCR 9.118 does not apply. Review of the hearing panel decision is by the Supreme Court as provided by MCR 9.122.

(C) **Investigation of Attorney Representing a Respondent or Witness in Proceedings Before Board or Commission.**

(1) *Request by a former client.* A request for investigation filed by an attorney or witness against his or her counsel for alleged misconduct occurring in a disciplinary investigation or proceeding, shall be treated under the procedures set forth in MCR 9.112.

(2) *Request by person other than former client.* If a person other than the attorney's former client requests an investigation for alleged misconduct committed during the course of that attorney's representation of a respondent or a witness in proceedings before the board or the commission, the procedures in subrule (A) shall be followed. A request for investigation that alleges misconduct of this type may be filed only by the chairperson of the commission, and only if the commission passes a resolution authorizing the filing by the chairperson.

(D) **Representation by Commission or Board Member or Employee.** A member or employee of the Attorney Grievance Commission or the Attorney Discipline Board and its hearing panels may not represent a respondent in proceedings before the commission, the board, or the Judicial Tenure Commission, including preliminary discussions with employees of the respective commission or board prior to the filing of a request for investigation.

Subchapter 9.200 Judicial Tenure Commission

Rule 9.200 Construction

An independent and honorable judiciary being indispensable to justice in our society, subchapter 9.200 shall be construed to preserve the integrity of the judicial system, to enhance public confidence in that system, and to protect the public, the courts, and the rights of the judges who are governed by these rules in the most expeditious manner that is practicable and fair.

Rule 9.201 Definitions

As used in this chapter, unless the context or subject matter otherwise requires

(A) "commission" means the Judicial Tenure Commission;

(B) "judge" means:

(1) a person who is serving as a judge of an appellate or trial court by virtue of election, appointment, or assignment;

(2) a magistrate or a referee; or

(3) a person who formerly held such office and is named in a request for investigation that was filed during the person's tenure, except that with respect to conduct that is related to the office, it is not necessary that the request for investigation be filed during the person's tenure; nothing in this paragraph deprives the attorney grievance commission of its authority to proceed against a former judge;

(C) "respondent" is a judge against whom a complaint has been filed;

(D) "chairperson" is the commission chairperson and includes the acting chairperson;

(E) "master" means one or more judges or former judges appointed by the Supreme Court at the commission's request to hold hearings on a complaint against a judge filed by the commission;

(F) "examiner" means the executive director or equivalent staff member or other attorney appointed by the commission to present evidence at a hearing before a master or the commission, or in proceedings in the Supreme Court;

(G) "request for investigation" is an allegation of judicial misconduct, physical or mental disability, or other circumstance that the commission may undertake to investigate under Const 1963, art 6, § 30, and MCR 9.207;

(H) "complaint" is a written document filed at the direction of the commission, recommending action against a judge and alleging specific charges of misconduct in office, mental or physical disability, or some other ground that warrants commission action under Const 1963, art 6, § 30.

Rule 9.202 Judicial Tenure Commission; Organization

(A) **Appointment of Commissioners.** As provided by Const 1963, art 6, § 30, the Judicial Tenure Commission consists of 9 persons. The commissioners selected by the judges shall be chosen by mail vote conducted by the state court administrator. The commissioners selected by the state bar members shall be chosen by mail vote conducted by the State Bar of Michigan. Both mail elections must be conducted in accordance with nomination and election procedures approved by the Supreme Court. Immediately after a commissioner's selection, the selecting authority shall notify the Supreme Court and the Judicial Tenure Commission.

(B) **Term of Office**. A commissioner's term of office shall be 3 years. To achieve staggered terms, the following terms shall expire in consecutive years:
  (1) one of the appointments of the Governor, the judge of a court of limited jurisdiction, and one of the attorneys selected by the state bar;
  (2) the other appointment of the Governor, the probate judge, and the other attorney selected by the state bar;
  (3) the Court of Appeals judge, the circuit judge, and the judge selected by the state bar.

(C) **Vacancy**.
  (1) A vacancy in the office of a commissioner occurs:
    (a) when a commissioner resigns or is incapable of serving as a member of the commission;
    (b) when a judge who is a member of the commission no longer holds the office held when selected;
    (c) when an attorney selected by state bar members is no longer entitled to practice in the courts of this state; and
    (d) when an appointee of the Governor becomes an attorney.
  (2) Vacancies must be filled by selection of a successor in the same manner required for the selection of the predecessor. The commissioner selected shall hold office for the unexpired term of the predecessor. Vacancies must be filled within 3 months after the vacancy occurs. If a vacancy occurs after the selection of a new commissioner but before that commissioner's term officially begins, the commissioner-elect shall fill that vacancy and serve the remainder of the unexpired term.
  (3) A member may retire by submitting a resignation in writing to the commission, which must certify the vacancy to the selecting authority.

(D) **Commission Expenses**.
  (1) The commission's budget must be submitted to the Supreme Court for approval.
  (2) The commission's expenses must be included in and paid from the appropriation for the Supreme Court.
  (3) A commissioner may not receive compensation for services but shall be paid reasonable and necessary expenses.

(E) **Quorum and Chairperson**.
  (1) The commission shall elect from among its members a chairperson, a vice-chairperson, and a secretary, each to serve 2 years. The vice-chairperson shall act as chairperson when the chairperson is absent. If both are absent, the members present may select one among them to act as temporary chairperson.
  (2) A quorum for the transaction of business by the commission is 5.
  (3) The vote of a majority of the members constitutes the adoption or rejection of a motion or resolution before the commission. The chairperson is entitled to cast a vote as a commissioner.

(F) **Meetings of Commission**. Meetings must be held at the call of the chairperson or the executive director, or upon the written request of 3 commission members.

(G) **Commission Staff**.
  (1) The commission shall employ an executive director or equivalent person or persons, and such other staff members as the commission concludes are warranted, to perform the duties that the commission directs, subject to the availability of funds under its budget.
  (2) The executive director or any other staff person who is involved in the investigation or prosecution of a judge
    (a) shall not be present during the deliberations of the commission or participate in any other manner in the decision to file formal charges or to recommend action by the Supreme Court with regard to that judge, and
    (b) shall have no substantive ex parte communication with the commission regarding a formal complaint that the commission has authorized.
  (3) Commission employees are exempt from the operation of Const 1963, art 11, § 5, as are employees of courts of record.

Rule 9.203 Judicial Tenure Commission; Powers; Review

(A) **Authority of Commission**. The commission has all the powers provided for under Const 1963, art 6, § 30, and further powers provided by Supreme Court rule. Proceedings before the commission or a master are governed by these rules. The commission may adopt and publish administrative rules for its internal operation and the administration of its proceedings that do not conflict with this subchapter and shall submit them to the Supreme Court for approval.

(B) **Review as an Appellate Court**. The commission may not function as an appellate court to review the decision of a court or to exercise superintending or administrative control of a court, but may examine decisions incident to a complaint of judicial misconduct, disability, or other circumstance that the commission may undertake to investigate under Const 1963, art 6, § 30, and MCR 9.207. An erroneous decision by a judge made in good faith and with due diligence is not judicial misconduct.

(C) **Control of Commission Action**. Proceedings under these rules are subject to the direct and exclusive superintending control of the Supreme Court. No other court has jurisdiction to restrict, control, or review the orders of the master or the commission.

(D) **Errors and Irregularities**. An investigation or proceeding under this subchapter may not be held invalid by reason of a nonprejudicial irregularity or for an error not resulting in a miscarriage of justice.

(E) **Jurisdiction Over Visiting Judges**. Notwithstanding MCR 9.116(B), the Attorney Grievance Commission may take action immediately with regard to a visiting judge who currently holds no other judicial office if the allegations pertain to professional or personal activities unrelated to the judge's activities as a judge.

Rule 9.204 Disqualification of Commission Member or Employee

(A) **Disqualification From Participation**. A judge who is a member of the commission or of the Supreme Court is disqualified from participating in that capacity in proceedings involving the judge's own actions or for any reason set forth in MCR 2.003(B).

(B) **Disqualification from Representation**. A member or employee of the commission may not represent

(1) a respondent in proceedings before the commission, including preliminary discussions with employees of the commission before the filing of a request for investigation; or

(2) a judge in proceedings before the Attorney Grievance Commission, or the Attorney Discipline Board and its hearing panels, as to any matter that was pending before the Judicial Tenure Commission during the member's or the employee's tenure with the commission.

Rule 9.205 Standards of Judicial Conduct

(A) **Responsibility of Judge**. A judge is personally responsible for the judge's own behavior and for the proper conduct and administration of the court in which the judge presides.

(B) **Grounds for Action**. A judge is subject to censure, suspension with or without pay, retirement, or removal for conviction of a felony, physical or mental disability that prevents the performance of judicial duties, misconduct in office, persistent failure to perform judicial duties, habitual intemperance, or conduct that is clearly prejudicial to the administration of justice. In addition to any other sanction imposed, a judge may be ordered to pay the costs, fees, and expenses incurred by the commission in prosecuting the complaint only if the judge engaged in conduct involving fraud, deceit, or intentional misrepresentation, or if the judge made misleading statements to the commission, the commission's investigators, the master, or the Supreme Court.

(1) Misconduct in office includes, but is not limited to:

(a) persistent incompetence in the performance of judicial duties;

(b) persistent neglect in the timely performance of judicial duties;

(c) persistent failure to treat persons fairly and courteously;

(d) treatment of a person unfairly or discourteously because of the person's race, gender, or other protected personal characteristic;

(e) misuse of judicial office for personal advantage or gain, or for the advantage or gain of another; and

(f) failure to cooperate with a reasonable request made by the commission in its investigation of a judge.

(2) Conduct in violation of the Code of Judicial Conduct or the Rules of Professional Conduct may constitute a ground for action with regard to a judge, whether the conduct occurred before or after the respondent became a judge or was related to judicial office.

(3) In deciding whether action with regard to a judge is warranted, the commission shall consider all the circumstances, including the age of the allegations and the possibility of unfair prejudice to the judge because of the staleness of the allegations or unreasonable delay in pursuing the matter.

Rule 9.206 Service

(A) **Judge**. When provision is made under these rules for serving a complaint or other document on a judge, the service must be made in person or by registered or certified mail to the judge's judicial office or last known residence. If an attorney has appeared for a judge, service may be on the attorney in lieu of service on the judge.

(B) **Commission**. Service on the commission must be made by personal delivery or by registered or certified mail to the executive director at the commission's office.

Rule 9.207 Investigation; Notice

(A) **Request for Investigation**. A request for investigation of a judge must be made in writing and verified on oath of the complainant. The commission also is authorized to act on its own initiative or at the request of the Supreme Court, the state court administrator, or the Attorney Grievance Commission.

(B) **Investigation**. Upon receiving a request for investigation that is not clearly unfounded or frivolous, the commission shall direct that an investigation be conducted to determine whether a complaint should be filed and a hearing held. If there is insufficient cause to warrant filing a complaint, the commission may:

(1) dismiss the matter,

(2) dismiss the matter with a letter of explanation or caution that addresses the respondent's conduct,

(3) dismiss the matter contingent upon the satisfaction of conditions imposed by the commission, which may include a period of monitoring,
(4) admonish the respondent, or
(5) recommend to the Supreme Court private censure, with a statement of reasons.

(C) **Adjourned Investigation**. If a request for investigation is filed less than 90 days before an election in which the respondent is a candidate, and the request is not dismissed forthwith as clearly unfounded or frivolous, the commission shall postpone its investigation until after the election unless two-thirds of the commission members determine that the public interest and the interests of justice require otherwise.

(D) **Notice to Judge**.

(1) Before filing a complaint or taking action under subrule (B)(5), the commission must give written notice to the judge who is the subject of a request for investigation. The purpose of the notice is to afford the judge an opportunity to apprise the commission, in writing within 28 days, of such matters as the judge may choose, including information about the factual aspects of the allegations and other relevant issues. The notice shall specify the allegations and may include the date of the conduct, the location where the conduct occurred, and the name of the case or identification of the court proceeding relating to the conduct.

(a) For good cause shown, the commission may grant a reasonable extension of the 28-day period.
(b) The Supreme Court may shorten the time periods prescribed in this and other provisions of this subchapter at its own initiative or at the request of the commission.

(2) Before taking action under subrule (B)(2)-(4), the commission must give written notice to the judge of the nature of the allegations in the request for investigation and afford the judge a reasonable opportunity to respond in writing.

(3) If a judge so requests in response to a written notice from the commission under this subrule, the commission may offer the judge an opportunity to appear informally before the commission to present such information as the judge may choose, including information about the factual aspects of the allegations and other relevant issues.

(4) On final disposition of a request for investigation without the filing of a formal complaint, the commission shall give written notice of the disposition to the judge who was the subject of the request. The commission also shall provide written notice to the complainant that the matter has been resolved without the filing of a formal complaint.

(5) If the commission admonishes a judge pursuant to MCR 9.207(B)(4):

(a) The judge may file 24 copies of a petition for review in the Supreme Court, serve two copies on the commission, and file a proof of service with the commission within 28 days of the date of the admonishment. The petition for review, and any subsequent filings, shall be placed in a confidential file and shall not be made public unless ordered by the Court.
(b) The executive director may file a response with a proof of service on the judge within 14 days of receiving service of the petition for review.
(c) The Supreme Court shall review the admonishment in accordance with MCR 9.225. Any opinion or order entered pursuant to a petition for review under this subrule shall be published and shall have precedential value pursuant to MCR 7.317.

(E) **Physical or Mental Examination**. In the course of an investigation, the commission may request the judge to submit to a physical or mental examination. Failure of the judge to submit to the examination may constitute judicial misconduct. MCR 2.311(B) is applicable to the examination.

(F) **Expediting Matters**. When the integrity of the judicial system requires, the Supreme Court may direct that the commission expedite its consideration of any investigation, and may set a deadline for the commission to submit any recommendation to the Court, notwithstanding any other provision in this subchapter.

Rule 9.208 Evidence

(A) **Taking of Evidence During Preliminary Investigation**. Before filing a complaint, the commission may take evidence before it or an individual member of the commission, or before the executive director or other member of the staff for purposes of the preliminary investigation.

(B) **Cooperation With Investigation**. A judge, clerk, court employee, member of the bar, or other officer of a court must comply with a reasonable request made by the commission in its investigation.

(C) **Discovery**.

(1) Pretrial or discovery proceedings are not permitted, except as follows:

(a) At least 21 days before a scheduled public hearing,

(i) the parties shall provide to one another, in writing, the names and addresses of all persons whom they intend to call at the hearing, a copy of all statements and affidavits given by those persons, and any material in their possession that they intend to introduce as evidence at the hearing, and

(ii) the commission shall make available to the respondent for inspection or copying all exculpatory material in its possession.

(b) The parties shall give supplemental notice to one another within 5 days after any additional witness or material has been identified and at least 10 days before a scheduled hearing.

(2) A deposition may be taken of a witness who is living outside the state or who is physically unable to attend a hearing.

(3) The commission or the master may order a prehearing conference to obtain admissions or otherwise narrow the issues presented by the pleadings.

If a party fails to comply with subrules (C)(1) or (2), the master may, on motion and showing of material prejudice as a result of the failure, impose one or more of the sanctions set forth in MCR 2.313(B)(2)(a)-(c).

Rule 9.209 Pleadings

The complaint and answer are the only pleadings allowed.

(A) **Complaint.**

(1) *Filing; Service.* A complaint may not be filed before the completion of a preliminary investigation. Upon concluding that there is sufficient evidence to warrant the filing of a complaint, the commission shall direct the executive director or equivalent staff member to do the following:

(a) enter the complaint in the commission docket, which is a public record;

(b) retain the complaint in the commission office; and

(c) promptly serve a copy of the complaint on the respondent.

(2) *Form of Complaint.* A complaint must be entitled: "Complaint Against _____, Judge. No. _____." A complaint must be in form similar to a complaint filed in a civil action in the circuit court.

(B) **Answer.**

(1) *Filing.* Within 14 days after service of the complaint, the respondent must file with the commission the original and 9 copies of an answer verified by the respondent.

(2) *Form.* The answer must be in form similar to an answer in a civil action in the circuit court, and must contain a full and fair disclosure of all facts and circumstances pertaining to the allegations regarding the respondent. Wilful concealment, misrepresentation, or failure to file an answer and disclosure are additional grounds for disciplinary action under the complaint.

(3) Affirmative defenses, including the defense of laches, must be asserted in the answer or they will not be considered.

Rule 9.210 Notice of Public Hearing; Appointment of Master and Examiners

(A) **Notice of Public Hearing**. Upon the filing of a complaint, the commission must set a time and a place of hearing before the commission and notify the respondent at least 21 days in advance, or request in writing that the Supreme Court appoint a master to hold the hearing. Such a request must be accompanied by a copy of the complaint.

(B) **Appointment of Master.**

(1) If the commission requests that the Supreme Court appoint a master to conduct the hearing, the Court shall do so within a reasonable period.

(2) The master shall set a time and a place for the hearing and shall notify the respondent and the examiner at least 28 days in advance. The master shall rule on all motions and other procedural matters incident to the complaint, answer, and hearing. Recommendations on dispositive motions shall not be announced until the conclusion of the hearing, except that the master may refer to the commission on an interlocutory basis a recommendation regarding a dispositive motion.

(3) MCR 2.003(B) shall govern all matters concerning the disqualification of a master.

(C) **Appointment of Examiners**. The executive director shall act as the examiner in a case in which a formal complaint is filed, unless the commission appoints another attorney to act as examiner.

Rule 9.211 Public Hearing

(A) **Procedure**. The public hearing must conform as nearly as possible to the rules of procedure and evidence governing the trial of civil actions in the circuit court. The hearing must be held whether or not the respondent has filed an answer or appears at the hearing. The examiner shall present the evidence in support of the charges set forth in the complaint, and at all times shall have the burden of proving the allegations by a preponderance of the evidence. A respondent is entitled to be represented by an attorney. Any employee, officer, or agent of the respondent's court, law enforcement officer, public officer or employee, or attorney who testifies as a witness in the hearing, whether called by the examiner or by the judge, is subject to cross-examination by either party as an opposite party under MCL 600.2161.

(B) **Effect of Failure to Comply**.

(1) The respondent's failure to answer or to appear at the hearing may not, standing alone, be taken as evidence of the truth of the facts alleged to constitute grounds for commission action.

(2) The respondent's failure to answer, to testify in his or her own behalf, or to submit to a medical examination requested by the commission or the

master, may be considered as an evidentiary fact, unless the failure was due to circumstances unrelated to the facts in issue at the hearing.

(C) **Record**. The proceedings at the hearing must be recorded by stenographic or mechanical means. A separate record must be made if the master or the commission declines to admit evidence.

(D) **Rulings**. When the hearing is before the commission, at least 5 members must be present while the hearing is in active progress. Procedural and other interlocutory rulings must be made by the chairperson and are taken as consented to by the other members of the commission unless a member calls for a vote, in which event a ruling must be made by a majority vote of those present.

Rule 9.212 Subpoenas

(A) **Issuance of Subpoenas**.

(1) Before the filing of a complaint, the commission may issue subpoenas for the attendance of witnesses to provide statements or produce documents or other tangible evidence exclusively for consideration by the commission and its staff during the preliminary investigation. Before the filing of a complaint, the entitlement appearing on the subpoena shall not disclose the name of a judge under investigation.

(2) After the filing of a complaint, the commission may issue subpoenas either to secure evidence for testing before the hearing or for the attendance of witnesses and the production of documents or other tangible evidence at the hearing.

(B) **Sanctions for Contempt; Disobedience by Respondent**.

(1) Contempt proceedings against a nonparty for failure to obey a subpoena issued pursuant to this rule may be brought pursuant to MCR 2.506(E) in the circuit court for the county in which the individual resides, where the individual is found, where the contempt occurred, or where the hearing is to be held.

(2) If a respondent disobeys a subpoena or other lawful order of the commission or the master, whether before or during the hearing, the commission or the master may order such sanctions as are just, including, but not limited to, those set forth in MCR 2.313(B)(2)(a)-(e).

Rule 9.213 Amendments of Complaint or Answer

The master, before the conclusion of the hearing, or the commission, before its determination, may allow or require amendments of the complaint or the answer. The complaint may be amended to conform to the proofs or to set forth additional facts, whether occurring before or after the commencement of the hearing. If an amendment is made, the respondent must be given reasonable time to answer the amendment and to prepare and present a defense against the matters charged in the amendment.

Rule 9.214 Report of Master

Within 21 days after a transcript of the proceedings is provided, the master shall prepare and transmit to the commission in duplicate a report that contains a brief statement of the proceedings and findings of fact and conclusions of law with respect to the issues presented by the complaint and the answer. The report must be accompanied by three copies of the transcript of the proceedings before the master. On receiving the report and the transcript, the commission must promptly send a copy of each to the respondent.

Rule 9.215 Objections to Report of Master

Within 28 days after copies of the master's report and the transcript are mailed to the respondent, the examiner or the respondent may file with the commission an original and 9 copies of a statement of objections to the report of the master, along with a supporting brief. A copy of a statement and brief must be served on the opposite party, who shall have 14 days to respond.

Rule 9.216 Appearance Before Commission

When the master files the report, the commission shall set a date for hearing objections to the report. The respondent and the examiner must file written briefs at least 7 days before the hearing date. The briefs must include a discussion of possible sanctions and, except as otherwise permitted by the Judicial Tenure Commission, are limited to 50 pages in length. Both the respondent and the examiner may present oral argument at the hearing.

Rule 9.217 Extension of Time

The commission or its chairperson may extend for periods not to exceed 28 days the time for the filing of an answer, for the commencement of a hearing before the commission, for the filing of the master's report, and for the filing of a statement of objections to the report of a master. A master may similarly extend the time for the commencement of a hearing.

Rule 9.218 Hearing Additional Evidence

The commission may order a hearing before itself or the master for the taking of additional evidence at any time while the complaint is pending before it. The order must set the time and place of hearing and indicate the matters about which evidence is to be taken. A copy of the order must be sent to the respondent at least 14 days before the hearing.

Rule 9.219 Interim Suspension

(A) **Petition**.

(1) After a complaint is filed, the commission may petition the Supreme Court for an order suspending a judge from acting as a judge until final adjudication of the complaint.

(2) In extraordinary circumstances, the commission may petition the Supreme Court for an order suspending a judge from acting as a judge in response to a request for investigation, pending a decision by the commission regarding the filing of a complaint. In such a circumstance, the documents filed with the Court must be kept under seal unless the petition is granted.

Whenever a petition for interim suspension is granted, the processing of the case shall be expedited in the commission and in the Supreme Court. The commission shall set forth in the petition an approximate date for submitting a final recommendation to the Court.

(B) **Contents; Affidavit or Transcript**. The petition must be accompanied by a sworn affidavit or court transcript, and state facts in support of the allegations and the assertion that immediate suspension is necessary for the proper administration of justice.

(C) **Service; Answer**. A copy of the petition and supporting documents must be served on the respondent, who may file an answer to the petition within 14 days after service of the petition. The commission must be served with a copy of the answer.

Rule 9.220 Commission Decision

(A) **Majority Decision**.

(1) The affirmative vote of 5 commission members who have considered the report of the master and any objections, and who were present at an oral hearing provided for in MCR 9.216, or have read the transcript of that hearing, is required for a recommendation of action with regard to a judge. A commissioner may file a written dissent.

(2) If the hearing was held without a master, the affirmative vote of 5 commission members who were present when the evidence was taken or who have read the transcript of that proceeding is required for such a recommendation. A commissioner may file a written dissent.

(3) It is not necessary that a majority agree on the specific conduct that warrants a recommendation of action with regard to a judge, or on the specific action that is warranted, only that there was some conduct that warrants such a recommendation.

(B) **Record of Decision**.

(1) The commission must make written findings of fact and conclusions of law along with its recommendations for action with respect to the issues of fact and law in the proceedings, but may adopt the findings of the master, in whole or in part, by reference.

(2) The commission shall undertake to ensure that the action it is recommending in individual cases is reasonably proportionate to the conduct of the respondent, and reasonably equivalent to the action that has been taken previously in equivalent cases.

(C) **Action With Respondent's Consent**. With the consent of the respondent and the commission, the Supreme Court may impose a sanction or take other action at any stage of the proceedings under these rules.

Rule 9.221 Confidentiality; Disclosure

(A) **Scope of Rule**. Except as provided in this rule, all papers filed with the commission and all proceedings before it are confidential in nature and are absolutely privileged from disclosure by the commission or its staff, including former members and employees, in any other matter, including but not limited to civil, criminal, legislative, or administrative proceedings. All the commission's investigative files and commission-generated documents are likewise confidential and privileged from disclosure. Nothing in this rule prohibits the respondent judge from making statements regarding the judge's conduct.

(B) **Before Filing a Formal Complaint**.

(1) Before a complaint is filed, neither a commissioner nor a member of the commission staff may disclose the existence or contents of an investigation, testimony taken, or papers filed in it, except as needed for investigative purposes.

(2) The commission may at any time make public statements as to matters pending before it on its determination by a majority vote that it is in the public interest to do so, limited to statements

(a) that there is an investigation pending,

(b) that the investigation is complete and there is insufficient evidence for the commission to file a complaint, or

(c) with the consent of the respondent, that the investigation is complete and some specified disciplinary action has been taken.

(C) **Discretionary Waiver of Confidentiality or Privilege**. The commission may waive the confidentiality or privilege protections if:

(1) the respondent waives, in writing, the right to confidentiality or privilege;

(2) the grievant waives, in writing, the right to confidentiality or privilege;

(3) the witness whose statement, testimony, or other evidentiary item will be disclosed waives, in writing, the right to confidentiality or privilege; and

(4) a majority of the commission determines that the public interest will be served by doing so.

(D) **After Filing of Formal Complaint**.

(1) When the commission issues a complaint, the following shall not be confidential or privileged:
  (a) the complaint and all subsequent pleadings filed with the commission or master, all stipulations entered, all findings of fact made by the master or commission, and all reports of the master or commission; however, all papers filed with and proceedings before the commission during the period preceding the issuance of a complaint remain confidential and privileged except where offered into evidence in a formal hearing; and
  (b) the formal hearing before the master or commission, and the public hearing provided for in MCR 9.216.
(2) This subrule neither limits nor expands a respondent's right to discovery under MCR 9.208(C).
(3) The confidentiality or privilege of any otherwise nonpublic disciplinary action is waived in any proceeding on a concurrent or subsequent formal complaint.

(E) **Disclosure to Grievant**.
(1) Upon completion of an investigation or proceeding on a complaint, the commission shall disclose to the grievant that the commission
  (a) has found no basis for action against the judge or determined not to proceed further in the matter,
  (b) has taken an appropriate corrective action, the nature of which shall not be disclosed, or
  (c) has recommended that the respondent be publicly censured, suspended, removed, or retired from office.

(F) **Public Safety Exception**. When the commission receives information concerning a threat to the safety of any person or persons, information concerning such person may be provided to the person threatened, to persons or organizations responsible for the safety of the person threatened, and to law enforcement or any appropriate prosecutorial agency.

(G) **Disclosure to State Court Administrator**.
(1) The commission may refer to the state court administrator requests for investigation and other communications received by the commission concerning the conduct of a judge if, in the opinion of the commission, the communications are properly within the scope of the duties of the administrator. The commission may provide the administrator with files, records, investigations, and reports of the commission relating to the matter. Such a referral does not preclude action by the commission if the judge's conduct is of such a nature as to constitute grounds for action by the commission, or cannot be adequately resolved or corrected by action of the administrator.
(2) The commission may disclose to the administrator, upon request, the substance of files and records of the commission concerning a former judge who has been or may be assigned judicial duties by the administrator; a copy of the information disclosed must be furnished to the judge.

(H) **Disclosure to Attorney Grievance Commission**. Notwithstanding the prohibition against disclosure in this rule, the commission shall disclose information concerning a judge's misconduct in office, mental or physical disability, or some other ground that warrants commission action under Const 1963, art 6, § 30, to the Attorney Grievance Commission, upon request. Absent a request, the commission may make such disclosure to the Attorney Grievance Commission. In the event of a dispute concerning the release of information, either the Attorney Grievance Commission or the Judicial Tenure Commission may petition the Supreme Court for an order resolving the dispute.

(I) **Disclosure to Chief Judge**. Notwithstanding the prohibition against disclosure in this rule, and except for those situations that involve a dismissal with explanation, the commission shall notify the chief judge of a court when the commission has taken action under MCR 9.207(B)(2)-(5) involving a magistrate or referee of that court. Upon the chief judge's request, the referee or magistrate shall provide the chief judge with a copy of the commission's written notice of disposition.

Rule 9.222 Record Retention

The commission shall develop a record-retention policy, which shall include a description of the materials that are to be stored, a list of the time for which specific materials must be maintained, and procedures for the disposal of records.

Rule 9.223 Filing and Service of Documents by Commission

Within 21 days after entering an order recommending action with regard to a respondent, the commission must take the action required by subrules (A) and (B).

(A) **Filings in Supreme Court**. The commission must file in the Supreme Court:
(1) the original record arranged in chronological order and indexed and certified;
(2) 24 copies of the order; and
(3) a proof of service on the respondent.

(B) **Service on Respondent**. The commission must serve the respondent with:
(1) notice of the filing under MCR 9.223(A)(1);
(2) 2 copies of the order;
(3) 2 copies of the index to the original record; and
(4) a copy of a portion of the original record not submitted by or previously furnished to the respondent.

Rule 9.224 Review by Supreme Court

(A) **Petition by Respondent**. Within 28 days after being served, a respondent may file in the Supreme Court 24 copies of
- (1) a petition to reject or modify the commission's recommendation, which must:
  - (a) be based on the record,
  - (b) specify the grounds relied on,
  - (c) be verified, and
  - (d) include a brief in support; and
- (2) an appendix presenting portions of the record that the respondent believes necessary to fairly judge the issues.

The respondent must serve the commission with 3 copies of the petition and 2 copies of the appendix and file proof of that service.

(B) **Brief of Commission**. Within 21 days after respondent's petition is served, the commission must file
- (1) 24 copies of a brief supporting its finding, and
- (2) proof that the respondent was served with 2 copies of the brief.

The commission may file 24 copies of an appendix containing portions of the record not included in the respondent's appendix that the commission believes necessary to fairly judge the issues.

(C) **Review in Absence of Petition by Respondent**. If the respondent does not file a petition, the Supreme Court will review the commission's recommendation on the record file. The Supreme Court may order that briefs be filed or arguments be presented.

(D) **Form of Briefs**. A brief filed under this subrule is to be similar to a brief filed in an appeal to the Supreme Court.

(E) **Additional Evidence**. The Supreme Court may, if cause is shown, order that further evidence be taken and added to the original record.

(F) **Submission**. The clerk will place the case on a session calendar under MCR 7.312. Oral argument may be requested.

Rule 9.225 Decision by Supreme Court

The Supreme Court shall review the record of the proceedings and file a written opinion and judgment, which may accept or reject the recommendations of the commission, or modify the recommendations by imposing a greater, lesser, or entirely different sanction. When appropriate, the Court may remand the matter to the commission for further proceedings, findings, or explication. If the respondent and the commission have consented to a course of action under subrule 9.220(C) and the Court determines to impose a greater, lesser, or entirely different sanction, the respondent shall be afforded the opportunity to withdraw the consent and the matter shall be remanded to the commission for further proceedings.

Rule 9.226 Motion for Rehearing

Unless the Supreme Court directs otherwise, the respondent may file a motion for rehearing within 14 days after the filing of the decision. If the Supreme Court directs in the decision that a motion for rehearing may not be filed, the decision is final on filing.

Rule 9.227 Immunity

A person is absolutely immune from civil suit for statements and communications transmitted solely to the commission, its employees, or its agents, or given in an investigation or proceeding on allegations regarding a judge, and no civil action predicated upon the statements or communications may be instituted against a complainant, a witness, or their counsel. Members of the commission and their employees and agents, masters, and examiners are absolutely immune from civil suit for all conduct in the course of their official duties.

Rule 9.228 Ethics Materials and Programs

The commission shall work with other groups and organizations, including the State Bar of Michigan, to develop educational materials and programs that are designed to assist judges in maintaining an awareness and understanding of their ethical obligations.

www.ingramcontent.com/pod-product-compliance
Lightning Source LLC
Chambersburg PA
CBHW061155240926
51846CB00006B/1017
* 9 7 8 1 9 4 2 8 4 2 0 0 2 *